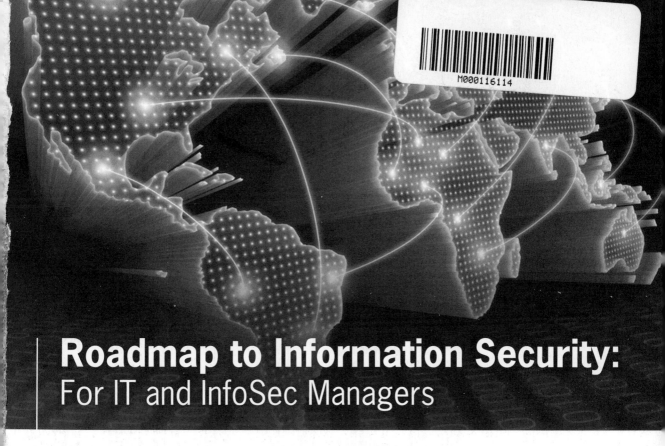

Roadmap to Information Security:
For IT and InfoSec Managers

Michael E. Whitman, Ph.D., CISM, CISSP

Herbert J. Mattord, CISM, CISSP

COURSE TECHNOLOGY
CENGAGE Learning™

Australia • Brazil • Japan • Korea • Mexico • Singapore • Spain • United Kingdom • United States

COURSE TECHNOLOGY
CENGAGE Learning™

Roadmap to Information Security:
  For IT and Infosec Managers
Michael E. Whitman and
  Herbert J. Mattord

Vice President, Editorial: Dave Garza

Director of Learning Solutions:
  Matthew Kane

Executive Editor: Steve Helba

Managing Editor: Marah Bellegarde

Senior Product Manager:
  Michelle Ruelos Cannistraci

Editorial Assistant: Jennifer Wheaton

Vice President, Marketing:
  Jennifer Ann Baker

Marketing Director: Deborah S. Yarnell

Senior Marketing Manager: Erin Coffin

Production Manager: Andrew Crouth

Senior Content Project Manager:
  Kara A. DiCaterino

Senior Art Director: Jack Pendleton

For product information and technology assistance, contact us at
Cengage Learning Customer & Sales Support, 1-800-354-9706

For permission to use material from this text or product,
submit all requests online at **cengage.com/permissions**
Further permissions questions can be emailed to
permissionrequest@cengage.com

Library of Congress Control Number: 2011925445

ISBN-13: 978-1-4354-8030-8
ISBN-10: 1-4354-8030-9

Course Technology
20 Channel Center Street
Boston, MA 02210
USA

Cengage Learning is a leading provider of customized learning solutions with office locations around the globe, including Singapore, the United Kingdom, Australia, Mexico, Brazil, and Japan. Locate your local office at: **international. cengage.com/region**

Cengage Learning products are represented in Canada by Nelson Education, Ltd.

For your lifelong learning solutions, visit **www.cengage.com/coursetechnology**

Purchase any of our products at your local college store or at our preferred online store **www.cengagebrain.com**

Visit our corporate website at **cengage.com**.

Printed in the United States of America
1 2 3 4 5 6 7 15 14 13 12 11

Brief Table of Contents

Introduction

Over the past twenty years the information security landscape has changed drastically into a maze of complicated and complex relationships among information technology (IT) specialists, users of IT, and general management. A myriad of books and articles on the subject have been published in response to this rapidly growing need of information and instruction concerning information security in business. In response to the call from businesses all over the country, colleges and universities are developing course curricula at high speed in order to educate the next generation of highly qualified information security specialists. In the meantime, many who are well established in the IT field, such as yourself, are finding themselves having the added burden of information security placed on their shoulders. Resources abound, but unlike many resources on this subject, this book is designed specifically to address those who are in need of more than just knowledge of information security, but are also in need of information on HOW to develop such a program in business. This book addresses both knowledge and know-how. The following material is targeted toward those of you who are tasked with the development of an information security program. But we encourage you to invite general managers and employees to also read this book as we believe that the more managers and employees become knowledgeable and understand this complex puzzle that you must piece together into an efficient and viable program, the more information security becomes the philosophical foundation of the business and the protection of its assets.

It is our philosophy that the responsibility for information security in every organization must always belong to the management team. The security of an organization's information assets is a problem that has important economic consequences and for which management will be held accountable. Therefore, the leadership needed for this effort must come from the top, but there are clearly defined roles for IT managers and information security (InfoSec) managers to fulfill these objectives. The solutions, when they are found, are not reserved for technology but are based on management action combined with technical controls where appropriate.

The successful development of an information security program in your organization need not rely only on the pool of current InfoSec practitioners when these specialists are unavailable. This is why you are reading this book! Unfortunately, there are few resources designed to assist you in addressing those challenges associated with developing a sound information security program in your organization. There are also only a few resources that provide you with concise guidance on assessing and improving an organization's security and furthering their security careers. This book pursues both of these objectives by providing a solid overview of information security and its relationship to the information needs of an organization, with specific content tailored to your needs when working in the information security context. This approach will allow you to handle an assignment in your information security role in ways that conform to the expectations of both new and existing information security programs, as well as supporting your needs and the new information security manager in the building and maintaining of a solid information security program.

You are not alone. As of 2010, a survey conducted for the International Information Systems Security Certification Consortium (ISC)2 estimated that there are over 2.28 million information security professionals world wide. The demand for infosec professionals is expected to reach 4.2 million by 2015. and already the U.S. Bureau of Labor Statistics reports over 3 million information technology workers in the United States alone (as of March 2006), with almost 10 percent of these being managers. The need for this book as a resource for IT managers to fill InfoSec expectations has never been greater.

We hope that you will find our book useful and that you will enter into a dialogue with us concerning any needs that you believe we have not sufficiently addressed. Such a dialogue can only help us continue to provide you with the valuable information you need in order to create and maintain what we believe the most important program in business.

APPROACH

While we appreciate the importance of management in its legal and fiscal roles of information security, this book, however, is about you—the person management has chosen to develop an information security program within your organization. Look at this book as your guide into the technical mazes of information security. We have designed this book with you in mind. We assume on your part little or no knowledge in the areas of information security, and we hope that this book will give you the tools you need in order to lay a solid foundation for information security in your organization.

What you will find in this book is a broad overview of the entire field of information security, background coverage of many related topics, and sufficient detail to ensure an understanding of this very important subject. It covers the terminology of the field, the history of the discipline, and an overview of how to develop and manage an information security program. In short, it is an inch deep and a mile wide.

Certified Security Professionals' Common Body of Knowledge

Since we hold the Certified Information Security Manager (CISM) and the Certified Information Systems Security Professional (CISSP) credentials, these knowledge domains have had a thorough influence on the design of this book. Although care has been taken to avoid producing another certification study guide, our backgrounds have influenced the way we handle the common body of knowledge (CBK) and its integration into this book.

FEATURES

Technical and Managerial Details Boxes—Interspersed throughout the book, these sections highlight interesting topics and detailed technical issues, giving you the option of delving further into selected topics.

The Information Security Manager's Checklist—Drawing on a number of sources, such as the NIST recommended practices and the ISO/IEC 27000 series of standards, we have pulled together a handy checklist of issues and factors that the information security manager should consider that were mentioned or referenced in that chapter. The checklist presents a number of subjects. Read the subject text mentioned and then consider your current state regarding that subject. The options are listed in increasing degree of information security program maturity—the most mature programs will answer that they have an "integrated" approach for that subject that is fully tested, validated against recognized standards, and fully integrated into routine business operations. The least mature organizations will answer "No" to the subject item indicating they have no formal allowance for that issue in their current information security program. We recommend that you review and complete this checklist as soon as possible after reading the chapter and then again, periodically, pull together all of the checklists and review your current status on each item at least once each year. It should be your goal to move your organization as far toward the "integrated" level of maturity as you can get with the resources you have available.

For Further Reading—Provides additional references that you can use to further your knowledge of the material covered.

At the end of the book you will find some additional resources you may find useful.

Hands-On Assessment Checklists—A set of program assessment questions offers you the opportunity to compare your developing program against national and international information security standards, such as ISO 17799 and NIST SP 800-26. Each checklist is independently developed based on these standards, but contains sufficient cross references for you to gauge whether your organization meets these standards in the design of a good security program. Using this model **will not** imply or infer that the organization is actually certifiable under these models but simply helps you to better understand both the standards and security programs assessed.

Security Professional Certification Map—A final resource is a map of the CISSP and CISM certification domains into the chapters and sections of the book that will facilitate review and study for those seeking certification. The two dominant certifications for managers, the CISM and the CISSP, are included in this map.

AUTHOR TEAM

Michael Whitman and Herbert Mattord have jointly developed this book by merging knowledge from the world of academic study with practical experience from the business world.

Michael Whitman, Ph.D., CISM, CISSP is a professor of Information Systems and Security in the Information Systems Department at Kennesaw State University, Kennesaw, Georgia, where he is also the coordinator of the Bachelor of Science in Information Security and Assurance and the director of the KSU Center for Information Security Education and Awareness (*infosec .kennesaw.edu*). Dr. Whitman is an active researcher in Information Security, Fair and Responsible Use Policies, Ethical Computing, and Information Systems Research Methods. He currently teaches graduate and undergraduate courses in Information Security. He has published articles in the top journals in his field, including *Information Systems Research*, the *Communications of the ACM, Information and Management*, the *Journal of International Business Studies*, and the *Journal of Computer Information Systems*. He is an active member of the Georgia Electronic Commerce Association's Information Security Working Group, the Association for Computing Machinery, and the Association for Information Systems. Dr. Whitman is also the coauthor of *Principles of Information Security, Management of Information Security, Principles of Incident Response and Disaster Recovery, Readings and Cases in the Management of Information Security*, Guide to Firewalls and VPNs and Principles of Network Security and *The Hands-On Information Security Lab Manual*, all published by Course Technology. Dr. Whitman has also conducted certification preparation classes (CISM/CISSP) in addition to dozens of professional presentations on information security education. While serving with the 1st Squadron, 2nd Armored Cavalry Regiment in German in the late 80's, he also assumed the responsibilities of the unit Automated Data Processing System Security Officer (ADPSSO).

Herbert Mattord, M.B.A. CISM, CISSP completed 24 years of IT industry experience as an application developer, database administrator, project manager, and information security practitioner before joining the faculty at Kennesaw State University in 2002. Professor Mattord is the operations manager of the KSU Center for Information Security Education and Awareness (*infosec.kennesaw.edu*), as well as the coordinator for the KSU Information Systems Department's Certificate in Information Security and Assurance. He is also currently pursuing a Ph.D. in Information Systems at Nova Southeastern University. During his career as an IT practitioner, he has been an adjunct professor at Kennesaw State University, Southern Polytechnic State University in Marietta, Georgia, Austin Community College in Austin, Texas, and Texas State University: San Marcos. He currently teaches undergraduate courses in Information Security. He was formerly a manager in the Corporate Information Technology Privacy and Security Department at Georgia-Pacific Corporation, where much of the practical knowledge found in this textbook was acquired. Professor Mattord is also the coauthor of *Principles of Information Security, Management of Information Security, Principles of Incident Response and Disaster Recovery, Readings and Cases in the Management of Information Security*, Guide to Firewalls and VPNs and Principles of Network Security and *The Hands-On Information Security Lab Manual*, all published by Course Technology. Professor Mattord has also conducted certification preparation classes (CISM/CISSP) in addition to dozens of professional presentations on information security education.

STRUCTURE

Roadmap to Information Security for IT and Infosec Managers is organized into nine parts, each of which are further divided into multiple chapters that flow from strategic to tactical to operational topics. This organizational approach is intended to offer each topic its own chapter, delivered with a concise treatment that is easily digestible, while continuing to serve as a ready reference for those of you already familiar with information security.

The following is an overview of each part in the book and an overall explanation of the information that you will find in the corresponding chapters.

PART I: OVERVIEW OF THE SECURITY LANDSCAPE

Part I includes Chapters 1–3 and addresses the basic foundation of information security. The chapters will provide important material on the key terms and concepts that are essential to understanding information security in the organization. In each of these chapters, you will be given detailed explanations of information security that you will be facing and will be responsible for finding the managerial and technical solutions current organizations need in order to secure their assets. The core concept that information security is primarily an issue of management and not technology is continuously emphasized, and you should apply best practices of technology only after considering the business needs.

PART II: STRATEGIC INFOSEC—SECURITY GOVERNANCE

Part II includes Chapters 4–7 will discuss the integration of strategic planning for IT and InfoSec into the organizational strategic planning process and the alignment of IT and InfoSec goals and objectives with those of the organization. Each of these chapters will help you to identify and describe the typical job titles and functions performed by key security personnel in the InfoSec program. The most important component of Part II is in its detailed explanation of how to plan and staff an organization's InfoSec program, based on organizational factors, as well as how to evaluate the internal and external factors that influence the activities and organization of an InfoSec program. Along with the development of this program, Part II will also provide you with a discussion on the processes necessary to conduct a fundamental security assessment, the procedures for identifying and prioritizing threats and assets, and identifying what controls are in place to protect these assets from threats.

PART III: STRATEGIC INFOSEC—RISK MANAGEMENT

Part III covers Chapters 8–11 and will focus on risk management. In the first chapter you will learn the definition of risk management and its role in the organization. Throughout each subsequent chapter, you will come to understand how to use risk management techniques in order to identify and prioritize risk factors for information assets. Quantitative versus qualitative risk management is also described, including the advantages and disadvantages of both. The risk management model presented in Part III assesses risk based on the likelihood of adverse events and the effects on information assets when events occur. We also believe it important to provide you with various approaches to risk management using two industry standards as the basis for understanding: the OCTAVE method from Carnegie Mellon and Microsoft's Risk Management Approach.

PART IV: STRATEGIC INFOSEC—STANDARDS, REGULATIONS, LAW, AND ETHICS

We believe it to be very important that anyone responsible for an information security program should know and understand the legal aspects that surround this field. Part IV, which covers Chapters 12–16, therefore, introduces and describes the components of the dominant InfoSec management models, including U.S. government-sanctioned and key international models, and discusses how to customize them for a specific organization's needs. You will also learn how to implement the fundamental elements of key InfoSec management practices. Many who enter into this field find it necessary to continue their training and education through the professional certification processes available. We describe the foundations and components of certification and accreditation of both public and private U.S. IT systems. We also include many of the requirements and responsibilities of individuals responsible for systems certification and accreditation and who use the NIST model as a foundation. As a fundamental part of the InfoSec process, we encourage you to carefully examine and consider our discussion of the current legislation, regulation, and common ethical expectations of both national and international entities found in Part IV. We have endeavored to provide you with key insights into the regulatory constraints that govern business. The laws that shape the field of Information Security are important for you to know and understand as they are the foundation for computer ethics necessary to better educate you in the implementation of information security. It has been well understood that *ignorance of the law is no excuse*, but better than negligence. The laws apply in either case. Business ethics in modern organizations remain the center of business and though we discuss and describe the several ethical issues that are commonly found in today's organizations, we do not believe our information is the substitute for continual professional certifications and participation in professional organizations.

PART V: TACTICAL INFOSEC—POLICIES AND PROGRAMS

Part V includes Chapters 17–20 and will define InfoSec policy and describe its central role in the successful implementation of such a program in business. Each chapter will explain InfoSec policy in its various facets, as well as demonstrate how to develop a program, implement it, and successfully maintain various types of InfoSec policies. The discussion of policy will focus on the organization's highest InfoSec policy—the Enterprise Information Security Policy (EISP). The implementation of employment policies and practices is also a crucial component of Part V, along with discussion concerning how information security policy affects, and is affected by, consultants, temporary workers, and outside business partners.

PART VI: TACTICAL INFOSEC—CONTINGENCY PLANNING

Chapters 21–24 in Part VI focus on the very crucial contingency planning for a disaster. Consideration and planning for fire and flood and other natural or man-made disasters must belong to any successful implementation of an information security program. In these chapters you will be provided with information concerning the need for contingency planning and its major components. The examination of contingency planning focuses on the establishment and creation of an incident response, disaster recovery, and business continuity planning committees and plans.

PART VII: OPERATIONAL INFOSEC—NETWORK SECURITY

Chapters 25–29 in Part VII will provide you with detailed discussions on the role of communications methods and protocols as a foundation of network security in business. Emphasis has been placed on the examination of the ISO OSI reference model, specifically the security and protocol components of each level. The detailed perspective on the configuration and use of technologies designed to segregate the organization from the insecure Internet will provide you with considerations for the evaluation and selection of firewall technology and architectures for the securing of business assets in such an open environment. Considerations such as the security precautions necessary to secure access points for organizations with older technology are also included. Intrusion and the technologies necessary to prevent, detect, react, and recover from intrusions as well as the specialized detection technologies that are designed to entice attackers into decoy systems are also explained.

PART VIII: OPERATIONAL INFOSEC—CRYPTOGRAPHY AND ACCESS CONTROLS

Building on the previous section, Part VIII covers Chapters 30–33 and provides a presentation of the underlying foundations of modern cryptosystems, as well as a discussion of their architectures. You will be given an understanding of the mathematical techniques that comprise cryptosystems, including hash functions. Implementations of modern cryptosystems and cryptographic algorithms are also discussed by comparing traditional symmetric encryption systems with more modern asymmetric encryption systems and Public Key Encryption systems. Access control methods and devices commonly deployed through modern operating systems and networks and new technologies in the area of biometrics will provide you with information on the execution of strong authentication to existing implementations.

PART IX: APPENDIX

Part IX is for you to use as a security self-assessment checklist, based in part on two dominant industry standards: ISO 17799 (soon to become ISO 27002) and NIST SP 800-27. The appendix in Part IX provides guidance on performing a continuous improvement assessment program, along with guidelines on implementing and interpreting the results of such an assessment. This section also contains information for those professionals interested in using this book's material as the beginning of a self-study program in pursuit of one of the two (ISC)^2 certifications: the CISSP and the SSCP. While this book **makes no claims** as to the level of preparation of a prospective certification candidate, it can serve as a starting point to determine the areas that might be in need of more study in order to optimize a chance of success.

Reference

1. http://www.net-security.org/secworld.php?id=10630

Cybercrime perpetrators are multiplying world-wide and overwhelming their victims, and information security is failing to stop them. For example, stolen identities for credit card and bank account fraud are counted in the millions and occurring in some cases to victims that are certified to have acceptable security. We are improving technological security and developing new security products, but the increased complexity, reliance on human frailties of trusted and privileged users, and inability to create adequately secure systems and application software defeat our efforts. In addition security is not keeping up with all of the fast-changing technological advances in information technology such as cloud computing, virtual systems, and mobile user endpoints. The greatest challenge may be to stop the victims and their stakeholders from misusing or failing to use the security available to them. It is generally accepted that the greatest and most difficult vulnerabilities to deal with are the insider people assigned to positions of trust and privilege violating their trust and outside people acquiring a position of trust to violate systems. The use of cloud computing and virtual systems is opening the door to more and greater vulnerabilities and increased complexity that hides vulnerabilities. Potential victims are forced to trust unknown people and systems out there in the cloud that they have little control over in performing their applications and sending and receiving data and instructions.

Security has always been at a disadvantage because of the asymmetric relationship between the adversaries and victims. Millions of potential adversaries have only one vulnerability that they create or exploit while the victims, not able to know what unknown adversaries are doing, must defend against attacks on all of their vulnerabilities. This includes the unknown vulnerabilities that they must discover and mitigate before adversaries discover and take advantage of them. Security is like playing a game in which your unknown intelligent opponents know your vulnerabilities and are making up the rules and keeping them secret as the game advances. You are not going to win under those conditions.

So what are victims to do? They can successfully stop or mitigate most of the frequent losses that they are unable to bear with available security. And with the currently accepted risk-based security strategy they try to identify, predict, and assess the risks of the perpetrators' more rare wrongdoings attempting to make good security decisions, justify investments, and set priorities to expend their limited resources to mitigate or eliminate the risks to an acceptable level. This obviously has not worked considering the mounting losses and underfunding of security efforts. Attempting to reduce the supposedly greatest risks merely causes adversaries to change their tactics to attack other vulnerabilities and create new and even greater risks, some of which the defenders are unaware of or have assigned to a low priority. When they install a new safeguard, has risk been reduced? There is no valid way to determine how risk has changed or the effect of the new safeguard. Because, if no attacks occur after installation, there is no conclusion to be reached about whether the risk was reduced, eliminated, or mitigated. The risk may have been increased for all we know, and if nothing bad happens, is the money spent for security wasted? If the attacks being mitigated don't occur, it is not possible to know whether increases or decreases of different attacks and increased or decreased risk are the result. If the attacks being mitigated still occur, you don't know how effective or ineffective the new safeguard is because you don't know what the adversary has done to counter or avoid it. After installation of new security the game has been changed in unknown ways, and there is a new environment and new rules and risks that users and stakeholders must adapt to. It is a losing battle, and the generally accepted but inadequate, incomplete, and invalid risk assessments and subsequent risk reduction strategy are the cause of the problem.

There is no complete or adequate solution. All of us including users, stakeholders, and security experts continue to be victims in this losing battle. Therefore, we must adopt a strategy of at least reducing this immeasurable problem in more effective ways. We can attempt to identify many of the risks and understand some of them, and we know the formula to estimate the future frequencies and impacts, but we don't have sufficient information about the potential adversaries and their plans to achieve valid risk estimates; so the next best thing is to adopt a different strategy to reduce the problem to a defensible position. Then when and if we suffer a loss, at the very least we can claim that we were diligent and met the requirements of state-of-the-art information security. We did the best that we could under the circumstances.

It is important that you know the risk-based concept of information security as described in this book. It is the prevailing methodology practiced for the past 40 years and is required by law, regulators, auditors, contracts, and many well-known security experts even though it has never been publicly demonstrated to be valid or effective (a sad commentary.) I propose that we abandon what I claim to be unworkable risk-based security and make no attempt to beat the potential adversaries at their unknown games. We must force them to play the game we want to play by our rules. I believe that we must abandon risk-based security and apply diligence, compliance, and enablement to advance security. I have done this successfully for more than 40 years. Diligence is based on facts, not on uncertain probabilities, including our and others' loss experience; vulnerability analysis; and developing, purchasing, and effectively installing generally accepted and experimental safeguards that are broad in their applications. Secondly, compliance with standards, laws, regulators, and auditors is necessary to avoid increasingly severe penalties. And third, apply enablement that is the security enhancement of products and services driven by competition. These three strategies that I include under the rubric of diligence at least challenges the potential adversaries, tends to make them fail, reduces errors and omissions, and possibly makes the perpetrators' attack efforts more costly than what they might gain (except for the many irrational perpetrators for which much of any strategy will rarely be successful). Adversaries are then more likely to pursue other, easier targets to solve their personal problems or advance their criminal livelihoods. And diligence leaves us in more defensible positions based on facts when losses do occur.

Regarding our technological safeguards, we need to move as much of the security as possible, such as cryptographic protection and firewalls, from vulnerable software into firmware and hardware where it is out of reach of perpetrators and transparent to users. Here is an example of one effort that had mixed results that provides important insights. Computer scientists at MIT and Honeywell (later acquired by General Electric) discovered and developed the design of a provably secure multi-access expandable computer system in 1964 called Multics. Security was encapsulated in a small operating system kernel that could be proven to have no vulnerabilities surrounded by a series of rings, each with its own security structure and leakage prevention from one ring to another. During many months of testing the prototype, a group of assigned U.S. Air Force computer hackers, as part of its development, led by Roger Schell routinely compromised the system almost weekly. Their successes were not based on the Multics' secure design (which everybody accepted as perfectly secure) but relied on the vulnerabilities left in the code from programming errors and shortcuts. When these problems were fixed, the system was virtually impregnable as far as the intensive testing could reasonably carry it out. Unfortunately, Multics was not a commercial success for several reasons. The product couldn't be maintained and serviced at the same sufficiently secure level in the field. The perfect security gradually deteriorated and the cost of production and attempts to maintain security were not competitive at the time, and there was one other insurmountable problem illustrated by the following incident. A large manufacturer installed a GE Multics system, and the users found the security too restrictive and difficult to use; so they gradually shut off most of the security features until they became happy with the results and ease of use. Management was happy with Multics because they had the most secure computer in the world, the users were happy with an easy-to-use system, but the auditors were the most unhappy people who saw what was going on. There are significant insights about the human side of security in this incident. The last Multics system was decommissioned in 2000.

After considering the failure of our risk-based strategy, the benefits of diligence-based security, and advances with technology-based security solutions, there remains possibly the most important and vulnerable aspect of security challenges. This is the role that humans play in making security work effectively. Whether in the context of diligence or risk management approaches, we must develop and increase the motives of all users and stakeholders to support the developed technological safeguards and especially to comply with rules-based safeguards. I include such rules addressing password usage, authentication, segregation of duties, avoidance of shoulder surfing, correct information classification, social engineering resistance, control over possession and content of mobile devises and flash memories, and so forth.

The greatest vulnerabilities arise because of the failure of human participation in protection. Security safeguards are often in place but ineffective because they interfere with stakeholders' job performance and cause them disliked and seemingly unneeded extra efforts such as secreting and using weak passwords, unauthorized obtaining of authority to use sensitive information, and limiting others from gaining and using information that they are not supposed to have. We all hate the constraints of security and secrecy in our work especially when we are not experiencing losses. Therefore, we take shortcuts around the safeguards and ignore the rules making them ineffective. If security is to be effective at all, it must become enthusiastically supported and a part of job performance with proper incentives instead of being in conflict with job performance. Every position of trust must include security responsibilities in its job description and must be a line item in every periodic performance review with real rewards and punishments. Violations of security must be confronted in effective ways, and rewards for exemplary security practice must be provided to motivate stakeholders and users. We must use both the carrot and the stick. Motivation must be established before any security awareness program will be successful. Otherwise, we are simply giving stakeholders and users information on how to avoid or overcome security. And part of the motivation and awareness that we need to promote should include urging stakeholders to read and refer to an excellent book such as this one.

ACKNOWLEDGMENTS

We would like to thank a few of the many who have enabled us to create this book. First, our editors at Cengage/Course Technology who have allowed us to propose and then execute this project. We appreciate the leap of faith required to move from textbooks to a trade/professional book. We would also like to thank Dr. Carola L. Mattord for here consultation on rhetorical approaches and some extensive help with the organization and structure of many of the chapters.

Any of the elements of this book that we get right are, no doubt, from the hard work and support of our team. Any errors or omissions are due to our own shortcomings. Also, thanks to Richard Austin for his interesting stories and broad perspective on the subject at hand.

A special thanks to Donn Parker for his foreword and his personal example of how to create a solid career in field of information security.

Overview of the Information Security Landscape

Part I of *Roadmap* will provide you with background information about this critical program in today's organizations. The following three chapters will explain the underlying basics of information security and why it has become a necessary component in business strategies across the country. If you are unfamiliar with the development and/or management of an InfoSec program, we highly recommend that you read all the chapters of Part I carefully before continuing to the more technical parts of this book because these will assume your knowledge of the terminology and standard InfoSec business practices. The chapters in Part I are intended to provide you with an overview of today's information security landscape. They will explain:

▸ information security and its terminology;

▸ guidelines for creating an organizational hierarchy based on InfoSec;

▸ an overview of threats to an organization's assets; and

▸ an overview of attacks on an organization's assets.

For those more familiar with InfoSec, the following chapters can be used as a reference tool on the issues that information security managers are currently facing when developing an InfoSec program.

Part Overview

Chapter 1—"Information Security" provides key terms and concepts essential to understanding information security in the organization. It will offer you guidelines to the creation of an organizational hierarchy based on InfoSec.

Chapter 2—"Risk Management and Information Assets" examines the various threats facing today's organizations and presents the process of ranking these threats in order to provide relative priority as the organization begins its security planning process.

Chapter 3—"Attacks on Information Assets" provides a detailed examination of the types of attacks that can occur based on these threats and their possible economic impact on the health of the organization and its information and systems.

Chapter **1**

Information Security

In today's global markets, the lifeblood of business operations is the information carried by a seemingly seamless network of technologies that enables its collection and use. But what happens when this informational flow is interrupted, even for just a little while? Business deals fall through, shipments are lost, customers leave, and business success suddenly eludes our grasp. Since the development of computer technology, the business manager's response to information flow problems has been to proclaim, "We have technology people to handle these problems!" This response might have been valid in the days when computer technology was confined to the glass-walled rooms of a centralized data processing facility. In the past twenty years, however, information and its supporting technology have been decentralized and now occupy every corner of the business environment. Today, business is conducted wherever employees and customers are located: from offices, in coffee shops in remote cities, from home, or even online in the virtual ether. Since conducting business has become more ubiquitous, the concept of *computer security* has evolved into the concept of *information security*. This new concept covers a broader range of issues than in the days of computer security. Information security is no longer the sole responsibility of an elite group of technology professionals; rather, it has become the joint responsibility of everyone in the organization, managers and employees alike.

Today's astute business managers increasingly recognize the importance of information security as the shield protecting the organization's critical information assets. In light of this growing awareness, businesses are creating managerial and technical positions to deal with information security issues. The emergence of technical managers, for example, allows for the creation of professionally managed information security teams whose main objective is the protection of an organization's information assets. In the current global climate, organizations are realizing that information security planning and budgeting must be added to the daily decision-making process and must not be limited to technical managers, such as information security managers or members of the information security team, but must include all levels of business management and employees with varying degrees of responsibility. Developing and managing a successful information security program can be a puzzle for many professionals when newly thrust into an information security role. As a newly promoted security manager or an IT manager with fresh accountabilities in the information security areas, you will find in this chapter explanation of information security and its terminology and explanations about the dynamics of the three communities of interest and the relationship among key managers and employees responsible for the organization's business practices.

Chapter Overview:

▶ Information security defined
▶ Critical terminology of information security

INFORMATION SECURITY DEFINED

Today, the general term **security** is defined as a quality or state of being secure—which means to be free from danger. However, most information security professionals would gladly delete that definition as it assumes that it is possible to achieve some ideal state where an organization and its assets are secure from all possible dangers at all times and in all places. In reality, information security is a never-ending process—a balancing act between the need to secure the information assets and the need to conduct business without any hindrances overshadowed by a limited set of human and financial resources. Within these limits of organizational objectives and resources, the risks to the organization's information assets must be mitigated to a level acceptable to management and its stakeholders. The term **information security (InfoSec)** assumes this balancing act as the protection of information and its critical elements, including the systems and hardware that use, store, and transmit that information, through the application of policy, training and awareness programs, and technology in order to balance as best as possible the need to secure and the need to gain access to the organization's assets.

CRITICAL TERMINOLOGY OF INFORMATION SECURITY

As in any other area of business, information security has its own terminology. Terms, such as *risk*, *asset*, and *threat*, for example, are applied to information security somewhat differently than their familiar use found in financial and/or general business practices. The following glossary, presented in Tables 1-1 and 1-2, will help you to navigate through the terminology as it applies to information security in general, as well as in its technical application. Each of the terms will be covered in later chapters with more detailed information and examples. At the end of the glossary, you will find Figure 1-1 illustrating some of these basic terms and their relation to one another as they are used in information security processes.

TABLE 1-1 General Terms

TERM	DEFINITION
Accountability	exists when a control provides assurance that every activity undertaken can be attributed to a named person or automated process. Accountability is often associated with auditability. For example, a database log that tracks each update or inserted record or deleted record and records who performed each activity might provide satisfactory accountability.
Asset	is the organization's possession or thing of value that the organization wants to (or must) protect. Assets can be physical objects, such as the accounts receivable database, or more abstract things, such as an organization's reputation or stock price. Assets are tied to (or valued by) owners whom the organization holds responsible for their appropriate use and protection.
Attack	means an act that takes advantage of a *vulnerability* to damage, steal, disclose, render unusable or available, or modify without the authorization of an asset.
Authenticity	the information must be real. What if a regulatory agency received two differing sets of financial records for a company? Authenticity would assure them which set was the real set of records.
Availability	is the characteristic of information that enables user access to information without interference or obstruction and in a useable format. Since the *integrity* and *confidentiality* of the asset must be protected, along with reducing its *vulnerabilities* to *threats* that can mount *attacks*, availability does not imply that the information is accessible to any user; rather, it means that the asset is available only to authorized users. In order to understand this concept more fully, consider access to the contents of a library—in particular, research libraries that require identification for access to the library as a whole or to certain collections. Library patrons must present the required identification before gaining access to the collection. Once patrons are granted access, they expect to be able to locate the resources easily and efficiently.
CIA triplet	are the three characteristics of information that give it value: *confidentiality*, *integrity*, and *availability*. Noted author Donn B. Parker adds three additional attributes: *utility*, *authenticity*, and *possession*.
Confidentiality	ensures that only those with authorization and a business-relevant need are allowed access to the *assets*. Confidentiality is breached when unauthorized individuals or systems can view information. To protect the confidentiality of information, a number of measures are used, including information classification, secure document storage, application of general security policies, education of information custodians and end users, and cryptography (encryption). Confidentiality of information is important for the protection of personal information about employees, customers, or patients. Not preserving confidential information can destroy the reputation of an organization and put it in danger of regulatory fines and serious litigation.

(continued)

TERM	DEFINITION
Countermeasures	are the methods imposed to mitigate (or reduce the effect of) *vulnerabilities*. A countermeasure, also known as a control, may be a logical measure, such as an acceptable use policy for company e-mail, or a hardware device, such as a firewall that makes it more difficult to gain unauthorized access to a network.
Integrity	is the quality or state of being whole, complete, and uncorrupted. A *threat* to the integrity of the *asset* occurs when it is exposed to corruption, damage, destruction, or other disruption of its authentic state. The corruption of a file does not necessarily result from deliberate *attacks*. An asset is *vulnerable* to corruption when it is simply being entered, stored, or transmitted during day-to-day processing. Faulty programming or even noise in the transmission channel or media can also cause data to lose its integrity. The key method for detecting an integrity failure of a file system from an *attack* by a virus or worm is to look for changes in the file's state as indicated by the file's size, or in a more advanced operating system, the file's *hash value* or checksum.
Possession	means control over the data or *asset* and is subtly different from *confidentiality*. Unlike confidentiality, possession deals with who has the information and, therefore, must assure its confidentiality. For example, a company can buy a client list, which means that once the client list is bought, the company has possession over it. But, only certain employees within that company will be authorized to have access to it, thereby ensuring the data's confidentiality from all other employees, or visitors, or any other individual unconnected with the company.
Privacy	means that when data is collected, used, and stored by an organization, it can only be used for the purposes stated by the data owner at the time it was collected. It governs what the organization can or cannot do with the information given. Privacy is often confused with *confidentiality*. Privacy is concerned with **uses** of the data, whereas confidentiality is concerned with the **access** to the data. For example, a company must respect the mandates of its customer if that customer does not wish its information (phone number, address, annual budget, etc.) to be sold to another company. In this instance, a breach of privacy would occur if the company sold the information of its customer without the customer's approval.
Risk	is the probability of an unwanted or undesirable event occurring, commonly used as an expression of potential loss. Risk is usually addressed through the implementation of controls; by transferring it to a third party, as in insurance or managed security services; by mitigating the damage if a loss occurs through effective contingency planning; or if the asset doesn't warrant additional protection, through simple acceptance. Residual risk is the risk that remains after all prudent measures have been taken. Risk appetite is the amount of risk the organization is willing to live with after it has completed a formal risk management program.
Threat	is a category of possible "bad things" that can happen to an *asset*. The use of the term *threat* means that the action has not yet occurred, but that the possibility of it occurring is within reason and experience (known as risk). The threat is different from the threat agent in that the hacker, for example, is the *threat agent*, but the threat (as defined here) is the action of the hacker. Therefore, the possible action of a hacker to gain access to an organization's internal network to delete critical tables is the threat to the asset(s), and not the hacker who is the agent of such a threat. Another example: A tornado is classified as the *threat agent*; its ferocious ability to wipe out a manufacturing plant is then classified as the *threat*.
Threat agents	are specific actors of threat categories, including but not limited to human attackers who seek to access or damage *assets* for financial gain or other reasons. Threat agents can also take other forms, such as forces of nature that might cause power outages, or a construction crew that unintentionally cuts the main network link to an ISP causing a network outage. *Assets* and *threats* are related to one another by risk—the assessment of how likely a particular "bad thing" (threat) is to occur and its resulting impact to some asset(s).

TERM	DEFINITION
Utility	means that the data must be available in a useful form. For example, consider an encrypted disk file. If the keying information required for decryption is lost or destroyed, the information is not useable even though you still have the disk file.
Vulnerabilities	are the "windows of opportunity" that allow threats to become a reality and affect assets. While many only think of technical vulnerabilities, such as defects in software, a vulnerability is a much broader concept that includes things such as failures in processes (deploying a firewall appliance with vendor default passwords in place). Another example: A vulnerability occurs when an employee continuously leaves unattended a sheet of paper with computer passwords on the desk, thereby allowing visitors easy access to these protections of the assets.

Course Technology/Cengage Learning

TABLE 1-2 Technical Terms

TERM	DEFINITION
Authentication	occurs when a control provides proof that a user possesses the *identification* that he or she claims. Examples include the use of cryptographic certificates, or the use of cryptographic hardware tokens like SecurID cards from RSA Security to confirm an identity.
Authorization	is a process that ensures that the user (person or a computer) has been specifically and explicitly authorized by the proper authority to perform an action. An example of this control is the activation and use of access control lists and authorization groups in a networking environment. Another example is a database authorization scheme to verify that the user of an application is authorized for specific functions, such as read, write, create, and delete.
File hashing	ensures information *integrity*. It is a special algorithm that evaluates the bits in a file and then computes a single representative number called a *hash value*; that is, essentially converting a variable length input into a fixed-length output, typically ranging from 56 to 256 bits.
Hash value	is the value resulting from a hashing calculation and will be different for each combination of bits. If the computer system performs the same hashing algorithm on the file and arrives at a different number each time than the file's recorded hash value, then the *integrity* of the file has been compromised.
HIDS	is an acronym for host intrusion detection system. These are devices installed on a computer system that monitor the status of files stored on that system to protect them from *attacks*. This technology is sometimes referred to as a host intrusion detection and prevention systems (HIDPS).
Identification	means that an information system is able to recognize individual users. Identification is the first step in gaining access to secured data, and it serves as the foundation for subsequent *authentication* and *authorization*. Identification and authentication are essential to establishing the level of access or authorization that an individual is granted. Identification is typically performed by means of a user name or other ID.
NIDS	is the acronym for network intrusion detection system. It is a collection of devices that work together to monitor and assess network activity for possible *attacks*.

Course Technology/Cengage Learning

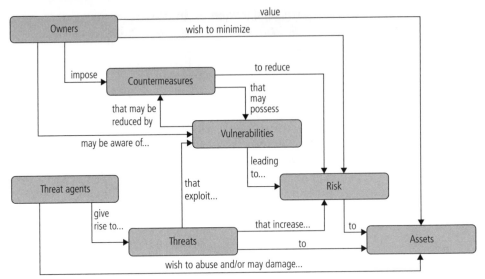

Figure 1-1 Security Terms and their Relationships
Course Technology/Cengage Learning

The Responsibility for Information Security

The process of securing information assets of an organization should involve three distinct groups of decision makers, or **communities of interest**:

▶ Information security managers and professionals
▶ Information technology managers and professionals
▶ Nontechnical general business managers and professionals

Through a process of organized communications, these three professional groups work to achieve consensus on an overall plan to protect the organization's information assets from threats and attacks.

The communities of interest fulfill the following roles:

▶ The **information security community** guides the protection of the organization's information assets from the many threats they face.
▶ The **information technology community** supports the business objectives of the organization by supplying and supporting information technology appropriate to the business's needs.
▶ The nontechnical **general business community** is focused on achieving the organization's objectives (making a profit, remaining competitive, in other words, "running the business"). In the final analysis, it is this community that largely controls the information security program through its setting of overall policy goals and control of the budget.

Working together, these communities of interest make collective decisions about how to most effectively secure an organization's information assets.

Information Security Categories

A successful information security program relies on several specialized areas that are perceived by many as separate business objectives. In fact, each of these categories work together to deliver a security net that collectively protects the organization's information assets. These categories are:

- **Physical security** encompasses strategies to protect people, physical assets, and the workplace from various threats including fire, unauthorized access, or natural disasters.
- **Operations security** focuses on securing the organization's ability to carry out its operational activities without interruption or compromise.
- **Communications security** encompasses the protection of an organization's communications media, technology, and content, and its ability to use these tools to achieve the organization's objectives.
- **Network security** addresses the protection of an organization's data networking devices, connections, and contents, and the ability to use that network to accomplish the organization's data communication functions.
- **Database security** encompasses the specific concerns arising from the storage of large amounts of information in a database store.
- **Storage security** deals with the specialized techniques for securing information stored in storage area networks (or SANs).

A Model for an Information Security Program

In the United States, the Committee on National Security System (CNSS) security model has become the comprehensive model of information security. Also known as the McCumber Cube after its developer John McCumber, this model is described in CNSS documents (see www .cnss.gov) and is illustrated in Figure 1-2. This figure shows the three dimensions central to the development of an information security program. The McCumber Cube is a 3 by 3 by 3 cube with 27 cells. Each of these cells represents an area of intersection among these three dimensions that must be addressed in any information security program. When using this model, you must make sure that each of the 27 cells is properly addressed by each of the three communities of

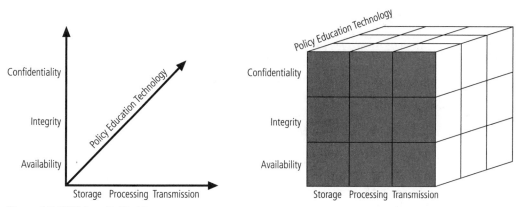

Figure 1-2 CNSS Security Model

Source: NSTISSC Security Model NSTISSI No. 4011 National Training Standard for Information Security (InfoSec) Professionals (see http://www.nsa.gov/ia/academia/cnsstesstandards.cfm)

interest. For example, the cell representing the intersection between the technology, integrity, and storage areas is expected to include controls or safeguards addressing the use of technology to protect the integrity of information while in storage. Such a control might consist of a host intrusion detection system (HIDS), which alerts the security administrators when a critical file is modified.

The main purpose of this model is to identify gaps in the coverage of an information security program. While the CNSS model covers the three dimensions of information security, it omits any discussion of detailed guidelines and policies that direct the implementation of information security controls. For this reason, merely having technical controls, policies, or education programs in place is inadequate. Another weakness of this model is when it is viewed from a single perspective. For example, the HIDS control that was described earlier addresses only the needs and concerns of the information security community without considering the needs and concerns of the broader IT and general business communities. In practice, thorough risk reduction requires that controls of all three types (policy, education, and technical) be created and communicated among all three communities of interest. These controls can come about only through a process that includes consensus building and constructive conflict to reflect the balancing act that each organization faces as it designs and executes an information security program.

The Information Security Manager's Checklist

At the end of each chapter, you will be provided with a checklist, such as the following one. Each checklist will highlight the major actions and deliverables necessary for the execution of those components found in that chapter. In general, the checklist is designed like this:

	No	Planned	In Progress	In Place	Integrated
This topic has been fully tested, validated, and integrated into organizational operations with formal performance measures in place (as appropriate).					
This topic has been implemented, but not fully tested, validated, and integrated into organizational operations.					
The implementation of this topic has begun, but is not yet complete.					
The formal planning for this topic has begun, but is not yet complete.					
This subject has not formally begun planning, or the organization has made a conscious decision not to pursue this topic.					
1. Subject					
Item 1					
Item 2					
Item 3					
. . .					

Your periodic review of the checklist should help you measure your program's progress toward the right-hand side of the list—indicating a move from a lack of critical security management tasks to a completely integrated, tested, and validated security management system. For the details on how to accomplish each item in the checklist, refer to the accompanying chapter.

For Further Reading

Fighting Computer Crime: A New Framework for Protecting Information by Donn B. Parker, Wiley, 1998.

Beyond Fear: Thinking Sensibly About Security in an Uncertain World by Bruce Schneier, Springer, 2003.

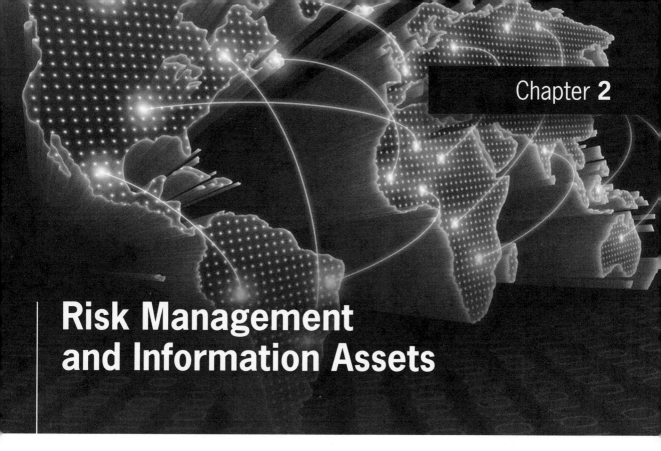

Chapter 2

Risk Management and Information Assets

Chapter 1 introduced information security and a simple program model—the McCumber Cube. Key considerations were addressed, such as critical terminology of information security, the responsibility for information security, and information security categories. Since information security is about the protection of the company's information assets, it requires a balancing act between defining and maintaining the various protections of assets, organizational needs to have uninterrupted access to those assets and limited resources. But in order for you to define and determine the balance of information security that is right for your company, it is important to become informed about the many hazards that your company can face and what can be done in order to minimize the risks these hazards represent to your company's information assets.

When we discuss the many hazards to the company's information assets, we are discussing what has been defined in this field as *risk*. Risk management is fundamental to any information security program. At its core are the identification of the many hazards that must be assessed and the determination of actions to be taken on account of these hazards in order to develop an information security program that minimizes possible disruptions. Experts in the field of information security have categorized and defined these hazards that face the company's information assets. Two major categories of risk are threats and attacks. This chapter will address threats. Chapter 3 will address attacks.

Chapter Overview:

▶ What is a threat?

▶ Threat categories

WHAT IS A THREAT?

As an information security manager it is important to understand that threats to your company's information assets are present 24/7 and that there is never a time when a threat is not present. That is why assessing threats and their hazard potential is one of the crucial cornerstones to any form of risk assessment. Recalling from Chapter 1, a threat can be any of one or more objects, persons, or other entities that has the potential to cause loss to the value or usability of an asset. Categorizing the types of threats facing the assets is the first step toward proactive planning and design of an information security program that works well with the business flow of your company. When considering risk to information assets, it is important to create a threat assessment that includes the specific threats facing your organization and the potential losses they represent. Based on your threat assessment, you will then put into place the necessary controls (managers, employees, policies and practices, and/or technology) that can hinder or minimize the damage to an asset, thereby saving your company time, energy, and money for recovery efforts.

THREAT CATEGORIES

While each organization's identification of threats will vary, in general, threats are well-documented and are well understood. In order for you to make good decisions concerning the identification and assessment of risks to your company, the following categorizations of various threats enable you to make sound business decisions based on their respective hazard potential. Your assessment of the specific threats represented by these categories will help you to determine necessary policy and practices for your organization, distribution of responsibility among managers and employees, budgeting, and acquisition or maintenance of the necessary technology controls. The following scheme consists of twelve general categories that represent real and present dangers to an organization's information and systems. These categories are listed with examples in Table 2-1 and described in more detail in Table 2-2. Some types of threats are shown in Figure 2-1.

Who is the biggest threat to your organization?

Dick Davis a.k.a.
"W4NN4_B_1337"

Harriet Allthumbs –
the employee who
accidentally deleted
the one copy of a
critical report

Tom Twostory
convicted burglar

Figure 2-1 Internal vs. External Threats
Course Technology/Cengage Learning

TABLE 2-1 Threats to Information Security[1]

CATEGORIES OF THREAT	EXAMPLES
1. Acts of human error or failure	Accidents, employee mistakes
2. Violations of intellectual property	Piracy, copyright infringement
3. Acts of trespass and espionage	Unauthorized access and/or data collection
4. Acts of information extortion	Blackmail or information disclosure
5. Acts of sabotage or vandalism	Destruction of systems or information
6. Acts of theft	Illegal confiscation of equipment or information
7. Software threats	Viruses, worms, macros, denial of service
8. Forces of nature	Fire, flood, earthquake, lightning
9. Deviations in services	ISP, power, or WAN service issues
10. Hardware failures or errors	Equipment failure
11. Software failures or errors	Bugs, code problems, unknown loopholes
12. Technological obsolescence	Antiquated or outdated technologies

Course Technology/Cengage Learning

TABLE 2-2 Description of Threat Categories

THREAT CATEGORY	DESCRIPTION
Acts of human error or failure	include acts performed without intent or malicious purpose by an authorized user. Inexperience, improper training, the making of incorrect assumptions, as well as the failure to follow specifications, policies, and regulations can turn the best of employees into threat-agents. Their mistakes can be a threat to the confidentiality, integrity, and availability of data—even, as Figure 2-1 suggests, relative to threats from outsiders. Leaving classified information in unprotected areas, such as a desk or desktop, Web site—even a trash can—poses as much a threat to the protection of the information asset as does the individual who intentionally seeks to exploit the information.

(continued)

THREAT CATEGORY	DESCRIPTION
Risk assessment of this category should include:	What is the state of information security training for all employees? Does the organization have clearly written policies and procedures? Does senior management support these polices? Are there ongoing awareness activities? What is the state of the technology controls that impact IT usage and quality assurance in the workplace?
Violations of intellectual property	is defined as "the ownership of ideas and control over the tangible or virtual representation of those ideas. Use of another person's intellectual property may or may not involve royalty payments or permission, but should always include proper credit to the source."[2] Intellectual property can include trade secrets, copyrights, trademarks, and patents. The unauthorized appropriation of a company's intellectual property constitutes a threat to information security. Software piracy is one of the most ubiquitous infractions of intellectual property today. Software licenses are strictly enforced by a number of regulatory and private organizations. In addition to the laws against software piracy, two watchdog organizations investigate allegations of software abuse: Software & Information Industry Association (SIIA) at www.siia.net and the Business Software Alliance (BSA) at www.bsa.org. A BSA survey in May 2006 revealed that as much as a third of all software in use globally is pirated.
Risk assessment of this category should include:	Are there established policies and procedures concerning the proper channels for the acquisition of company software and hardware? Does the organization comply with applicable end-user license agreements (EULA)?
Acts of trespass and espionage	is a well-known and broad category of electronic and human activity that can breach the confidentiality of information. Threat-agents use many different methods to access the information assets. Some use techniques that are quite legal, for example, using a Web browser to perform market research. These legal techniques are called **competitive intelligence**. When threat-agents employ techniques that cross the threshold of the legal or ethical boundary, they are conducting **industrial espionage**. Some forms of espionage are relatively low-tech. One example is **shoulder surfing**, an activity used in public or semipublic settings by unauthorized people who are looking over the shoulder of the authorized individual in order to gain access to the information asset from a distance. The classic perpetrator is the hacker. **Hackers** are "people who use and create computer software [to] gain access to information illegally."[3] There are generally two recognized skill levels among hackers as is shown in Figure 2-2. The first is the **expert hacker**, sometimes called an **elite hacker**, who develops software scripts and program exploits for personal use or sale to criminal organizations. The expert hacker is usually a master of several programming languages, networking protocols, and operating systems, and also exhibits a mastery of the technical environment of the chosen targeted system. The expert hacker also publicly posts intrusion technology for use by those in the second category, the **unskilled hacker**. Novice hackers act as **script kiddies**—hackers of limited skill who use expertly written software to attack a system—or **packet monkeys**—script kiddies who "ape" experts in using automated exploits to engage in distributed denial-of-service attacks. The good news is that if an expert hacker can post a script tool where a script kiddie or packet monkey can find it, then systems and security administrators can find it as well.
Risk assessment of this category should include:	Sound policies and procedures requiring authentication and authorization practices to help organizations protect valuable information and systems. These control methods and technologies employ multiple layers or factors to protect against unauthorized access—known as **defense in depth**. Are there provisions to keep the technical control systems current? The developers of defensive software and hardware and the service providers keep current on the latest exploit scripts and usually provide them to their customers.

Traditional hacker profile:
Age 13–18, male with limited
parental supervision spends all his
free time at the computer

Modern hacker profile:
Age 12–60, male or female, unknown
background, with varying technological
skill levels; may be internal or external
to the organization

Figure 2-2 The Changing Definition of the Hacker?
Course Technology/Cengage Learning

THREAT CATEGORY	DESCRIPTION
Acts of information extortion	occur when an attacker or trusted insider steals information from a computer system and demands compensation for its return, or for an agreement not to disclose the information. Extortion is common in credit card number theft and can also be carried out by malware (discussed later in this chapter) as in the case of file encryption. In this type of extortion, the user is manipulated into installing/running a piece of malware that encrypts their files (usually concentrating on commonly valuable files, such as documents, music files, and pictures). The user is then offered the decryption key in return for a monetary payment.[4]
Risk assessment of this category should include:	Are information protection technologies such as file encryption and data classification in place? Are employee background checks performed for all employees with varying degrees of thoroughness, depending on the role of the employee? Is there a periodic assessment of which persons have access to which data to maintain the principle of **least privilege**? Least privilege makes an assurance that users have access only to the information and systems required to perform their assigned duties.
Acts of sabotage or vandalism	involve the deliberate sabotage of a computer system or business, or acts of vandalism to either destroy an asset or damage the image of an organization. These acts can range from petty vandalism by employees to organized sabotage against an organization. Vandalism to a Web site can erode consumer confidence, thus reducing an organization's sales and net worth, as well as its reputation. Compared to Web site defacement, vandalism within a network is more malicious in intent and less public. Today, security experts are noticing a rise in another form of online vandalism, **hacktivist** or **cyberactivist** operations, which interfere with or disrupt systems to protest the operations, policies, or actions of an organization or government agency. A much more sinister form of hacking is **cyberterrorism**. The United States and other governments are developing security measures intended to protect the critical computing and communications networks as well as the physical and power utility infrastructure against cyberterrorism. Some industry observers have taken the position that cyberterrorism is not a real threat, and instead is merely hype that distracts from the more concrete and pressing information security issues that do need attention.[5]
Risk assessment of this category should include:	Is your organization a part of the critical infrastructure defined by the national or local government? If it is, is your organization in compliance with the regulations and standards that are applied to those systems?

(continued)

THREAT CATEGORY	DESCRIPTION
Acts of theft	are the unauthorized taking of another's property. Within an organization, property is considered to be physical, electronic, or intellectual. The property's value is diminished when it is copied and/or taken away without the owner's knowledge.
Risk assessment of this category should include:	Does the organization have sufficient controls to eliminate physical theft? These may range from locked doors to trained security personnel, to the installation of alarm systems and authentication of authorized personnel. Are there adequate controls to limit the risk from electronic theft of information?
Software threats	are those that deal with the computer programs that are developed intentionally for the purpose of damaging, destroying, or denying service to your company's systems and/or information assets and are called malicious code or malicious software, or sometimes malware. When we think of information security, we tend to think of this category before many others. Some malicious code can be defined as either a virus or a worm, while other definitions may combine the two. Malware can present itself to potential victims in a number of ways, including Trojan horses, logic bombs, and back doors. Today, the term "crimeware" better reflects the intent to conduct criminal activity resulting in financial gain for its perpetrators rather than doing damage to systems and information assets.[6] Information technology practices should be assessed to make sure the following types of software intrusion and attack are anticipated and controlled: **Computer virus**: segments of code that perform malicious actions. Similar to a viral pathogen attacking animals and plants, the computer virus attaches itself to an existing program and takes control of that program's access to the targeted computer. The virus-controlled target program then carries out the virus's plan, by replicating itself into additional targeted systems. The macro virus and the boot virus are the most common with the former automatically executing macro code used by word processors, spreadsheets, and database applications, and the latter infecting the key operating system files located in a computer's boot sector. **Worms**: named for the tapeworm in John Brunner's novel *The Shockwave Rider*, a worm is a malicious program that replicates itself independently, without requiring another program. Worms can continue replicating themselves until they completely fill available resources, such as memory, hard drive space, and network bandwidth. Modern worms combine multiple modes of attack into a single package. These worm variants often contain multiple exploits (so-called blended threats) that can use any of the many predefined infection vectors to programmatically distribute the worm. **Trojan horses**: are software programs that hide their true nature and reveal their designed behavior only when activated. Frequently disguised as helpful, interesting, or necessary pieces of software, such as readme.exe files, Trojan horses are often included with shareware or freeware packages, screensavers, video codecs, etc. Only when brought into a system will it become active. **Back Door** or **Trapdoor**: A virus or worm can have a payload that installs a back door or trapdoor component in a system, which allows the attacker to access the system at will with special privileges. Examples of these kinds of payloads include Sub7 and Back Orifice. **Polymorphism**: A polymorphic threat is one that over time changes the way it appears to antivirus software programs, making it undetectable by techniques that look for preconfigured signatures. These viruses and worms actually evolve, changing their size and other external file characteristics to elude detection by antivirus software programs.

THREAT CATEGORY	DESCRIPTION
	Rootkits: take their name from their historical development as malicious replacements for common UNIX administrative tools (thus, their name as "rootkits" since the default administrative user on a UNIX system is root). The characteristic of these modified tools was that while they appeared to function exactly as expected, they did not reveal any information about themselves. For example, the ps command will normally display a list of all running processes, but a "rootkit ps" will display all running processes, except the malicious ones included in the compromise. Rootkits are now widely available (e.g., backorifice, etc.) for most platforms and are intended to hide a malicious companion, such as a remote access facility or keylogger, from administrators and antivirus products.
	Phishing: are hybrids that combine both social engineering and malicious software. One of the very common tactics is to use spoofed e-mails from eBay, PayPal, banking sites, etc., that try to con the user into clicking on an embedded Web link that takes them to a spoofed malicious site that looks identical to the real site. The user will then enter his or her credentials to "fix an account," "validate a fraudulent charge," "reset their password," etc., and the credentials are harvested and sent to the unauthorized user. Once the user's credentials have been acquired, the unauthorized user can fraudulently order merchandise, transfer funds, etc.
	Virus and Worm Hoaxes: More time and money has been spent on resolving virus hoaxes, which are notices from well-meaning individuals who distribute e-mail warnings concerning fictitious viruses or worms. When individuals fail to follow virus-reporting procedures, the network becomes overloaded, and much time and energy is wasted as users forward the warning messages to everyone they know, post the messages on bulletin boards, and try to update their antivirus protection software. For the latest information on real threatening viruses and hoaxes, along with other relevant and current security information, visit the CERT Coordination Center at www.cert.org. For a more entertaining approach to the latest virus, worm and hoax information, visit the Urban Legend Reference Pages at *www.snopes.com/ inboxer/hoaxes/hoaxes.asp* or the Hoax Busters Web page at *hoaxbusters.ciac.org*.
Risk assessment of this category should include:	Is there adequate malicious code control at the gateway to the organization, such as spam filtering, e-mail attachment filtering, SMS text filtering, etc.? Is there adequate desktop end-point security in place, such as traditional antivirus software or some other configuration control mechanism that can detect a virus or other malware?
Forces of nature	also known as *force majeure*, or acts of God, can present some of the most dangerous threats because they usually occur with little warning and are beyond the control of people. The threats listed below can disrupt not only the lives of individuals, but also the storage, transmission, and use of information assets. Most of these threat instances can usually be mitigated with fire casualty insurance and/or business interruption insurance. The management and IT practices of the organization should be assessed to determine their ability to manage the risk from these threats from natural disasters:
	Fire: damages a building and/or computing equipment that comprises all or part of the information assets, as well as smoke damage and/or water damage from sprinkler systems or firefighters.
	Flood: The overflow of water causes direct damage to all or part of the information system, or to the building that houses all or part of the information assets.
	Earthquake: may cause stresses to foundations that could damage or destroy structures which house information assets and/or information systems. Volcanic activity is also included in this category.
	Lightning: an abrupt, discontinuous natural electric discharge in the atmosphere, lightning usually damages all or part of the information system and/or its power distribution components. It can also cause fires or other damage.

(continued)

THREAT CATEGORY	DESCRIPTION
Forces of nature (*continued*)	**Landslide or mudslide**: can directly damage all or part of the information system or, more likely, the building that houses it.
	Tornado or severe windstorm: can cause electrical disruption to the information systems, or partially or completely damage the building in which the information assets are housed.
	Hurricane or typhoon: This severe tropical storm of the Pacific usually involves heavy rains and hurricane gale forces that can cause damage to the building, disrupt electrical services, or completely destroy an organization's physical complex.
	Tsunami: caused by an underwater earthquake or volcanic eruption, these events can directly damage all or part of the information system or, more likely, the building that houses it.
	Electrostatic discharge (ESD): Usually static electricity and ESD are little more than a nuisance. Unfortunately, however, the mild static shock we receive when walking across a carpet can be costly or dangerous when it damages valuable electronic components. Static electricity can draw dust into clean-room environments or cause products to stick together.
	Dust contamination: Excessive presence of foreign material on hardware preventing normal operation or impeding function.
Risk assessment of this category can include:	Assessment of these types of forces of nature should include procedures, controls, and a disaster recovery plan aimed at minimizing the disruption of the business flow of a company. Sound policies, procedures, and regularly planned disaster avoidance activities raise awareness of these unpredictable forces. Preparation of contingency plans for continued operations, such as disaster recovery plans, business continuity plans, and incident response plans to limit losses in the face of these threats is a necessary part of an information security program.
Deviations in services	can disrupt an organization's information system since it requires the successful functioning of many interdependent support systems, including power grids, telecom networks, parts suppliers, service vendors, and even the janitorial staff and garbage haulers. Any one of these support systems can be interrupted by forces of nature, employee illnesses, or other unforeseen events. Threats that result in deviations in quality of service can manifest in attacks, such as a backhoe taking out a fiber-optic link for an ISP. This degradation of service is a form of **availability disruption**. Irregularities in Internet service, communications, and power supplies can dramatically affect the availability of information and systems.
Risk assessment of this category should include:	Are Internet service providers managed to reduce the impact to your organization from their failures? ISP failures can considerably undermine the availability of information. Many organizations have sales staff and telecommuters working at remote locations. When these off-site employees cannot contact the host systems, manual procedures must be used to continue operations. Are Web hosting service providers managed to reduce the impact to your organization from their failures? These types of services are usually arranged with an agreement providing minimum service levels known as a **Service Level Agreement (SLA)**. When a service provider fails to meet the SLA, the provider may accrue fines to cover losses incurred by the client, but these payments seldom cover the losses generated by the outage. Are basic utilities managed properly? Telephone, water, wastewater, trash pickup, cable television, natural or propane gas, and custodial services are commonly provisioned using contractors. The loss of any or all of these services can impair the business flow of an organization. Is electrical power managed to minimize losses from normal variations in service? Irregularities from power utilities are common and can lead to fluctuations, such as power excesses, power shortages, and/or power losses. When voltage levels **spike** (experience a momentary increase), or **surge** (experience a prolonged increase), the extra voltage can severely damage or destroy equipment. Equally disruptive are power shortages from a lack of available power.

THREAT CATEGORY	DESCRIPTION
	A momentary low voltage or **sag**, or a more prolonged drop in voltage, known as a **brownout**, can cause systems to shut down or reset, or otherwise disrupt availability. Complete loss of power for a moment is known as a **fault**, and a more lengthy loss as a **blackout**. Because sensitive electronic and computing equipment is vulnerable to fluctuations, controls should be applied to manage power quality. Uninterruptable power supplies (UPS) can protect against spikes and surges as well as against sags and even blackouts of limited duration.
Hardware failures or errors	are faults that occur when a manufacturer distributes equipment containing a known or unknown flaw. These defects can cause the system to perform outside of expected parameters, resulting in unreliable service or lack of availability. Some errors are terminal—that is, they result in the unrecoverable loss of the equipment. Some errors are intermittent, in that they only periodically manifest themselves, resulting in faults that are not easily repeated, and thus, equipment can sometimes stop working, or work in unexpected ways.
Risk assessment of this category should include:	Does the organization have the proper service contracts in place to manage the risk from hardware failures? As in any matter involving contracts for goods or services, consultation with a trusted expert is always recommended.
Software failures or errors	are often threats since large quantities of computer code are written, debugged, published, and sold before all their bugs are detected and resolved. Sometimes, combinations of certain software and hardware reveal new bugs. These failures range from bugs to untested failure conditions. Sometimes these bugs are not errors, but rather purposeful shortcuts left by programmers for benign or malign reasons. Collectively, shortcut access routes into programs that bypass security checks are called trapdoors and can cause serious security breaches. Software bugs are so commonplace that entire Web sites are dedicated to documenting them. Among the most often used is Bugtraq, found at *http://www.securityfocus.com*, which provides both up-to-the-minute information on the latest security vulnerabilities, and a very thorough archive of past bugs.
Risk assessment of this category should include:	Does the organization have a fully functional change management and change control process? Change management deals with the general processes used by an organization to manage change. Change control is a mechanism of coordinating changes throughout the organization to reduce the impact from technical change when systems are updated whether to meet the needs of patching for bugs or updating to meet business requirements.
Technological obsolescence	can occur when antiquated or outdated infrastructure leads to unreliable and untrustworthy systems. Management must recognize that when technology becomes outdated, there is a risk of loss of data integrity from potential attacks.
Risk assessment of this category should include:	What critical technologies are at risk from obsolescence? Organizations may want to perform an analysis of the technology currently in use. Ideally, proper planning by management should prevent technology from becoming obsolete, but when obsolescence is identified, management must take immediate action. IT professionals play a large role in the identification of probable obsolescence.

The Information Security Manager's Checklist

	No	Planned	In Progress	In Place	Integrated
This topic has been fully tested, validated, and integrated into organizational operations with formal performance measures in place (as appropriate).					
This topic has been implemented, but not fully tested, validated, and integrated into organizational operations.					
The implementation of this topic has begun, but is not yet complete.					
The formal planning for this topic has begun, but is not yet complete.					
This subject has not formally begun planning, or the organization has made a conscious decision not to pursue this topic.					
2. Threats	No	Planned	In Progress	In Place	Integrated
All threats to your information assets identified					
Threat evaluation criteria identified					
Threat evaluation criteria weighted					
Threats ranked based on criteria					

For Further Reading

Threat Modeling by Frank Swiderski and Window Snyder, Microsoft Press, 2004.

Threat Assessment and Management Strategies: Identifying the Howlers and Hunters by Frederick S. Calhoun and Stephen W. Weston J.D., CRC Press, 2008.

References

1. Michael Whitman. "Enemy at the Gates: Threats to Information Security." *Communications of the ACM*, 46(8) August 2003, pp. 91–96.

2. FOLDOC. "Intellectual Property." *FOLDOC Online*, 27 March 1997. Accessed 15 February 2007 from foldoc.org/index.cgi?query=intellectual+property

3. Merriam-Webster. "hackers." *Merriam-Webster Online*. [Cited 15 February 2004]. Available from the World Wide Web <http://www.m-w.com>

4. http://www.viruslist.com/en/weblog?weblogid=208187524 Accessed 23 June 2008.

5. April Brousseau. "Cybersecurity Threat Evaluated." *2001 MEDiA Student Group Online*. Accessed 1 February 2002 from media.sa.utoronto.ca/jup460/april.pdf

6. Markus Jakobsson and Zulfikar Ramzan. *Crimeware: Understanding New Attacks and Defense.* Upper Saddle River: Addison-Wesley, 2008.

Chapter 3

Attacks on Information Assets

This chapter explains attacks, how they occur, and the suggested courses of action to be taken in order to eliminate or minimize the damage to your company's assets. While threats represent risk (the *potential* for loss), in order for the loss to an asset to actually occur, the threat must be *accomplished* through an attack. The major difference between a threat and an attack is that the former is an attack in theory while the latter is an attack in reality. For example, the *threat* of someone breaking into the company's warehouse and stealing an asset is ever present, but an *attack* and its associated threat of loss exist when someone commits the act of breaking in. Another example of an attack on information assets is the deletion of data by an employee, either intentional or unintentional. An intentional attack, for example, is when an angry employee deletes all the payroll files in retaliation for not having received an expected raise in salary. An unintentional attack is when an employee hits delete instead of cancel and current payroll data has been lost. In either case, the attack caused damage or loss of information assets, and these types of situations need to be evaluated during the threat assessment phase that was discussed in Chapter 2 and a plan developed to eliminate or minimize such damage or losses during an attack.

As the above examples indicate, attacks usually occur when an individual or application causes loss to an asset. These can range from an unauthorized user pretending to be a "confused new employee" calling the help desk to get a password, to various types of malware that are intended to subvert information systems in various ways, to an individual physically breaking into the company and stealing data and/or other organization assets. Understanding common attack modes is critical toward the formulation of an information security program as these determine the characteristics of the controls that must be implemented in order to ensure the protection of the company's information assets. Your prioritized threat assessment will help you with determining the most likely instances of when and how attacks will occur and producing a reasonable budget, as well as policies and procedures that will address these areas of concern for your company.

Chapter Overview:

▶ Attacks, exploits, and vulnerabilities

ATTACKS, EXPLOITS, AND VULNERABILITIES

An **attack** is the act that takes advantage of a vulnerability to compromise an asset, thus resulting in a loss. It is accomplished by a **threat–agent** that denies, damages, or steals an organization's information or physical asset. A **vulnerability** is an identified weakness in a system, where controls are not present or not effective, or have become obsolete. Table 3-1 presents information about attacks, exploits and vulnerabilities.

TABLE 3-1 Attacks, Exploits, and Vulnerabilities

ATTACK	DESCRIPTION
Malicious code (or malware)	is an attack program that exploits multiple vulnerabilities in commonly used software. Malicious code also makes use of polymorphism, or the ability to assume multiple forms (e.g., by varying their "packers"), in order to evade the signature-based detection used by many anti-malware products.[1] A malware infection is not static. It spreads to other systems using a variety of infection vectors: ▶ *IP scan and attack*—the infected system scans a random or local range of IP addresses and targets any of several vulnerabilities known to hackers or left over from previous exploits such as Code Red, Back Orifice, or PoizonBox. ▶ *Web browsing*—if the infected system has write access to any Web pages, it makes all Web content files (.html, .asp, .cgi, and others) infectious, so that users who browse to those pages become infected. Also known as a "drive-by infection." ▶ *Virus*—each infected machine infects certain common executable or script files on all computers to which it can write with virus code that can cause infection. ▶ *Unprotected shares*—using vulnerabilities in file systems and the way many organizations configure them, the infected machine copies the viral component to all locations it can reach. ▶ *Mass mail*—by sending e-mail infections to addresses found in the address book, the infected machine infects many users, whose mail-reading programs also automatically run the program and infect other systems.

ATTACK	DESCRIPTION
	Other forms of malware include covert software applications—bots, spyware, and adware. A **bot** (an abbreviation of robot) is "an automated software program that executes certain commands when it receives a specific input. Bots are often the technology used to implement Trojan horses, logic bombs, back doors, and spyware."[2] **Spyware** is "any technology that aids in gathering information about a person or organization without their knowledge.... The various types of spyware include (1) a Web bug, a tiny graphic on a Web site that is referenced within the Hypertext Markup Language (HTML) content of a Web page or e-mail to collect information about the user viewing the HTML content; (2) a tracking cookie, which is placed on the user's computer to track the user's activity on different Web sites and create a detailed profile of the user's behavior."[3] **Adware**—"any software program intended for marketing purposes such as that used to deliver and display advertising banners or popups to the user's screen or tracking the user's online usage or purchasing activity."[4] Each of these hidden code components can be used to collect information from or about the user, which could then be used in a social engineering or identity theft attack.
Suggested controls:	The obvious controls are good vulnerability management (e.g., installing patches on a regular basis), up-to-date antivirus, anti-spyware, etc., but there are also policy and awareness controls that guide user's behavior (e.g., don't click on links in e-mails).
Hoaxes with an attached virus	are a more devious attack on computer systems since the transmission of a virus hoax also adds a social engineering aspect to the attack to get the victim to act along *with a real virus attached*. When the attack is masked in a seemingly legitimate message, unsuspecting users more readily distribute it. Even though these users are trying to do the right thing to avoid infection, they end up sending the attack on to their coworkers and friends and infecting many users along the way.
Suggested controls:	As noted for malware with an emphasis on awareness activities.
Back doors	are used by an attacker to can gain access to a system or network resource through a software feature that bypasses ordinary security controls. Sometimes these entries are left behind by system designers or maintenance staff, and may be called trapdoors.[5] A trapdoor is hard to detect, because very often the programmer who puts it in place also makes the access exempt from the usual audit logging features of the system. As noted in Chapter 2, many trapdoors utilize rootkit technologies to hide themselves from detection. Attackers may choose to install their own back door into a system once it has been compromised to make the return to control of the system easier on subsequent visits.
Suggested controls:	Policy controls that forbid trapdoors in production code and proper awareness training to make the policies effective.
Password attacks	are those attacks that exploit weaknesses in authentication practices that rely on passwords for authentication. Many systems store user passwords in hashed files, the Windows SAM file being one example. If attackers discover these hashed files, they may be able to learn the passwords contained in these files. By gaining access to one system through breaching password protection, an attacker may be able to use the same information to gain access to other systems, creating a domino effect in system breach. Three of the more common types of password attacks are **password cracking**, **brute force attacks**, and **dictionary attacks**.

Password attacks are rarely successful against systems that have adopted the manufacturers' recommended security practices. |

(continued)

ATTACK	DESCRIPTION
Suggested controls:	Avoid *password cracking*—an attempt to reverse-calculate a password—by protecting your password hash files and using password salting values. If a password file is "unsalted," it is easy to reverse the hash into the corresponding password. A randomly chosen candidate password is hashed using the same algorithm and compared to the hashed results. If they are the same, the password has been cracked. By using a constant value for each organization called a salting value, an attacker must know the salting value in advance in order to perform password cracking. A newer technique to crack passwords uses precomputed "rainbow tables" developed by cryptographer Philippe Oecshlin.[6] The tables are made up of precomputed hashes for password sequences and allow very rapid matching of a hash value to its source. The use of salt values eliminates the rainbow table attack method.
	Avoid *brute force*—an attempt to try every possible combination of options for a password—by putting controls in place that limit the number of unsuccessful access attempts allowed per unit of elapsed time are very effective against brute force attacks. If attackers can narrow the field of target accounts, they can devote more time and resources to these accounts. That is one reason to always change the manufacturer's default passwords before placing a software or hardware product into production.
	Avoid *dictionary attack*—a variation of the brute force attack that narrows the field selecting specific target accounts and using a list of commonly used passwords (the dictionary) instead of random combinations—by disallowing passwords during the reset process and thus guarding against easy-to-guess passwords. In addition, rules requiring additional numbers and/or special characters make the dictionary attack less effective.
Denial-of-service (DoS) and distributed denial-of-service (DDoS) attacks	occur when the attacker sends a large number of connection or information requests to a target (see Figure 3-1) that will either crash or overload the system and cannot respond to legitimate requests for service. A **distributed denial of service (DDoS)** is an attack in which a coordinated stream of requests is launched against a target from many locations at the same time. Most DDoS attacks are preceded by a preparation phase in which many systems, perhaps thousands, are compromised. The compromised machines are turned into **zombies**, machines that are directed remotely (usually by a transmitted command) by the attacker to participate in the attack. Any system connected to the Internet and providing TCP-based network services (such as a Web server, FTP server, or mail server) is vulnerable to denial-of-service attacks. DoS attacks can also be launched against routers or other network server systems if these hosts enable (or turn on) other TCP services (e.g., echo).
Suggested controls:	DDoS attacks are among the most difficult to defend against, and there are presently no controls that any single organization can apply. There are, however, some cooperative efforts to enable DDoS defenses among groups of service providers; among them is the Consensus Roadmap for Defeating Distributed Denial of Service Attacks.[7] To use a popular metaphor, DDoS is considered a weapon of mass destruction on the Internet.[8]
Spoofing	is a class of attacks used to gain unauthorized access to computers by pretending to be another person or computer. The intruder sends messages with a source IP address that has been forged to indicate that the messages are coming from a trusted host. To engage in IP spoofing, hackers use a variety of techniques to obtain trusted IP addresses, and then modify the packet headers (see Figure 3-2) to insert these forged addresses.[9]
Suggested controls:	Sound architecture and implementation practices when implementing routers and firewalls can offer protection against IP spoofing (e.g., ingress and egress filters).

In a denial-of-service attack, a hacker compromises a system and uses that system to attack the target computer, flooding it with more requests for services than the target can handle.

In a distributed denial-of-service attack, dozens or even hundreds of computers (known as zombies) are compromised, loaded with DoS attack software, and then remotely activated by the hacker to conduct a coordinated attack.

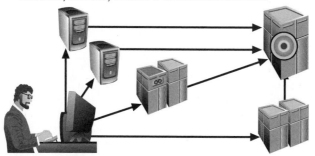

Figure 3-1 Denial of Service Attacks
Course Technology/Cengage Learning

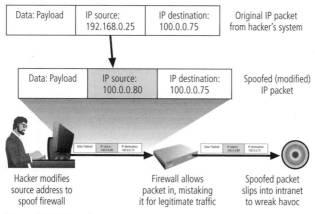

Figure 3-2 IP Spoofing
Course Technology/Cengage Learning

ATTACK	DESCRIPTION
Man-in-the-middle (MITM)	is a form of attack that allows an intruder to become an intermediary in the communications between two parties. This can be done in a variety of ways such as **TCP hijacking** where an attacker monitors (or sniffs) packets from the network, modifies them, and inserts them back into the network. This type of attack uses IP spoofing to enable an attacker to impersonate another entity on the network. It allows the attacker to eavesdrop as well as to change, delete, reroute, add, forge, or divert data.[10] Phishing is a common tactic as well; while **pharming** is an attack for implementing an MITM attack where the host's file on the client system is modified to resolve the target address (say *www.mybank.com*) to the address of the hostile intermediary.

(continued)

ATTACK	DESCRIPTION
Suggested controls:	Deny the attacker physical access to the intervening network through good physical security controls (locked wiring closets, etc.) and logical access through vulnerability management, anti-malware, policy, and awareness training. Strong design and operation of a network's naming services (such as DNS) can also play a role in controlling MITM attacks.
Spam	is the receipt of unsolicited commercial e-mail. Many have considered spam a trivial nuisance rather than a serious attack; however, it has been used as a means of making malicious code attacks more effective. In March 2002, for example, there were reports of malicious code embedded in MP3 files that were included as attachments to spam.[11] Far less the nuisance, spam has become a significant enabler of Internet crime as it can be used to implement phishing attacks, install malware (through malicious attachments), or conduct frauds such as the "Nigerian 419 scams" or the more recent lottery scams described later in this chapter. The **mail bomb** is a DoS attack in which large quantities of e-mail are routed to the targeted system through either social engineering or by exploiting various technical flaws in the Simple Mail Transport Protocol (SMTP). By sending large e-mails with forged header information, attackers can take advantage of poorly configured e-mail systems on the Internet and trick them into sending many e-mails to an address chosen by the attacker. If many such systems are tricked into participating in the event, the target e-mail address is buried under thousands or even millions of unwanted e-mails.
Suggested controls:	Spam is a tough problem because there are just so many ways to generate it and many nefarious purposes for its use. Many of today's spam messages originate from bot networks where the individual bots are compromised systems. Good anti-malware and vulnerability management help prevent creation of new bots; extrusion detection helps identify existing bots within an organization; spam filters on e-mail gateways can block many of the messages and good policy and awareness can help prevent users from falling victim to phishing scams.
Sniffer	is a program or device that monitors data traveling over a network. Unauthorized sniffers are extremely dangerous to a network's security because they are virtually impossible to detect and can be inserted almost anywhere. Sniffers often work on TCP/IP networks, where they're sometimes called **packet sniffers**.[12] Many systems and users send information on local networks in clear text. A sniffer program shows all the data going by, including passwords, the data inside files—such as word processing documents—and screens full of sensitive data from applications. The freeware tools Ethereal and Wireshark provide useful services to both InfoSec professional and attacker alike.
Suggested controls:	Use policy and awareness procedures to communicate when a sniffer may be used on a network and by whom. Carefully consider the sensitivity of information before allowing it to transit ANY network in unencrypted (clear-text) form.
Social engineering	is a process that convinces systems insiders that an attacker is a legitimate and authorized entity. The infamous hacker Kevin Mitnick once stated: "People are the weakest link. You can have the best technology; firewalls, intrusion-detection systems, biometric devices… and somebody can call an unsuspecting employee. That's all she wrote, baby. They got everything."[13] Attackers are some of the best social engineers in that they possess the ability to convince people in revealing credentials or other valuable information in order to gain access to the information assets. Social engineering attacks involve individuals posing as higher-level employees or new employees or as current employees pathetically requesting assistance to prevent getting fired. Sometimes attackers threaten, cajole, or beg to sway the target. *Advance fee fraud* (AFF)—internationally known as the "4-1-9" fraud—is named after a section of the Nigerian penal code. The perpetrators are often named as important sounding, but fictitious companies, such as the Nigerian National Petroleum Company, or other governmental

ATTACK	DESCRIPTION
	or nongovernmental agencies in order to steal funds from gullible individuals. In the past, these 4-1-9 schemes have involved kidnapping, extortion, and murder, and, according to the Secret Service, they have bilked over $100 million from unsuspecting Americans.
	Phishing—these attacks use three primary techniques, often in combination with one another: URL manipulation, Web site forgery, and phone phishing. In URL manipulation, attackers send an html embedded e-mail message, or a hyperlink whose HTML code opens a forged Web site. Phishers usually use the names of large banks or retailers so that users who do business with them will click on the link without giving it a lot of thought. For example, in one phishing e-mail, a link to "RegionsNetOnline" actually links the user to a Web site elsewhere. While this attack may seem crude to experienced users, the fact is that *many* e-mail users have fallen for these tricks.
	Phone phishing—is a traditional form of social engineering. The attacker calls a victim on the telephone and pretends to be someone they are not (a practice sometimes called **pretexting**) in order to gain access to private or confidential information, such as health or employment records or financial information. They will impersonate a person known to the potential victim by reputation only.
	Go to *http://www.ftc.gov/bcp/conline/pubs/alerts/nigeralrt.htm* and CERT Advisory CA-91.03
Suggested controls:	While some technical controls can help keep insiders from straying, the basic approach is to get authorized users to take actions on behalf of unauthorized attackers. The best chance for success is in strong policies coupled with aggressive awareness training.
Timing attack	exploits the contents of a Web browser's cache and stores a malicious form of cookie on the client's system. The cookie allows the intruder to collect information on how to access password-protected sites.[14] Another attack by the same name involves the interception of cryptographic elements to determine keys and encryption algorithms.[15]
Suggested controls:	Mandate proper hardening of browser configurations through policy and awareness. Carefully control physical access to sensitive devices such as cryptographic appliances.
Theft or encroachment of intellectual property	Many organizations create or support the development of intellectual property (IP) as part of their business operations. As already discussed in Chapter 2, use of another person's intellectual property may or may not involve royalty payments or permission, but should always include proper credit to the source.[16] Intellectual property examples include trade secrets, copyrights, trademarks, and patents. Once a piece of intellectual property has been properly identified, its unauthorized appropriation constitutes a threat to information security.
Suggested controls:	Employees may have access privileges to the various types of IP and may be required to use the IP to conduct day-to-day business. Therefore, it is important to implement strong policies and use aggressive awareness training.
Human error	Employees are categorized as threat-agents because of their daily use of data in business activities. Unlike the various attacks discussed above, employee mistakes become unintentional attacks against the information assets. Employee mistakes easily lead to revelation of classified data, entry of erroneous data, accidental deletion or modification of data, storage of data in unprotected areas, and failure to protect information or other company assets.
Suggested controls:	Much human error or failure can be prevented with training and ongoing awareness activities, but also with controls, ranging from simple procedures, such as requiring the user to type a critical command twice, to more complex procedures, such as the verification of commands by a second party. An example of the latter is the performance of key recovery actions in PKI systems. Many military applications have robust, dual-approval controls built in. Some systems that have a high potential for data loss or system outages use expert systems to monitor human actions and request confirmation for critical inputs.

The Information Security Manager's Checklist

	No	Planned	In Progress	In Place	Integrated
This topic has been fully tested, validated, and integrated into organizational operations with formal performance measures in place (as appropriate).					
This topic has been implemented, but not fully tested, validated, and integrated into organizational operations.					
The implementation of this topic has begun, but is not yet complete.					
The formal planning for this topic has begun, but is not yet complete.					
This subject has not formally begun planning, or the organization has made a conscious decision not to pursue this topic.					
3. Attacks					
Threat methods of attack identified					
Threat-attack vectors identified					
Organization information assets evaluated for threat-attack vectors					

For Further Reading

Computers Under Attack: Intruders, Worms and Viruses by Peter J. Denning, Addison-Wesley Professional, 1990.

Gray Hat Hacking, Second Edition: The Ethical Hacker's Handbook by Shon Harris, Allen Harper, Chris Eagle, and Jonathan Ness, McGraw-Hill Osborne Media, 2007.

Phishing and Countermeasures by Markus Jakobsson and Steven Myers, Wiley-Interscience, 2007.

Extrusion Detection: Security Monitoring for Internal Intrusions by Richard Bejtlich, Addison-Wesley Professional, 2006.

Crimeware: Understanding New Attacks and Defenses by Markus Jakobsson and Zulfikar Ramzan, 2008.

References

1. Peter Szor. *Computer Virus Research and Defense.* Upper Saddle River: Addison-Wesley, 2005.
2. Samuel T. Redwine, Jr., ed. *Software Assurance: A Guide to the Common Body of Knowledge to Produce, Acquire, and Sustain Secure Software Version 1.1.* U.S. Department of Homeland Security, September 2006.
3. Ibid.
4. Ibid.

5. SANS Institute. "Back Door NSA Glossary of Terms Used in Security and Intrusion Detection." *SANS Institute Online.* Accessed 15 February 2004 from www.sans.org/resources/glossary.php.

6. Philippe Oecshlin. *Making a Faster Cryptanalytical Time-Memory Trade-Off.* Advances in Cryptology—CRYPTO 2003, 23rd Annual International Cryptology Conference, Santa Barbara, California, 17–21 August 2003. A web-based demonstration of this technique is available at http://www.objectif-securite.ch/en/products.php.

7. SANS Institute. "Consensus Roadmap for Defeating Distributed Denial of Service Attacks: A Project of the Partnership for Critical Infrastructure Security." *SANS Institute Online.* 23 February 2000. Accessed 15 February 2004 from www.sans.org/dosstep/roadmap.php.

8. Paul Brooke. "DDoS: Internet Weapons of Mass Destruction." *Network Computing* 12, no. 1 (January 2001): 67.

9. Webopedia. "IP spoofing." *Webopedia Online,* 4 June 2002. Accessed 15 February 2004 from www.webopedia.com/TERM/I/IP_spoofing.html.

10. Bhavin Bharat Bhansali. "Man-in-the-Middle Attack: A Brief." *SANS Institute Online,* 16 February 2001. Accessed 15 February 2004 from www.giac.org/practical/gsec/Bhavin_Bhansali_GSEC.pdf.

11. James Pearce. "Security Expert Warns of MP3 Danger." *ZDNet News Online,* 18 March 2002. Accessed 15 February 2004 from zdnet.com.com/2100-1105-861995.html.

12. Webopedia. "Sniffer." *Webopedia Online,* 5 February 2002. Accessed 7 April 2007 from www.webopedia.com/TERM/s/sniffer.html.

13. Elinor Abreu. "Kevin Mitnick Bares All." *NetworkWorldFusion News Online,* 28 September 2000. Accessed 7 April 2007 from www.nwfusion.com/news/2000/0928mitnick.html.

14. Princeton University. "Standard Feature of Web Browser Design Leaves Opening for Privacy Attacks." *Science Daily Online,* 8 December 2000. Accessed 7 April 2007 from www.sciencedaily.com/releases/2000/12/ 001208074325.htm.

15. Gaël Hachez, François Koeune, and Jean-Jacques Quisquater. "Timing Attack: What Can Be Achieved by a Powerful Adversary?" (Proceedings of the 20th Symposium on Information Theory in the Benelux, May 1999), 63–70.

16. FOLDOC. "Intellectual Property." *FOLDOC Online,* 27 March 1997. Accessed 15 February 2007 from foldoc.org/index.cgi?query=intellectual+property.

Strategic Information Security: Security Governance

Part II of *Roadmap* will provide you with greater details concerning governance and the procedural structure of an InfoSec program. The following chapters will explain such important issues as the alignment of an InfoSec program with the organization's strategic plan and identify staffing requirements. If you are unfamiliar with the development and/or management of an InfoSec program, we highly recommend that you read all the chapters of Part II carefully before continuing to the technical parts of this book because we assume your knowledge of the terminology and standard InfoSec business practices. The chapters in Part II are intended to provide you with an overview
of today's information security landscape. They will explain:

► information security strategic planning;

► guidelines for creating an organizational hierarchy based on InfoSec;

► an overview of threats to an organization's assets; and

► an overview of attacks on an organization's assets.

For those more familiar with InfoSec, the following chapters can be used as a reference for that information security managers are currently facing when developing such a program.

Part Overview

Chapter 4—"Information Technology and Information Security Governance" discusses the integration of strategic planning for information technology (IT) and InfoSec into the organizational, strategic planning process and the alignment of IT and InfoSec goals and objectives with those of the organization.

Chapter 5—"Information Security Roles and Responsibilities" identifies and describes the typical job titles and the functions performed in the InfoSec program and includes an exploration of key security personnel. The skills and requirements for InfoSec positions will be examined, as well as key concepts of data ownership and responsibilities. The chapter also explores the various InfoSec professional requirements and identifies which skills are vital for each position. The chapter then continues with an examination of current security certifications dominant in the field.

In **Chapter 6**—"Positioning the Information Security Function," the reader learns how to plan and staff an organization's InfoSec staff, based on organizational factors, as well as how to evaluate the internal and external factors that influence the activities and organization of an InfoSec program.

Chapter 7—"Conducting an Information Security Assessment" examines the processes necessary to conduct a fundamental security assessment by describing the procedures for identifying and prioritizing threats and assets and identifying what controls are in place to protect these assets from threats.

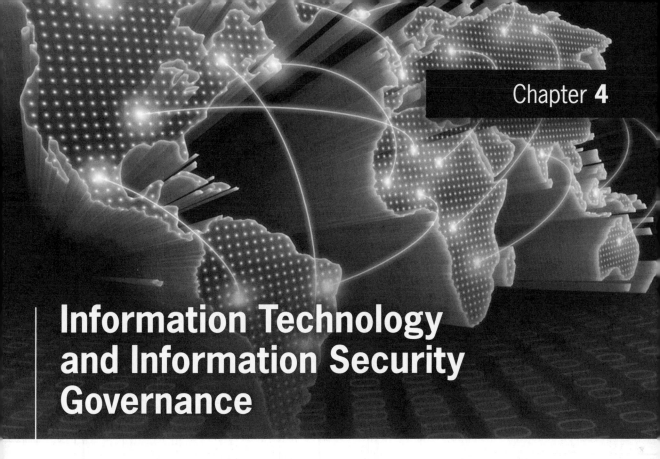

Chapter 4

Information Technology and Information Security Governance

Many times those working in an organization have the best intentions when it comes to figuring out the best strategy for handling information security. Unfortunately, for the practicing security professional, there remains a tendency to jump straight to engineering without spending time planning out the resources, scheduling, and budgeting. Without adequate foresight there may be no budget for the acquisition of a critical piece of software or hardware, or some other shortfall in resources or staffing or management. To avoid these problems, it is critical that the information security program fit into and become a part of the vision and mission of the organization and the regular processes used for organizational planning and management of ongoing operations—in other words, **governance**.

Is the term *governance* just the latest in corporate-speak buzzwords or the latest trendy approach that consultants use to generate billable hours? Not necessarily, but exploring the concept of governance and a look at a bit of its history might help to bring context to how we want you to understand the term in this chapter. Corporate governance became a hot topic in the wake of the corporate accounting scandals of the early 2000s. The intent of governance in that setting was to provide transparent processes and standards for corporate management as a method for restoring investor confidence. Information technology (IT) governance became the natural outgrowth from these same processes and controls. As in the rest of the organization structure, they are now applied to the IT function. This leads to one definition of IT governance as "specifying the decision rights and accountability framework to encourage desirable behavior in the use of IT."[1]

Many organizations that experience rapid growth will find themselves with a technology function that has more or less grown organically to support the growing business with little formal planning or structure. The IT budget likely began as a small expense that was hardly noticeable on the accounting ledgers. But, as the business grew, IT came to play an even more critical part in its operations, and the budget grew as well until it, too, became as significant a part of the business's operations as any other. During this time of unchecked growth, there were likely few controls and formal processes to guide the IT function toward alignment with the rest of the business. Acquisitions at this phase of IT growth would likely have been reactive rather than proactive: In other words, the staff responsible for the IT function would see a need, put together a budget, and ask senior management for the resources. IT governance, therefore, responds to the need for the management structure to recognize IT as a significant investment that impacts the flow of business. It really needs to be included in the same processes as other business units. Where IT is concerned, such a philosophical change in an organization can be a painful adjustment away from the way things have always been done.

Information security governance often evolved in much the same way. In the early days of information security, the assertion of "we need it for security" was an acceptable justification for an investment and implementation. However, as security budgets grew, important questions, fiscal and strategic questions, started to be raised about what the organization was really getting for those investments and how they were connected to achieving the overall business goals. The basic objective of functional alignment comes to the fore as everyone on the management team is directed to align the priorities of the supporting groups of IT and information security with the objectives of the revenue-generating business units.

Chapter Overview:

▶ The link between governance and planning
▶ The role of planning
▶ Precursors to planning
▶ Strategic planning
▶ Planning for information security implementation
▶ The security life cycle

THE LINK BETWEEN GOVERNANCE AND PLANNING

As with all business planning, InfoSec planning begins with a very simple question: "With our limited time and budget, what are the most advantageous things we can do to achieve our organization's objectives?" In the information security arena, the answers to this question should include securing information assets during normal operation (the subject of this chapter) and contingency planning (the subject of the next chapter). Figure 4-1 illustrates this concept.

Figure 4-1 Information Security and Planning
Course Technology/Cengage Learning

The essential nature of InfoSec planning in business and organizational management can't be overstated. In the resource-constrained setting where modern business operates, good planning enables an organization to make the most out of the resources at hand. Some Chief Information Security Officers (CISOs) find themselves locked in a never-ending cycle of firefighting where they are continually responding to immediate threats (the "hamster wheel of pain"[2]). Though it is a hard lesson, the only real way out of the fire zone is by allocating a portion of their resources to routine planning. The challenge lies in balancing the degree of planning with the resource costs of the planning effort.

THE ROLE OF PLANNING

InfoSec planning usually involves many interrelated groups and organizational processes. The groups involved in planning represent the three communities of interest discussed in previous chapters: They may be internal or external to the organization, and can include employees, management, stockholders, and other outside stakeholders. Among the other factors that affect InfoSec planning are the physical, political and legal, competitive, and technological forces in the environment.

Planning done by members of the information security community of interest uses processes common to the general management and IT management communities of interest. Because the information security community of interest seeks to influence the whole organization in protecting valuable assets, an effective InfoSec planner should know how the organizational planning process works so that participation in this process can yield the desired results. Before we can explore the positioning of information security within an organization's planning processes, however, we must understand organizational planning.

As the dominant means of managing resources in modern organizations, planning entails the enumeration of a sequence of actions intended to achieve specific goals over a defined period of time and then controlling the implementation of these steps. Planning provides direction for the organization's future. Without specific and detailed planning, organizational units attempt to meet objectives independently, under guidance of its own initiatives and ideas. Such an uncoordinated effort may not only fail to meet the objectives, but would result in an inefficient use of resources.

PRECURSORS TO PLANNING

An InfoSec plan is rooted in the entrepreneurial, philosophical, and ethical principles of the organization. These principles may be explicitly embodied in position papers or may be part of the generally understood organizational culture. The more clearly defined the organization's principles, the easier it is to conduct InfoSec planning in accordance with them.

An important issue with organizational principles is that they must reflect reality; if not, they will be ineffective as guidance to your planning process. For example, if an organization advertises in its principles that "ethical behavior is a core value," yet, in fact, the organization pursues competitive advantage by any means possible, an InfoSec plan that emphasizes ethics in business conduct would be out of step with the organization's stated values and would be effectively ignored by the communities of interest.

Statement of Values

An important first step is a **statement of values** that identifies which aspects of its operations an organization regards as most important and, therefore, hopes to exhibit in its operations. Developing a statement of values is not an empty exercise because it helps garner the trust of both stockholders and the public through a formal set of organizational principles and qualities, as well as benchmarks for measuring behavior against these published values. These values make the organization's conduct and performance standards meaningful for its employees and the public and works as the foundational principle for InfoSec planning. Value statements must also go beyond vague, abstract "motherhood and apple pie" statements to serve as concrete and effective purpose in shaping an organization's culture demonstrated in the following steps of the planning process and, most importantly, in the actual behavior of the organization.

Mission Statement

The **mission statement** explicitly declares the business of the organization and its intended areas of operations. It is, in a sense, the organization's identity card. A mission statement should be concise, should reflect both internal and external operations, and should be robust enough to remain valid for a period of at least four to six years. Simply put, the mission statement must explain *what* the organization does and for *whom*.

Vision Statement

The second underpinning of organizational planning is the **vision statement**. In contrast to the mission statement, which expresses what the organization is, the vision statement expresses what the organization wants to become. Vision statements should be ambitious; after all, they are meant to express the aspirations of the organization and to serve as a means for visualizing its future. In other words, the vision statement is the desired end-state for the organization's future.

While these precursors to planning may seem like the glossy front matter of an annual report, they serve a very useful purpose in defining the philosophical foundation of how the business operates and what its overall purpose is to be, two very important guides when developing the InfoSec culture within the larger scope of the organization.

STRATEGIC PLANNING

In general, **strategy**, or **strategic planning**, lays out the long-term business direction to be taken by the organization. Strategic planning guides organizational efforts and focuses resources toward specific, clearly defined goals, in the midst of an ever-changing environment. As an InfoSec planner, we recommend that you also take these attributes of strategic planning into account. As described earlier, a clearly directed strategy flows from top to bottom, and a systematic approach is required to translate it into a program that can articulate and lead all levels of the organization. As shown in Figure 4-2, strategic plans formed at the highest levels of the organization are translated into more specific strategic plans for intermediate layers of management. These plans are then converted into tactical planning for supervisory managers and eventually provide direction for the operational plans undertaken by the nonmanagement members of the organization. This multilayered approach encompasses two key objectives: general strategy and overall strategic planning. First, general strategy is translated into specific strategy; second, overall strategic planning is translated into lower-level tactical and operational planning. Each of these steps is discussed below.

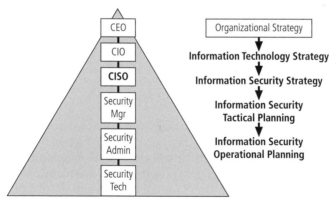

Figure 4-2 Strategic Planning Process
Course Technology/Cengage Learning

Creating the InfoSec Strategic Plan

After an organization develops a general strategy, it must create an overall strategic plan by extending that general strategy into specific strategic objectives for major divisions. Each level of each division implements its objectives by translating its objectives into more specific objectives for the level below. To execute this broad strategy and turn the general statement into action, the executive team must first define individual responsibilities. This successive waterfall of concrete objectives helps assure that the overall strategic goals are translated into meaningful actions at each level of the organization. However, this translation of goals is more art than science. It relies on the management at each level's ability to know and understand the strategic goals they are given, to know and appreciate the strategic and tactical abilities of each unit within their organization, and to negotiate with peers, superiors, and subordinates.

Planning Levels

Once the organization's overall strategic plan is translated into strategic goals for each major division or operation, the next step is to implement these objectives through tasks with specific, measurable, achievable, and time-bound objectives. Strategic planning then begins a transformation from general, sweeping statements toward more specific and applied objectives. Strategic plans are used to create tactical plans, which are in turn used to develop operational plans.

Tactical planning has a more short-term focus than strategic planning, usually six months to one year. It breaks down each applicable strategic goal into a series of incremental objectives. Each objective should be concrete with a specific delivery date. Budgeting, resource allocation, and manpower are critical components of the tactical plan. Although these components may be discussed in general terms at the strategic planning level, they are crucial at the tactical level because they must be in place before the tactical plan can be translated into the operational plan. Tactical plans often include project plans and resource acquisition planning documents (such as product specifications), project budgets, project reviews, and monthly and annual reports.

Because tactical plans are often created for specific projects, some organizations no longer call this process tactical planning; instead, they refer to it as project planning or intermediate planning. The CISO and the security managers use the tactical plan to organize, prioritize, and acquire resources necessary for the major projects required to achieve the overall strategic goals.

Managers and employees use operational plans, which are derived from the tactical plans, to organize the ongoing, day-to-day performance of tasks. An operational plan includes clearly identified coordination activities that span department boundaries, communications requirements, weekly meetings, summaries, progress reports, and associated tasks.

InfoSec Planning and the CISO

The first priority of the CISO and the information security management team should be the structure of a strategic plan. While each organization may have its own format for the design and distribution of a strategic plan, the fundamental elements of planning are the same for all types of enterprises. Following is a brief outline showing the basic structure of a strategic plan.

    I. Executive Summary

    II. Mission Statement and Vision Statement

    III. Organizational Profile and History

    IV. Strategic Issues and Core Values

    V. Program Goals and Objectives

    VI. Management/Operations Goals and Objectives

    VII. Appendices (optional) [strengths, weaknesses, opportunities, and threats (SWOT) analyses, surveys, budgets, etc.]"[3]

PLANNING FOR INFORMATION SECURITY IMPLEMENTATION

The Chief Information Officer (CIO) and CISO play important roles in translating overall strategic planning into tactical and operational information security plans. Depending on the information security function's placement within the organizational chart, the roles of the CIO and the CISO may differ. Most commonly, the CISO directly reports to the CIO. In that case, the CIO charges the CISO and other IT department heads with creating and adopting plans that are consistent and supportive of the entire organizational strategy. The CIO must also ensure that the various IT functional areas in the organization provide broad support for the plan, and that no areas are omitted or ignored.

The CISO plays a more active role in the development of the planning details than does the CIO. Once the organization's overall strategic plan has been translated into IT and information security departmental objectives by the CIO, and then further translated into tactical and operational plans by the CISO, the implementation of information security can begin.

Implementation of information security can be accomplished in two ways: bottom-up or top-down. The **bottom-up approach** might begin as a grassroots effort in which systems administrators attempt to improve the security of their systems (and may be quite common in growing organizations where there has not been a previous information security function). This approach can be quite challenging because it lacks a number of critical features, such as coordinated planning from upper-level management, coordination between departments, and the provision of sufficient resources. However, as the Chinese philosopher Confucius once said, "A journey of a thousand miles begins with a single step," and sometimes that single step begins with the administrators responsible for an organization's information systems recognizing that there is something seriously wrong and attempting to do something about it.

The **top-down approach**, in contrast, features strong upper-level management support, a dedicated champion, assured funding, a clear planning and implementation process, and the ability to influence organizational culture. High-level managers provide resources; give direction; issue policies, procedures, and processes; dictate the goals and expected outcomes of the project; and determine who is accountable for each of the required actions. The most successful top-down approach also incorporates formal processes such as a systems development life cycle.

The success of information security plans can be enhanced by using the processes of system analysis and design, a discipline that is an integral part of most academic curricula in the field of information technology. The following sections provide a brief treatment of this topic, but are not designed to replace a more thorough study of the discipline.

THE SECURITY LIFE CYCLE

In general, a **systems development life cycle (SDLC)** is a methodology for the design and implementation of an information system in an organization. Using a **methodology** ensures a rigorous process and increases the likelihood of achieving the desired final objective ontime and within budget. A variation of the SDLC methodology, used to create a comprehensive security posture, is called the **security life cycle (SLC)**.

System projects may be initiated in response to specific conditions or combinations of conditions. The impetus to begin an SDLC-based project may be **event-driven**—that is, a response to some event in the business community, inside the organization, or within the ranks of employees, customers, or other stakeholders. Alternatively, it may also be **plan-driven**—that is, the result of a carefully developed planning strategy. Either way, once an organization recognizes the need for a project, the use of a methodology can ensure that development proceeds in an orderly, comprehensive fashion. At the end of each phase, a **structured review** or *reality check* takes place, during which the team and its management-level reviewers decide whether the project should be continued, discontinued, outsourced, or postponed until additional expertise or organizational knowledge is acquired.

An approach that makes use of six phases in a traditional waterfall model SDLC will illustrate the SLC in the sections that follow. The SLC process involves the identification of specific threats and the risks that they represent, and the subsequent design and implementation of specific controls to counter those threats and assist in the management of the risk. It turns information security into a coherent program rather than a series of responses to individual threats and attacks. Figure 4-3 shows the phases in the SLC.

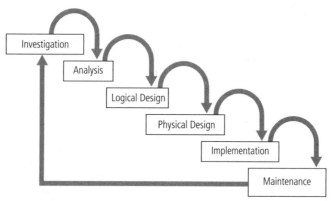

Figure 4-3 Phases of the SLC
Course Technology/Cengage Learning

Investigation in the SLC

The investigation phase of the SLC begins with a trigger, such as a directive, from upper management, specifying the process, outcomes, and goals of the project, as well as its budget and other constraints. Regardless of the trigger, subsequent actions should be guided by a structured process beginning with the affirmation or creation of security policies on which the security program is or will be founded. Teams of managers, employees, and consultants are assembled to analyze problems, define their scope, specify goals and objectives, and identify any additional constraints not covered in the enterprise security policy. Finally, an organizational feasibility analysis determines whether the organization has the resources and commitment to conduct a successful security analysis and design.

Analysis in the SLC

In the analysis phase, the documents from the investigation phase are studied. The development team created during the investigation phase conducts a preliminary analysis of existing security policies or programs, along with documented current threats and associated controls. This phase also includes an analysis of relevant legal issues that could affect the design of the security solution. Risk management also begins in this stage. Risk management is the process of identifying, assessing, and evaluating the levels of risk facing the organization—specifically, the threats to the organization's assets, such as the information stored and processed by the organization. Risk management is examined in more detail in later chapters.

Design in the SLC

The SLC design phase actually consists of two distinct phases: the logical design and the physical design. In the logical design phase, team members create and develop the blueprint for security, and they examine and implement key policies that influence later decisions. At this stage, critical contingency plans for incident response are developed. Next, a feasibility analysis determines whether the project should continue in-house or should be outsourced. In the physical design phase, team members evaluate the technology needed to support the security blueprint, generate alternative solutions, and agree on a final design. During the logical and physical design phases, a security manager may seek to use established security models to guide the design process. Security models provide frameworks for ensuring that all areas of security are addressed; organizations can adapt or adopt a framework to meet their own information security needs. A number of information security frameworks have been published including the National Institute for Standards and Technology Special Publications, the ISO 27000 series, and Control Objectives for Information Technology (COBIT).

As the design phase continues, attention turns to the design of the controls and safeguards used to protect information from threats and attacks. The terms **control** and **safeguard** are often used interchangeably. There are three broad categories of controls: managerial controls, operational controls, and technical controls. **Managerial controls** cover security processes that are designed by the strategic planners and performed by security administration of the organization. They set the direction and scope of the security process and provide detailed guidance for its conduct. **Operational controls** deal with the operational functionality of security in the organization. They cover management functions and lower-level planning, such as disaster recovery and incident response planning. **Technical controls** address those tactical and technical issues related to designing and implementing security in the organization. Whereas operational controls address specific operational issues, such as developing controls and integrating them into the business functions, technical controls address the specifics of technology selection and the acquisition (make or buy) of certain technical components, including logical access controls, such as those related to identification, authentication, authorization, and accountability.

Another element of the design phase is the creation of essential preparedness documents, contingency planning, discussed in the next chapter. As the design phase progresses, attention turns to **physical security**, which addresses the design, implementation, and maintenance of countermeasures intended to protect the physical resources of an organization.

Implementation in the SLC

The SLC implementation phase specifies how security solutions are acquired (made or bought), tested, implemented, and retested. Personnel issues are evaluated and specific training and education programs are conducted. Finally, the entire tested package is presented to upper management for final approval.

The information security systems software or application systems selection process is not appreciably different from that for general IT needs. Vendors should be provided with detailed specifications; they should in turn provide detailed information about products and costs. As in IT system implementation, it is essential to establish clear specifications and rigorous test plans to assure a high-quality implementation.

Perhaps the most important element of the implementation phase is the management of the project plan. While it has not been mentioned until this point, project management is a process that underlies all phases of the SLC. The execution of the project plan proceeds in three steps:

1. Planning the project
2. Supervising the tasks and action steps within the project plan
3. Wrapping up the project plan

Maintenance and Change in the SLC

Once the information security program is implemented, it must be operated, properly managed, and kept up-to-date by means of established procedures. If the program is not adjusting adequately to the changes in the internal or external environment, it may be necessary to begin the cycle again. The CISO determines whether the information security group can adapt adequately and maintain the information security profile of the organization, or whether the macroscopic process of the SLC must start over to redevelop a fundamentally different information security profile. It is less expensive and more effective when an information security program is able to deal with change.

While a systems management model is designed to manage and operate systems, a maintenance model is intended to complement a systems management model and focus organizational effort on system maintenance. Figure 4-4 presents one recommended approach for dealing with information security maintenance.

External Monitoring The objective of external monitoring within the maintenance model shown in Figure 4-4 is to provide early awareness of new and emerging threats, threat-agents, vulnerabilities, and attacks, thereby enabling the creation of an effective and timely defense.

Internal Monitoring The primary goals of internal monitoring are to maintain an informed awareness of the state of all of the organization's networks, information systems, and information security defenses. This status must be communicated and documented, especially the status of the parts of information systems that are connected to the external network.

Planning and Risk Assessment The primary objective of planning and risk assessment is to keep a wary eye on the entire information security program. It is achieved in part by identifying and planning ongoing information security activities that further reduce risk. Also, the risk assessment group identifies and documents risks introduced by both IT projects and information security projects. Furthermore, it identifies and documents risks that may be latent in the present environment.

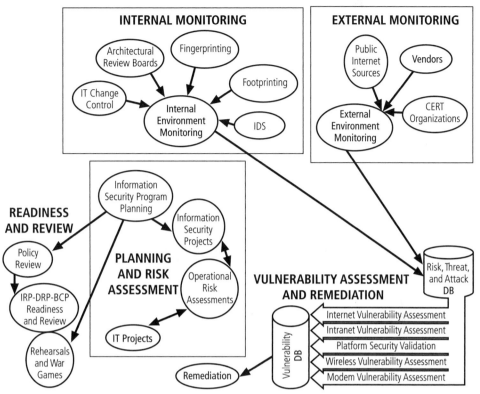

Figure 4-4 Information Security Maintenance
Course Technology/Cengage Learning

Vulnerability Assessment and Remediation
The primary goal of vulnerability assessment and remediation is the identification of specific, documented vulnerabilities and their timely remediation. It is accomplished by:

▶ Using documented vulnerability assessment procedures to safely collect intelligence about networks (internal and public-facing), platforms (servers, desktops, and process control), dial-in modems, and wireless network systems;

▶ Documenting background information and providing tested remediation procedures for the reported vulnerabilities; and

▶ Tracking, communicating, and reporting to management the itemized facts about the discovered vulnerabilities and the success or failure of the organization to remediate them.

Readiness and Review
The primary objectives of readiness and review are to keep the information security program functioning as designed and, it is hoped, continuously improve it over time.

Performance Measures

Measurement of success is a critical component in the management of any organizational project including information security. One of the oft-leveled criticisms of information security programs is that they are a "black hole" that absorbs massive amounts of money and resources with little to show for it other than a larger resource request next year. For example, a public corporation will measure its success by earnings per share and its marketing function will report its increased sales based on the investment in a new marketing program. However, the successful information security program often has nothing to report: no intrusions, no hacked systems, no data breaches, etc.

Developing meaningful performance measures, commonly referred to as metrics, to measure and report the progress of a security program can be challenging. Sometimes the challenge is avoiding the easily collected, yet meaningless, metrics such as the number of antivirus signatures in an organization's antivirus product (if it's higher, it must be better, right?). A much more meaningful metric would be the number of viruses/spyware items detected and eliminated in incoming e-mail[4] since this demonstrates effectiveness in mitigating a threat. Couple this metric with metrics describing the incidence of malware on an organization's servers, desktops, and laptops and a good picture can be painted of how well defended the organization actually is against malware. When setting the objectives during the planning process, the wise security manager will ask himself how he will be able to measure progress and effectiveness in achieving the objectives. This will avoid finding oneself in the position of a homeowner irritating her neighbors by beating a large gong in her front yard with the explanation of "It's to keep tigers away!" When assured there are no tigers in the area, she responds "See how well it's working!" For information on developing and implementing meaningful performance measures refer to the NIST SP 800-55 Revision 1 which is available from http://csrsc.nist.gov/publications.

Whether the organization has a formalized governance framework or uses a more ad hoc process, there will always be a method used to prioritize the allocation and management of corporate resources, such as people and money, in accomplishing the organization's objectives. The information security function competes for these scarce resources with other functions such as marketing, manufacturing, produce development, etc. In order to develop and implement a successful information security program, the security manager must be able to understand the governance process of their particular organization and be able to articulate their program using the language and constructs of that governance process. The degree to which an InfoSec leader succeeds in obtaining the budget and resources necessary to carry out the program depends very much on a mastery of the governance process.

The Information Security Manager's Checklist

This topic has been fully tested, validated, and integrated into organizational operations with formal performance measures in place (as appropriate).

This topic has been implemented, but not fully tested, validated, and integrated into organizational operations.

The implementation of this topic has begun, but is not yet complete.

The formal planning for this topic has begun, but is not yet complete.

This subject has not formally begun planning, or the organization has made a conscious decision not to pursue this topic.

3. Attacks	No	Planned	In Progress	In Place	Integrated
InfoSec received appropriate recognition and support from executive management					
InfoSec roles and responsibilities for executive management defined and promoted					
InfoSec strategy developed and implemented					
InfoSec strategy aligned with business strategy					
InfoSec strategy aligned with IT strategy					
Appropriate InfoSec metrics/performance measures in place and periodically analyzed and presented					

For Further Reading

Information Security Governance by S. H. von Solms and Rossouw von Solms, Springer, 2010.

Board Briefing on IT Governance, Second Edition by IT Governance Institute, Available from www.isaca.org, 2003.

Security Metrics Guide for Information Technology Systems by the U.S. National Institute of Standards and Technology, Available from cscrc.nist.gov/publications, 2008.

References

1. P. Weill. *IT Governance: How Top Performers Manage IT Decision Rights for Superior Results.* Boston: Harvard Business School Publishing, 2004, p. 8.

2. A. Jaquith. *Security Metrics: Replacing Fear, Uncertainty and Doubt.* Upper Saddle River, NJ: Addison-Wesley, 2007.

3. Ibid.

4. Ibid.

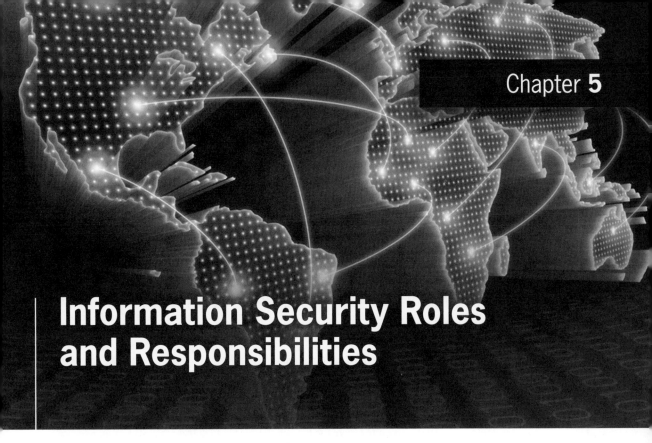

Information Security Roles and Responsibilities

One of the most confusing things for new information security managers is getting a solid understanding of where they fit into the organization. Is information security part of audit, or part of IT, or does it belong better in HR, or even in compliance? There is not a single right answer because it really depends on the preferences of organizational management. Regardless of where the security function reports in the organizational hierarchy, it is always cross functional and should be designed with such an organizational role in mind. Because it touches so many aspects of the organization, you as the information security manager will be responsible for affecting the behavior of many departments and individuals that do not report to you. Achieving success in this cross-functional role will challenge your technical knowledge as well as your understanding of the business and, perhaps most importantly, your ability to relate and sell the information security program across the organization. Despite the plethora of responsibilities and organizational challenges, there are common themes that run through the structure of successful information security programs that can be translated into the particular structure appropriate to a particular organization.

Chapter Overview:

▶ Information security positions

▶ Credentials for information security professionals

INFORMATION SECURITY POSITIONS

Titles abound in information security: chief information security officer, senior security analyst, business compliance architect, firewall technician, security administrator, etc. And, unfortunately, these titles tend to say more about the organizations that produce them rather than the actual functions they entail. Most information security programs, however, do include a consistent set of roles that are mapped to these positions. Schwartz, Erwin, Weafer, and Briney studied the general problem of structuring an information security program and identified three main roles as follows:

> **Definers** *provide the policies, guidelines and standards. . . . They're the people who do the consulting and the risk assessment, who develop the product and technical architectures. These are senior people with a lot of broad knowledge, but often not a lot of depth. . . .* **Builders** *are the real techies, who create and install security solutions. . . .* **Administrators** *operate and administrate the security tools [and] the security monitoring function and . . . continuously improve the processes, performing all the day-to-day . . . work. . . . We often try to use the same people for all of these roles. We use builders all the time. . . . If you break your infosec professionals into these three roles, you can recruit them more efficiently, with the policy people being the more senior people, the builders being more technical and the operating people being those you can train to do a specific task.*[1]

The Toxic Waste Dump

Sometimes an organization treats its security program as a toxic waste dump where all the unpleasantness is tossed and promptly forgotten. When further problems crop up, the information security manager is castigated, disciplined, and sometimes replaced. You can most effectively combat this perception by assuring upper management's understanding and support of the program as an important part of the daily flow of business. Otherwise, information security managers might face some real challenges here—perhaps they have been promoted from outside the IT organization into a CISO role, but it is not clear what the chain of authority is and/or how they relate to the IT teams. Fostering a relationship between the information security program and IT is critical since they are the most active partners in making the mission of protecting the organization's information assets a great success. This means that you are placed in a position that requires the "selling" of the information security program both to senior management and to the IT professionals who will carry it out.

These roles are commonly expressed in the following titles.

Chief Information Security Officer (CISO or CSO)

This is typically the top information security officer in the organization (or, if physical security, executive protection, loss prevention, etc., are also included as duties, the title of chief security officer or CSO is common). The CISO may or may not be an executive-level position and sometimes the person in this role reports to the chief information officer (or the chief financial officer, or even internal audit). Though CISOs are usually business managers first and technologists second, they must be conversant in all areas of information security, including the technical, planning, and policy areas. In many cases, the CISO is the major definer or architect of the information security program. The CISO performs the following functions:

- ▶ Manages the overall information security program for the organization
- ▶ Drafts or approves information security policies
- ▶ Works with other senior managers on strategic, tactical, and operational plans
- ▶ Develops information security budgets based on available funding
- ▶ Sets priorities for the purchase and implementation of information security projects and technology
- ▶ Makes decisions or recommendations on the recruiting, hiring, and firing of security staff
- ▶ Acts as the organizational champion and spokesperson for the information security team

A qualification for this type of position is the Certified Information Systems Security Professional (CISSP) certification, which is described later in this chapter. A graduate degree is also often required, although it may be from a number of possible disciplines, including information systems, computer science, criminal justice, military science, business, or other fields related to the broader topic of security. To qualify for this position, the candidate must demonstrate experience as a security manager (see the description of this position in the next section), and present experience with planning, policy, and budgets. As mentioned earlier, some organizations prefer to hire individuals with law enforcement experience (particularly when physical security and loss control is of particular importance). The following is an example of a typical job description for a CISO:

Information Security Department Manager

Job Title: Chief information security officer

Reports to: Chief information officer

Summary: The information security department manager directs, coordinates, plans, and organizes information security activities throughout Company X. He or she acts as the focal point for all communications related to information security, both with internal staff and third parties. The manager works with a wide variety of people from different internal organizational units, bringing them together to manifest controls that reflect workable compromises as well as proactive responses to current and future information security risks.

Responsibilities and Duties: The information security department manager is responsible for envisioning, planning, and taking steps to implement the controls needed to protect both Company X information as well as information that has been entrusted to Company X by third parties. The position involves overall Company X responsibility for information security regardless of the form that the information takes, the information handling technology employed, or the people involved.

Security Manager

Security managers are accountable for the day-to-day operation of all or part of the information security program. They accomplish objectives identified by the CISO and resolve issues identified by technicians. Management of technology requires an understanding of the technology administered, but does not necessarily require proficiency in the technology's configuration, operation, and fault resolution. (Note that there are a number of positions with titles that contain the word *manager* or other language suggesting management responsibilities, but only those people responsible for management functions, such as scheduling, setting relative priorities, or administering budgetary control, should be considered true managers.)

It is not uncommon for a candidate for this position to have a CISSP. Traditionally, managers earn the CISSP or CISM, and technical professionals earn Global Information Assurance Certifications (GIAC). (A number of certifications that are common in the information security field, such as CISSP, CISM, and GIACs, are discussed in the section on certification.) Security managers must have the ability to draft middle- and lower-level policies, as well as standards and guidelines. They must have experience in traditional business matters: budgeting, project management, hiring, and firing. They must also be able to manage technicians, both in the assignment of tasks and in the monitoring of activities. Experience with business continuity planning is usually a plus.

The following is an example of a typical security manager job description. Note that there are several different types of security managers, since the security manager position is much more specialized than that of CISO.

Information Security Manager

Job description: This management position reports to the chief information security officer. The successful candidate will manage the development of the information security programs and control systems in conformance with organizational policy and standards across the organization. This is a high-visibility role that involves the day-to-day management of IT security staff and their career development. The principal accountabilities for this role are as follows:

- ▶ Develop and manage information security programs and control systems under the supervision of the CISO in conjunction with the evolving information security architecture of the organization.
- ▶ Monitor performance of information security programs and control systems to maintain alignment with organizational policy and common industry practices for emerging threats and technologies.
- ▶ Prepare and communicate risk assessments for business risk in software developments as well as ongoing systems events (to include merger, acquisition, and divestiture) and ensure effective risk management across the organization's IT systems.
- ▶ Represent the information security organization in the organization's change management process.

- ► Perform assigned duties in the area of incident response management and disaster recovery response.
- ► Supervise assigned staff and perform other general management tasks as assigned including budgeting, staffing, and employee performance reviews.

Security Technician

Security technicians are the technically qualified individuals tasked to configure firewalls, deploy IDSs, implement security software, diagnose and troubleshoot problems, and coordinate with systems and network administrators to ensure that an organization's security technology is properly implemented. The position of security technician is often entry level; but, to be hired in this role, candidates must possess some technical skills. This often poses a dilemma for applicants since many seeking to enter a new field find it is difficult to get a job without experience—which they can only attain by getting a job. Just as in the networking arena, security technicians tend to be specialized, focusing on one major security technology group (firewalls, IDSs, servers, routers, or software) and further specializing in one particular software or hardware package, such as Check Point firewalls, Cisco firewalls, or Trip Wire IDSs. These areas are sufficiently complex to warrant a high level of specialization, but to move up in the corporate hierarchy, security technicians must expand their knowledge horizontally—that is, gain an understanding of the general organizational issues related to information security, as well as its technical areas.

The technical qualifications and position requirements for a security technician vary. Organizations prefer expert, certified, proficient technicians. Regardless of the area, the particular job description covers some level of experience with a particular hardware and software package. Sometimes familiarity with a technology secures an applicant an interview; however, actual experience in using the technology is usually required. The following is a typical job announcement for a security technician:

Firewall Engineering Consultant

Job Description: Working for an exciting customer-focused security group within one of the largest managed network providers in Europe, this person will have the opportunity to expand his or her experience and gain all the technical and professional support to achieve within the group. This person must have experience in third-line technical support of firewall technologies, be Cisco certified, and have experience in Acme systems.

Because overtime and on-call pay are listed, this is probably an hourly position rather than a salaried one, which is commonly the case for security technician positions.

CREDENTIALS FOR INFORMATION SECURITY PROFESSIONALS

As mentioned earlier, many organizations seek industry-recognized certifications to screen candidates for the required level of technical proficiency. Unfortunately, most of the existing certifications are relatively new and not fully understood by many hiring organizations. The certifying bodies are working hard to educate employers and potential professionals on the value and qualifications of their certification programs. In the meantime, employers are trying to understand the match between certifications and position requirements, and hopeful professionals are trying to gain meaningful employment based on their newly received certifications.

(ISC)² Certifications

The International Information Systems Security Certification Consortium (ISC)² (*www.isc2.org*) is considered one of the foremost organizations offering information security certifications today. Currently, (ISC)² offers three primary certifications and three specializations for its flagship certification. (ISC)² also offers an intermediate, or in-progress, certification to allow candidates who have not completed the experiential requirements of a certification to provide evidence of progress toward completing the certification, Certified Information Systems Security Professional (CISSP). The CISSP candidate must focus on ten areas (or domains) that make up the (ISC)² "common body of knowledge":

- ▶ Access Control
- ▶ Application Security
- ▶ Business Continuity and Disaster Recovery Planning
- ▶ Cryptography
- ▶ Information Security and Risk Management
- ▶ Legal, Regulations, Compliance, and Investigations
- ▶ Operations Security
- ▶ Physical (Environmental) Security
- ▶ Security Architecture and Design
- ▶ Telecommunications and Network Security

CISSP Concentrations In recent years, the CISSP certification program has added a set of concentration exams—the Information Systems Security Engineering Professional (ISSEP), Information Systems Security Architecture Professional (ISSAP), and Information Systems Security Management Professional (ISSMP). These certification extensions are designed to work in tandem with the CISSP credential. To qualify for any of these concentrations, one must be a CISSP professional in good standing and pass a supplemental examination on the specialized body of knowledge.

Systems Security Certified Practitioner (SSCP) Given the difficulty involved in mastering all ten domains, many information security professionals seek other, less rigorous, certifications. In response, (ISC)² developed the Systems Security Certified Practitioner, or SSCP. SSCP was designed to recognize mastery of an international standard for information security and a common body of knowledge (sometimes called the CBK). The SSCP certification is oriented toward the security administrator. Like the CISSP, the SSCP certification is more applicable to the information security manager than the technician because most questions focus on the operational nature of information security. In other words, the SSCP focuses "on practices, roles, and responsibilities as defined by experts from major IS industries."[2] Even so, an information security technician seeking advancement can benefit from acquiring this certification. The SSCP certification focuses on seven areas:

- ▶ Access controls
- ▶ Administration
- ▶ Audit and monitoring
- ▶ Risk, response, and recovery

- ▸ Cryptography
- ▸ Data communications
- ▸ Malicious code and malware

Associate of (ISC)² The Associate of (ISC)² program is geared toward those who want to take the CISSP or SSCP exams before obtaining the requisite experience for full certification: "The Associate of (ISC)² program is a mechanism for information security professionals, who are still in the process of acquiring the necessary experience to become CISSPs or SSCPs, to become associated with (ISC)2 and obtain career-related support during this early period in his or her information security career."[3] Once candidates pass the examination and subscribe to the (ISC)² Code of Ethics, they receive the Associate Certification indicating satisfactory progress toward a certification. Once the experiential requirements have been met, they receive their CISSP or SSCP.

ISACA Certifications

The Information Systems Audit and Control Association (ISACA) was founded by a group of individuals with similar jobs in computer auditing, who sought to provide a centralized source of information and guidance. Today ISACA offers two well-recognized and well-respected certifications: the CISA certification for auditing, networking, and security professionals, and the CISM certification for information security management professionals.

Certified Information Systems Auditor (CISA) Although it does not primarily focus on information security certification, the Certified Information Systems Auditor or CISA certification covers many information security components including the IS audit process, IT governance, systems and infrastructure life cycle, IT service delivery and support, protection of information assets and business continuity, and disaster recovery.[4]

Certified Information Security Manager (CISM) The second ISACA certificate program is the CISM. This certificate is awarded to those who have passed the CISM requirements, which are different from those of the CISA. The applicant must demonstrate knowledge of information security governance, information risk management, information security program management, information security program development, and incident management and response. Many industry professionals consider the CISM to be the top managerial certification in information security, or at least as desirable as the CISSP.

SANS Global Information Assurance Certifications (GIAC)

The System Administration, Networking, and Security Organization, better known as SANS (*www.sans.org*), developed a series of technical security certifications in 1999 that are known as the Global Information Assurance Certifications or GIAC family of certifications (see *www.giac.org*). When the GIAC was established, no technical certifications were available elsewhere—anyone who wished to be certified to work in the technical security field could obtain only vendor-specific networking or computing certifications, such as the MCSE (Microsoft Certified Systems Engineer) or CNE (Certified Novell Engineer). Now, you can choose to attain the various GIAC certifications separately, or to pursue a comprehensive certification known as the GIAC Security Engineer (GSE). The GIAC Information Security Officer (GISO) is an overview certification that combines basic technical knowledge with an understanding of threats, risks, and best practices, similar to the SSCP. The GIAC Security Expert is considered the pinnacle of GIAC security-related certifications.

CompTIA's Security+

CompTIA (*www.comptia.org*) introduced the first truly vendor-neutral technical professional IT certifications—the A+ series. Offered as part of the A+ program, the Security+ certification focuses on the key skills that are necessary to perform security, but is not tied to a particular software or hardware vendor package. According to the CompTIA Web site, "the CompTIA Security+ certification tests for security knowledge mastery of an individual with two years on-the-job networking experience, with emphasis on security. The exam covers industry-wide topics, including communication security, infrastructure security, cryptography, access control, authentication, external attack and operational and organization security."[5]

Certification Costs

Certifications cost money, and the better certifications can be quite expensive to attain. Some certification exams can run as much as $500 per examination, and their entire educational track can cost several thousand dollars. The cost of the formal training required to prepare for the certification can also be significant. While these courses should not serve as a candidate's only means of preparation, they can help round out knowledge and fill in gaps. As mentioned earlier, some of the exams, such as the CISSP, are very broad and others very technical. Even an experienced professional would find it difficult to sit for one of these exams without some preparation. Certifications are designed to recognize experts in their respective fields, and the cost of certification is meant to limit the number of candidates who take exams just to see if they can pass. Most examinations admit only candidates with two and three years of expertise in the skills being tested.

Entering the Information Security Profession

Many information security professionals enter the field after having prior careers in law enforcement or the military, or careers in other IT areas, such as networking, programming, database administration, or systems administration. Recently, college graduates who have

Paper Certifications

One of the challenges in any certification program lies in establishing and maintaining the value of the certification. Many once well-respected certifications have lost much of their luster by becoming vulnerable to memorization and exam "brain dump" training that teach a candidate to pass the exam without having much real knowledge of the underlying field.

This has given rise to the growing trend for certification to require both exam performance as well as a documented work history in the field. (ISC)² requires five years of documented experience and includes random audits to assure validity. SANS requires practical projects as conditions for certification in addition to the exam. Perhaps the "gold standard" for this type of requirement is the Cisco Certified Internetworking Engineer (CCIE), which requires successful performance on several exams and completion of a multi-day practical examination. The wise information security manager will carefully consider the requirements for achieving a certification when assessing the weight a certification should be given as qualification for a class of positions.

tailored their degree programs to specialize in information security have begun to enter the field in appreciable numbers.

Many information technologists believe that information security professionals must have an established track record in some other IT specialty. However, IT professionals who move into information security tend to focus on technical problems and solutions to the exclusion of general information security issues. Organizations can foster greater professionalism in the information security discipline by clearly defining their expectations and establishing explicit position descriptions.

Structuring a new information security program is a complex undertaking that involves understanding the structure of the hosting organization as well as the types of positions required for its successful function. Structuring the program based on the role filled by the positions rather than their title can be a valuable timesaver. Once the roles of the positions are defined and understood, the new information security manager can evaluate and make use of industry certifications and prior work experience to identify appropriate candidates for those positions.

The Information Security Manager's Checklist

	No	Planned	In Progress	In Place	Integrated
This topic has been fully tested, validated, and integrated into organizational operations with formal performance measures in place (as appropriate).					
This topic has been implemented, but not fully tested, validated, and integrated into organizational operations.					
The implementation of this topic has begun, but is not yet complete.					
The formal planning for this topic has begun, but is not yet complete.					
This subject has not formally begun planning, or the organization has made a conscious decision not to pursue this topic.					
5. InfoSec Roles and Responsibilities					
InfoSec personnel (managers, administrators, technicians) have roles and responsibilities clearly delineated.					
InfoSec personnel have roles and responsibilities evaluated in annual job performance reviews.					
All InfoSec positions have an appropriate level of expectation with regard to required knowledge, skills, and abilities (including certifications).					
All non-InfoSec personnel are briefed on their InfoSec roles and responsibilities.					
All personnel with InfoSec responsibilities have them reflected in annual job performance reviews.					

For Further Reading

Information Security Roles & Responsibilities Made Easy by Charles Cresson Wood, Information Shield, 2005.

The Executive MBA in Information Security by John J. Trinckes Jr., CRC Press, 2009.

References

1. Eddie Schwartz, Dan Erwin, Vincent Weafer, and Andy Briney. "Roundtable: Infosec Staffing Help Wanted!" *Information Security Magazine Online.* (April 2001) Accessed 5 July 2007 from infosecuritymag.techtarget.com/articles/april01/features_roundtable.shtml.

2. International Information Systems Security Certification Consortium, Inc. "About SSCP Certification." ISC² Online. Accessed 5 July 2007 from www.isc2.org/cgi-bin/content.cgi?page=815.

3. International Information Systems Security Certification Consortium, Inc. "Associate of (ISC)² Designation." ISC² Online. Accessed 5 July 2007 from www.isc2.org/cgi-bin/content.cgi?page=824.

4. ISACA. "June 2007 CISA Exam Bulletin of Information." WWW Document viewed 26 April 2007 from http://www.isaca.org/Template.cfm?Section=Exam_Information&Template=/ContentManagement/ContentDisplay.cfm&ContentID=27640.

5. CompTIA. "CompTIA Security+ Certification." Accessed 25 April 2007 from certification.comptia .org/security/default.aspx.

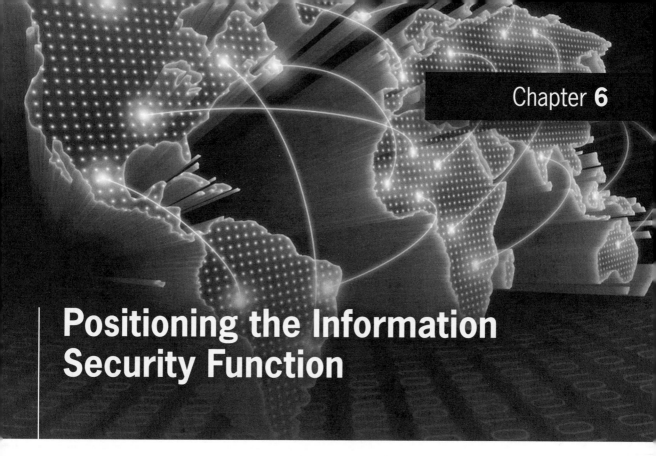

Positioning the Information Security Function

Why is this chapter important? The operations of businesses are forever in flux. Companies down-size, restructure, reorganize, get bought out, or go through bankruptcy to name a few issues that can cause a flux in business flow. Any of these shifts in business can greatly affect the function of information security. That's why positioning the information security program in a shifting business climate requires some thought and planning. The answers to where the information security program should be positioned are not simple. To help you make a strategic decision, the following will provide you with a number of options for locating the information security function within your organization. Some are more common than others, but each has its advantages and disadvantages.

Chapter Overview:

- ▶ Organizing for security
- ▶ Does Size Matter?
- ▶ Placing information security within the organization

ORGANIZING FOR SECURITY

Among the variables that determine how an organization chooses to structure its information security program are organizational culture, size, security personnel budget, and security capital budget. The first and most influential of these variables is the organizational culture. If upper management and staff believe that information security is a waste of time and resources, the information security program will remain small and poorly supported. Efforts made by the information security staff will be viewed as contrary to the mission of the organization and detrimental to the organization's productivity. The organization will spend its time and resources locked in a never-ending struggle to contain fire after fire with a self-fulfilling prophecy that the information security programs cannot protect the organization. Conversely, where there is a strong, positive view of information security, the information security program is likely to be larger and well supported.

The organization's size and available resources also directly affect the size and structure of the information security program. Organizations with complex IT infrastructures and sophisticated system users are likely to require more information security support. Large, complex organizations may have entire divisions dedicated to information security, including a CISO, multiple security managers, multiple administrators, and many technicians. Such divisions might have specialized staff focusing on specific issues—for example, policy, planning, firewalls, and intrusion detection systems (IDSs). In general, the larger the organization is, the larger the information security program is. Smaller organizations, by contrast, may have a single security administrator, or they may assign the information security responsibilities to a systems or network administrator.

Another variable is the personnel budget for the information security program. The size of the information security budget typically corresponds to the size of the organization. Although no standard exists for the size of the information security budget and/or the number of security personnel in any given organization, measured industry averages are available. Industry averages vary widely and may be expressed in terms of information security budget per unit of revenue, in terms of information security staff per number of total employees in the organization, or as information security budget per unit of IT budget. Determining the industry average in any given case may be a challenge, but the reality is that regardless of the industry average, it is the management of the particular organization that has the most influence over this variable, for better or worse. In general, security programs are understaffed for the tasks they have been assigned. Top security managers must constantly struggle to create policy and policy plans, manage personnel issues, plan training, and keep the administrative and support staff focused on their assigned responsibilities and tasks. According to the article "Does Size Matter?,"

> As organizations get larger in size, their security departments are not keeping up with the demands of increasingly complex organizational infrastructures. Security spending per user and per machine declines exponentially as organizations grow, leaving most handcuffed when it comes to implementing effective security procedures.[1]

Office politics, the economy, and budget forecasts are just some of the factors that cause upper management to juggle with staffing levels. In today's environment, the information security programs in most organizations do not yet receive the support they need to function properly. That situation may change, however, because the current political climate and the many reported events regarding information security breaches are rapidly forcing organizational cultures to view information security as another critical function.

It's an old truism in engineering school that any fool can build a bridge. It takes an engineer to build just enough bridge to meet its requirements. Similarly, given unlimited budget and resources, most any fool can run a successful information security program. Budgets and resources are never boundless in the real world and it takes a skilled security professional to manage their budget and resources to address the most serious risks in the most cost-effective manner. The real challenge for the security manager is to make sure they always provide "just enough security."

Another important variable is the capital and expense budget for physical resources dedicated to information security. This budget includes allocation of offices, computer labs, and testing facilities, as well as the general information security expense budget. Because the information security staff handles confidential information regarding security plans, policies, structures, designs, and a host of other items, it is prudent to provide this group with its own secured physical resources, including office space.

DOES SIZE MATTER?

While many IT professionals may think they would be better off in the big IT departments of nationally renowned organizations, the fact is they may be better off at a smaller organization. Big organizations have large staffs, full-time and part-time security professionals, and more problems than the typical smaller organization. This section defines small, medium, large, and very large organizations and describes the problems inherent in each and how they are staffed to deal with them.

- ▶ The small organization has 10 to 100 computers. Most small organizations have a simple, centralized IT organizational model and spend disproportionately more on security, averaging almost 20 percent of the total IT budget. The typical security staff in this organization is usually only one person (the lone ranger!), if in fact there is a full-time security professional. Much more frequently, information security is an additional duty of one of the IT staffers. However, the small organizations, the ones with the smallest budgets, spend more per user than medium- and large-sized organizations. "More than two-thirds say all or most of their security decisions are guided by management-approved policies, and 57 percent say that all or most of their responses to incidents were guided by a predefined IR plan."[2]

- ▶ The medium-sized organization has 100 to 1,000 computers and has a smaller budget (averaging about 11 percent of the total IT budget), about the same security staff, and a larger need than the small organization. The medium-sized organization's security people must rely on help from IT staff to carry out security plans and practices. "Their ability to set policy, handle incidents in a regular manner and effectively allocate resources are, overall, worse than any other group. Considering their size, the number of incidents they recognize is skyrocketing. Some 70 percent of them had damages from security breaches, a 48 percent increase over small organizations."[3]

- ▶ The large organization has 1,000 to 10,000 computers. Organizations of this size have generally integrated planning and policy into the organizational culture;

"eight in 10 organizations say at least some of their security decisions are guided by them."[4] Unfortunately, the large organization tends to spend substantially less on security (only about 5% of the total IT budget on average) creating issues across the organization, especially in the "people" areas.

▶ The very large organization has more than 10,000 computers, and large information security budgets, which may grow faster than IT budgets. However, in these multimillion-dollar security budgets, the average amount per user is still less than in any other type of organization because of economies of scale. "Where small organizations spend more than $5,000 per user on security, very large organizations spend about one-eighteenth of that, roughly $300 per user"; or approximately 6 percent of the total IT budget. The very large organization does a better job in the policy and resource management areas, although "only about a third of organizations in this demographic handled incidents according to an IR plan."[5]

Organizing an information security program poses several managerial challenges. Although the size of an organization influences the organization of its information security program, certain basic functions should occur in every organization, and thus these functions should be included in any budget allocation. Table 6-1 outlines the suggested functions for a successful information security program. These functions are not necessarily performed within the information security department, but they must be performed somewhere within the organization.

TABLE 6-1 Functions of the Information Security Program

FUNCTION	DESCRIPTION	COMMENTS
Risk Assessment	Evaluates risk present in IT initiatives and/or systems	Identifies the sources of risk and may offer advice on controls that can reduce risk
Risk Management	Implements or oversees use of controls used to reduce risk	Often paired with the risk assessment team
Systems Testing	Evaluates patches used to close software vulnerabilities and acceptance testing of new systems to assure compliance with policy and assure effectiveness	Usually part of the incident response and/or risk management functions
Policy	Maintains and promotes information security policy across the organization	Must be coordinated with organization-wide policy processes
Legal Assessment	Maintains awareness of planned and actual laws and their impact, and coordinates with outside legal counsel and law enforcement agencies	Almost always external to the information security and IT departments
Incident Response	Handles initial response to potential incidents, manages escalation of actual incidents, and coordinates the earliest responses to incidents and disasters	Often cross functional, drawn from multiple departments and should include middle management to manage escalation processes
Planning	Researches, creates, maintains, and promotes information security plans; often takes a project management approach to planning as contrasted with strategic planning for the whole organization	Must coordinate with organization-wide policy processes

FUNCTION	DESCRIPTION	COMMENTS
Measurement	Uses existing control systems (and perhaps specialized data collection systems) to measure all aspects of the information security environment	Management relies on timely and accurate statistics to make informed decisions
Compliance	Verifies that system and network administrators repair identified vulnerabilities promptly and correctly	Poses problems for good customer service since it is difficult to be customer-focused and to force compliance at the same time
Centralized Authentication	Manages the granting and revocations of network and system credentials for all members of the organization	Often delegated to the help desk or else staffed in conjunction and colocated with the help desk function
System Security Administration	Administers the configuration of computer systems, which are often organized into groups by the operating system they run	Many organizations may have originally assigned all security functions to these groups; this can be a source of conflict when organizations update their information security program
Training	Trains general staff in information security topics, IT staff in specialized technical controls, and internal information security staff in specialized areas of information security, including both technical and managerial topics	Some or all of this may be done in conjunction with the corporate training department
Network Security Administration	Administer configuration of computer networks, often organized into groups by logical network area (WAN, LAN, DMZ, etc.) or geographic location	Many organizations may have originally assigned some security functions to these groups, which may require close coordination or reassignment
Vulnerability Assessment	Locates exposure within information assets so they can be repaired before weaknesses are exploited	Sometimes called the penetration testing team or the ethical hacking unit; often outsourced to consultant "tiger teams"

Course Technology/Cengage Learning

How Much Should You Be Spending?

One of the most pernicious myths in information security is that there is a fixed percentage of IT budget that should be spent on security (1%, 5%, 10%, etc). The information security budget should be based on the results of the risk analysis, not an arbitrary number pulled out of a glossy magazine.

Industry averages can be used as ballpark estimates but organizational management is becoming increasingly leery of information security budgets that are sized based on fixed percentages. The core issue is that the organization doesn't really have a way to tie the investment to results—they just toss some percentage of the budget into the gaping maw labeled "information security" as if they are making a propitiating sacrifice to a primitive idol in the hope that evil events will be forestalled.

By basing the information security budget on the results of the risk analysis, the CISO is much better positioned to answer tough questions about what the organization can expect to receive in return for those investments.

Security in Large Organizations

Large organizations, which have more than 1,000 devices requiring security management, are likely to be staffed and funded at a level that enables them to accomplish most of the functions identified in Table 6-1. They often create an internal organization to deal with the specific information security challenges they face. Not surprisingly, the security functions and organizational approaches implemented by larger organizations are as diverse as the organizations themselves. Information security departments in such organizations tend to dynamically form and re-form focused internal groups to meet long-term challenges even as they handle day-to-day security operations. Thus, functions are likely to be split into groups in larger organizations; in contrast, smaller organizations typically create fewer groups, perhaps only having one general group representing the whole department.

Security in Medium-Sized Organizations

Medium-sized organizations have between 100 and 1,000 machines requiring security management. These organizations may still be large enough to implement the multitiered approach to security described previously for large organizations, though perhaps with fewer dedicated groups and more functions assigned to each group. In a medium-sized organization, more of the functional areas from Table 6-1 are assigned to other departments within IT, but outside of the information security department. Also, the central authentication function often gets handed off to systems administration personnel within the IT department.

Medium-sized organizations tend to ignore some of the functions from Table 6-1—in particular, when the information security department cannot staff a certain function and the IT or other department is not encouraged or required to perform that function in its stead. In these cases, the CISO must improve the collaboration among these groups and must provide leadership in advocating decisions that stretch the capabilities of the organization.

Security in Small Organizations

Smaller organizations—those with fewer than 100 systems to supervise—face many challenges. Information security in the small organization often becomes the responsibility of a *jack-of-all-trades,* a single security administrator with perhaps one or two assistants for managing the technical components. It is not uncommon in smaller organizations to have the systems or network administrators play these many roles. Such organizations frequently have little in the way of formal policy, planning, or security measures, and they commonly outsource their Web presence or electronic commerce operations. As a result, the security administrator most often deals with desktop management, virus protection, and local area network security issues.

In small organizations, security training and awareness is most commonly conducted on a one-on-one basis, with the security administrator providing advice to users as needed. Any published policies are likely to be issue-specific policies—for example, on Web and Internet use, and fair-and-responsible use of office equipment. Formal planning, when it happens, is usually part of the IT planning conducted by the director of information systems or the CIO.

Threats from insiders are also less likely in an environment where every employee knows every other employee. In general, the less anonymity an employee has, the less likely he or she feels able to get away with mischief, abuse, or misuse of company assets.

PLACING INFORMATION SECURITY WITHIN THE ORGANIZATION

Although there are other valid models for placing the information security department within an organization, in large organizations this department is often located within the information technology department, headed by the CISO who reports directly to the top computing executive, or the CIO. Such a structure implies that the goals and objectives of the CISO and the CIO are closely aligned. In reality, this is not always the case. By its very nature, an information security program is sometimes at odds with the goals and objectives of the information technology department as a whole. On the one hand, the CIO, as the executive in charge of the organization's technology, focuses on the processing efficiency and ease of accessing the organization's information. Anything that limits access or slows information processing directly contradicts the CIO's mission. On the other hand, the CISO functions more like an internal auditor, with the information security department examining existing systems to discover information security faults and flaws in technology, software, and employees' activities and processes. At times, these activities may disrupt the processing and accessing of the organization's information. Because the goals and objectives of the CIO and the CISO may come in conflict, it is not difficult to understand the current movement to separate information security from the IT division. The article "Where the Chief Security Officer Belongs" perhaps states this point more succinctly: "The people who do and the people who watch shouldn't report to a common manager."[6] The challenge is to design a reporting structure for the information security program that balances the competing needs of the communities of interest.

There are many ways to position the information security program within an organization. In his book *Information Security Roles and Responsibilities Made Easy*,[7] Charles Cresson Wood has compiled many of the best practices on information security program positioning from many industry groups.

> *In successful organizational structures, the [Information Security] Department reports high up in the management hierarchy. Reporting directly to top management is advisable for the Information Security Department Manager [or CISO] because it fosters objectivity and the ability to perceive what's truly in the best interest of the organization as a whole, rather than what's in the best interest of a particular department (such as the Information Technology Department). A highly placed executive in charge of information security will also be more readily able to gain management's attention, and this in turn will increase the likelihood that the Information Security Department will obtain the necessary budget and staffing resources. An Information Security Department that reports high up on the management ladder will also be more readily able to force compliance with certain requirements, such as a standard specifying consistent implementation of certain encryption technology.*[8]

Charles Cresson Wood uses six reporting relationships to show the most common reporting relationships of the information security function in modern organizations.

> *"The six [relationships] are illustrative of real-world organizations and are not in any way meant to be hypothetical or normative. [. . .] Because these options are based on real-world experience, you can be assured that any one of these six initial options could be effective within your organization.*

OPTION 1: INFORMATION TECHNOLOGY

In the first option, the Information Security Department Manager reports directly to the Chief Information Officer (CIO), or the Vice President of Information Systems. In this option, you will find the most common organizational structure. Various statistical studies show that over 50% of organizations use this reporting relationship. This option is desirable because the manager to whom the Information Security Department Manager reports generally has clout with top management, and understands (in broad and general terms) the information systems technological issues. . . . Nonetheless, this option is flawed because it includes an inherent conflict of interest. When confronted with resource allocation issues, or when required to strike a trade-off, the CIO is likely to discriminate against the information security function. . . . Another drawback of this option involves the implied conclusion that information security is strictly a technological issue, which clearly it is not. Although common, this organizational structure is not as desirable as several of the other options, and for that reason is not particularly recommended.

OPTION 2: SECURITY

Another popular option, which again is not necessarily recommended, involves the Information Security Department reporting to a Security Department. In this case, the information security function is perceived to be primarily protective in nature, and therefore comparable to the Physical Security Department as well as the Personnel Security and Safety Department. Where this organizational design prevails, you may occasionally find the Information Security Department is instead referred to as the Information Protection Department. This approach is desirable because it facilitates communication with others who have both a security perspective and related security responsibilities. This may help with incident investigations as well as reaching practical solutions to problems like laptop computer theft (which involves a combination of physical and information security).

Nonetheless, there are some problems with this structure. Although the information security and physical security functions may at first seem to be philosophically aligned, there is a significant cultural difference between the two. For example, information security staff see themselves as high-tech workers, while physical security staff see themselves as participants in the criminal justice system. This option is moreover undesirable because, at most firms, the budget for physical security has not increased much over the last few years, but the budget for information security has rapidly escalated; by combining these two departments under the Security Department umbrella, top management may underestimate the resources that the information security function will need.

OPTION 3: ADMINISTRATIVE SERVICES

Another way to do things, which is a significant improvement over both Option 1 and 2, has the Information Security Department reporting to the Administrative Services Department (which may also be called Administrative Support). In this case, the Information Security Department Manager reports to the Administrative Services Department Manager or the Vice President of Administration. This approach assumes that the Information Security Department is advisory in nature (also called a staff function), and performs services for workers throughout the organization, much like the Human Resources Department. This option is desirable because it acknowledges that information and information systems are found everywhere throughout the organization, and that workers throughout the organization are expected to work with the Information Security Department. This option is also attractive because it supports efforts to secure information no matter what form it takes (on paper, verbal, etc.), rather than viewing the information security function as strictly a computer- and network-oriented activity.

In many cases, depending on who fills the Administrative Services Vice President position, this option suffers because the Vice President doesn't know much about information systems technology, and this in turn may hamper his or her efforts to communicate with the CEO about information security.

OPTION 4: INSURANCE AND RISK MANAGEMENT

The Information Security Department can report to the Insurance and Risk Management Department. With this approach, the Information Security Department Manager would typically report to the Chief Risk Manager (CRM) or the Vice President of Risk and Insurance Management. This option is desirable because it fosters what is often called an integrated risk management perspective. With this viewpoint, a centralized perspective prioritizes and compares all risks across the organization.

The CRM is also likely to be prevention oriented, adopt a longer-term viewpoint, and is able to engage the CEO in intelligent discussions about risk acceptance (doing nothing), risk mitigation (adding controls), and risk transfer (buying insurance). A CRM is also likely to be comfortable thinking about the future and generating scenarios reflecting a number of different possibilities, including information security scenarios such as a denial-of-service (DoS) attack. The CRM, however, is often not familiar with information systems technology, and so may need some special coaching or extra background research from the Information Security Department Manager to make important points with the CEO. Another problem with this approach is that its focus is strategic, and the operational and administrative aspects of information security (such as changing privileges when people change jobs) may not get the attention that they deserve from the CRM.

OPTION 5: STRATEGY AND PLANNING

Here the Information Security Department reports to the Strategy and Planning Department. In this case, the Information Security Department Manager reports directly to the Vice President of Strategy and Planning. This option views the information security function as critical to the success of the organization. This option would be appropriate for an Internet merchant (a "dot-com" enterprise) or a credit card company, both of which are critically dependent on the success of the information security function.

Option 5 is [also] desirable because it underscores the need for documented information security requirements (policies, standards, procedures, etc.) that apply to the entire organization. . . . Another desirable aspect of this approach is that it implicitly communicates that information security is very importantly a management and people issue, not just a technological issue.

This same advantage can be a disadvantage if workers in the Information Technology Department consider the staff in the Information Security Department to be management oriented, and out of touch when it comes to the technology. One problem with this approach is that the focus is strategic, and the operational and administrative aspects of information security (such as changing privileges when people change jobs) may not get the attention that they deserve from the Vice President of Strategy and Planning.

OPTION 6: LEGAL

[While not common,] in this case the Information Security Department reports to the Legal Department. This option correctly emphasizes that information is the asset of primary concern, not information systems. This option thus places great emphasis on copyrights, patents, trademarks, and related intellectual property protection mechanisms. As they should, contracts—such as nondisclosure agreements (NDAs) and outsourcing agreements—will also get great attention with this organizational *structure. With this option there is also great emphasis on compliance with laws, regulations, and ethical standards (like privacy). Information security is increasingly mandated by law, regulated, and affected by ethical standards, so Option 6 is really an organizational structure for the future. If your organization happens to be in a highly regulated industry, such as credit bureaus or defense contractors, then this organizational structure could be appropriate today. . . . This reporting structure is also advisable because the members of the Legal Department are comfortable with, and spend a lot of time developing, documentation such as policies and procedures; and documentation showing that the organization is in compliance with the information security standard of due care is increasingly important.*

On the downside of Option 6 is the potential overemphasis on compliance, with the potential consequential underemphasis on other aspects of information security, such as access control administration. This organizational structure might also inadvertently lead to the Information Security Department doing compliance checking work, which presents a clear conflict of interest. Compliance checking should be performed by an Internal Auditing Department, not the Information Security Department.

OTHER OPTIONS

Other, less desirable, options could include:

Option 7: Internal Audit: where the Information Security Manager reports to the Internal Auditing Department Manager.

Option 8: Help Desk: where the Information Security Department Manager reports to the Help Desk Department Manager.

Option 9: Accounting and Finance Through IT: where the Information Security Manager reports to the Accounting and Finance Manager through the Information Technology Department.

Option 10: Human Resources: where the Information Security manager reports to the Human Resources manager.

Option 11: Facilities Management: where the Information Security manager reports to the Facilities Management (sometimes called Buildings and Grounds) manager.

Option 12: Operations: where the Information Security Department manager reports to the Chief Operating Officer (COO).

SUMMARY OF REPORTING RELATIONSHIPS

The Information Security Department at many organizations has been an unwelcome stepchild, handed back and forth between various groups, none of which felt as though they were its proper home. [. . .]

Smaller organizations will want to have a part-time Information Security Coordinator or Information Security Manager. [. . .] Small to medium-sized organizations will often require at least one full-time person, and medium-sized to large organizations will often require several full-time information security staff. [. . .] Since so few people are involved, in smaller organizations, the formal designation of a separate department will be considered to be unwarranted. But for all other organizations, no matter where the information security function happens to report, it is desirable to designate a separate department that has been formally recognized by top management. [. . .][9]

It's an unfortunate fact of life that the information security manager has very little control over where his or her organization is positioned, at least in the beginning. This requires him or her to understand the focus, biases, and reporting relationships of the organization where he or she is placed and adapt efforts to work within them. This often requires impeccable people skills in order to build the relationships, educate the other managers about information security, and acquire the resources in order to achieve the information security manager's objective of protecting the organization's information assets.

This chapter provided an overview of the various places where information security has often been grafted into the organizational tree and presented the special concerns and challenges accompanying this graft. The new information security manager should take heart from the fact that these examples were drawn from real-life organizations and where the manager in each case was able to develop a functioning security program despite the challenges posed by the organizational location.

The Information Security Manager's Checklist

	No	Planned	In Progress	In Place	Integrated
This topic has been fully tested, validated, and integrated into organizational operations with formal performance measures in place (as appropriate).					
This topic has been implemented, but not fully tested, validated, and integrated into organizational operations.					
The implementation of this topic has begun, but is not yet complete.					
The formal planning for this topic has begun, but is not yet complete.					
This subject has not formally begun planning, or the organization has made a conscious decision not to pursue this topic.					
6. Positioning the Security Function					
Position of InfoSec in the organization has been specifically implemented and reviewed.					
CISO or equivalent manager has appropriate reporting relationships (both formal and informal).					
InfoSec position does not threaten viability of information asset protection profile.					
InfoSec department has appropriate staff to accomplish assigned mission.					

For Further Reading

Information Security Roles & Responsibilities Made Easy by Charles Cresson Wood, Information Sheild, 2005.

References

1. Andrew Briney and Frank Prince. Does Size Matter? *Information Security,* September 2002, 36–54.

2. Ibid.

3. Ibid.

4. Ibid.

5. Ibid.

6. M. Hayes. Where the Chief Security Officer Belongs. *InformationWeek*, 25 February 2002. Accessed 4 May 2003. http://www.informationweek.com/story/showArticle.jhtml?articleID=6500913.

7. Charles Cresson Wood. *Information Security Roles and Responsibilities Made Easy.* Houston: PentaSafe, 2002: 95–105. Used with permission.

8. Ibid.

9. Ibid.

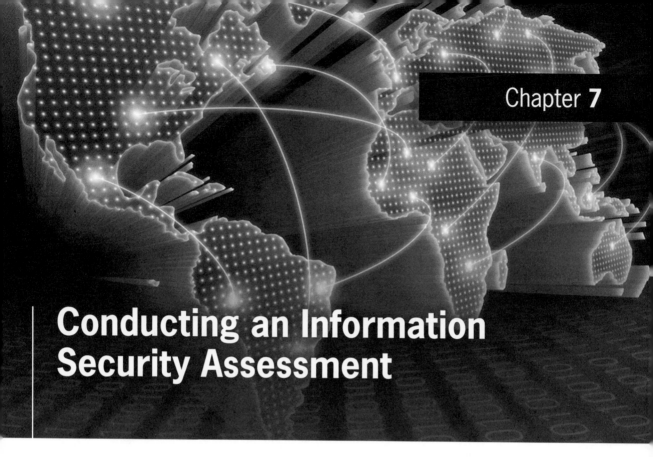

Chapter 7

Conducting an Information Security Assessment

At some point in your role as the information security professional, you will need to look at the big picture—to examine the entire organization's security efforts from the perspective of overall business operations. This may be part of an initial assessment, where you have new responsibilities, and you need to determine how effective the organization is currently protecting its information assets. Or, it may be part of a periodic reassessment to determine how effective recent efforts in risk management have been in implementing new controls. In some cases this effort is triggered by an event that makes an assessment necessary to see if there are critical deficiencies that need immediate attention. When it comes to information security program assessments, few organizations have effective tools in place to make this a straightforward and repeatable process.

Chapter Overview:

- ▶ Conducting security assessments
- ▶ Security controls
- ▶ Performing the assessment
- ▶ Using the results

CONDUCTING SECURITY ASSESSMENTS

A number of tools could be used to conduct this assessment, ranging from proprietary check-lists provided by consulting companies to those derived from publicly available information, like the ISO 27000 series and the NIST (National Institute of Standards and Technology) documents. There are also sources of specific industry guidance, for example, the PCI-DSS (Payment Card Industry Data Security Standard). What is most important is that you find a comprehensive checklist relevant to your industry or environment so that you can fully assess not just the technical security implementation, but also the effectiveness of security planning, policy, and program efforts. Equally important is that the results of the assessment are used regularly to improve the security program, and that the assessment is repeated regularly to determine whether or not the organization is improving. This use of a baseline, described in later chapters, results in what is known as a Gap Analysis—the comparison of what was to what is—with improvements and shortfalls noted. In fact, the security professional should create two Gap Analyses, one comparing the organization's past performance to the current performance, and one comparing the organization's current performance to Standards of Due Care—that level of effort that a prudent organization should be displaying. Fortunately both can be performed with the same assessment, once a measure of what the "prudent organization" should be doing is determined.

The first step is to determine what controls the organization should have in place and then to assess compliance with those controls. The following sections provide a sample set of controls, derived from the NIST Documents Special Publication 800-53 Revision 1, Recommended Security Controls for Federal Information Systems. While these documents are binding guidance only on U.S. federal information systems, they are a public source of a fairly comprehensive set of security controls that apply in many private sector organizations as well. No single organization will likely need to apply all these controls, but starting with a comprehensive list and eliminating the inapplicable one is a good tactic for making sure that something is not overlooked.

SECURITY CONTROLS

The NIST security controls are broken down into three classes with a total of seventeen control families. The three classes correspond to the NIST approach of management, operational, and technical control groups. The remainder of this chapter is adapted and in some cases quoted directly from NIST SP 800-53 Rev 1. Detailed guidance for assessing the degree of compliance with each of the items is provided in NIST SP 800-53A "Guide for Assessing the Security Controls in Federal Information Systems."

Access Controls (AC)

Access control is a family within the technical class that deals with who will have which access to an organization's information assets. This includes specification of purpose for access, scope of access, roles and responsibilities, management commitment, coordination across organizational boundaries as well as the demonstration of compliance.

AC-1 Access Control Policy and Procedures—The organization has and periodically reviews a formal, documented access control policy and has formal documented procedures that implement the policy.

AC-2 Account Management—The organization manages information system accounts; their creation, activation, modification, review, disabling, and deletion. The accounts are reviewed periodically and at least annually.

AC-3 Account Enforcement—The information system enforces authorizations in controlling access to the system in accordance with policy.

AC-4 Information flow Enforcement—The system enforces authorizations in controlling information flows within the system and between interconnected systems in accordance with policy.

AC-5 Separation of Duties—The system enforces separation of duties through assigned access authorizations. The intent is to preclude activities such as fraud by requiring two or more individuals to participate in an action that neither can perform alone.

AC-6 Least Privilege—The system enforces the minimal set of privileges required to perform a specific task.

AC-7 Unsuccessful Logon Attempts—The system enforces a specified limit on the number of invalid access attempts by a user over a specified period of time. When the limit is exceeded, the system will either lock the affected account or impose a delay before another logon can be attempted.

AC-8 System Use Notification—The system displays an approved system use notification message before granting system access. This notification may take the form of a login banner that informs the user that this is a private system, access is by permission only, activities may be monitored and recorded, etc.

AC-9 Previous Logon Notification—The system notifies the user upon successful logon of the date and time of the last successful logon and the number of unsuccessful logon attempts since that successful logon. This is an optional control.

AC-10 Concurrent Session Limit—The system limits the number of concurrent sessions to a specified limit.

AC-11 Session Lock—After a specified period of inactivity, the system prevents further access by initiating a session lock that remains in effect until the user reestablishes access using appropriate identification and authorization procedures.

AC-12 Session Termination—After a specified period of inactivity, the system automatically terminates a remote session.

AC-13 Supervision and Review—Access Control—The organization supervises and reviews the activities of users with respect to the enforcement and usage of access controls.

AC-14 Permitted Actions without Identification or Authentication—The organization identifies and documents specific user actions that can be performed without identification or authentication.

AC-15 Automated Marking—The system marks output using standard naming conventions to identify any special dissemination, handling, or distribution restrictions. This is an optional control.

AC-16 Automated Labeling—The system appropriately labels information in storage (at rest), in process (in use), and in transmission (in flight). This is an optional control.

AC-17 Remote Access—The organization authorizes, monitors, and controls all methods of remote access to the information system.

AC-18 Wireless Access Restrictions—The organization both establishes usage restrictions and implementation guidance for wireless technologies and authorizes, monitors, and controls wireless access.

AC-19 Access Controls for Portable and Mobile Devices—The organization: (i) establishes usage restrictions and implementation guidance for wireless technologies; and (ii) authorizes, monitors, and controls wireless access to the information system.

AC-20 Use of External Information Systems—The organization: (i) establishes usage restrictions and implementation guidance for organization-controlled portable and mobile devices; and (ii) authorizes, monitors, and controls device access to organizational information systems.

Awareness and Training Controls (AT)

Awareness and training is a family within the operational controls class that seeks to assure that the organization's employees understand its security policies and the rationale behind them.

AT-1 Security Awareness and Training Policy and Procedures—The organization develops, disseminates, and periodically reviews/updates: (i) a formal, documented, security awareness and training policy that addresses purpose, scope, roles, responsibilities, management commitment, coordination among organizational entities, and compliance; and (ii) formal, documented procedures to facilitate the implementation of the security awareness and training policy and associated security awareness and training controls.

AT-2 Security Awareness—The organization provides basic security awareness training to all information system users (including managers and senior executives) before authorizing access to the system, when required by system changes, and periodically thereafter.

AT-3 Security Training—The organization identifies personnel that have significant information system security roles and responsibilities during the system development life cycle, documents those roles and responsibilities, and provides appropriate information system security training: (i) before authorizing access to the system or performing assigned duties; (ii) when required by system changes; and (iii) periodically thereafter.

AT-4 Security Training Records—The organization documents and monitors individual information system security training activities including basic security awareness training and specific information system security training.

AT-5 Contacts with Security Groups and Associations—The organization establishes and maintains contacts with special interest groups, specialized forums, professional associations, news groups, and/or peer groups of security professionals in similar organizations to stay up to date with the latest recommended security practices, techniques, and technologies and to share the latest security-related information including threats, vulnerabilities, and incidents. This is an optional control.

Audit and Accountability Controls (AU)

Audit and accountability controls are concerned with maintaining a record of what events occurred and assuring that those events can be traced to a specific identity. For example, changing the access control list on the account master file would create an audit event documenting the change and the time it occurred, thus recording that the change was performed by Joe Jones on March 23, 2011 at 3:54 PM. Other details might also be recorded about where the request came from within the network.

AU-1 Audit and Accountability Policy and Procedures—The organization develops, disseminates, and periodically reviews/updates: (i) a formal, documented, audit and accountability policy that addresses purpose, scope, roles, responsibilities, management commitment, coordination among organizational entities, and compliance; and (ii) formal, documented procedures to facilitate the implementation of the audit and accountability policy and associated audit and accountability controls.

AU-2 Auditable Events—The information system generates audit records for the specified events. Moderate impact systems must additionally periodically review and update the list of auditable events.

AU-3 Content of Audit Records—The information system produces audit records that contain sufficient information to establish what events occurred, the sources of the events, and the outcomes of the events.

AU-4 Audit Storage Capacity—The organization allocates sufficient audit record storage capacity and configures auditing to reduce the likelihood of such capacity being exceeded.

AU-5 Response to Audit Processing Failures—The information system alerts appropriate organizational officials in the event of an audit processing failure and takes specified actions (e.g., shut down the system, overwrite oldest log records, etc.).

AU-6 Audit Monitoring, Analysis, and Reporting—The organization regularly reviews/ analyzes information system audit records for indications of inappropriate or unusual activity, investigates suspicious activity or suspected violations, reports findings to appropriate officials, and takes necessary actions.

AU-7 Audit Reduction and Report Generation—The information system provides an audit reduction and report generation capability.

AU-8 Time Stamps—The information system provides time stamps for use in audit record generation.

AU-9 Protection of Audit Information—The information system protects audit information and audit tools from unauthorized access, modification, and deletion.

AU-10 Nonrepudiation—The information system provides the capability to determine whether a given individual took a particular action. This is a core support for providing accountability.

AU-11 Audit Record Retention—The organization retains audit records for an appropriate, specified period of time to provide support for after-the-fact investigations of security incidents and to meet regulatory and organizational information retention requirements.

Certification, Accreditation, and Security Assessments (CA)

The certification, accreditation, and security assessment controls are a family in the management class and are concerned with accrediting (authorizing use of) information systems, certifying their compliance with policy and regular assessment of their security controls.

CA-1 Certification, Accreditation, and Security Assessment Policies and Procedures—
The organization develops, disseminates, and periodically reviews/updates: (i) formal,

documented, security assessment and certification and accreditation policies that address purpose, scope, roles, responsibilities, management commitment, coordination among organizational entities, and compliance; and (ii) formal, documented procedures to facilitate the implementation of the security assessment and certification and accreditation policies and associated assessment, certification, and accreditation controls.

CA-2 Security Assessments—The organization conducts an assessment of the security controls in the information system on a regular basis to determine the extent to which the controls are implemented correctly, operating as intended and producing the desired outcome with respect to meeting the security requirements for the system.

CA-3 Information System Connections—The organization authorizes all connections from the information system to other information systems outside of the accreditation boundary through the use of system connection agreements and monitors/controls the system connections on an ongoing basis.

CA-4 Security Certification—The organization conducts an assessment of the security controls in the information system to determine the extent to which the controls are implemented correctly, operating as intended and producing the desired outcome with respect to meeting the security requirements for the system.

CA-5 Plan of Action and Milestones—The organization develops and updates periodically a plan of action and milestones for the information system that documents the organization's planned, implemented, and evaluated remedial actions to correct deficiencies noted during the assessment of the security controls and to reduce or eliminate known vulnerabilities in the system.

CA-6 Security Accreditation—The organization authorizes (i.e., accredits) the information system for processing before operations and updates the authorization periodically or when there is a significant change to the system. A senior organizational official signs and approves the security accreditation.

CA-7 Continuous Monitoring—The organization monitors the security controls in the information system on an ongoing basis.

Configuration Management Controls (CM)

Configuration management controls are a family within the operational class that are concerned with how systems are configured in their initial deployment and how changes in that configuration are managed over time. This area is often overlooked with the result that systems and equipment are deployed in an insecure state (e.g., with vendor default users and passwords still in effect), or a secure initial baseline configuration is gradually "unhardened" by a sequence of changes that happen over time without any thought or analysis of the overall effect of the change history. Changes to a running system are also a major source of downtime when consequences of the change have not been carefully considered and analyzed.

CM-1 Configuration Management Policy and Procedures—The organization develops, disseminates, and periodically reviews/updates: (i) a formal, documented, configuration management policy that addresses purpose, scope, roles, responsibilities, management commitment, coordination among organizational entities, and compliance; and (ii) formal, documented procedures to facilitate the implementation of the configuration management policy and associated configuration management controls.

CM-2 Baseline Configuration—The organization develops, documents, and maintains a current baseline configuration of the information system.

CM-3 Configuration Change Control—The organization authorizes, documents, and controls changes to the information system.

CM-4 Monitoring Configuration Changes—The organization monitors changes to the information system conducting security impact analyses to determine the effects of the changes.

CM-5 Access Restrictions for Change—The organization: (i) approves individual access privileges and enforces physical and logical access restrictions associated with changes to the information system; and (ii) generates, retains, and reviews records reflecting all such changes.

CM-6 Configuration Settings—The organization: (i) establishes mandatory configuration settings for information technology products employed within the information system; (ii) configures the security settings of information technology products to the most restrictive mode consistent with operational requirements; (iii) documents the configuration settings; and (iv) enforces the configuration settings in all components of the information system.

CM-7 Least Functionality—The organization configures the information system to provide only essential capabilities and specifically prohibits and/or restricts the use of the following functions, ports, protocols, and/or services: [Assignment: organization-defined list of prohibited and/or restricted functions, ports, protocols, and/or services].

CM-8 Information System Component Inventory—The organization develops, documents, and maintains a current inventory of the components of the information system and relevant ownership information.

Contingency Planning Controls (CP)

Contingency planning controls are a family within the operational class that deal with how the organization plans to handle unexpected events when they occur.

CP-1 Contingency Planning Policy and Controls—The organization develops, disseminates, and periodically reviews/updates: (i) a formal, documented contingency planning policy that addresses purpose, scope, roles, responsibilities, management commitment, coordination among organizational entities, and compliance; and (ii) formal, documented procedures to facilitate the implementation of the contingency planning policy and associated contingency planning controls.

CP-2 Contingency Plan—The organization develops and implements a contingency plan for the information system addressing contingency roles, responsibilities, assigned individuals with contact information, and activities associated with restoring the system after a disruption or failure. Designated officials within the organization review and approve the contingency plan and distribute copies of the plan to key contingency personnel.

CP-3 Contingency Training—The organization trains personnel in their contingency roles and responsibilities with respect to the information system and provides refresher training on a periodic basis (at least annually).

CP-4 Contingency Plan Testing and Exercises—The organization: (i) tests and/or exercises the contingency plan for the information system periodically (at least annually) using appropriate tests and exercise scenarios to determine the plan's effectiveness and the organization's readiness to execute the plan; and (ii) reviews the contingency plan test/exercise results and initiates corrective actions.

CP-5 Contingency Plan Update—The organization reviews the contingency plan for the information system periodically (at least annually) and revises the plan to address system/organizational changes or problems encountered during plan implementation, execution, or testing.

CP-6 Alternate Storage Site—The organization identifies an alternate storage site and initiates necessary agreements to permit the storage of information system backup information.

CP-7 Alternate Processing Site—The organization identifies an alternate processing site and initiates necessary agreements to permit the resumption of information system operations for critical mission/business functions within a specified time when the primary processing capabilities are unavailable.

CP-8 Telecommunications Services—The organization identifies primary and alternate telecommunications services to support the information system and initiates necessary agreements to permit the resumption of system operations for critical mission/business functions within a specified time when the primary telecommunications capabilities are unavailable.

CP-9 Information Systems Backup—The organization conducts backups of user-level and system-level information (including system state information) contained in the information system periodically and protects backup information at the storage location.

CP-10 Information Systems Recovery and Reconstitution—The organization employs mechanisms with supporting procedures to allow the information system to be recovered and reconstituted to a known secure state after a disruption or failure.

Identification and Authentication Controls (IA)

The identification and authentication controls are a family within the technical class that are concerned with the means used to assert and prove an identity.

IA-1 Identification and Authentication Policy and Procedures—The organization develops, disseminates, and periodically reviews/updates: (i) a formal, documented identification and authentication policy that addresses purpose, scope, roles, responsibilities, management commitment, coordination among organizational entities, and compliance; and (ii) formal, documented procedures to facilitate the implementation of the identification and authentication policy and associated identification and authentication controls.

IA-2 User Identification and Authentication—The information system uniquely identifies and authenticates users (or processes acting on behalf of users).

IA-3 Device Identification and Authentication—The information system identifies and authenticates specific devices before establishing a connection.

IA-4 Identifier Management—The organization manages user identifiers by: (i) uniquely identifying each user; (ii) verifying the identity of each user; (iii) receiving authorization to issue a user identifier from an appropriate organization official; (iv) issuing the user identifier to the intended party; (v) disabling the user identifier after a specified period of inactivity; and (vi) archiving user identifiers.

IA-5 Authenticator Management—The organization manages information system authenticators by: (i) defining initial authenticator content; (ii) establishing administrative procedures for initial authenticator distribution, for lost/compromised or damaged authenticators, and for revoking authenticators; (iii) changing default authenticators upon information system installation; and (iv) changing/refreshing authenticators periodically.

IA-6 Authenticator Feedback—The information system obscures feedback of authentication information during the authentication process to protect the information from possible exploitation/use by unauthorized individuals.

IA-7 Cryptographic Module Authentication—The information system employs authentication methods that meet the requirements of applicable laws, executive orders, directives, policies, regulations, standards, and guidance for authentication to a cryptographic module.

Incident Response Controls (IR)

The incident response controls are a family within the operational class that are concerned with how security incidents are detected and handled within an organization.

IR-1 Incident Response Policy and Procedures—The organization develops, disseminates, and periodically reviews/updates: (i) a formal, documented incident response policy that addresses purpose, scope, roles, responsibilities, management commitment, coordination among organizational entities, and compliance; and (ii) formal, documented procedures to facilitate the implementation of the incident response policy and associated incident response controls.

IR-2 Incident Response Training—The organization trains personnel in their incident response roles and responsibilities with respect to the information system and provides refresher training on a periodic basis (at least annually).

IR-3 Incident Response Testing and Exercises—The organization tests and/or exercises the incident response capability for the information system periodically (at least annually) using appropriate tests and exercise scenarios to determine the incident response effectiveness and documents the results.

IR-4 Incident Handling—The organization implements an incident handling capability for security incidents that includes preparation, detection and analysis, containment, eradication, and recovery.

IR-5 Incident Monitoring—The organization tracks and documents information system security incidents on an ongoing basis.

IR-6 Incident Reporting—The organization promptly reports incident information to appropriate authorities.

IR-7 Incident Response Assistance—The organization provides an incident response support resource that offers advice and assistance to users of the information system for the handling and reporting of security incidents. The support resource is an integral part of the organization's incident response capability.

Maintenance Controls (MA)

Maintenance controls are a family within the operational class that are concerned with how regular and preventive maintenance activities are managed within the organization.

MA-1 System Maintenance Policy and Procedures—The organization develops, disseminates, and periodically reviews/updates: (i) a formal, documented information system maintenance policy that addresses purpose, scope, roles, responsibilities, management commitment, coordination among organizational entities, and compliance; and (ii) formal, documented procedures to facilitate the implementation of the information system maintenance policy and associated system maintenance controls.

MA-2 Controlled Maintenance—The organization schedules, performs, documents, and reviews records of routine preventative and regular maintenance (including repairs) on the components of the information system in accordance with manufacturer or vendor specifications and/or organizational requirements.

MA-3 Maintenance Tools—The organization approves, controls, and monitors the use of information system maintenance tools and maintains the tools on an ongoing basis.

MA-4 Remote Maintenance—The organization authorizes, monitors, and controls any remotely executed maintenance and diagnostic activities, if employed.

MA-5 Maintenance Personnel—The organization allows only authorized personnel to perform maintenance on the information system.

MA-6 Timely Maintenance—The organization obtains maintenance support and spare parts for key information system components within specified time since failure.

Media Protection Controls (MP)

Media protection controls are a family within the operational class and are concerned with how information media are handled and protected.

MP-1 Media Protection Policy and Procedures—The organization develops, disseminates, and periodically reviews/updates: (i) a formal, documented media protection policy that addresses purpose, scope, roles, responsibilities, management commitment, coordination among organizational entities, and compliance; and (ii) formal, documented procedures to facilitate the implementation of the media protection policy and associated media protection controls.

MP-2 Media Access—The organization restricts access to information system media to authorized individuals.

MP-3 Media Labeling—The organization: (i) affixes external labels to removable information system media and information system output indicating the distribution limitations, handling caveats and applicable security markings (if any) of the information; and (ii) exempts a specified list of media from labeling as long as they remain within a specified protected environment.

MP-4 Media Storage—The organization physically controls and securely stores information system media within controlled areas.

MP-5 Media Transport—The organization protects and controls information system media during transport outside of controlled areas and restricts the activities associated with transport of such media to authorized personnel.

MP-6 Media Sanitization and Disposal—The organization sanitizes information system media, both digital and nondigital, prior to disposal or release for reuse.

Physical and Environmental Protection Controls (PE)

The physical and environmental protection controls are a family within the operational class and are concerned with providing a safe physical environment for information systems and their operations.

PE-1 Physical and Environmental Protection Policy and Procedures—The organization develops, disseminates, and periodically reviews/updates: (i) a formal, documented physical and environmental protection policy that addresses purpose, scope, roles, responsibilities, management commitment, coordination among organizational entities, and compliance; and (ii) formal, documented procedures to facilitate the implementation of the physical and environmental protection policy and associated physical and environmental protection controls.

PE-2 Physical Access Authorizations—The organization develops and keeps current a list of personnel with authorized access to the facility where the information system resides (except for those areas within the facility officially designated as publicly accessible) and issues appropriate authorization credentials. Designated officials within the organization review and approve the access list and authorization credentials on a periodic basis (and at least annually).

PE-3 Physical Access Control—The organization controls all physical access points (including designated entry/exit points) to the facility where the information system resides (except for those areas within the facility officially designated as publicly accessible) and verifies individual access authorizations before granting access to the facility. The organization controls access to areas officially designated as publicly accessible, as appropriate, in accordance with the organization's assessment of risk.

PE-4 Access Control for Transmission Medium—The organization controls physical access to information system distribution and transmission lines within organizational facilities.

PE-5 Access Control for Display Medium—The organization controls physical access to information system devices that display information to prevent unauthorized individuals from observing the display output.

PE-6 Monitoring Physical Access—The organization monitors physical access to the information system to detect and respond to physical security incidents.

PE-7 Visitor Control—The organization controls physical access to the information system by authenticating visitors before authorizing access to the facility where the information system resides other than areas designated as publicly accessible.

PE-8 Access Records—The organization maintains visitor access records to the facility where the information system resides (except for those areas within the facility officially designated as publicly accessible) that includes: (i) name and organization of the person visiting; (ii) signature of the visitor; (iii) form of identification; (iv) date of access; (v) time of entry and departure; (vi) purpose of visit; and (vii) name and organization of person visited. Designated officials within the organization review the visitor access records on a regular basis.

PE-9 Power Equipment and Power Cabling—The organization protects power equipment and power cabling for the information system from damage and destruction.

PE-10 Emergency Shutoff—The organization provides, for specific locations within a facility containing concentrations of information system resources, the capability of shutting off power to any information system component that may be malfunctioning or threatened without endangering personnel by requiring them to approach the equipment.

PE-11 Emergency Power—The organization provides a short-term uninterruptible power supply to facilitate an orderly shutdown of the information system in the event of a primary power source loss.

PE-12 Emergency Lighting—The organization employs and maintains automatic emergency lighting that activates in the event of a power outage or disruption and that covers emergency exits and evacuation routes.

PE-13 Fire Protection—The organization employs and maintains fire suppression and detection devices/systems that can be activated in the event of a fire.

PE-14 Temperature and Humidity Controls—The organization regularly maintains, within acceptable levels, and monitors the temperature and humidity within the facility where the information system resides.

PE-15 Water Damage Protection—The organization protects the information system from water damage resulting from broken plumbing lines or other sources of water leakage by providing master shutoff valves that are accessible, working properly, and known to key personnel.

PE-16 Delivery and Removal—The organization authorizes and controls information system–related items entering and exiting the facility and maintains appropriate records of those items.

PE-17 Alternate Work Site—The organization employs appropriate management, operational, and technical information system security controls at alternate work sites.

PE-18 Location of Information System Components—The organization positions information system components within the facility to minimize potential damage from physical and environmental hazards and to minimize the opportunity for unauthorized access.

PE-19 Information Leakage—The organization protects the information system from information leakage due to electromagnetic signals' emanations.

Planning Controls (PL)

Planning controls are a family within the management class that are concerned with how the organization does its planning and how those plans are documented.

PL-1 Security Planning Policy and Procedures—The organization develops, disseminates, and periodically reviews/updates: (i) a formal, documented security planning policy that addresses purpose, scope, roles, responsibilities, management commitment, coordination among organizational entities, and compliance; and (ii) formal, documented procedures to facilitate the implementation of the security planning policy and associated security planning controls.

PL-2 System Security Plan—The organization develops and implements a security plan for the information system that provides an overview of the security requirements for the system and a description of the security controls in place or planned for meeting those requirements. Designated officials within the organization review and approve the plan.

PL-3 System Security Plan Update—The organization reviews the security plan for the information system on a periodic basis (and at least annually) and revises the plan to address system/organizational changes or problems identified during plan implementation or security control assessments.

PL-4 Rules of Behavior—The organization establishes and makes readily available to all information system users a set of rules that describes their responsibilities and expected behavior with regard to information and information system usage. The organization receives signed acknowledgment from users indicating that they have read, understand, and agree to abide by the rules of behavior, before authorizing access to the information system and its resident information.

PL-5 Privacy Impact Assessment—The organization conducts a privacy impact assessment on the information system in accordance with OMB policy (or other regulations that may apply).

PL-6 Security-Related Activity Planning—The organization plans and coordinates security-related activities affecting the information system before conducting such activities in order to reduce the impact on organizational operations (i.e., mission, functions, image, and reputation), organizational assets, and individuals.

Personnel Security Controls (PS)

Personnel security controls are a family in the operational class that address how the organization handles the human component of the information system to assure compliance with security policies.

PS-1 Personnel Security Policy and Procedures—The organization develops, disseminates, and periodically reviews/updates: (i) a formal, documented personnel security policy that addresses purpose, scope, roles, responsibilities, management commitment, coordination among organizational entities, and compliance; and (ii) formal, documented procedures to facilitate the implementation of the personnel security policy and associated personnel security controls.

PS-2 Position Categorization—The organization assigns a risk designation to all positions and establishes screening criteria for individuals filling those positions. The organization reviews and revises position risk designations on a regular basis.

PS-3 Personnel Screening—The organization screens individuals requiring access to organizational information and information systems before authorizing access.

PS-4 Personnel Termination—The organization, upon termination of individual employment, terminates information system access, conducts exit interviews, retrieves all organizational information system-related property, and provides appropriate personnel with access to official records created by the terminated employee that are stored on organizational information systems.

PS-5 Personnel Transfer—The organization reviews information systems/facilities' access authorizations when personnel are reassigned or transferred to other positions within the organization and initiates appropriate actions.

PS-6 Access Agreements—The organization completes appropriate signed access agreements for individuals requiring access to organizational information and information systems before authorizing access and reviews/updates the agreements on a regular basis.

PS-7 Third-Party Personnel Security—The organization establishes personnel security requirements including security roles and responsibilities for third-party providers and monitors provider compliance.

PS-8 Personnel Sanctions—The organization employs a formal sanctions process for personnel failing to comply with established information security policies and procedures.

Risk Assessment Controls (RA)

Risk assessment controls are a family within the management class that are concerned with how risk is determined (assessed) so that the proper risk management decisions can be made.

RA-1 Risk Assessment Policy and Procedures—The organization develops, disseminates, and periodically reviews/updates: (i) a formal, documented risk assessment policy that addresses purpose, scope, roles, responsibilities, management commitment, coordination among organizational entities, and compliance; and (ii) formal, documented procedures to facilitate the implementation of the risk assessment policy and associated risk assessment controls.

RA-2 Security Categorization—The organization categorizes the information system and the information processed, stored, or transmitted by the system in accordance with applicable laws, executive orders, directives, policies, regulations, standards, and guidance and documents the results (including supporting rationale) in the system security plan. Designated senior-level officials within the organization review and approve the security categorizations.

RA-3 Risk Assessment—The organization conducts assessments of the risk and magnitude of harm that could result from the unauthorized access, use, disclosure, disruption, modification, or destruction of information and information systems that support the operations and assets of the agency (including information and information systems managed/operated by external parties).

RA-4 Risk Assessment Update—The organization updates the risk assessment on a periodic basis or whenever there are significant changes to the information system, the facilities where the system resides, or other conditions that may impact the security or accreditation status of the system.

RA-5 Vulnerability Scanning—The organization scans for vulnerabilities in the information system on a regular basis or when significant new vulnerabilities potentially affecting the system are identified and reported.

System and Services Acquisition Controls (SA)

System and services acquisition controls are a family within the management class that are concerned with how systems and services are acquired by the organization.

SA-1 System and Services Acquisition Policy and Procedures—The organization develops, disseminates, and periodically reviews/updates: (i) a formal, documented system and services acquisition policy that includes information security considerations and that addresses purpose, scope, roles, responsibilities, management commitment, coordination among organizational entities, and compliance; and (ii) formal, documented procedures to facilitate the implementation of the system and services acquisition policy and associated system and services acquisition controls.

SA-2 Allocation of Resources—The organization determines, documents, and allocates as part of its capital planning and investment control process, the resources required to adequately protect the information system.

SA-3 Life Cycle Support—The organization manages the information system using a system development life cycle methodology that includes information security considerations.

SA-4 Acquisitions—The organization includes security requirements and/or security specifications, either explicitly or by reference, in information system acquisition contracts based on an assessment of risk and in accordance with applicable laws, executive orders, directives, policies, regulations, and standards.

SA-5 Information System Documentation—The organization obtains, protects as required, and makes available to authorized personnel, adequate documentation for the information system.

SA-6 Software Usage Restrictions—The organization complies with software usage restrictions.

SA-7 User-Installed Software—The organization enforces explicit rules governing the installation of software by users.

SA-8 Security Engineering Principles—The organization designs and implements the information system using security engineering principles.

SA-9 External Information System Services—The organization: (i) requires that providers of external information system services employ adequate security controls in accordance with applicable laws, executive orders, directives, policies, regulations, standards, guidance, and established service-level agreements; and (ii) monitors security control compliance.

SA-10 Developer Configuration Management—The organization requires that information system developers create and implement a configuration management plan that controls changes to the system during development, tracks security flaws, requires authorization of changes, and provides documentation of the plan and its implementation.

SA-11 Developer Security Testing—The organization requires that information system developers create a security test and evaluation plan, implement the plan, and document the results.

System and Communication Protection Controls (SC)

System and communication protection controls are a family in the technical class and are concerned with how the systems and their communications are protected while in operation.

SC-1 System and Communications Protection Policy and Procedures—The organization develops, disseminates, and periodically reviews/updates: (i) a formal, documented system and communications protection policy that addresses purpose, scope, roles, responsibilities, management commitment, coordination among organizational entities, and compliance; and (ii) formal, documented procedures to facilitate the implementation of the system and communications protection policy and associated system and communications protection controls.

SC-2 Application Partitioning—The information system separates user functionality (including user interface services) from information system management functionality.

SC-3 Security Function Isolation—The information system isolates security functions from nonsecurity functions.

SC-4 Information Remnance—The information system prevents unauthorized and unintended information transfer via shared system resources.

SC-5 Denial-of-Service Protection—The information system protects against or limits the effects of relevant or common denial-of-service attacks.

SC-6 Resource Priority—The information system limits the use of resources by priority.

SC-7 Boundary Protection—The information system monitors and controls communications at the external boundary of the information system and at key internal boundaries within the system.

SC-8 Transmission Integrity—The information system protects the integrity of transmitted information.

SC-9 Transmission Confidentiality—The information system protects the confidentiality of transmitted information.

SC-10 Network Disconnect—The information system terminates a network connection at the end of a session or after a specified period of inactivity.

SC-11 Trusted Path—The information system establishes a trusted communications path between the user and significant security functions.

SC-12 When cryptography is required and employed within the information system, the organization establishes and manages cryptographic keys using automated mechanisms with supporting procedures or manual procedures.

SC-13 Use of Cryptography—For information requiring cryptographic protection, the information system implements cryptographic mechanisms that comply with applicable laws, executive orders, directives, policies, regulations, standards, and guidance.

SC-14 Public Access Protections—The information system protects the integrity and availability of publicly available information and applications.

SC-15 Collaborative Computing—The information system prohibits remote activation of collaborative computing mechanisms and provides an explicit indication of use to the local users.

SC-16 Transmission of Security Parameters—The information system reliably associates security parameters with information exchanged between information systems.

SC-17 Public Key Infrastructure Certificates—The organization issues public key certificates under an appropriate certificate policy or obtains public key certificates under an appropriate certificate policy from an approved service provider.

SC-18 Mobile Code—The organization: (i) establishes usage restrictions and implementation guidance for mobile code technologies based on the potential to cause damage to the information system if used maliciously; and (ii) authorizes, monitors, and controls the use of mobile code within the information system.

SC-19 Voice over Internet Protocol—The organization: (i) establishes usage restrictions and implementation guidance for Voice over Internet Protocol (VoIP) technologies based on the potential to cause damage to the information system if used maliciously; and (ii) authorizes, monitors, and controls the use of VoIP within the information system.

SC-20 Secure Name /Address Resolution Service (Authoritative Source)—The information system that provides name/address resolution service provides additional data origin and integrity artifacts along with the authoritative data it returns in response to resolution queries.

SC-21 Secure Name /Address Resolution Service (Recursive or Caching Resolver)—The information system that provides name/address resolution service for local clients performs data origin authentication and data integrity verification on the resolution responses it receives from authoritative sources when requested by client systems.

SC-22 Architecture and Provisioning for Name /Address Resolution Service—The information systems that collectively provide name/address resolution service for an organization are fault tolerant and implement role separation.

SC-23 Session Authenticity—The information system provides mechanisms to protect the authenticity of communications sessions.

System and Information Integrity Controls (SI)

System and information integrity controls are a family in the operational class that are concerned with how the integrity of systems and information are assured.

SI-1 System and Information Integrity Policy and Procedures—The organization develops, disseminates, and periodically reviews/updates: (i) a formal, documented system and information integrity policy that addresses purpose, scope, roles, responsibilities, management commitment, coordination among organizational entities, and compliance; and (ii) formal, documented procedures to facilitate the implementation of the system and information integrity policy and associated system and information integrity controls.

SI-2 Flaw Remediation—The organization identifies, reports, and corrects information system flaws.

SI-3 Malicious Code Protection—The information system implements malicious code protection.

SI-4 Information System Monitoring Tools and Techniques—The organization employs tools and techniques to monitor events on the information system, detect attacks, and provide identification of unauthorized use of the system.

SI-5 Security Alerts and Advisories—The organization receives information system security alerts/advisories on a regular basis, issues alerts/advisories to appropriate personnel, and takes appropriate actions in response.

SI-6 Security Functionality Verification—The information system verifies the correct operation of security functions periodically as needed and takes appropriate action when anomalies are discovered. An example of an anomaly would be a cryptographic appliance that suddenly began transmitting clear text instead of cipher text.

SI-7 Software and Information Integrity—The information system detects and protects against unauthorized changes to software and information.

SI-8 Spam Protection—The information system implements spam protection.

You may be feeling like you should start looking for a new line of work after our presentation of the wide variety of security controls that your organization may need to implement. However, remember this list is not a recipe for how to secure a system or an organization but it is a fairly comprehensive list of security controls that you will need to examine. This is part of the risk assessment process and your particular organization's needs and environment will decide which controls are applicable in your setting.

It is this pared down list that meets your own local needs that you should actually use to assess where you are in compliance and where there is more work to be done. Also, you may, depending on your budget and resources, need to prioritize the list in order to address the more important controls first.

Assuring the security of your organization's information assets may be a difficult task but it is not impossible.

SI-9 Information Input Restrictions—The organization restricts the capability to input information to the information system to authorized personnel.

SI-10 Information Accuracy, Completeness, Validity, and Authenticity—The information system checks information for accuracy, completeness, validity, and authenticity.

SI-11 Error Handling—The information system identifies and handles error conditions in an expeditious manner without providing information that could be exploited by adversaries.

SI-12 Information Output Handling and Retention—The organization handles and retains output from the information system in accordance with applicable laws, executive orders, directives, policies, regulations, standards, and operational requirements. The new Federal Rules of Civil Procedure (FRCP) explicitly recognize the importance of electronically stored information (ESI) and this creates a responsibility on a party to a lawsuit to preserve all relevant ESI. Thus, the organization must have policy and procedures in place to modify retention requirements for ESI relevant to pending litigation.

PERFORMING THE ASSESSMENT

Once you've identified the list of controls that are relevant and important to your organization, it is time to assess your organization's success in implementing the control. This section makes use of NIST SP 800-53A "Guide for Assessing the Security Controls in Federal Information Systems." This document is organized the same way as the security controls were presented and this makes it fairly easy to move back and forth between the two. For each control, the assessment procedure describes the control, presents detailed supplemental guidance on the control, and then provides a series of assessment objectives.

For example, let's assume that you have determined that the control within RA-5 called "vulnerability scanning" is an important control in your environment and ties in well with the results of your risk assessment. On page F-211 of SP800-53A we see:

ASSESSMENT PROCEDURE	
RA-5	**VULNERABILITY SCANNING**
	Control: The organization scans for vulnerabilities in the information system [*Assignment: organization-defined frequency*] or when significant new vulnerabilities potentially affecting the system are identified and reported.
	Supplemental Guidance: Vulnerability scanning is conducted using appropriate scanning tools and techniques. The organization trains selected personnel in the use and maintenance of vulnerability scanning tools and techniques. Vulnerability scans are scheduled and/or random in accordance with organizational policy and assessment of risk. The information obtained from the vulnerability scanning process is freely shared with appropriate personnel throughout the organization to help eliminate similar vulnerabilities in other information systems. Vulnerability analysis for custom software and applications may require additional, more specialized approaches (e.g., vulnerability scanning tools for applications, source code reviews, static analysis of source code). NIST Special Publication 800-42 provides guidance on network security testing. NIST Special Publication 800-40 (Version 2) provides guidance on patch and vulnerability management.
RA-5.1	ASSESSMENT OBJECTIVE:
	Determine if:
	(i) the organization defines in the security plan, explicitly or by reference, the frequency of vulnerability scans within the information system;
	(ii) the organization scans for vulnerabilities in the information system in accordance with the organization-defined frequency and/or random in accordance with organizational policy and assessment of risk, or when significant new vulnerabilities potentially affecting the system are identified and reported;
	(iii) the organization uses appropriate scanning tools and techniques to conduct the vulnerability scans;
	(iv) the organization trains selected personnel in the use and maintenance of vulnerability scanning tools and techniques; and
	(v) the organization freely shares the information obtained from the vulnerability scanning process with appropriate personnel throughout the organization to help eliminate similar vulnerabilities in other information systems.

The Checkbox Mentality

As Adam Shoostack and Andrew Stewart note in their book *The New School of Information Security*,[1] "Checklists compress complex issues into a list of simple questions. Someone using a checklist therefore may think he has done the right thing, when in fact he has not addressed the problem in depth" (p. 35f). It is a real danger that one may get caught up in a "check the box" mentality devoted to passing the audit or assessment and forget that one's real task is protection of the organization's information assets.

Sadly, several high-profile data breaches were in progress while the affected organization passed a security audit against a well-known industry standard. When using the NIST assessment, ISO27002, PCI-DSS, OWASP, or any other assessment instrument, always remember that the assessment is a guide on how to evaluate your information security efforts, not a magical ritual to make the hackers pass you by.

The assessment objective defines five items that must be present in order for the control to be considered as successfully implemented. The authors of the publication deliberately avoided checkbox questions such as "Perform vulnerability scans" and delve deeper into the policy and organizational support necessary to assure that the vulnerability scanning efforts achieve their objective in helping to secure the organization's information assets.

USING THE RESULTS

Once you have completed assessing each of these areas, the results can be used to support planning for future modifications and changes to the security program or profile. Documenting the current level of preparedness will serve to provide valuable insight into the organization's security efforts, past and present. Just the process of conducting the assessment is valuable in and of itself.

The security assessment tool presented is not designed to represent the state-of-the-art assessment tool or methodology, but provide a starting point where none may currently exist. Some audit checklists may provide a better, more customized approach to determining what the organization is doing well, and what it is not. What is important is not what tool is being used, but that something proactive is being done to continually assess and improve security in the organization.

This chapter has presented a publicly available catalog of security controls and a matching assessment procedure that can be used to assess the security controls needed by a particular organization. There are many other checklists and assessment procedures available but these easily accessible ones are both useful and give a flavor of the assessment process itself.

The wise security professional will always carefully weigh any assessment instrument as to its applicability and real meaning in helping determine how well her organization's information assets are being protected. Don't fall for the checkbox mentality because the innovative criminals and other attackers will likely remind you that the purpose of assessment is to acquire strategic knowledge not from a form filled with checked boxes.

The Information Security Manager's Checklist

	This topic has been fully tested, validated, and integrated into organizational operations with formal performance measures in place (as appropriate).				
	This topic has been implemented, but not fully tested, validated, and integrated into organizational operations.				
	The implementation of this topic has begun, but is not yet complete.				
	The formal planning for this topic has begun, but is not yet complete.				
	This subject has not formally begun planning, or the organization has made a conscious decision not to pursue this topic.	No	Planned	In Progress	In Place	Integrated
7. Conducting InfoSec Program Assessment					
Candidate InfoSec program assessment criteria identified (ISO/NIST/etc.).					
Program assessment criteria developed from candidates.					
Periodic assessment scheduled and conducted.					
Assessment results presented to appropriate executive management.					
Current results compared to previous results to identify improvements and performance gaps.					
Plan to remediate performance gaps developed and implemented.					
Appropriate recognition for improved performance conducted.					
Assessment program periodically reviewed for effectiveness of assessment methods and criteria.					

For Further Reading

NIST SP 800-53A "Guide for Assessing the Security Controls in Federal Information Systems." National Institute of Standards and Technology, 2008.

Reference

1. A. Shostack and A. Stewart. *The New School of Information Security*. Boston: Addison-Wesley, 2008.

Part III

Strategic Information Security: Risk Management

Information security in a modern organization exists primarily to manage risks to the organization's information assets. Managing risk is one of the key responsibilities of every manager within an organization. In any well-developed risk management program, two formal processes are at work. The organizational will to implement risk management is essential. The primary objective must be to make risk management an element of every important decision made across the organization. Optimally, the bigger the decision, the more importance is assigned to the risk management aspects of the choices. One of the better controls to reduce operational risk in an organization is project management, and the project management and systems development methodologies of the organization should both have elements and structures in them that help assess (or identify) and then manage (or control) the risks from each and every decision.

The chapters in Part III are intended to provide you with information about risk management. They will explain:

▶ why we must identify all significant information assets;

▶ how to assess or estimate the relative value of each of the information assets;

▶ why understanding the risks and threats facing the assets is essential; and

▶ how the various risk control strategies can be employed to reduce overall risks facing the organization.

Part Overview

Chapter 8—"Risk Management" defines risk management and its role in the organization, demonstrating how to use risk management techniques to identify and prioritize risk factors for information assets. It also discusses information valuation as a foundation for quantitative versus qualitative risk management.

Chapter 9—"Risk Management: Risk Assessment" explores the risk assessment aspects of risk management. This approach assesses risk based on the likelihood of adverse events and the effects on information assets when untoward events occur. The chapter also includes a discussion on how to document the results of the risk identification process.

Chapter 10—"Risk Management: Risk Control" provides a discussion of the various types of risk control mechanisms available and identifies the steps involved in performing the initial risk assessment. The chapter continues by defining risk management as the process of identifying, assessing, and reducing risk to an acceptable level and implementing effective control measures to maintain that level of risk.

Chapter 11—"Alternate Approaches to Risk Management" discusses alternative approaches to risk management using two industry standards as the basis for understanding: The OCTAVE method from Carnegie Mellon and Microsoft's risk management approach.

Chapter 8

Risk Management

At the heart of information security is the management of risk. Risk, an inevitable consequence of business operations, is the chance that an undesired event will cause a loss. In managing an information security program, you should strive to plan for this eventuality, work to reduce, or even eliminate the probability of a loss, and prepare strategies for the eventuality. The undesired event that you are trying to avoid is the unauthorized modification, damage, or loss of information or an information asset. As you will learn in this section, it is not practical to reduce risk to zero. Some element of risk will always remain. In this chapter we will examine what you can do to begin the process of reducing risk through risk management.

Chapter Overview:

▶ Risk management

▶ Creating an inventory of information assets

▶ Listing assets in order of importance

▶ Threat identification

▶ The TVA worksheet

RISK MANAGEMENT

As you know and understand in your day-to-day business activities, modern businesses require connectivity. This connectivity to customers, suppliers, business partners, or others is required to enable business to function and grow. But, all too often, this business connectivity can increase risk. A critical part of understanding and controlling that risk is the information security risk assessment, which identifies an organization's critical assets, the threats those assets face, and ways that those threats can be countered. Sun Tzu, an ancient Chinese general, offers this advice:

> If you know the enemy and know yourself, you need not fear the result of a hundred battles. If you know yourself but not the enemy, for every victory gained you will also suffer a defeat. If you know neither the enemy nor yourself, you will succumb in every battle.[1]

Sun Tzu recommends that the wise organization (1) know itself and (2) know its enemy. This means that managers from all three communities of interest discussed in previous chapters must locate the weaknesses of the organization's operations; understand how the organization's information is processed, stored, and transmitted; and identify what resources are available to secure them from the threat of losses. Only then can a strategic plan of defense be developed. Another great military thinker, Carl von Clausewitz, put it this way: "from the character, the institutions, the situation and the circumstances of the adversary, each side will draw its conclusions, in accordance with the laws of probability, as to what the actions of the other will be and determine its own accordingly."[2] Clausewitz points out that organizations are engaged in a struggle where the adversary (hackers, disgruntled employees, competitors, etc.) will adapt and innovate their strategies of attack. This requires the organization to assess and reassess their defensive posture in light of attacks. Whichever sage speaks most cogently to you, the way that information security managers "know themselves" and make decisions about the probable actions of the adversary is through the risk assessment process.

Know Ourselves

For your organization to properly manage risk, it should understand what information it is responsible for, where it is stored, how it is transmitted, and how it is currently protected. Once you are armed with this knowledge from the organization, you can then initiate an in-depth risk management program for the organization. Note that the mere existence of a risk management program is not sufficient. Frequently, risk management mechanisms are implemented but not maintained and kept current. Risk management is a process, which means the safeguards and controls that are devised and implemented are not install-and-forget devices, but must be continually assessed and reassessed, updated, and maintained.

Know the Enemy

Once you become aware of the weaknesses present in the defenses surrounding your organizations, you can then take up Sun Tzu's second dictum: know the enemy. This means identifying, examining, and understanding the threats facing your organization's information assets. As the information security manager, you must be prepared to fully identify those threats that pose risks to the organization's information assets and determine how those risks can be controlled or mitigated. For this reason, risk analysis is among the most important processes you can use to identify and assess the various levels of risk to the information assets of your organization.

CREATING AN INVENTORY OF INFORMATION ASSETS

The risk identification process begins with the identification of information assets, including people, procedures, data and information, software, hardware, and networking elements. This step should be done independent of the value of each asset as values will be assigned later in the process. The following list outlines identified assets, which are subcategorized into risk management components:

▶ *People* are divided into insiders (employees) and outsiders (nonemployees). Insiders may hold trusted roles and have correspondingly greater authority and accountability, or may be regular staff without any special privileges. Outsiders consist of others who have some access to the organization's information assets (which in a Web-enabled world may include the majority of the human race).

▶ *Procedures* are assets since they are used to create value for the organization. They are split into two categories: IT and business *standard procedures*, and IT and business *sensitive procedures*. Sensitive procedures have the potential to enable an attack or to otherwise introduce risk to the organization. For example, the procedure to create a new user for an information system is a sensitive procedure because it grants authorized access to some portion of the organization's assets.

▶ *Data* components account for information in all states: transmission (in flight), processing (in use), and storage (at rest). These categories expand the conventional use of the term "data," which is usually associated with databases, not the full range of information used by modern organizations.

▶ *Software* elements can be inventoried in one of three general categories: applications, operating systems, or security. Software components that provide security controls may fall into the operating systems or applications category, but are differentiated by the fact that they are part of the information security control environment and must be more stringently protected.

▶ *Hardware* is split into two categories: the usual systems devices and their peripherals, and the devices that are part of information security control systems. The latter must be protected more stringently than the former.

▶ *Networking* components are extracted from software and hardware because networking subsystems are often an important vector for attacks against a system. You will have to make a judgment call as to whether a device is primarily a computer or primarily a networking device. A server computer that is used exclusively as a proxy server or bastion host may be classified as a networking component, while an identical server configured as a database server may be classified as hardware.

Identifying Hardware, Software, and Network Assets

It is likely that your organization has purchased an asset inventory system to keep track of hardware, network, and perhaps software components. While numerous packages are available in the market today, it is up to the CISO or CIO to determine which package best serves the needs of the organization. If you use a tool to collect your inventory facts or you choose to perform this task by hand, you should be certain that the key attributes are recorded and tracked. For example, the following is a list of commonly tracked asset attributes:

- Name
- Asset tag
- IP address
- MAC address
- Asset type—for example:
  - DeviceClass = S (Server)
  - DeviceOS = W2K (Windows 2000)
  - DeviceCapacity = AS (Advanced Server)
- Serial number
- Manufacturer name
- Manufacturer's model or part number:
- Software/firmware version, update revision, or field change order number
- Physical location
- Logical location
- Controlling entity

You should have a process in place that keeps the asset inventory current as the infrastructure of your organization changes and evolves. As with many other facets of an information security program, an asset inventory is not a one-time-for-all event but must be updated on a regular basis to reflect reality. This recurring update capability is one of the core advantages of an automated asset discovery and tracking system.

Identifying People, Procedures, and Data Assets

Unlike hardware and software, human resources, documentation, and data information assets are not as easy to identify and document. For this reason, the responsibility for identifying, describing, and evaluating people as information assets should be assigned to managers who possess the necessary knowledge, experience, and judgment. As you identify these assets, record via a reliable data-handling process like the one used for hardware and software. The recordkeeping system should also be flexible, allowing you to link assets to attributes based on the nature of the information asset being tracked. Some basic attributes for various classes of assets are:

People

- Position name/number/ID: Avoid names; use position titles, roles, or functions
- Supervisor name/number/ID: Avoid names; use position titles, roles, or functions
- Security clearance level
- Special skills

Procedures

▶ Description

▶ Intended purpose

▶ Software/hardware/networking elements to which it is tied

▶ Location where it is stored for reference

▶ Location where it is stored for update purposes

Data

▶ Classification

▶ Owner/creator/manager

▶ Size of data structure

▶ Data structure used: for example, sequential or relational

▶ Online or off-line

▶ Location

▶ Backup procedures

Classifying and Categorizing Assets

Once the initial inventory is assembled, you must determine whether its asset categories are meaningful to the organization's risk management program. Such a review may cause managers to further subdivide the categories listed earlier or to create new categories that better meet the needs of the risk management program. Your inventory should also reflect the sensitivity and security priority assigned to each information asset. A classification scheme should be developed (or reviewed, if already in place) that categorizes these information assets based on their sensitivity and security needs. A more detailed discussion of classification schemes is provided later in this chapter in the section entitled "Data Classification Model."

Data and E-discovery

In December of 2006, the new U.S. Federal Rules of Civil Procedure (FRCP) went into effect and one of their major changes was to recognize the importance of electronically stored information (ESI) to the litigation process. ESI poses special demands and risks on organizations who become involved in litigation and require that the organization be able to identify and preserve *all* information relevant to the litigation. Failure to do so can hamper the case (if one is the plaintiff) or generate huge fines and damage awards (if one is the respondent).

For example, consider e-mail: While an organization may automatically delete all e-mails after they are 90 days old using an automated process, unless they are very careful in their asset inventory, they may overlook the copies of e-mails on backup tapes or other archives, which could likely lead to expensive sanctions. E-discovery has significantly raised the importance of an organization's having a good handle on its data assets and all the places where they squirrel copies away.

Classification categories must be comprehensive and mutually exclusive. **Comprehensive** means that all inventoried assets are assigned to a category; **mutually exclusive** means that each asset is found in only one category. For example, an organization may have a public key infrastructure certificate authority, which is a software application that provides cryptographic key management services. Using a purely technical standard, a manager could categorize the application in the asset list as *software,* a general grouping with no special classification priority. Because the certificate authority must be carefully protected as part of the information security infrastructure, it should be categorized into a higher priority classification, such as *software/security component/cryptography*, and it should be verified that no overlapping category exists, such as *software/security component/PKI*.

Assessing Values for Information Assets

As each information asset is identified, categorized, and classified, a relative value must also be assigned to it. Relative values are comparative judgments intended to ensure that the most valuable information assets are given the highest priority when managing risk. It may be impossible to know in advance—in absolute economic terms—what losses will be incurred if an asset is compromised; however, a relative assessment helps to ensure that the higher-value assets are protected first.

As each information asset is assigned to its proper category, posing the following basic questions can help you develop the weighting criteria to be used for information asset valuation or impact evaluation. It may be useful to refer to the information collected in the Business Impact Analysis process (discussed later under "Contingency Planning") in order to help you assess a value for an asset. You can use a worksheet, such as the one shown in Figure 8-1, to collect the answers for later analysis.

It may also be helpful to use these questions when determining the relative worth of an information asset:

- ▶ Which information asset is the most critical to the success of the organization?
- ▶ Which information asset generates the most revenue?
- ▶ Which information asset generates the highest profitability?
- ▶ Which information asset is the most expensive to replace?

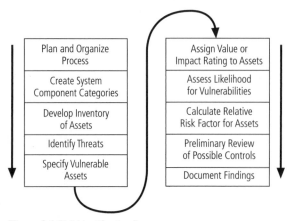

Figure 8-1 Risk Identification Process
Course Technology/Cengage Learning

- ► Which information asset is the most expensive to protect?
- ► Which information asset's loss or compromise would be the most embarrassing or cause the greatest liability?

You may also need to identify and add other institution-specific questions to the evaluation process.

NOTE

Throughout this chapter numbers are assigned to example assets in order to illustrate the concepts being discussed. This highlights one of the challenging issues in risk management. While other industries use actuarially derived sources to make estimates, information security risk management usually lacks such data. Many organizations use a variety of estimating methods to assess values. Some in the industry question the use of "guessed at" values in calculations with other estimated values, claiming this degree of uncertainty undermines the entire risk management endeavor. Research in this field is ongoing and you are encouraged to study those chapters of this text where alternative, qualitative risk management techniques are discussed.

LISTING ASSETS IN ORDER OF IMPORTANCE

The next step in the risk identification process is the ordering of assets by importance. This goal can be achieved by using a weighted factor analysis worksheet similar to the one shown in Table 8-1. In this process, each information asset is assigned a score for each critical factor.

TABLE 8-1 Example Weighted Factor Analysis Worksheet

INFORMATION ASSET	CRITERIA 1: IMPACT TO REVENUE	CRITERIA 2: IMPACT TO PROFITABILITY	CRITERIA 3: PUBLIC IMAGE IMPACT	WEIGHTED SCORE
Criterion Weight (1–100) Must total 100	30	40	30	
EDI Document Set 1—Logistics BOL to outsourcer (outbound)	0.8	0.9	0.5	75
EDI Document Set 2—Supplier orders (outbound)	0.8	0.9	0.6	78
EDI Document Set 2—Supplier fulfillment advice (inbound)	0.4	0.5	0.3	41
Customer order via SSL (inbound)	1.0	1.0	1.0	100
Customer service request via e-mail (inbound)	0.4	0.4	0.9	55

Notes: EDI: Electronic Data Interchange
SSL: Secure Sockets Layer

Course Technology/Cengage Learning

Table 8-1 uses the NIST SP 800-30 recommended values of 0.1 to 1.0. Each criterion has an assigned weight, showing its relative importance in the organization.

A quick review of Table 8-1 shows that the Customer order via SSL (inbound) data flow is the most important asset on this worksheet, and that the EDI Document Set 2—Supplier fulfillment advice (inbound) is the least critical asset.

Data Classification Model

Corporate and military organizations use a variety of classification schemes. As you might expect, the military relies on a more complex categorization system than the schemes of most corporations. Most organizations do not need the detailed level of classification used by the military or federal agencies. Nevertheless, you may find it necessary to classify data to provide protection. A simple scheme can allow an organization to protect its sensitive information such as marketing or research data, personnel data, customer data, and general internal communications. A scheme such as the following could be adopted:

- ▶ Public: For general public dissemination, such as an advertisement or press release.
- ▶ For official use only: Not for public release but not particularly sensitive, such as internal communications.
- ▶ Sensitive: Important information that could embarrass the organization or cause loss of market share if compromised.
- ▶ Classified: Essential and confidential information, disclosure of which could severely damage the well-being of the organization.

Security Clearances

The other half of the data classification scheme is the personnel security clearance structure, in which each user of an information asset is assigned an authorization (or trust) level that indicates the level of information classification he or she can access. Beyond a simple reliance on the security clearance of the individual is the **need-to-know** principle. Regardless of one's security clearance, an individual is not allowed to view data simply because it falls within that individual's level of clearance. That is, after being granted a security clearance but before viewing a specific set of data, a person must also meet the need-to-know requirement. This extra requirement ensures that the confidentiality of information is properly maintained.

Management of the Classified Information Asset

Managing an information asset includes all aspects of its life cycle: from specification, design, acquisition, implementation, use, storage, distribution, backup, recovery, retirement, to destruction. An information asset, such as a report, that has a classification designation other than unclassified or public must be clearly marked as such. The U.S. government, for example, uses color-coordinated cover sheets to protect classified information from the casual observer. Every classified document should also contain the appropriate security designation at the top and bottom of each page. Classified documents must be available only to authorized individuals, which usually require locking file cabinets, safes, or other such protective devices for hard copies and systems. When an individual carries a classified report, it should be inconspicuous

Digital information is surprisingly resilient and as Simson Garfinkel showed by examining used disk drives purchased off e-Bay and other sites,[3] a lot of sensitive information is left on discarded/recycled media through a lack of media sanitization. With the increasing awareness of privacy and the threat of criminal misuse of personal information, an organization must recognize that the tools of digital forensics are available to both the "good" and the "bad" people. Thus, data destruction (or sanitization) must destroy the information beyond the capability of forensics tools to recover it, not by simply erasing, reformatting, or overwriting the directory information.

and kept in a locked briefcase or portfolio, and in compliance with appropriate policies (for example, requirements for double-sealed envelopes, tamper-proof seals, etc.).

When copies of classified information are no longer valuable or too many copies exist, care should be given to destroy them properly, usually after double signature verification. Documents should be destroyed by means of shredding, burning, or transfer to a service offering authorized document destruction. Data stored electronically must receive the same care in its destruction at end-of-life. NIST has published SP 800-88 "Guidelines for Media Sanitization" to provide guidance in this area. Policy should ensure that no classified information is inappropriately disposed of in trash or recycling areas. Otherwise, people who engage in **dumpster diving** may retrieve information and thereby compromise the security of the organization's information assets.

THREAT IDENTIFICATION

As mentioned at the beginning of this chapter, the ultimate goal of risk identification is to assess the circumstances and setting of each information asset to expose any vulnerabilities. Armed with a properly classified inventory, you can assess potential weaknesses in each information asset—a process known as **threat identification**.

Any organization typically faces a wide variety of threats. If you assume that every threat can and will attack every information asset, then the project scope becomes too complex. To make the process less unwieldy, each step in the threat identification and vulnerability identification processes is managed separately and then coordinated at the end. At every step the manager is called upon to exercise good judgment and draw on experience to make the process function smoothly.

Identify and Prioritize Threats and Threat-Agents

Earlier, we identified twelve categories of threats to information security. Each of these threats presents a unique challenge to information security and can be mitigated by specific controls that address the particular threat and the threat-agent's attack strategy. Before threats can be assessed in the risk identification process, however, each threat must be further examined to determine its potential to affect the targeted information asset. In general, this process is referred to as threat assessment. Posing the following questions can help you understand the threat and its potential effects on an information asset:

- ▶ Which threats present a danger to this organization's information assets in its current environment?
- ▶ Which threats represent the gravest danger to the organization's information assets?
- ▶ Which threat could cause the most financial damage if successful? Public relations damage?
- ▶ Which threat has the highest probability of occurrence? of success?
- ▶ How much would it cost to recover from a successful attack from this threat?
- ▶ Which threats would require the greatest expenditure to prevent?

Vulnerability Assessment

Once you have identified the information assets of the organization and documented some threat assessment criteria, you can begin to review every information asset for each threat. This review leads to the creation of a list of vulnerabilities (specific avenues that threat-agents can exploit to attack an information asset) that pose potential risks to the organization. For example, Table 8-2 analyzes the threats to and possible vulnerabilities of a DMZ router.

A list like the one in Table 8-2 must be created for each information asset to document its exposure to each possible or likely attack. This list is usually long and shows all the vulnerabilities of the information asset. Some threats manifest themselves in multiple ways, yielding multiple vulnerabilities for that asset–threat pair. Of necessity, the process of listing vulnerabilities is somewhat subjective and is based on the experience and knowledge of the people who create the list. Therefore, the process works best when groups of people with diverse backgrounds work together in a series of brainstorming sessions. For instance, the team that reviews the vulnerabilities for networking equipment should include networking specialists, the systems management team that operates the network, information security risk specialists, and even technically proficient users of the system.

THE TVA WORKSHEET

At the end of the risk identification process, an organization should have a prioritized list of assets and their vulnerabilities. This list serves as the starting point (with its supporting documentation from the identification process) for the next step in the risk management process—risk assessment. Another list prioritizes threats facing the organization based on the weighted table discussed earlier. These two lists can be combined into a Threats-Vulnerabilities-Assets (TVA) worksheet, in preparation for the addition of vulnerability and control information during risk assessment. Along one axis lies the prioritized set of assets. Table 8-3 shows the placement of assets along the horizontal axis, with the most important asset at the left. The prioritized list of threats are placed along the vertical axis, with the most important or most dangerous threat listed at the top. The resulting grid provides a convenient method of examining the "exposure" of assets, allowing a simplistic vulnerability assessment. We now have a starting point for our risk assessment, along with the other documents and forms.

TABLE 8-2 Vulnerability Assessment of a DMZ Router

THREAT	POSSIBLE VULNERABILITIES
Deliberate Software Attacks	▶ Internet protocol is vulnerable to denial-of-service attack. ▶ Outsider IP fingerprinting activities can reveal sensitive information unless suitable controls are implemented.
Act of Human Error or Failure	▶ Employees or contractors may cause outage if configuration errors are made.
Technical Software Failures or Errors	▶ Vendor-supplied routing software could fail and cause an outage.
Technical Hardware Failures or Errors	▶ Hardware can fail and cause an outage. ▶ Power system failures are always possible.
Quality of Service Deviations from Service Providers	▶ Unless suitable electrical power conditioning is provided, failure is probable over time.
Deliberate Acts of Espionage or Trespass	▶ Router has little intrinsic value, but other assets protected by this device could be attacked if it is compromised.
Deliberate Acts of Theft	▶ Router has little intrinsic value, but other assets protected by this device could be attacked if it is compromised.
Deliberate Acts of Sabotage or Vandalism	▶ Internet protocol is vulnerable to denial-of-service attacks. ▶ Device may be subject to defacement or cache poisoning.
Technological Obsolescence	▶ If it is not reviewed and periodically updated, the device may fall too far behind its vendor support model to be kept in service.
Forces of Nature	▶ All information assets in the organization are subject to forces of nature unless suitable controls are provided.
Compromises to Intellectual Property	▶ Router has little intrinsic value, but other assets protected by this device could be attacked if it is compromised.
Deliberate Acts of Information Extortion	▶ Router has little intrinsic value, but other assets protected by this device could be attacked if it is compromised.

Course Technology/Cengage Learning

As you begin the risk assessment process, it will help to create a list of the TVA "triples" to facilitate your examination of the severity of the vulnerabilities. For example, between Threat 1 and Asset 1 there may or may not be a vulnerability. After all, not all threats pose risk to all assets. For example, if a pharmaceutical company's most important asset is its research and development database, and that database resides on a stand-alone network (i.e., one that is not connected to the Internet), then there may be no vulnerability to external hackers. If the intersection of T1 and A1 has no vulnerability, then the risk assessment team simply crosses out that box. It is much more likely, however, that one or more vulnerabilities exist between the two, and as these vulnerabilities are identified they are categorized as follows:

T1V1A1—Vulnerability 1 that exists between Threat 1 and Asset 1

T1V2A1—Vulnerability 2 that exists between Threat 1 and Asset 1

T1V1A2—Vulnerability 1 that exists between Threat 1 and Asset 2 and so on . . .

TABLE 8-3 Sample TVA Spreadsheet

	Asset 1	Asset 2	...	...	...	...	...	...	...	...	...	Asset n
Threat 1												
Threat 2												
...												
...												
...												
...												
...												
...												
...												
...												
Threat n												
Priority of Controls	1		2		3		4		5		6	

These bands of controls should be continued through all threat–asset pairs.

Course Technology/Cengage Learning

In the risk assessment phase, discussed in the next chapter, not only are the vulnerabilities examined, but the assessment team also examines any existing controls that protect the asset from the threat or mitigate the losses that may occur. Cataloging and categorizing these controls is the next step in the TVA spreadsheet.

In order to plan an effective information security program, the organization must understand how the program protects its assets. The critical process for this understanding is the risk assessment. The risk assessment process identifies the organization's assets, their value, and threats that might affect those assets and the vulnerabilities that might allow a threat to be realized.

This risk relationship is often summarized in the equation $Risk = F(t, v, a)$ or risk is a function of the threat, vulnerability, and asset. The TVA worksheet is a useful tool for identifying which threats have the capability of affecting which assets and forms a valuable input to later stages of the risk management process.

The Information Security Manager's Checklist

	This subject has not formally begun planning, or the organization has made a conscious decision not to pursue this topic.	The formal planning for this topic has begun, but is not yet complete.	The implementation of this topic has begun, but is not yet complete.	This topic has been implemented, but not fully tested, validated, and integrated into organizational operations.	This topic has been fully tested, validated, and integrated into organizational operations with formal performance measures in place (as appropriate).
8. Risk Identification	No	Planned	In Progress	In Place	Integrated
Threat prioritization (from Ch. 2) conducted					
Information assets identified and inventoried					
Information assets classified and security clearances implemented (if appropriate)					
Information assets ranked					
Ranked TVA spreadsheet developed					

For Further Reading

Against the Gods: The Remarkable Story of Risk by Peter Bernstein, John Wiley & Sons, 1996.

Beating IT Risks by Ernie Jordan and Luke Silcock, John Wiley & Sons, 2005.

Risk Management Guide for Information Technology Systems by Stoneburner, Gogien and Feringa. National Instritute of Standards and Technology (Special Publication 800-30), 2002.

References

1. Sun Tzu. *The Art of War*. Translation by Samuel B. Griffith. Oxford, UK: Oxford University Press, 1988.

2. Carl von Clausewitz. (1993). *On War*. Translation by M. Howard and P. Paret. New York: Alfred A. Knopf, p. 90.

3. S. Garfinkel. http://www.blackhat.com/presentations/bh-federal-06/BH-Fed-06-Garfinkel.pdf, 2006. Accessed 19 July 2008.

Chapter 9

Risk Management:
Risk Assessment

Assessing and communicating the relative risks that you will face while protecting your organization's information assets is accomplished through a process called *risk assessment*. Risk assessment strives to assign a risk rating or score to each specific possible loss. While this rating number will likely not mean anything in absolute terms, it does enable you to gauge the relative risk associated with each vulnerable information asset, which facilitates the creation of comparative ratings later in the risk control process. There are many methodologies available for performing this process including OCTAVE,[1] Factor Analysis of Information Risk (FAIR),[2] Microsoft's Security Risk Management Guide,[3] and NIST SP 800-30.[4] The specific methodology you choose to use is less important than your comfort with it and your ability to defend its results to management.

Chapter Overview:

► Vulnerability risk model

► Approaches to risk assessment

► Documenting The Results of Risk Assessment

VULNERABILITY RISK MODEL

In many ways, a risk assessment is simply finding good sources for the values you can use to estimate risk. When these values are plugged into a risk assessment model, you will compare the risks the information assets face and then choose your course of action to reduce risk. Unfortunately, there are obstacles to your ability to get good values for these inputs to the risk assessment process. For instance, the newness of the information security profession means that there are few, if any, commercial sources for underwriting data. Also, information security is characterized by having a code of professional secrecy that discourages information sharing. The evolving nature of the information security threat environment makes the process of finding and sharing data about risks even more challenging. Figure 9-1 shows the factors that go into the risk-rating estimate for each of the vulnerabilities.

The goal at this point is to identify a method you can use to assess the relative risk associated with each vulnerability that you have identified on your ranked information asset list from the risk identification process. Later, in Chapter 10, we will describe how to determine more precise cost estimates for vulnerabilities as well as projected expenses for the controls that reduce the risks. For now, let's use the simpler risk model shown in Figure 9-1 to evaluate the risk for each information asset. The next section describes the factors used to calculate the relative risk for each vulnerability.

Risk is
The **likelihood** of the occurrence of a vulnerability
Multiplied by
The **value** of the information asset
Minus
The percentage of risk mitigated by **current controls**
Plus
The **uncertainty** of current knowledge of the vulnerability

---

Figure 9-1 Factors of Risk
Course Technology/Cengage Learning

APPROACHES TO RISK ASSESSMENT

There are three general approaches to conducting a risk assessment:

- ▶ Quantitative—uses numeric values for impacts and probabilities
- ▶ Qualitative—uses ratings (high, medium, low) for impacts and probabilities
- ▶ Hybrid—uses a combination of the two approaches

The quantitative approach is the most appealing because it is quite simple to use. The problem with this approach is that the numbers are very hard to come by (e.g., what is the exact probability of an uncontained virus outbreak in your organization this year?). The qualitative approach recognizes this difficulty and uses ratings (very likely, very unlikely, etc.) rather than absolute numbers. The results of a qualitative approach are by definition "fuzzy" but have the advantage that they can be developed through structured surveys and other techniques. They are also in many ways easier to defend as senior management is usually quite accustomed to working with projections in qualitative terms. The hybrid approach is the most flexible as it allows use of quantitative methods when the data is available and qualitative methods when it is not. Regardless of which approach you decide to take, the factors identified in Figure 9-1 need to have values assessed or assigned.

Likelihood

As you approach risk assessment, you need to consider the factors previously mentioned, often starting with the probability of the loss. Likelihood is the overall rating—a value on a defined scale—reflecting the probability that a specific vulnerability will be exploited. NIST recommends in its Special Publication 800-30 that vulnerabilities be assigned a likelihood rating between 0.1 (low) and 1.0 (high). For example, the likelihood of an employee or system being struck by a meteorite while indoors would be rated 0.1, while the likelihood of receiving at least one e-mail containing a virus or worm in the next year would be rated 1.0. You could also choose to use a number between 1 and 100, but not zero, since vulnerabilities with a zero likelihood should have already been removed from the asset–vulnerability list.

The Microsoft Risk Management Guide suggests the probability ratings:[5]

▶ High—one or more impacts within one year

▶ Medium—within two to three years

▶ Low—not expected within three years

Whatever rating system you employ for assigning likelihood, use professionalism, experience, and judgment to determine the rating—and use it consistently. Whenever possible, use external references for likelihood values, after reviewing and adjusting them for your specific circumstances. For many asset–vulnerability combinations, existing sources have already determined their likelihood. For example,

▶ The likelihood of a fire has been estimated actuarially for each type of structure.

▶ The likelihood that any given e-mail will contain a virus or worm has been researched.

▶ The number of network attacks can be forecast depending on how many network addresses the organization has assigned.

Assessing Potential Loss

Using the information documented during the risk identification process, you can assign weighted scores based on the value of each information asset to the business. The actual value used will vary according to the needs of the organization. Some groups use a scale of 1 to 100, with 100 being reserved for those information assets whose loss would stop company operations within a few minutes. Other recommended scales, including the one in NIST SP 800-30, use assigned weights in broad categories, with all-important assets having a value of 100, low-criticality assets having a value of 1, and all other assets having a medium value of 50. Still other scales employ weights from 1 to 10, or assigned values of 1, 3, and 5 to represent low-, medium-, and high-valued assets, respectively. Alternatively, you can use "high impact" to represent those events that would "stop the business" and so on.

To be effective, the values must be assigned by asking the questions listed in Chapter 8 in the section entitled "Identify and Prioritize Threats and Threat-Agents." These questions are restated here for easy reference:

> ▶ Which threats present a danger to this organization's assets in the given environment?
>
> ▶ Which threats represent the most danger to the organization's information?
>
> ▶ How much would it cost to recover from a successful attack?
>
> ▶ Which threats would require the greatest expenditure to prevent?

After reconsidering these questions, use the background information from the risk identification process and add to that information by posing yet another question:

> ▶ Which of the aforementioned questions is the most important to the protection of information from threats within this organization?

The answer to this question determines the priorities used in the assessment of vulnerabilities. Which is the most important to the organization—the cost to recover from a threat attack or the cost to protect against a threat attack? More generally, which of the threats has the highest probability of successful attack? Recall that the purpose of risk assessment is to look at the threats an organization faces in its current state. Once these questions are answered, move to the next step in the process: examining how current controls can reduce the risk faced by specific vulnerabilities.

Percentage of Risk Mitigated by Current Controls

If a vulnerability is fully managed by an existing control, it can be set aside. If it is partially controlled, estimate what percentage of the vulnerability has been controlled. This result is called the exposure of the asset to this vulnerability (if there are no controls in place, the asset is fully exposed).

Uncertainty

It is not possible to know everything about each and every vulnerability, such as how likely is an attack against an asset, or how great would be the impact of a successful attack. The degree to which a current control can reduce risk is also subject to estimation error. A factor that accounts for uncertainty must always be added to the assessment; it consists of an estimate made by the manager using good judgment and experience.

Risk Determination

Using this equation illustrated in Figure 9-1 we can then view some sample scenarios:

▶ Information asset A has a value score of 50 and has one vulnerability: Vulnerability 1 has a likelihood of 1.0 with no current controls. You estimate that assumptions and data are 90 percent accurate.

▶ Information asset B has a value score of 100 and has two vulnerabilities: Vulnerability 2 has a likelihood of 0.5 with a current control that addresses 50 percent of its risk; vulnerability 3 has a likelihood of 0.1 with no current controls. You estimate that assumptions and data are 80 percent accurate.

The resulting ranked list of risk ratings for the three vulnerabilities described above is as follows [(value times likelihood) minus risk mitigated plus uncertainty]:

▶ Asset A: Vulnerability 1 rated as 55 = (5021.0) – ((5021.0)2.2) + ((5021.0)2.1)

▶ Asset B: Vulnerability 2 rated as 35 = (10020.5) – ((10020.5)2.5) + ((10020.5)2.2)

▶ Asset B: Vulnerability 3 rated as 12 = (10020.1) – ((10020.5)2.0) + ((10020.5)2.2)

Ratings can be combined in similar ways by defining the result of particular combinations. For example, a "high" rating for an asset with a medium exposure level results in a "high" impact rating. As mentioned before, the results for such a qualitative analysis are "fuzzy" in that there are really only a few "buckets" for the values to fall into. However, the use of ratings avoids the problem of gratuitous accuracy mentioned earlier and is sometimes the easiest to defend with senior management. In other words, it is much easier to defend a "medium" rather than engage in a prolonged debate over whether the number should have been a "4" or a "5."

Identify Possible Controls

For each threat and its associated vulnerabilities that have residual risk, create a preliminary list of control ideas. The purpose of this list, which begins with the identification of existing controls, is to identify areas of residual risk that may nor may not need to be reduced. Residual risk is the risk that remains even after the existing control has been applied.

Controls, safeguards, and *countermeasures* are all terms used to describe security mechanisms, policies, and procedures. These mechanisms, policies, and procedures counter attacks, reduce risk, resolve vulnerabilities, and otherwise improve the general state of security within an organization.

Three general categories of controls exist: policies, programs, and technical controls. You learned about policies earlier. **Programs** are activities performed within the organization to improve security; they include security education, training, and awareness programs. Technical controls—also known as security technologies—are the technical implementations of the policies defined by the organization. These controls, whether in place or planned, should be added to the TVA worksheet as they are identified.

Access Controls

Access controls specifically address the admission of users into a trusted area of the organization. These areas can include information systems, physically restricted areas such as computer rooms, and even the organization in its entirety. Access controls usually consist of a combination of policies, programs, and technologies.

A number of approaches to, and categories of, access controls exist. They can be mandatory, nondiscretionary, or discretionary.

Mandatory Access Controls (MACs) MACs are structured and coordinated with a data classification scheme (such as the U.S. government's "Confidential," "Secret," and "Top Secret"). When MACs are implemented, users and data owners have limited control over their access to information resources. MACs use a data classification scheme that rates each collection of information. Each user is also rated to specify the level of information that he or she may access. These ratings are often referred to as sensitivity levels.

In a variation of this form of access control called **lattice-based access control**, users are assigned a matrix of authorizations for particular areas of access. The level of authorization may vary depending on the classification authorizations that individuals possess for each group of information assets or resources. The lattice structure contains subjects and objects, and the boundaries associated with each subject–object pair are clearly demarcated. Lattice-based access control then specifies the level of access each subject has to each object, if any. With this type of control, the column of attributes associated with a particular object (such as a printer) is referred to as an **access control list (ACL)**. The row of attributes associated with a particular subject (such as a user) is referred to as a **capabilities table**.

Nondiscretionary Controls Nondiscretionary controls are determined by a central authority in the organization and can be based on roles—called **role-based access controls**[6]— or on a specified set of tasks—called **task-based controls**. Task-based controls can, in turn, be based on lists maintained on subjects or objects. Role-based controls are tied to the role that a

particular user fills in an organization, whereas task-based controls are tied to a particular assignment or responsibility.

The role- and task-based controls make it easier to maintain controls and restrictions, especially if the individual performing the role or task changes often. Instead of constantly assigning and revoking the privileges of individuals who come and go, the administrator simply assigns the associated access rights to the role or task. When individuals are subsequently assigned to that role or task, they automatically receive the corresponding access. The administrator can easily remove individuals' associations with roles and tasks, thereby revoking their access.

Discretionary Access Controls (DACs)
DACs are implemented at the discretion or option of the data user. The ability to share resources in a peer-to-peer configuration allows users to control and possibly provide access to information or resources at their disposal. The users can allow general, unrestricted access, or they can allow specific individuals or sets of individuals to access these resources. As an example, suppose a user has a hard drive containing information to be shared with office coworkers. This user can elect to allow access to specific individuals by listing their names in the share control function.

Technical Controls
Technical controls are technologies such as TLS/SSL, firewalls, intrusion protection systems, etc. They are a core part of any security program but are just a part of it. A firewall is useless unless there are policies and procedures defined that specify what types of traffic are allowed to pass and the processes for approving and implementing new firewall rules.

An access control system may be implemented using a RADIUS server but again, unless there are policies that define which classes of users may have accounts, how their credentials are managed, etc., the investment in the technical control will be ineffective.

There is an almost frightening tendency in security programs to install a new whiz-bang appliance to solve a particular security problem only to have it rendered ineffective by misconfiguration and a lack of proper support and management. It is imperative that technical controls be supported by proper policy and procedure to assure their successful function in protecting the organization's assets.

DOCUMENTING THE RESULTS OF RISK ASSESSMENT

The goal of the risk management process so far has been to identify information assets and their vulnerabilities and to rank them according to the need for protection. In preparing this list, a wealth of factual information about the assets and the threats they face is collected. Also, information about the controls that are already in place is collected. The final summarized document is the ranked vulnerability risk worksheet, as shown in Table 9-1. This document is an extension of the TVA spreadsheet discussed in Chapter 8 in Table 8-3, showing only the assets and relevant vulnerabilities. A review of this worksheet reveals similarities to the weighted factor analysis worksheet depicted in Chapter 8 in Table 8-1. The columns in the worksheet shown in Table 9-1 are used as follows:

- ▶ Asset: List each vulnerable asset.
- ▶ Asset Impact: Show the results for this asset from the weighted factor analysis worksheet. In our example, this value is a number from 1 to 100.

TABLE 9-1 Ranked Vulnerability Risk Worksheet

ASSET	ASSET IMPACT	VULNERABILITY	VULNERABILITY LIKELIHOOD	RISK-RATING FACTOR
Customer service request via e-mail (inbound)	55	E-mail disruption due to hardware failure	0.2	11
Customer service request via e-mail (inbound)	55	E-mail disruption due to software failure	0.2	11
Customer order via Secure Sockets Layer (SSL) (inbound)	100	Lost orders due to Web server hardware failure	0.1	10
Customer order via SSL (inbound)	100	Lost orders due to Web server ISP service failure	0.1	10
Customer service request via e-mail (inbound)	55	E-mail disruption due to SMTP mail relay attack	0.1	5.5
Customer service request via e-mail (inbound)	55	E-mail disruption due to ISP service failure	0.1	5.5
Customer service request via e-mail (inbound)	55	E-mail disruption due to power failure	0.1	5.5
Customer order via SSL (inbound)	100	Lost orders due to Web server denial-of-service attack	0.025	2.5
Customer order via SSL (inbound)	100	Lost orders due to Web server software failure	0.01	1
Customer order via SSL (inbound)	100	Lost orders due to Web server buffer overrun attack	0.01	1

Course Technology/Cengage Learning

- ▶ Vulnerability: List each uncontrolled vulnerability.
- ▶ Vulnerability Likelihood: State the likelihood of the realization of the vulnerability by a threat-agent as indicated in the vulnerability analysis step. In our example, the potential values range from 0.1 to 1.0.
- ▶ Risk-Rating Factor: Enter the figure calculated by multiplying the asset impact and its likelihood. In our example, the calculation yields a number ranging from 0.1 to 100.

Looking at Table 9-2, you may be surprised that the most pressing risk requires making the mail server or servers more robust. Even though the impact rating of the information asset represented by the customer service e-mail is only 55, the relatively high likelihood of a hardware failure makes it the most pressing problem.

Now that the risk identification process is complete, what should the documentation package look like? In other words, what are the deliverables from this stage of the risk management project? The risk identification process should designate what function the reports serve, who is responsible for preparing them, and who reviews them. The ranked vulnerability risk worksheet

TABLE 9-2 Risk Identification and Assessment Deliverables

DELIVERABLE	PURPOSE
Information asset classification worksheet	Assembles information about information assets and their impact on or value to the organization
Weighted criteria analysis worksheet	Assigns a ranked value or impact weight to each information asset
Ranked vulnerability risk worksheet	Assigns a risk-rating ranked value to each uncontrolled asset–vulnerability pair

Course Technology/Cengage Learning

is the initial working document for the next step in the risk management process: assessing and controlling risk. Table 9-2 shows an example list of the worksheets that should have been prepared by an information asset risk management team to this point.

In the last stage of the risk analysis (identification and assessment) process, you use the TVA worksheet, along with the other worksheets created, to develop a prioritized list of tasks. Obviously the presence of uncontrolled vulnerabilities in high-ranking assets are the first priority for the implementation of new controls, as part of the risk management process discussed in the next chapter. Before any additional controls are added, though, you must determine the levels of risk that your organization is willing to accept, based on a cost-benefit analyses.

Repeat as Required

Unfortunately, though a risk assessment process is in many ways daunting and painful, it must be repeated on a regular basis to assure its continued accuracy. Some of the factors that drive this repetition are:

- ▶ New technologies—If Sequential had not created their Web site with its applications, it might have been much more difficult for them to have been compromised. However, they would have also foregone the increase in business revenue the Web site enabled.
- ▶ New ways of doing business—If Sequential were to issue laptops to their field sales personnel, then they will need to consider the risks posed by these mobile assets.
- ▶ New attacks—Adversaries are continuing to innovate to find new ways of attacking an organization's assets.

Given these factors, you must repeat the risk assessment process on a regular basis (perhaps at least annually). In addition, the information security function must insinuate itself into the business so that new technologies or business methods can be identified before they are deployed so that risk assessments and appropriate controls can be put into place.

The risk assessment process is concerned with developing a defensible understanding of the threats and vulnerabilities of an organization's information assets. This understanding includes estimates of the likelihood of a threat being realized and its resulting impact. This combination of likelihood, threat, and impact represents the risk to the information asset. This risk may be mitigated by various types of controls but can probably never be reduced to 0. The challenge for the information security professional is to mitigate this residual risk to the point that it is less than the risk appetite of the organization.

The Information Security Manager's Checklist

	No	Planned	In Progress	In Place	Integrated
This topic has been fully tested, validated, and integrated into organizational operations with formal performance measures in place (as appropriate).					
This topic has been implemented, but not fully tested, validated, and integrated into organizational operations.					
The implementation of this topic has begun, but is not yet complete.					
The formal planning for this topic has begun, but is not yet complete.					
This subject has not formally begun planning, or the organization has made a conscious decision not to pursue this topic.					
9. Risk Assessment					
Threats–asset couples evaluated					
Vulnerabilities identified for each threat–asset couple					
TVA triples identified					
TVA control shortcomings identified					

For Further Reading

A Practical Guide to Security Assessments by Sudhanshu Kairab, Auerbach Publications, 2005.

Managing Information Security Risks: The OCTAVE Approach by C. Alberts and A. Dorofee, Addison-Wesley Professional, 2003.

Risk Management Guide for Information Technology Systems by Stoneburner, Gogien and Feringa. National Instritute of Standards and Technology (Special Publication 800-30), 2002.

References

1. C. Alberts and A. Dorofee. *Managing Information Security Risks: The OCTAVE^SM Approach*. Boston: Addison-Wesley, 2003.

2. J. A. Jones. *An Introduction to Factor Analysis of Information Risk (FAIR)*, no date.

3. Microsoft Corporation. *The Security Risk Management Guide*. http://www.microsoft.com/downloads/details.aspx?FamilyID=c782b6d3-28c5-4dda-a168-3e4422645459&displaylang=en, 2006. Accessed 19 July 2008.

4. Risk Management Guide for Information Technology Systems, NIST SP 800-30. Viewed 30 September 2008 from http://csrc.nist.gov/publications/nistpubs/800-30/sp800-30.pdf.

5. Ibid., p. 48.

6. D. F. Ferraiolo, D. R. Kuhn, and C. Ramaswarmy. *Role-Based Access Control* (2d ed). Boston: Artech House, 2007.

Risk Management: Risk Control

An important challenge in the risk management process emerges when it is time to select the strategy that you will use to address the estimated risks. While there are only four strategies to choose from, the art lies in selecting the one most appropriate for a particular risk confronting a specific asset–vulnerability pair. The organizational culture and the corresponding risk appetite of the organization can influence this choice. In this chapter, you'll discover a commonly used technique, cost-benefit analysis, which can provide a framework for making these decisions.

Chapter Overview:

▶ Risk control strategies

▶ Managing risk

▶ Feasibility studies and cost-benefit analysis

▶ Defending risk control decisions

RISK CONTROL STRATEGIES

When an organization determines that risks from information security threats are unacceptable, it typically falls on the information technology and security organizations to make recommendations on how to control those risks. Once the ranked vulnerability worksheet is created (see Chapter 7), one of four basic strategies must be chosen to control those risks:

▶ Self-Protection: Applying updates, new or revised practices, and adding or updating technical safeguards that eliminate or reduce the remaining uncontrolled risks

▶ Risk Transfer: Shifting the risks to other areas or to outside entities

▶ Self-Insurance: Reducing the impact should an attacker successfully exploit the vulnerability, including informed choices to do nothing, choices that accept the consequences and the risk without any attempts at control or mitigation, and/or choices that prepare for loss eventualities through contingency planning

▶ Avoidance: Choosing not to engage in types of business activity that exposes the organization and its information systems to risks that are not otherwise controllable or finding ways to move

Self-Protection

Self-protection attempts to prevent the exploitation of the vulnerability. It is the preferred approach, because it seeks to avoid risk rather than deal with it. This strategy is accomplished through one or more of the following techniques:

▶ Application of policy: the application of policy (discussed in additional detail in Chapters 17 and 18) allows all levels of management to mandate that certain procedures always be followed. Obviously the policy must be implemented and enforced to achieve its purpose in avoiding the risk.

▶ Application of training and education: Distributing a policy to employees is not usually sufficient to assure compliance. Awareness training and education are essential to achieving the necessary changes in end-user behavior.

▶ Countering threats: Risks can be avoided by countering the threats facing an asset or by eliminating its exposure to threats.

Risk Transfer

Risk transfer attempts to shift the risk elsewhere (usually outside the organization). This goal may be accomplished by rethinking how services are offered, revising deployment models, outsourcing to other organizations, purchasing insurance, or implementing service contracts with providers.

In the popular book *In Search of Excellence*, management consultants Tom Peters and Robert Waterman present a series of case studies of high-performing corporations. They assert that one of the eight characteristics of excellent organizations is that they "stick to their knitting" by staying reasonably close to their businesses' core competencies.[1] This means that companies should focus energy and resources on what they do best while relying on third parties for other types of expertise, like Web site development.

Organizations should consider this approach whenever they begin to expand their operations, including information and systems management, and even information security. If an organization does not have adequate security management and administration experience, it should consider outsourcing. Outsourcing, of course, is not without its own risks. It is up to the owner of the information asset, IT management, and the information security team to ensure that security requirements are included in the outsourcing contract and have been met.

Self–Insurance

Self-insurance is the control approach that attempts to reduce, by means of contingency planning and preparation, the damage caused by the exploitation of vulnerability, or the approach to acknowledge that some risks may not be controllable and the loss from them will be absorbed should they occur. The choice to do nothing to protect an information asset from risk, and to accept the outcome from any resulting exploitation, while it is a perfectly legitimate risk control strategy, must always be a conscious business decision based on a careful process that includes the following steps:

▶ Determined the level of risk posed to the information asset

▶ Assessed the probability of attack and the likelihood of a successful exploitation of a vulnerability

▶ Approximated the likelihood of occurrence of such an attack

▶ Estimated the potential loss that could result from attacks

▶ Performed a thorough cost-benefit analysis

▶ Evaluated controls using each appropriate type of feasibility analysis report

▶ Determined that the particular function, service, information, or asset does not justify the cost of protection

The acceptance of the risk of loss without contingency planning assumes that it can be a prudent business decision to examine the alternatives and conclude that the cost of protecting an asset does not justify the security expenditure. Suppose it would cost an organization $100,000 per year to protect a server. The security assessment determines that for $10,000 the

Choosing a Strategy

A common piece of advice when playing poker is to "Know when to hold 'em" and similar advice applies to risk control. Not all risks will need to be controlled and in some cases the cost of control may exceed the value of the asset. Resource constraints (time, budget, technology, personnel) will limit the number and types of risks the organization can attempt to control. This has been the real background purpose in conducting the risk assessment: to identify the most serious risks so that the organization's limited resources may be dedicated appropriately.

organization could replace the information contained in the server, replace the server itself, and cover associated recovery costs. Under this scenario the organization may legitimately choose to take its chances and save the money that would otherwise be spent on protecting this particular asset.

Avoidance

Avoidance is the risk management strategy that directs the organization to avoid those business activities that introduce uncontrollable risks. If an organization studies the risks from implementing business-to-consumer e-commerce operations and determines that the risks of this type of activity are not sufficiently offset by the potential benefits of the activity, the organization may seek an alternate mechanism to meet customer needs—perhaps developing new channels for product distribution or new partnership opportunities.

MANAGING RISK

It is extremely unlikely that risk can ever be reduced to zero. A strategic goal to "eliminate risk" is likely doomed from the outset. The practical goal is to reduce the risk to a level that is acceptable to the organization (in other words, is acceptable considering the organization's risk appetite).

Risk appetite (also known as **risk tolerance**) describes the quantity and nature of risk that organizations are willing to accept, as they evaluate the trade-offs between the limits of perfect security (e.g., sealed in a concrete shell and sunk to the bottom of the Marianas Trench) and unlimited accessibility. For instance, a financial services company may be conservative by nature and seek to apply every reasonable control and even some invasive controls to protect its information assets. Other, less closely regulated organizations may also be conservative, and thus seek to avoid the negative publicity and perceived loss of integrity caused by exploitation of a vulnerability. A firewall vendor might install a set of firewall rules that are far more stringent than necessary, simply because becoming a hacking victim would jeopardize its reputation in the market. Other organizations with a corporate culture of aggressively pursuing new business methods and opportunities may have a more relaxed attitude and accept a higher degree of risk (e.g., deploying a new Web technology before its security implications and weaknesses are understood). The reasoned approach to risk is one that balances the expense against the possible losses.

When vulnerabilities have been controlled as much as possible, there is usually remaining risk that has not been completely removed, shifted, or planned for—in other words, residual risk. To express it another way, "**Residual risk** is a combined function of (1) a threat less the effect of threat-reducing safeguards; (2) a vulnerability less the effect of vulnerability-reducing safeguards; and (3) an asset less the effect of asset value-reducing safeguards."[2] Residual risk persists even after safeguards are implemented.

Although it might seem counterintuitive, the goal of information security is not to bring residual risk to zero; rather, it is to bring residual risk within an organization's risk appetite. If decision makers have been informed of uncontrolled risks and the proper authority groups within the communities of interest decide to leave residual risk in place, then the information security program has accomplished its primary goal.

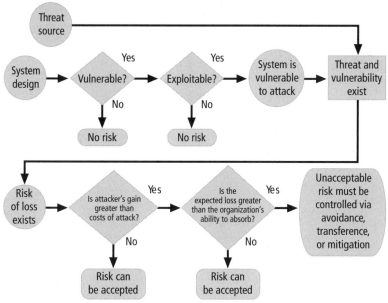

Figure 10-1 Risk Handling Action Points
Course Technology/Cengage Learning

Figure 10-1 illustrates the process of choosing among the four risk control strategies. The first step is determining whether the system has vulnerabilities that can be exploited (while it is a truism that all systems have vulnerabilities one must still identify which one in particular applies in a given situation). If a viable threat exists, examine what an attacker would gain from a successful attack. Then, estimate the expected loss the organization will incur if the vulnerability is successfully exploited. If this loss is within the range of losses the organization can absorb, or if the attacker's gain is less than the likely cost of executing the attack, the organization may choose to accept the risk. Otherwise, you must select one of the other control strategies.

For further guidance, some rules of thumb on strategy selection are presented below. When weighing the benefits of the various strategies, keep in mind that the level of threat and the value of the asset should play a major role in strategy selection.

▶ When a vulnerability (flaw or weakness) exists: Implement security controls to reduce the likelihood of a vulnerability being exercised.

▶ When a vulnerability can be exploited: Apply layered protections, architectural designs, and administrative controls to minimize the risk or prevent the occurrence of an attack.

▶ When the attacker's potential gain is greater than the costs of attack: Apply protections to increase the attacker's cost, or reduce the attacker's gain, by using technical or managerial controls.

▶ When the potential loss is substantial: Apply design principles, architectural designs, and technical and nontechnical protections to limit the extent of the attack, thereby reducing the potential for loss.[3]

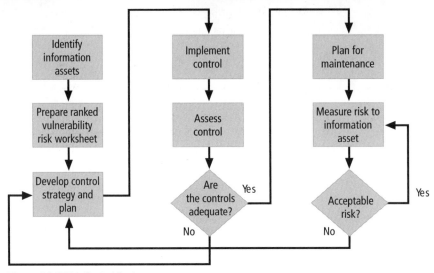

Figure 10-2 Risk Control Cycle
Course Technology/Cengage Learning

Once a control strategy has been selected and implemented, controls should be monitored and measured on an ongoing basis to determine their effectiveness and to estimate the remaining risk. Figure 10-2 shows how this cyclical process ensures that risks are controlled. This is a critical process as the tendency is to soften security controls over time. For example, one large organization had a very sophisticated firewall architecture designed to protect access to its internal network. Unfortunately, it did not have a good change management process for controlling changes to the firewall configuration and rule set. Over time, as new applications and business functions came online, more and more traffic was permitted through the firewall until a later penetration test revealed that over time, the firewall configuration had been so softened that it was essentially "turned off."

At a minimum, each information asset–threat pair should have a documented control strategy that clearly identifies any residual risk that remains after the proposed strategy has been executed. This control strategy articulates which of the four fundamental risk-reducing approaches will be used, how the various approaches might be combined, and justifies the findings by referencing the feasibility studies.

Some organizations document the outcome of the control strategy for each information asset–threat pair in an action plan. This action plan includes concrete tasks, with accountability for each task being assigned to an organizational unit or to an individual. It may include hardware and software requirements, budget estimates, and detailed timelines.

FEASIBILITY STUDIES AND COST-BENEFIT ANALYSIS

Before deciding on the strategy (self-protection, risk transfer, self-insurance, or avoidance) for a specific vulnerability, an organization must determine the economic and noneconomic consequences of the vulnerability. This exploration attempts to answer the question, "What are the actual and perceived advantages of implementing a control as opposed to the actual and perceived disadvantages of implementing the control?"

There are a number of ways to identify the advantages of a specific control, though the primary means is to determine the value of the information assets that it is designed to protect. There are also many ways to identify the disadvantages associated with specific risk controls. The following sections describe some of the more commonly used techniques for making these choices. Note that some of these techniques use dollar-denominated expenses and savings from economic cost avoidance, while others use noneconomic feasibility criteria. **Cost avoidance** is the money saved by avoiding, via the implementation of a control, the financial ramifications of an incident.

Cost-Benefit Analysis

The principle of a cost-benefit analysis (CBA) is quite simple: How much bang will I get for my buck? Or to put it another way, for each dollar invested in a particular security control, what benefits will accrue? The desire is to determine where it makes the most sense to invest the organization's limited resources in order to obtain the best protection. A CBA can be performed using either quantitative or qualitative methods (just like the risk assessment). When using the quantitative method, estimates of benefits will be in numerical terms. When using a qualitative method, the estimates usually will be in the form of a rating scale (e.g., high to low). The problem with the quantitative CBA is the same as it was with a quantitative risk assessment: The numbers can be devilishly hard to come by and very tricky to defend. However, the inherent "fuzziness" of a qualitative CBA may be hard for some organizations to accept. The most flexible approach is to use what is called a hybrid methodology: Use quantitative methods where the data is available and qualitative methods when it's not.

Cost Just as it is difficult to determine the value of information, so it is difficult to determine the cost of safeguarding it. Among the items that contribute to the cost of a control or safeguard are the following:

- ▶ Cost of development or acquisition of hardware, software, and services
- ▶ Training fees (cost to train personnel)
- ▶ Cost of implementation (installing, configuring, and testing hardware, software, and services)
- ▶ Service costs (vendor maintenance and upgrades)
- ▶ Cost of maintenance (labor expense to verify and continually test, maintain, train, and update)

Benefit The **benefit** is the value to the organization of using controls to prevent losses associated with a specific vulnerability. It is usually determined by valuing the information asset or assets exposed by the vulnerability and then determining how much of that value is at risk, and how much risk exists for the asset. This result is expressed as the annualized loss expectancy (on average, the amount the organization can expect to lose per year), which is defined later in this chapter.

Asset Valuation **Asset valuation** is the process of assigning financial value or worth to each information asset. As you learned in Chapter 8, the value of information differs within organizations and between organizations. Some argue that it is virtually impossible to accurately determine the true value of information and information-bearing assets, which is perhaps one reason why insurance underwriters currently have no definitive valuation tables for information assets. Asset valuation can draw on the assessment of information assets performed as part of the risk identification process you learned about in Chapter 8.

Asset valuation can involve the estimation of real or perceived costs. These costs can be selected from any or all of those associated with the design, development, installation, maintenance, protection, recovery, and defense against loss or litigation. Some costs are easily determined, such as the cost to replace a network switch, or the hardware needed for a specific class of server. Other costs are almost impossible to determine, such as the dollar value of the loss in market share if information on a firm's new product offerings were released prematurely and the company lost its competitive edge. A further complication is that some information assets acquire over time value that is beyond their **intrinsic value**—the essential worth—of the asset under consideration. This higher **acquired value** is the more appropriate value in most cases.

Asset valuation must account for the following:

- ▶ Value retained from the cost of creating the information asset: Information is created or acquired at a cost that can be calculated or estimated.
- ▶ Value retained from past maintenance of the information asset: It is estimated that for every dollar spent to develop an application or to acquire and process data, many more dollars are spent on maintenance over the useful life of the data or software.
- ▶ Value implied by the cost of replacing the information: The costs associated with replacing information should include the human and technical resources needed to reconstruct, restore, or regenerate the information from backups, independent transactions logs, or even hard copies of data sources.
- ▶ Value from providing the information: Separate from the cost of developing or maintaining the information is the cost of providing the information to those users who need it.
- ▶ Value acquired from the cost of protecting the information: The value of an asset is based in part on the cost of protecting it, and the amount of money spent to protect an asset is based in part on the value of the asset.
- ▶ Value to owners: How much is your Social Security number worth to you?
- ▶ Value of intellectual property: Related but separate are intellectual properties known as trade secrets. These intellectual information assets are the primary assets of some organizations.
- ▶ Value to adversaries: How much would it be worth to an organization to know what the competition is doing?
- ▶ Loss of productivity while the information assets are unavailable: For example, when a power failure occurs, effective use of UPS equipment can prevent data loss, but users cannot create additional information.
- ▶ Loss of revenue while information assets are unavailable: Many organizations have all but abandoned manual backups for automated processes. Sometimes, businesses may even have to turn away customers because their automated payments systems are inoperative.

- What damage could occur, and what financial impact would it have?
- What would it cost to recover from the attack, in addition to the financial impact of damage?
- What is the single loss expectancy for each risk?

A **single loss expectancy (SLE)** is a function used to estimate or calculate a value associated with the most likely loss from an single attack. This function should take into account both the value of the asset and the expected percentage of loss that would occur from a particular attack:

$$SLE = F(\text{asset value } (AV), \text{ exposure factor } (EF))$$

where AV is the asset value and EF is the percentage loss that would occur from a given vulnerability being exploited. When using quantitative techniques, the function is a simple multiplication of the two values ($AV \times EF$). For example, if a Web site has an estimated value of $1,000,000 (as determined by asset valuation), and a sabotage or vandalism (hacker defacement) scenario indicates that 10% of the Web site would be damaged or destroyed in such an attack (the exposure factor), then the SLE for this Web site would be $1,000,000 \times .10 = \$100,000$. When using a qualitative method, it is common to use a table lookup where a "high" asset value with a "low" exposure factor would produce a "moderate" SLE.[4]

Usually, the probability of a threat occurring is depicted as a table that indicates how frequently an attack from each threat type is likely to occur within a given time frame (for example, once every ten years). This value is commonly referred to as the **annualized rate of occurrence (ARO)**. ARO is simply how often you expect a specific type of attack to occur in a year. For example, if a successful act of sabotage or vandalism occurs about once every two years, then the ARO would be 50 percent (0.5). A network attack that can occur multiple times per second might be successful once each month and would have an ARO of 12. Qualitative methods use ratings such as "high" meaning one or more occurrences in a single year and "low" meaning not expected to occur within three years.

Once you determine the loss from a single attack (SLE), and the likely frequency of successful attacks (ARO), you can calculate the overall loss potential per risk expressed as an **annualized loss expectancy (ALE)** using the values for the ARO and SLE from the previous sections.

$$ALE = (SLE \times ARO)$$

As before, for the quantitative method, the function is a simple multiplication: if $SLE = \$100,000$ and $ARO = 0.5$, then

$$ALE = \$100,000 \times 0.5$$
$$ALE = \$50,000$$

Thus, the organization can expect to lose $50,000 per year, every year, unless it increases its Web security.

The qualitative method would use a table lookup again to determine with a "moderate" SLE and a "medium" probability, the result would be "moderate." At this point, the qualitative method will have given a ranking of the particular asset and vulnerability but has not produced a dollar estimate of the risk. To "hybridize" this process, some defensible decisions have to be made

While the lack of exact knowledge regarding the dollar value of assets, frequency of threats, and exact monetary consequences of vulnerability exploitation may force us to use qualitative methods, control costs are always quantitative. Since control costs represent expenditures of organizational resources (personnel, time, money), you must be able to produce accurate cost figures. While executives are confortable dealing with risks in terms of high to low, they are very unlikely to "buy a pig in a poke" by giving you a blank check to control those risks.

about the general meaning of "high" asset values, etc. The Microsoft Risk Management Guide suggests that a value be set on a high asset value of "M," "moderate" value is "M/2," and "low" is "M/4." This allows the value to "trickle down" through the analysis and give an estimate for the ALE. Again, the reason why qualitative methods are used in the absence of hard data is that it is much easier to get a group of hard-headed executives to agree that a specific asset is of "high" or "moderate" value without spending hours debating whether the customer order application is worth $5,000,000 or $6,000,000.

Now, armed with a figure to justify its expenditures for controls and safeguards, the information security design team can deliver a budgeted value for planning purposes. Note that sometimes noneconomic factors are considered in this process, so even when ALE amounts are not large, control budgets can still be justified using factors like defending the organization's reputation or public image.

The Cost-Benefit Analysis Formula CBA (or economic feasibility) determines whether a control alternative is worth its associated cost. Such analyses may be performed before implementing a control or safeguard, or after controls have been in place for a time. Observation over time adds precision to the evaluation of the benefits of the safeguard and the determination of whether the safeguard is functioning as intended. While many CBA techniques exist, it is most easily calculated using the ALE from earlier assessments.

$$CBA = ALE \text{ (pre-control)} - ALE \text{ (post-control)} - ACS$$

where
ALE (pre-control) = ALE of the risk before the implementation of the control
ALE (post-control) = ALE examined after the control has been in place for a period of time
ACS = annual cost of the safeguard

Once the controls are implemented, it is crucial to continue to examine their benefits, to determine when they must be upgraded, supplemented, or replaced.

Other Feasibility Studies

Information security controls work in the context of an overall information technology and organizational ecology. An important step in planning a control program is to consider the organizational, operational, technological, and political feasibility of implementing those controls. This can be particularly challenging for those organizations that have undeveloped information security programs since they will have had little previous security experience and may be responding to events that have created embarrassment from a significant security breach.

Organizational Feasibility

Organizational feasibility analysis examines how the proposed information security alternatives will contribute to the efficiency, effectiveness, and overall operation of an organization. In other words, the proposed control approach must mesh with the organization's strategic objectives. How does the implementation align with the strategic planning for the information systems? Does it require deviation from the planned expansion and management of the current systems?

Operational Feasibility

Operational feasibility refers to user acceptance and support, management acceptance and support, and the system's compatibility with the requirements of the organization's stakeholders. Operational feasibility is also known as **behavioral feasibility**.

Organizations should *communicate* with system users, sharing timetables and implementation schedules, plus the dates, times, and locations of upcoming briefings and training. The affected parties must know the purpose of the proposed changes and how they will enable everyone to work more securely.

In addition, users should be *educated* and trained on how to work under the new constraints while avoiding any negative performance consequences. One of the most frustrating things for users is the implementation of a new program that prevents them from accomplishing their duties, with only a promise of eventual training.

Finally, those making changes should *involve* users by asking them what they want, or what they will tolerate, from the new systems. One way to do so this is to include representatives from the various constituencies in the development process.

Communication, education, and involvement can reduce *resistance* to change and build *resilience* for change—that ethereal quality that allows workers to embrace it as a necessary part of the job.

Technical Feasibility

Unfortunately, many organizations rush to acquire new safeguards, without thoroughly examining what is required to implement and use them effectively. Because the implementation of technological controls can be extremely complex, the project team must consider their **technical feasibility**, that is, examine whether the organization has or can acquire the technology necessary to implement and support them. Technical feasibility analysis also examines whether the organization has the technological expertise needed to manage the new technology. Does the staff include individuals who are qualified (and possibly certified) to install and manage a new firewall system? If not, can staff be spared from their current obligations to attend formal training and education programs to prepare them to administer the new systems? Or must personnel be hired? In the current environment, how difficult is it to find qualified personnel?

Political Feasibility

Politics has been defined as "the art of the possible."[5] **Political feasibility** analysis considers what can and cannot occur based on the consensus and relationships among the communities of interest. The limits imposed by the information security controls must fit within the realm of the possible before they can be effectively implemented, and that realm includes the availability of staff resources. Some organizations may find that the structure of the information security governance model can cause resistance to implementation of plans. When those perceived as outsiders direct change that affect how things are done in those organizations it may result in poor outcomes or unintended consequences.

Alternatives to Feasibility Analysis

Rather than using cost-benefit analysis or some other feasibility reckoning to justify risk controls, an organization might look to alternative models. Many of these have been described in earlier chapters (especially in Chapter 6). A short list of alternatives is provided here:

- ▶ Benchmarking is the process of seeking out and studying the practices used in other organizations that produce the results you desire in your organization. When benchmarking, an organization typically uses either metrics-based measures or process-based measures.
- ▶ Due care and due diligence occur when an organization adopts a certain minimum level of security as what any *prudent* organization would do in similar circumstances.
- ▶ Best business practices are considered those thought to be among the best in the industry, balancing the need to access information with adequate protection.
- ▶ Government recommendations and best practices are useful for organizations that operate in industries that are regulated by governmental agencies; government recommendations are, in effect, requirements.
- ▶ Government regulations can also serve as excellent sources for information about what some organizations may be doing, or are required to do, to control information security risks.
- ▶ A baseline is derived by comparing measured actual performance against established standards for the measured category.

DEFENDING RISK CONTROL DECISIONS

Risk management decisions must be defensible—as the information security professional, you will be competing with other organizational entities for budget and personnel resources. As you may already know, this competition can be fierce and the former excuse of "it's for security" is no longer the golden key to the corporate coffers. But, if you follow the practices we've outlined, you will be well positioned to present sound reasoning for your risk management decisions to your senior management.

A final factor to consider in your plan is that IT is very much an ecology where each control or safeguard affects more than one asset–threat pair. If a new $50,000 firewall is installed to protect the Internet connection infrastructure from hackers' mapping the network by port scanning, the same firewall may also protect other information assets from other threats and attacks. The final choice may call for a balanced mixture of controls that provides the greatest value for as many asset–threat pairs as possible. This example reveals another facet of the problem: Information security professionals manage a dynamic matrix covering a broad range of threats, information assets, controls, and identified vulnerabilities. Each time a control is added to the matrix, it undoubtedly changes the ALE for the information asset vulnerability for which it has been designed, and it also may alter the ALE for other information asset vulnerabilities. To put it more simply, if you put in one safeguard, you decrease the risk associated with all subsequent control evaluations. To make matters worse, the action of implementing a control may change the values assigned or calculated earlier in the risk management process.

Between the difficult task of valuing information assets and the dynamic nature of the ALE calculations, it's no wonder that organizations look for a more straightforward method of implementing controls. This preference has prompted an ongoing search for ways to design security architectures that go beyond the direct application of specific controls for specific information asset vulnerabilities. This is an active area of research and is a space definitely worth watching.

Choosing the methods for controlling risk is where "the rubber meets the road" in information security because this is where you make the hard decisions about what you will do in order to protect your organization's information assets. The decisions you make must be based on sound reasoning so that they will be defensible when competing with other parts of the organization for budget and resources. The ability to articulate the risk management plan in terms of concrete business consequences is a core skill of the successful information security professional.

The Information Security Manager's Checklist

	No	Planned	In Progress	In Place	Integrated
This topic has been fully tested, validated, and integrated into organizational operations with formal performance measures in place (as appropriate).					
This topic has been implemented, but not fully tested, validated, and integrated into organizational operations.					
The implementation of this topic has begun, but is not yet complete.					
The formal planning for this topic has begun, but is not yet complete.					
This subject has not formally begun planning, or the organization has made a conscious decision not to pursue this topic.					
10. Risk Control					
TVA shortcomings evaluated for additional control strategies					
Those TVAs requiring avoidance have additional controls developed and implemented					
Those TVAs requiring transference have auxiliary sources identified					
Those TVAs requiring mitigation have additional plans developed					
Those TVAs requiring acceptance have been reviewed against all other strategies and been determined not to warrant additional controls					

For Further Reading

Risk Management for Projects: How to Deal with over 150 Issues and Risks by Bennet Lientz and Lee Larssen, Butterworth-Heinemann, 2006.

References

1. Thomas J. Peters and Robert H.Waterman. *In Search of Excellence: Lessons from America's Best-Run Companies.* New York: Harper and Row, 1982.

2. Gamma Secure Systems. First measure your risk. *Gamma Online,* 2 January 2002. Accessed 19 June 2002 from www.gammassl.co.uk/inforisk/.

3. National Institute of Standards and Technology. *Risk Management Guide for Information Technology Systems.* SP 800-30. January 2002.

4. As illustrated in the Microsoft Security Risk Management Guide, referenced earlier.

5. Thomas Mann. Politics is often defined as the art of the possible. Speech in the Library of Congress, Washington, DC, May 29, 1945.

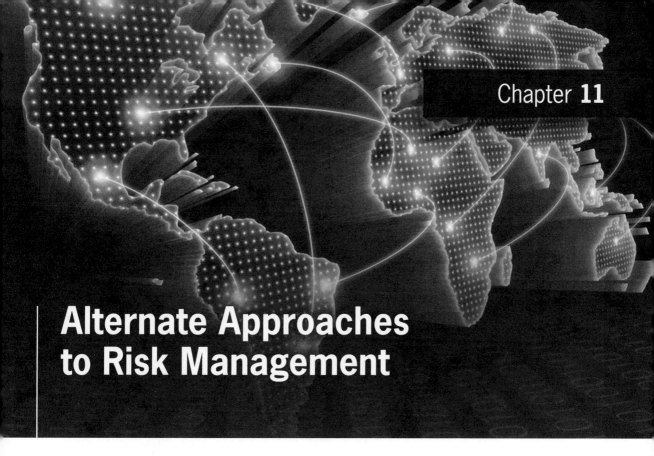

Chapter 11

Alternate Approaches to Risk Management

Up till now, we've offered a "risk management smorgasbord" to provide a number of perspectives on the different ways to approach risk management. This chapter will take a detailed look at two specific approaches to the risk management process, which are both well known and publicly available. There are, of course, many others, ranging from other public frameworks to proprietary tools developed by various consulting organizations. However, a detailed look at these two will provide you with informed insight into choosing the right methodology you eventually choose for your company.

Chapter Overview:

► The OCTAVE method
► The Microsoft risk management approach

THE OCTAVE METHOD*

The OCTAVE method is an InfoSec risk evaluation methodology that allows organizations to balance the protection of critical information assets against the costs of providing protective and detection controls. It enables an organization to measure itself against known or accepted good security practices, and then establish an organization-wide protection strategy and information security risk mitigation plan. If, after reading the following section, you want more information, you can download the OCTAVE method implementation guide from www.cert .org/octave/omig.html.[1] In addition to the OCTAVE method described here, there are two variants of OCTAVE: OCTAVE-S (for smaller organizations) and OCTAVE-Allegro (a streamlined version of OCTAVE). The following sections represent an excerpt of the OCTAVE method, reprinted with permission.

The Operationally Critical Threat, Asset, and Vulnerability Evaluation (OCTAVE) method defines the essential components of a comprehensive, systematic, context-driven, self-directed information security risk evaluation.[2] By following the OCTAVE method, an organization can make information-protection decisions based on risks to the confidentiality, integrity, and availability of critical information technology assets. Using a three-phase approach, the OCTAVE method examines organizational and technology issues to assemble a comprehensive picture of the information security needs of an organization. The phases are described below:

- ▶ *Phase 1: Build Asset-Based Threat Profiles. This is an organizational evaluation. Key areas of expertise within the organization are examined to elicit important knowledge about information assets, the threats to those assets, the security requirements of the assets, what the organization is currently doing to protect its information assets, and weaknesses in organizational policies and practice.*

- ▶ *Phase 2: Identify Infrastructure Vulnerabilities. This is an evaluation of the information infrastructure. The key operational components of the information technology infrastructure are examined for weaknesses (technology vulnerabilities) that can lead to unauthorized action.*

- ▶ *Phase 3: Develop Security Strategy and Plans. Risks are analyzed in this phase. The information generated by the organizational and information infrastructure evaluations (Phases 1 and 2) is analyzed to identify risks to the organization and to evaluate the risks based on their impact to the organization's mission. In addition, an organization protection strategy and risk mitigation plans for the highest priority risks are developed.*

Important Aspects of the OCTAVE Method

1. *The OCTAVE method is self-directed. A small, interdisciplinary team of the organization's personnel (called the analysis team) manages the process and analyzes all information. Thus, the organization's personnel are actively involved in the decision-making process.*

2. *The OCTAVE method requires an analysis team to conduct the evaluation and to analyze the information. The analysis team is an interdisciplinary team (typically*

---

*From Appendix D of *OCTAVE Method Implementation Guide Version 2.0* by C. Alberts and A. Dorofee, June 2001. Reprinted here with permission.

3–5 members) comprising representatives from both the mission-related and information technology areas of the organization. The basic tasks of the analysis team are:

▶ To facilitate the knowledge elicitation workshops of Phase 1

▶ To gather any supporting data that are necessary

▶ To analyze threat and risk information

▶ To develop a protection strategy for the organization

▶ To develop mitigation plans to address the risks to the organization's critical assets

3. The OCTAVE method uses a workshop-based approach for gathering information and making decisions. In Phase 1, key areas of expertise within the organization are examined in facilitated workshops (also called knowledge elicitation workshops). The result is the identification of important information assets, the threats to those assets, the security requirements of the assets, what the organization is currently doing to protect its information assets (current protection strategy), and weaknesses in organizational policies and practice (organizational vulnerabilities). The remainder of Phase 1, as well as Phases 2 and 3, include consolidation and analysis workshops to consolidate and analyze the information gathered during the Phase 1 knowledge elicitation workshops.

4. The OCTAVE method relies upon the following major catalogs of information:

▶ Catalog of practices: A collection of good strategic and operational security practices

▶ Threat profile: The range of major sources of threats that an organization needs to consider

▶ Catalog of vulnerabilities: A collection of vulnerabilities based on platform and application

Phases, Processes, and Activities

Each phase of the OCTAVE method contains two or more processes. Each process is made of activities. Each of these is described in more detail in the following sections.

Preparing for the OCTAVE Method

Preparing for the OCTAVE method creates the foundation for a successful or unsuccessful evaluation. Getting senior management sponsorship, the selection of the analysis team, scoping of the project and the selection of the participants are all key to a successful evaluation: The preparation activities for the OCTAVE method address the issues listed above. The following are the activities required when preparing to conduct the OCTAVE method:

1. Obtain senior management sponsorship of OCTAVE.

2. Select analysis team members.

3. Train analysis team.

4. Select operational areas to participate in OCTAVE.

5. Select participants.

6. Coordinate logistics.

7. Brief all participants.

Once the preparation is completed, the organization is ready to start the evaluation.

Phase 1: Build Asset-Based Threat Profiles

The OCTAVE method enables decision makers to develop relative priorities based on what is important to the organization. This involves examining both organizational practices and the installed technology base to identify risks to the organization's important information assets.[3]

During Phase 1, the analysis team facilitates workshop interviews with staff from multiple organizational levels. During these workshops, the participants identify important assets and discuss the impact on the organization if the assets are compromised. These knowledge elicitation workshops are held separately for senior management, middle management, and staff (including IT staff). The purpose of the knowledge elicitation workshops is to identify the following information from each organizational perspective:

- ▶ *Important assets and their relative values*
- ▶ *Perceived threats to the assets*
- ▶ *Security requirements*
- ▶ *Current protection strategy practices*
- ▶ *Current organizational vulnerabilities*

The OCTAVE method requires workshop participants to examine the relative priority of assets, based on the impact to the organization if the asset is lost. Participants are asked to examine threats to the highest-priority assets that they have identified. The participants create threat scenarios based on known sources of threat and typical threat outcomes (from the threat profile). Participants next examine security requirements. Security requirements outline the qualities of information assets that are important to an organization. The following processes illustrate the information collected in the workshops:

- ▶ *Identify assets and relative priorities.*
- ▶ *Identify areas of concern.*
- ▶ *Identify security requirements for the most important assets.*
- ▶ *Capture knowledge of protection strategy practices and organizational vulnerabilities.*

This information is collected through the first three processes:

- ▶ *Process 1: Identify Senior Management Knowledge*
- ▶ *Process 2: Identify Operational Area Management Knowledge*
- ▶ *Process 3: Identify Staff Knowledge*

During Process 4, the information elicited from the different organizational levels during the previous processes is grouped, critical assets are chosen, and a threat profile is created for each critical asset. The following are the activities of Process 4:

- ▶ *Group assets, security requirements, and areas of concern by organizational level.*
- ▶ *Select critical assets.*
- ▶ *Refine security requirements for critical assets*
- ▶ *Identify threats to critical assets.*

After completion of the organization view, or Phase 1 of the OCTAVE method, the organization is ready to move to the technological view. Phase 2 of the evaluation examines the organization's information technology infrastructure.

Phase 2: Identify Infrastructure Vulnerabilities

Each information technology system or component will have many specific technology vulnerabilities against which it can be benchmarked. The OCTAVE method requires that technology be measured against a catalog of vulnerabilities. The Common Vulnerabilities and Exposures (CVE) is a list or dictionary that provides common names for publicly known vulnerabilities.[4] It enables open and shared information without any distribution restrictions.

Technology vulnerability evaluations target weaknesses in the installed technology base of the organization, including network services, architecture, operating systems, and applications. The following basic activities are performed during a technology vulnerability evaluation:

- ▶ Identify key information technology systems and components.
- ▶ Examine systems and components for technology weaknesses.

The focus of a vulnerability evaluation of systems and components is to identify and evaluate the configuration and strength of devices on the organization network(s). The following list includes examples of tests performed during a technology vulnerability evaluation:

- ▶ Reviewing firewall configuration
- ▶ Checking the security of public Web servers
- ▶ Performing a comprehensive review of all operating systems
- ▶ Identifying services running and/or available on hosts and systems
- ▶ Listing all system user accounts
- ▶ Identifying known vulnerabilities in routers, switches, remote access servers, operating systems, and specific services and applications
- ▶ Identifying configuration errors
- ▶ Looking for existing signs of intrusion (Trojan horses, backdoor programs, integrity checks of critical system files, etc.)
- ▶ Checking file ownership and permissions
- ▶ Testing password usage and strength

The participants in Process 5 (identify Key Components) are the analysis team and selected members of the information technology (IT) staff. During Process 5, components to be evaluated for technology vulnerabilities are selected using these activities:

- ▶ Identify system of interest.
- ▶ Identify key classes of components.
- ▶ Identify infrastructure components to examine.

The participants in Process 6 (Evaluate Selected Components) are the analysis team and selected members of the IT staff who review the results of the evaluation during the workshop in these activities:

- ▶ Run vulnerability evaluation tools on selected infrastructure components.
- ▶ Review technology vulnerabilities and summarize results.

After the organization completes the technology view, or Phase 2 of the evaluation, it is ready to develop a protection strategy and mitigation plans. During Phase 3 of the OCTAVE method, the analysis team identifies the risks to its critical assets, develops a protection strategy for the organization, and develops mitigation plans for the risks to the critical assets.

Phase 3: Develop Security Strategy and Plans

Once the assets, threats, and vulnerabilities have been identified, an organization is positioned to analyze the information and to identify the information security risks. The analysis of risks in the OCTAVE method is based on scenario planning. The analysis team constructs a range of risk scenarios, or a risk profile, for each critical asset. The risk profile for a critical asset comprises the threat profile for the critical asset and a narrative description of the resulting impact(s) to the organization.[5] After the risk analysis has been completed, the goal is to reduce risk through a combination of these actions:

- ▶ Implementing new security practices within the organization
- ▶ Taking the actions necessary to maintain the existing security practices
- ▶ Fixing identified vulnerabilities

The following are the activities of Process 7:

- ▶ Identify the impact of threats to critical assets.
- ▶ Create risk evaluation criteria.
- ▶ Evaluate the impact of threats to critical assets.

Process 8 consists of two workshops. The goal of Process 8 is to develop a protection strategy for the organization, mitigation plans for the risks to the critical assets, and an action list of near-term actions. The following are the activities of the first workshop of Process 8:

- ▶ Consolidate protection strategy information.
- ▶ Create protection strategy.
- ▶ Create mitigation plans.
- ▶ Create action list.

In the second workshop of Process 8, the analysis team presents the proposed protection strategy, mitigation plans, and action list to senior managers in the organization. The senior managers review and revise the strategy and plans as necessary and then decide how the organization will build on the results of the evaluation. The following are the activities of the second workshop of Process 8:

- ▶ Review risk information.
- ▶ Review and refine protection strategy, mitigation plans, and action list.
- ▶ Create next steps.

After the organization has developed the protection strategy and risk mitigation plans, it is ready to implement them. This completes the OCTAVE method.

MICROSOFT RISK MANAGEMENT APPROACH

Microsoft has published its own Security Risk Management Guide, located at: http://technet .microsoft.com/en-us/library/cc163143.aspx. Since this version is comprehensive, easily scalable and repeatable, it is summarized here with permission.[6]

Microsoft asserts that risk management is not a stand-alone subject and should be part of a general governance program to allow the organizational general management community of interest to evaluate the organization's operations and make better, more-informed decisions. The purpose of the risk management process is to prioritize and manage security risks. Microsoft presents four phases in their security risk management process:

1. Assessing Risk
2. Conducting Decision Support
3. Implementing Controls
4. Measuring Program Effectiveness

These four phases provide an overview of a program which is similar to the methods presented earlier in the OCTAVE approach. Microsoft, however, breaks the phases into fewer, more manageable pieces.

Assessing Risk

The first phase of the Microsoft Security Risk Management program is the same first step taken in both the OCTAVE method and in Chapter 7: Risk assessment—the identification and prioritization of the risks facing the organization.

1. Plan data gathering. Discuss keys to success and preparation guidance.
2. Gather risk data. Outline the data collection process and analysis.
3. Prioritize risks. Outline prescriptive steps to qualify and quantify risks.

Conducting Decision Support

The second step is simply the identification and evaluation of controls available to the organization. Methods used to evaluate the controls could include both the qualitative and quantitative methods discussed earlier, including cost-benefit analyses, which Microsoft stresses.

1. Define functional requirements. Define functional requirements to mitigate risks.
2. Select possible control solutions. Outline approach to identify mitigation solutions.
3. Review solution. Evaluate proposed controls against functional requirements.
4. Estimate risk reduction. Endeavor to understand reduced exposure or probability of risks.

5. Estimate solution cost. Evaluate direct and indirect costs associated with mitigation solutions.

6. Select mitigation strategy. Complete the cost-benefit analysis to identify the most cost-effective mitigation solution.

Implementing Controls

The next step involves the deployments and operation of the controls selected from the cost-benefit analyses and other mitigating factors from the previous step.

1. Seek holistic approach. Incorporate people, process, and technology in mitigation solution.

2. Organize by defense in depth. Organize mitigation solutions across the business.

Measuring Program Effectiveness

The last and first step in the rest of the program is the ongoing assessment of the effectiveness of the risk management program. As controls are used, as the organization and its environment changes and evolves, the process must be closely monitored to ensure the controls continue to provide the desired level of protection.

1. Develop risk scorecard. Understand risk posture and progress.

2. Measure program effectiveness. Evaluate the risk management program for opportunities to improve.

These steps are illustrated in Figure 11-1.

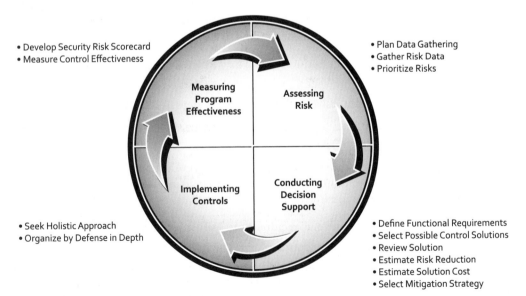

Figure 11-1 Security Risk Management Guide
Course Technology/Cengage Learning

Before You Start

Now that you understand what's involved in a risk management process, there are some things you need to consider before you start down this path. Microsoft recommends that the organization consider the level of effort involved, and the need to lay a good foundation. While the amount of work involved in the early stages declines initially, as the organization enters the detailed risk analysis phase, the relative amount of work increases quickly, and could derail the program if the appropriate resources are not available. The critical need is to make sure you have laid the appropriate groundwork so that your organization is in for "the long haul" and won't abandon the effort half-way through because it's "too much work."

Next comes determining the organization's "risk management maturity." Microsoft uses the concept of the "well-formed risk statement" in their work, and, as illustrated in Figure 11-2, this risk statement is based on both the probability and impact components of risk. While impact is based on the assets and threats facing those assets, probability in turn is based upon vulnerabilities and any mitigation (e.g., controls) the organization currently employs. From this we can derive the Microsoft definition of risk as "risk is the probability of a vulnerability being exploited in the current environment, leading to a degree of loss of confidentiality, integrity, or availability, of an asset."[7] Communicating the impact and probability of a risk can be accomplished using a complex metric; however, a simple method of using high, moderate, or low provides a more usable method. It is up to the organization's risk management team to define these.

Figure 11-2 The Well-formed Risk Statement
Course Technology/Cengage Learning

The organization's risk management maturity level describes the experience the organization has with risk management. If an organization previously implemented a different risk management process, this points to a general understanding of risk and risk management, as well as

One of the challenges in starting a new information security program is that the organization will likely score quite poorly on the maturity index. This low maturity score does not mean that the risk management process does not need to be done, but it does indicate that you have a lot of groundwork to lay before the process can be used effectively. Some organizations face difficult situations because the organization's assets have already been plundered. These organizations may, in fact, have a head start on immediate remediation ("stopping the bleeding") because of the efforts that may have been undertaken in the response to the triggering incident.

What will make or break an information security program at an organization that has suffered losses is how well it transitions from the "stop the pain" to a continuing cycle of risk assessment and management. There will be a terrible temptation on the part of the organization to say "Whew! That's over and we're secure" but as we've seen throughout this book, that is a prescription for a future disaster.

The maturity assessment both helps you understand where your organization is on the road to mature risk management and also offers guidance on the tasks you should undertake to move your organization along that road. Many risk management efforts are ineffective because they neglected this first step of determining how prepared the organization was to implement meaningful risk management.

to the existence of policies and procedures. One method the organization can use to gauge its maturity is to refer to the CoBIT method. Additional information on how to use the CoBIT model are provided in the Microsoft Risk Management Guide.[8]

Roles and Responsibilities

Microsoft's next step is the definition and assignment of the roles and responsibilities of individuals who will participate in the risk management process. The primary roles that are involved include many of the same players described earlier, including the following:

- ▶ Executive sponsor
- ▶ Business owner
- ▶ Information security group
- ▶ Information technology group
- ▶ Security risk management team
- ▶ Risk assessment facilitator
- ▶ Risk assessment note taker
- ▶ Mitigation owners
- ▶ Security steering committee
- ▶ Stakeholder

The first step is to ensure that everyone knows their roles and responsibilities in the risk management process. Even if some of these players were involved in previous efforts, the application of a different methodology requires a detailed discussion on what is expected.

To summarize, the Executive Sponsor is ultimately accountable for defining acceptable risk and provides guidance to the Security Risk Management Team in terms of ranking risks to the business. The Security Risk Management Team is responsible for assessing risk and defining functional requirements to mitigate risk to an acceptable level. The Security Risk Management Team then collaborates with the IT groups who own mitigation selection, implementation, and operations. The final relationship defined below is the Security Risk Management Team's oversight of measuring control effectiveness. This usually occurs in the form of audit reports, which are also communicated to the Executive Sponsor.

Figure 11-3 illustrates the relationship between these individuals.

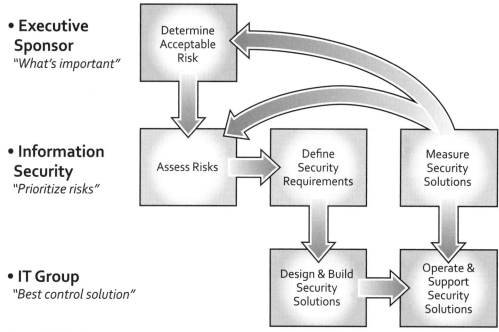

Figure 11-3 Risk Management Roles and Responsibilities
Course Technology/Cengage Learning

Depending on the size and complexity of your organization, not all these roles will be necessary in the sense that there must be a person assigned to each role (there may not even be that many employees in your organization). However, when eliminating roles, take a good look at the function that role fulfills before deciding that you don't really need it. For example, the dedicated "note taker" may be an obvious elimination for the smaller organization but someone will still need to capture details of important discussions and decisions to avoid later disagreements and confusion.

This chapter gave a high-level overview of two common risk management processes. The fundamental purpose of a risk management methodology is to make sound decisions about how to use the organization's scarce resources in protecting its assets to the best level possible. Another sound takeaway from both methodologies is that risk management is never a one-time affair but is a cycle that must be repeated on a regular basis in order to assure that the organization's resources and protections remain in an optimal relationship.

The Information Security Manager's Checklist

	This topic has been fully tested, validated, and integrated into organizational operations with formal performance measures in place (as appropriate).				
	This topic has been implemented, but not fully tested, validated, and integrated into organizational operations.				
	The implementation of this topic has begun, but is not yet complete.				
	The formal planning for this topic has begun, but is not yet complete.				
	This subject has not formally begun planning, or the organization has made a conscious decision not to pursue this topic.	No	Planned	In Progress	In Place	Integrated
11. Alternate Appropriate to Risk Management					
Alternative strategies identified					
Each strategy evaluated for "fit" with organization					
Alternate strategy selected and implemented					
Alternate strategy reviewed for continued value to organization					

For Further Reading

Managing Information Security Risks: The OCTAVE Approach by C. Alberts and A. Dorofee, Addison-Wesley Professional, 2003.

Security Risk Management Guide by Microsoft available from http://www.microsoft.com/technet/security/topics/complianceandpolicies/secrisk/default.mspx, 2004.

References

1. Another good reference on OCTAVE is: C. Alberts and A. Dorofee. *Managing Information Security Risks: The OCTAVE^SM Approach.* Boston: Addison-Wesley, 2003.

2. Christopher J. Alberts, Sandra G. Behrens, Richard D. Pethia, and William R. Wilson. *Operationally Critical Threat, Asset, and Vulnerability Evaluation (OCTAVE) Framework, Version 1.0* (CMU/SEI-99-TR-017, ADA 367718). Pittsburgh, PA: Software Engineering Institute, Carnegie Mellon University, June 1999.

3. U.S. General Accounting Office. *Executive Guide: Information Security Management* (GAO/AIMD-98-68). Washington, DC: GAO, May 1998.

4. M. S. Merkow and J. Breithaupt. *The Complete Guide to Internet Security.* New York: AMACOM, American Management Association, 2000, 95–109.

5. Kees Van der Heijden. *Scenarios: The Art of Strategic Conversation.* Chichester, UK: John Wiley & Sons, 1997.

6. Microsoft Security Risk Management Guide, 15 March 2006. Accessed 15 August 2006 from www .microsoft.com/technet/security/topics/complianceandpolicies/secrisk/srsgch03.mspx.

7. Microsoft, Security Risk Management Guide: Chapter 3: Security Risk Management Overview, 15 March 2006. Accessed 15 August 2006 from www.microsoft.com/technet/security/topics/ complianceandpolicies/secrisk/srsgch03.mspx.

8. Ibid.

Strategic Information Security: Standards, Regulations, Law, and Ethics

Part IV of *Roadmap to Information Security for IT and InfoSec Managers* will explore the area of strategic information security. This will encompass regulations and standards frequently encountered by InfoSec managers as well as other legal and ethical issues.

Part Overview

Chapter 12—"Standards for Managing the Information Security Program" describes the components of the dominant InfoSec management models, including U.S. government-sanctioned and key international models, and discusses how to customize them for a specific organization's needs. Readers also learn how to implement the fundamental elements of key InfoSec management practices.

Chapter 13—"Emerging Trends in Certification and Accreditation" describes the foundations and components of certification and accreditation of public and private U.S. IT systems. It defines and examines the requirements and responsibilities of individuals responsible for systems certification and accreditation and uses the NIST model as a foundation.

Chapter 14—"Dealing with Regulatory Compliance and Other Legal Issues" observes that a fundamental part of the InfoSec process is a careful examination of current legislation, regulation, and common ethical expectations of both national and international entities. This will provide key insights into the regulatory constraints that govern business. The chapter focuses on the dominant subjects facing most IT and InfoSec managers: SOX, HIPAA, GLB, and PCI.

Chapter 15—"Key Laws for Every IT Security Manager" examines several key laws that shape the field of information security and presents a detailed examination of computer ethics necessary to better educate those implementing security. Although ignorance of the no excuse, negligence (knowing and doing nothing) is equally inexcusable.

Chapter 16—"Ethics in IT and InfoSec-Who Watches the Watchers?" presents an overview of ethics in modern organizations and discusses several ethical issues that are commonly found in today's organizations, as well as formal and professional organizations that promote ethics and legal responsibility.

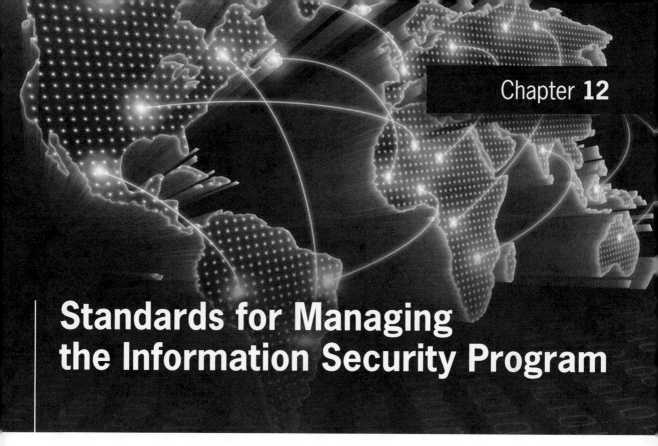

Chapter 12

Standards for Managing the Information Security Program

Up until this point, the previous chapters helped you to build a policy foundation for an information security program. Using the results of the risk assessments from Part 3, you and your security team can now develop the blueprint for the implementation of the organization's information security program. This **security blueprint** is the basis for the design, selection, and implementation of all security program elements including policy implementation, ongoing policy management, risk management programs, education and training programs, technical controls, and maintenance of the security program. The security blueprint, built on top of the organization's information security policies, is a scalable, upgradeable, comprehensive plan to meet the organization's current and future information security needs. It is the detailed version of the **security framework**, which is an outline of the overall information security strategy for the organization and a roadmap for planned changes to the information security environment of the organization. The blueprint specifies the tasks in the order in which they are to be accomplished by you and your team.

When selecting a methodology upon which to develop an information security blueprint, a good place to start is an already published information security model or framework. This framework can be an outline of steps to take to design and implement information security in the organization. There are a number of published information security frameworks, including ones from the government sources presented later in this chapter. Because each information security environment is unique, the security team will usually need to adapt and customize pieces from several already existing frameworks. Experience has shown that what works well for one organization may not precisely fit another.

Chapter Overview:

► The ISO 27000 Series

► NIST security models

► Other models

► Baselining and best business practices

THE ISO 27000 SERIES

One of the most widely referenced security models is the *Information Technology—Code of Practice for Information Security Management*, which was originally published as British Standard BS7799. In 2000, this Code of Practice was adopted as an international standard framework for information security by the International Organization for Standardization (ISO) and the International Electrotechnical Commission (IEC) as ISO/IEC 17799. The document was revised in 2005 (becoming ISO 17799:2005), and it was then renamed ISO 27002 in 2007, to align it with the document ISO 27001, discussed later in this chapter. While the details of ISO/IEC 27002 are available to those who purchase the standard, its structure and general organization are well known. For a summary description, see Table 12-1. For more details on ISO/IEC Sections, see *http://www.27000.org*.

TABLE 12-1 The Sections of the ISO/IEC 27002[1]

1. Risk Assessment and Treatment
2. Security Policy
3. Organization of Information Security
4. Asset Management
5. Human Resource Security
6. Physical and Environmental Security
7. Communications and Operations
8. Access Control
9. Information Systems Acquisition, Development, and Maintenance
10. Information Security Incident Management
11. Business Continuity Management
12. Compliance

Course Technology/Cengage Learning

The stated purpose of ISO/IEC 27002 is to "give recommendations for information security management for use by those who are responsible for initiating, implementing, or maintaining security in their organization. It is intended to provide a common basis for developing organizational security standards and effective security management practice and to provide confidence in inter-organizational dealings."[2] Where ISO/IEC 27002 is focused on a broad overview of the various areas of security, providing information on 127 controls over ten broad areas, ISO/IEC 27001 provides information on how to implement ISO/IEC 27002 and how to set up an information security management system (ISMS). The overall methodology for this process and its major steps are presented in Figure 12-1.

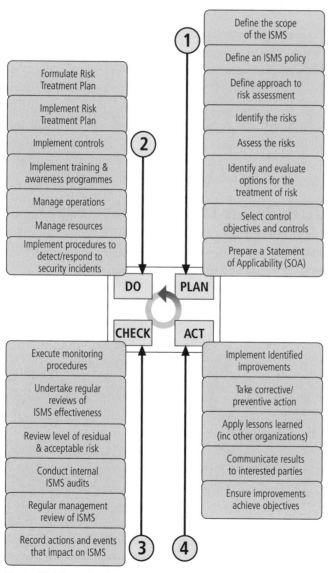

Figure 12-1 The Major Steps of ISO 27002
Course Technology/Cengage Learning

In the United Kingdom, correct implementation of these standards, as determined by a BS7799-certified evaluator, allowed organizations to obtain system (ISMS) certification and accreditation. When the standard first came out, several countries including the United States, Germany, and Japan refused to adopt it, claiming that there were several fundamental problems, including:

- The global information security community has not defined any justification for a code of practice as was identified in the ISO/IEC 17799.
- ISO/IEC 17799 lacked "the necessary measurement precision of a technical standard."[3]
- There is no reason to believe that ISO/IEC 17799 was more useful than any other approach.
- ISO/IEC 17799 was not as complete as other frameworks.
- ISO/IEC 17799 was hurriedly prepared given the tremendous impact its adoption could have on industry information security controls.[4]

It is also speculated that there was a certain amount of national pride involved in these objections. For example, in the United States, NIST is generally considered responsible for providing security guidance and there was reluctance to accept an externally developed standard. Though few organizations outside of businesses that operate in the European Union are likely to seek formal certification under the 27000 framework, it is a useful framework for managing an information security program, and becoming increasingly popular in the U.S.

ISO/IEC 27001:2005: The Information Security Management System

ISO/IEC 27001 provides implementation details using a plan-do-check-act cycle, as described in Table 12-2 and shown in Figure 12-2 in abbreviated form:

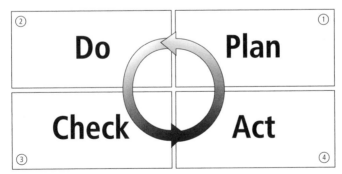

Figure 12-2 Plan-Do-Check-Act
Course Technology/Cengage Learning

Although ISO/IEC 27001 provides some implementation information, it simply specified *what* must be done—not *how* to do it. As noted by Gamma Secure Systems, "The standard has an appendix that gives guidance on the use of the standard, in particular to expand on the Plan-Do-Check-Act concept. It is important to realize that there will be many Plan-Do-Check-Act

TABLE 12-2 The ISO/IEC 27001:2005 Plan-Do-Check-Act Cycle[5]

Plan:
1. Define the scope of the ISMS.
2. Define an ISMS policy.
3. Define the approach to risk assessment.
4. Identify the risks.
5. Assess the risks.
6. Identify and evaluate options for the treatment of risk.
7. Select control objectives and controls.
8. Prepare a Statement of Applicability (SOA).

Do:
9. Formulate a Risk Treatment Plan.
10. Implement the Risk Treatment Plan.
11. Implement controls.
12. Implement training and awareness programs.
13. Manage operations.
14. Manage resources.
15. Implement procedures to detect and respond to security incidents.

Check:
16. Execute monitoring procedures.
17. Undertake regular reviews of ISMS effectiveness.
18. Review the level of residual and acceptable risk.
19. Conduct internal ISMS audits.
20. Undertake regular management review of the ISMS.
21. Record actions and events that impact an ISMS.

Act:
22. Implement identified improvements.
23. Take corrective or preventive action.
24. Apply lessons learned.
25. Communicate results to interested parties.
26. Ensure improvements achieve objectives.

Course Technology/Cengage Learning

cycles within a single ISMS all operating asynchronously at different speeds."[6] As stated earlier, ISO/IEC 27001's primary purpose is to enable organizations that adopt it to obtain certification, and thus serves better as an assessment tool than as an implementation framework.

In 2007, the International Standards Organization announced the plans for the numbering of current and impending standards related to information security issues and topics. It is expected that over the next few years the standards that are shown in Table 12-3 will be published in the areas shown.

TABLE 12-3 ISO 27000 Series Current and Planned Standards

ISO 27000 SERIES STANDARD	PUB DATE	TITLE OR TOPIC	COMMENT
27000	2009	Series Overview and Terminology	Defines terminology and vocabulary for the standard series
27001	2005	Information Security Management System Specification	Drawn from BS 7799:2
27002	2007	Code of Practice for Information Security Management	Renamed from ISO/IEC 17799; drawn from BS 7799:1
27004	2009	ISMS Risk Management	
27005	2008		Supports 27001, but doesn't recommend any specific risk method
27006	2007	Requirements for Bodies Providing Audit and Certification of an ISMS	Largely intended to support the accreditation of certification bodies providing ISMS certification
PLANNED 27000 SERIES STANDARDS			
27003	Planned	Information Security Management Systems Implementation Guidelines	Expected in 2010
27007	Planned	Guideline for ISMS Auditing	Focuses on management systems
27008	Planned	Guideline for Information Security Auditing	Focuses on security controls
27013	Planned	Guideline on the Integrated Implementation of ISO/IEC 20000-1 and ISO/IEC 27001	
27014	Planned	Information Security Governance Framework	
27015	Planned	Information Security Management Guidelines for Finance and Insurance Sectors	

Course Technology/Cengage Learning

NIST SECURITY MODELS

Another approach to information security management is described in the many documents available from the Computer Security Resource Center of the National Institute for Standards and Technology (*csrc.nist.gov*). Because the NIST documents are publicly available at no charge and have been available for some time, they have been broadly reviewed by government and industry professionals, and are among the references cited by the federal government when it decided not to select the ISO/IEC 17799 standards. The following NIST documents can assist in the design of a security framework:

- ▶ SP 800-12: *An Introduction to Computer Security: The NIST Handbook*
- ▶ SP 800-14: *Generally Accepted Security Principles and Practices for Securing Information Technology Systems*
- ▶ SP 800-18 Rev. 1: *Guide for Developing Security Plans for Federal Information Systems*
- ▶ SP 800-53 A Rev. 1: *Guide for Assessing Security Controls in Federal Information Systems and Organizations, Building Effective Security Assessment Plans*
- ▶ SP 800-30: *Risk Management Guide for Information Technology Systems*

Many of these documents have been referenced earlier in this book as sources of information for the management of security. The following sections examine these documents as they apply to the blueprint for information security.

NIST Special Publication 800-12

SP 800-12, *An Introduction to Computer Security: The NIST Handbook,* is an excellent reference and guide for the security manager or administrator in the routine management of information security. It provides little guidance, however, on design and implementation of new security systems, and therefore should be used only as a precursor to understanding an information security blueprint.

NIST Special Publication 800-14

Generally Accepted Principles and Practices for Securing Information Technology Systems provides best practices and security principles that can direct the security team in the development of a security blueprint. In addition to detailing security best practices across the spectrum of security areas, it provides philosophical principles that the security team should integrate into the entire information security process. Table 12-4 presents the table of contents of the NIST SP 800-14. The document can guide the development of the security framework and should be combined with other NIST publications providing the necessary structure to the entire security process.

TABLE 12-4 NIST SP 800-14 Generally Accepted Principles and Practices for Securing Information Technology Systems Table of Contents[7]

2. Generally Accepted System Security Principles
2.1   Computer Security Supports the Mission of the Organization
2.2   Computer Security Is an Integral Element of Sound Management
2.3   Computer Security Should Be Cost-Effective
2.4   Systems Owners Have Security Responsibilities Outside Their Own Organizations
2.5   Computer Security Responsibilities and Accountability Should Be Made Explicit
2.6   Computer Security Requires a Comprehensive and Integrated Approach
2.7   Computer Security Should Be Periodically Reassessed
2.8   Computer Security Is Constrained by Societal Factors

(continued)

TABLE 12-4 *(continued)*

3. Common IT Security Practices
   3.1   Policy
          3.1.1 Program Policy
          3.1.2 Issue-Specific Policy
          3.1.3 System-Specific Policy
          3.1.4 All Policies
   3.2   Program Management
          3.2.1 Central Security Program
          3.2.2 System-Level Program
   3.3   Risk Management
          3.3.1 Risk Assessment
          3.3.2 Risk Mitigation
          3.3.3 Uncertainty Analysis
   3.4   Life Cycle Planning
          3.4.1 Security Plan
          3.4.2 Initiation Phase
          3.4.3 Development/Acquisition Phase
          3.4.4 Implementation Phase
          3.4.5 Operation/Maintenance Phase
          3.4.6 Disposal Phase
   3.5   Personnel/User Issues
          3.5.1 Staffing
          3.5.2 User Administration
   3.6   Preparing for Contingencies and Disasters
          3.6.1 Business Plan
          3.6.2 Identify Resources
          3.6.3 Develop Scenarios
          3.6.4 Develop Strategies
          3.6.5 Test and Revise Plan
   3.7   Computer Security Incident Handling
          3.7.1 Uses of a Capability
          3.7.2 Characteristics
   3.8   Awareness and Training
   3.9   Security Considerations in Computer Support and Operations
   3.10 Physical and Environmental Security
   3.11 Identification and Authentication
          3.11.1 Identification
          3.11.2 Authentication
          3.11.3 Passwords
          3.11.4 Advanced Authentication
   3.12 Logical Access Control
          3.12.1 Access Criteria
          3.12.2 Access Control Mechanisms
   3.13 Audit Trails
          3.13.1 Contents of Audit Trail Records
          3.13.2 Audit Trail Security
          3.13.3 Audit Trail Reviews
          3.13.4 Keystroke Monitoring
   3.14 Cryptography

The scope of NIST SP 800-14 is broad. It is important to consider each of the security principles it presents, and therefore the following sections examine some of the more significant points in more detail:

2.1 Security Supports the Mission of the Organization: Failure to develop an information security system based on the organization's mission, vision, and culture guarantees the failure of the information security program.

2.2 Security Is an Integral Element of Sound Management: Effective management includes planning, organizing, leading, and controlling.

2.3 Security Should Be Cost-Effective: The costs of information security should be considered part of the cost of doing business, much like the cost of the computers, networks, and voice communications systems. These are not profit-generating areas of the organization and may not lead to competitive advantages. Information security should justify its own costs. The use of security measures that do not justify their cost must have a strong business justification (such as a legal requirement).

2.4 Systems Owners Have Security Responsibilities Outside Their Own Organizations: Whenever systems store and use information from customers, patients, clients, partners, or others, the security of this information becomes the responsibility of the owner of the systems. Each system's owners are expected to diligently work with those who have systems that are interconnected with their own to assure the confidentiality, integrity, and availability of the entire value chain of interconnected systems.

2.5 Security Responsibilities and Accountability Should Be Made Explicit: Policy documents should clearly identify the security responsibilities of users, administrators, and managers. To be legally binding, the policies must be documented, disseminated, read, understood, and agreed to. As noted in Chapter 3, ignorance of the law is no excuse, but ignorance of policy is. Organizations should also provide information about relevant laws in issue-specific security policies.

2.6 Security Requires a Comprehensive and Integrated Approach: Security personnel alone cannot effectively implement security. As emphasized throughout this textbook, *security is everyone's responsibility*. The three communities of interest (information technology management and professionals, information security management and professionals, and users, managers, administrators, and other stakeholders) should participate in the process of developing a comprehensive information security program.

2.7 Security Should Be Periodically Reassessed: Information security that is implemented and then ignored is considered negligent, the organization having not demonstrated due diligence. Security is an ongoing process. To be effective against a constantly shifting set of threats and a changing user base, the security process must be periodically repeated. Continuous analyses of threats, assets, and controls must be conducted and new blueprints developed. Only thorough preparation, design, implementation, eternal vigilance, and ongoing maintenance can secure the organization's information assets.

2.8 Security Is Constrained by Societal Factors: There are a number of factors that influence the implementation and maintenance of security. Legal demands, shareholder requirements, even business practices affect the implementation of security controls and safeguards. For example, security professionals generally prefer to isolate information assets from the Internet, which is the leading avenue of threats to the assets, but the business requirements of the organization may preclude this control measure.

TABLE 12-5 Principles for Securing Information Technology Systems

NIST SP 800-14 Generally Accepted Principles and Practices for Securing Information Technology Systems[8]

Principle 1.	Establish a sound security policy as the foundation for design.
Principle 2.	Treat security as an integral part of the overall system design.
Principle 3.	Clearly delineate the physical and logical security boundaries governed by associated security policies.
Principle 4.	Reduce risk to an acceptable level.
Principle 5.	Assume that external systems are insecure.
Principle 6.	Identify potential trade-offs between reducing risk and increased costs and decrease in other aspects of operational effectiveness.
Principle 7.	Implement layered security (ensure no single point of vulnerability).
Principle 8.	Implement tailored system security measures to meet organizational security goals.
Principle 9.	Strive for simplicity.
Principle 10.	Design and operate an IT system to limit vulnerability and to be resilient in response.
Principle 11.	Minimize the system elements to be trusted.
Principle 12.	Implement security through a combination of measures distributed physically and logically.
Principle 13.	Provide assurance that the system is, and continues to be, resilient in the face of expected threats.
Principle 14.	Limit or contain vulnerabilities.
Principle 15.	Formulate security measures to address multiple overlapping information domains.
Principle 16.	Isolate public access systems from mission critical resources (e.g., data, processes, etc.).
Principle 17.	Use boundary mechanisms to separate computing systems and network infrastructures.
Principle 18.	Where possible, base security on open standards for portability and interoperability.
Principle 19.	Use common language in developing security requirements.
Principle 20.	Design and implement audit mechanisms to detect unauthorized use and to support incident investigations.
Principle 21.	Design security to allow for regular adoption of new technology, including a secure and logical technology upgrade process.
Principle 22.	Authenticate users and processes to ensure appropriate access control decisions both within and across domains.
Principle 23.	Use unique identities to ensure accountability.
Principle 24.	Implement least privilege.
Principle 25.	Do not implement unnecessary security mechanisms.
Principle 26.	Protect information while being processed, in transit, and in storage.
Principle 27.	Strive for operational ease of use.
Principle 28.	Develop and exercise contingency or disaster recovery procedures to ensure appropriate availability.
Principle 29.	Consider custom products to achieve adequate security.
Principle 30.	Ensure proper security in the shutdown or disposal of a system.
Principle 31.	Protect against all likely classes of "attacks."
Principle 32.	Identify and prevent common errors and vulnerabilities.
Principle 33.	Ensure that developers are trained in how to develop secure software.

Course Technology/Cengage Learning

Table 12-5 presents the "Principles for Securing Information Technology Systems," which is part of NIST SP 800-14. You can use this document to make sure the key elements needed for a successful effort are factored into the design of an information security program, and to produce a blueprint for an effective security architecture.

TABLE 12-6

Guide for Developing Security Plans
for Federal Information Systems Partial Table of Contents[9]

2. System Boundary Analysis and Security Controls
    2.1   System Boundaries
    2.2   Major Applications
    2.3   General Support Systems
    2.4   Minor Applications
    2.5   Security Controls
        2.5.1 Scoping Guidance
        2.5.2 Compensating Controls
        2.5.3 Common Security Controls
3. Plan Development
    3.1   System Name and Identifier
    3.2   System Categorization
    3.3   System Owner
    3.4   Authorizing Official
    3.5   Other Designated Contacts
    3.6   Assignment of Security Responsibility
    3.7   System Operational Status
    3.8   Information System Type
    3.9   General Description/Purpose
    3.10 System Environment
    3.11 System Interconnection/Information Sharing
    3.12 Laws, Regulations, and Policies Affecting the System
    3.13 Security Control Selection
    3.14 Minimum Security Controls
    3.15 Completion and Approval Dates
    3.16 Ongoing System Security Plan Maintenance
Appendix A: Sample Information System Security Plan Template

Course Technology/Cengage Learning

NIST Special Publication 800-18 Rev. 1

The Guide for Developing Security Plans for Federal Information Systems can be used as the foundation for a comprehensive security blueprint and framework. This publication provides detailed methods for assessing, designing, and implementing controls and plans for applications of varying size. SP 800-18 Rev. 1 can serve as a useful guide to the activities described in this chapter and as an aid in the planning process. It also includes templates for major application security plans. As with any publication of this scope and magnitude, SP 800-18 Rev.1 must be customized to fit the particular needs of an organization. The table of contents for Publication 800-18 Rev.1 is presented in Table 12-6.

OTHER MODELS

IETF Security Architecture

The Security Area Working Group acts as an advisory board for the protocols and areas developed and promoted by the Internet Society and the Internet Engineering Task Force (IETF), and while the group endorses no specific information security architecture, one of its requests for comment (RFC), RFC 2196: *Site Security Handbook*, provides a good functional discussion of important security issues. RFC 2196: *Site Security Handbook* covers five basic areas of security with detailed discussions on development and implementation. There are also chapters on such important topics as security policies, security technical architecture, security services, and security incident handling. The chapter on architecture begins with a discussion of the importance of security policies, and continues with an examination of services, access controls, and other relevant areas.

The chapter on architecture begins with a discussion of the importance of security policies, and continues with an examination of services, access controls, and other relevant areas.

INCITS/CS1 Small Organization Baseline Information Security Handbook (SOBISH)

The specialized needs of small and medium businesses and organizations have long been ignored by standards bodies that have focused on the enterprise space. In recognition of the importance of protecting the information assets in these smaller organizations, INCITS/CS1 has recently chartered a project to produce a baseline information security handbook targeted specifically at these organizations. Though the project is still in the very early stages, this will be an important project for the future.

BASELINING AND BEST BUSINESS PRACTICES

Baselining and best practices are reliable methods used by some organizations to assess security practices. Baselining and best practices don't provide a complete methodology for the design and implementation of all the practices needed by an organization; however, it is possible to piece together the desired outcome of the security process, and therefore to work backwards toward an effective design. You can also use these approaches to help refine one of the broader ISM approaches to make it fit your needs more precisely. The Federal Agency Security Practices (FASP) site, *http://csrc.nist.gov/groups/SMA/fasp/index.html*, is a popular place to look up best practices. FASP is designed to provide best practices for public agencies, but these practices can be adapted easily to private institutions. The documents found in this site include specific examples of key policies and planning documents, implementation strategies for key technologies, and position descriptions for key security personnel. Of particular value is the section on program management, which includes the following:

- ▶ A summary guide: public law, executive orders, and policy documents
- ▶ Position description for computer system security officer
- ▶ Position description for information security officer
- ▶ Position description for computer specialist
- ▶ Sample of an information technology (IT) security staffing plan for a large service application (LSA)
- ▶ Sample of information technology (IT) security program policy
- ▶ Security handbook and standard operating procedures
- ▶ Telecommuting and mobile computer security policy

Specific Guidance

It is one of the core challenges facing information security that we are faced with both a continually changing threat landscape as well as an evolving technological enterprise. As we've seen in the running case of Sequential, their security problems came to a head when they changed their business model to include a Web component without considering the risks in that technology.

Standards provide good overall guidance but they must be general to avoid providing specific advice that is rendered inapplicable because "we don't do it that way anymore." New technologies will be deployed well in advance of the security guidance that makes them "safe" and will be in use for a substantial time before their specific issues make it into a standard.

Some technology industry groups have recognized this issue and have begun providing security guidance to accompany the new technologies. For example, the Storage Networking Industry Association (SNIA) provides its technical position on "Best Common Practices for Storage Security," available at www .snia.org/forums/ssif/programs/best_practices/ SNIATechnicalProposal-Security-BCPs.080904.pdf. Similarly, the Open Web Application Security Project (OWASP) provides guidance on the deployment of new Web technologies at www.owasp.org.

These technology groups' guidance are critical supplements to the general guidance of standards and recommendations and should be consulted when these newer technologies are deployed in practice.

In the later stages of creating an information security blueprint, these policy documents are particularly useful.

A number of other public and semipublic institutions provide information on best practices—one of the best known groups is the CERT® Coordination Center (formerly known as the Computer Emergency Response Team Coordination Center) at Carnegie Mellon University (www.cert.org). CERT/CC provides detailed and specific assistance on how to implement a sound security methodology.

Professional societies often provide information on best practices for their members. The Technology Manager's Forum (www.techforum.com) has an annual best practice award in a number of areas, including information security. The Information Security Forum (www .isfsecuritystandard.com) has a free publication titled "Standard of Good Practice." This publication outlines information security best practices.

Many organizations hold seminars and classes on best practices for implementing security; in particular, the Information Systems Audit and Control Association (www.isaca.org) hosts regular seminars. The International Association of Professional Security Consultants (www.iapsc .org) has a listing of best practices, as does the Open Grid Forum (www.ogf.org). At a minimum, information security professionals can peruse Web portals for posted security best practices. There are several free portals dedicated to security that have collections of best practices, such as SearchSecurity.com, and NIST's Computer Resources Center. These are but a few of the many public and private organizations that promote solid best security practices. Investing a few hours searching the Web reveals dozens of locations for additional information.

While the reference documents we've mentioned may seem like a mass of conflicting detail taken from wildly differing viewpoints, there are general themes that are common to all the documents that make up the broad skeleton of a successful information security program. Critical to success is the idea of a process (the plan-do-check-act cycle) that is a continuous repetition of planning, implementation, and review. In the constantly evolving threat landscape faced by the modern organization, this is a core requirement to assure that the information security plan as currently implemented provides the best protection possible for the organization's information assets.

The ISO27001/27002 and NIST frameworks provide good *starting points* for producing a comprehensive management plan that avoids overlooking important details. Coupling their guidance with a good continuous improvement process will assure that the information security program functions in a self-tuning manner that matches the protections to the threats within the limits of organizational resources.

This chapter has reviewed the broad outlines of the widely accepted patterns for an information security management program. These patterns are not "to do" lists to be followed blindly but are important source documents that must be customized to fit the specific organization where they will be applied. The standards also provide a useful basis for comparison to assure that the management system you develop covers the common bases. You may choose to ignore a particular section or recommendation but the comparison will help assure that the choice is a reasoned decision, taken after mature deliberation, and not a "I didn't think of that. . . ."

The Information Security Manager's Checklist

This topic has been fully tested, validated, and integrated into organizational operations with formal performance measures in place (as appropriate).					
This topic has been implemented, but not fully tested, validated, and integrated into organizational operations.					
The implementation of this topic has begun, but is not yet complete.					
The formal planning for this topic has begun, but is not yet complete.					
This subject has not formally begun planning, or the organization has made a conscious decision not to pursue this topic.	No	Planned	In Progress	In Place	Integrated
12. Standards for Managing the InfoSec Program					
Relevant standards identified					
Each standard evaluated for "fit" with organization					
Standard selected and best practices adopted					
Standard reviewed for continued value to organization					

For Further Reading

ISO IEC 27002 (17799) Information Security Library by Praxiom Research Group Limited, accessed on-line at http://www.praxiom.com/iso-home.htm

ISO27000 and Information Security: A Combined Glossary by Alan Calder and Steve Watkins, IT Governance Publishing, 2010.

References

1. National Institute of Standards and Technology. *Information Security Management, Code of Practice for Information Security Management.* ISO/IEC 17799. (6 December 2001).

2. Ibid.

3. Ibid.

4. Ibid.

5. T. Humphries. *The Newly Revised Part 2 of BS 7799.* Accessed May 27, 2003. *http://www.gammassl .co.uk/bs7799/The%20Newly%20Revised%20Part%202%20of%20BS%207799ver3a.pdf.*

6. *How 7799 Works.* WWW Document [Cited 27 May 2003] available from *http://www.gammassl. co.uk/bs7799/works.html.*

7. National Institute of Standards and Technology. *Generally Accepted Principles and Practices for Securing Information Technology Systems.* SP 800-14. (September 1996).

8. Ibid.

9. M. Swanson, J. Hash, and P. Bowen. *National Institute of Standards and Technology SP 800-18 Rev. 1. Guide for Developing Security Plans for Federal Information Systems.* Accessed February 2006 from *http://csrc.nist.gov/publications/nistpubs/800-18-Rev1/sp800-18-Rev1-final.pdf.*

\

Chapter **13**

Emerging Trends in Certification and Accreditation

Certification and accreditation (C&A) are concerned with assuring that a piece of software or equipment has the appropriate features and capabilities to meet an organization's needs. For example, the U.S. government has extensive procedures for C&A based on the type of organization and how the items will be used. In the private sector, guidance is much less structured and often left to the discretion of the individual organization. For this reason, the U.S. governmental and international standards are reviewed in order to provide a basis for development of a C&A program for your organization.

Chapter Overview:

▶ Information systems security certification and accreditation

▶ NIST guidance on the certification and accreditation of federal information technology systems

▶ CNSS guidance on certification and accreditation

▶ ISO 27002 guidance on systems certification and accreditation

INFORMATION SYSTEMS SECURITY CERTIFICATION AND ACCREDITATION

At first glance it may seem that only systems handling secret government data require security certification or accreditation. However, organizations are increasingly finding that in order to comply with the myriad of new federal regulation protecting personal privacy, their systems need to have some formal mechanism for verification and validation.

Certification versus Accreditation

In security management, **accreditation** authorizes an IT system to process, store, or transmit information. It is issued by the organization's management and serves as a means of assuring that systems are appropriate for the organization's needs. It also challenges managers and technical staff to find the best methods to assure security, given technical constraints, operational constraints, and mission requirements. In the same vein, **certification** is defined as "the comprehensive evaluation of the technical and nontechnical security controls of an IT system to support the accreditation process that establishes the extent to which a particular design and implementation meets a set of specified security requirements."[1] Organizations pursue accreditation or certification when required by law or to gain a competitive advantage, or provide assurance or confidence for their customers. Federal systems require accreditation under OMB Circular A-130 and the Computer Security Act of 1987. Accreditation demonstrates that management has identified an acceptable risk level and provided resources to control unacceptable risk levels.

Accreditation and certification are not permanent. Just as standards of due diligence and due care require an ongoing maintenance effort, most accreditation and certification processes require reaccreditation or recertification every few years (typically every three to five years).

In the private sector, certification and accreditation is somewhat less clear. Some organizations must meet certain criteria in order to engage in particular types of business activities. For example, if the organization processes credit card payments, it must usually certify under the Payment Card Industry (PCI) Data Security Standard. Outside of those types of requirements, organizations are pretty much left on their own devices to develop their own certification and accreditation processes appropriate to their environment.

The following sections will review the available guidance furnished by several U.S. government documents and the guidance contained in the ISO27002 standard to provide a general overview of the types of processes and decisions that go into performing certification and accreditation.

NIST GUIDANCE ON THE CERTIFICATION AND ACCREDITATION OF FEDERAL INFORMATION TECHNOLOGY SYSTEMS

Two C&A documents provide guidance for the certification and accreditation of federal information systems: SP 800-37: *Guidelines for the Security Certification and Accreditation of Federal Information Technology Systems*, and CNSS Instruction-1000: *National Information Assurance Certification and Accreditation Process (NIACAP)*.

Information processed by the federal government is grouped into one of three categories: National Security Information (NSI), non-NSI, and intelligence community (IC). National security information is processed on national security systems (NSS). NSS systems are managed and operated by the Committee for National Systems Security (CNSS), and non-NSS systems are managed and operated by the National Institute of Standards and Technology (NIST). Intelligence community (IC) information is yet another category and is handled according to guidance from office of the Director of National Intelligence (DNI).

An NSS is defined as any information system (including any telecommunications system) used or operated by an agency or by a contractor of any agency, or other organization on behalf of an agency, the function, operation, or use of which:

1. Involves intelligence activities;
2. Involves cryptologic activities related to national security;
3. Involves command and control of military forces;
4. Involves equipment that is an integral part of a weapon or weapon system;
5. Subject to subparagraph (B), is critical to the direct fulfillment of military or intelligence missions; or is protected at all times by procedures established for information that have been specifically authorized under criteria established by an Executive Order or an Act of Congress to be kept classified in the interest of national defense or foreign policy.

Subparagraph (B) states: Does not include a system that is to be used for routine administration and business applications (including payroll, finance, logistics, and personnel management applications) (Title 44 US Code Section 3542, Federal Information Security Management Act of 2002).

National security information must be processed on NSSs, which have more stringent requirements. NSSs (which process a mix of NS and non-NS information) are accredited using CNSS guidance. Non-NSS systems follow NIST guidance. More than a score of major government agencies store, process, or transmit NSI, and some of them have both NSSs and non-NSSs. You can learn more about the CNSS community and how NSSs are managed and operated at *www.cnss.gov*.[2]

To support the C&A process for these non-NSSs, NIST has developed and promotes a System Certification and Accreditation Project designed to achieve three goals:

▸ Develop standard guidelines and procedures for certifying and accrediting federal IT systems.
▸ Define essential minimum security controls for federal IT systems.
▸ Promote the development of public- and private-sector assessment organizations and the credentialing of individuals capable of providing cost-effective, high-quality security reviews based on standard guidelines and procedures.

The security certification and accreditation (C&A) initiative offers several specific benefits:

▸ More consistent, comparable, and repeatable certifications of IT systems
▸ More complete, reliable information for authorizing officials, leading to better understanding of complex IT systems and their associated risks and vulnerabilities, and, therefore, to more informed decisions by management
▸ Greater availability of competent security evaluation and assessment services
▸ More secure federal government IT systems

Figure 13-1 shows the relationship between the primary publication SP 800-37 and other NIST publications.

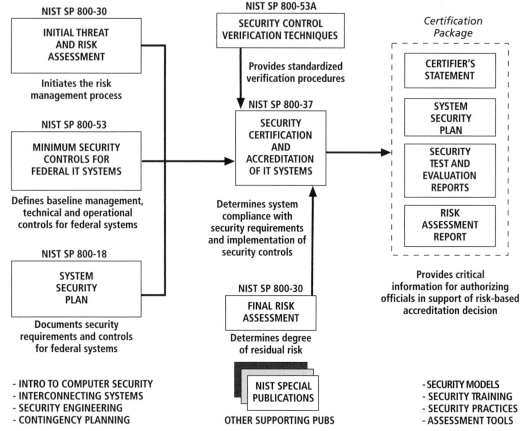

Figure 13-1 Special Publications Supporting SP 800-37
Course Technology/Cengage Learning

NIST SP 800-37 states that "The security certification and accreditation process consists of four distinct phases:

▶ Initiation Phase;
▶ Security Certification Phase;
▶ Security Accreditation Phase; and
▶ Continuous Monitoring Phase."

As illustrated in Figure 13-2, each phase in the security certification and accreditation process consists of a set of well-defined tasks and subtasks that are to be carried out, as indicated, by responsible individuals—the chief information officer, authorizing official, authorizing official's designated representative, senior agency information security officer, information system owner, information owner, information system security officer, certification agent, and user representatives.

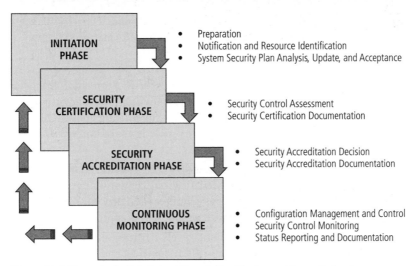

Figure 13-2 Phases in the U.S. Federal Security Certification and Accreditation Process
Course Technology/Cengage Learning

The initiation phase consists of three tasks: (1) preparation; (2) notification and resource identification; and (3) system security plan analysis, update, and acceptance. The purpose of this phase is to ensure that the authorizing official and senior agency information security officer approve the system security plan, including the system's documented security requirements, before the certification agent begins the assessment of the security controls in the information system.

The security certification phase consists of two tasks: (1) security control assessment and (2) security certification documentation. The purpose of this phase is to determine whether the security controls in the information system are implemented correctly, operating as intended, and meeting the security requirements for the system. This phase also addresses specific actions taken or planned to correct deficiencies in the security controls and to reduce or eliminate known vulnerabilities in the information system. Upon successful completion of this phase, the authorizing official will have enough information to determine the risk to agency operations, agency assets, or individuals—and thus will be able to render a security accreditation decision for the information system.

The security accreditation phase consists of two tasks: (1) security accreditation decision and (2) security accreditation documentation. The purpose of this phase is to determine if the remaining known vulnerabilities in the information system (after the implementation of an agreed-upon set of security controls) pose an acceptable level of risk to agency operations, agency assets, or individuals. Upon successful completion of this phase, the information system owner will have: (1) authorization to operate the information system, (2) an interim authorization to operate the information system under specific terms and conditions, or (3) denial of authorization to operate the information system.

The continuous monitoring phase consists of three tasks: (1) configuration management and control, (2) security control monitoring, and (3) status reporting and documentation. The purpose of this phase is to provide oversight and monitoring of the security controls in the information system on an ongoing basis and to inform the authorizing official when changes occur that may have an impact on the security of the system. The activities in this phase are performed continuously throughout the life cycle of the information system.

Systems are classified into one of three security certification levels:

▸ Security Certification Level 1: The entry-level certification appropriate for low-priority (concern) systems. SCL-1 certifications typically employ agency-directed, independent assessments or basic security reviews of IT systems using questionnaires or specialized checklists, intended to demonstrate proper levels of implementation for these low levels of concern.

▸ Security Certification Level 2: The mid-level certification appropriate for moderate-priority (concern) systems. SCL-2 certifications call for independent assessments of IT systems building on the verification techniques and procedures from SCL-1 and adding more substantial techniques and procedures, as appropriate.

▸ Security Certification Level 3: The top-level certification appropriate for high-priority (concern) systems. SCL-3 certifications call for independent assessments of IT systems building on the verification techniques and procedures from SCL-1 and SCL-2 and employing the most rigorous verification techniques, as appropriate.

Completing a security accreditation ensures that an information system will be operated with appropriate management review, that there is ongoing monitoring of security controls, and that reaccreditation occurs periodically in accordance with federal or agency policy and whenever there is a significant change to the system or its operational environment.

CNSS GUIDANCE ON CERTIFICATION AND ACCREDITATION

National Security Interest Systems have their own security certification and accreditation standards, which also follow the guidance of OMB Circular A-130. The Committee on National Systems Security (CNSS) (formerly known as the National Security Telecommunications and Information Systems Security Committee or, NSTISSC) document is titled the NSTISS Instruction 1000: *National Information Assurance Certification and Accreditation Process (NIACAP)*; see *http://www.cnss.gov/Assets/pdf/nstissi_1000.pdf*. The following section contains excerpts from this document, and provides an overview of the purpose and process of this certification and accreditation program:

1. National Security Telecommunications and Information Systems Security Instruction (NSTISSI) No. 1000, *National Information Assurance Certification and Accreditation Process (NIACAP)*, establishes the minimum national standards for certifying and accrediting national security systems. This process provides a standard set of activities, general tasks, and a management structure to certify and accredit systems that will maintain the information assurance (IA) and security posture of a system or site. This process focuses on an enterprise-wide view of the information system (IS) in relation to the organization's mission and the IS business case.

2. The NIACAP is designed to certify that the IS meets documented accreditation requirements and will continue to maintain the accredited security posture throughout the system life cycle.

The key to the NIACAP is the agreement between the IS program manager, Designated Approving Authority (DAA), certification agent (certifier), and user representative. (DAA is also referred to as the accreditor in this document.) These individuals resolve critical schedule, budget, security, functionality, and performance issues.

The NIACAP agreements are documented in the System Security Authorization Agreement (SSAA). The SSAA is used to guide and document the results of the Certification and Accreditation (C&A). The objective is to use the SSAA to establish an evolving yet binding agreement on the level of security required before the system development begins or changes to a system are made. After accreditation, the SSAA becomes the baseline security configuration document.

The minimum NIACAP roles include the program manager, DAA, certifier, and user representative. Additional roles may be added to increase the integrity and objectivity of C&A decisions. For example, the information systems security officer (ISSO) usually performs a key role in the maintenance of the security posture after the accreditation and may also play a key role in the C&A of the system.

The SSAA:

- ▶ Describes the operating environment and threat.
- ▶ Describes the system security architecture.
- ▶ Establishes the C&A boundary of the system to be accredited.
- ▶ Documents the formal agreement among the DAA(s), certifier, program manager, and user representative.
- ▶ Documents all requirements necessary for accreditation.
- ▶ Minimizes documentation requirements by consolidating applicable information into the SSAA (security policy, concept of operations, architecture description, test procedures, etc.).
- ▶ Documents the NIACAP plan.
- ▶ Documents test plans and procedures, certification results, and residual risk.
- ▶ Forms the baseline security configuration document.

The NIACAP is composed of four phases shown in Figure 13-3: These phases are definition, verification, validation, and post accreditation.

Phase 1, definition, determines the necessary security measures and effort level to achieve certification and accreditation. The objective of Phase 1 is to agree on the security requirements, C&A boundary, schedule, level of effort, and resources required.

Phase 2, verification, verifies the evolving or modified system's compliance with the information in the SSAA. The objective of Phase 2 is to ensure the fully integrated system is ready for certification testing.

Phase 3, validation, validates compliance of the fully integrated system with the security policy and requirements stated in the SSAA. The objective of Phase 3 is to produce the required evidence to support the DAA in making an informed decision to grant approval to operate the system [accreditation or Interim Approval to Operate (IATO)].

Phase 4, post accreditation, starts after the system has been certified and accredited for operations. Phase 4 includes those activities necessary for the continuing operation of the accredited

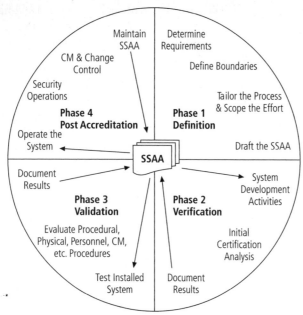

Figure 13-3 Overview of the NIACAP Process
Course Technology/Cengage Learning

IS and manages the changing threats and small-scale changes a system faces through its life cycle. The objective of Phase 4 is to ensure secure system management, operation, and maintenance to sustain an acceptable level of residual risk.

The accreditation process itself is so complex that professional certifiers must be trained. The CNSS has a set of training standards for federal information technology workers who deal with information security. One of these documents, NSTISSI 4015, provides a National Training Standard for Systems Certifiers (see *www.cnss.gov/Assets/pdf/nstissi_4015.pdf*).

A qualified system certifier must be formally trained in the fundamentals of INFOSEC, and have field experience. It is recommended that system certifiers have system administrator and/or basic information system security officer (ISSO) experience, and be familiar with the knowledge, skills, and abilities (KSAs) required of the DAA (see *www.cnss.gov/Assets/pdf/nstissi_4015.pdf*). Once these professionals complete training based on NSTISSI-4015, which includes material from NSTISSI-1000, they are eligible to be a federal agency systems certifier. Note: NSTISSI-1000 is currently under revision, and a revised version could be available within the next few years.

ISO 27002 GUIDANCE ON SYSTEMS CERTIFICATION AND ACCREDITATION

Entities outside the United States apply the standards provided under the International Standards Organization standard ISO 17799 and 27001, discussed in Chapter 5. Recall that the standards were originally created to provide a foundation for British certification of Information Security Management Systems (ISMS). It should be noted that while ISO27001 spells out the requirements, ISO27002 spells out the actual evaluation requirements. Organizations wishing to demonstrate their systems have met this international standard and followed the certification process, which includes the following phases:

The first phase of the process involves your company preparing and getting ready for the certification of your ISMS: developing and implementing your ISMS, using and integrating your ISMS into your day to day business processes, training your staff, and establishing an ongoing program of ISMS maintenance.

The second phase involves employing one of the accredited certification bodies to carry out an audit of your ISMS.

The certificate that is awarded will last for three years after which the ISMS needs to be re-certified. Therefore, there is a third phase of the process (assuming the certification has been successful and a certificate has been issued), which involves the certification body visiting your ISMS site on a regular basis (e.g., every 6–9 months) to carry out a surveillance audit.[3]

Figure 13-4 shows the process flow of ISMS certification and accreditation in Japan.

Certification and accreditation is basically a process for assuring that a particular piece of equipment or software provides the appropriate capabilities to be successfully used within an organization. For governmental agencies, there are specific requirements that must be met in making this decision but except for a few industries, in the private sector guidance is much more limited. As the review of the government documents showed, the basic process is developing a clear understanding of the requirements, specifying criteria and process for deciding how well the requirements are met and a process to assure regular review and evaluation. Organizations should develop a C&A process to assure that the technologies they deploy provide appropriate security features and will work within the context of the organization. Though the C&A process may be much less formal than that of a governmental body, the process itself must both exist and be followed.

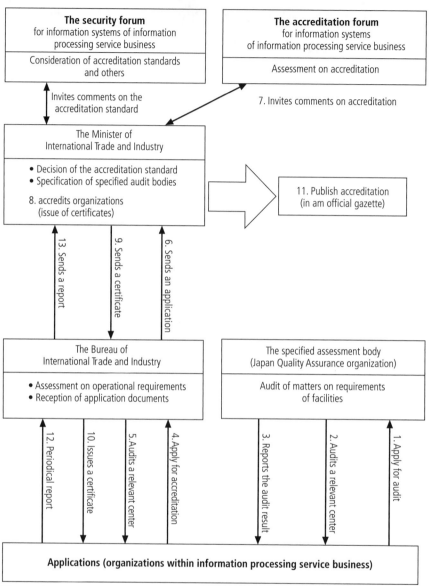

Figure 13-4 Japanese ISMS Certification and Accreditation
Course Technology/Cengage Learning

The Information Security Manager's Checklist

	This topic has been fully tested, validated, and integrated into organizational operations with formal performance measures in place (as appropriate).						Integrated
	This topic has been implemented, but not fully tested, validated, and integrated into organizational operations.					In Place	
	The implementation of this topic has begun, but is not yet complete.				In Progress		
	The formal planning for this topic has begun, but is not yet complete.			Planned			
	This subject has not formally begun planning, or the organization has made a conscious decision not to pursue this topic.		No				
13. C&A		No	Planned	In Progress	In Place	Integrated	
C & A requirements determined							
C & A preferences identified							
C & A criteria identified							
System compared to specified criteria							
Criteria gaps identified							
Criteria gaps resolved							

For Further Reading

Building and Implementing a Security Certification and Accreditation Program: OFFICIAL (ISC)² GUIDE to the CAPcm CBK by Patrick D. Howard, (ISC)² Press, 2005.

IT Governance: A Manager's Guide to Data Security and ISO 27001 / ISO 27002 by Alan Calder and Steve Watkins, 2008.

References

1. National Institute of Standards and Technology. *Background.* Accessed 27 May 2003 from *csrc.nist .gov/sec-cert/ca-background.html.*

2. Conversations with an expert from the NIACAP program, 24 April 2007.

3. ISMS Certification Process. ISMS International User Group Ltd. Accessed 22 April 2007 from *www .iso27001certificates.com/certification_directory.htm.*

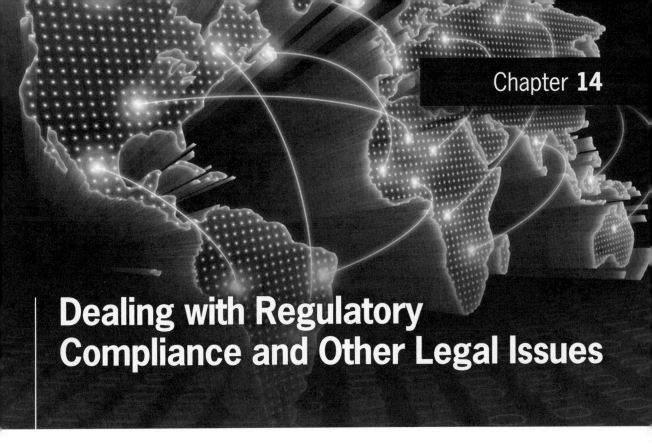

Dealing with Regulatory Compliance and Other Legal Issues

Unfortunately many enterprises have shown themselves to be poor stewards of the information they collect and store. The daily newspapers, trade press, and blogosphere are littered with tales of yet another data breach where personally identifiable information (PII) on thousands or millions of people have been lost or otherwise disclosed. In fact, so much information is available on the PII black market that prices are reported to have dropped tenfold over the past decade.[1] With the public frustration over loss of their information and financial losses due to fraud, laws and regulations have been developed to deal with the situation. In a somewhat related area, accounting scandals have resulted in more regulation over financial records.

The net result has been an increasing complex regulatory environment dealing with information. The security professional sits at the nexus of the regulatory environment as one of their core tasks is control over the organization's information assets. This chapter focuses on the major regulatory issues that affect the management of information in an organization today.

Chapter Overview:

▶ Law and ethics in information security
▶ Major regulatory issues today

LAW AND ETHICS IN INFORMATION SECURITY

In general, people elect to trade some aspects of personal freedom for social order. As Jean-Jacques Rousseau explains in *The Social Contract or Principles of Political Right*[2] (1762), the rules the members of a society create to balance the right of the individual to self-determination with the needs of the society as a whole are called *laws*. **Laws** are rules that mandate or prohibit certain behavior in society; they are drawn from **ethics**, which define socially acceptable behaviors. The key difference between laws and ethics is that laws carry the sanctions of a governing authority and ethics do not. Ethics in turn are based on **cultural mores**: the fixed moral attitudes or customs of a particular group. Some ethics are recognized as universal. For example, murder, theft, assault, and arson are commonly accepted as actions that deviate from ethical and legal codes in the civilized world. However, it must be recognized that ethics and law are distinct and that, in fact, ethics is a stronger concept than law because many activities that may be considered legal are considered unethical. This tension between "what is legal" and "what is ethical" can present significant challenges in the practice of information security.

Ethics is a core requirement for information security professionals because of their privileged position within the organization. Being responsible for the protection of the organization's information assets, they have wide-ranging access to that information and with that special level of access comes a potential for severe abuse. Adherence to a sound code of professional ethics is a critical control on the behavior of the information security professional.

Organizational Liability and the Need for Counsel

What if an organization does not demand or even encourage strong ethical behavior from its employees? What if an organization does not behave ethically? Even if there is no breach of criminal law, there can still be liability. **Liability** is the legal obligation of an entity that extends beyond criminal or contract law; it includes the legal obligation to make **restitution**, or to compensate, for wrongs committed by an organization or its employees. The bottom line is that if an employee, acting with or without the authorization of the organization, performs an illegal or unethical act that causes some degree of harm, the organization can be held financially liable for that action. An organization increases its liability if it refuses to take measures known as due care. **Due care** has been taken when an organization makes sure that every employee knows what is acceptable or unacceptable behavior, and knows the consequences of illegal or unethical actions. **Due diligence** requires that an organization make a valid effort to protect others and continually maintain this level of effort. Given the Internet's global reach, those who could be injured or wronged by an organization's members could be anywhere, in any state, any country around the world. Under the U.S. legal system, any court can impose its authority over an individual or organization if it can establish **jurisdiction**—that is, the court's right to hear a case if the wrong was committed in its territory or involving its citizenry. This is sometimes referred to as **long arm jurisdiction**—the long arm of the law reaching across the country or around the world to pull an accused individual into its court systems. Trying a case in the injured party's home area is usually favorable to the injured party.[3]

Policy versus Law

Within an organization, information security professionals help maintain security via the establishment and enforcement of policies. These **policies**—a body of expectations that describe acceptable and unacceptable employee behaviors in the workplace—function as organizational laws, complete with penalties, judicial practices, and sanctions to require compliance. Because these policies function as laws, they must be crafted with the same care, to ensure that they are complete, appropriate, and fairly applied to everyone in the workplace. The difference between a policy and a law, however, is that ignorance of a policy is an acceptable defense. Thus, for a policy to become enforceable, it must meet five criteria:

- ▶ Dissemination (distribution)—The organization must be able to demonstrate that the relevant policy has been made readily available for review by the employee. Common dissemination techniques include hard-copy and electronic distribution.

- ▶ Review (reading)—The organization must be able to demonstrate that it disseminated the document in an intelligible form, including versions for illiterate, non-English reading, and reading-impaired employees. Common techniques include recordings of the policy in English and alternate languages.

- ▶ Comprehension (understanding)—The organization must be able to demonstrate that the employee understood the requirements and content of the policy. Common techniques include quizzes and other assessments.

- ▶ Compliance (agreement)—The organization must be able to demonstrate that the employee agrees to comply with the policy, through act or affirmation. Common techniques include log-on banners, which require a specific action (mouse click or keystroke) to acknowledge agreement, or a signed document clearly indicating the employee has read, understood, and agreed to comply with the policy.

- ▶ Uniform enforcement—The organization must be able to demonstrate that the policy has been uniformly enforced, regardless of employee status or assignment.

Only when all of these conditions are met can an organization penalize employees who violate the policy, without fear of legal retribution.

Types of Law

Civil law represents a wide variety of laws that govern a nation or state and deal with the relationships and conflicts between organizational entities and people. **Criminal law** addresses violations harmful to society and is actively enforced by the state. The categories of laws that affect the individual in the workplace are private law and public law. **Private law** regulates the relationship between the individual and the organization, and encompasses family law, commercial law, and labor law. **Public law** regulates the structure and administration of government agencies and their relationships with citizens, employees, and other governments. Examples of public law include criminal, administrative, and constitutional law.

MAJOR REGULATORY ISSUES TODAY

As a fundamental part of the InfoSec process, a careful examination of current legislation, regulation, and common ethical expectations of both national and international entities provides key insights into the regulatory constraints that govern business. The chapter focuses on the dominant subjects facing most IT and InfoSec managers: Privacy and HIPAA, SOX, GLB, and PCI.

Privacy and HIPAA

The issue of privacy has become one of the hottest topics in information security at the beginning of the twenty-first century. Many organizations are collecting, swapping, and selling personal information as a commodity, and many people are looking to governments for protection of their privacy. The ability to collect information, combine facts from separate sources, and merge it all with other information has resulted in databases of information that were previously impossible to set up. One technology that could be used by others to monitor or track private communications is the Clipper Chip. The Clipper Chip uses an algorithm with a two-part key that was to be managed by two separate government agencies, and it was reportedly designed to protect individual communications while allowing the government to decrypt suspect transmissions.[4] This technology was the focus of discussion between advocates for personal privacy and those seeking to enable more effective law enforcement. Consequently, this technology was never implemented by the U.S. government.

In response to the pressure for privacy protection, the number of statutes addressing an individual's right to privacy has grown. It must be understood, however, that **privacy** in this context is not absolute freedom from observation, but rather is a more precise "state of being free from unsanctioned intrusion."[5] To help you better understand this rapidly evolving issue, some of the more relevant privacy laws are presented here.

Privacy of Customer Information
Some regulations in the U.S. legal code stipulate the responsibilities of common carriers (organizations that process or move data for hire) to protect the confidentiality of customer information, including that of other carriers. The **Privacy of Customer Information Section** of the common carrier regulation states that any proprietary information shall be used explicitly for providing services, and not for any marketing purposes, and that carriers cannot disclose this information except when necessary to provide their services. The only other exception is when a customer requests the disclosure of information, and then the disclosure is restricted to that customer's information only. This law does allow for the use of aggregate information, as long as the same information is provided to all

common carriers and all carriers possessing the information engage in fair competitive business practices. **Aggregate information** is created by combining pieces of nonprivate data—often collected during software updates, and via cookies—that when combined may violate privacy.

While common carrier regulation regulates public carriers in order to protect individual privacy, **The Federal Privacy Act of 1974** regulates government agencies and holds them accountable if they release private information about individuals or businesses without permission. The following agencies, regulated businesses, and individuals are exempt from some of the regulations so that they can perform their duties:

- ▶ Bureau of the Census
- ▶ National Archives and Records Administration
- ▶ Congress
- ▶ Comptroller General
- ▶ Federal courts with regard to specific issues using appropriate court orders
- ▶ Credit reporting agencies
- ▶ Individuals or organizations that demonstrate that information is necessary to protect the health or safety of that individual

The **Electronic Communications Privacy Act of 1986** is a collection of statutes that regulate the interception of wire, electronic, and oral communications. These statutes work in conjunction with the **Fourth Amendment of the U.S. Constitution**, which protects individuals from unlawful search and seizure.

The **Health Insurance Portability and Accountability Act of 1996 (HIPAA)**, also known as the **Kennedy-Kassebaum Act**, protects the confidentiality and security of health care data by establishing and enforcing standards and by standardizing electronic data interchange. HIPAA affects all health care organizations, including doctors' practices, health clinics, life insurers, and universities, as well as some organizations that have self-insured employee health programs. HIPAA specifies stiff penalties for organizations that fail to comply with the law, with fines up to $250,000 and/or 10 years imprisonment for knowingly misusing client information. Organizations were required to comply with the act by April 14, 2003.[6]

How does HIPAA affect the field of information security? Beyond the basic privacy guidelines, the act requires organizations that retain health care information to use information security mechanisms to protect this information, as well as policies and procedures to maintain this security. It also requires a comprehensive assessment of the organization's information security systems, policies, and procedures. Electronic signatures have become more common, and HIPAA provides guidelines for the use of these signatures based on security standards that ensure message integrity, user authentication, and nonrepudiation. There is no specification of particular security technologies for each of the security requirements, only that security must be implemented to ensure the privacy of the health care information.

The privacy standards of HIPAA severely restrict the dissemination and distribution of private health information without documented consent. The standards provide patients with the right to know who has access to their information and who has accessed it. The standards also restrict the use of health information to the minimum necessary for the health care services required.

HIPAA has five fundamental principles:

1. Consumer control of medical information
2. Boundaries on the use of medical information
3. Accountability for the privacy of private information
4. Balance of public responsibility for the use of medical information for the greater good measured against impact to the individual
5. Security of health information

Identity Theft Related to the legislation on privacy is the increasing body of law on identity theft. The Federal Trade Commission defines identity theft as "occurring when someone uses your personally identifying information, like your name, Social Security number, or credit card number, without your permission, to commit fraud or other crimes."[7] The FTC estimates that perhaps as many as 9 million Americans are faced with identity theft each year. Many people, among them perhaps someone you know or even you, have been affected by some form of identity theft.[8] Organizations can also be victims of identity theft, as described in the sections in Chapter 2 on URL Manipulation and DNS redirection. This type of crime has caught the attention of the president of the United States: In May of 2006, President Bush signed an Executive Order creating the Identity Theft Task Force. The goals of this group are to create a strategic plan to improve efforts of the government and private organizations and individuals in combating identity theft. The group is seeking better coordination among groups, more effective prosecution of criminals engaged in these activities, and methods to increase restitution made to victims.[9]

While numerous states have passed identity theft laws, at the federal level the primary legislation is the **Fraud and Related Activity in Connection with Identification Documents, Authentication Features, and Information** (Title 18, U.S.C. § 1028), which criminalizes creation, reproduction, transfer, possession, or use of unauthorized or false identification documents or document-making equipment. The penalties for such offenses range from one to twenty-five years in prison and fines as determined by the courts.

The Federal Trade Commission recommends four steps people can take when they suspect a theft of identity has occurred:

1. Report to the three dominant consumer reporting companies that your identity is threatened so that they may place a fraud alert on your record. This informs current and potential creditors to follow certain procedures before taking credit-related actions.
2. If you know which accounts have been compromised, close them. If new accounts are opened using your identity without your permission, the U.S. FTC has provided a document template online that may be used to dispute these new accounts. The ID Theft Affidavit can be downloaded as a 56 KB PDF file from *http://www.consumer .gov/idtheft/pdf/affidavit.pdf.*
3. Register your concern with the U.S. FTC. You may use the FTC-provided complaint form at *https://rn.ftc.gov/pls/dod/widtpubl$.startup?Z_ORG_CODE=PU03.*
4. Report the incident to either your local police or police in the location where the identity theft occurred. Use your copy of the FTC ID Theft complaint form to make the report. Once your police report has been filed, be sure to get a copy of it or else acquire the police report number.[10]

Financial Reporting and SOX

In the wake of the Enron and WorldCom (among others) financial scandals and the damage done to financial markets from criminal violations of the federal securities laws, the U.S. Congress enacted a law designed to enforce accountability for the financial recordkeeping and reporting at publicly traded corporations. While this law on its face would not seem to affect information security or even general IT functions, in fact its effects are being felt throughout the organizations to which it applies.

The law requires that the CEO and chief financial officer (CFO) assume direct and personal accountability for the completeness and accuracy of a publicly traded organization's financial reporting and recordkeeping systems. As these executives attempt to ensure that the reporting and recording systems are sound—often relying upon the expertise of CIOs and CISOs to do so—they also must maintain the availability and confidentiality of information. The provisions include:

- ▶ Creation of the Public Company Accounting Oversight Board (PCAOB)
- ▶ A requirement that public companies evaluate and disclose the effectiveness of their internal controls as they relate to financial reporting, and that independent auditors for such companies "attest" (i.e., agree, or qualify) to such disclosure
- ▶ Certification of financial reports by chief executive officers and chief financial officers
- ▶ Auditor independence, including outright bans on certain types of work for audit clients and precertification by the company's audit committee of all other nonaudit work
- ▶ A requirement that companies listed on stock exchanges have fully independent audit committees that oversee the relationship between the company and its auditor
- ▶ Ban on most personal loans to any executive officer or director
- ▶ Accelerated reporting of trades by insiders
- ▶ Prohibition on insider trades during pension fund blackout periods
- ▶ Additional disclosure
- ▶ Enhanced criminal and civil penalties for violations of securities law
- ▶ Significantly longer maximum jail sentences and larger fines for corporate executives who knowingly and willfully misstate financial statements, although maximum sentences are largely irrelevant because judges generally follow the federal sentencing guidelines in setting actual sentences
- ▶ Employee protections allowing those corporate fraud whistle-blowers who file complaints with OSHA within ninety days, to win reinstatement, back pay and benefits, compensatory damages, abatement orders, and reasonable attorney fees and costs

These systems "need to be assessed, along with other important processes for compliance with Sarbanes-Oxley Act. So, although the act signals a fundamental change in business operations and financial reporting, and places responsibility in corporate financial reporting on the CEO and CFO, the CIO plays a significant role in the sign-off of financial statements."[11]

PCI and GLB

Financial services regulation are perhaps some of the oldest and best understood regulations present in the information processing area. In 1999, the Financial Services Modernization Act updated several outdated regulations, specifically focusing on customer privacy. The Payment Card Industry has a long history of leading the way in developing information protection standards, dating back decades. Today, PCI compliance is required of all organizations that process credit card information. This section will examine the regulation and expectations of both regulations.

GLB Regulations

The **Financial Services Modernization Act** or **Gramm-Leach-Bliley Act of 1999** contains a number of provisions focusing on facilitating affiliation among banks, securities firms, and insurance companies. Specifically, this act requires all financial institutions to disclose their privacy policies on the sharing of nonpublic personal information. It also requires due notice to customers, so that they can request that their information not be shared with third parties. In addition, the act ensures that the privacy policies in effect in an organization are both fully disclosed when a customer initiates a business relationship, and distributed at least annually for the duration of the professional association.

PCI and the PCI Data Security Standard

Organizations that rely on credit card processing are most likely already familiar with the PCI Data Security Standard (DSS). The standard, available from the PCI Security Standards Council (*www.pcisecuritystandards.org*) is described here:

> *The PCI DSS, a set of comprehensive requirements for enhancing payment account data security, was developed by the founding payment brands of the PCI Security Standards Council, including American Express, Discover Financial Services, JCB International, MasterCard Worldwide and Visa Inc. International, to help facilitate the broad adoption of consistent data security measures on a global basis.*

> *The PCI DSS is a multifaceted security standard that includes requirements for security management, policies, procedures, network architecture, software design and other critical protective measures. This comprehensive standard is intended to help organizations proactively protect customer account data. [. . .]*

> *The core of the PCI DSS is a group of principles and accompanying requirements, around which the specific elements of the DSS are organized:*

> **Build and Maintain a Secure Network:**

> *Requirement 1: Install and maintain a firewall configuration to protect cardholder data*

> *Requirement 2: Do not use vendor-supplied defaults for system passwords and other security parameters*

> **Protect Cardholder Data**

> *Requirement 3: Protect stored cardholder data*

> *Requirement 4: Encrypt transmission of cardholder data across open, public networks*

> **Maintain a Vulnerability Management Program**

> *Requirement 5: Use and regularly update anti-virus software*

> *Requirement 6: Develop and maintain secure systems and applications*

> **Implement Strong Access Control Measures**

> *Requirement 7: Restrict access to cardholder data by business need-to-know*

Requirement 8: Assign a unique ID to each person with computer access

Requirement 9: Restrict physical access to cardholder data

Regularly Monitor and Test Networks

Requirement 10: Track and monitor all access to network resources and cardholder data

Requirement 11: Regularly test security systems and processes

Maintain an Information Security Policy

Requirement 12: Maintain a policy that addresses information security

(Source: www.pcisecuritystandards.org/security_standards/pci_dss.shtml)

In support of the standard, there is also a certification and accreditation method, including directions on becoming quality security assessors (QSAs) and approved scanning vendors (ASVs).

The specification itself can be downloaded from the PCI Security Standards Council Web site. Even organizations that do not use credit card processing can use these standards as best practices to improve their overall security posture.

This chapter has provided an overview of the legal and ethical issues facing the protection of information. In today's current regulatory environment, it is important that the issues discussed in this chapter be fully understood and addressed in information security planning and management.

The Information Security Manager's Checklist

		This topic has been fully tested, validated, and integrated into organizational operations with formal performance measures in place (as appropriate).				
	This topic has been implemented, but not fully tested, validated, and integrated into organizational operations.					
	The implementation of this topic has begun, but is not yet complete.					
	The formal planning for this topic has begun, but is not yet complete.					
This subject has not formally begun planning, or the organization has made a conscious decision not to pursue this topic.						
14. Regulatory Issues and Laws	No	Planned	In Progress	In Place	Integrated
Organization aware of applicable federal regulations					
Organization aware of applicable industry regulations					
Employees familiarized with dominant relevant, federal, technology-related laws					
Organization monitors and ensures compliance with privacy requirements					

For Further Reading

Readings & Cases in Information Security: Law & Ethics by Michael E. Whitman; Herbert J. Mattord, Cengage/Course Technology, 2010.

Business Ethics: A Stakeholder and Issues Management Approach, by Joseph W. Weiss, South-Western College Publishing, 2009.

References

1. Taylor Buley, *Hackonomics*. *http://www.forbes.com/security/2008/10/25/credit-card-theft-tech-security-cz_tb1024theft.html*. Accessed 2 November 2008.

2. John B. Noone. *Rousseau's Social Contract: A Conceptual Analysis*. Athens: University of Georgia Press, 1981.

3. Robert J. Alberts, Anthony M. Townsend, and Michael E. Whitman. "The Threat of Long-arm Jurisdiction to Electronic Commerce." *Communications of the ACM* 41, no. 12 (December 1998): 15–20.

4. EPIC. *The Clipper Chip*. Accessed 6 March 2004 from *www.epic.org/crypto/clipper/*.

5. American Heritage Dictionary. "privacy." *The American Heritage Dictionary of the English Language Online*. Accessed 22 February 2007 from *www.bartleby.com/61/87/P0568700.html*.

6. HIPA Advisory. "HIPAA primer." *HIPAAdvisory Online*. Accessed 31 January 2007 from *www .hipaadvisory.com/REGS/HIPAAprimer.htm*.

7. FTC. *About Identity Theft*. Accessed 22 February 2007 from *www.ftc.gov/bcp/edu/microsites/idtheft/ consumers/about-identity-theft.html*.

8. Ibid.

9. FTC. *The President's Identity Theft Task Force*. Accessed 22 February 2007 from *www.ftc.gov/bcp/ edu/microsites/idtheft/taskforce.htm*.

10. FTC. "If You Think Your Identity has Been Stolen, Here's What To Do." Accessed 22 February 2007 from *www.ftc.gov/bcp/edu/microsites/idtheft/*.

11. Wikipedia: The Free Encyclopedia. Information Technology and SOX. Accessed 28 August 2006 from *en.wikipedia.org/wiki/Sarbanes-Oxley_Act#Information_technology_and_SOX_404*.

Chapter **15**

Key Laws for Every IT Security Manager

This chapter focuses on the legislation and regulations that affect the management of information in an organization. Use this chapter both as a reference to the legal aspects of information security and as an aide in the continued planning of your information security career. As a future information security professional, it is important to understand the scope of an organization's legal and ethical responsibilities. You will play an important role in an organization's approach to controlling liability for privacy and security risks. To minimize liability and reduce risks from electronic and physical threats, and to reduce all losses from legal action, you must thoroughly understand the current legal environment, stay current with laws and regulations, and watch for new issues as they emerge. By educating the management and employees of your organization on their legal and ethical obligations and the proper use of information technology and information security, you in your role as security information manager can help keep an organization focused on its primary objectives.

Chapter Overview:

▶ Relevant U.S. laws

▶ International laws and legal bodies

RELEVANT U.S. LAWS

Historically, the United States has been a leader in the development and implementation of information security legislation to prevent misuse and exploitation of information and information technology. The implementation of information security legislation contributes to a more reliable business environment, which, in turn, enables a stable economy. In its global leadership capacity, the United States has demonstrated a clear understanding of the problems facing the information security field and has specified penalties for individuals and organizations that fail to follow the requirements set forth in the U.S. civil statutes. The sections that follow present the most important U.S. laws that apply to information security.

General Computer Crime Laws

There are several key laws relevant to the field of information security and of particular interest to those who live and/or work in the United States.

This discussion of information security–related laws is supplemented in Table 15-1.

TABLE 15-1 Key U.S. Laws of Interest to Information Security Professionals

ACT	SUBJECT	DATE	WEB RESOURCE LOCATION	DESCRIPTION
Communications Act of 1934, updated by Telecommunications Deregulation and Competition Act of 1996	Tele-communications	1934 (amended 1996 and 2001)	www.fcc.gov/ Reports/1934new.pdf	Regulates inter-state and foreign telecommunications
Computer Fraud and Abuse Act [also known as Fraud and Related Activity in Connection with Computers (18 U.S.C. 1030)]	Threats to computers	1986 (amended 1994, 1996, and 2001)	www.usdoj.gov/criminal/ cybercrime/1030_new.html	Defines and formalizes laws to counter threats from computer-related acts and offenses
Computer Security Act of 1987	Federal Agency Information Security	1987	www.cio.gov/Documents/ computer_security_act_ Jan_1998.html	Requires all federal computer systems that contain classified information to have surety plans in place, and requires periodic security training for all individuals who operate, design, or manage such systems
Economic Espionage Act of 1996	Trade secrets	1996	http://www.usdoj.gov/ criminal/cybercrime/eea.html	Designed to prevent abuse of information gained by an individual working in one company and employed by another

ACT	SUBJECT	DATE	WEB RESOURCE LOCATION	DESCRIPTION
Federal Privacy Act of 1974	Privacy	1974	www.usdoj.gov/oip/privstat.htm	Governs federal agency use of personal information
Gramm-Leach-Bliley Act of 1999 (GLB) or Financial Services Modernization Act	Banking	1999	http://banking.senate.gov/conf/	Focuses on facilitating affiliation among banks, insurance, and securities firms; it has significant impact on the privacy of personal information used by these industries
Health Insurance Portability and Accountability Act (HIPAA)	Health care privacy	1996	www.hhs.gov/ocr/hipaa/	Regulates collection, storage, and transmission of sensitive personal health care information
Sarbanes-Oxley Act of 2002	Financial Reporting	2002	http://fl1.findlaw.com/news.findlaw.com/hdocs/docs/gwbush/sarbanesoxley072302.pdf	Affects how public organizations and accounting firms deal with corporate governance, financial disclosure, and the practice of public accounting
Security and Freedom Through Encryption Act of 1999	Use and sale of software that uses or enables encryption	1999	http://thomas.loc.gov/cgi-bin/query/z?c106:H.R.850.IH	Clarifies use of encryption for people in the United States and permits all persons in the United States to buy or sell any encryption product and states that the government cannot require the use of any kind of key escrow system for encryption products
U.S.A. Patriot Act of 2001 (H.R. 3162)	Terrorism	2001	http://www.legal-database.com/patriot-act.htm	Defines stiffer penalties for prosecution of terrorist crimes

Course Technology/Cengage Learning

The **Computer Fraud and Abuse Act of 1986 (CFA Act)** is the cornerstone of many computer-related federal laws and enforcement efforts. It was amended in October 1996 by the **National Information Infrastructure Protection Act of 1996**, which modified several sections of the previous act and increased the penalties for selected crimes. The punishment for offenses prosecuted under this statute varies from fines to imprisonment up to twenty years, or both.

The severity of the penalty depends on the value of the information obtained and whether the offense is judged to have been committed:

1. For purposes of commercial advantage
2. For private financial gain
3. In furtherance of a criminal act

The previous law was further changed when the **U.S.A. PATRIOT Act of 2001** modified a wide range of existing laws to provide law enforcement agencies with broader latitude in order to combat terrorism-related activities. The laws modified by the Patriot Act include some of the earliest laws created to deal with electronic technology. In 2006, this act was amended further with the **USA PATRIOT Improvement and Reauthorization Act**, which made permanent fourteen of the sixteen expanded powers of the Department of Homeland Security, and the FBI in investigating terrorist activity. The act also reset the date of expiration written into the law as a so-called *sunset clause* for certain wiretaps under the Foreign Intelligence Surveillance Act of 1978 (FISA), and revised many of the criminal penalties and procedures associated with criminal and terrorist activities.[1]

Another key law is the **Computer Security Act of 1987**. It was one of the first attempts to protect federal computer systems by establishing minimum acceptable security practices. The National Bureau of Standards, in cooperation with the National Security Agency, became responsible for developing these security standards and guidelines.

Export and Espionage Laws

The need for national security, and to protect trade secrets and a variety of other state and private assets, has led to several laws restricting what information and information management and security resources may be exported from the United States. These laws attempt to stem the theft of information by establishing strong penalties for these crimes.

In an attempt to protect American ingenuity, intellectual property, and competitive advantage, the U.S. Congress passed the **Economic Espionage Act (EEA)** in 1996. This law attempts to prevent trade secrets from being illegally shared.

The **Security and Freedom through Encryption Act of 1999** provides guidance on the use of encryption, and provides measures of protection from government intervention. The acts include provisions that:

▶ Reinforce an individual's right to use or sell encryption algorithms, without concern for regulations requiring some form of key registration. Key registration is the storage of a cryptographic key (or its text equivalent) with another party to be used to break the encryption of data. This is often called "key escrow."

▶ Prohibit the federal government from requiring the use of encryption for contracts, grants, and other official documents, and correspondence.

▶ State that the use of encryption is not probable cause to suspect criminal activity.

▶ Relax export restrictions by amending the Export Administration Act of 1979.

▶ Provide additional penalties for the use of encryption in the commission of a criminal act.

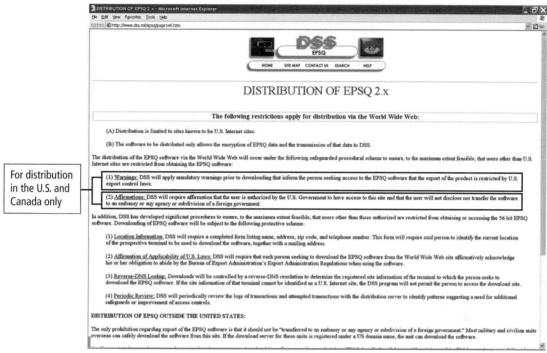

Figure 15-1 Export and Espionage
Course Technology/Cengage Learning

As illustrated in Figure 15-1, the distribution of many software packages is restricted to approved organizations, governments, and countries.

U.S. Copyright Law

Intellectual property is recognized as a protected asset in the United States. The U.S. copyright laws extend this privilege to the published word, including electronic formats. Fair use of copyrighted materials includes their use to support news reporting, teaching, scholarship, and a number of other related activities, so long as the use is for educational or library purposes, not for profit, and is not excessive. As long as proper acknowledgment is provided to the original author of such works, including a proper description of the location of source materials (citation), and the work is not represented as one's own, it is entirely permissible to include portions of someone else's work as reference. For more detailed information on copyright regulations, visit the U.S. Copyright Office Web site at *http://www.copyright.gov*.

Freedom of Information Act of 1966 (FOIA)

The **Freedom of Information Act** allows any person to request access to federal agency records or information not determined to be a matter of national security. Agencies of the federal government are required to disclose any requested information on receipt of a written request. This requirement is enforceable in court. Some information is, however, protected from disclosure, and the act does not apply to state or local government agencies or to private businesses or individuals, although many states have their own version of the FOIA.

State and Local Regulations

In addition to the national and international restrictions placed on organizational use of computer technology, each state or locality may have a number of its own applicable laws and regulations. Information security professionals must, therefore, understand state laws and regulations and ensure that the organization's security policies and procedures comply with those laws and regulations.

For example, in 1991 the state of Georgia passed the **Georgia Computer Systems Protection Act**, which seeks to protect information, and which establishes penalties for the use of information technology to attack or exploit information systems.

INTERNATIONAL LAWS AND LEGAL BODIES

It is important for IT professionals and information security practitioners to realize that when their organizations do business on the Internet, they do business globally. As a result, you must be sensitive to the laws and ethical values of many different cultures, societies, and countries. While it may be impossible to please all of the people all of the time, dealing with the laws of other states and nations is one area where it is certainly *not* easier to ask for forgiveness than for permission.

A number of different security bodies and laws are described in this section. Because of the political complexities of the relationships among nations, and the differences in culture, there are currently few international laws relating to privacy and information security. The laws discussed below are important, but are limited in their enforceability. The American Society of International Law is an example of a typical American institution that deals in international law (see *http://www.asil.org*).

European Council Cyber-Crime Convention

The Council of Europe adopted the **European Council Cyber-Crime Convention** in 2001. It provides for the creation of an international task force to oversee a range of security functions associated with Internet activities for standardized technology laws across international borders. It also attempts to improve the effectiveness of international investigations into breaches of technology law. This convention has been well received by advocates of intellectual property rights because of its emphasis on copyright infringement prosecution. However, many supporters of individual rights are opposed to the adoption of the convention because they think it unduly infringes on freedom of speech and threatens the core civil liberties of U.S. residents.

While thirty-four countries attended the signing in November, 2001, only eighteen nations, including the United States, have ratified the convention as of February 2007. These include Albania, Armenia, Bosnia and Herzegovina, Bulgaria, Croatia, Cyprus, Denmark, Estonia, France, Hungary, Lithuania, Netherlands, Norway, Romania, Slovenia, the former Yugoslav Republic of Macedonia, the Ukraine, and the United States of America. The United States is technically not a "member state of the council of Europe" but does participate in the convention.

As is true with much complex international legislation, the Cyber-Crime Convention lacks any realistic provisions for enforcement. The overall goal of the convention is to simplify the acquisition of information for law enforcement agencies in certain types of international crimes. It also simplifies the extradition process. The convention has more than its share of skeptics, who see it as an overly simplistic attempt to control a complex problem.

Agreement on Trade-Related Aspects of Intellectual Property Rights

The **Agreement on Trade-Related Aspects of Intellectual Property Rights (TRIPS)**, created by the World Trade Organization (WTO), and negotiated over the years 1986–94, introduced intellectual property rules into the multilateral trade system. It is the first significant international effort to protect the intellectual property rights of individuals and of sovereign nations. It outlines requirements for governmental oversight and legislation of WTO member countries to provide minimum levels of protection for intellectual property. The WTO TRIPS agreement covers five issues:

1. "how basic principles of the trading system and other international intellectual property agreements should be applied
2. how to give adequate protection to intellectual property rights
3. how countries should enforce those rights adequately in their own territories
4. how to settle disputes on intellectual property between members of the WTO
5. special transitional arrangements during the period when the new system is being introduced."[2]

Digital Millennium Copyright Act (DMCA)

The **Digital Millennium Copyright Act (DMCA)** is the American contribution to an international effort by the World Intellectual Properties Organization (WIPO) to reduce the impact of copyright, trademark, and privacy infringement, especially when accomplished via the removal of technological copyright protection measures. This American law was created in response to the 1995 adoption of **Directive 95/46/EC** by the European Union, which added protection for individuals with regard to the processing of personal data and the use and movement of such data. The United Kingdom has also already implemented a version of this law called the **Database Right**, in order to comply with Directive 95/46/EC.

United Nations Charter

To some degree the **United Nations Charter** makes provisions for information security during information warfare. **Information warfare (IW)** involves the use of information technology by a sovereign state to conduct organized and lawful military operations. IW is a relatively new type of warfare, although the military has been conducting electronic warfare and counter warfare operations for decades by jamming, intercepting, and spoofing enemy communications. You can access the UN's Web site at *www.un.org* for information on UN International Law.

This chapter has reviewed the impact that key U.S. and international laws have on the practicing information security professional. With the growing amount of information that is harvested and stored comes a significant responsibility for its proper protection and management. This responsibility may be imposed by legal mandates imposed on the professional. It is thus important for the professional to be aware of the international, national, and state laws that affect their roles and responsibilities.

The Information Security Manager's Checklist

	No	Planned	In Progress	In Place	Integrated
This topic has been fully tested, validated, and integrated into organizational operations with formal performance measures in place (as appropriate).					
This topic has been implemented, but not fully tested, validated, and integrated into organizational operations.					
The implementation of this topic has begun, but is not yet complete.					
The formal planning for this topic has begun, but is not yet complete.					
This subject has not formally begun planning, or the organization has made a conscious decision not to pursue this topic.					
15. Other Laws					
Employees familiarized with other federal, state, and local laws relevant to the business					
Employees familiarized with other federal laws relevant to the business					
Employees familiarized with federal, state laws relevant to the business					
Employees familiarized with local laws relevant to the business					

For Further Reading

Harboring Data: Information Security, Law, and the Corporation by Andrea Matwyshyn, Stanford Law Books, 2009.

Information Security and Privacy: A Guide to Federal and State Law and Compliance, 2009 ed., by Andrew Serwin, Thomson/Reuters, 2009.

References

1. B Yeh and C. Doyle. "USA PATRIOT Improvement and Reauthorization Act of 2005: A Legal Analysis," CRS Report for Congress. Accessed 22 February 2007 from *www.fas.org/sgp/crs/intel/RL33332.pdf*.

2. WTO Understanding the TRIPS Agreement. Accessed 22 February 2007 from *www.wto.org/english/thewto_e/whatis_e/tif_e/agrm7_e.htm*.

Chapter 16

Ethics in IT and InfoSec—Who Watches the Watchers?

Most people have an understanding of the concept of "ethics" but have some difficulty in actually defining it. In its simplest form, ethics is what we fall back on when laws and policies leave gray areas where there are several courses of action and we must choose the "best" course of action. Thus, some consider ethics to be the organized study of how humans ought to act. Others consider ethics to be a consideration of rules we should live by.

Chapter Overview:

▶ Ethics and motives

▶ Differences in ethical concepts

▶ Ethics and education

▶ Professional organizations and their codes of ethics

▶ Unified ethical framework

ETHICS AND MOTIVES

Because of their privileged position in the organization and their wide access to information, information security professionals are expected to withstand a higher degree of scrutiny regarding their personal and professional behavior. One useful model for thinking about ethical matters is the "motive-act-consequences" model shown in Figure 16-1.[1]

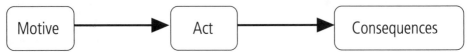

Figure 16-1 Motive-Act-Consequences
Course Technology/Cengage Learning

Motive deals with the "whys" of an action and deal with the motivations underlying the act. The act itself is what is done and the consequences are the ensuing results. For example, consider the example of a software engineer who wishes to make some money to start her own company.[2] This motive is ethically neutral since it is neither good nor bad. The engineer conducts research identifying software vulnerabilities in widely deployed software products and sells the information to the highest bidder. This action could be questionable but really depends on the ensuing consequences for its characterization as good or bad. If the vulnerability information was to be purchased by the affected vendor or a reputable security firm, it could be a "good" act that would result in better quality software or successful defense of existing installations of the vulnerable software. If the vulnerability information was purchased by a criminal organization, it could be used to craft damaging exploits. Since the engineer could not control how the winning bidder would use the information, he would conclude that selling the information to the highest bidder would be ethically questionable and limit his marketing to the affected vendor or a reputable security firm.

This simple model is quite useful because it covers "most of the bases" when we think about what we should do in a particular situation. Most of the ethical codes we review in the following sections apply quite well with this model and provide guidance to the professional in making ethical choices.

The Ten Commandments of Computer Ethics are a useful guide to the field's ethical standards:

The Ten Commandments of Computer Ethics—from The Computer Ethics Institute[3]

1. Thou shalt not use a computer to harm other people.
2. Thou shalt not interfere with other people's computer work.
3. Thou shalt not snoop around in other people's computer files.
4. Thou shalt not use a computer to steal.
5. Thou shalt not use a computer to bear false witness.
6. Thou shalt not copy or use proprietary software for which you have not paid.
7. Thou shalt not use other people's computer resources without authorization or proper compensation.
8. Thou shalt not appropriate other people's intellectual output.
9. Thou shalt think about the social consequences of the program you are writing or the system you are designing.
10. Thou shalt always use a computer in ways that ensure consideration and respect for your fellow humans.

DIFFERENCES IN ETHICAL CONCEPTS

Studies reveal that individuals of different nationalities have different views on the ethics of computer use. Difficulties arise when one nationality's ethical behavior does not correspond to that of another national group. For example, Westerners view some of the ways in which Asians use computer technology as software copyright piracy.[4] This conflict arises from Asian traditions of collective ownership, which clashes with the Western notions of intellectual property.

The Nine Country Study

A recent study has examined computer-use ethics among eight countries: Singapore, Hong Kong, United States, Great Britain, Australia, Sweden, Wales, and the Netherlands. This study selected a number of computer-use vignettes (see "Offline: The Use of Scenarios in Computer Ethics Studies" later in this chapter) and presented them to students in universities in these nine countries. This study did not categorize or classify the responses as ethical or unethical, but indicated a degree of "ethical sensitivity" about the performance of the individuals in the short case studies. The results were grouped into three categories of ethical computer use: software license infringement, illicit use, and misuse of resources. The following sections are taken from the study, "Cross-National Differences in Computer-Use Ethics: A Nine Country Study," published in *The Journal of International Business Studies*.[5]

Software License Infringement
Overall, most of the countries studied had similar attitudes toward software piracy. Statistically speaking, only the United States and the Netherlands had attitudes that differed substantially from the other countries examined. The United States was significantly less tolerant of piracy, while the Netherlands was significantly more permissive. Although a number of studies have reported that the Pacific Rim countries of Singapore and Hong Kong are software piracy hotbeds, the study found their tolerance for copyright infringement to be moderate, as were the attitudes of England, Wales, Australia, and Sweden. This could mean that the individuals surveyed understood what software license infringement was, but either felt their use was not piracy, or that their society permitted it anyway. Peer pressure, the lack of legal disincentives, the lack of punitive measures, or any one of a number of other reasons could also explain why these reported piracy centers were not oblivious to intellectual property laws.

Although the Netherlands displayed a more permissive attitude towards piracy, which reflects their general culture, they only ranked third in piracy rates of the countries represented in this study.

Illicit Use
All of the individuals studied condemned viruses, hacking, and other forms of system abuse as unacceptable behavior. There were, however, differences in groups as to just how tolerant individuals were. Singapore and Hong Kong proved to be significantly more tolerant than the United States, Wales, Great Britain, and Australia. Sweden and the Netherlands were also significantly more tolerant than Wales and Australia and significantly less tolerant than Hong Kong. The low overall degree of tolerance for illicit system use may be a function of the easy association between the common crimes of breaking and entering, trespassing, theft, and destruction of property to their computer-related counterparts.

Misuse of Corporate Resources
The scenarios used to examine the levels of tolerance in this category each represented different kinds of personal use of corporate assets,

with no indication of established policy toward personal use of company resources. In general, individuals displayed a rather lenient view of personal use of company equipment. Only Singapore and Hong Kong view personal use of company equipment as unethical. There were several substantial national differences in this category, with the Netherlands reporting the most lenient view. Regardless of cultural background, many individuals feel that if an organization does not specifically forbid the use of its computing resources for personal use, then such use is acceptable. In fact, only the two Asian samples, Singapore and Hong Kong, reported generally intolerant attitudes toward personal use of organizational computing resources. The reasons behind this are unknown. Perhaps the formal Asian work ethic provides stricter guidance on duty to the company versus personal rights and privileges.

Overall, the researchers found that there is a general agreement among nationalities as to what is acceptable or unacceptable computer use. There is however, a range of degrees of tolerance of unethical behavior.

> *Thus, the results of this study underscore inter-cultural similarities as much as they describe inter-cultural differences. The study also found little to support, from an ethical perspective, the popular media's portrayal of Asians as "digital bandits." In fact, the Hong Kong and Singapore respondents were not consistently the most permissive nationalities among those studied. As noted earlier, the higher piracy rates in Singapore and Hong Kong may be less a function of ethical difference and more a function of the lack of legal and financial disincentive to engage in software copyright infringement. The only country that consistently ranked as "most tolerant" was the Netherlands. However, this level of tolerance does not seem to have completely manifested itself in action; although the Netherlands has a higher piracy rate than the United States, Australia, Wales, England, and Sweden, it still ranks behind Singapore and Hong Kong.[6]*

Vulnerability Research and Disclosure

Research in software vulnerabilities has become a thriving endeavor where academic, corporate, and independent researchers evaluate widely deployed software products to identify vulnerabilities and disclose them in various ways. Most of the controversy in this area revolves around the disclosure process and there are three general approaches to disclosing vulnerabilities:[7]

- ▶ No disclosure—no details are released regarding the vulnerability. This is quite common when a vendor identifies a vulnerability in their own product.
- ▶ Partial disclosure—the existence of the vulnerability and a workaround or fix is publicly disclosed.
- ▶ Full disclosure—full details of the vulnerability are publicly disclosed.

However, the debate over disclosure methods is becoming less relevant with the increasing financial component of cyber-crime. As cyber-crime has grown to a larger and larger economic force, the financial rewards that can be reaped from vulnerability discovery have dwarfed the philosophical debates over the proper way to disclose vulnerabilities. As will be discussed later in the section on ethics, this is a critical area for ethical concerns.

ETHICS AND EDUCATION

Differences in computer use ethics are not exclusively cultural. Differences are found among individuals within the same country, within the same social class, and within the same company. Key studies reveal that the overriding factor in leveling the ethical perceptions within a small population is education. Employees must be trained and kept up to date on information security topics, including the expected behaviors of an ethical employee. This is especially important in areas of information security, as many employees may not have the formal technical training to understand that their behavior is unethical or even illegal. Proper ethical and legal training is vital to creating an informed, well-prepared, and low-risk system user.

Deterring Unethical and Illegal Behavior

It is the responsibility of information security personnel to deter unethical and illegal acts, using policy, education and training, and technology as controls or safeguards to protect the information and systems. Many security professionals understand technological means of protection, but many underestimate the value of policy. There are three general categories of unethical behavior that organizations and society should seek to eliminate:

1. Ignorance: As you learned earlier, ignorance of the law is no excuse, but ignorance of policies and procedures is. The first method of deterrence is education. Organizations must design, publish, and disseminate organizational policies and relevant laws, and employees must explicitly agree to abide by them. Reminders, training, and awareness programs support retention, and one hopes, compliance.

2. Accident: Individuals with authorization and privileges to manage information within the organization have the greatest opportunity to cause harm or damage by accident. The careful placement of controls can help prevent accidental modification to systems and data.

3. Intent: Criminal or unethical intent refers to the state of mind of the individual committing the infraction. A legal defense can be built upon whether or not the accused acted out of ignorance, by accident, or with the intent to cause harm or damage. Deterring those with criminal intent is best done by means of litigation, prosecution, and technical controls. As you learned in earlier chapters, intent is only one of several factors to consider when determining whether a computer-related crime has occurred.

Deterrence is the best method for preventing an illegal or unethical activity. Laws, policies, and technical controls are all examples of deterrents. However, laws and policies and their associated penalties only deter if three conditions are present.

1. Fear of penalty: Threats of informal reprimand or verbal warnings may not have the same impact as the threat of imprisonment or forfeiture of pay.

2. Probability of being caught: There must be a strong possibility that perpetrators of illegal or unethical acts will be caught.

3. Probability of penalty being administered: The organization must be willing and able to impose the penalty.

The security professional may feel that this is a "bet my job" situation where they should draw the line that if management doesn't comply with the PCI-DSS, they will resign. While this is an admirable attitude, a more nuanced approach is more appropriate. In the final analysis, it is management's decisions that drive implementation of the information security program for the organization. If the security professional has clearly articulated the risks, costs, and consequences of both compliance and noncompliance to management, they are on fairly sound ethical grounds with whatever management decides.

In other words, the security professional is ethically required to assure that management has the most complete and accurate information accompanied with appropriate recommendations to support their decision making. Security decisions are really no different than any other type of business decision and the final responsibility falls on management as long as the professional has fulfilled her responsibility to provide the best advice possible.

As one of the authors' favorite quote goes, "As a consultant, my duty is to provide the best advice I can. Feel free to ignore my advice as I can always use you as a bad example to your replacement." Unfortunately, too many consultants prefer the quote "if you're not part of the solution, there's good money to be made in prolonging the problem."[8]

PROFESSIONAL ORGANIZATIONS AND THEIR CODES OF ETHICS

A number of professional organizations have established codes of conduct and/or codes of ethics that members are expected to follow. Codes of ethics can have a positive effect on an individual's judgment regarding computer use.[9] Unfortunately, many employers do not encourage their employees to join these professional organizations. The loss of accreditation or certification due to a violation of a code of conduct can be a deterrent, as it can dramatically reduce the individual's marketability and earning power.

In general, research has shown that some certifications have little impact on the long-term earning potential of practitioners, while other certifications, notably those in information security, have a lingering effect on the economic prospects of certificate holders.[10] The long-term value of an information security certification adds leverage to the certification granting authority to exert influence over its members, including influence in matters of ethical responsibility.

Ethics and the Profession

What exactly does it mean to say that information security is a profession? One definition of a profession requires four components:[11]

- ▶ A common body of knowledge
- ▶ A governing body
- ▶ Certification authority (whether self or government created) within the profession
- ▶ A code of ethics with an oversight body with authority to enforce the provisions of the code

While some might debate that the field is not mature enough to meet some of these requirements, the need for a code of ethics to govern professional behavior cannot be overlooked. The next section reviews several of the ethical codes established by organizations with "some skin in the game" for information security.

It remains the individual responsibility of security professionals to act ethically and according to the policies and procedures of their employers, their professional organizations, and the laws of society. It is likewise the organization's responsibility to develop, disseminate, and enforce its policies. The following sections describe several of the relevant professional associations.

Association of Computing Machinery (ACM)

The ACM (*www.acm.org*) is a respected professional society, originally established in 1947, as the world's first educational and scientific computing society. It is one of the few organizations that strongly promotes education and provides discounted membership for students. The ACM's code of ethics requires members to perform their duties in a manner befitting an ethical computing professional. The code contains specific references to protecting the confidentiality of information, causing no harm (with specific references to viruses), protecting the privacy of others, and respecting the intellectual property and copyrights of others. The ACM also publishes a wide variety of professional computing publications, including the highly regarded *Communications of the ACM*.

International Information Systems Security Certification Consortium, Inc. (ISC)²

The (ISC)² (*www.isc2.org*) is not a professional association in the strictest sense and has no member or membership services. It is a nonprofit organization that focuses on the development and implementation of information security certifications and credentials. The (ISC)² manages a body of knowledge on information security and administers and evaluates examinations for information security certifications. The code of ethics put forth by (ISC)² is primarily designed for information security professionals who have earned one of their certifications. This code includes four mandatory canons:

1. Protect society, the commonwealth, and the infrastructure.
2. Act honorably, honestly, justly, responsibly, and legally.
3. Provide diligent and competent service to principals.
4. Advance and protect the profession.[12]

Through this code, (ISC)² seeks to provide sound guidance that will enable reliance on the ethicality and trustworthiness of the information security professional as the guardian of the information and systems.

System Administration, Networking, and Security Institute (SANS)

The System Administration, Networking, and Security Institute, or SANS (*www.sans.org*), is a professional organization with a large membership dedicated to the protection of information and systems. Founded in 1989, SANS is a professional research and education cooperative organization. For individuals who seek one of SANS's many GIAC certifications they must agree to comply with the organization's code of ethics:

Respect for the Public

▶ *I will accept responsibility in making decisions with consideration for the security and welfare of the community.*

▶ *I will not engage in or be a party to unethical or unlawful acts that negatively affect the community, my professional reputation, or the information security discipline.*

Respect for the Certification

▶ *I will not share, disseminate, or otherwise distribute confidential or proprietary information pertaining to the GIAC certification process.*

▶ *I will not use my certification, or objects or information associated with my certification (such as certificates or logos) to represent any individual or entity other than myself as being certified by GIAC.*

Respect for My Employer

▶ *I will deliver capable service that is consistent with the expectations of my certification and position.*

▶ *I will protect confidential and proprietary information with which I come into contact.*

▶ *I will minimize risks to the confidentiality, integrity, or availability of an information technology solution, consistent with risk management practice.*

Respect for Myself

▶ *I will avoid conflicts of interest.*

▶ *I will not misuse any information or privileges I am afforded as part of my responsibilities.*

▶ *I will not misrepresent my abilities or my work to the community, my employer, or my peers.*[13]

Information Systems Audit and Control Association (ISACA)

The Information Systems Audit and Control Association, or ISACA (*www.isaca.org*), is a professional association with a focus on auditing, control, and security. The membership comprises both technical and managerial professionals. ISACA focuses on providing IT control practices and standards. They offer the certified information systems auditor (CISA) certification, which does not focus exclusively on information security but does contain many information security components.

The ISACA also has the following code of ethics:

Members and ISACA certification holders shall:

1. *Support the implementation of, and encourage compliance with, appropriate standards, procedures and controls for information systems.*

2. *Perform their duties with objectivity, due diligence and professional care, in accordance with professional standards and best practices.*

3. *Serve in the interest of stakeholders in a lawful and honest manner, while maintaining high standards of conduct and character, and not engage in acts discreditable to the profession.*

4. Maintain the privacy and confidentiality of information obtained in the course of their duties unless disclosure is required by legal authority. Such information shall not be used for personal benefit or released to inappropriate parties.

5. Maintain competency in their respective fields and agree to undertake only those activities which they can reasonably expect to complete with professional competence.

6. Inform appropriate parties of the results of work performed; reveal all significant facts known to them.

7. Support the professional education of stakeholders in enhancing their understanding of information systems security and control.[14]

Information Systems Security Association

The **Information Systems Security Association (ISSA)** (*www.issa.org*) is a nonprofit society of information security professionals. Its primary mission is to bring together qualified practitioners of information security for information exchange and educational development. ISSA provides conferences, meetings, publications, and information resources to promote information security awareness and education.[15] ISSA also promotes a code of ethics, similar to those of (ISC)[2], ISACA, and the ACM, "promoting management practices that will ensure the confidentiality, integrity, and availability of organizational information resources."[16]

▶ Perform all professional activities and duties in accordance with all applicable laws and the highest ethical principles;

▶ Promote generally accepted information security current best practices and standards;

▶ Maintain appropriate confidentiality of proprietary or otherwise sensitive information encountered in the course of professional activities;

▶ Discharge professional responsibilities with diligence and honesty;

▶ Refrain from any activities that might constitute a conflict of interest or otherwise damage the reputation of employers, the information security profession, or the association; and

▶ Not intentionally injure or impugn the professional reputation or practice of colleagues, clients, or employers.[17]

UNIFIED ETHICAL FRAMEWORK

Because each professional association has its own code of ethics, there is the possibility for confusion and possibly even conflict when it comes to practicing within these multiple codes. For that reason, ISSA, (ISC)[2], and SANS collaborated in the Unified Ethics Working Group (*http://www.ethics-wg.org/*) to define a single ethical framework that would meet the needs for the information security profession:

Unified Framework of Professional Ethics for Security Professionals[18]

Integrity

Perform duties in accordance with existing laws, exercising the highest moral principles.

▶ Refrain from activities that would constitute a conflict of interest.

▶ Act in the best interests of stakeholders consistent with public interest.

▶ Act honorably, justly, responsibly, and legally in every aspect of your profession.

Objectivity

Perform all duties in a fair manner and without prejudice

- ▶ Exercise independent professional judgment, in order to provide unbiased analysis and advice.
- ▶ When an opinion is provided, note it as opinion rather than fact.

Professional Competence and Due Care

Perform services diligently and with professionalism

- ▶ Act with diligence and promptness in rendering service.
- ▶ Render only those services for which you are fully competent and qualified.
- ▶ Ensure that work performed meets the highest professional standards. Where resource constraints exist, ensure that your work is both correct and complete within those limits. If, in your professional judgment, resources are inadequate to achieve an acceptable outcome, so inform clients and principals.
- ▶ Be supportive of colleagues, and encourage their professional development. Recognize and acknowledge the contributions of others, and respect the decisions of principals and coworkers.
- ▶ Keep stakeholders informed regarding the progress of your work.
- ▶ Refrain from conduct that would damage the reputation of the profession, or the practice of colleagues, clients, and employers.
- ▶ Report ethical violations to the appropriate governing body in a timely manner.
- ▶ Participate in learning throughout your career, to maintain the skills necessary to function effectively as a member of the profession.

Confidentiality

Respect and safeguard confidential information and exercise due care to prevent improper disclosure.

- ▶ Maintain appropriate confidentiality of proprietary and otherwise confidential information encountered in the course of professional activities, unless such action would conceal, or result in, the commission of a criminal act, is otherwise required by law, or is authorized by the principal.

Enforcement

The existence of an accepted ethical code is an important step but as noted earlier, it is much more valuable when there exists a process for enforcing the provisions of the code. Thus, it is up to the individual security professional to police the discipline. Because InfoSec professionals are trusted with the most valuable of assets—information, we must be above reproach with regard to our ethics and morals. If management and the users can't trust security, where will they go for help?

Ethics is a requirement for professional practice, particularly in information security, because there will always be "corner cases" that arise where both law and policy are silent. Information security professionals have highly privileged access to the organization's information assets and must conform to the highest ethical standards in their activities. The ethical code provides guidance for the information security professional in analyzing the motive, act, and consequences for the situation to produce a decision that will be defensible under scrutiny as "ethical."

There is a certain amount of confusion in the information security ethical space because each professional organization has its own code of ethics, which though they have a common goal in assuring ethical behavior, their wording is slightly different. For this reason, some organizations have collaborated in defining a unified ethical framework to guide the profession.

The Information Security Manager's Checklist

This topic has been fully tested, validated, and integrated into organizational operations with formal performance measures in place (as appropriate).

This topic has been implemented, but not fully tested, validated, and integrated into organizational operations.

The implementation of this topic has begun, but is not yet complete.

The formal planning for this topic has begun, but is not yet complete.

This subject has not formally begun planning, or the organization has made a conscious decision not to pursue this topic.

16. Ethics	No	Planned	In Progress	In Place	Integrated
IT and InfoSec professional aware of appropriate codes of ethics					
Company has established values statement					
All employees aware of their responsibilities under the company values statement					

For Further Reading

Understanding Privacy by Daniel J. Solove, Harvard University Press, 2010.

Computer Network Security and Cyber Ethics, 2d ed., by Joseph Migga Kizza, McFarland & Company, 2001.

References

1. B. MacKinnon. *Ethics: Theory and Contemporary Issues* (4th ed). Belmont, CA: Wadsworth, 2004.

2. Adapted from Richard Austin. "Righteous Money the Wrong Way." *ISSA Journal* 6 (August 2008), p. 8.

3. Computer Professionals for Social Responsibility. The Ten Commandments of Computer Ethics. Referenced October 14, 2006. Available on the World Wide Web from *www.cpsr.org/issues/ethics/cei*.

4. Mike Magee. Software piracy in Asia exposed. *The Inquirer*. Accessed 14 October 2006. *www .theinquirer.net/default.aspx?article=2385*.

5. M. E. Whitman, A. M. Townsend, and A. R. Hendrickson. "Cross-National Differences in Computer-Use Ethics: A Nine Country Study." *The Journal of International Business Studies*, 30(4), 1999, 673–687.

6. Ibid.

7. Ari Takanen, Jared Demott, and Charles Miller. *Fuzzing for Software Testing and Quality Assurance*. Boston: Artech House, 2008.

8. Despair, Inc. Web page viewed 10 November 2008 from *http://www.despair.com/consulting.html*.

9. S. J. Harrington. "The Effects of Codes of Ethics and Personal Denial of Responsibility on Computer Abuse Judgment and Intentions." *MIS Quarterly* (September 1996), 257–278.

10. Foote Partners, LLC. Press release, 18 August 2003, New Canaan, CT.

11. *http://www.ethics-wg.org/* accessed 3 November 2008.

12. (ISC)². *Code of Ethics*. Accessed 14 October 2006 from *www.isc2.org/cgi-bin/content.cgi?category=12*.

13. GIAC. *Code of Ethics*. Accessed August 28. 2006 from *www.giac.org/overview/ethics.php*

14. ISACA. *Code of Ethics*. AccessedAugust 28. 2006 from *www.isaca.org/Template.cfm?Section= Code_of_Professional_Ethics*

15. ISSA. *What is ISSA*. Accessed October 14, 2006 from *http://www.issa.org/aboutissa.html*

16. ISSA. *Code of Ethics*. Accessed October 14, 2006 from *www.issa.org/codeofethics.html*

17. ISSA. *Code of Ethics*. Accessed November 3, 2008 from *www.issa.org/codeofethics.html*

18. *http://www.ethics-wg.org/* accessed November 3, 2008.

Tactical Information Security: Policies and Programs

Part V of *Roadmap to Information Security for IT and InfoSec Managers* will examine the impact of policy, procedures, and operational programs developed to improve the security of information assets frequently encountered in the area of IT-related security.

Part Overview

Chapter 17—"Information Security Policy Development and Implementation" defines InfoSec policy and describes its central role in a successful InfoSec program. There are three major types of InfoSec policy, and the chapter explains what goes into each type, and demonstrates how to develop, implement, and maintain these various types of InfoSec policies.

Chapter 18—"Information Security Policy Types: EISP, ISSP, and SysSP" continues the discussion on policy, focusing on the organization's highest InfoSec policy—the EISP. The chapter examines the critical components of the development and implementation of this policy document. This chapter continues with the discussion of the organization's other critical InfoSec policies—the ISSP and SysSP. The chapter examines the critical components of the development and implementation of these policy documents.

Chapter 19—"Employment Policies and Practices" examines the implementation of employment policies and practices. It also discusses how security policy affects, and is affected by, consultants, temporary workers, and outside business partners.

Chapter 20—"Security Education Training and Awareness (SETA)" examines the development of one of the organization's most visible InfoSec programs: the SETA program. The chapter examines the components needed for the successful design, development, and implementation of such a program along with considerations for each major component.

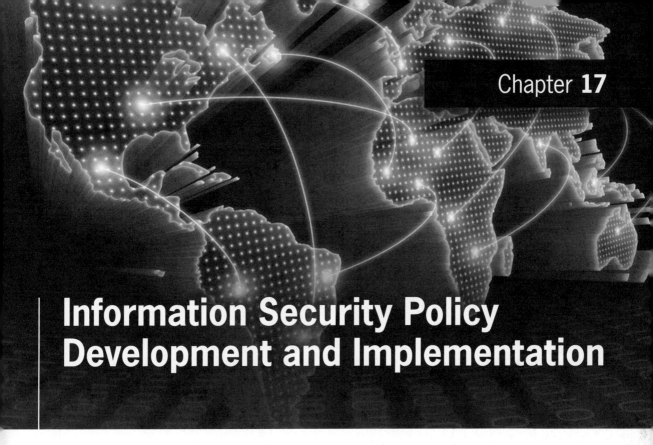

Chapter 17

Information Security Policy Development and Implementation

As previously discussed, the creation of an information security program begins with good policy. This is usually the result of a lot of work to make and keep the policy process effective. If you are assigned to this task, we recommend that you begin a review of the organization's information security policies, standards, and practices, followed by the selection or creation of information security architecture and a detailed information security blueprint. If these documents and practices do not exist, they will have to be designed, developed, and deployed. If they do exist, the odds are good that they will need to be refreshed. An organization's information security effort can be successful only if it operates under a complete and consistent information security policy. Without policy, blueprints, and planning, the organization will be unable to meet the information security needs of the various communities of interest. The role of planning in the modern organization is hard to overemphasize. All but the smallest organizations undertake at least some planning: strategic planning to manage the allocation of resources, and contingency planning to prepare for the uncertainties of the business environment.

Chapter Overview:

- ▶ Information security policy, standards, and practices
- ▶ Enterprise information security policy (EISP)
- ▶ Policy management

INFORMATION SECURITY POLICY, STANDARDS, AND PRACTICES

The centrality of policy to an information security program sometimes mystifies the more technical information security professionals. Policies seem general, fuzzy, and really unrelated to the processes of hardening assets and protecting network traffic. However, policy in its purest form sets the overall goal and direction for the information security program. For example, most everyone would agree that every Internet-connected organization needs a firewall. But without policy, there's no real guidance as to how that firewall should be configured, what traffic it should pass or block, what information should be logged, how changes to its configuration should be managed, etc. In other words, without a policy to specify that only business critical network services are to be exposed on the Internet, etc., the firewall becomes just a magic totem, erected on the path into the organization in the hopes that it will magically frighten bad things away. Policy is basically management's specification of what is to be done and serves as the overall motivation and basis for the information security program.

Management from all communities of interest, including general staff, information technology, and information security, must make policies the foundation for all information security planning, design, and deployment. Policies direct how issues should be addressed and technologies

Management Has No Clue

One of the frustrations that greets many new information security professionals is that, though they have been trained to believe that management sets overall direction and policy for the security program, management has no real idea of what is involved in a security program or what policies they need. Unfortunately, this is a fairly common situation, particularly in organizations starting up their first information security program.

In these situations it falls on you, the information security professional, to consult with management and educate them on issues and requirements, work with them to develop the required policies, and then shepherd the policies through the approval process. This work can be both tedious and filled with controversy but is the critical first step in the security program. Because of the cross-functional nature of information security (in other words, to be successful, you must have the help and cooperation of people who do not work for you and whose management is not even in the same chain of command as yours). Without a clear statement of management's intentions expressed in policy, the security program will be a continual battle over turf lines, resource priorities, etc.

should be used. Policies do not specify the proper operation of equipment or software—this information should be placed in the standards, procedures, and practices of users' manuals and systems documentation. In addition, *policy may never contradict law*, because this can create a significant liability for the organization and its management.

Quality information security programs begin and end with policy.[1] Because information security is primarily a management problem, not a technical one, policy obliges personnel to function in a manner that adds to the security of information assets, rather than threatening them. It is interesting to note that security policies are the least expensive control to develop, but the most difficult to implement *properly*. They are the lowest cost in that their creation and dissemination requires only the time and effort of the management team. Even if the management team hires an outside consultant to assist in the development of policy, the costs are minimal compared to those of technical controls. However, shaping policy is difficult because policy must:

- ▶ Never conflict with laws
- ▶ Be defensible if challenged in court
- ▶ Be properly and consistently administered through dissemination and documented acceptance

For a policy to be effective and thus legally enforceable, it must meet the following criteria:

- ▶ Dissemination (distribution)—The organization must be able to demonstrate that the relevant policy has been made readily available for review by the employee. Common dissemination techniques include hard-copy and electronic distribution.
- ▶ Review (reading)—The organization must be able to demonstrate that it disseminated the document in an intelligible form, including versions for illiterate, non-English reading, and reading-impaired employees. Common techniques include recordings of the policy in English and alternate languages.
- ▶ Comprehension (understanding)—The organization must be able to demonstrate that the employee understood the requirements and content of the policy. Common techniques include quizzes and other assessments.
- ▶ Compliance (agreement)—The organization must be able to demonstrate that the employee agrees to comply with the policy, through act or affirmation. Common techniques include log-on banners that require a specific action (mouse click or keystroke) to acknowledge agreement, or a signed document clearly indicating the employee has read, understood, and agreed to comply with the policy.
- ▶ Uniform enforcement—The organization must be able to demonstrate that the policy has been uniformly enforced, regardless of employee status or assignment.

Definitions

Before examining the various types of information security policies, it is important to understand exactly what policy is and how it can and should be used.

A **policy** is a plan or course of action used to convey intent from an organization's senior-most management to those who make decisions, take actions, and perform other duties. Policies

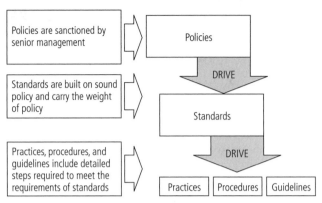

Figure 17-1 Policies, Standards, and Practices
Course Technology/Cengage Learning

function as organizational laws in that they define acceptable and unacceptable behavior within the organization. Like laws, policies define what is right, and what is wrong, what the penalties are for violating policy, and what the appeal process is. (These topics are explored further in the following sections.) **Standards**, on the other hand, are more detailed statements of what must be done to comply with policy. They have the same requirements for compliance as policies. The standards may be informal, or part of an organizational culture, as in **de facto standards**. Or standards may be published, scrutinized, and ratified by a group, as in formal or **de jure standards**. Finally, practices, procedures, and guidelines effectively explain how to comply with policy. Figure 17-1 shows policies as the force that drives standards, which in turn drive practices, procedures, and guidelines.

Policies are put in place to support the mission, vision, and strategic planning of an organization. The **mission** of an organization is a written statement of an organization's purpose. The **vision** of an organization is a written statement about the organization's goals—where will the organization be in five years? In ten? **Strategic planning** is the process of moving the organization toward its vision.

To be effective, a policy must be thoroughly disseminated—via printed personnel manuals, organization intranets, and periodic supplements. All members of the organization must read, understand, and agree to the policies. But keep in mind that policies are living documents, in that they require constant modification and maintenance as the needs of the organization evolve.

The meaning of the term **security policy** depends on the context in which it is used. Governmental agencies discuss security policy in terms of national security and national policies to deal with foreign states. A security policy can also represent a credit card agency's method for processing credit card numbers. In general, a security policy is a set of rules that protect an organization's assets. An **information security policy** provides rules for the protection of the information assets of the organization. As stated in Chapter 1, the task of information security professionals is to protect the confidentiality, integrity, and availability of information and information systems, during transmission, storage, and processing. This is accomplished by applying policy, education and training programs, and technology.

Management must define three types of security policy according to the National Institute of Standards and Technology's Special Publication 800-14 (a publication that was discussed in detail in Chapter 12):

1. Enterprise information security policies
2. Issue-specific security policies
3. Systems-specific security policies

Each of these management policies is examined in greater detail in the pages that follow.

ENTERPRISE INFORMATION SECURITY POLICY (EISP)

An **enterprise information security policy (EISP)** is also known as a general security policy, IT security policy, or information security policy. The EISP is based on and directly supports the mission, vision, and direction of the organization and sets the strategic direction, scope, and tone for all security efforts. The EISP is an executive-level document, usually drafted by, or in cooperation with, the chief information officer of the organization. This policy is usually only two to ten pages long and deals with the philosophy of security in the IT environment. The EISP usually needs to be modified only when there is a change in the strategic direction of the organization.

The EISP guides the development, implementation, and management of the security program. It contains the requirements to be met by the information security blueprint or framework. It defines the purpose, scope, constraints, and applicability of the security program in the organization. It also assigns responsibilities for the various areas of security, including systems administration, maintenance of the information security policies, and the practices and responsibilities of the users. Finally, it addresses legal compliance. According to the National Institute of Standards, the EISP typically addresses compliance in two areas:

> 1) General compliance to ensure meeting the requirements to establish a program and the responsibilities assigned therein to various organizational components and 2) the use of specified penalties and disciplinary action.[2]

When the EISP has been developed, the CISO (chief information security officer) begins forming the security team and initiating the necessary changes to the information security program.

EISP Elements

Although the specifics of EISPs vary from organization to organization, most EISP documents should include the following elements:

- ▶ An overview of the corporate philosophy on security
- ▶ Information on the structure of the information security organization and individuals who fulfill the information security role
- ▶ Fully articulated responsibilities for security that are shared by all members of the organization (employees, contractors, consultants, partners, and visitors)
- ▶ Fully articulated responsibilities for security that are unique to each role within the organization

The components of a good EISP are shown in Table 17-1.[3]

TABLE 17-1 Components of the EISP

COMPONENT	DESCRIPTION
Statement of Purpose	Answers the question, "What is this policy for?" Provides a framework that helps the reader to understand the intent of the document. Can include text such as the following: "This document will: ▶ Identify the elements of a good security policy ▶ Explain the need for information security ▶ Specify the various categories of information security ▶ Identify the information security responsibilities and roles ▶ Identify appropriate levels of security through standards and guidelines This document establishes an overarching security policy and direction for our company. Individual departments are expected to establish standards, guidelines, and operating procedures that adhere to and reference this policy while addressing their specific and individual needs."[4]
Information Technology Security Elements	Defines information security. For example: "Protecting the confidentiality, integrity, and availability of information while in processing, transmission, and storage, through the use of policy, education and training, and technology. . . ." This section can also lay out security definitions or philosophies to clarify the policy.
Need for Information Technology Security	Provides information on the importance of information security in the organization and the obligation (legal and ethical) to protect critical information whether regarding customers, employees, or markets.
Information Technology Security Responsibilities and Roles	Defines the organizational structure designed to support information security within the organization. Identifies categories of individuals with responsibility for information security (IT department, management, users) and their information security responsibilities, including maintenance of this document.
Reference to Other Information Technology Standards and Guidelines	Lists other standards that influence and are influenced by this policy document, perhaps including relevant laws (federal and state) and other policies.

Course Technology/Cengage Learning

POLICY MANAGEMENT

Policies are living documents that must be managed and nurtured so they evolve with the organization they support. It is unacceptable to create such an important set of documents and then shelve them. These documents must be properly disseminated (distributed, read, understood, and agreed to) and managed. How they are managed relates directly to the policy management section of the issue-specific policy described earlier. Good management practices for policy development and maintenance make for a more resilient organization. For example, all policies, including security policies, undergo tremendous stress when corporate mergers and divestitures occur; in such situations employees are faced with uncertainty and many distractions. System vulnerabilities can arise if, for instance, incongruent security policies are implemented in different parts of a new, merged organization. When two companies merge but retain separate policies, the difficulty of implementing security controls increases. Likewise, when one company with unified policies splits in two, each new company may require different policies.

To remain viable, security policies must have responsible individuals, a schedule of reviews, a method for making recommendations for reviews, and a policy issuance and revision date. Each of these is examined in additional detail below.

Responsible Individual

Just as information systems and information security projects must have champions and managers, so must policies. The policy champion and manager is called the **policy administrator**. Typically the policy administrator is a mid-level staff member and is responsible for the creation, revision, distribution, and storage of the policy. Note that the policy administrator does not necessarily have to be technically oriented. While practicing information security professionals require extensive technical knowledge, policy management and policy administration requires only a moderate technical background. It is good practice, however, for policy administrators to solicit input both from the technically adept information security experts and from the business-focused managers in each community of interest when making revisions to security policies. The administrator should also notify all affected members of the organization when the policy is modified. It is disheartening when a policy that required hundreds of staff-hours to develop and document is ignored. Thus, someone must be responsible for placing that policy and all subsequent revisions into the hands of those who are accountable for its implementation. The policy administrator must be clearly identified on the policy document as the primary point of contact for additional information or for revision suggestions to the policy.

Schedule of Reviews

Policies can only retain their effectiveness in a changing environment if they are periodically reviewed for relevancy and accuracy and modified to reflect these changes. Policies that are not kept current can become liabilities, as outdated rules are enforced (or not), and new requirements are ignored. In order to demonstrate due diligence, an organization must actively seek to meet the requirements of the market in which it operates. This applies equally to both public (government, academic, and nonprofit) and private (commercial and for-profit) organizations. A properly organized schedule of reviews should be defined and published as part of the document. Typically a policy should be reviewed at least annually to ensure that it is still an effective control.

The Policy Manual

One of the saddest findings in a security audit was the response to the question "Where are your security policies?" The person smiled brightly and produced a very professional-looking binder filled with a colorfully tabbed document still in shrink-wrap. The organization had spent a large amount of time and money developing a set of security policies, publishing them and promptly forgetting about them. An unread book of security policies is useless except as a paper weight or door stop. In order to achieve their purpose as expressing management's intention of how the security program will work, they must be taken out of the binder and into the way employees conduct business.

Review Procedures and Practices

To facilitate policy reviews, the policy manager should implement a mechanism by which individuals can comfortably make recommendations for revisions. Recommendation methods can involve e-mail, office mail, and an anonymous drop box. If the policy is controversial, the policy administrator may feel that anonymous submission of information is the best way to solicit staff opinions. Many employees are intimidated by management and hesitate to voice honest opinions about a policy unless they can do so anonymously. Once the policy has come up for review, all comments should be examined and management-approved improvements should be implemented. Additional review methods can include representative users in the revision process and solicit direct comment on the revision of the policy. In reality, most policies are drafted by a single, responsible individual and are then reviewed by a higher-level manager. But even this method should not preclude the collection and review of employee input.

Policy and Revision Date

The simple action of dating the policy is often skipped. When policies are drafted and published without dates, confusion can arise. If policies are not reviewed and kept current, or if members of the organization are following undated versions, disastrous results and legal headaches can ensue. These problems are particularly common in a high-turnover environment. It is, therefore, important that the policy contain the date of origin, along with the date(s) of any revisions. Some policies may also need a **sunset clause** indicating their expiration date. This can be particularly important for policies governing information use in short-term business associations or agencies that are involved with the organization. Establishing a policy end date prevents a temporary policy from mistakenly becoming permanent, and it also enables an organization to gain experience with a given policy before adopting it permanently.

When Business Outruns Policy

Policy revision can be triggered by changes in how the organization conducts its business. One organization discovered this to its detriment when the marketing department decided to equip its sales representatives with laptops to improve their productivity. Unfortunately, no one in the marketing department realized that this might have security implications and the information security department was not consulted nor were any policies developed to cover the types of information allowed to be on these mobile assets, any required protections, etc.

Not too surprisingly, one of the laptops was stolen and later investigation revealed that it had contained complete customer lists, purchasing histories, product roadmaps, and other highly confidential information. Further, the laptop did not even require its user to enter a password to log on.

Though as far as the organization knew, the thief was interested in the laptop and not its information, the episode produced a great deal of consternation and had career limiting implications for some of the managers involved.

This story illustrates the important rule that information security must be integrated into the business strategy process so that changes in the way business is conducted does not expose information assets.

Automated Policy Management

Recent years have seen the emergence of a new category of software for the management of information security policies. This type of software was developed in response to needs articulated by information security practitioners. While there have been many software products that meet the need for a specific technical control, there is now software to meet the need for automating some of the busywork of policy management. Automation can streamline the repetitive steps of writing policy, tracking the workflow of policy approvals, publishing policy once it is written and approved, and tracking when individuals have read the policy. Using techniques from computer-based training and testing, organizations can train staff members and also improve the organization's awareness program.

This chapter has introduced the centrality of policy to a successful information security program and introduced the broad types of policies a typical organization will need to develop. Policies are living documents that must change and evolve along with the organization they support and processes must be put in place to assure regular review and modification of policy. This policy review can be either a manual or automated process.

The Information Security Manager's Checklist

	No	Planned	In Progress	In Place	Integrated
This topic has been fully tested, validated, and integrated into organizational operations with formal performance measures in place (as appropriate).					
This topic has been implemented, but not fully tested, validated, and integrated into organizational operations.					
The implementation of this topic has begun, but is not yet complete.					
The formal planning for this topic has begun, but is not yet complete.					
This subject has not formally begun planning, or the organization has made a conscious decision not to pursue this topic.					
17. InfoSec Policies					
All policies distributed					
All employees able to read policy					
All employees able to understand policy					
All employees agree to comply with policy and compliance documented					
Policies reviewed periodically					
Policies uniformly enforced					

For Further Reading

Information Security Policy Made Easy by Charles Cresson Wood, Information Shield, 2008.

Writing Information Security Policies by Scott Barman, New Riders Publishing, 2002.

References

1. Charles Cresson Wood. "Integrated Approach Includes Information Security." *Security* 37, no. 2 (February 2000): 43–44.

2. National Institute of Standards and Technology. *An Introduction to Computer Security: The NIST Handbook.* SP 800-12.

3. Derived from a number of sources, the most notable of which is *http://www.wustl.edu/policies/infosecurity.html*.

4. Robert J. Alberts, Anthony M. Townsend, and Michael E. Whitman. "Considerations for an Effective Telecommunications Use Policy." *Communications of the ACM* 42, no. 6 (June 1999): 101–109.

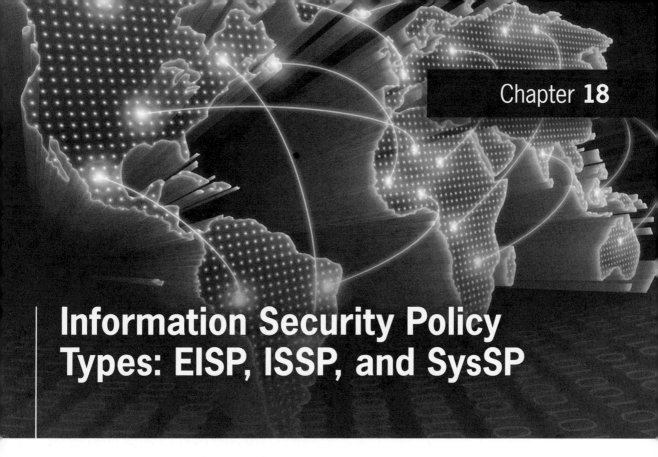

Information Security Policy Types: EISP, ISSP, and SysSP

As noted in the previous chapter, the enterprise information security policy (EISP) sets the general overall direction and tone for the security program. However, this is not the end of the policy story. From the EISP will flow other types of policies that delve into additional portions of the overall program. Two of these other types of policies issue-specific security policy (ISSP) dealing with specific issues such as e-mail and system-specific security policy (SysSP) dealing with, for example, how a firewall might be configured.

Chapter Overview:

▶ Issue-specific security policy
▶ System-specific security policy

ISSUE-SPECIFIC SECURITY POLICY (ISSP)

As you and your team execute various technologies and processes to support routine operations, you must also guide employees toward the proper use of these technologies and processes. In general, the **issue-specific security policy**, or **ISSP**, (1) addresses specific areas of technology as listed below, (2) requires frequent updates, and (3) contains a statement on the organization's position on a specific issue.[1] An ISSP may cover the following topics, among others:

- ▶ Electronic mail
- ▶ Use of the Internet
- ▶ Specific minimum configurations of computers to defend against worms and viruses
- ▶ Prohibitions against hacking or testing organization security controls without authorization
- ▶ Home use of company-owned computer equipment
- ▶ Use of personal equipment on company networks
- ▶ Use of telecommunications technologies (fax and phone)
- ▶ Use of photocopy equipment
- ▶ Requirement that all software used for business purposes be properly licensed for such use

There are a number of approaches to creating and managing ISSPs within an organization. Three of the most common are to create the following types of ISSP documents:

1. Independent ISSP documents, each tailored to a specific issue
2. A single comprehensive ISSP document covering all issues
3. A modular ISSP document that unifies policy creation and administration, while maintaining each specific issue's requirements

The independent ISSP document typically has a scattershot effect. Each department responsible for a particular application of technology creates a policy governing its use, management, and control. While the local autonomy of this approach is appealing, it may fail to cover all of the necessary issues, and can lead to poor policy distribution, management, and enforcement.

The single comprehensive ISSP is centrally managed and controlled. With formal procedures for the management of ISSPs in place, the comprehensive policy approach establishes guidelines for overall coverage of necessary issues and clearly identifies processes for the dissemination, enforcement, and review of these guidelines. Usually, these policies are developed by those responsible for managing the information technology resources. Unfortunately, because of their attempt to be all inclusive, these policies may overgeneralize and miss important issues. Because the comprehensive ISSP addresses so many issues, keeping it up to date can be a very complex process with various pieces undergoing revision at different times. One wry complaint often heard about the comprehensive ISSP is "it will be a great policy IF we ever finish it." So, be prepared. It will never be finished, but remain in flux by being constantly updated to meet the needs of organizational change.

The optimal balance between the independent and comprehensive ISSP is the modular ISSP. It is also centrally managed and controlled but tailored to the individual technology issues. The modular approach provides a balance between issue orientation and policy management. The policies created with this approach comprise individual modules, each created and updated by individuals responsible for the issues addressed. These individuals report to a central policy administration group that incorporates specific issues into an overall comprehensive policy.

Table 18-1 is an outline of a sample ISSP, which can be used as a model. An organization should add to this structure the specific details that dictate security procedures not covered by these general guidelines.

The components of each of the major categories presented in the sample issue-specific policy shown in Table 18-1 are discussed below. Even though the details may vary from policy to policy and some sections of a modular policy may be combined, it is essential for management to address and complete each section.

TABLE 18-1 Considerations for an Effective Telecommunications Use Policy

1. Statement of policy
   a. Scope and applicability
   b. Definition of technology addressed
   c. Responsibilities

2. Authorized access and usage of equipment
   a. User access
   b. Fair and responsible use
   c. Protection of privacy

3. Prohibited usage of equipment
   a. Disruptive use or misuse
   b. Criminal use
   c. Offensive or harassing materials
   d. Copyrighted, licensed, or other intellectual property
   e. Other restrictions

4. Systems management
   a. Management of stored materials
   b. Employer monitoring
   c. Virus protection
   d. Physical security
   e. Encryption

5. Violations of policy
   a. Procedures for reporting violations
   b. Penalties for violations

6. Policy review and modification
   a. Scheduled review of policy and procedures for modification

7. Limitations of liability
   a. Statements of liability or disclaimers

Statement of Policy

The policy should begin with a clear statement of purpose. Consider a policy that covers the issue of fair and responsible Internet use. The introductory section of this policy should outline these topics: What is the scope of this policy? Who is responsible and accountable for policy implementation? What technologies and issues does it address?

Authorized Access and Usage of Equipment

This section of the policy statement addresses *who* can use the technology governed by the policy, and *what* it can be used for. Remember that an organization's information systems are the exclusive property of the organization, and users have no particular rights of use. Each technology and process is provided for business operations. Use for any other purpose may constitute misuse of equipment and services. This section defines "fair and responsible use," and should also address key legal issues, such as protection of personal information and privacy.

Prohibited Use of Equipment

Unless a particular use is clearly prohibited, the organization cannot penalize its employees for misuse. The following can be prohibited: personal use, disruptive use or misuse, criminal use, offensive or harassing materials, and infringement of copyrighted, licensed, or other intellectual property. As an alternative approach, categories 2 and 3 of Table 18-1 can be collapsed into a single category—appropriate use. Many organizations use an ISSP titled "Appropriate Use" to cover both categories.

Systems Management

The systems management section of the ISSP policy statement focuses on the users' relationship to systems management. Specific rules from management include regulating the use of e-mail, the storage of materials, authorized monitoring of employees, and the physical and electronic scrutiny of e-mail and other electronic documents. It is important that all such responsibilities are clearly assigned to either the systems administrator or the users, otherwise both parties may infer that the responsibility belongs to the other party.

Rights and Wrongs

Sometimes the view develops that policy is a "tail-covering" activity to assure the organization is not held responsible for the actions of its employees. While this can be one use of policy, it is far from an optimal use. Remember that the purpose of policy is to clearly state management's intention of what should be done. This should embrace both the desired behavior as well as the consequences of undesired behavior. We clearly want employees, contractors, etc., to know what they should do in a given situation and this is the best use of policy.

Do not let yourself fall into the trap of defining long lists of punitive measures for violations without spending equal (or even more) time communicating what is the desired behavior.

Violations of Policy

Once guidelines have been outlined and responsibilities have been assigned, the individuals to whom the policy applies must understand the consequences of violating the policy. Violations of policy should carry appropriate, not draconian, penalties. This section of the policy statement should contain not only the specifics of the penalties for each category of violation but also instructions on how individuals in the organization can report observed or suspected violations. Many people think that powerful individuals in the organization can discriminate, single out, or otherwise retaliate against someone who reports violations. Allowing anonymous submissions is often the only way to convince users to report the unauthorized activities of other, more influential employees.

Policy Review and Modification

Because policy must evolve with the organization it supports, each policy should contain procedures and a timetable for periodic review. As the needs and technologies change in the organization, so must the policies that govern their use. This section should contain a specific methodology for the review and modification of the policy, to assure that the policy stays current and does not become a virtual appendix that is routinely ignored because it is obsolete.

Limitations of Liability

If an employee is caught conducting illegal activities with organizational equipment or assets, management does not want the organization held liable. So the policy should state that if employees violate a company policy or any law using company technologies, the company will not defend them, and will not assume liability for their actions. It is inferred that such a violation would be without knowledge or authorization by the organization.

SYSTEM-SPECIFIC SECURITY POLICY (SysSP)

While issue-specific policies are formalized as written documents readily identifiable as policy, system-specific security policies (SysSPs) sometimes have a different look. SysSPs often function as instructions or procedures to be used when configuring or maintaining systems. For example, a SysSP might describe the configuration and operation of a network firewall, encryption applicance, etc. This document could include a statement of managerial intent and guidance on selection, configuration, and operation. SysSPs can be separated into two general groups, **managerial guidance** and **technical specifications**, or they can be combined into a single policy document.

Managerial Guidance SysSPs

A managerial guidance SysSP document is created by management to guide the implementation and configuration of technology as well as to address the behavior of people in the organization in ways that support the security of information. For example, while the method for implementing a firewall belongs in the technical specifications SysSP, the firewall's configuration must follow guidelines established by management. For example, the firewall must block all incoming traffic not expressly permitted and required for an authorized business function.

Firewalls are not the only technology that may require system-specific policies. Another example policy would be that all public key encryption (PKI) certificates used in the organization must be traceable to the organization's root certificate.

Any system that affects the confidentiality, integrity, or availability of information must be assessed to evaluate the trade-off between improved the business impact of appropriate restrictions and the improvements in security posture those restrictions provide. System-specific policies can be developed at the same time as ISSPs, or they can be prepared in advance of their related ISSPs. Before management can craft a policy informing users what they can do with the technology and how they are supposed to do it, it might be necessary for system administrators to configure and operate the system. Some organizations may prefer to develop ISSPs and SysSPs in tandem, so that operational procedures and user guidelines are created simultaneously.

Why do we need managerial guidance SysSPs? Suppose a technician from an academic institution where the general protection focus was on the free and open exchange of information was recently hired at a major DOD contract or organization manufacturing remote guidance systems for missiles. If a new firewall came in, and the new technician was asked to configure it, he or she may use their personal experiences to configure the device—with few restrictions or prohibitions. This would be completely counter to the ultra-strict security posture desired at the contractor organization. Clear and specific guidance from management on how the system should be configured will prevent potentially costly mistakes.

Technical Specifications SysSPs

While a manager can work with a systems administrator to create managerial policy as described in the preceding section, the system administrator may in turn need to create a policy to implement the managerial policy. Each type of equipment requires its own set of policies, which are used to translate the management intent for the technical control into an enforceable technical approach. For example, an ISSP may require that user passwords be changed quarterly; a systems administrator can implement a technical control to enforce this policy. Another ISSP might mandate access controls for critical information (a configuration file) or interfaces (such as the management port on a network router). There are two general methods of implementing such technical controls: access control lists and configuration rules.

Access Control Lists
Access control lists (ACLs) consist of the user access lists, matrices, and capability tables that govern the rights and privileges of users. ACLs can control access to file storage systems, software components, or network communications devices. A capability table specifies which subjects and objects users or groups can access; in some systems, capability tables are called user profiles or user policies. These specifications frequently take the form of complex matrices, rather than simple lists or tables. The access control matrix includes a combination of tables and lists, such that organizational assets are listed along the column headers, while users are listed along the row headers. The resulting matrix contains ACLs in columns for a particular device or asset, while a row would contain the capability table for a particular user.

Most operating systems translate ACLs into sets of configurations that administrators use to control access to their systems. The level of detail may differ from system to system, but in general ACLs can restrict access for a particular user, computer, time, duration—even a particular file. This specificity provides powerful control to the administrator. In general ACLs regulate:

- *Who* can use the system
- *What* authorized users can access
- *When* authorized users can access the system
- *Where* authorized users can access the system from

The *who* of ACL access may be determined by a person's identity or by a person's membership in a group. Restricting *what* authorized users are permitted to access—whether by type (printers, files, communication devices, or applications), name, or location—is achieved by adjusting the resource privileges for a person or group to one of read, write, create, modify, delete, compare, or copy. To control *when* access is allowed, some organizations implement time-of-day and/or day-of-week restrictions for some network or system resources. To control *where* resources can be accessed from, many network-connected assets block remote usage and also have some levels of access that are restricted to locally connected users. When these various ACL options are applied concurrently, the organization has the ability to govern how its resources can be used.

Configuration Rule Policies Configuration rule policies are the specific instructions entered into a security system that govern how it reacts to the data it receives. Rule-based policies are more specific to the operation of a system than ACLs are, and they may or may not deal with users directly. Many security systems, for example, firewalls, intrusion detection systems (IDSs), and proxy servers, use specific configuration scripts that represent the configuration rule policy to determine how the system handles each data element they process.

Combination SysSPs

Many organizations create a single document that combines the management guidance SysSP and the technical specifications SysSP. While this document can be somewhat confusing to casual users, it is practical to have the guidance from both managerial and technical perspectives in a single place. If this approach is employed, care should be taken to clearly articulate the required actions. Some might consider this type of policy document a procedure, but it is actually a hybrid that combines policy with procedural guidance for the convenience of the implementers of the system being managed. This approach is best used by organizations that have multiple technical control systems of different types, and by smaller organizations that are seeking to document policy and procedure in a compact format.

Keep in mind that the management guidance SysSP will change much less frequently than the technology dependent technical specifications SysSP (which, for example, might change with each new release of router firmware).

This chapter has followed the implementation of the EISP in the much more focused and specific ISSPs and SysSPs. The intent of these policies is to guide employees, contractors, etc., in behaving in accordance with management's intention of what should be done and ensuring that failure to follow that guidance has appropriate consequences.

Because these policies are more specific, they will need to be subject to more frequent review to assure that they continue to be relevant to the business of the evolving organization.

The Information Security Manager's Checklist

	This topic has been fully tested, validated, and integrated into organizational operations with formal performance measures in place (as appropriate).				
	This topic has been implemented, but not fully tested, validated, and integrated into organizational operations.				
	The implementation of this topic has begun, but is not yet complete.				
	The formal planning for this topic has begun, but is not yet complete.				
	This subject has not formally begun planning, or the organization has made a conscious decision not to pursue this topic.				
18. InfoSec Policy Types	No	Planned	In Progress	In Place	Integrated
Organization-wide security policy contains appropriate components					
Appropriate issue-specific security policies developed with needed components					
Needed system-specific security policies developed with appropriate components					

For Further Reading

An Introduction to Computer Security: The NIST Handbook, SP 800-12, U.S. National Institute of Standards and Technology, 1995.

Management of Information Security by Michael Whitman and Herbert Mattord, Cengage/Course Technology, 2010.

Reference

1. National Institute of Standards and Technology. *An Introduction to Computer Security: The NIST Handbook.* SP 800-12.

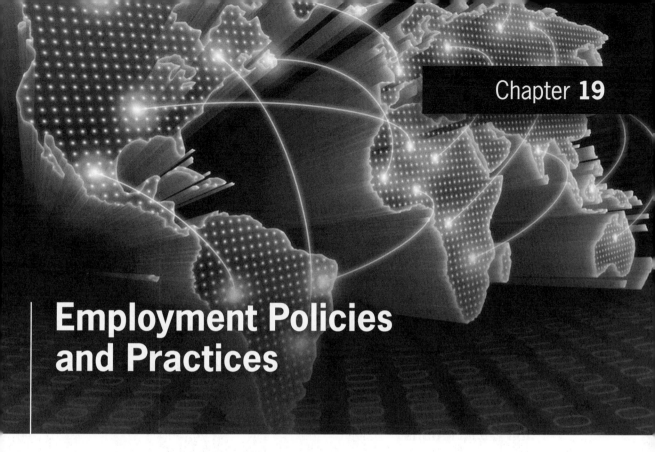

Employment Policies and Practices

Chapter **19**

For you to ensure that information security is taken seriously in your organization, make information security a documented part of every employee's job description. In other words, have solid information security concepts integrated into your organization's employment policies and practices. The chapter that follows examines the important information security–related issues associated with recruiting, hiring, firing, and managing human resources in an organization.

Chapter Overview:

► Personnel and security
► Security considerations for nonemployees
► Internal control strategies
► Privacy and the security of personnel data

Fixing technology is fairly easy, but changing the way people behave is hard. This is why many people are convinced that "security is a people problem rather than a technology problem." Technology does matter, but it is a lot easier for an attacker to "social engineer" a way into an organization or to retrieve confidential information discarded in a dumpster than to compromise a heavily defended network.

Attackers are creatures of opportunity and will exploit any weakness in an organization's defenses whether that be an improperly configured router or an employee who doesn't shred confidential waste. For this reason, proper employee behavior is critical, and ensuring this proper behavior starts during the hiring process.

PERSONNEL AND SECURITY

From an information security perspective, the hiring of employees is a responsibility laden with potential security pitfalls. Therefore, the CISO and information security manager should establish a dialogue with the human resources department to provide information security input to the guidelines used for hiring all personnel.

Job Descriptions

The process of integrating information security perspectives into the hiring process begins with reviewing and updating all job descriptions. To prevent people from applying for positions based solely on access to sensitive information, the organization should avoid revealing access privileges to prospective employees when it advertises open positions. This can be somewhat tricky as statements such as "must pass criminal background check" or "must pass security clearance" in a position posting are pretty clear indications that sensitive information is involved yet are required to assure the proper pool of candidates.

Interviews

Some interviews with job candidates are conducted with members of the human resources staff, and others include members of the department for which the new position is being offered. A very common practice is for the HR department to "vet" applications against the requirements from the position description and then pass only those qualified applicants on to the hiring manager. An opening within the information security department creates a unique opportunity for the security manager to educate HR on the various certifications and the specific experience each certification requires, as well as the qualifications of a good candidate. In all other areas of the organization, information security should, for the same reason mentioned during the discussion of job descriptions, advise HR to limit the information provided to the candidate about the responsibilities and access rights that the new hire would have. For those organizations that include on-site visits as part of their initial or follow-up interviews, it is important to exercise caution when showing a candidate around the facility. Avoid tours through secure and restricted sites. Candidates who are shown around may be able to retain enough information about the operations or information security functions to become a threat.

Background Checks

Some sort of background check should be conducted during the hiring process. These checks come in all shapes and sizes ranging from fairly simple public records checks that look for criminal records to extensive reviews that investigate credit histories, verify qualifications and experience, etc. The reason why background checks are very important from a security perspective is that employees are "insiders" and regardless of their level within the organization enjoy access to facilities and information not available to the general public. Past behavior (such as a criminal record) can indicate a likelihood of future criminal behavior. There are a number of government regulations that govern what the organization can investigate, and how much of the information uncovered can be allowed to influence the hiring decision. The security manager and HR manager should discuss these matters with legal counsel to determine what state and federal (and perhaps international) regulations impact the hiring process.

The level of detail in a background check should reflect the level of trust placed in the position. For example, in the Department of Defense and the military, background checks determine the individual's level of security classification, a requirement for many positions. People being considered for security positions should expect to be subjected to a moderately high-level background check. Those considering careers in law enforcement or high-security positions may even be required to submit to polygraph tests. The following is a list of various types of background checks with the type of information each looks into:

- Identity checks: Validation of identity and Social Security number
- Education and credential checks: Validation of institutions attended, degrees and certifications earned, and certification status
- Previous employment verification: Validation of where candidates worked, why they left, what they did, and for how long
- Reference checks: Validation of references and integrity of reference sources
- Worker's compensation history: Investigation of claims from worker's compensation
- Motor vehicle records: Investigation of driving records, suspensions, and DUIs
- Drug history: Screening for drugs and drug usage, past and present
- Credit history: Investigation of credit problems, financial problems, and bankruptcy
- Civil court history: Investigation of involvement as the plaintiff or defendant in civil suits
- Criminal court history: Investigation of criminal background, arrests, convictions, and time served

As mentioned, there are federal regulations regarding the use of personal information in employment practices, including the Fair Credit Reporting Act (FCRA), which governs the activities of consumer credit reporting agencies and the uses of the information procured from these agencies.[1] These credit reports generally contain information on a job candidate's credit history, employment history, and other personal data.

Among other things, the FCRA prohibits employers from obtaining these reports unless the candidate is informed in writing that such a report will be requested as part of the employment process. FCRA also allows the candidate to request information on the nature and type of reporting used in the making of the employment decision and subsequently enables the candidate to learn the content of these reports. The FCRA also restricts the periods of time these reports can address. If the candidate earns less than $75,000 per year, the report can contain only seven years' worth of negative credit information. If the candidate earns $75,000 or more per year, there is no time limitation. Note that "any person who knowingly and willfully obtains information on a consumer from a consumer reporting agency under false pretenses shall be fined under title 18, United States Code, imprisoned for not more than two years, or both."[2]

Employment Contracts

Once a candidate has accepted a job offer, the employment contract becomes an important security instrument. Many of the policies discussed in previous chapters, specifically the ISSPs, require an employee to agree in writing to monitoring and nondisclosure agreements. If an existing employee refuses to sign these contracts, the security personnel are placed in a difficult situation. They may not be able to force the employee to sign, nor to deny the employee access to the systems necessary to perform his or her duties. With new employees, however, security personnel are in a different situation provided the procedural step of policy acknowledgment is to be made a condition of employment. Policies that govern employee behavior and are applied to all employees may be classified as "employment contingent upon agreement." This classification means the employee is not actually employed until he or she agrees in a written affidavit to comply with these binding organizational policies. Some organizations choose to execute the remainder of the employment contract *after* the candidate has signed the security agreements. Although this may seem harsh, it is a necessary component of the security process. Employment contracts may also contain restrictive clauses regarding the creation and ownership of intellectual property while the candidate is employed by the organization. These provisions may require the employee to protect the information assets of the organization actively—especially those assets that are critical to security.

New Hire Orientation

When new employees are introduced into the organization's culture and workflow, they should receive as part of their employee orientation an extensive information security briefing. All major policies should be explained, along with the procedures for performing necessary security operations and the new position's other information security requirements. In addition, the levels of authorized access should be outlined for the new employees, and training should be provided to them regarding the secure use of information systems. By the time new employees are ready to report to their positions, they should have been thoroughly briefed on the security component of their particular jobs, as well as the rights and responsibilities of all personnel in the organization.

On-the-Job Security Training

Encourage your organization to integrate security awareness education as described in Chapter 5 into a new hire's ongoing job orientation, and make it a part of every employee's on-the-job security training. Keeping security at the forefront of employees' minds helps minimize employee mistakes and is, therefore, an important part of the information security team's mission. Formal external and informal internal seminars should also be used to increase the security awareness level of employees, especially that of security employees. An example of the importance of proper and ongoing security training awareness of employees can be found in *The 9/11 Commission Report*, which is a congressional examination (published in 2004) of the terrorist attacks of September 11, 2001. As the following excerpt shows, upon reviewing the videotapes made at the security checkpoints in airports when the terrorists were passing through, security investigators found the security process inadequate, not from a technological standpoint, but from a human one:

> When the local civil aviation security office of the Federal Aviation Administration (FAA) later investigated these security screening operations, the screeners recalled nothing out of the ordinary. They could not recall that any of the passengers they screened were CAPPS selectees. We asked a screening expert to review the videotape of the hand-wanding, and he found the quality of the screener's work to have been "marginal at best." The screener should have "resolved" what set off the alarm; and in the case of both Moqed and Hazmi, it was clear that he did not.[3]

This excerpt illustrates how physical security is dependent on the human element. The maintenance of information security also depends heavily on the consistent vigilance of people. In many information security breaches, the hardware and software usually accomplished what they were designed to do, but people failed to make the correct decisions and follow-up choices. Education and regular training of employees and authorized users are important elements of information security—and therefore cannot be ignored.

Evaluating Performance

To heighten information security awareness and minimize workplace behavior that poses risks to information security, you should also have information security components incorporated into employee performance evaluations. For example, if employees have been observed writing system passwords on notes stuck to their monitor, they should be warned, and if such behavior continues, they should be reminded of their failure to comply with the organization's information security regulations during their annual performance review. In general, employees pay close attention to job performance evaluations, and are more likely to be motivated to take information security seriously if their performance with respect to information security tasks and responsibilities is documented in these evaluations.

Termination

Leaving the organization may or may not be a decision made by the employee. Organizations may downsize, be bought out or taken over, shut down, run out of business, or simply be forced to lay off, fire, or relocate their workforce. In any event, when an employee leaves an organization, there are a number of security-related issues that arise. Key among these is the continuity of protection of all information to which the employee had access. Therefore, when an employee prepares to leave an organization, the following tasks must be performed:

- ▸ Access to the organization's systems must be disabled.
- ▸ Removable media must be returned.
- ▸ Hard drives must be secured.
- ▸ File cabinet locks must be changed.
- ▸ Office door lock must be changed.
- ▸ Keycard access must be revoked.
- ▸ Personal effects must be removed from the organization's premises.

After the employee has delivered keys, keycards, and other business property, he or she should be escorted from the premises.

Preserving Information

We live in a litigious society and an important part of the termination process is to assure that the organization retains copies of information in the former employee's possession that may be or may become relevant to a legal action. In times past, it was sufficient to just wipe and reinstall a formal employee's workstation or laptop and then reissue it to someone else.

However, with the increased awareness of electronically stored information (ESI) in the legal process,

the organization must carefully consider its responsibilities for preserving information or it may find itself facing severe sanctions for spoliation of relevant information.

Many organizations as part of their exit process now collect disk images of employee digital assets (workstation, laptop, etc.) and hold them for a period of time to assure they will not become relevant to a pending or future litigation.

In addition to the tasks listed above, many organizations use an **exit interview** to remind the employee of contractual obligations, such as nondisclosure agreements, and to obtain feedback on the employee's tenure in the organization. At this time, the employee should be reminded that should he or she fail to comply with contractual obligations, civil or criminal action may be initiated.

In reality, most employees are allowed to clean out their own offices and collect their personal belongings, and simply asked to return their keys. From a security standpoint, these procedures are/would be considered risky and lax, for they expose the organization's information to disclosure and theft. To minimize such risks, an organization should ideally have security-minded termination procedures that are followed consistently—in other words, they are followed regardless of what level of trust the organization had placed in the employee and what level of cordiality is generally maintained in the office environment. But this kind of universally consistent approach is a difficult and awkward practice to implement (which is why it's not often applied). Given the realities of workplaces, the simplest and best method for handling the outprocessing of an employee may be to select, based on the employee's reasons for leaving, one of the scenarios that follows.

Hostile Departures

Hostile departures include termination for cause, permanent downsizing, temporary layoff, or leaving to work for a competitor. Before the employee knows that he or she is leaving, or as soon as the hostile resignation is tendered, the security staff should terminate all logical and keycard access. In the case of involuntary terminations, the employee should be escorted into the supervisor's office for the bad news. Upon receiving the termination notice, or tendering a hostile resignation, the employee should be escorted to his or her office, cubicle, or personal area and allowed to collect personal effects. No organizational property should be allowed to be taken from the premises, including company-owned digital media, pens, papers, and books. Regardless of the claim the employee has on organizational property, he or she should not be allowed to take it from the premises. If there is property that the employee strongly wishes to retain, the employee

Commingling of Information

As our society becomes more digital, the possibility of organizational information on personal equipment becomes a real problem in the termination process. Sorting out which information on an employee's PDA, memory stick, or smartphone belongs to the organization and which is private can be a nightmare.

As with many other things in the security world, it is better to deal with the issue in advance through both policy and the provision of all *needed* equipment at organization expense. Organizations should carefully consider their needs in this area and assure that employment agreements and accepted policies assure that the organization will be able to retrieve its information from employee-owned assets without running afoul of "expectation of privacy" barriers.

should be informed that he or she can submit, in writing, a list of the particular items and the reasons why he or she should be allowed to retain them. After the employee's personal property has been gathered, the employee should be asked to surrender all company property such as (but not limited to) keys, keycards, organizational identification, physical access devices, PDAs, pagers, cell phones, and portable computers. The employee should then be escorted out of the building.

Friendly Departures *Friendly departures* include resignation, retirement, promotion, or relocation. In this case, the employee may have tendered notice well in advance of the actual departure date. This scenario actually makes it much more difficult for the security team to maintain positive control over the employee's access and information usage. Employee accounts are usually allowed to continue to exist, though an expiration date can be set for the employee's declared date of departure. Another complication associated with friendly departures is that until their departure date employees can come and go at will, which means they are usually collecting their own belongings and leaving under their own cognizance. As with hostile departures, employees should be asked to drop off all organizational property on their final way out and usually sign a written agreement that they have returned or destroyed all company information in their possession.

In either circumstance (hostile or friendly), the offices and information used by the employee must be inventoried, files must be stored or destroyed, and all property must be returned to organizational stores. It is possible in either situation that the employees foresee their departure well in advance and, perhaps thinking that such items may be valuable in their future employment, start taking home organizational information such as files, reports, and data from databases. This may be impossible to prevent. Only by scrutinizing systems logs after the employee has departed and sorting out authorized actions from systems misuse or information theft can the organization determine if there has been a breach of policy or a loss of information. In the event that information is illegally copied or stolen, the action should be declared an incident and the appropriate policy followed.

SECURITY CONSIDERATIONS FOR NONEMPLOYEES

Contractors, temporary employees, business partners, vendor service personnel, etc., who are not subject to rigorous screening, contractual obligations, and eventual secured termination, often have access to sensitive organizational information. As outlined in the sections that follow, relationships with individuals in this category should be carefully managed to prevent a possible information leak or theft.

Temporary Employees

Temporary employees are hired by the organization to serve in a temporary position or to supplement the existing workforce. These employees do not work for the organization where they are performing their duties, but instead are usually the paid employees of a "temp agency" or organization that provides qualified individuals at the paid request of another company. Temps typically provide secretarial or administrative support, and thus may be exposed to a wide range of information. As they are not employed by the host organization, they are often not subject to the contractual obligations or general policies of other employees. If temps violate a policy or cause a problem, the strongest action the host organization can take is to terminate the relationships and request that they be censured. The employing agency is under no contractual obligation to do this, however, though it may censure the employee to appease an important client.

From a security standpoint, temporary employees' access to information should be limited to that which is necessary for them to perform their duties. The organization can attempt to have temporary employees sign nondisclosure agreements and fair use policies, but the temp agency may refuse, forcing the host organization to choose between arranging for a new temp agency, going without the assistance of a temp worker, or allowing the temp to work without the agreement. This can create a potentially awkward and dangerous situation, as temporary workers may inadvertently gain access to information that does not directly relate to their responsibilities. The only way to combat this threat is to ensure that the temp's supervisor restricts the information to which the temp has access and makes sure all employees follow good security practices, especially clean desk policies and the security of classified data. Temps can provide great benefits to the host organization, but should not be employed at the cost of sacrificing information security.

Contract Employees

Contract employees are typically hired to perform specific services for the organization. In such cases, the host company often makes a contract with a parent organization rather than with an individual for a particular task. Typical contract employees include groundskeepers, maintenance service people, electrical contractors, mechanical service contractors, and other service repair people. Although some individuals may require access to virtually all areas of the organization to do their jobs, they seldom need access to information or information resources, except in the case where the organization has leased computing equipment or has contracted with a disaster recovery service. Contract employees may also need access to various facilities, but this does not mean they should be allowed to wander freely in and out of buildings. To maintain a secure facility, all contract employees should be escorted from room to room, as well as into and out of the facility. When these employees report for maintenance or repair services, the first step security personnel should take is to verify that these services are actually scheduled or called for. As indicated in earlier chapters, it is not unheard of for an attacker to dress up as a telephone repairman, maintenance technician, or janitor to gain physical access to a building, and therefore, direct supervision of contract employees is a necessity.

Another necessary aspect of hiring contract employees is making certain that restrictions or requirements are negotiated into the contract agreements when they are activated. The following regulations should be negotiated well in advance: The facility requires twenty-four to forty-eight hours notice of a maintenance visit; the facility requires all on-site personnel to undergo background checks; and the facility requires advance notice for cancellation or rescheduling of a maintenance visit.

Consultants

Sometimes on-site contracted employees are self-employed or they are employees of an organization hired for a specific, one-time purpose. These people are typically referred to as consultants, and they have their own security requirements and contractual obligations. Consultants should have all specific requirements for information or facility access integrated into their contracts before these individuals are allowed into the workplace. Security and technology consultants especially must be prescreened, escorted, and subjected to nondisclosure agreements to protect the organization from possible intentional or accidental breaches of confidentiality. It is human nature (and a trait often found among consultants) to brag about the complexity of a particular job or an outstanding service provided to another client. If the organization does not want the consultant to mention its relationship with the consultant, or to disclose the least detail about its particular system configuration, the organization must write these restrictions into the contractual agreement. It should be noted that consultants typically request permission to present their work to other companies as part of their resumes, but a client organization is not obligated to grant this permission and can even explicitly deny permission in writing. Organizations should also remember that just because they are paying an information security consultant, this doesn't mean the protection of their information is the consultant's number one priority.

Business Partners

On occasion, businesses find themselves in strategic alliances with other organizations wishing to exchange information, integrate systems, or simply discuss operations for mutual advantage. In these situations, there must be a prior business agreement that specifies the level of exposure both organizations are willing to endure. Sometimes, one division of a company enters a strategic partnership with an organization that directly competes with another one of the company's own divisions. If the strategic partnership evolves into an integration of the systems of both companies, there is a chance that competing groups may exchange information that neither parent organization expected to share. As a result, there must be a meticulous, deliberate process of determining what information is to be exchanged, in what format, and to whom. Nondisclosure agreements must be in place. And as discussed in earlier chapters, the level of security of both systems must be examined before any physical integration takes place, because when systems are connected, the vulnerability of any one system becomes the vulnerability of all.

INTERNAL CONTROL STRATEGIES

Among several internal control strategies, separation of duties is a cornerstone in the protection of information assets and in the prevention of financial loss. **Separation of duties** is used to reduce the chance of an individual violating information security and breaching the confidentiality, integrity, or availability of information. The control stipulates that the completion of a significant task that involves sensitive information should require at least two people, neither of which can perform the task alone. The idea behind this separation is that if only one person had the authorization to access a particular set of information, there may be nothing the organization can do to prevent this individual from copying the information and removing it from the premises. Separation of duties is especially important, and thus commonly implemented, when the information in question is financial. Consider, for example, how in a bank two people are required to issue a cashier's check. The first is authorized to prepare the check, acquire the numbered financial document, and ready the check for signature. The process then requires a second person, usually a supervisor, to sign the check. Only then can the check be issued. If one person had the authority to perform both functions, that person could write a number of checks, sign them, and steal large sums from the bank. The same level of control should be applied to critical data. One person may create updates for the system while another person must actually apply those updates to the production environment. Or, a critical cryptographic key could be split into two halves and given to two separate individuals—each must install their half of the key before the new key can take effect.

Related to the concept of separation of duties is that of **two-man control**, the requirement that two individuals review and approve each other's work before the task is categorized as finished. This is distinct from separation of duties, in which the two people work in sequence. In two-man control, each person completely finishes the necessary work, and then submits it to the other coworker. Each coworker then examines the work performed, double-checking the actions performed, and making sure no errors or inconsistencies exist. Figure 19-1 illustrates these operations.

Another control used to prevent personnel from misusing information assets is job rotation. **Job rotation** or **task rotation** is the requirement that every employee be able to perform the work of

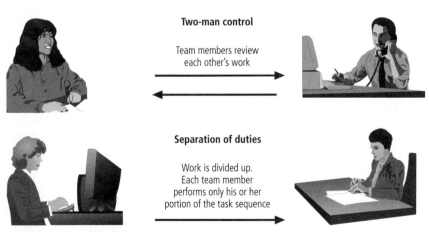

Two-man control

Team members review each other's work

Separation of duties

Work is divided up. Each team member performs only his or her portion of the task sequence

Figure 19-1 Internal Control Strategies
Course Technology/Cengage Learning

another employee. If it is not feasible that one employee learn the entire job of another, then the organization should at least try to ensure that for each critical task it has multiple individuals on staff that are capable of performing it. Job or task rotations such as these can greatly increase the chance that an employee's misuse of the system or abuse of the information will be detected by another. They also ensure that no one employee is performing actions that cannot be physically audited by another employee. In general, this method makes good business sense. One threat to information is the inability of an organization to perform the tasks of one employee in the event that the employee is unable or unwilling to perform his or her duties. If everyone knows at least part of the job of another person (thus serves, in effect, as part of a human Redundant Array of Independent Disks (RAID) system), the organization can survive the loss of any one employee.

This leads to a control measure that may seem surprising: mandatory vacations. Why should a company *require* its employees to take vacations? A mandatory vacation, of at least one week, provides the organization with the ability to audit the work of an individual. Individuals who are stealing from the organization or otherwise misusing information or systems are, in general, reluctant to take vacations, for fear that their actions will be detected. Therefore, all employees should be required to take at least one one-week vacation, so that their jobs can be audited. All this is not meant to imply that employees are untrustworthy, but rather to show how organizations must be creative—even consider the security situation as a potential attacker would—with the control measures they apply. The mandatory vacation policy is effective because it ensures that employees who want to abuse the system know that there is a strong probability of being caught. Information security professionals who think this practice impugns the character of their coworkers should note that in some industries bonding authorities, auditing agencies, or oversight boards not only require mandatory vacations, but apply this requirement universally (i.e., to all employees).

One final control measure: Employees should be provided access to the minimal amount of information for the minimal amount of time necessary for them to perform their duties. In other words, there is no need for everyone in the organization to have access to all information. This principle is called **least privilege**. Similar to the concept of need-to-know, least privilege ensures that no unnecessary access to data exists, and that only those individuals who must access the data do so. The whole purpose of information security is to allow those people with a need to use the information contained in a given system to do so without being concerned about the system's ability to maintain the confidentiality, integrity, and availability of the information. Organizations should keep in mind that everyone who can access data probably will, and that such a situation can have devastating consequences for the organization's information security.

PRIVACY AND THE SECURITY OF PERSONNEL DATA

Organizations are required by law to protect employee information that is sensitive or personal, as you learned in Chapter 3. This includes employee addresses, phone numbers, Social Security numbers, medical conditions, and even names and addresses of family members. While personnel data is, in principle, no different from other data that an organization's information security group must protect, there is a great deal more regulation covering its protection. As a result, information security groups should ensure that this data receives at least the same level of protection as does the other important data in the organization—such as intellectual property, strategic planning, and other business-critical information.

Many security surveys and reviews of actual security incidents have shown that one of the largest threats to an organization is the organization's own employees, contractors, etc. While employees may "go bad" only rarely, when they do, their access to the organization can create a huge impact. For this reason, security must be an integral part of the hiring process to assure that the organization minimizes its risk. One of the significant components in minimizing this risk is education in what the new employees' responsibilities are regarding information security and assuring those responsibilities are understood.

The risk arising from employee behavior does not end with the hiring decision and important techniques such as separation of duties, least privilege, and job rotation should be applied to security-significant operations within the organization. Similarly, security concerns must play an active role in the termination process to assure that insider access is terminated and all organization assets are returned to its control.

The Information Security Manager's Checklist

	No	Planned	In Progress	In Place	Integrated
This topic has been fully tested, validated, and integrated into organizational operations with formal performance measures in place (as appropriate).					
This topic has been implemented, but not fully tested, validated, and integrated into organizational operations.					
The implementation of this topic has begun, but is not yet complete.					
The formal planning for this topic has begun, but is not yet complete.					
This subject has not formally begun planning, or the organization has made a conscious decision not to pursue this topic.					
19. Personnel Security					
All jobs reviewed for least privilege/need to know					
HR Hiring process reviewed by InfoSec					
Appropriate background checks on employees and applicants					
Termination procedures					
Employee actions auditable					

For Further Reading

Information Security Policies Made Easy Version 11 by Charles Cresson Wood, Information Shield, 2009.

Background Checks: A Guide for HR, Security, and Investigations by Ted L. Moss, CRC Press, 2011.

References

1. Background Check International, LLC. "BCI," *BCI Online*. Accessed 7 July 2007 from *www.bcint .com/legal.html*.

2. Federal Trade Commission. *Fair Credit Reporting Act,* 2002. 15 U.S.C., S. 1681 et seq.

3. *September 11th Commission Final Report*, July 2004.

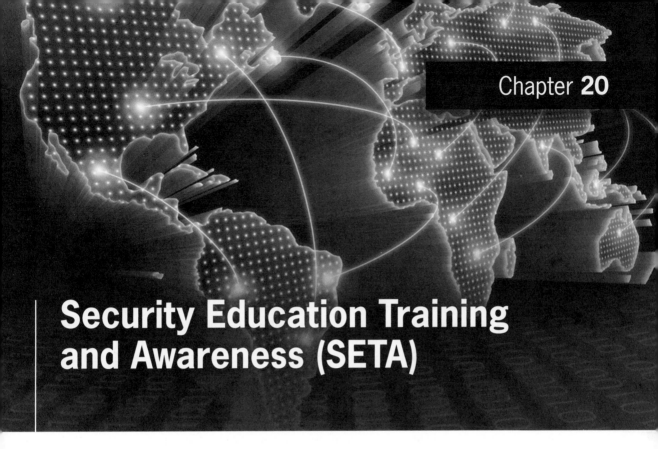

Chapter 20

Security Education Training and Awareness (SETA)

As you may have heard before, a book of the best security policies in the world is useless if all it does is sit on a shelf. In order to repay the time and effort spent in developing policies, they must be brought out of the book and made to affect the behavior of the people within the organization. One of the most effective ways to make this happen is through **security education, training, and awareness (SETA)** programs.

Chapter Overview:

► SETA overview
► Security education
► Security training
► Security awareness

Too many times the SETA program is an endless catalog of all the acts that will get you fired; this misses the point of the SETA program. The SETA program should leave no doubt that violations of security policy are a serious matter with grave consequences but its primary purpose is that none of those consequences will ever come to bear because there will be no policy violations.

The SETA program's goal is to teach employees how to behave in accordance with policy. An effective program will spend most of its training time on how employees should behave in certain situations (based on policy) rather than endlessly cataloging the ways security policy allows an employee to be terminated.

SETA OVERVIEW

The SETA program is the responsibility of the CISO and is designed to reduce the incidence of accidental security breaches by members of the organization, including employees, contractors, consultants, vendors, and business partners who come into contact with its information assets. As mentioned in earlier chapters, *acts of human error or failure* (known generally as *errors*) are among the top threats to information assets.

Awareness, training, and education programs offer three major benefits:

1. They can guide employees to act in accordance with policy.
2. They can inform members of the organization about where to report violations of policy.
3. They enable the organization to hold employees accountable for their actions.

Employee accountability is necessary to ensure that the acts of an individual do not threaten the long-term viability of the entire company. When employees recognize that the organization protects itself by enforcing accountability, they will be less likely to view these programs as punitive. In fact, when an organization does not enforce accountability, it increases the risk of incurring a substantial loss that might cause it to fail, putting the entire workforce out of jobs.

SETA programs enhance general education and training programs by focusing on information security. For example, if an organization finds that many employees are using e-mail attachments in an unsafe manner, then e-mail users must be educated in the safe ways to use e-mail attachments. As a matter of good practice, all systems development life cycles include user training during both the implementation and maintenance phases. Information security projects are no different; they require initial training programs as systems are deployed and occasional retraining as needs arise.

A SETA program consists of three elements: security education, security training, and security awareness. An organization may not be able or willing to undertake the development of all of these components in-house, and may outsource them to local educational institutions or specialized consultancies. The purpose of SETA is to enhance security in three ways:

1. By building in-depth knowledge, as needed, to design, implement, or operate security programs for organizations and systems

TABLE 20-1 Framework of Security Education Training and Awareness

	AWARENESS	TRAINING	EDUCATION
Attribute	"What"	"How"	"Why"
Level	Information	Knowledge	Insight
Objective	Recognition	Skill	Understanding
Teaching Method	▶ Media videos ▶ Newsletters ▶ Posters, Inc.	▶ Practical Instruction lecture ▶ Case study workshop ▶ Hands-on practice	▶ Theoretical Instruction Discussion seminar ▶ Background reading
Test Measure	True/False Multiple Choice (identify learning)	Problem Solving (apply learning)	Essay (interpret learning)
Impact Timeframe	Short-term	Intermediate	Long-term

Source: National Institute of Standards and Technology. An Introduction to Computer Security: The NIST Handbook. *SP 800-12.* http://csrc.nist.gov/publications/nistpubs/800-12/

2. By developing skills and knowledge so that computer users can perform their jobs while using IT systems more securely
3. By improving awareness of the need to protect system resources[1]

Table 20-1 shows the features of security education, training, and awareness within the organization.

SECURITY EDUCATION

Where information security is concerned, some organizations may have employees who are not properly prepared for their roles. These employees should be encouraged to acquire formal education in the area of information security. Resources that describe information security training programs include the NIST training and education site at *http://csrc.nist.gov/groups/SMA/ate/index.html*, the Virginia Alliance for Security Computing and Networking (VA SCAN) at *http://www.vascan.org*, and the National Security Agency (NSA)—identified Centers of Academic Excellence in Information Assurance Education (CAEIAE) at *http://www.nsa.gov/ia/academia/acade00001.cfm*. Local resources might also provide information and services in educational areas. Local companies and/or educational institutions can be used.

Information security training programs must address the following issues:

▶ The information security educational components required of all *information security* professionals

▶ The general educational requirements that all *information technology* professionals must have

A number of institutions of higher learning, including colleges and universities, provide formal coursework in information security. Unfortunately, a recent review found that the majority of information security or computer security degrees (bachelor's or master's) are, in reality, computer science or information systems degrees that include a few courses in information security. While some programs do offer depth and breadth in information security education, prospective students must carefully examine the curriculum before enrolling. Those planning for careers in information security should carefully review the number of courses offered, as well as the content of those courses.

The general IT educational curriculum needs to prepare students to work in an environment that values a secure and ethical computing environment. As noted by Irvin, Chin, and Frinke in the article "Integrating Security into the Curriculum," "An educational system that cultivates an appropriate knowledge of computer security will increase the likelihood that the next generation of IT workers will have the background needed to design and develop systems that are engineered to be reliable and secure."[2]

The need for improved information security education is so great that in May 1998 President Clinton issued Presidential Decision Directive 63, the Policy on Critical Infrastructure Protection. Among other things, the directive required the NSA to establish outreach programs like the CAEIAE. The CAEIAE program goal is "to reduce vulnerabilities in our National Information Infrastructure by promoting higher education in information assurance, and producing a growing number of professionals with IA expertise."[3] These initiatives are intended to increase not only the number of information security professionals, but also the information security awareness and educational knowledge of all technologists.

Developing Information Security Curricula

Hybrid information technology/security programs have emerged to fill the gap created by the lack of formal guidance from established curricula bodies. Established organizations that have developed and promoted standardized curricula, such as the Association of Computing Machinery (ACM), the Institute of Electrical and Electronics Engineers (IEEE), and the Accreditation Board for Engineering and Technology (ABET), do not have formal information security curricula models. For two-year institutions, however, the National Science Foundation (NSF) and the American Association of Community Colleges sponsored a workshop in 2002 that drafted recommendations for a report entitled *The Role of Community Colleges in Cybersecurity Education*. This report serves as a starting point for community colleges developing curricula in the field. A similar effort is currently underway for four-year institutions, but remains in its infancy.

Because many institutions have no frame of reference for which skills and knowledge are required for a particular job area, frequently they refer to the certifications offered in that field. A managerial program would examine certifications like the CISSP, CISM, or GISO; a technical program would examine the specific GIAC or Security+ certifications. A balanced program takes the best of both programs and then maps the knowledge areas from each specialty area backward to specific courses.

Busy professionals may not have time to pursue even part-time coursework at an educational institution and may opt for professional seminars, industry courses, etc. Many of these courses are excellent and immerse the trainee in a saturated presentation of the material. However, this

Outsource or In-House

The decision to develop training in-house or to outsource it is a complex one. Outsourcing to a group of training professionals is an attractive option but needs to be carefully considered. The expense of the training program will depend on the amount of custom material that must be developed—if the organization wants a curriculum tailored to its particular needs, it will pay a premium to support that development. If the organization can select from a menu of predeveloped courseware, this will be much cheaper but will be less relevant to the organization's unique needs. Also the outsourcing of security training will require sharing a lot of information about the security posture and operations of the organization with the outside party.

For these reasons, many organizations decide to develop their own training programs but the capabilities of the organization in developing quality training materials must be carefully evaluated. Unfortunately, the direct and indirect costs of a security incident that was preventable through proper training can easily dwarf the investment in quality outsourced training.

Choosing an option is not always clear-cut but the guiding principle must be which option will most effectively lead to employees acting in accordance with policy?

compressed time frame does have its limitations because there is no way to compress years of university-level coursework into the few weeks of an intense seminar. While the educational institutions have been slow to recognize the need for significant security coursework in their business and technology degree programs, many of them are racing ahead to remedy this lack and an information security professional will overlook the advantages of this resource at the peril of their career development.

SECURITY TRAINING

Security training involves providing members of the organization with detailed information and hands-on instruction to enable them to perform their duties securely. Management of information security can develop customized in-house training or outsource all or part of the training program.

Alternatively, organizations can subsidize or underwrite industry training conferences and programs offered through professional agencies such as SANS (*www.sans.org*), (ISC)2 (*www.isc2 .org*), ISSA (*www.issa.org*), and CSI (*www.gocsi.org*). Many of these programs are too technical for the average employee, but they may be ideal for the continuing education requirements of information security professionals.

A number of resources can help organizations put together SETA programs. The Computer Security Resource Center at NIST, for example, provides several very useful documents free of charge in its special publications area (*http://csrc.nist.gov*). Among the most useful of these documents for information security practitioners and those developing training programs is

NIST Special Publication 800-16 (and the new Draft 800-16, Rev 1). This comprehensive manual with extensive appendices describes training with an emphasis on training criteria or standards, rather than on specific curricula or content. The training criteria are established according to trainees' role(s) within their organizations and are measured by their on-the-job performance. This emphasis on roles and results, rather than on fixed content, gives the training requirements "flexibility, adaptability, and longevity. . . ."[4]

This approach makes the document a durable and useful guide. Although it is directed toward federal agencies and organizations, its overall approach applies to all kinds of organizations: "Federal agencies and organizations cannot protect the integrity, confidentiality, and availability of information in today's highly networked systems environment without ensuring that each person involved understands their roles and responsibilities and is adequately trained to perform them."[5]

Also available from NIST is Special Publication 800-50: *Building an Information Technology Security Awareness and Training Program*, which provides an overview for structuring a complete SETA program.

The Computer Security Act of 1987 requires federal agencies to provide mandatory periodic training in computer security awareness and accepted computer practices to all employees involved with the management, use, or operation of their computer systems. Other federal requirements for computer security training are contained in OMB Circular A-130, Appendix III, and OPM regulations.

Customizing Training by User

Training is most effective when it is designed for a specific category of user. The more closely the training is designed to match specific needs of the user, the more effective it is. Training includes teaching users not only what they should or should not do, but also how they should do it.

There are two methods for customizing training for users. The first is by functional background: general user, managerial user, and technical user. The second is by skill level: novice, intermediate, and advanced. Because traditional training models are accustomed to using skill level as course customization criteria, the more detailed discussion that follows focuses on the development of training by functional area.

Training for General Users
One method of ensuring that policies are read and understood by general users is to provide training on those policies. This strategy allows users to ask questions and receive specific guidance, and it allows the organization to collect the required letters of compliance. These general users also require training on the technical details of how to do their jobs securely, including good security practices, password management, specialized access controls, and violation reporting.

A convenient time to conduct this type of training is during employee orientation. During this critical time, employees are educated on a wide variety of organizational policies and on the expectations that the organization has for its employees. Because employees should have no preconceived notions or established methods of behavior at that point, they are more likely to be receptive to this instruction. This openness is balanced against their lack of familiarity with

"We didn't think of that!"

Though not normally considered as part of the policy review process, user training can be a surprisingly good source of ideas for policy revision. New employees without an extensive indoctrination into "how things are done here" are a good source for areas that were overlooked because of organizational tunnel vision.

Trainers should as a matter of course feed information gleaned from trainee questions and suggestions back into the policy review process. Some of the ideas will be useless but occasionally a true golden nugget will come through.

the systems or their jobs, so any particular issues that they might have questions about will not have arisen yet.

Training for Managerial Users

Management may have the same training requirements as the general user, but managers typically expect a more personal form of training, characterized by smaller groups and more interaction and discussion. In fact, managers often resist organized training of any kind. This is another area in which a champion can exert influence. Support at the executive level can convince managers to attend training events, which in turn reinforces the entire training program.

Management as a Risk

Management, unfortunately, sometimes has the attitude that since they run the organization, they by definition know how to do everything correctly. However, they also have very privileged access to organizational information and other resources and

are becoming a real target for attacks (for example, "spear phishing"). Unless management has a sound grounding in the security policies and the reasons behind them, they can constitute a serious risk to the organization's assets.

Training for Technical Users

Technical training for IT staff, security staff, and technically competent general users is more detailed than general user or managerial training and may therefore require the use of consultants or outside training organizations. There are three methods for selecting or developing advanced technical training:

1. By job category—for example, technical users versus managers
2. By job function—for example, accounting versus marketing versus operations functional areas
3. By technology product—for example, e-mail client, database

Training Techniques

Good training techniques are as essential to successful training as thorough knowledge of the subject area. As explained by Charles Trepper in his article "Training Developers More Efficiently,"

> Using the wrong method can actually hinder the transfer of knowledge and lead to unnecessary expense and frustrated, poorly trained employees. Good training programs, regardless of delivery method, take advantage of the latest learning technologies and best practices. Recent developments include less use of centralized public courses and more on-site training. Training is often needed for one or a few individuals, not necessarily for a large group. Waiting until there is a large-enough group for a class can cost companies lost productivity. Other best practices include the increased use of short, task-oriented modules and training sessions, available during the normal work week, that are immediate and consistent. Newer concepts in training also provide students with the training they need when they need it—a practice often called just-in-time training.[6]

Delivery Methods Selection of the training delivery method is not always based on the best outcome for the trainee. Often other factors—most usually budget, scheduling, and needs of the organization—come first. Table 20-2 lists the most common delivery methods.

Selecting the Training Staff To provide employee training, an organization can use a local training program, a continuing education department, or another external training agency. Alternatively, it can hire a professional trainer, a consultant, or someone from an accredited institution to conduct on-site training. It can also organize and conduct training in-house using its own employees. This last option should not be undertaken without careful consideration. Effective training requires a special set of skills and abilities. Teaching a class of five or more peers (or subordinates) is very different from offering friendly advice to coworkers.

Implementing Training While each organization develops its own strategy based on the techniques discussed above, the following seven-step methodology generally applies:

Step 1: Identify program scope, goals, and objectives.

Step 2: Identify training staff.

Step 3: Identify target audiences.

Step 4: Motivate management and employees.

Step 5: Administer the program.

Step 6: Maintain the program.

Step 7: Evaluate the program.

This methodology, and the material that follows, is drawn from the previously referenced NIST document, SP 800-12: *An Introduction to Computer Security: The NIST Handbook.*

Identify Program Scope, Goals, and Objectives The scope of the security training program should encompass all personnel who interact with information systems. Because users need training that relates directly to their use of particular systems, an organization-wide training program may need to be supplemented by more specific programs targeted at specific groups. Generally, the goal of a security training program is to sustain an appropriate level of protection for computer resources by increasing employee awareness of, and ability to fulfill, computer security responsibilities. More specific goals may need to be established as well. Objectives should be defined to meet the organization's specific goals.

TABLE 20-2 Training Delivery Methods

METHOD	ADVANTAGES	DISADVANTAGES
One-on-One: A dedicated trainer works with each trainee on the areas specified.	▶ Informal ▶ Personal ▶ Customized to the needs of the trainee ▶ Can be scheduled to fit the needs of the trainee	▶ Resource intensive, to the point of being inefficient
Formal Class: A single trainer works with multiple trainees in a formal setting.	▶ Formal training plan, efficient ▶ Trainees can learn from each other ▶ Interaction with trainer is possible ▶ Usually considered cost-effective	▶ Relatively inflexible ▶ May not be sufficiently responsive to the needs of all trainees ▶ Difficult to schedule, especially if more than one session is needed
Computer-Based Training (CBT): Prepackaged software that provides training at the trainee's workstation.	▶ Flexible, no special scheduling requirements ▶ Self-paced, can go as fast or as slow as the trainee needs ▶ Can be very cost-effective	▶ Software can be very expensive ▶ Content may not be customized to the needs of the organization
Distance Learning/Web Seminars: Trainees receive a seminar presentation at their computers. Some models allow teleconferencing for voice feedback; others have text questions and feedback.	▶ Can be live, or can be archived and viewed at the trainee's convenience ▶ Can be low- or no-cost	▶ If archived, can be very inflexible, with no mechanism for trainee feedback ▶ If live, can be difficult to schedule
User Support Group: Support from a community of users is commonly facilitated by a particular vendor as a mechanism to augment the support for products or software.	▶ Allows users to learn from each other ▶ Usually conducted in an informal social setting	▶ Does not use a formal training model ▶ Centered on a specific topic or product
On-the-Job Training: Trainees learn the specifics of their jobs while working, using the software, hardware, and procedures they will continue to use.	▶ Very applied to the task at hand ▶ Inexpensive	▶ A sink-or-swim approach ▶ Can result in substandard work performance until trainee gets up to speed
Self-Study (Noncomputerized): Trainees study materials on their own, usually when not actively performing their jobs.	▶ Lowest cost to the organization ▶ Places materials in the hands of the trainee ▶ Trainees can select the material they need to focus on the most ▶ Self-paced	▶ Shifts responsibility for training onto the trainee, with little formal support

Course Technology/Cengage Learning

Identify Training Staff Whether the trainer is an in-house expert or a hired professional, the organization should carefully match the capabilities of the training to the needs of the class. It is also vital that the trainer knows how to effectively communicate information and ideas.

Identify Target Audiences A security training program that distinguishes between groups of people and that presents only the information needed by the particular audience and omits irrelevant information yields the best results. In larger organizations, some individuals will fit into more than one group. In smaller organizations, it may not be necessary to draw distinctions between groups.

You can divide employees into groups for training as follows:

> ▶ *By level of awareness*—Separating individuals into groups according to level of awareness may require research to determine how well employees follow computer security procedures or understand how computer security fits into their jobs.

> ▶ *By general job task or function*—Individuals may be grouped as data providers, data processors, or data users.

> ▶ *By specific job category*—Many organizations assign individuals to job categories. As each job category generally has different job responsibilities, training for each will necessarily be different. Examples of job categories include general management, technology management, applications development, and security.

> ▶ *By level of computer knowledge*—Computer experts may find a program containing highly technical information more valuable than one covering management issues in computer security. Conversely, a computer novice would benefit more from a training program that presents fundamentals.

> ▶ *By types of technology or systems used*—Security techniques used for each off-the-shelf product or application system usually vary. The users of major applications normally require training specific to that application.

Motivate Management and Employees To successfully implement an awareness and training program, it is important to gain the *support* of both management and employees. For this reason, consideration should be given to using motivational techniques as part of the SETA program. Motivational techniques should demonstrate to management and employees how participation in the security training program benefits the organization. To motivate managers, for example, make them aware of the potential for losses and the role of training in computer security. Employees must understand how computer security benefits them and the organization and how it relates to their jobs.

Administer the Program Several important considerations apply when administering the security training program:

> ▶ *Visibility*—The visibility of a security training program plays a key role in its success. Efforts to achieve a highly prominent place in the organization should begin during the early stages of security training program development.

> ▶ *Training methods*—The methods used in the security training program should be consistent with the material presented and should be tailored to the specific audience's needs. Some training and awareness methods and techniques were listed earlier in the "Training Techniques" section.

SETA Must Be Organic

To be effective in helping staff behave in accordance with security policy, SETA must be an organic part of the organization's operations. This includes major initiatives or evolutionary changes in how the business operates. As noted earlier, as part of the planning for these initiatives, the security policies must be reviewed and updated but these new policies must be embodied and communicated through the SETA program.

▶ *Training topics*—Topics should be selected based on the audience's requirements.

▶ *Training materials*—In general, higher-quality training materials are more favorably received, but are more expensive. To reduce costs, you can obtain training materials from other organizations. Modifying existing materials is usually cheaper than developing them from scratch.

▶ *Training presentation*—Presentation issues to consider include the frequency of training (for example, annually or as needed), the length of presentations (for example, twenty minutes for general presentations, one hour for updates, or one week for an off-site class), and the style of presentation (for example, formal, informal, computer-based, humorous).

Maintain the Program Efforts should be made to keep current of changes in computer technology and security requirements. A training program that meets an organization's needs today may become ineffective if the organization begins using a new application or changes its business practices, such as by connecting to the Internet or issuing laptops to field marketing personnel. Likewise, an awareness program can become obsolete if laws, organizational policies, or common usage practices change. For example, if an awareness program uses examples from Eudora (a popular e-mail client program) to train employees about a new policy for e-mail usage, when the organization actually uses the e-mail client Outlook, employees may discount the security training program, and by association the importance of computer security.

Consider the organization that decides to issue laptops to field marketing personnel so that they can have access to customer information, enter orders, etc., while on the road. While planning for the technicalities of ordering laptops, providing network infrastructure to support mobile access, and training the sales reps in how to use the new technology, security may not even be an afterthought. In this scenario, policy must be updated to specify what types of information should be on those laptops, how communications are to be secured, etc. These policy revisions must also be embedded in the SETA program and communicated to the sales reps, if they are to be effective in avoiding unauthorized access to or disclosure of information.

Evaluate the Program Organizations can evaluate their training programs by ascertaining how much information is retained, to what extent computer security procedures are being followed, and the attitudes toward computer security. The results of such an evaluation should help identify and correct problems. Some popular evaluation methods (which can be used in conjunction with one another) are:

▶ Using student evaluations to collect feedback from the trainees

▶ Observing how well employees follow recommended security procedures after being trained

- Testing employees on material after it has been covered in training
- Monitoring the number and kind of computer security incidents reported before and after the training program is implemented

SECURITY AWARENESS

One of the least frequently implemented, but most effective security methods, is the periodic security awareness program. As noted in the NIST document Special Publication 800-12, "Security awareness programs: (1) set the stage for training by changing organizational attitudes to realize the importance of security and the adverse consequences of its failure; and (2) remind users of the procedures to be followed."[7]

A security awareness program keeps information security at the forefront of users' minds on a daily basis. Awareness serves to instill a sense of responsibility and purpose in employees who handle and manage information, and it leads employees to care more about their work environment. When developing an awareness program, be sure to:

- Focus on people both as part of the problem and as part of the solution.
- Refrain from using technical jargon; speak the language the users understand.
- Use every available venue to access all users.
- Define at least one key learning objective, state it clearly, and provide sufficient detail and coverage to reinforce the learning of it.
- Keep things light; refrain from "preaching" to users.
- Don't overload users with too much detail or too great a volume of information.
- Help users understand their roles in information security and how a breach in that security can affect their jobs.
- Take advantage of in-house communications media to deliver messages.
- Make the awareness program formal; plan and document all actions.
- Provide good information early, rather than perfect information late.

As Susan Hansche indicates in her article "Designing a Security Awareness Program," good security awareness programs should be:

supported and led by example from management, simple and straightforward, a continuous effort. They should repeat important messages to ensure they get delivered. They should be entertaining, holding the users' interest and humorous where appropriate in order to make slogans easy to remember. They should tell employees what the dangers are (threats) and how they can help protect the information vital to their jobs.[8]

Hansche continues by noting that awareness programs should focus on topics that the employees can relate to, including:

threats to physical assets and stored information, threats to open network environments, [and] federal and state laws they are required to follow, including copyright violations or privacy act information. It can also include specific organization or department policies and information on how to identify and protect sensitive or classified information, as well as how to store, label, and transport information. This awareness information should also address who they should report security incidents to, whether real or suspect.[9]

Employee Behavior and Awareness

Security awareness and security training are designed to modify any employee behavior that endangers the security of the organization's information. By teaching employees how to properly handle information, use applications, and operate within the organization, you minimize the risk of accidental compromise, damage, or destruction of information. Making employees aware of threats to information security, the potential damage that can result from these threats, and the ways that these threats can occur increases the probability that they will take such threats seriously. By making employees aware of policy, the penalties for failure to comply with policy, and the mechanism by which policy violations are discovered, you reduce the probability that an employee will try to get away with intentional misuse and abuse of information. Penalties for policy violations are effective only when (1) employees fear the penalty, (2) employees believe they may be caught, and (3) employees believe that, if caught, they will be penalized.

Security training and awareness activities can be undermined, however, if management does not set a good example. Failure of management—and especially upper management—to follow organizational policy is quickly mirrored by the actions and activities of all employees. For example, suppose Random Widget Works has a policy that all employees must wear identification badges in a visible location at all times. If, over time, employees observe that senior executives do not wear badges, then soon no one will wear a badge, and attempts to penalize employees for this failure will be compromised. Policy breaches by upper management are always perceived as a lack of support for the policy. For that reason, management must always lead by example.

Employee Accountability

Effective training and awareness programs make employees accountable for their actions. The legal defense *ignorantia legis neminem excusat* (ignorance of the law excuses no one) may not be valid in a criminal courtroom, but it does protect employees who are fighting policy violation penalties in labor disputes, administrative law hearings, or civil court cases. Comprehensive and properly disseminated policies enable organizations to require employee compliance. Dissemination and enforcement of policy become easier when training and awareness programs are in place.

Demonstrating **due care** and **due diligence**—warning employees that misconduct, abuse, and misuse of information resources will not be tolerated and that the organization will not defend employees who engage in this behavior—can help indemnify the institution against lawsuits. Lawyers tend to seek compensation from employers, which have more assets than employees, and thus attempt to prove that the alleged conduct was not clearly prohibited by organizational policy, thereby making the organization liable for it.

Awareness Techniques

The NIST document Special Publication 800-12, *An Introduction to Computer Security: The NIST Handbook,* describes the essentials of developing effective awareness techniques:

> Awareness can take on different forms for particular audiences. Appropriate awareness for management officials might stress management's pivotal role in establishing organizational attitudes toward security. Appropriate awareness for other groups, such as system programmers or information analysts, should address the need for security as it relates to their job. In today's systems environment, almost everyone in an organization may have access to system resources and therefore may have the potential to cause harm.

A security awareness program can use many methods to deliver its message, including video tapes, newsletters, posters, bulletin boards, flyers, demonstrations, briefings, short reminder notices at log-on, talks, or lectures. Awareness is often incorporated into basic security training and can use any method that can change employees' attitudes. Effective security awareness programs need to be designed with the recognition that people tend to practice a tuning out *process (also known as* acclimation). *For example, after a while, a security poster, no matter how well designed, will be ignored; it will, in effect, simply blend into the environment. For this reason, awareness techniques should be creative and frequently changed.*[10]

Developing Security Awareness Components

Many security awareness components are available at low cost, or virtually no cost, except for the time and energy of the developer. Others can be very expensive if purchased externally. Security awareness components include the following items:

- ▶ Videos
- ▶ Posters and banners
- ▶ Lectures and conferences
- ▶ Computer-based training
- ▶ Newsletters
- ▶ Brochures and flyers
- ▶ Trinkets ("loot" such as coffee cups, pens, pencils, T-shirts)
- ▶ Bulletin boards

The key is to keep the security message fresh and constantly in front of the users.

This chapter dealt with one of the most difficult parts of a security program—communicating security policy in such a way that staff understands its requirements so they can act in accordance with it. The SETA program is a critical component in assuring that policies don't remain in a book on the shelf, taken down only to show auditors once a year or to justify the disciplining of a violator.

The SETA program can be developed in-house, outsourced, or provided by a local educational institution depending on the particular needs and capabilities of the organization.

After the initial training component of the SETA program, a regular awareness program through newsletters, security events, etc., can help maintain awareness of the importance of security to successful business operations. However, awareness programs must be evaluated on their real effects, not the number of newsletters published, events held, etc.

The Information Security Manager's Checklist

		No	Planned	In Progress	In Place	Integrated
This topic has been fully tested, validated, and integrated into organizational operations with formal performance measures in place (as appropriate).						
This topic has been implemented, but not fully tested, validated, and integrated into organizational operations.						
The implementation of this topic has begun, but is not yet complete.						
The formal planning for this topic has begun, but is not yet complete.						
This subject has not formally begun planning, or the organization has made a conscious decision not to pursue this topic.						
20. SETA Program						
New employees receive SETA during in-processing						
All employees receive routine security training and awareness						
All SETA efforts documented						

For Further Reading

Managing the Human Factor in Information Security: How to Win over Staff and Influence Business Managers by David Lacey, Wiley, 2009.

Building an Information Technology Security Awareness and Training Program by NIST at *http://csrc.nist .gov/publications/nistpubs/800-50/NIST-SP800-50.pdf*

Success Strategies for Security Awareness by Tech Republic at *http://articles.techrepublic.com.com/ 5100-10878_11-5193710.html*

DRAFT Information Security Training Requirements: A Role- and Performance-Based Model NIST SO 800-16, Rev. 1 at *http://csrc.nist.gov/publications/PubsDrafts.html#SP-800-16-Rev.%201*

References

1. National Institute of Standards and Technology. *An Introduction to Computer Security: The NIST Handbook*. SP 800-12. *http://csrc.nist.gov/publications/nistpubs/800-12/*.

2. C. Irvine, S-K. Chin, and D. Frincke. Integrating security into the curriculum. *Computer*, 31, no. 12 (December 1998): 25–30.

3. National InfoSec Education and Training Program (NIETP). Centers of Academic Excellence in Information Assurance Education. Accessed February 6, 2001. *http://www.nsa.gov/isso/programs/ coeiae/index.htm*.

4. National Institute of Standards and Technology. *Information Technology Security Training Requirements: A Role- and Performance-Based Model. http://csrc.nist.gov/publications/nistpubs/800-16/800-16.pdf.*

5. Ibid.

6. Charles Trepper. Training developers more efficiently. *InformationWeekOnline. http://www.informationweek.com/738/38addev.htm.*

7. National Institute of Standards and Technology. *An Introduction to Computer Security: The NIST Handbook.* SP 800-12. *http://csrc.nist.gov/publications/nistpubs/800-12/.*

8. Susan Hansche. Designing a security awareness program: Part I. *Information Systems Security,* 9, no. 6 (January/February 2001): 14–23.

9. Ibid.

10. National Institute of Standards and Technology. *An Introduction to Computer Security: The NIST Handbook.* SP 800-12. *http://csrc.nist.gov/publications/nistpubs/800-12/.*

Tactical Information Security: Contingency Planning

Part VI of *Roadmap to Information Security for IT and InfoSec Managers* will focus on the critical topics of contingency planning. Many IT professionals may already have experience in many aspects of contingency planning since data processing has long been coupled to disaster recovery and business continuity. However, should you be new to InfoSec, you may find the concept of incident response preparations a new twist.

Chapters in Part VI

Chapter 21—"Contingency Planning—Preparing for the Worst" provides an introduction to contingency planning, describes the need for contingency planning, and explores the major components of contingency planning. It also examines the requirements to set up a CP team, and begin CP planning for the three subordinate plans, the IRP, DRP, and BCP. The chapter further illustrates how to create a simple set of contingency plans using business impact analysis, and how to prepare and execute a test of contingency plans.

Chapter 22—"The Incident Response Plan" continues the examination of contingency planning focusing on the establishment and conduct of an incident response planning committee. It further examines the components of an effective incident response plan and reviews the process of implementing, testing, and maintaining it.

Chapter 23—"The Disaster Recovery Plan" continues the examination of contingency planning focusing on the establishment and conduct of a disaster recovery planning committee. It further examines the components of an effective disaster recovery plan and reviews the process of implementing, testing, and maintaining it.

Chapter 24—"The Business Continuity Plan" continues the examination of contingency planning focusing on the establishment and conduct of a business continuity planning committee. It further examines the components of an effective business continuity plan and reviews the process of implementing, testing, and maintaining it.

Contingency Planning—Preparing for the Worst

Contingency is a simple word that hides a vast expanse of complex detail for the security professional. It can be difficult enough to keep a security program running correctly in normal circumstances but these difficulties multiply when events such as an intrusion incident or fire or natural disaster occurs. Information security is charged with protecting the C-I-A of information assets from all relevant threats; whether those threats be compromise by an attacker or a hurricane. Planning to deal with these contingencies that may interrupt normal business operations is the subject of this chapter. Because business increasingly depends on technology, planning for an unexpected event must include staff from both the information technology and information security communities of interest, who analyze the entire technological infrastructure of the organization considering the mission statement and current organizational objectives. But, like other plans in information security, contingency planning depends on the support of all members of the organization and must be sanctioned and actively supported by the organization's management.

Chapter Overview:

- ▶ What is contingency planning?
- ▶ Components of contingency planning
- ▶ Testing contingency plans

WHAT IS CONTINGENCY PLANNING?

The need to have a plan in place that systematically addresses how to identify, contain, and resolve an unexpected event is nothing new. The latest modification to the approaches taken toward these issues is noted in the 1998 NIST Special Publication 800-18, *Guide for Developing Security Plans for Information Technology Systems*, when an unexpected event occurs, "Procedures are required that will permit the organization to continue essential functions if information technology support is interrupted."[1] Some organizations—particularly, for national security reasons, federal agencies—are charged by law or other mandate to have such procedures in place at all times.

Business organizations of whatever size must prepare for the unexpected. In general, a business organization's ability to weather losses caused by an unexpected event depends on proper planning and execution of such a plan; without a workable plan, an unexpected event can cause severe damage to an organization's information resources and assets from which it may never recover. As noted by The Hartford Insurance Company: "On average, over 40% of businesses that don't have a disaster plan go out of business after a major loss like a fire, a break-in, or a storm."[2] In 1991, for instance, national news outlets reported that two key executives of the Bruno's supermarket chain, Angelo and Lee Bruno, were killed in a plane crash. While it will never be known for certain, the steady growth of the firm since its founding during the Great Depression seems to have reversed course at that point. The fortunes of the company declined and it went through bankruptcy in 2000. While the brand continues in a few southern markets, the business as it operated before the crash no longer exists. The development of a plan for handling unexpected events should be a high priority for all managers. That plan should take into account the possibility that key members of the organization will not be available to assist in the recovery process.

The overall process of preparing for unexpected events is called **contingency planning (CP)**. CP is the process by which the information technology and information security communities of interest position their organizations to prepare for, detect, react to, and recover from events that threaten the security of information resources and assets, both human and natural. The main goal of CP is to restore normal modes of operation with minimal cost and disruption to normal business activities after an unexpected event—in other words, to make sure things get back to the way they were within a reasonable period of time. Ideally, CP should ensure continuous information systems availability to the organization even in the face of the unexpected.

CP consists of four major components:

- ▶ Business impact analysis (BIA)
- ▶ Incident response plan (IRP)
- ▶ Disaster recovery plan (DRP)
- ▶ Business continuity plan (BCP)

The BIA is a preparatory activity that is common to both CP and risk management, a topic that is covered in earlier chapters. It helps the organization determine which business functions and information systems are the most critical to the success of the organization. The IR plan focuses on the immediate response to an incident. Any unexpected event is treated as an incident, unless and until a response team deems it to be a disaster. Then the DR plan, which focuses on restoring operations at the primary site, is invoked. If operations at the primary site cannot be quickly restored—for example, when the damage is major or will affect the organization's functioning over the long term—the BC plan occurs concurrently with the DR plan, enabling the business to continue at an alternate site, until the organization is able to resume operations at its primary site or select a new primary location.

Depending on the size and business philosophy of an organization, information technology and information security managers can either (1) create and develop these three CP components as one unified plan or (2) create the three separately in conjunction with a set of interlocking procedures that enable continuity. Typically, larger, more complex organizations create and develop the CP components separately, because the functions of each component differ in scope, applicability, and design. Smaller organizations tend to adopt a one-plan method, consisting of a straightforward set of recovery strategies.

Ideally, the CIO, systems administrators, CISO, and key IT and business managers should be actively involved during the creation and development of all CP components, as well as during the distribution of responsibilities among the three communities of interest. The elements required to begin the CP process are a planning methodology; a policy environment to enable the planning process; an understanding of the cause and effects of core precursor activities, known as the business impact analysis; and access to financial and other resources, as articulated and outlined by the planning budget. Each of these is explained in the sections that follow. Once formed, the **contingency planning management team (CPMT)** begins developing a CP document using the following process:

1. Develop the contingency planning policy statement: A formal department or agency policy provides the authority and guidance necessary to develop an effective contingency plan.
2. Conduct the business impact analysis: The BIA helps to identify and prioritize critical IT systems and components. A template for developing the BIA is also provided [in NIST Special Publication 800-34] to assist the user.
3. Identify preventive controls: Measures taken to reduce the effects of system disruptions can increase system availability and reduce contingency life cycle costs.
4. Develop recovery strategies: Recovery strategies ensure that the system may be recovered quickly and effectively following a disruption.
5. Develop an IT contingency plan: The contingency plan should contain detailed guidance and procedures for restoring a damaged system.
6. Plan testing, training, and exercises: Testing the plan identifies planning gaps, whereas training prepares recovery personnel for plan activation; both activities improve plan effectiveness and overall agency preparedness.
7. Plan maintenance: The plan should be a living document that is updated regularly to remain current with system enhancements.[3]

Four teams of individuals are involved in contingency planning and contingency operations:

- The *CP team* collects information about information systems and the threats they face, conducts the business impact analysis and then creates the contingency plans for incident response, disaster recovery, and business continuity. The CP team often consists of a coordinating manager and representatives from each of the other three teams.

  The CP team should include the following personnel:

  - Champion: As with any strategic function, the CP project must have a high-level manager to support, promote, and endorse the findings of the project. This **champion** could be the CIO, or ideally the CEO/President.

  - Project manager: A champion provides the strategic vision and the linkage to the power structure of the organization, but does not manage the project. A **project manager**—possibly a mid-level manager or even the CISO—leads the project, putting in place a sound project planning process, guiding the development of a complete and useful project, and prudently managing resources.

  - Team members: The **team members** should be the managers or their representatives from the various communities of interest: business, information technology, and information security who will function as subject matter experts supplying the detailed knowledge of their particular areas. Business managers supply details of their activities and insight into those functions critical to running the business. Information technology managers supply information about the at-risk systems and provide technical content for IRP, DRP, and BCP. Information security managers oversee the security planning and provide information on threats, vulnerabilities, attacks, and recovery requirements. A representative from the legal affairs or corporate counsel's office helps keep all planning steps within legal and contractual boundaries. A member of the corporate communications department makes sure the crisis management and communications plan elements are consistent with the needs of that group.

- The *incident response team* manages and executes the incident response plan by detecting, evaluating, and responding to incidents.

- The *disaster recovery team* manages and executes the disaster recovery plan by detecting, evaluating, and responding to disasters, and by reestablishing operations at the primary business site.

- The *business continuity team* manages and executes the business continuity plan by setting up and starting off-site operations in the event of an incident or disaster.

As indicated earlier, in larger organizations these teams are distinct entities, with non-overlapping membership, although the latter three teams have representatives on the CP team. In smaller organizations, the four teams may include overlapping groups of people. The core takeaway is to focus on the role filled by each entity and assuring that role is filled, whether by a single person or a team from the appropriate area.

Many organizations' contingency plans are woefully inadequate. Some might claim that most fall short of what they could be. CP often fails to receive the high priority necessary for the efficient and timely recovery of business operations during and after an unexpected event. The fact that many organizations do not place an adequate premium on CP does not mean that it is unimportant, however. The Computer Security Resource Center (CSRC) at the National Institute for Standards and Technology (NIST) describes the need for this type of planning as follows:

> These procedures (contingency plans, business interruption plans, and continuity of operations plans) should be coordinated with the backup, contingency, and recovery plans of any general support systems, including networks used by the application. The contingency plans should ensure that interfacing systems are identified and contingency/disaster planning coordinated.[4]

As you learn more about CP, you may notice that it shares certain characteristics with common approaches to risk management . Many information technology and information security managers are already familiar with these processes; they can transfer that knowledge to the CP process.

COMPONENTS OF CONTINGENCY PLANNING

As noted earlier, CP includes four major components: the business impact analysis, incident response, disaster recovery, and business continuity plans. Whether an organization adopts the one-plan method or the multiple-plan method with interlocking procedures, each of these CP components must be addressed and developed in its entirety. The following sections describe each component in detail, and discuss when and how each should be used. They also consider how to determine which plan is best suited for the identification, containment, and resolution of any given unexpected event. Figure 21-1 depicts the major project modules performed during contingency planning efforts.

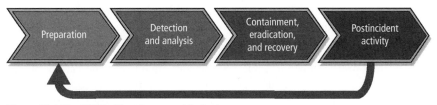

Figure 21-1 The NIST Incident Response Life Cycle
Source: NIST SP 800-61 (2004)

Business Impact Analysis

The **business impact analysis (BIA)**, the first phase in the CP process, provides the CP team with information about systems and the threats they face. The BIA is a crucial component of the initial planning stages, because it provides detailed scenarios of the effects that each potential attack could have on the organization.

One of the fundamental differences between a BIA and the risk management processes discussed in Chapters 7 and 8 is that risk management focuses on identifying the threats, vulnerabilities, and attacks to determine which controls can protect the information. The BIA assumes that these controls have been bypassed, have failed, or have otherwise proved ineffective, and that the attack succeeded.

The CP team conducts the BIA in the following stages, which are shown in Figure 21-2 and described in the sections that follow:

1. Threat attack identification and prioritization
2. Business unit analysis
3. Attack success scenario development
4. Potential damage assessment
5. Subordinate plan classification

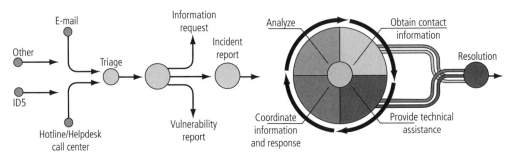

Figure 21-2 Major Tasks in Contingency Planning

Source: CSIRT 77. Retrieved January 24, 2011 from http://www.cert.org/archive/pdf/csirt-handbook.pdf

Threat Attack Identification and Prioritization
An organization that has followed an effective risk management process will have already identified and prioritized threats facing it. To conduct the BIA, these organizations simply update the threat list and add one piece of information, the attack profile.

An **attack profile** is a detailed description of the activities that occur during an attack. The example attack profile shown in Table 21-1 includes preliminary indications of the attack, as well as the actions taken and the outcome. Such a profile must be developed for every serious threat that the organization faces, whether natural or human-made, deliberate or accidental. This document is useful in later planning stages to provide indicators of attacks. It is used here to determine the extent of damage that could result to a business unit if the attack were successful.

Business Unit Analysis
The second major BIA task is the analysis and prioritization of business functions within the organization. Each business department, unit, or division must be independently evaluated to determine how important its functions are to the organization as a whole. For example, recovery operations would probably focus on the IT department and network operation before turning to the personnel department's hiring activities. Likewise, recovering a manufacturing company's assembly line is more urgent than recovering its maintenance tracking system. This is not to say that personnel functions and assembly-line maintenance are not important to the business, but unless the organization's main revenue-producing operations can be restored quickly, other functions are irrelevant.

Attack Success Scenario Development
Once the threat attack profiles have been developed and the business functions prioritized, the BIA team must create a series of scenarios depicting the effects of an occurrence of each threat on each prioritized functional

TABLE 21-1

DATE OF ANALYSIS:	JUNE 23, 2012
Attack name/description:	*Malicious code via e-mail*
Threat/probable threat agents:	▶ *Vandalism/script kiddies* ▶ *Theft/experienced hacker*
Known or possible vulnerabilities:	▶ *Emergent weakness in e-mail clients* ▶ *Inappropriate actions by employees, contractors, and visitors using e-mail clients* ▶ *Emergent weakness in e-mail servers or gateways*
Likely precursor activities or indicators:	*Announcements from vendors and bulletins*
Likely attack activities or indicators of attack in progress:	▶ *E-mail volume measurements may show variances* ▶ *Unusual system failures among clients* ▶ *Unusual system failures among servers* ▶ *Notification from e-mail recipients who may be ahead of us in atack life cycle*
Information assets at risk from this attack:	*All connected systems due to blended attack model now prevalent*
Damage or loss to information assets likely from this attack:	▶ *Denial-of-service for some clients almost certain* ▶ *Denial-of-service for servers possible* ▶ *Possible losses of data depending on nature of attack*
Other assets at risk from this attack:	*None likely*
Damage or loss to other assets likely from this attack:	*None likely*
Immediate actions indicated when this attack is under way:	▶ *Disconnect e-mail gateway(s)* ▶ *Update e-mail gateway filtering patterns and apply* ▶ *Update and distribute client filtering patterns* ▶ *Isolate all infected servers* ▶ *Isolate all infected clients* ▶ *Begin server recovery actions for infected servers* ▶ *Begin client recovery actions for infected clients*
Follow-up actions after this attack was successfully executed against our systems:	*Review pattern update timing and procedure to assure adequacy*
Comments:	*None at this time*

Course Technlology/Cengage Learning

area. This step can be a long and detailed process, as such occurrences may have implications for many functions. Attack profiles should include scenarios depicting a typical attack, including its methodology, indicators of an attack, and broad consequences. Once the attack profiles are completed, the business function details can be integrated with the attack profiles. Then **attack success scenarios** with more detail are added to the attack profile, including alternative outcomes—best, worst, and most likely. This level of detail allows planners to address each possibility in turn.

Potential Damage Assessment

From these detailed scenarios, the BIA planning team must estimate the cost of the best, worst, and most likely outcomes by preparing an **attack scenario end case**. This allows the organization to identify what must be done to recover from each possible case. (At this time the team does not attempt to determine how much to spend on the protection of business units—this issue is analyzed during risk management.) The costs include accounting for the time required by the response team members to perform the required actions—described in the following sections—to effectively recover from any incident or disaster. These cost estimates can persuade management representatives throughout an organization of the importance of planning and recovery efforts.

Subordinate Plan Classification

Once the potential damage has been assessed, and each scenario and attack scenario end case has been evaluated, a subordinate plan must be developed or identified from among existing plans already in place. Some of these related plans may already be part of standard operating procedures, such as file recovery from backup. Other plans may be in place as part of existing DRP or BCP projects. Because most attacks are not disastrous and therefore fall into the category of incident response, the BIA team will likely develop a number of subordinate plans that are meant to be exclusively used at the incident level. Those scenarios that do qualify as disastrous are likely addressed in the DR plan or BC plan.

Each attack scenario end case is categorized as disastrous or not. The difference between the two classifications reflects whether the organization is able to take effective action during the event to combat the attack's effects. Attack end cases that are disastrous find members of the organization waiting out the attack and planning to recover from it after the attack ends.

What Is Most Important?

Preparing the BIA may be the most contentious part of the CP effort because it requires a realistic assessment of what is most important to a business. Organizational turf, the charisma of the involved managers, and unrealistic expectations all play together in a drama that can resemble a daytime soap opera.

However, it is critical that this drama reach an acceptable denouement in the final form of the BIA.

The BIA is the critical assessment that undergirds the remainder of the CP process and guides the prioritization of recovery operations. During the trauma of recovering business operations after a disaster is no time to reopen the debate over whose systems should be recovered first.

It is therefore critical that these issues be hashed out and resolved during preparation of the BIA.

In a typical disaster recovery operation, the lives and welfare of the employee are the highest priority, since most disasters involve fires, floods, hurricanes, tornadoes, and the like. Other disasters might include the following events as a sample of the many possible disasters that could arise:

- ▶ Electrical blackouts affecting a city or region
- ▶ Attacks on service providers that result in a loss of communications to the organization (either telephone or Internet)
- ▶ Massive, malicious-code attacks that sweep through the organization before they can be contained

Timing and Sequence of CP Elements

As indicated earlier, the IR plan focuses on immediate response, but if the incident escalates into a disaster, the IR plan may give way to the DR plan and BC plan, as illustrated in Figure 21-3. The DR plan typically focuses on restoring systems after disasters occur, and therefore is closely associated with the BC plan. The BC plan occurs concurrently with the DR plan when the damage is major or long term, requiring more than simple restoration of information and information resources, as illustrated in Figure 21-3.

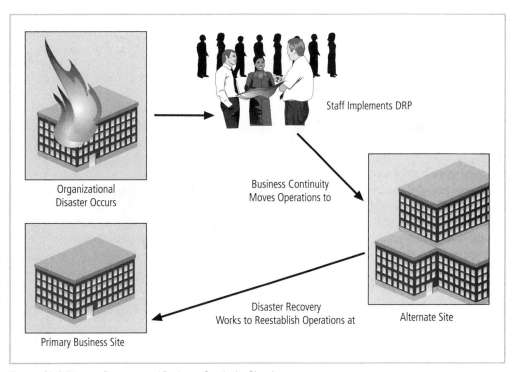

Organizational Disaster Occurs

Staff Implements DRP

Business Continuity Moves Operations to

Primary Business Site

Disaster Recovery Works to Reestablish Operations at

Alternate Site

Figure 21-3 Disaster Recovery and Business Continuity Planning
Course Technology/Cengage Learning

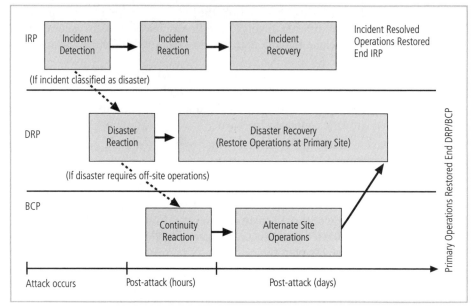

Figure 21-4 Contingency Planning Implementation Timeline
Course Technology/Cengage Learning

Some experts argue that the three elements of CP are so closely linked that they are indistinguishable. In fact, each has a distinct place, role, and planning requirement. Furthermore, each component (IR, DR, and BC) comes into play at a specific time in the life of an incident. Figure 21-4 illustrates this sequence and shows the overlap that may occur. How the plans interact and the ways in which they are brought into action are discussed in the sections that follow.

Friction

Carol von Clausewitz in his classic book *On War* describes the concept of friction—a factor that arises due to unexpected events, fatigue, and other matters that collectively cause a unit to perform much slower than its theoretical capability. Friction is just as important a factor in CP where personnel may be "shell shocked" by a natural disaster, worried about their families, fatigued after long hours of work under strenuous circumstances, etc. For example, in normal operation, a new server may be built and put into production within 8 hours. But in a CP scenario, this activity may require much longer because of the friction that affects the administrators' ability to perform their jobs.

Just as a general planning a major battle, the contingency planning team must consider the effects of friction on the timelines for their recovery efforts.

TESTING CONTINGENCY PLANS

Very few plans are executable as initially written; instead, they must be tested to identify vulnerabilities, faults, and inefficient processes. Once problems are identified during the testing process, improvements can be made, and the resulting plan can be relied on in times of need. Five strategies[5] can be used to test contingency plans:

- ▶ Desk check—The simplest kind of validation involves distributing copies of the appropriate plans to all individuals who will be assigned roles during an actual incident. Each of these people performs a **desk check** by reviewing the plan and creating a list of correct and incorrect components. While not a true test, this strategy is a good way to review the perceived feasibility and effectiveness of the plan.

- ▶ Structured walk-through—In a **structured walk-through**, all involved individuals walk through the steps they would take during an actual event. This exercise can consist of an on-site walk-through, in which everyone discusses their actions at each particular location and juncture, or it may be more of a "talk-through" or "chalk talk," in which all involved individuals sit around a conference table and discuss in turn their responsibilities as the incident unfolds.

- ▶ Simulation—In a **simulation**, each person works individually, rather than in a group setting, to simulate the performance of each task. The simulation stops short of performing the actual physical tasks required, such as installing the backup data or disconnecting a communications circuit. The major difference between a walk-through and a simulation is that individuals work on their own tasks and are responsible for identifying the faults in their own procedures.

- ▶ Parallel testing—In **parallel testing**, individuals act as if an actual incident occurred, and begin performing their required tasks and executing the necessary procedures, without interfering with the normal operations of the business. Great care must be taken to ensure that the procedures performed do not halt the operations of the business functions, thereby creating an actual incident.

- ▶ Full interruption—In **full-interruption** testing, the individuals follow each and every procedure, including the interruption of service, restoration of data from backups, and notification of appropriate individuals. This exercise is often performed after normal business hours in organizations that cannot afford to disrupt or simulate the disruption of business functions. Although full-interruption testing is the most rigorous testing strategy, it is unfortunately too risky for most businesses.

At a minimum, organizations should conduct periodic walk-throughs (or chalk talks) of each of the CP component plans. A failure to update these plans as the business and its information resources change can erode the team's ability to respond to an incident, or possibly cause greater damage than the incident itself. If this sounds like a major training effort, note that the author Richard Marcinko, a former Navy SEAL, provides a few relevant statements[6] to motivate teams:

- The more you sweat in training, the less you bleed in combat.
- Training and preparation hurts.
- Lead from the front, not the rear.
- You don't have to like it; just do it.
- Keep it simple.
- Never assume.
- You are paid for your results, not your methods.

One often-neglected aspect of training is cross-training. In a real incident or disaster, the people assigned to particular roles are often not available. In some cases, alternate people must perform the duties of personnel who have been incapacitated by the disastrous event that triggered the activation of the plan. The testing process should train people to take over in the event that a team leader or integral member of the execution team is unavailable.

Just as in all organizational efforts, iteration results in improvement. A formal implementation of this methodology is continuous process improvement (CPI). Each time the organization rehearses its plans, it should learn from the process, improve the plans, and then rehearse again. Each time an incident or disaster occurs, the organization should review what went right and what went wrong. Through the ongoing evaluation and improvement, the organization continues to move forward, and continually improves upon the process, so that it can strive for an even better outcome.

Planning for the unexpected is a necessary component of the information security program because it assures the CIA of assets even when unexpected events occur. This planning must follow a defined procedure and enjoy the support of senior management in order to succeed.

One of the most contentious parts of the CP process is preparation of the BIA, which identifies the most critical resources for the organization and sets the priorities for their recovery. Because these priorities may be at odds with organizational turf, the egos of the affected managers may get in the way.

Timelines in CP must anticipate the effects of friction, which are the factors that come into play and slow the progress of activities due to fatigue and stress. Contingency plans must be tested on a regular basis to assure that they are practical and will stand the test of plan meeting reality.

The Information Security Manager's Checklist

	No	Planned	In Progress	In Place	Integrated
This topic has been fully tested, validated, and integrated into organizational operations with formal performance measures in place (as appropriate).					
This topic has been implemented, but not fully tested, validated, and integrated into organizational operations.					
The implementation of this topic has begun, but is not yet complete.					
The formal planning for this topic has begun, but is not yet complete.					
This subject has not formally begun planning, or the organization has made a conscious decision not to pursue this topic.					
21. Contingency Planning					
CP management team formed					
CP policy					
CP plan					
Business impact analysis conducted periodically					
Subordinate teams formed					

For Further Reading

Total Contingency Planning for Disasters: Managing Risk . . . Minimizing Loss . . . Ensuring Business by Kenneth N. Myers, John Wiley and Sons, 1996.

IT Disaster Recovery Planning for Dummies by Peter Gregory CISA CISSP, John Wiley and Sons, 2007.

Principles of Incident Response and Disaster Recovery by Michael E. Whitman & Herbert J. Mattord, Cengage/Course Technology, 2006.

SP 800-34 Rev. 1 May 2010 Contingency Planning Guide for Federal Information Systems at http://csrc.nist.gov/publications/nistpubs/800-34-rev1/sp800-34-rev1_errata-Nov11-2010.pdf

References

1. NIST. *Special Publication 800-18: Guide for Developing Security Plans for Information Technology Systems.* December 1998. Accessed 13 May 2003, from http://csrc.nist.gov/publications/nistpubs/800-18/Planguide.doc, p. 31.

2. *Why You Need a Disaster Recovery Plan.* Accessed 13 May 2003, from http://sb.thehartford.com/reduce_risk/disaster_recovery.asp.

3. M. Swanson, A. Wohl, L. Pope, T. Grance, J. Hash, and R. Thomas. "Contingency Planning Guide for Information Technology Systems," NIST Special Publication 800-34. Accessed 13 June 2005, from http://csrc.nist.gov/publications/nistpubs/800-34/sp800-34.pdf.

4. NIST. *Special Publication 800-18: Guide for Developing Security Plans for Information Technology Systems.* December 1998. Accessed 13 May 2003, from http://csrc.nist.gov/publications/nistpubs/800-18/Planguide.doc, p. 31.

5. Ronald L. Krutz and Russell Dean Vines. *The CISSP Prep Guide: Mastering the Ten Domains of Computer Security.* New York: John Wiley and Sons, 2001:288.

6. Richard Marcinko and John Weisman. *Designation Gold.* New York: Pocket Books, 1998: preface.

Chapter 22

The Incident Response Plan

One of the first problems to confront the security professional is accepting that security incidents deal with two classes of problems:

1. Natural forces such as weather, earthquake, etc.
2. Human forces such as deliberate intrusion or attack

The differences between the two are significant. A natural force is not "out to get you" and will not change its actions based on what defensive measures you employ. A flood, for example, will not suddenly decide to pull in more water so that it can overtop your three-foot flood wall. On the other hand, a human attacker can deliberately attack your organization and will study your defenses and adapt attacks based on your defensive measures.

Incident response is really all about how the organization will identify and respond to security incidents in a way to contain and minimize damage to its assets. The process of incident response is based on the incident response plan.

- ▶ Incident response planning
- ▶ Law enforcement involvement

INCIDENT RESPONSE PLANNING

The **incident response plan (IR plan)**[1] comprises a detailed set of processes and procedures that anticipate, detect, and mitigate the effects of an unexpected event that might compromise information resources and assets. **Incident response planning (IRP)** is, therefore, the preparation for such an event. In CP, an unexpected event is called an **incident**. An incident occurs when an attack (natural or human-made) affects information resources and/or assets, causing actual damage or other disruptions. **Incident response (IR)**, then, is a set of procedures that commence when an incident is detected. IR must be carefully planned and coordinated, because organizations depend heavily on the quick and efficient containment and resolution of incidents. The IR plan is usually activated when an incident causes minimal damage—according to criteria set in advance by the organization—with little or no disruption to business operations.

Incident Response Policy

Prior to the development of each plan outlined in this chapter, the CP team should work to develop a policy for that component (IR, DR, BC). These policies provide guidance on the structure of the subordinate teams and the philosophy of the organization, and assist in the structuring of the plan. As the planning committee forms a **security incident response team (SIRT)**, key SIRT representatives join the IR planning committee in the development of policy to define the operations of the team, articulate the organizational response to various types of incidents, and advise end users on how to contribute to the effective response of the organization, rather than contributing to the problem at hand. You will learn more about SIRT's roles and composition later in this section.

The incident response policy is similar in structure to other policies used by the organization. Just as the enterprise information security policy defines the information security roles and responsibilities for the entire enterprise, the incident response policy defines the roles and responsibilities for incident response for the SIRT and others who will be mobilized in the activation of the plan. The *Computer Security Incident Handling Guide* from the National Institute on Standards and Technology (NIST SP 800-61, Rev. 1) identifies the following as key components of a typical IR policy:[2]

- ▶ Statement of management commitment
- ▶ Purpose and objectives of the policy
- ▶ Scope of the policy (to whom and what it applies and under what circumstances)
- ▶ Definition of information security incidents and their consequences within the context of the organization
- ▶ Organizational structure and delineation of roles, responsibilities, and levels of authority; should include the authority of the incident response team to confiscate or disconnect equipment and to monitor suspicious activity, and the requirements for reporting certain types of incidents

- Prioritization or severity ratings of incidents
- Performance measures (as discussed in later chapters)
- Reporting and contact forms

IR policy, like all policies, must gain the full support of top management and be clearly understood by all affected parties. It is especially important to gain the support of those communities of interest that will be required to alter business practices or make changes to their information technology infrastructures. For example, if the SIRT determines the only way to stop a massive denial-of-service attack is to sever the organization's connection to the Internet, they should have a signed document locked in an appropriate filing cabinet preauthorizing such an action. This ensures that the SIRT team is performing authorized actions, and protects both the SIRT team members and the organization from misunderstanding and potential liability.

The Incident Response Plan

Those members of the organization who have an understanding of the technical underpinnings of the business processes used must become involved in assessing impact when the unexpected becomes reality. The initial assessment is critical since if the outcome is trivial, it can be accommodated with routine actions. But when outcomes are nontrivial they will involve the activation of a well-considered incident response plan. In fact, when it is apparent that an event is actually a disaster, the incident response plan may be skipped in favor of activating a disaster response plan as well as a business continuity plan if needed. The boundaries between routine events, incidents, and disasters should be well defined and well understood by the decision makers who will be asked to make such choices. All of these planning options are discussed in this chapter.

When a threat turns into an attack, it is classified as an information security incident, but only if it has all of the following characteristics:

- It is directed against information assets.
- It has a realistic chance of success.
- It threatens the confidentiality, integrity, or availability of information resources and assets.

The prevention of threats and attacks has been intentionally omitted from this discussion because guarding against such possibilities is primarily the responsibility of the information security department, which works with the rest of the organization to implement sound policy, effective risk controls, and ongoing training and awareness programs. It is important to understand that *IR is a reactive measure, not a preventive one.*

The responsibility for creating an organization's IR plan usually falls to the CISO. With the aid of other managers and systems administrators on the CP team, the CISO should select members from each community of interest to form an independent IR team, which executes the IR plan. The roles and responsibilities of the members of the IR team should be clearly documented and communicated throughout the organization. The IR plan also includes an alert roster, which lists certain critical agencies to be contacted during the course of an incident.

Using the multistep CP process discussed in the previous section, the CP team can use it as a model to create the IR plan. During this planning process the IR procedures take shape. For every incident scenario, the CP team creates three sets of incident-handling procedures:

1. During the incident: The planners develop and document the procedures that must be performed during the incident. These procedures are grouped and assigned to individuals. Systems administrators' tasks differ from managerial tasks, so members of the planning committee must draft a set of function-specific procedures.

2. After the incident: Once the procedures for handling an incident are drafted, the planners develop and document the procedures that must be performed immediately after the incident has ceased. Again, separate functional areas may develop different procedures.

3. Before the incident: The planners draft a third set of procedures, those tasks that must be performed to prepare for the incident. These procedures include the details of the data backup schedules, disaster recovery preparation, training schedules, testing plans, copies of service agreements, and business continuity plans, if any. At this level, the business continuity plan could consist of just additional material on a service bureau that stores data off-site via electronic vaulting, with an agreement to provide office space and lease equipment as needed.

Preparing to Plan

Planning for an incident and the responses to it require a detailed understanding of the information systems and the threats they face. The business impact analysis (BIA) provides the data used to develop the IR plan. The IR planning team seeks to develop a series of predefined responses that will guide the team and information security staff through the incident response steps. Predefining incident responses enables the organization to react to a detected incident quickly and effectively, without confusion or wasted time and effort.

The execution of the IR plan typically falls to the SIRT. As was noted previously, the SIRT is a subset of the IR team and is composed of technical and managerial information technology and information security professionals prepared to diagnose and respond to an incident. In some organizations the SIRT may simply be a loose or informal association of IT and InfoSec staffers who would be called up if an attack was detected on the organization's information assets. At some level, every member of an organization is a member of the SIRT team, since every action they take can cause or avert an incident.

The SIRT should be available for contact by anyone who discovers or suspects that an incident involving the organization has occurred. One or more team members, depending on the magnitude of the incident and availability of personnel, then handles the incident. The incident handlers analyze the incident data, determine the impact of the incident, and act appropriately to limit the damage to the organization and restore normal services. Although the SIRT may have only a few members, the team's success depends on the participation and cooperation of individuals throughout the organization.

The SIRT consists of professionals who are capable of handling the information systems and functional areas affected by an incident. For example, imagine a firefighting team responding to an emergency call. Rather than responding to the fire as individuals, each member of the team has a specific role to perform, so that the team acts as a unified body that assesses the situation, determines the appropriate response, and coordinates the response. Similarly, each member of the IR team must know his or her specific role, work in concert with other team members, and execute the objectives of the IR plan.

Incident Detection

The challenge for every IR team is determining whether an event is the product of routine systems use or an actual incident. Many anomalous conditions occur during normal operation of a business and these conditions must be filtered, correlated, and evaluated to determine if they define an actual incident. Some organizations define this process in three tiers:

Indications → Events → Incident

Indications are the raw notifications (an alert from an IDS, an invalid log-on attempt, etc.) and these are filtered to determine if they define an event (e.g., five invalid log-on attempts from the same IP address within a 2-minute period). Events are then correlated and evaluated to see if they indicate an incident (for example, five invalid log-on events against three different accounts over a 5-minute period).

Incident Classification

Incident classification is the process of examining a possible incident, or **incident candidate**, and determining whether it constitutes an actual incident. Classifying an incident is the responsibility of the IR team. Initial reports from end users, intrusion detection systems, host- and network-based virus detection software, and systems administrators are some of the ways to track and detect incident candidates. Careful training in the reporting of an incident candidate allows end users, the help desk staff, and all security personnel to relay vital information to the IR team. Once an actual incident is properly identified, the members of the IR team can effectively execute the corresponding procedures from the IR plan.

A number of occurrences signal the presence of an incident candidate. Unfortunately, these same events can result from an overloaded network, computer, or server, and some are similar to the normal operation of these information assets. Other incident candidates mimic the actions of a misbehaving computing system, software package, or other less serious threat. To help make the detection of actual incidents more reliable, D. L. Pipkin has identified three categories[3] of incident indicators: possible, probable, and definite.

Possible Indicators The following four types of incident candidates are considered *possible* actual incidents:

1. Presence of unfamiliar files: For example, users might discover unfamiliar files in their home directories or on their office computers. Administrators might also find unexplained files that do not seem to be in a logical location or owned by an authorized user.

2. Presence or execution of unknown programs or processes: For example, users or administrators might detect unfamiliar programs running, or processes executing, on office machines or network servers.

3. Unusual consumption of computing resources: For example, consumption of memory or hard disk space might suddenly spike or fall. Many computer operating systems,

including Windows, Linux, and UNIX variants, allow users and administrators to monitor CPU and memory consumption. Most computers also have the ability to monitor hard drive space. In addition, servers maintain logs of file creation and storage.

4. Unusual system crashes: Computer systems can crash. Older operating systems running newer programs are notorious for locking up or spontaneously rebooting whenever the operating system is unable to execute a requested process or service. You are probably familiar with systems error messages such as "Unrecoverable Application Error," "General Protection Fault," and the infamous Windows NT "Blue Screen of Death." However, if a computer system seems to be crashing, hanging, rebooting, or freezing more frequently than usual, the cause could be an incident candidate.

Probable Indicators The four types of incident candidates described below are *probable* indicators of actual incidents:

1. Activities at unexpected times: If traffic levels on the organization's network exceed the measured baseline values, an incident candidate is probably present. If this activity surge occurs when few members of the organization are at work, this probability becomes much higher.

2. Presence of new accounts: Periodic review of user accounts can reveal an account (or accounts) that the administrator does not remember creating or that is not logged in the administrator's journal. Even one unlogged new account is an incident candidate. An unlogged new account with root or other special privileges has an even higher probability of being an actual incident.

3. Reported attacks: If users of the system report a suspected attack, there is a high probability that an attack has occurred, which constitutes an incident. The technical sophistication of the person making the report should be considered.

4. Notification from IDS: If the organization has installed and correctly configured a host- or network-based intrusion detection system (IDS), then notification from the IDS indicates that an incident might be in progress. However, the administrator must determine whether the notification is real, a false positive, or the result of a routine operation by a user or other administrator.

Definite Indicators The six types of incident candidates described below are *definite* indicators of an actual incident. That is, they clearly signal that an incident is in progress or has occurred. In these cases, the corresponding IR must be activated immediately.

1. Use of dormant accounts: Many network servers maintain default accounts, and there often exist accounts from former employees, employees on a leave of absence or sabbatical without remote access privileges, or dummy accounts set up to support system testing.

2. Changes to logs: The smart systems administrator backs up system logs as well as system data. As part of a routine incident scan, systems administrators can compare these logs to the online versions to determine whether they have been modified. If they have, and the systems administrator cannot determine explicitly that an authorized individual modified them, an incident has occurred. One significant indicator is a hole (missing record) in the log record, which may indicate deletion in an attempt to conceal an attacker's actions.

3. Presence of hacker tools: Network administrators sometimes use system vulnerability and network evaluation tools to scan internal computers and networks to determine what a hacker can see. These tools are also used to support research into attack profiles. All too often, however, they are used by employees, contractors, or outsiders with local network access to hack into systems. To combat this problem, many organizations explicitly prohibit the use of these tools without written permission from the CISO, making any unauthorized installation a policy violation.

4. Notifications by partner or peer: If a business partner or another connected organization reports an attack from your computing systems, then an incident has occurred.

5. Notification by hacker: Some hackers enjoy taunting their victims. If an organization's Web pages are defaced, it's an incident. If an organization receives an extortion request for money in exchange for its customers' credit card files, an incident is in progress.

6. Use of unusual protocols: Richard Bejtlich in his book Extrusion Detection[4] makes the point that much can be learned from the traffic leaving the network. For example, an outgoing FTP session from the Web tier should set off alarms as that activity should never occur (FTP sessions would likely only be into the Web tier).

Given the number of indication sources in the modern enterprise, managing the incoming flood of indications is a challenging task. This challenge has given rise to an entire class of security event management (SEM) applications. SEM applications are becoming increasingly critical given the speed with which an incident can unfold. For example, the exponential spread of a virulent worm within an organization can require effective response within a matter of seconds if the spread is to be contained.

Occurrences of Actual Incidents
When the following actual incidents are confirmed, the corresponding IR must be immediately activated:

1. Loss of availability: Information or information systems become unavailable.

2. Loss of integrity: Users report corrupt data files, garbage where data should be, or data that just looks wrong.

3. Loss of confidentiality: You are notified of sensitive information leaks, or information you thought was protected has been disclosed.

4. Violation of policy: If organizational policies addressing information or information security have been violated, an incident has occurred.

5. Violation of law or regulation: If the law has been broken and the organization's information assets are involved, an incident has occurred.

Incident Response

Once an actual incident has been confirmed and properly classified, the IR plan moves from the detection phase to the reaction phase.

The steps in the IR are designed to stop the incident, mitigate its effects, and provide information for the recovery from the incident. In the incident response phase, a number of action steps are taken by the SIRT, and others must occur quickly and may take place concurrently. An effective IR plan prioritizes and documents these steps to allow for efficient reference in the midst of an incident. These steps include notification of key personnel, the assignment of tasks, and documentation of the incident.

Not the Time to Plan

People in stressful situations don't have time to think and react in accordance with their training and experience. This knowledge will serve an organization well in incident response. IR is one of the most stressful times for an organization and is no time for any involved person to be standing around wondering what it is they should be doing right now.

The IR plan must be clearly communicated and spell out what the duties of staff are in responding to the incident. The staff must be trained in how to carry out the plan so that when an incident occurs, action is rapid and effective.

An acquaintance of the authors received a crash course in incident response from a NASA contractor over a very intense weekend. A new computer system was installed and found to have a severe software incompatibility.

The old system was going to have to be put back into production in order to meet a tight mission-critical processing schedule. Members of the staff were called into a room, the manager asked them to open their procedures manual to the appropriate section, told they were going to perform the procedure, and asked if they had any questions. None did; the staff left and the old system was brought uneventfully back into operation.

Though few organizations will have as much experience dealing with the unexpected as NASA, this situation shows the attributes a successful IR must have: There must be a plan; the staff must have the plan, understand it, and be able to follow it; and the plan must be able to achieve its objective, if followed. This is the IR performance we should all strive to achieve.

Notification of Key Personnel As soon as the SIRT determines that an incident is in progress, the right people must be notified in the right order. Most response organizations, such as firefighters or the military, maintain an alert roster for all emergencies. An **alert roster** is a document containing contact information on the individuals to be notified in the event of an actual incident.

The **alert message** is a scripted description of the incident and consists of just enough information so that each responder, SIRT or otherwise, knows what portion of the IR plan to implement without impeding the notification process. It is important to recognize that not everyone is on the alert roster—only those individuals who must respond to a specific actual incident. As with any part of the IR plan, the alert roster must be regularly maintained, tested, and rehearsed if it is to remain effective.

The Duty Roster

One of the most frustrating things to occur during IR is to have an inaccurate contact list. A good practice is for the alert roster to be defined as a set of roles to be activated when a particular part of the IR plan is activated. A duty roster is maintained that specifies who will fill that role over a particular time period and their contact information. The alert roster is static and spelled out in the policy. The duty roster is dynamic and changes on a regular basis, as needed.

During this phase, other key personnel not on the alert roster, such as general management, must be notified of the incident as well. This notification should occur only after the incident has been confirmed, but before media or other external sources learn of it. Among those likely to be included in the notification process are members of the legal, communications, and human resources departments. In addition, some incidents are disclosed to the employees in general, as a lesson in security, and some are not, as a measure of security. Furthermore, other organizations may need to be notified, if it is determined that the incident is not confined to internal information resources, or if the incident is part of a larger-scale assault. In general, the IR planners should determine in advance whom to notify and when, and should offer guidance about additional notification steps to take as needed.

Documenting an Incident

Documenting an Incident As soon as an incident has been confirmed and the notification process is under way, the team should begin to document it. The documentation should record the *who, what, when, where, why,* and *how* of each action taken while the incident is occurring. This documentation serves as a case study after the fact to determine whether the right actions were taken and if they were effective. It also proves, should it become necessary, that the organization did everything possible to prevent the spread of the incident. Legally, the standards of due care may offer some protection to the organization should an incident adversely affect individuals inside and outside the organization, or other organizations that use the target organization's systems. Incident documentation can also be used as a simulation in future training sessions on future versions of the IR plan.

Incident Containment Strategies

Incident Containment Strategies One of the most critical components of IR is stopping the incident or containing its scope or impact. Incident containment strategies vary depending on the incident, and on the amount of damage caused. Before an incident can be stopped or contained, however, the affected areas must be identified. Now is not the time to conduct a detailed analysis of the affected areas; those tasks are typically performed after the fact, in the forensics process. Instead, simple identification of what information and systems are involved determines the containment actions to be taken. Incident containment strategies focus on two tasks: stopping the incident and recovering control of the affected systems.

The SIRT can stop the incident and attempt to recover control by means of several strategies. If the incident originates outside the organization, the simplest and most straightforward approach is to disconnect the affected communication circuits. Of course, if the organization's lifeblood runs through that circuit, this step may be too drastic; if the incident does not threaten critical functional areas, it may be more feasible to monitor the incident and contain it another way. One approach used by some organizations is to dynamically apply filtering rules to limit certain types of network access. For example, if a threat agent is attacking a network by exploiting a vulnerability in the Simple Network Management Protocol (SNMP), then applying a blocking filter for the commonly used IP ports for that vulnerability will stop the attack without compromising other services on the network. Depending on the nature of the attack and the organization's technical capabilities, ad hoc controls can sometimes gain valuable time to devise a more permanent control strategy. Other containment strategies include the following:

- ▶ Disabling compromised user accounts
- ▶ Segmenting the network to contain malware's spread
- ▶ Reconfiguring a firewall to block the problem traffic

- ▶ Temporarily disabling the compromised process or service
- ▶ Taking down the conduit application or server—for example, the e-mail server
- ▶ Stopping all computers and network devices

Obviously, the final strategy is used only when all system control has been lost, and the only hope is to preserve the data stored on the computers so that operations can resume normally once the incident is resolved. The SIRT, following the procedures outlined in the IR plan, determines the length of the interruption.

Consider how many people aren't there on a regular basis. Many businesses require employees to travel, with members of the organization going off-site to meetings, seminars, training, vacations, or other activities. In considering these possibilities, the importance of preparedness becomes clear. Everyone should know how to handle an incident, not just the CISO and systems administrators.

Incident Escalation An incident may increase in scope or severity to the point that the IR plan cannot adequately handle it. An important part of knowing how to handle an incident is knowing at what point to escalate the incident to a disaster, or to transfer the incident to an outside authority such as law enforcement or another public response unit. Each organization will have to determine, during the business impact analysis, the point at which an incident is deemed a disaster. These criteria must be included in the incident response plan. The organization must also document when to involve outside responders, as discussed in other sections. Escalation is one of those things that once done cannot be undone, so it is important to know when and where it should be used.

Incident Recovery

Once the incident has been contained, and system control has been regained, incident recovery can begin. As in the incident response phase, the first task is to inform the appropriate human resources. Almost simultaneously, the SIRT must assess the full extent of the damage so as to determine what must be done to restore the systems. Each individual involved should begin recovery operations based on the appropriate incident recovery section of the IR plan.

The immediate determination of the scope of the breach of confidentiality, integrity, and availability of information and information assets is called **incident damage assessment**. Incident

Preserving Information

If a critical server is compromised, there is a great deal of pressure to get that server back into operation by doing a "bare metal" recovery. However, destroying the information on the server may severely impede future investigation of how the intrusion occurred, etc. A useful compromise is to take a forensic image of the server before recovery begins. If the organization is properly prepared, the delay to collect the forensic image is minimal and will preserve the information required for a full incident investigation and future legal action.

damage assessment can take days or weeks depending on the extent of the damage. The damage can range from minor (a curious hacker snooped around) to severe (hundreds of computer systems infected by a worm or virus). System logs, intrusion detection logs, configuration logs, and other documents, as well as the documentation from the incident response, provide information on the type, scope, and extent of damage. Using this information, the SIRT assesses the current state of the information and systems, and compares it to a known state. Individuals who document the damage from actual incidents must be trained to collect and preserve evidence, in case the incident is part of a crime or results in a civil action.

Once the extent of the damage has been determined, the recovery process begins. This process involves the following steps:[5]

- ▶ Identify the vulnerabilities that allowed the incident to occur and spread. Resolve them.
- ▶ Address the safeguards that failed to stop or limit the incident, or were missing from the system in the first place. Install, replace, or upgrade them.
- ▶ Evaluate monitoring capabilities (if present). Improve detection and reporting methods, or install new monitoring capabilities.
- ▶ Restore the data from backups. The IR team must understand the backup strategy used by the organization, restore the data contained in backups, and then use the appropriate recovery processes from incremental backups or database journals to recreate any data that was created or modified since the last backup.
- ▶ Restore the services and processes in use. Compromised services and processes must be examined, cleaned, and then restored. If services or processes were interrupted in the course of regaining control of the systems, they need to be brought back online.
- ▶ Continuously monitor the system. If an incident happened once, it could easily happen again. Hackers frequently boast of their exploits in chat rooms and dare their peers to match their efforts. If word gets out, others may be tempted to try the same or different attacks on your systems. It is therefore important to maintain vigilance during the entire IR process.
- ▶ Restore the confidence of the members of the organization's communities of interest. Management, following the recommendation from the SIRT, may wish to issue a short memorandum outlining the incident, and assuring all that the incident was handled and the damage was controlled. If the incident was minor, say so. If the incident was major or severely damaged systems or data, reassure the users that they can expect operations to return to normal as soon as possible. The objective of this communication is to prevent panic or confusion from causing additional disruption to the operations of the organization.

Before returning to its routine duties, the SIRT must conduct an **after-action review (AAR) or post mortem**. The after-action review entails a detailed examination of the events that occurred from first detection to final recovery. All key players review their notes and verify that the IR documentation is accurate and precise. All team members review their actions during the incident and identify areas where the IR plan worked, didn't work, or should improve. This exercise allows the team to update the IR plan. The AAR can serve as a training case for future staff. It also brings the SIRT's actions to a close.

LAW ENFORCEMENT INVOLVEMENT

When an incident violates civil or criminal law, it is the organization's responsibility to notify the proper authorities. Selecting the appropriate law enforcement agency depends on the type of crime committed. Each state, county, and city in the United States has its own law enforcement agencies. These agencies enforce all local and state laws and handle suspects and security crime scenes for state and federal cases. Local law enforcement agencies rarely have computer crimes task forces, but the investigative (detective) units are quite capable of processing crime scenes and handling most common criminal violations, such as physical theft or trespassing, damage to property, and the apprehension and processing of suspects in computer-related crimes.

Involving law enforcement agencies has both advantages and disadvantages. Such agencies are usually much better equipped to process evidence than a business. Unless the security forces in the organization have been trained in processing evidence and computer forensics, they may do more harm than good when attempting to extract information that can lead to the legal conviction of a suspected criminal. Law enforcement agencies are also prepared to handle the warrants and subpoenas necessary when documenting a case. They are adept at obtaining statements from witnesses, affidavits, and other required documents. For all these reasons, law enforcement personnel can be a security administrator's greatest allies in prosecuting a computer crime. It is therefore important to become familiar with the appropriate local and state agencies, before you have to make a call announcing a suspected crime.

The disadvantages of law enforcement involvement include possible loss of control of the chain of events following an incident, including the collection of information and evidence, and the prosecution of suspects. An organization that wishes to simply reprimand or dismiss an employee should not involve a law enforcement agency in the resolution of an incident. Additionally, the organization may not hear about the case for weeks or even months due to heavy caseloads or resource shortages. A very real issue for commercial organizations when involving law enforcement agencies is the taking of equipment vital to the organization's business as evidence. Assets can be removed, stored, and preserved to prepare the criminal case. Despite these difficulties, if the organization detects a criminal act, it has the legal obligation to notify the appropriate law enforcement officials. Failure to do so can subject the organization and its officers to prosecution as accessories to the crimes or for impeding the course of an investigation. It is up to the security administrator to ask questions of law enforcement agencies to determine when each agency wishes to be involved, and specifically which crimes will be addressed by each agency.

Incident response is one of the most critical functions in the information security program because it deals with how the organization responds to situations where its defenses have proved inadequate and have been compromised. During this critical time, there must be a well-defined plan in place to guide staff through appropriate notifications and actions to identify, contain, and recover the incident.

The Information Security Manager's Checklist

This topic has been fully tested, validated, and integrated into organizational operations with formal performance measures in place (as appropriate).

This topic has been implemented, but not fully tested, validated and integrated into organizational operations.

The implementation of this topic has begun, but is not yet complete.

The formal planning for this topic has begun, but is not yet complete.

This subject has not formally begun planning, or the organization has made a conscious decision not to pursue this topic.

22. Incident Response Plan	No	Planned	In Progress	In Place	Integrated
Develop the IR planning policy statement					
Review the business impact analysis (BIA)					
Identify preventive IR controls					
Develop data backup and recovery strategies					
Develop the IR plan document					
Plan testing, training, and exercises					
Plan maintenance					

For Further Reading

Building a Business Impact Analysis (BIA) Process: A Hands-On Blueprint by Barry Cardoza, K & M Publishers, Inc. , 2006.

Effective Business Impact Analysis—The Handbook by Institute for Business Continuity Training, 2008.

Leadership and Training for the Fight: A Few Thoughts on Leadership and Training from a Former Special Operations Soldier by Paul R. Howe, AuthorHouse, 2005.

SP 800-61 Rev. 1 Mar 2008 Computer Security Incident Handling Guide at http://csrc.nist.gov/publications/nistpubs/800-61-rev1/SP800-61rev1.pdf

References

1. The IR plan may also be called the "incident detection and response (ID&R) plan."

2. Tim Grance, Karen Kent, and Brian Kim. *Computer Security Incident Handling Guide,* Special Publication SP 800-61 (National Institute of Standards and Technology, 2004).

3. Donald L. Pipkin. *Information Security: Protecting the Global Enterprise.* Upper Saddle River, NJ: Prentice Hall PTR, 2000: 256.

4. Richard Bejtlich. *Extrusion Detection: Security Monitoring for Internal Intrusions.* Boston: Addison-Wesley, 2005.

5. Donald L. Pipkin. *Information Security: Protecting the Global Enterprise.* Upper Saddle River, NJ: Prentice Hall PTR, 2000: 285.

Chapter 23

The Disaster Recovery Plan

When incident response planning is well underway, the next vital step in the contingency planning process is disaster recovery planning. Though the IT and information security communities are often made responsible for disaster recovery planning, this planning includes many aspects that are not necessarily technology based. Some organizations have dedicated, corporate-level processes and staff to manage the disaster readiness of the organization.

Chapter Overview:

- ▶ What is disaster recovery?
- ▶ DR policy
- ▶ Disaster classification
- ▶ Planning for disaster
- ▶ Crisis management
- ▶ Sample disaster recovery plan

WHAT IS DISASTER RECOVERY?

Disaster recovery planning (DRP) entails the preparation for and recovery from a disaster, whether natural or human-made. In some cases, actual incidents detected by the IR team may escalate to the level of disaster, and the IR plan may no longer be able to handle the effective and efficient recovery from the loss. For example, if a malicious program evades containment actions and infects and disables many or most of an organization's systems and impairs its ability to function, the DR plan is activated. Sometimes events are by their nature immediately classified as disasters, such as an extensive fire, flood, damaging storm, or earthquake.

The CP team is responsible for creating the DR plan. In general, a disaster has occurred when either of two criteria is met: (1) the organization is unable to contain or control the impact of an incident, or (2) the level of damage or destruction from an incident is so severe that the organization cannot quickly recover from it. The distinction between an incident and a disaster is often subtle and deciding when to transition from the IR plan to the DR plan requires careful up-front planning. The CP team must document in the DR plan whether an event is classified as an incident or a disaster. This determination is critical because it determines which plan is activated. The key role of a DR plan is defining how to reestablish operations at the location where the organization is usually located.

The planning process for the DR plan should be tied to, but distinct from, the IR plan. In some cases, a disaster may be the natural progression of an incident when it spirals out of control. It is important that the planning processes be tightly integrated so that the reaction teams can easily make the transition from incident response to disaster recovery and business continuity planning (the subject of the next chapter).

You learned in an earlier chapter about a planning process recommended by NIST that uses seven steps. In the broader context of organizational contingency planning, these steps form the overall CP process. These process steps are used again here within the narrower context of the DRP process:

1. Develop the DR planning policy statement: A formal department or agency policy provides the authority and guidance necessary to develop an effective contingency plan.
2. Review the business impact analysis (BIA): The BIA was prepared to help identify and prioritize critical IT systems and components. A review of these determinations is an important step in the process.
3. Identify preventive controls: Measures taken to reduce the effects of system disruptions can increase system availability and reduce contingency life-cycle costs.
4. Develop recovery strategies: Thorough recovery strategies ensure that the system can be recovered quickly and effectively following a disruption.
5. Develop the disaster recovery plan document: The plan should contain detailed guidance and procedures for restoring a damaged system.
6. Plan testing, training, and exercises: Testing the plan identifies planning gaps, whereas training prepares recovery personnel for plan activation; both activities improve plan effectiveness and overall agency preparedness.
7. Plan maintenance: The plan should be a living document that is updated regularly to remain current with system enhancements.

DR POLICY

The DR team, led by the business manager designated as the DR team leader, begins with the development of the DR policy. The policy presents an overview of an organization's philosophy on the conduct of disaster recovery operations and serves as the guide for the development of the DR plan. The DR policy itself may have been created by the organization's CP team and handed down to the DR team leader. Alternatively, the DR team may be assigned the role of developing the DR policy. In either case, the disaster recovery policy contains the following key elements:

- ▶ Purpose—The purpose of the disaster recovery program is to provide for the direction and guidance of any and all disaster recovery operations. In addition, the program provides for the development and support for the disaster recovery plan. In everyday practice those responsible for the program must also work to emphasize the importance of creating and maintaining effective disaster recovery functions. As with any major enterprise-wide policy effort, it is important for the disaster recovery program to begin with a clear statement of executive vision.

- ▶ Scope—This section of the policy identifies the organizational units and groups of employees to which the policy applies. This clarification is important if the organization is geographically dispersed or is creating different policies for different organizational units.

- ▶ Roles and responsibilities—This section of the DR policy identifies the roles and responsibilities of the key players in the disaster recovery operation. It can include a delineation of the responsibilities of the executive management down to the individual employee. Note that some sections of the DR policy may be duplicated from the organization's overall contingency planning policy. In smaller organizations, this redundancy can be eliminated, since many of the functions are performed by the same group.

- ▶ Resource requirements—An organization can allocate specific resources to the development of disaster recovery plans here. While this may include directives for individuals, it can be separated from the previous section for emphasis and clarity.

- ▶ Training requirements—This section defines and highlights the training requirements for the units within the organization and the various categories of employee.

- ▶ Exercise and testing schedules—This section stipulates the testing intervals of the DR plan, as well as the type of testing and the individuals involved.

- ▶ Plan maintenance schedule—This section states the review and update intervals of the plan, and identifies who is involved in the review. It is not necessary for the entire DR team to be involved, but the review can be combined with a periodic test of the DR plan as long as the resulting discussion includes areas for improvement for the plan.

- ▶ Special considerations (such as information storage and maintenance).

DISASTER CLASSIFICATION

A DR plan can classify disasters in a number of ways. The most common method is to separate natural disasters from human-made disasters. *Acts of terrorism*, including cyberterrorism or hactivism, *acts of war*, and *acts of man* that may begin as incidents and escalate into disasters are all examples of human-made disasters. Another way of classifying disasters is by speed of development. **Rapid-onset disasters** occur suddenly, with little warning, possibly taking the lives of people and destroying the means of production. Rapid-onset disasters may be caused by earthquakes, floods, storm winds, tornadoes, mud flows, or even an especially virulent worm that affects a majority of the organization's systems before it can be contained. **Slow-onset disasters** occur over time and slowly degrade the capacity of an organization to withstand their effects. Hazards causing these disaster conditions typically include droughts, famines, environmental degradation, desertification, deforestation, and pest infestation.[1]

PLANNING FOR DISASTER

To plan for disaster, the CP team engages in scenario development and impact analysis, along the way categorizing the level of threat that each potential disaster poses. When generating a disaster recovery scenario, start first with the most important asset—people. Do you have the human resources with the appropriate organizational knowledge to restore business operations? Organizations must cross-train their employees to ensure that operations and a sense of normalcy can be restored. In addition, the DR plan must be tested regularly so that the DR team can lead the recovery effort quickly and efficiently. The key elements that the CP team must build into the DR plan include the following:

1. Clear delegation of roles and responsibilities: Everyone assigned to the DR team should be aware of his or her duties during a disaster. Some team members may be responsible for coordinating with local services, such as fire, police, and medical personnel. Some may be responsible for the evacuation of company personnel, if required. Others may be assigned to simply pack up and leave.

2. Execution of the alert roster and notification of key personnel: These notifications may extend outside the organization to include the fire, police, or medical services mentioned earlier, as well as insurance agencies, disaster teams such as those of the Red Cross, and management teams.

3. Clear establishment of priorities: During a disaster response, the first priority is always the preservation of human life. Data and systems protection is subordinate when the disaster threatens the lives, health, or welfare of the employees or members of the community. Only after all employees and neighbors have been safeguarded can the disaster recovery team attend to protection of other organizational assets.

4. Procedures for documentation of the disaster: Just as in an incident response, the disaster must be carefully recorded from the onset. This documentation is used later to determine how and why the disaster occurred.

5. Action steps to mitigate the impact of the disaster on the operations of the organization: The DR plan should specify the responsibilities of each DR team member, such as the evacuation of physical assets or making sure that all systems are securely shut down, to prevent further loss of data.

6. Alternative implementations for the various systems components, should primary versions be unavailable: These components include stand-by equipment, either purchased, leased, or under contract with a disaster recovery service agency. Developing systems with excess capacity, fault tolerance, auto-recovery, and

fail-safe features facilitates a quick recovery. Something as simple as using Dynamic Host Control Protocol (DHCP) to assign network addresses instead of using static addresses can allow systems to quickly and easily regain connectivity without technical support. Networks should support dynamic reconfiguration; restoration of network connectivity should be planned. Data recovery requires effective backup strategies as well as flexible hardware configurations. System management should be a top priority. All solutions should be tightly integrated and developed in a strategic plan to provide continuity. Piecemeal construction can result in a disaster after the disaster, since incompatible systems are unexpectedly thrust together.

There are a number of options available to an organization to protect their information and assist in getting operations up and running quickly:

▶ Traditional data backups: The use of a combination of on-site and off-site media (tape, disk, optical, etc.) backup methods, in a variety of rotation schemes. Because the backup point is sometime in the past, recent data is potentially lost. Newer data backup schemes may involve remote data replication or disk-to-disk-to-tape methods.

▶ Electronic vaulting: The bulk batch-transfer of data to an off-site facility. This transfer is usually conducted via dedicated network links or secure Internet connections. The receiving server archives the data as it is received. Some disaster recovery companies specialize in **electronic vaulting** services.

▶ Remote journaling: The transfer of live transactions to an off-site facility. It differs from electronic vaulting in two ways: (1) Only transactions are transferred, not archived data, and (2) the transfer takes place online and in much closer to real time. While electronic vaulting is akin to a traditional backup, with a dump of data to the off-site storage, **remote journaling** involves online activities on a systems level, much like server fault tolerance, where data is written to two locations simultaneously.

▶ Database shadowing: The storage of duplicate online transaction data, along with the duplication of the databases at the remote site on a redundant server. **Database shadowing** combines electronic vaulting with remote journaling, by writing multiple copies of the database simultaneously in two separated locations.

Food, Water, and Toilet Tissue

DRP planning is another of those areas where technical people love to immediately jump to the engineering of technical controls. However, the people component of disaster recovery cannot be overlooked. During DR, the organization's employees will be working long hours in very stressful circumstances for possibly an extended period of time.

Napoleon is credited with the insight that "an army moves on its stomach" and the DR planners will neglect this piece of wisdom at their peril. The DR plan must also provide for food, water, sanitary facilities, and common consumables such as toilet tissue, paper towels, etc.

DR is a complex area and often organizations spend vast amounts of resources developing and distributing lengthy manuals to all employees. While this is a worthwhile effort in some cases, a manual that was destroyed along with the building is useless in a DR situation.

For this reason, the critical, immediate knowledge and information should be distilled down to a wallet card that employees can keep in their possession. It won't hold a lot of information but what it does hold will likely be available to the employee when a disaster strikes.

As part of DR plan readiness, each employee should have two types of emergency information cards in his or her possession at all times. The first lists personal emergency information—the person to notify in case of an emergency (next of kin), medical conditions, and a form of identification. The second comprises a set of instructions on what to do in the event of an emergency. This snapshot of the DR plan should contain a contact number or hotline for calling the organization during an emergency, emergency services numbers (fire, police, medical), evacuation and assembly locations (storm shelters, for example), the name and number of the disaster recovery coordinator, and any other needed information.

CRISIS MANAGEMENT

The DR plan must also include reference to another process that many organizations plan for separately—**crisis management**, or the action steps that affect the people both inside and outside the organization that are taken during and after a disaster. The DR team works closely with the crisis management team to assure complete and timely communication during a disaster. According to Gartner Research, the crisis management team is responsible for managing the event from an enterprise perspective and covers the following major activities:

- ▶ Supporting personnel and their loved ones during the crisis
- ▶ Determining the event's impact on normal business operations and, if necessary, making a disaster declaration
- ▶ Keeping the public informed about the event and the actions being taken to ensure the recovery of personnel and the enterprise
- ▶ Communicating with major customers, suppliers, partners, regulatory agencies, industry organizations, the media, and other interested parties[2]

The crisis management team should establish a base of operations or command center near the site of the disaster as soon as possible. It should include individuals from all functional areas of the organization to facilitate communications and cooperation. The crisis management team is charged with two key tasks:

1. Verifying personnel status: Everyone must be accounted for, including individuals who are on vacations, leaves of absence, and business trips.
2. Activating the alert roster: Alert rosters and general personnel phone lists are used to notify individuals whose assistance may be needed, or to simply tell employees not to report to work, until the disaster is over.

The crisis management team should plan an approach for releasing information in the event of a disaster, and should perhaps even have boilerplate scripts prepared for press releases. Advice from Lanny Davis, former counselor to President Bill Clinton, is very clear. When beset by damaging events, tell the whole story as soon as possible directly to the affected audience. This can be summed up with the pithy statement, "Tell It Early, Tell It All, Tell It Yourself," which is the subtitle of Davis's memoir.[3]

Responding to the Disaster

When a disaster strikes, actual events can at times overwhelm even the best of DR plans. To be prepared, the CP team should incorporate a degree of flexibility into the plan. If the physical facilities are intact, the DR team should begin the restoration of systems and data to work toward full operational capability. If the organization's facilities are destroyed, alternative actions must be taken until new facilities can be acquired. When a disaster threatens the viability of an organization at the primary site, the disaster recovery process becomes a business continuity process, which is described in detail in the next chapter.

SAMPLE DISASTER RECOVERY PLAN

Figure 23-1 shows another example of what may be found in a disaster recovery plan. This document provides a sample disaster recovery plan adapted from one provided by the Texas State Library and Archives State and Local Records Management Division.[4]

The plan has nine major sections, each of which is outlined below. Many organizations—particularly ones with multiple locations and hundreds of employees—would find this plan too simple. Nevertheless, the basic structure provides a solid starting point for any organization.

1. Name of agency: The first section identifies the department, division, or institution to which this particular plan applies. This identification is especially important in organizations that are large enough to require more than one plan.

2. Date of completion or update of the plan and test date.

3. Agency staff to be called in the event of a disaster: This roster should be kept current; it will not help the organization to have a list of employees who are no longer with the company. This section should also identify key support personnel such as building maintenance supervisors, physical security directors, legal council, and the starting points on the alert roster. A copy of the alert roster (also known as the telephone tree) should be attached.

4. Emergency services to be called (if needed) in event of a disaster: While dialing 911 will certainly bring police, fire, and ambulance services, the organization may have equally pressing needs for emergency teams from the gas, electric, and water companies. This section should also list electricians, plumbers, locksmiths, and software and hardware vendors.

5. Locations of in-house emergency equipment and supplies: This section should include maps and floor plans with directions to all critical in-house emergency materials, including shut-off switches and valves for gas, electric, and water. It should also provide directions to key supplies including first aid kits, fire extinguishers, flashlights,

batteries, and a stash of office supplies. It is a good idea to place a disaster pack on every floor in an unlocked closet or readily accessible location. These items should be inventoried and updated as needed.

6. Sources of off-site equipment and supplies: These items include contact sources for mobile phones, dehumidifiers, industrial equipment such as forklifts and portable generators, and other safety and recovery components.

7. Salvage priority list: While the IT director may have just enough time to grab the last on-site backup before darting out the door in the event of a fire, most likely additional materials can be salvaged if recovery efforts permit. In this event, recovery teams should know what has priority. This list should specify whether to recover hard copies or if the effort should be directed toward saving equipment. Similarly, it specifies whether the organization should focus on archival records or recent documents. The plan should include the locations and priorities of all items of value to the organization. When determining priorities, ask questions such as the following: Are these records archived elsewhere (i.e., off-site), or is this the only copy? Can these records be reproduced if lost, and if so, at what cost? Is the cost of replacement more or less than the cost of the value of the materials? It may be useful to create a simple rating scheme for materials. Data classification labels can be adapted to include disaster recovery information. For example, some records may be labeled "Salvage at all costs," "Salvage if time and resources permit," or "Do not salvage."

8. Agency disaster recovery procedures: This very important section outlines the specific assignments given to key personnel, including the disaster recovery team, to be performed in the event of a disaster. If these duties differ by type of disaster, it may be useful to create multiple scenarios, each listing the duties and responsibilities of the parties involved. It is equally important to make sure that all personnel identified in this section have a copy of the DRP stored where they can easily access it, and that they are familiar with their responsibilities.

9. Follow-up assessment: The final section details what is to be accomplished after disaster strikes—specifically, what documentation is required for recovery efforts, including mandatory insurance reports, required photographs, and the after-action review format.

This chapter introduced the important topic of disaster recovery planning, which is a critical process in protecting an organization's ability to continue its operation in the face of a natural or human-caused disaster.

The DR plan must address organizational, technical, and human issues if it is to be effective in recovering from a disaster. A sometimes overlooked but very important component of this plan deals with crisis management—the actions that are taken immediately after the disaster occurs to locate personnel; to communicate with family, business partners, and the general public; and to begin the notification process for initiating the DR plan.

EXAMPLE DISASTER RECOVERY PLAN

1. Name of agency_____

2. Date of completion or update of the plan_____

3. Agency staff to be called in the event of a disaster:

   Disaster Recovery Team:

   Name: Numbers: Position:

   _____

   _____

   _____

   Building Maintenance_____

   Building Security_____

   Legal Advisor_____

   Note below who is to call whom upon the discovery of a disaster (Telephone Tree):

Figure 23-1 Sample Disaster Recovery Plan
Course Technology/Cengage Learning

4. Emergency services to be called (if needed) in event of a disaster:

Service:	Contact Person:	Number:

Ambulance_____

Carpenters_____

Data Processing Backup_____

Electrician_____

Emergency Management Coordinator _____

Exterminator_____

Fire Department_____

Food Services_____

Locksmith_____

Plumber_____

Police _____

Security Personnel (extra)_____

Software Vendor_____

Temporary Personnel_____

Utility Companies:

   Electric _____

   Gas _____

   Water_____

Others:

Figure 23-1 (Continued)

5. Locations of in-house emergency equipment and supplies (attach map or floor plan with locations marked):

Batteries_____

Badges (employee identification)_____

Camera /Film_____

Cut-off Switches and Valves:

Electric_____

Gas_____

Water_____

Sprinkler System (if separate) _____

Extension Cords (heavy-duty)_____

Fire Extinguishers_____

Flashlights_____

Ladders_____

Mops/Sponges/Buckets/Brooms_____

Nylon Monofilament_____

Packing Tape/String/Sissors_____

Paper Towels (white)_____

Plastic Trash Bags_____

Rubber Gloves_____

Transistor Radio (battery powered)_____

3

6. Sources of off-site equipment and supplies (if maintained on-site, note location):

    Item: Contact/Company: Number:

    Cellular Phone_____

    Dehumidifiers_____

    Drying Space_____

    Dust Masks_____

    Fans_____

    Fork Lift_____

    Freezer/Wax Paper_____

    Freezer Space/Refrigeration Truck_____

    Fungicides_____

    Generator (portable)_____

    Hard Hats_____

    Pallets_____

    Plastic Milk Crates_____

    Pumps (submersion)_____

    Rubber Boots_____

    Safety Glasses_____

    Trash Can (all sizes)_____

    Vacuum/Freeze Drying Facilities_____

    Waterproof Clothing_____

    Wet-Dry Vacuum_____

Figure 23-1 (Continued)

7. Salvage Priority List:

    Attach a copy of the records retention schedule identifying all vital/essential records series. The location and record medium of the preservation duplicate for each vital records series should be noted.

    It is also very helpful if other records series are reviewed to determine their priority for salvage should a disaster occur. The following questions can be helpful in determining priorities:

    1. Can the records be replaced? At what cost?
    2. Would the cost of replacement be less or more than restoration of the records?
    3. How important are the records to the agency?
    4. Are the records duplicated elsewhere?

    To simplify this process, priorities may be assigned as follows:

    1. Salvage at all costs.
        (example, records that are historically valuable or non-vital records that are important to agency operations and very difficult to recreate)

    2. Salvage if time and resources permit.
        (example, records that are less important to the agency or somewhat easier to recreate)

    3. Dispose of as part of general cleanup.
        (example, records that do not need to be salvaged because they are convenience copies and the record copy is at another location)

8. Agency Disaster Recovery Procedures:

    Attach a list of specific procedures to be followed in the event of a disaster in you agency, including responsibilities of in-house recovery team members.

9. Follow-up Assessment:

    A written report, including photographs, should be prepared after recovery and attached to a copy of the disaster plan. The report should note the effectiveness of the plan, and should include an evaluation of the sources of supplies and equipment, and of any off-site facilities used.

    (Adapted from *Basic Guidelines for Disaster Planning in Oklahoma*)

The Information Security Manager's Checklist

	This topic has been fully tested, validated, and integrated into organizational operations with formal performance measures in place (as appropriate).				
	This topic has been implemented, but not fully tested, validated, and integrated into organizational operations.				
	The implementation of this topic has begun, but is not yet complete.				
	The formal planning for this topic has begun, but is not yet complete.				
	This subject has not formally begun planning, or the organization has made a conscious decision not to pursue this topic.				
23. Disaster Recovery Plan	No	Planned	In Progress	In Place	Integrated
Develop the DR planning policy statement					
Review the business impact analysis (BIA)					
Identify preventive controls					
Develop recovery strategies					
Develop the disaster recovery plan document					
Plan testing, training, and exercises					
Plan maintenance					

For Further Reading

The Disaster Recovery Handbook: A Step-by-Step Plan to Ensure Business Continuity and Protect Vital Operations, Facilities, and Assets by Michael Wallace and Lawrence Webber, AMACOM, 2010.

Business Continuity and Disaster Recovery Planning for IT Professionals by Susan Snedaker, Syngress, 2007.

IT Disaster Recovery Planning for Dummies by Peter and Philip Jan Rothstein, International Data Group (IDG), 2007.

References

1. International Federation of Red Cross and Red Crescent Societies. *Disaster Preparedness Training Programme*. Accessed 1 March 2003, from http://www.ifrc.org/what/dp/manual/introdp.pdf.

2. Roberta Witty. What is crisis management? *Gartner Online*. 19 September 2001. [Cited 26 June 2002]. Available from the World Wide Web at http://security1.gartner.com/story.php.id.152.jsp.

3. Lanny J. Davis. *Truth to Tell: Tell It Early, Tell It All, Tell It Yourself: Notes from My White House Education*. New York: Free Press, May 1999.

4. Texas State Library and Archives State and Local Records Management Division. *Example Disaster Recovery Plan*. Accessed 21 May 21 2003, from http://www.tsl.state.tx.us/slrm/disaster/recovery_plan.pdf.

Chapter 24

The Business Continuity Plan

Business continuity planning (BCP) ensures that critical business functions can continue if a disaster occurs. Unlike the DR plan, which is usually managed by the IT community of interest, the business continuity plan (BC plan) is most properly managed by the CEO of an organization. The BC plan is activated and executed concurrently with the DR plan when the disaster is major or long term and requires fuller and complex restoration of information and IT resources. If a disaster has rendered the current business location unusable, there must be a plan to allow the business to continue to function. While the BC plan reestablishes critical business functions at an alternate site, the DR plan team focuses on the reestablishment of the technical infrastructure and business operations at the primary site. Not every business needs such a plan, or such facilities. Some small companies or fiscally sound organizations may be able to simply cease operations until the primary facilities are restored. Manufacturing and retail organizations, however, depend on continued operations for revenue. Thus, these entities must have a BC plan in place in order to quickly relocate operations with minimal loss of revenue.

BC is an element of contingency planning, and it is best accomplished using a repeatable process or methodology. If you would like to get additional background on contingency planning, access a copy of NIST Special Publication 800-34, the *Contingency Planning Guide for Information Technology Systems*, from the Internet. It includes guidance for planning for incidents, disasters, and situations calling for business continuity. The approach used in that document has been adapted for BC use here.

Chapter Overview:

▶ Business resumption planning

▶ Continuity strategies

▶ Implementing the BC strategy

BUSINESS RESUMPTION PLANNING

Because the DR and BC plans are closely related, most organizations prepare them at the same time, and may combine them into a single planning document called the **business resumption plan** (or BR plan). Such a comprehensive plan must be able to support the reestablishment of operations at two different locations—one immediately at an alternate site, and one eventually back at the primary site. Therefore, although a single planning team can develop the BR plan, execution of the plan requires separate execution teams.

The first step in all contingency efforts is to verify that the proper policy is in place to enable the necessary processes. If it is not in place, or it is deficient, it will need to be brought up to speed. The next step is to plan. In some organizations the policy development and planning process may happen at the same time when development of policy is a function of planning. Others place policy before planning as a separate process. For our purposes, the BC policy should be developed prior to the BC plan; the development of both are part of BC planning. The development process includes:

1. Develop the BC planning policy statement: A formal organizational policy provides the authority and guidance necessary to develop an effective continuity plan. As with any enterprise-wide policy process, it is important to begin with the executive vision.

2. Review the business impact analysis: The BIA helps to identify and prioritize critical IT systems and components.

3. Identify preventive controls: Measures taken to reduce the effects of system disruptions can increase system availability and reduce continuity life-cycle costs.

4. Develop relocation strategies: Thorough relocation strategies ensure that critical system functions may be recovered quickly and effectively following a disruption.

5. Develop the continuity plan: The continuity plan should contain detailed guidance and procedures for restoring a damaged system.

6. Plan testing, training, and exercises: Testing the plan identifies planning gaps, whereas training prepares recovery personnel for plan activation; both activities improve plan effectiveness and overall agency preparedness.

7. Plan maintenance: The plan should be a living document that is updated regularly to remain current with system enhancements.

BC Planning Policy Statement

BC planning begins with the development of the BC policy, which reflects the organization's philosophy on the conduct of business continuity operations and serves as the guiding document for the development of the BC planning. The BC team leader might receive the BC policy from the CP team, or might guide the BC team in developing one. The BC policy contains the following key sections:

- ▶ Purpose—What is the purpose of the business continuity program? To provide the necessary planning and coordination to facilitate the relocation of critical business functions should a disaster prohibit continued operations at the primary site.

- ▶ Scope—This section identifies the organizational units and groups of employees to which the policy applies. This is especially useful in organizations that are geographically dispersed, or that are creating different policies for different organizational units.

- ▶ Roles and Responsibilities—This section identifies the roles and responsibilities of the key players in the business continuity operation, from executive management down to individual employees. In some cases, sections may be duplicated from the organization's overall contingency planning policy. For smaller organizations, this redundancy can be eliminated because many of the functions are performed by the same group of individuals.

- ▶ Resource Requirements—Organizations can allocate specific resources to the development of business continuity plans. Although this may include directives for individuals, it can be separated from the Roles and Responsibilities section for emphasis and clarity.

- ▶ Training Requirements—This section specifies the training requirements for the various employee groups.

- ▶ Exercise and Testing Schedules—This section stipulates the frequency of BC plan testing, and can include both the type of exercise or testing and the individuals involved.

- ▶ Plan Maintenance Schedule—This section specifies the procedures and frequency of BC plan reviews, and identifies the personnel who will be involved in the review. It is not necessary for the entire BC team to be involved; the review can be combined with a periodic test of the BC (as in a talk-through) as long as the resulting discussion includes areas for improvement for the plan.

- ▶ Special Considerations—As described earlier, in extreme situations the DR and BC plans overlap. Thus, this section provides an overview of the information storage and retrieval plans of the organization. While the specifics do not have to be elaborated in this document, at a minimum the plan should identify where more detailed documentation is kept, which individuals are responsible, and any other information needed to implement the strategy.

You may have noticed that this structure is virtually identical to that of the disaster recovery policy and plans. The processes are generally the same, with minor differences in implementation.

The identification of critical business functions and the resources to support them is the cornerstone of a BC plan. When a disaster strikes, these functions are the first to be reestablished at the alternate site. The CP team needs to appoint a group of individuals to evaluate and compare the various alternatives and to recommend which strategy should be selected and implemented.

What's the Goal?

A question that must be carefully answered revolves around the goal of BC planning. It is a perfectly acceptable BC goal for the organization to shut its doors and cease operations if its primary site is damaged beyond timely repair. It is a sign of wisdom that an organization recognizes that it is not able (or does not choose) to invest the time and resources to plan and execute a BC operation.

However, this decision should not be taken lightly and in any case should be an explicit decision on the part of management rather than the result of either a lack of planning or poor execution of a plan.

The strategy selected usually involves an off-site facility, which should be inspected, configured, secured, and tested on a periodic basis. The selection should be reviewed periodically to determine whether a better alternative has emerged or whether the organization needs a different solution.

Many organizations with operations in New York City had their business continuity efforts (or lack thereof) tested critically on September 11, 2001. Similarly, organizations located in the Gulf Coast region of the United States had their BCP effectiveness tested during the 2005 hurricane season. When these organizations considered how much business continuity they wanted to have, they were faced with establishing two design parameters for their BC planning process: the recovery time objective (RTO) and the recovery point objective (RPO). The **recovery time objective (RTO)** is the amount of time that passes before an infrastructure is available once the need for BC is declared. Reducing RTO requires mechanisms to shorten start-up time or provisions to make data available online at a failover site. The **recovery point objective (RPO)** is the point in the past to which the recovered applications and data at the alternate infrastructure will be restored. In database terms, this is the amount of data loss that will be experienced as a result of the resumption at the alternate site. Reducing RPO requires mechanisms to increase the synchronicity of data replication between production systems and the backup implementations for those systems.

Return to Access

Being that Cisco is a networking company, they add a third design parameter of return to access (RTA) to specify the time before the organization's information resources are network accessible. For any organization that includes network access for external customers a part of its business model, this would be a significant factor in planning.

The factors that contribute to RTA include network connectivity, updates to external DNS servers to reflect any address changes for the alternate facility, etc.

CONTINUITY STRATEGIES

A CP team can choose from several strategies in its planning for business continuity. The determining factor is usually cost. In general, three exclusive-use options exist:

Hot Sites

A **hot site** is a fully configured computer facility, with all services, communications links, and physical plant operations. It duplicates computing resources, peripherals, phone systems, applications, and workstations. Essentially, this duplicate facility needs only the latest data backups and the personnel to function. If the organization uses one of the data services listed in the following sections, a hot site can be fully functional within minutes. Not surprisingly, it is the most expensive alternative available. Other disadvantages include the need to provide maintenance for all the systems and equipment at the hot site, as well as physical and information security. However, if the organization requires a 24/7 capability for near real-time recovery, the hot site is the optimal strategy.

Warm Sites

A **warm site** provides many of the same services and options as the hot site, but, typically, software applications are not included or are not installed and configured. It frequently includes computing equipment and peripherals with servers but not client workstations. A warm site offers many of the advantages of a hot site at a lower cost. The disadvantage is that it requires several hours—perhaps days—to make a warm site fully functional.

Cold Sites

A **cold site** provides only rudimentary services and facilities. No computer hardware or peripherals are provided. All communications services must be installed after the site is occupied. A cold site is an empty room with standard heating, air-conditioning, and electrical service. Everything else is an added cost option. Despite these disadvantages, a cold site may be better than nothing. Its primary advantage is its low cost. The most useful feature of this approach is that it ensures an organization has floor space should a widespread disaster strike, but some organizations are prepared to struggle to lease new space rather than pay maintenance fees on a cold site.

Shared-Use Options

In addition to the exclusive use options just discussed, there are also three shared-use contingency options:

Time-Shares A **time-share** operates like one of the three sites described above, but is leased in conjunction with a business partner or sister organization. It allows the organization to provide a disaster recovery/business continuity option, while reducing its overall costs. The primary disadvantage is the possibility that more than one time-share participant might need the facility simultaneously. Other disadvantages include the need to stock the facility with the equipment and data from all organizations involved, the complexity of negotiating the time-share with the sharing organizations, and the possibility that one or more parties might exit the agreement or sublease their options. Operating under a time-share is much like agreeing to co-lease an apartment with a group of friends. One can only hope that the organizations remain on amicable terms, since they all could potentially gain physical access to each other's data.

Service Bureaus A **service bureau** is a service agency that provides a service for a fee. In the case of disaster recovery/continuity planning, this service is the provision of physical facilities in the event of a disaster. Such agencies also frequently provide off-site data storage for a fee. Contracts with service bureaus can specify exactly what the organization needs under what circumstances. A service agreement usually guarantees space when needed; the service bureau must acquire additional space in the event of a widespread disaster. In this sense, it resembles the rental car provision in a car insurance policy. The disadvantage is that service contracts must be renegotiated periodically and rates can change. It can also be quite expensive.

Mutual Agreements A **mutual agreement** is a contract between two organizations in which each party agrees to assist the other in the event of a disaster. It stipulates that each organization is obligated to provide the necessary facilities, resources, and services until the receiving organization is able to recover from the disaster. This arrangement can be a lot like moving in with relatives or friends—it doesn't take long for an organization to wear out its welcome. Many organizations balk at the idea of having to fund (even in the short term) duplicate services and resources. Still, mutual agreements between divisions of the same parent company, between subordinate and senior organizations, or between business partners may be a cost-effective solution when both parties to the agreement have a mutual interest in each other's continued operations and both have similar capabilities and capacities.

In addition to these six basic strategies, some specialized alternatives are available, such as a **rolling mobile site** configured in the payload area of a tractor/trailer or externally stored resources, such as a rental storage area containing duplicate or older equipment. These alternatives are similar to the Pre-positioning of Overseas Material Configured to Unit Sets (POM-CUS) sites of the Cold War era, in which caches of materials to be used in the event of an emergency or war were stored. An organization might arrange with a pre-fabricated building contractor for immediate, temporary facilities (mobile offices) on-site in the event of a disaster.

The Human Element

One of the reasons that BC plans fail in practice is that they do not consider the human element in their implementation. For example, when business operations move to an alternate site, how will employees find the site and once there, find their way around to where it is that they are supposed to work?

Another significant factor revolves around the myriad of services that were present at the main site and may be lacking in the alternate site. For example, finding a T-15 Torx may have been as simple as walking down the hall to borrow one at the main site but may be a significant obstacle in the alternate site when the helpful group isn't there. Even simple services such as shipping and receiving, mail handling, food service, and janitorial service require careful planning to assure that they will be available at the alternate site.

The important takeaway is that BC planning doesn't just revolve around assuring that hardware, software, data, and network connectivity will be present when needed. Careful planning must be done to assure that the people who "make that technology happen" are present, adequately supplied and able to do their jobs in some modicum of comfort.

IMPLEMENTING THE BC STRATEGY

The BC plan includes detailed guidance and procedures for moving into the contracted alternate site. The procedures developed and tested previously are documented and formalized in the plan. Just as with the DR plan, the responsibility for creating the BC plan does not usually fall to the CISO. The BC team leader is most likely a general manager from the operations or production division, appointed by the chief operations officer, chief finance officer, or chief executive officer. This officer guides the management team in the development of specific plans to execute once the CEO declares such a move to be necessary. In most cases, the trigger for such a decision is the evaluation of the damage to the primary site, conducted by the DR team, and reported to the CP team, who in turn advises the organization's executive management group.

Once the trigger has been tripped, the extent of the BC move depends on the extent of damage to the organization. This is why subordinate BC plans are so important. An organization may sustain sufficient damage to move some, but not all of its functions. Each subordinate group must then be prepared to pack whatever they can salvage and then relocate to the alternate site. The BC team should have already arrived and begun designating the locations for each function.

Executing the BC plan consists of three distinct phases of operation, the first of which must be done prior to any disaster requiring relocation. These phases are preparation for BC actions, relocation to the alternate site, and return to primary site.

Preparation for BC Actions

The developers of the BC plan must first specify what must be done before the relocation occurs. Unlike the DR plan, the type of disaster does not affect the method of relocation, nor does the selection of services, only the extent of the disaster does. The more devastating the disaster (or the more damage caused by it), the more an organization must be relocated to the alternate site.

In this phase of the BC plan the organization specifies what type of relocation services is desired and what type of data management strategies is deployed to support relocation.

From the variety of relocation services available—hot, warm, or cold sites, as well as the three time-share and the mobile site options—the plan specifies what type of resources is needed and desired to support ongoing operations.

Relocation to the Alternate Site

This phase of the BC plan is the official beginning of actual BC operations. The plan should specify under what conditions and how the organization relocates from the primary site to the alternate. Some of the items to be covered include the following:

- ▶ Identification of advance party and departure point: At a minimum the BCP should specify the BC team serving as the advance party (the group responsible for the process of initiating the occupation of the alternate facility) to initiate the preparation of the location. It should also include information as to what the trigger is that signals the relocation of the advance party to the BC site. This is usually done by verbal directive of the CP team leader, as directed by the CEO.

- Notification of service providers: One of the first tasks the advance party must do is notify a number of individuals, including all necessary service providers (power, water, gas, telephone, Internet) as well as the BC site owner so that they can begin activating the necessary resources to get the BC site up and running. The plan should contain this critical information as well as designate who should notify the service providers and when. As the BC advance party arrives at the BC site, they should meet with the site manager and conduct a detailed walk-through to assess the status of the facility and identify any problems. This is the same type of inspection performed when leasing an apartment or home. If the organization does not identify any preexisting problems, they may be charged for the repairs when they leave. Of course, the contract stipulates whether this is necessary.

- Notification of BC team to move to BC site: The next group to relocate to the BC site is the main body of the BC team. While the two or three individuals who make up the BC advance party move to the site first, the remainder of the team follows as soon as the BC team leader directs them to do so. The BCP should reflect this information.

- Acquisition of supplies, materials, and equipment: Before the BC team arrives at the site, some members may have preliminary tasks, such as purchasing supplies, materials, and equipment or acquiring them from off-site storage. The BCP should contain information on what materials should be purchased or obtained from off-site storage, and who is responsible for acquiring what. Some of this material may need to be ordered from a vendor, such as replacement computing equipment. The BCP should also contain this information, and ensure that preapproved purchasing orders or purchasing cards are available to the BC team.

Some organizations may wish to have all BC team members meet at the BC site prior to beginning their procurement activities. This method allows the BC team leader to conduct a face-to-face coordination to ensure everyone knows their responsibilities and to issue the purchasing orders or cards. If this is the case, the BCP should contain this information. In any case, to prevent the misuse of this emergency procurement operation, it may be best to have all BC team members working in two-person teams, one with acquisition authority and the other with approval authority.

- Notification of employees to relocate to BC site: At some point during the BC, the rest of the organization employees report to the BC site. These individuals receive this notification through a predetermined mechanism at a predetermined time, both of which must be specified in the BCP. It is also useful to have a summary document or card issued to each employee containing the location of the BC site along with directions to get there and the phone numbers of at least a few of the individuals who will be already on-site, in case additional information is needed.

- Organization of incoming employees: The move of employees for medium and large organizations to the BC site will typically not be done at one time. For larger organizations there may need to be a schedule indicating what groups are to move in what sequence to prevent too many employees trying to get into the BC site at one time. As a result, any scheduling of employee movement is contained in the BC plan. This information varies depending on whether the organization experiences a disaster requiring relocation during the business day or after business hours.

Some organizations prefer to simply send employees home until such time that they determine that the BC site is ready to be occupied. At that time, they begin notifying employees to arrive at a specific date and time, based on the criticality of business functions those employees fill.

As employees arrive at the new site, it is helpful to have a reception area established where each employee is provided information on where their new work area is located, and to provide them with any other needed information. To facilitate this, it is useful to have an in-processing packet prepared, or stored electronically off-site. This way the organization can quickly draft the needed instructions to the individual employees. As all employees may not know the extent of the damage to the organization's facilities, an inclusion of a disaster summary and the assessed damage should be provided to employees as soon as possible, perhaps in this document set. Supplementary information, including what organizational elements have been relocated and what their contact numbers are, should also be either directly distributed or placed in the new work areas. Preprinted signage can be used to direct incoming employees as they wander into the new site.

Each new employee, in addition to their in-processing package, should receive a briefing to answer any questions not covered in the document set. This briefing should at a minimum include safety issues, including emergency relocation from the BC site, parking recommendations, locations of facilities, and regional food or scheduled food services for the new work area. It should conclude with a positive message about the ability of the organization to survive due to the proactive BC planning, and a hearty "get to work."

The BCP should provide an overview of which of these options are adopted by the organization and who is responsible for overseeing and implementing them.

Return to the Primary Site

At some point, the organization is notified that the primary site has been restored to working order. At that time, the organization prepares to relocate individuals back to the primary site. To accomplish this in a orderly fashion, the BCP should have procedures documented for "clearing" the BC site and redirecting employees back to their normal work offices. Overall, the operations that must be specified in the BC plan to support return to the primary site include the following:

- ▶ Scheduling of employee move: Note that not all business functions may return at the same time, just as not all will relocate to the BC site in the same order or time. The organization may have the most critical functions continue to work out of the BC site until all support personnel are relocated and support services are functional at the primary site. The organization may also want to wait for a natural break in the business week, like the weekend. In any case the BCP should contain information on who will begin directing the move back to the primary site, and generally what order the business functions and associated personnel will move.

- ▶ Vanguard clearing responsibilities: The term *clearing* is used in the military and government sectors to represent the process of moving out of temporary facilities and returning them back to the owners or managers. The concept is the same here. The BC team, as temporary stewards of the facilities, is responsible for coordinating the shutdown of services, packing and moving the temporary equipment and supplies, and the return of the facilities to the BC site owner. The BC plan should contain these critical details. The subordinate activities include the following:

- ▶ Disconnecting services: Each of the service providers contacted during the move-in need to be notified of the date the organization will no longer need the services. Again these include power, water, gas, telephone, and Internet, as needed. Not all services may be needed, depending on the arrangements with the BC site owners.

- ▶ Breakdown of equipment: All of the equipment used by the organization while at the BC site must be made ready for transportation back to the primary site or to the storage locations. The timing on this shutdown is critical, since the organization most likely requires a backup to off-site storage before shutting down the equipment so that the DR team at the primary site can then bring their equipment online and download the most recent backups, thus preventing loss of information in transition.

- ▶ Pack up and place in storage or transport to primary: All of the supplies, materials, and equipment purchased or obtained while at the BC site need to be packed up and shipped back to the primary site or to storage in anticipation for the next relocation. Unless the BCP includes details on who is responsible for what, valuable materials may be lost in the shuffle. Prior to packing, a detailed inventory must also be made to prevent pilferage and to assess any damage that may occur in transit.

An important item to consider is whether individuals will be permitted to relocate their own supplies and materials. Although it may be easier to allow individual employees to clean out their own offices, taking their supplies back to the primary site using their personal vehicles, the damage, loss, and liability issues associated with such an action may make it prohibitive. If an individual were injured loading or unloading equipment from personal vehicles, or equipment was damaged, destroyed, or stolen from a personal vehicle, complications may arise. The organization may prefer to hire professional movers or at least lease moving vehicles. This too must be specified in the BC plan.

- ▶ Transfer of building to BC service provider and clearing: The final activity that occurs at the BC site is the walk-through with the site manager to identify any damage to the facility that was caused by the organization. The BC team then documents their findings, compares them with the list made during the move-in, and coordinates any needed expenses with the manager. Once all parties are satisfied with the clearing, the keys are returned to the manager and the BC team moves back to the primary site.

BC After-Action Review

Just as was performed by the IR and DR teams, before returning to routine duties, the BC team must also conduct an after-action review (AAR). All key players review their notes and verify that the BC documentation is accurate and precise. All team members review their actions during the incident and identify areas where the BC plan worked, didn't work, or should improve. This allows the team to update the BCP. The BCP AAR is then stored to serve as a training case for future staff. This formally ends the BC team's responsibilities for this business continuity event.

Business continuity planning addresses how the organization may continue its operations when its primary site is rendered inoperable for some significant period of time. While choosing to cease business when such an event occurs is an option, most organizations will choose to attempt to survive in spite of the disaster.

BC planning includes both significant technological and social challenges in assuring that business operations can be resumed within the RTO/RTA and at the RPO as required by the organization. The social challenges of relocating a workforce and its supporting infrastructure in a timely and effective fashion requires careful consideration and will be neglected at the organization's peril.

The Information Security Manager's Checklist

	No	Planned	In Progress	In Place	Integrated
This topic has been fully tested, validated, and integrated into organizational operations with formal performance measures in place (as appropriate).					
This topic has been implemented, but not fully tested, validated, and integrated into organizational operations.					
The implementation of this topic has begun, but is not yet complete.					
The formal planning for this topic has begun, but is not yet complete.					
This subject has not formally begun planning, or the organization has made a conscious decision not to pursue this topic.					
24. Business Continuity Plan					
Develop the BC planning policy statement					
Review the business impact analysis (BIA)					
Develop alternate site operations strategies					
Develop the BC plan document					
Plan testing, training, and exercises					
Plan maintenance					

For Further Reading

NIST Special Publication 800-34, *Contingency Planning Guide for Information Technology Systems*, *National Institute of Standards and Technology*, 2010.

Business Continuity and Disaster Recovery Planning for IT Professionals by Susan Snedaker, Syngress, 2007.

Business Continuity Planning for Data Centers and Systems: A Strategic Implementation Guide by Ronald H. Bowman, John Wiley and Sons, 2008.

Operational Information Security: Network Security

Part VII of *Roadmap to Information Security for IT and InfoSec Managers* will explore the world of technical controls used to manage the risk from operating information systems. Technical controls are often viewed as the only way to solve information security problems. While they are often the most visible aspect of a complete information security strategy, especially to those outside an organization, they are not always the most critical layer of a sound, multi-layered, defense-in-depth strategy.

Chapters in Part VII

Chapter 25—"Communications and Operations Management" provides a detailed discussion of the role of communications methods and protocols as a foundation of network security. The emphasis is an examination of the ISO OSI reference model, specifically discussing the security and protocol components of each level. The chapter begins with a primer on modern networking

Chapter 26—"Firewalls" provides a detailed perspective on the configuration and use of technologies designed to segregate the organization from the insecure Internet. This chapter examines the various definitions and categorizations of firewall technologies and the architectures under which firewalls may be deployed. The chapter continues with a discussion of the rules and guidelines associated with the proper configuration and use of firewalls.

Chapter 27—"Remote Access Protection" discusses the need for security in dial-up remote access network systems, and the precautions necessary to secure this access point for organizations with this older technology still deployed. The chapter continues with a presentation of content filtering capabilities and considerations.

Chapter 28—"Intrusion Detection and Prevention Systems" examines the concept of intrusion and the technologies necessary to prevent, detect, react, and recover from intrusions. Specific types of Intrusion Detection Systems (IDSs)—the Host IDS, Network IDS, and Application IDS—and their respective configurations and uses are also presented and discussed. The chapter continues with an examination of the specialized detection technologies that are designed to entice attackers into decoy systems (and thus, away from critical systems) or simply to identify the attackers' entry into these decoy areas known as Honey Pots, Honey Nets, and Padded Cell Systems.

Chapter 29—"Scanning and Analysis Tools" continues with a detailed examination of some of the key security tools an InfoSec professional can use to examine the current state of his or her organization's systems, and to identify any potential vulnerabilities or weaknesses that may exist in the systems or the organization's overall security posture. Also examined are trace-back systems, which are designed to track down the true address of attackers who were lured into decoy systems.

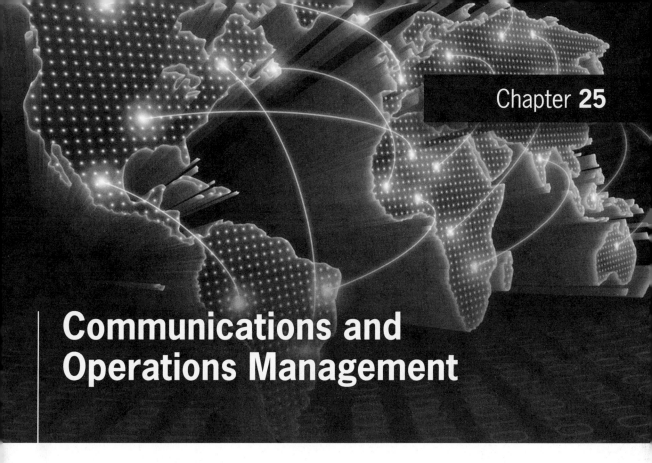

Chapter 25

Communications and Operations Management

Data communications and modern networking seem to have a language all their own and it can be quite daunting for a newly appointed security professional to get up to speed quickly. A substantial technical knowledge base is needed to operate and secure the data communications network that is the implementing infrastructure of a current-generation information system. Information security professionals are not typically expected to function as network professionals (any more than they are expected to be application development professionals or database professionals), but they must be familiar enough with the basics of data communication technology in order to communicate with the subject matter experts.

This chapter provides enough of an introduction to computer networking so that the security professional will be able to grasp the broad outlines of how networks are structured, their major protocols, and how they operate as well as providing a solid introduction to the specialized language used in the field. Before learning about firewalls and how they are deployed to help secure a network, you must know the basics of how computer networks function.

Chapter Overview:

▶ Networking fundamentals

▶ OSI reference model and security

▶ The Internet and TCP/IP

▶ Configuration and change management

NETWORKING FUNDAMENTALS

Data communications and networking go hand in hand. Data communications is the exchange of messages across a medium, and networking is the interconnection of groups or systems with the purpose of exchanging information. Though they seem similar, a useful informal distinction is that data communications is the "physics" that allows networking to occur. Networking is more concerned with the plumbing (routers, switches) and protocols that allow two systems to talk to each other. There are a number of reasons to build a network:

1. To exchange information.
2. To share scarce or expensive resources.
3. To allow distributed organizations to act as if centrally located.

Communications have evolved to the point where the individual really does not need to care about where their peers are, but only if they are able to get responses in a timely manner.

Types of Networks

One of the most common methods of describing networks is by size. Originally, network sizes were described as either local area or wide area. The Institute of Electrical and Electronics Engineers' (IEEE) first specifications for a local area network (LAN) was less than three miles of total cabling. The current definition of a LAN is a network containing a dedicated server (unlike a P2P network) that connects systems within or between a few buildings, over a small geographic space. LANs are typically owned by a single organization and used to support its internal communications.

The next size up in networks is the metropolitan area network (MAN). A MAN is a network that typically covers a region the size of a municipality, county, or district. The informal definition is a network that is larger than a LAN, but smaller than a WAN.

A wide area network (WAN) is a very large network that covers a vast geographic region like a state, a country, or even the planet. There are two dominant WANs—the public telephone network, and the Internet. (Note that the Internet is identified with a capital I, while an internet— an internetwork or network of networks—begins with a lowercase i.) A WAN can actually comprise a collection of LANs and MANs.

Networks are commonly implemented by topology. A topology is the geometric association of components of a network in relation to each other. The topology can be physical or logical. Physical topology describes how the network is cabled, while logical topology describes how the network functions. The dominant physical topologies are ring, bus, star, hierarchy, mesh, and hybrid. Figure 25-1 illustrates the physical topologies.

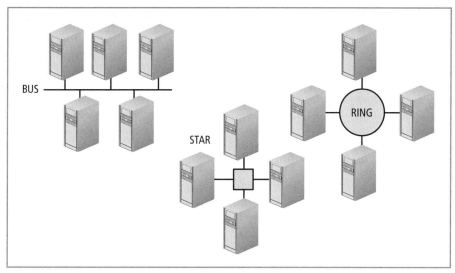

Figure 25-1 Physical Network Topologies
Course Technology/Cengage Learning

The dominant logical topologies are bus and star. A bus is simply a linear communication channel (for example, a single long cable) with all associated nodes, while the star connects a central node to other nodes. A bus transmits messages from a single station or node at a time with each node taking turns; messages can travel in both directions (in the case of a physical bus) or in one direction (in the case of a physical ring). In a star logical topology, each station or node transmits to the central node, which then retransmits the message to all attached nodes.

Networks incorporate a variety of media type. Media typically fall into two categories—guided and unguided, also known as wired and wireless. Wired media networks typically use electricity or light waves over cables to transmit messages, whereas wireless media networks use radio or infrared electromagnetic energy to transmit messages.

Network Standards

A number of organizations promote standardized components of data communications. Some seek to standardize the use of communications, while others work on standardizing the design of data communications technologies and protocols—that is, the rules for communications. Protocols that are widely accepted become standards. Some standards are formal, or *de jure*; these formal standards have been reviewed by a group of experts, and endorsed by a standards body. Other standards are informal, or *de facto*, and have simply been widely adopted without having been formally reviewed. The Internet standards such as TCP/IP are de facto standards, while Ethernet standards (IEEE 802.3) are de jure standards.

Among the agencies that work on data communications standards are the Internet Society (ISOC), the American National Standards Institute (ANSI), the International Telecommunications Union (ITU), the Institute of Electrical and Electronics Engineers (IEEE), the Telecommunications Industry Association, and the International Standards Organization (ISO).

OSI REFERENCE MODEL AND SECURITY

In 1982 the ISO and the International Telecommunication Union Standardization Sector (ITU-T) began working to develop a vendor-neutral, nonproprietary set of network standards, in an effort to establish a method of creating networking components that used common protocols. This effort was based on an Open Systems Interconnection (OSI) basic reference model developed in 1977, which rapidly became the dominant method of teaching the functions of a network protocol. The OSI reference model allocates the functions of network communications into seven distinct layers, each layer with its own specific functions and protocols. Figure 25-2 provides an overview of the OSI reference model layers and functions.

As shown in Figure 25-3, the fundamental premise of the model is that information sent from one host is translated and encoded through the various layers, from the application layer to

OSI Model			
	Data Unit	**Layer**	**Function**
Host layers	Data	7. Application	Network process to application
		6. Presentation	Data representation and encryption
		5. Session	Interhost communication
	Segments	4. Transport	End-to-end connections and reliability (TCP)
Media layers	Packets	3. Network	Path determination and logical addressing (IP)
	Frames	2. Data Link	Physical addressing (MAC & LLC)
	Bits	1. Physical	Media, signal, and binary transmission

Figure 25-2 OSI Reference Model
Course Technology/Cengage Learning

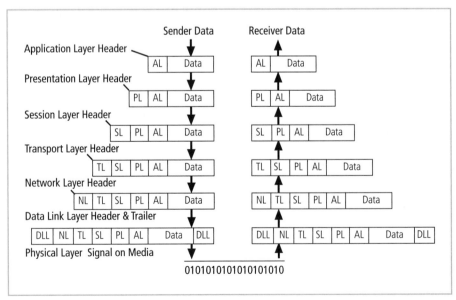

Figure 25-3 OSI Reference Model in Action
Course Technology/Cengage Learning

the physical layer. The physical layer then initiates the transmission across the network to a receiver. The receiver then translates and decodes the message in the reverse order. The receiver interprets the information by processing each layer, thus providing a header with specific information on the function of that layer, and passes the data and header to the next level in turn.

The Physical Layer

The primary function of the physical layer is to place the transmission signal carrying the message onto the communications media—that is, to put "bits on a wire." The functions of the physical layer are:

▶ Establish and terminate the physical and logical connection to the media

▶ Manage the flow and communication on the media

▶ Embed the message onto the signal carried across the physical media

Embedding the Message The method used to embed the message on the signal depends on the type of message and type of signal. As shown in Figure 25-4, there are two types of message (or information). Analog information, such as voice communications, is a continuously varying source, while digital information, such as computer communications, is discrete between a few values—in this case between 1s and 0s. Analog signals, such as those carried on the public phone network, use continuously varying waveforms, while discrete signals, such as those carried on computer networks, use discrete values in defined voltage levels.

Multiplexing combines several circuits for a high-bandwidth stream to carry multiple signals long distances. The three dominant multiplexing methods are frequency division multiplexing (FDM), time division multiplexing (TDM), and wave division multiplexing (WDM). FDM is used in analog communications to combine voice channels and works by temporarily shifting channels to higher frequencies, and then moving them back on the far end of the high-capacity connection. TDM, which is used in digital communications, assigns a time block to each client,

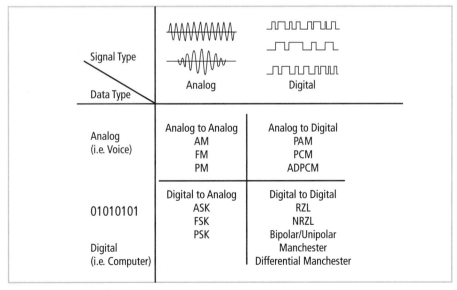

Figure 25-4 Data and Signals
Course Technology/Cengage Learning

and then polls each in turn to transmit a unit of information. Each station sends its information, which is recompiled into a cohesive data stream on the receiving end of the communication channel. If a station has no data to send, that time slot goes empty. A variant of TDM—statistical TDM—eliminates the dedicated time slots by adding header information to each packet, allowing any station with traffic to transmit on an as-needed basis. WDM, used exclusively in fiber optic communications, uses different frequencies (colors) of laser light to allow multiple signals to travel on the same fiber optic cable. This is a derivative of FDM, but only applies to fiber optic networks.

Managing Communication Bit (or signal) flow down the media can be conducted in a number of ways:

- ▶ Simplex transmissions flow one way through a media (i.e., broadcast television and radio).
- ▶ Half-duplex transmissions can flow either way, but in only one direction at a time (i.e., walkie-talkie radio).
- ▶ Full-duplex transmissions can flow both ways at the same time (i.e., telephone).
- ▶ Serial transmissions flow one bit at a time down a single communications channel.
- ▶ Parallel transmissions flow multiple bits at a time down multiple channels.
- ▶ Asynchronous (or timing independent) data transmissions formulate the data flow so that each byte or character has its own start and stop bit.
- ▶ Synchronous (or timing dependent) data transmissions use computer clocking to transmit data in a continuous stream between the two systems. Computer clock synchronization makes it possible for end nodes to identify the start and end of the data flow.

Data Link Layer

The data link layer (DLL) is the primary networking support layer. It is sometimes referred to as the first "subnet" layer because it provides addressing, packetizing, media access control, error control, and some flow control for the local network. In LANs, it handles client-to-client and client-to-server communications. The DLL is further divided into two sublayers:

- ▶ The LLC sublayer is designed primarily to support multiplexing and demultiplexing protocols transmitted over the MAC layer. It also provides flow control and error detection and retransmission.
- ▶ The MAC sublayer is designed to manage access to the communications media—in other words, to regulate which clients are allowed to transmit and when.

DLL Protocols The dominant protocol for local area networking is Ethernet for wired networks and Wi-Fi for wireless networks. Other DLL LAN protocols include Token Ring, FDDI, PPP, PPTP, and L2TP. WANs typically use ATM and Frame Relay.

Ethernet The most common LAN protocol, original versions of IEEE standard 802.3 Ethernet worked at 10 Mbps, over coaxial cable and UTP. The subsequent iterations of Ethernet are shown in Table 25-1.

TABLE 25-1 Modern Ethernet Variants

ETHERNET VARIANT	DESCRIPTION
100BaseTX	100 Mbps Ethernet over UTP (a.k.a. Fast Ethernet)
100BaseFX	100 Mbps Ethernet over fiber-optic cable
100BaseT4	100 Mbps Ethernet over low-grade UTP
1000BaseX	Generic Term for 1000 Mbps Ethernet (a.k.a Gigabit Ethernet)
1000BaseSX	1000 Mbps Ethernet over multimode fiber-optic cable
1000BaseLX	1000 Mbps Ethernet over single mode fiber-optic cable
1000BaseCX	1000 Mbps Ethernet over balanced copper cable (obsolete)
1000BaseT	1000 Mbps Ethernet over UTP

Course Technology/Cengage Learning

Most UTP installations have limits of 100 m for the cables from the client to a powered repeater or switch.

For its MAC sublayer, Ethernet uses the Carrier Sense Multiple Access with Collision Detection for its wired protocols, and Carrier Sense Multiple Access with Collision Avoidance for its wireless protocols; both are described later in this chapter.

Wireless Ethernet Standardized as IEEE 802.11, wireless communications use basically the same Ethernet functions as their wired counterparts. The primary difference between the two lies in the data rates obtainable, and the MAC methods employed. Note that the range estimates assume the use of standard receivers and antennas and do not set a maximum range beyond which the signal cannot be intercepted by specialized receivers or antennas.

Forming Packets
The first responsibility of the DLL is converting the Network layer packet into a DLL frame. Unlike higher levels, the DLL adds not only a header component but also a trailer. When necessary, the packet is fragmented into one or more frames, with corresponding information embedded into the frame header.

Addressing
Addressing at the data link layer is accomplished with a number embedded in the network interface card (NIC) by the manufacturer. This number, known as the MAC address, Ethernet hardware address, or simply hardware address, allows packets to be delivered to an end point. This 48-bit number is typically denoted in hexadecimal format (i.e., 00-00-A3-6A-B2-1A). The first three octets (or hex sets) are assigned by IEEE as part of their Organizationally Unique Identifier or Company_id. The database of these addresses can be viewed at *http://standards.ieee.org/cgi-bin/ouisearch*.

Media Access Control
One of the primary functions of the DLL is the control of the flow of traffic—that is, determining which station is allowed to transmit when. There are two general approaches to this task, control (or deterministic) and contention (stochastic).

There are a number of ways to implement the control approach. The first is a controlled network in which the client must request permission to transmit. In roll call polling, the central control unit, usually a server, polls a client to determine if it has traffic to transmit. If it does, it is then permitted to send that data. If not, the next client on the list is polled. In go-ahead polling, the first client on the list transmits data if it needs to, but if not, it notifies the next client that it may transmit data. Token-passing rings and busses work on this principle, using the token as the control mechanism. Control approaches maintain a well-regulated network where traffic is transmitted in an orderly fashion, maintaining an optimal data rate. They also facilitate a priority system, in that key clients or servers can be polled more frequently than others. Token-based systems can also incorporate a priority set of bits that allows assignment of different classes to facilitate the transmission of important and time-sensitive data, like video.

Clients wishing to transmit on a network using a contention approach simply listen to determine if the network is currently being used. If the channel is free, the station transmits. Because it is possible for more than one station to attempt to transmit at virtually the same time, contention approaches must have mechanisms to deal with the resulting event, which is referred to as a collision. Carrier Sense Multiple Access (CSMA) is the dominant contention mechanism. CSMA requires that each station listen to the media (Carrier Sense), and that all stations have equal access (Multiple Access). CSMA with collision detection (CSMA/CD) systems are set up so that if a collision is detected, both stations immediately emit a jamming signal to warn all other clients that a collision has occurred and must be resolved. How do clients know a collision has occurred? A client transmitting a specific voltage level on a wire receives a voltage spike when more voltage is detected than is being transmitted. When these stations recognize a collision, they begin the binary exponential back-off algorithm—beginning with one bit, which has two values (zero or one), each client randomly selects a value and waits that amount of time in milliseconds, then attempts to retransmit. If the two clients choose the same value, they move to two bits (four values) and try again. The clients continue until they either are able to transmit or reach sixteen bits, at which time they give up and send an error message to their systems.

Collision avoidance differs from collision detection in that before a client transmits, it sends a short "intent to transmit" message warning other clients not to transmit. The client then waits a short time to ensure that the channel is clear, and then transmits its message, and waits for acknowledgment of receipt.

Switches and Bridges
To connect networks at the data link layer, specific technologies are employed. While the hub connects networks at the physical layer, connecting two networks with a hub results in one large network (or collision domain). Connecting them with a Layer 2 switch, which is capable of bridging, maintains separate collision domains. Bridging is the process of connecting networks with the same DLL protocols while maintaining the integrity of each network, and only passing messages that need to be transmitted between the two.

Network Layer
The network layer is the primary layer for communications between networks. This layer has three key functions: packetizing, addressing, and routing.

Packetizing
The network layer takes the segments sent from the transport layer and organizes them into one or more packets for transmission across a network.

Addressing
The network layer uses a network-layer address to uniquely identify a destination across multiple networks. A typical address consists of multiple components: the

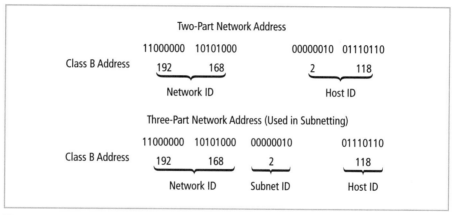

Figure 25-5 Multi-Part Addresses
Course Technology/Cengage Learning

network ID, and the host ID, as shown in Figure 25-5. In TCP/IP, the IP address is the network-layer address. The IP address contains a source-and-destination IP address along with additional information on the packet.

Addresses are maintained by the Internet Assigned Numbers Authority (IANA) and issued on an as-needed basis. In early years, these addresses were distributed as shown in Table 25-2.

TABLE 25-2 IP Address Classes

CLASS	EXAMPLE ADDRESS RANGE	SUPPORTS
Class A	1.0.0.1 to 1.255.255.254 (1.X.X.X)	16 million hosts on each of 127 networks.
Class B	1.0.0.1 to 1.0.255.254 (1.0.X.X)	65,000 hosts on each of 16,000 networks.
Class C	1.0.0.1 to 1.0.0.254 (1.0.0.X)	254 hosts on each of 2 million networks.
Class D	224.0.0.1 to 227.255.255.254	Reserved for multicast groups.
Class E	248.0.0.1 to 255.255.255.254	Reserved.

Course Technology/Cengage Learning

In practice this assignment method proves very inefficient. For example, a typical university was issued a Class B address, but may have at its peak only 4000–5000 devices needing a network address, which means that 61,000 or more addresses are not used. This is one reason that the Internet is moving to a new version of IP, IPv6, which uses a 128-bit address, instead of a 32-bit address. This substantially increases the number of available addresses (by a factor of 2128). The "classful" method of assigning addresses shown in Table 25-2 is rather inflexible, because the size of the address blocks are determined by the "class" of the address. For example, a Class C address can only accommodate up to 254 hosts. If an organization needs 500 hosts, they need two Class C blocks, and thus two entries in all routing tables, and other supporting network infrastructure including Domain Name System, Mail Exchange addressing and every other higher-order protocol. The solution to this problem is Classless Inter Domain Routing (CIDR), in which the netmask is specified rather than taken from the class of the address. For example, a normal Class C address would be specified as 192.168.16.0/24 in CIDR notation, which specifies that the network ID is the first 24 bits of the address. An organization that needs a block of 500 hosts might be assigned the CIDR address block 192.168.16.0/23. This "steals" one of the netmask bits of the Class C address and makes it part of the host address (more about the details of how this works in the subnet section). This allows the single CIDR address block 192.168.16.0/23 to actually refer to the two Class C network blocks 192.168.16.0 and 192.168.17.0 with a single network address.

Instead of assigning fixed addresses to each network entity, addresses can be assigned dynamically. Dynamic addressing assigns a pool of addresses to an address assignment server. When a system boots, it requests and receives an address and additional network configuration information, including the gateway address and the addresses of DNS servers. The advantages of this method are ease of administration and that it allows a large group of systems to use a smaller number of addresses. When a system shuts down, it returns the address to the pool, where it can be reused by another system.

Network Address Translation (NAT)   NAT, a network layer mechanism that helps systems manage addresses, uses a device like a router to segregate the external Internet from an internal intranet or network. The device is provided with the addresses assigned to the organization. The device then maps these addresses to different addresses inside the intranet. This provides security but can also maximize network address assignment when combined with Port Address Translation (PAT), which is described later in this chapter. The internal addresses could be any address, but specific IP addresses are reserved for use in private (nonroutable) networking (RFC1918). These include:

10.0.0.0—Class A networks

172.16.0.0 through 172.31.0.0—Class B networks

192.168.0.0—Class C networks

Routing   Routing is the process of moving a network layer packet across multiple networks. The devices that connect networks are called routers. Routers work at the network layer to receive packets and direct them toward their ultimate destination. The transmission links between routers work at the data link layer. In other words, the router has one or more types of data link layer protocols represented by an interface or network card. A router could have different types of data link protocols, since it receives the frame carrying the network layer packet, and creates a new frame once it determines the outbound interface that represents the direction the packet needs to go. Routers accomplish this through the use of routing tables. A routing table contains information on destination addresses, outbound interfaces toward that address, and additional information such as the cost of using that route.

There are a number of categories of routing protocols:

- ▶ Static versus Dynamic: Static routing requires an administrator to manually enter the routing table information, while dynamic routing is accomplished by a router capable of updating its own table. Routers do this by transmitting their router tables to their neighbors and updating their own tables with the information they receive.
- ▶ Internal Routing Protocols. Internal routing protocols are used inside an autonomous system (AS). An AS is a system owned or managed by a single entity, and generally consisting of analogous technologies. The two dominant internal routing methods are distance-vector

routing protocols and link-state routing protocols. Distance-vector protocols base their routing decisions on a simple determination of the number of hops between the router and the destination. A hop is one connection from router to router. The two dominant distance-vector protocols are the Routing Information Protocol (RIP) and the Interior Gateway Routing Protocol (IGRP). RIP is more widely used, although implementations are rapidly being replaced by link-state protocols. RIP routers originally transmitted their entire router tables every 30 seconds, resulting in a significant amount of network traffic.

▶ Link-state protocols contain information about not only the distance to the destination but also about the states of the links, including traffic, throughput, and other components. The dominant link-state routing protocols are Open Shortest Path First (OSPF) and Intermediate System to Intermediate System (IS-IS). OSPF is superior to RIP in that the entire router table is not transmitted, only information on the immediate neighbor routers. OSPF also includes information on time to transmit and receive an update. OSPF also doesn't broadcast routing information on a regular basis; instead, it selectively sends routing updates to select devices.

▶ External Gateway Routing Protocols. External routing protocols are used to communicate between ASs. They provide translation among different internal routing protocols. The dominant external routing protocol is the Border Gateway Protocol (BGP). When used as an Internal Gateway Protocol, it is referred to as IBGP, and when used externally, as EBGP.

Transport Layer

The primary function of the transport layer is to provide reliable end-to-end transfer of data between user applications. While the lower layers focus on networking and connectivity, the upper layers, beginning with the transport layer, focus on application-specific services. The transport layer can also provide support for a virtual circuit, which is an extension of the connection-oriented model. In a connectionless model, *individual segments* (the term for packets at this level) are transmitted, each with its own addressing information. Individual segments may take different paths but end up at the same destination, where they are reassembled into the correct order. In a connection-oriented model, a connection is established between two points, and all communication occurs over that dedicated end-to-end connection. With virtual circuits, each segment has the path as well as the destination embedded into the packet, insuring that the segment will follow the predesigned path, without the overhead of establishing an actual connection. The transport layer is also responsible for end-to-end error control, flow control, and several other functions.

Error Control
Error control is the process of handling problems with the transfer process, which might result in modified or corrupted segments. Error control is broken into two components, error detection and error correction. Errors typically comprise one of two formats. A single bit error affects only a single bit—typically changing a 1 to a 0 or vice versa. Single bit errors are easily detected. Multiple bit errors are more complex in that they affect more than one bit, and even bits in more than one location in the segment. Bit errors are most likely the result of noise interference. Errors are detected through one of several common schemes:

▶ Repetition—data is transmitted redundantly. Each block of data is repeated a predetermined number of times. Any errors may not affect each block and thus allow an error to be detected. This overly simplistic method is inefficient, and only catches basic errors.

- Parity—additional bits are provided at the end of each byte of data; these additional "check bits" provide a measure of error detection. With odd parity, the sum of the values in a bit is expected to be odd. If they are, a 0 is added to the block; if not, then a 1 is added, making the block sum odd. Similarly, with even parity the check bits are added to make the sum even.

- Redundancy—parity is calculated for blocks of data rather than for an individual byte. Longitudinal redundancy checking (LRC) examines a long row of blocks, and then adds a byte of parity for the row. LRC is often used with vertical redundancy checking (VRC), which does the same task for a column of data. By placing the data into blocks and incorporating both LRC and VRC data, it becomes possible to detect even multibit errors easily. Cyclic redundancy checking (CRC) uses a long division computation, where the remainder becomes a block of data included with the segment. CRCs are often 16, 32, and 64 bits long. The receiver performs the same computation at its end and if the remainder is different, then there is a problem with the segment, and a retransmission is requested.

For advanced error detection, especially at the message level, redundancy checking has given way to message authentication codes, where hash values of the entire message are appended onto the message.

Errors are most commonly corrected by retransmission of the damaged segment. The dominant error correction techniques are automatic repeat requests (ARQs). The three most common ARQs are Stop-and-Wait ARQ, Go-Back-N ARQ, and Selective Repeat ARQ. Stop-and-Wait ARQ works on a 1-datagram (or packet) premise. For each segment transmitted there must be acknowledgment by the receiver before another segment is transmitted. This one-to-one operation is very slow and intensive. However, it is very reliable in that if an error is detected, the bad segment is requested for retransmission—most commonly by reacknowledging the last good segment received.

Go-Back-N ARQ requires that a number of packets be transmitted before an acknowledgment is received. The exact number—called the window size—is negotiated between the two stations, as part of the sliding window protocol described in the following section. Once the number of packets that is set by the window size is transmitted, an acknowledgment is received, and additional segments are transmitted. If an error is detected, then the recipient acknowledges the last good segment received before the error, and all segments after that point are retransmitted. While this is somewhat wasteful, in that all segments received since the bad segment are discarded, it is still much more efficient than Stop-and-Wait ARQ. Selective Repeat ARQ only retransmits those segments that are determined to be bad.

Flow Control Along with the error correction schemes, the transport layer also provides for flow control for end-to-end transfers. The purpose of flow control is to prevent a receiver from being overwhelmed with segments preventing effective processing of each received segment. Some error correction techniques, like Stop-and-Wait ARQ, provide built-in flow control. Other techniques require some mechanism to regulate the traffic. The dominant technique for flow control is the sliding window protocol, which provides a mechanism by which a receiver can specify the number of segments (or number of bytes) it can receive before the sender must wait. In TCP this is implemented as a WIN value. A typical WIN value is 4096 (or 4 K). If the sender and receiver are using a maximum segment size of 1 K, then the sender could send four segments before waiting for permission to continue transmitting. As a receiver gains efficiency—possibly through the reduction in number of concurrent sessions, it could enlarge the window size. As the receiver gets overwhelmed with additional connection requests, it could reduce the window size, slowing down each connection.

Other functions The transport layer is also responsible for the assignment of ports, which identify the service requested by the user. The combination of network layer address and port is referred to as a socket. When a client wishes to establish a connection with a particular service, such as HTTP, it sends a connection request to the destination on well-known port address 80. This tells the receiving server, which may provide more than one type of service, the specific application layer service that is requested. The client system usually assigns a random port number outside of the well-known port range (that is, above 1023) as the source port of its socket, so that the response can find its way to the corresponding application. This socket combination allows an individual to open multiple versions of an application, such as multiple Web browsers. Similarly, this allows a home Internet user to have multiple systems working off of a single dynamic IP address. The home router performs Port Address Translation, and assigns a unique socket to each client request, along with an internal IP address. The transport layer is responsible for directing the traffic sent to these various ports to make sure they reach the correct service.

Tunneling protocols also work at the transport layer. These protocols work with data link layer protocols to provide secure connections. You learn more about tunneling later in this book.

Session Layer

The session layer is responsible for establishing, maintaining, and terminating communications sessions between two systems. It also regulates whether communications are preformed in a simplex (one way only), half-duplex (one way at a time), or full-duplex (bidirectional) mode. In other words, when one station wishes to request services from a server, it requests a session, much as a person dials a telephone. The dialing, ringing, and opening conversation ("Hello, may I speak with Mr. Smith?") are part of the establishment of a communications session. As data is transferred, the session layer maintains the connection. Once both parties are finished communicating, the session is closed. In TCP/IP this is referred to as a half-close, because even though the client may have completed its data transfer, the server may still have data to transmit.

Presentation Layer

The presentation layer is responsible for data translation and other functions such as some types of encryption. For example, if one system is using the standard ASCII (American Standard Code for Information Interchange) and another system is using EBCDIC (Extended Binary Coded Decimal Interchange Code), then the presentation layer performs the translation. Encryption can also be part of this layer's operations. The presentation layer also encapsulates the application layer message prior to passing it down to the transport layer.

Application Layer

At the application layer, the user is provided with a number of services, perhaps most aptly called application protocols. The TCP/IP protocol suite includes applications such as e-mail (SMTP and POP), the World Wide Web (HTTP and HTTPS), file transfer (FTP and SFTP), and others.

THE INTERNET AND TCP/IP

The Internet incorporates millions of small independent networks, connected by most of the major common carriers (AT&T, ITT, MCI, Sprint, etc.). Most of the services we associate with the Internet are based on application layer protocols like e-mail, the Web, FTP, and instant messaging (IM). Because the subject of the Internet and the World Wide Web are so vast, this section will only provide a brief overview of the Internet and its primary protocols, TCP and IP. In June 2008, Internet World Stats reported that 1.463 billion people were using the Internet.[1]

TCP/IP is actually a suite of protocols used to facilitate communications across the Internet. Developed before the OSI reference model, the TCP/IP suite is similar in concept, but different in detail, as shown in Table 25-3.

The TCP/IP model is less formal than the OSI reference model. Each of the four layers of the TCP/IP model represents a section of one or more layers of the OSI model.

Application Layer

The TCP/IP application layer consists of the utility protocols that provide value to the end user. Data from the users and use of these utilities are passed down to the transport layer for processing. A wide variety of application layer protocols support Internet users—SMTP and POP for e-mail, FTP for data transfer, and HTTP for the transfer of Web content. The application layers on each host interact directly with corresponding applications on the other hosts to provide the requisite communications support.

Transport Layer

The transport layer is responsible for the basic capacity of transferring messages including resolution of errors, managing necessary fragmentation and the control of message flow regardless of the underlying network. At this layer, two basic message approaches are used: (1) a connection-oriented approach such as that implemented in the Transmission Control Protocol (TCP); or (2) a connectionless-oriented approach such as the one used in the User Datagram Protocol (UDP). The

TABLE 25-3 TCP/IP Layers Compared to OSI Layers

	OSI LAYERS	INCLUDED PROTOCOLS		TCP/IP LAYERS
7	Application	SNMP	FTP	
6	Presentation	TFTP NFS	Telnet Finger	Application
5	Session	DNS BOOTP	SMTP POP	
4	Transport	UDP	TCP	Host-to-Host Transport
3	Network	IP		Internet
2	Data Link	Network Interface Cards		Subnet (LAN) Layers
1	Physical	Transmission Media		

Course Technology/Cengage Learning

transport layer can be considered literally as a mechanism of transport, perhaps like a delivery truck that takes on the responsibility for the delivery of its contents (goods) to the specified destination without risk, unless a higher or lower layer is responsible for that sure delivery. The transport layer provides the service of connecting applications through the use of the ports and the transport layer is the lowest layer of the TCP/IP stack to offer any form of reliability.

TCP is a connected protocol that tackles many questions of reliability. It provides a reliable mechanism such that data packets will arrive in sequence, with a minimum level of errors, without redundancy, without loss, and able to handle congestion concerns found in networks.

UDP is a connectionless protocol. Like the IP, it is a best-effort or an unreliable protocol. UDP is typically employed for applications such as streaming media (audio, video, Voice over IP) where the on-time arrival is more important than reliability, or for simple query/response functions such as those found in DNS, where the overhead to install a reliable connection is disproportionately large.

Internetwork Layer

The internetwork layer addresses the problem of moving packets in a single network. Examples of such protocols are X.25, and the ARPANET's Host/IMP Protocol. The Internet Protocol (IP) performs the basic task of moving packets of data from a source host to a destination host. IP carries data for many different upper-layer protocols.

Some of the protocols carried by IP, such as the Internet Control Management Protocol (ICMP) (which is used to transmit diagnostic information about IP transmission) and the Internet Group Management Protocol (IGMP) (which is used to manage IP Multicast data), function on top of IP but perform other internetwork layer functions. This illustrates an incompatibility between the Internet model (and its implementation as the IP stack) and OSI model. All routing protocols are also part of the network layer.[2] Discussions about the specifics on IP packets are provided in other chapters throughout the text.

Subnet Layers

The TCP/IP subnet layers include the data link and physical layers. TCP/IP relies on whatever native network subnet layers are present. If the user's network is Ethernet, then the IP packets are encapsulated into Ethernet frames. As such, TCP/IP provides no specification for the data link layer or physical layer.

CONFIGURATION AND CHANGE MANAGEMENT

One of the critical components of ongoing information security operations management is the ability to assess and inventory assets (as part of the risk assessment process) and to manage the changes to those assets. **Configuration management** is the administration of the configuration of information security program components. **Change management** is the administration of changes in the strategy, operation, or components of the information security program.

Both configuration and change management administration involve nontechnical as well as technical changes. Nontechnical changes are those that do not affect the technology, but instead affect two other system components—people and procedures. IT managers and professionals are responsible for the organization's information-processing systems. The information security community, however, should ensure that the technical systems of information security are managed independently from traditional IT equipment, except when there is overlap. In cases of overlap (as there would be, for example, with a filtering router), joint management is necessary. The ultimate goal is to ensure that all information technology is properly managed, particularly those systems directly affecting the success of the information security program.

Technical Configuration Management

Just as documents should have version numbers, revision dates, and other features designated to monitor and administer the changes made to them, so should the technical components of systems, such as software, hardware, and firmware. Several terms used in the management of configuration and change in technical components are as follows:

- ▶ Configuration item: A hardware or software item that is to be modified and revised throughout its life cycle.
- ▶ Version: The recorded state of a particular revision of a software or hardware configuration item. The version number is often noted in a specific format: M.N.b. In this notation, "M" is the major release number, and "N.b" can represent various minor releases or builds within that major release.
- ▶ Major release: A significant revision of the version from its previous state.
- ▶ Minor release (update or patch): A minor revision of the version from its previous state.
- ▶ Build: A snapshot of a particular version of software assembled (or linked) from its various component modules.
- ▶ Build list: A list of the versions of components that make up a build.
- ▶ Configuration: A configuration is a collection of components that make up a configuration item.
- ▶ Revision date: The date associated with a particular version or build.
- ▶ Software library: A collection of configuration items that is usually controlled and that developers use to construct revisions and to issue new configuration items.

Both product developers and users participate in configuration management. The developers focus on managing the build list and keeping up with the development of major and minor releases, while the users monitor the implementation of versions and track the latest releases as well as which computers in their organizations are running each of the released versions.

Four steps are associated with configuration management.[3]

1. Configuration identification: The identification and documentation of the various components, implementations, and states of configuration items
2. Configuration control: The administration of changes to the configuration items and the issuance of versions
3. Configuration status accounting: The tracking and recording of the implementation of changes to configuration items
4. Configuration audit: Auditing and controlling the overall configuration management program

While the other three steps/procedures can be performed by any organization that uses technology to solve problems, configuration control is usually only performed by an entity that actually develops its own versions.

In general, configuration management should not interfere with the use of the technology. One person on the security team should be appointed as the configuration manager and made responsible for maintaining the appropriate data elements in the organization's cataloging mechanism, such as the specific version, revision date, and build associated with each piece of hardware and software implemented. In some cases, it may be better to have someone outside the implementation process document the process, so this person is not distracted by the installation, configuration, and troubleshooting of the new implementation. In the case of minor revisions, it may be simpler to have a procedure in place that involves documenting the machines on which a revision is installed, the date and time of the installation, and the name of the installer. While the documentation procedures required for the configuration and change management processes may seem onerous, they enable security teams to quickly and accurately determine exactly which systems are affected when a new vulnerability arises. When stored in a comprehensive database along with risk, threat, and attack information, configuration information enables organizations to respond quickly to new and rapidly changing threats and attacks.

Technical Change Management

Technical change management programs control the modifications to the configuration of the technical systems. As such, many organizations merge the change management and configuration management functions. An example of a specifically focused technical change management program is the Patch and Vulnerability Management Program. NIST Special Publication SP 800-40 v2 includes recommendations for establishing this type of program. This process integrates configuration management as the first aspect of inventorying assets, then addresses the steps in evaluating, vetting, and implementing recommended changes to the technical configuration of organizational information systems through a controlled process, such as that described later in this section.

Nontechnical Configuration and Change Management

When implementing changes to the information security program, the organization also probably needs to implement a number of new policies and procedures. Consequently, the implementation effort produces documents that must be updated or replaced when they are insufficient, outdated, or inaccurate. To support this process, a document manager should maintain a master copy of each document, record and archive the revisions made, and keep copies of the revisions, along with editorial comments on what was added, removed, or modified. A library of these sorts of documents can become unwieldy; the organization may wish to implement online archives to maintain the documents and revisions. It is important to be able to track changes to these documents, and to determine why and by whom the changes were made. It is also important that the record include insight into the environment that caused the change. Without this type of recordkeeping, organizations may find that some members are working from older versions of critical policy or procedural documents.

When these policies are revised, the updated versions must be disseminated to all involved personnel, and documented user agreement must be obtained. The management of the agreement documentation presents an administrative challenge, because many security policies and procedures contain sensitive information that the organization may not wish to disclose. The most effective way to manage changes to documents is to include the version number in the header, along with the file name and revision date, and to physically distribute the documents to all parties affected. In accordance with the classified document management program, as the new documents are distributed, all older versions should be collected and destroyed. When employees receive new versions of a policy (and return old versions), the distribution should be documented, including collecting the employees' signatures indicating receipt. Employees should also be given a confirmation form that states that they have read the policies and that they agree to them, and they must be required to return the confirmation form by a specified date.

Modern Web-based software can help organizations manage the creation of policy content, modification of policy content, dissemination of policy, and the processes used for recordkeeping of agreement documentation.

Establishing a Change Management Process

In order to prevent unwanted or untested modification to both technical and nontechnical components of the information security program, the organization will want to establish a formal program to manage change. Each **Request for Change (RFC)** should be properly reviewed, tested, and approved before being implemented. This will require the establishment of a Change Approval Board (CAB), which will serve as the approval authority on all technical and nontechnical changes. While many organizations will delegate nontechnical changes (i.e., policy revisions) to an appropriate manager, most organizations have formal or informal procedures for handling technical changes. Organizations that do not frequently find themselves with unauthorized and unwanted changes to technical systems, including security systems, leading to the potential for incidents.

The primary activities of the CAB include the following:

> ► Development of policy to guide the change management process
> ► Development of procedures to follow in requesting changes to information assets
> ► Drafting of RFC forms
> ► Periodic review of submitted RFCs
> ► Development of procedures for testing requested changes
> ► Approval and implementation procedures for changes
> ► Establishment of variances for immediate or emergency changes

While most of these steps are self-explanatory, the need for the last item is most crucial. Critical patches and updates to high-profile and mission critical systems may require the organization to conduct immediate or expedited review processes, rather than waiting for the next scheduled CAB meeting. Some organizations only hold their CAB meetings once per month for routine changes, others hold them more frequently. However, a critical update may require an immediate bypass or exception to change review. In these cases, the organization must have established policy and procedures to handle these situations.

A typical RFC will look similar to the following:

ABC Co IT/InfoSec Technical Request for Change

Requested by: Date:

Reviewed by: Date:

Tested by: Date:

Approved by: Date:

Request Description:

Request Justification:

Alternative Solutions:

Impact Assessment: (Note potential impacts of implementing or not implementing this change on other systems)

Recommended implement by date:

CAB use only:

Recommendation:

This chapter has provided a whirlwind introduction to the field of data communications networks to enable the information security professional to better communicate with the experts in the networking field. Since much of the modern organization's information is transmitted over some form of network during its lifetime, familiarity with networking models (ISO, TCP/IP), functions (routing), and addressing are necessary skills for the security professional. As has been said, the security professional does not also have to be a networking professional, but he or she had better be able to speak their language.

The Information Security Manager's Checklist

	This topic has been fully tested, validated, and integrated into organizational operations with formal performance measures in place (as appropriate).						
	This topic has been implemented, but not fully tested, validated, and integrated into organizational operations.						
	The implementation of this topic has begun, but is not yet complete.						
	The formal planning for this topic has begun, but is not yet complete.						
	This subject has not formally begun planning, or the organization has made a conscious decision not to pursue this topic.			No	Planned	In Progress	In Place	Integrated
25. Communications and Operations Management							
Employees familiar with fundamental functionality of modern telecommunications							
Organization develops policies on use of telecommunications							
IT employees trained on organization telecommunications and telecommunications threats							
Organization develops configuration management policy							
Organization develops configuration management plan							
Organization develops change management policy							
Organization develops change management plan							
Configuration and change management plans implemented							
Configuration and change management plans periodically reviewed							

For Further Reading

Network Know-How: An Essential Guide for the Accidental Admin by John Ross, 2009.

Networking: A Beginner's Guide, Fifth Edition (Networking Professional's Library) by Bruce A. Hallberg, No Starch Press, 2009.

Networking for Dummies by Doug Lowe, International Data Group (IDG), 2009.

References

1. http://www.internetworldstats.com/stats.htm.

2. http://en.wikipedia.org/wiki/TCP/IP_model.

3. R. L. Krutz and R. D.Vines. *The CISSP Prep Guide.* (New York: Wiley 2001), p. 253.

Firewalls

A physical firewall in a building is a concrete or masonry wall running from the basement through the roof to prevent fire in one section from spreading to another. In information security, a firewall is any device that controls (usually by blocking) information flows between a less trusted network (e.g., the Internet), and a more trusted network (such as the application tier of the internal network). The firewall may be a separate computer system, a service running on an existing router or server, or a separate network containing a number of supporting devices. Since many modern networks are divided into several trust domains (the Web tier, the application tier, the data management tier, etc.), there may be many firewalls present with each functioning to control the traffic that flows between the various domains.

Chapter Overview:

▶ The development of firewalls

▶ Firewall architectures

▶ Managing firewalls

THE DEVELOPMENT OF FIREWALLS

Firewalls have made significant advances since their earliest implementations. The first generation[1] of firewalls, **packet filtering firewalls**, are simple networking devices that filter packets by examining every incoming and, in some cases, outgoing packet header. They can selectively filter packets based on values in the packet header, accepting or rejecting packets as needed. These devices can be configured to filter based on IP address, type of packet, port request, and/or other elements present in the packet header. The filtering process examines packets for compliance with or violation of rules configured into the firewall's database. The rules most commonly implemented in packet filtering firewalls are based on a combination of IP source and destination address, direction (inbound or outbound), and/or source and destination port requests. Figure 26-1 shows how such a firewall typically works.

The ability to restrict a specific service is now considered standard in most modern routers (AKA filtering routers, and is invisible to the user. Unfortunately, filtering rules can be evaded by modifying the packet headers as is done in IP spoofing attacks.

Early firewall models examined one aspect of the packet header: the destination address and the source address. For example, consider the rules listed in Table 26-1.

This table uses special, nonroutable (RFC-1918) IP addresses in the rules for this example. In reality, a firewall that connects to a public network will use routable address ranges for the external addresses.

With the rules shown in Table 26-1, any attempt to make a connection from any computers or network devices in the 10.10.x.x address range is blocked from all services offered at the network with the address 172.16.126.x. This first rule might be used to block objectionable content found at that particular address, for example. At the same time, the fourth rule allows all other 10.10 addresses to access any HTTP services at any other address. The second rule blocks any devices in the 192.168 network from any access to the 10.10 network, effectively blacklisting that external network from connecting to this network. The third rule allows a specific computer found at 172.16.121.1 to access a certain FTP server found at 10.10.10.22. The fourth rule allows all internal users to browse the entire Internet, unless blocked by an earlier rule, and

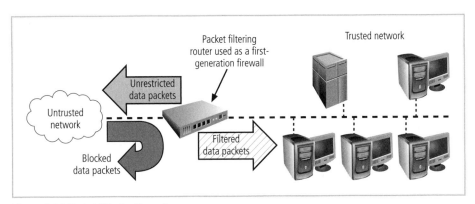

Figure 26-1 Packet Filtering Firewall
Course Technology/Cengage Learning

TABLE 26-1 Packet Filtering Example Rules

SOURCE ADDRESS	DESTINATION ADDRESS	SERVICE PORT	ACTION
10.10.x.x	172.16.126.x	Any	Deny
192.168.x.x	10.10.x.x	Any	Deny
172.16.121.1	10.10.10.22	FTP	Allow
10.10.x.x	x.x.x.x	HTTP	Allow
x.x.x.x	10.10.10.25	HTTP	Allow
x.x.x.x	10.10.10.x	Any	Deny

Note: These rules apply to a network at 10.10.x.x.
Course Technology/Cengage Learning

the fifth rule allows any outside user to access the Web server at 10.10.10.25 unless otherwise blocked by an earlier rule. The final rule enforces an exclusionary policy that blocks all access not specifically allowed.

The second generation of firewalls, known as **application-level firewalls**, often consists of dedicated computers kept separate from the first filtering router (called an edge router); they are commonly used in conjunction with a second or internal filtering router. This second router is often called a **proxy server**, because it serves as a proxy for external service requests to internal services.

With this configuration, the proxy server, rather than the Web server, is exposed to the outside world from within a network segment called the **demilitarized zone (DMZ)**. The DMZ is an intermediate area between a trusted network and an untrusted network (see Figure 26-4 later in this chapter). Using this model, additional filtering routers are placed between the proxy server and internal systems, thereby restricting access to internal systems to the proxy server alone. If these servers store the most recently accessed pages in their internal caches, they may also be called **cache servers (or a caching proxy)**.

Suppose an external user wanted to view a Web page from an organization's Web server. Rather than expose the Web server to direct traffic from the users and potential attackers, the organization can install a proxy server, configured with the registered domain's URL. This proxy server receives Web page requests, accesses the Web server on behalf of external clients, and then returns the requested pages to users.

The primary disadvantage of application-level firewalls is that they are designed for a specific protocol, and cannot be easily reconfigured to work with other protocols.

The third generation of firewalls, **stateful inspection firewalls**, keeps track of each network connection established between internal and external systems using a **state table**. State tables track the state and context of each exchanged packet by recording which station sent which packet and when. Like first-generation firewalls, stateful inspection firewalls perform packet filtering, but where simple packet filtering firewalls merely allow or deny certain packets based on their addresses, a stateful inspection firewall can restrict incoming packets by restricting access to packets that constitute responses to internal requests. If the stateful inspection firewall receives an incoming packet that it cannot match in its state table, then it defaults to its ACL to determine whether to allow the packet to pass. You can think of the state table as a window—when an internal system makes a request to an external system, a window is opened to allow the external system to respond to that request. The advantage is that external requests to internal systems that are not permitted by an opened window are blocked (for example, if an attacker were scanning your organization's address range to identify active hosts).

The primary disadvantage of this type of firewall is the additional processing requirements of managing and verifying packets against the state table, which can possibly lead to a DoS attack. In such an attack, the firewall is subjected to a large number of external packets, slowing it down as it attempts to compare all of the incoming packets first to the state table and then to the ACL. On the positive side, these firewalls can track connectionless packet traffic such as User Datagram Protocol (UDP) and remote procedure call (RPC) traffic.

Whereas static filtering firewalls, such as those in the first and third generations, allow entire sets of one type of packet to enter in response to authorized requests, a fourth-generation firewall, called a **dynamic packet filtering firewall**, allows only a particular packet with a specific source, destination, and port address to pass through the firewall. It does so by understanding how the protocol functions, and by opening and closing "doors" in the firewall based on the information contained in the packet header.[2] Dynamic packet filters are an intermediate form, between traditional static packet filters and application proxies.

FIREWALL ARCHITECTURES

Each of the firewall generations can be implemented in a number of architectural configurations, either alone or sometimes in combination. The configuration that works best for a particular organization depends on the uses of its network, the organization's ability to develop and implement the architectures, and the available budget. Although literally hundreds of variations exist, four architectural implementations of firewalls are especially common: packet filtering routers, screened-host firewalls, dual-homed host firewalls, and screened-subnet firewalls.

Router or Firewall?

The decision on whether to implement the filtering at the router or firewall really boils down to the hardware in use and the amount of traffic. Routers are designed to move traffic between networks with minimal delay. Adding filtering requires resources and that can come to limit the total throughput the router can support (more filtering, less resources to support routing traffic). Since high-traffic routers are some of the most expensive pieces of networking equipment, it can make sense to dedicate their resources to moving traffic and leave filtering to a dedicated firewall.

However, there is no single "best" answer and the choice will depend on the particular circumstances in your organization.

Packet Filtering Routers

Most organizations with an Internet connection use some form of router between their internal networks and the external service provider. Many of these routers can be configured to block packets that the organization does not allow into the network. This is a simple but effective means of lowering the organization's risk of external attack. Such an architecture lacks auditing and strong authentication, and the complexity of the access control lists used to filter the packets can grow and degrade network performance. An example of this type of architecture was illustrated in Figure 26-1.

Screened-Host Firewalls

Screened-host firewall systems combine the packet filtering router with a separate, dedicated firewall such as an application proxy server. This approach allows the router to screen packets to minimize the network traffic and load on the internal proxy. The application proxy examines an application layer protocol, such as HTTP, and performs the proxy services. This separate host, which is often referred to as a **bastion host**, represents a single, rich target for external attacks, and should be very thoroughly secured. Because it stands as the point of access on the network perimeter, it is also commonly referred to as the **sacrificial host**.

Even though the bastion host/application proxy actually contains only cached copies of the internal Web documents, it can still present a promising target. An attacker that infiltrates the bastion host can discover the configuration of internal networks and possibly provide external sources with internal information. To its advantage, the proxy requires the external attack to compromise two separate systems before the attack can access internal data. As a consequence, the bastion host protects the data more fully than the router alone. Figure 26-2 shows a typical configuration of a screened-host architectural approach.

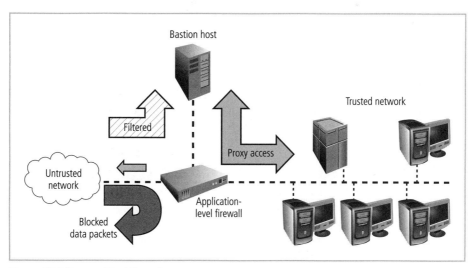

Figure 26-2 Screened-Host Firewall
Course Technology/Cengage Learning

Dual-Homed Host Firewalls

The next step up in firewall architectural complexity is the dual-homed host. In this configuration, the bastion host contains two network interfaces: one that is connected to the external network, and one that is connected to the internal network. All traffic *must* go through the firewall to move between the internal and external networks.

A technology known as **network-address translation (NAT)** is often implemented with this architecture. NAT is a method of converting multiple real, valid, external IP addresses to special ranges of internal IP addresses. A related approach called port-address translation (PAT) converts single real, valid, external IP addresses to special ranges of internal IP addresses. Both of these approaches create a barrier to internal intrusion because these internal addresses cannot be routed over the public network. These special, nonroutable addresses have three possible ranges:

- ▶ Organizations that need very large numbers of local addresses can use the 10.x.x.x range, which has more than 16.5 million usable addresses.

- ▶ Organizations that need a moderate number of addresses can use the 192.168.x.x range, which has more than 65,500 addresses.

- ▶ Organizations with smaller needs can use the 172.16.0.0 to 172.16.15.0 range, which has approximately 4000 usable addresses.

Taking advantage of NAT prevents external attacks from reaching internal machines with addresses in specified ranges. This type of translation works by dynamically assigning addresses to internal communications and tracking the conversations with sessions to determine which incoming message is a response to which outgoing traffic. Figure 26-3 shows a typical configuration of a dual-homed host firewall that uses NAT and proxy access to protect the internal network.

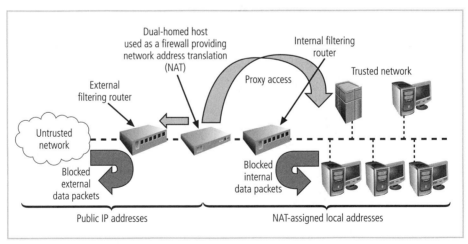

Figure 26-3 Dual-Homed Host Firewall
Course Technology/Cengage Learning

Since a dual-homed host includes a complete network stack on both interfaces, it is able to translate between the protocols of two different data link layers, such as Ethernet and asynchronous transfer method (ATM). This approach has two disadvantages, however:

▶ If the dual-homed host is compromised, it can take out the connection to the external network.

▶ As traffic volume increases, the dual-homed host can become overloaded.

Overall, however, this architecture provides strong protection with minimal expense compared to more complex solutions.

Screened-Subnet Firewalls (with DMZ)

The screened-subnet firewall consists of one or more internal bastion hosts located behind a packet filtering router, with each host protecting the trusted network. Many variants of the screened-subnet architecture exist. The first general model uses two filtering routers, with one or more dual-homed bastion hosts between them. In the second general model, as illustrated in Figure 26-4, the connections are routed as follows:

▶ Connections from the outside or untrusted network are routed through an external filtering router.

▶ Connections from the outside or untrusted network are routed into—and then out of—a routing firewall to the separate network segment known as the DMZ.

▶ Connections into the trusted internal network are allowed only from the DMZ bastion host servers.

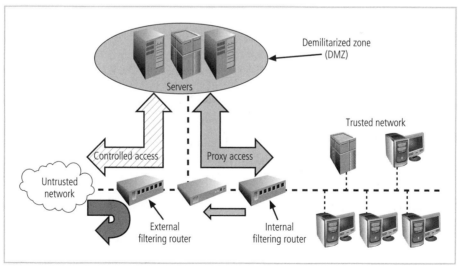

Figure 26-4 Screened-Subnet (DMZ)
Course Technology/Cengage Learning

As depicted in Figure 26-4, the screened subnet is an entire network segment that performs two functions: It protects the DMZ systems and information from outside threats, and it protects the internal networks by limiting how external connections can gain access to internal systems. Although extremely secure, the screened subnet can be expensive to implement and complex to configure and manage; the value of the information it protects must justify the cost.

The screened-subnet firewall architecture provides an intermediate area between the trusted network and the untrusted network—that is, a DMZ. This DMZ can be a dedicated port on the firewall device linking a single bastion host or it can be connected to a screened subnet or DMZ as shown in Figure 26-4. The servers providing Internet-facing services can be located in the DMZ or may be "fronted" by a proxy in the DMZ. This design decision will be based on the performance and scalability needs of the application.

Selecting the Right Firewall

When evaluating a firewall for your networks, you should ask the following questions:[3]

1. What type of firewall technology offers the right balance between protection, performance, and cost for the needs of the organization?

2. What features are included in the base price? What features are available at extra cost? Are all cost factors known and accounted for?

3. How easy is it to set up and configure the firewall? How accessible are the staff technicians who can competently configure and manage the firewall?

4. Can the candidate firewall adapt to the growing network in the target organization?

Question 2 addresses the second most important issue, cost. The cost of a firewall may put a certain make, model, or type out of reach for a particular security solution. As with all security decisions, the budgetary constraints stipulated by management must be taken into account.

MANAGING FIREWALLS

Any firewall device—whether a packet filtering router, bastion host, or other firewall implementation—must have its own set of configuration rules that regulate its actions. With packet filtering firewalls, these rules may be simple statements regulating source and destination addresses, specific protocol or port usage requests, or decisions to allow or deny certain types of requests. In all cases, a policy regarding the use of a firewall should be articulated before it is made operable.

In practice, configuring firewall rule sets can be something of a nightmare. Logic errors in the preparation of the rules can cause unintended behavior, such as allowing access instead of denying it, specifying the wrong port or service type, or causing the network to misroute traffic. These and a myriad of other mistakes can turn a device designed to protect communications into a choke point. For example, a novice firewall administrator might improperly configure a virus screening e-mail gateway (think of it as a type of e-mail firewall), resulting in the blocking of all incoming e-mail, instead of screening only e-mail that contains malicious code. Even worse, poor change control over time can reduce the effectiveness of the firewall (or even result in its being effectively disabled). Each firewall rule must be carefully crafted, placed into the list in the proper sequence, debugged, and tested. The proper rule sequence ensures that the more resource-intensive actions are performed after the more restrictive ones, thereby reducing the number of packets that undergo intense scrutiny.

The ever-present need to balance performance against restrictions imposed by security practices is very obvious in the use of firewalls. If users can't work due to a security restriction, then the security administration will most likely be told by management to remove it. Organizations are much more willing to live with a potential risk than certain failure.

Using a computer to protect a computer is fraught with problems that must be managed by careful preparation and continuous evaluation. Automated control systems, including firewalls, for the most part cannot learn from mistakes, and they cannot adapt to changing situations. They are limited by the constraints of their programming and rule sets in the following ways:

- ▶ Firewalls are not creative and cannot make sense of human actions outside the range of their programmed responses.
- ▶ Firewalls deal strictly with defined patterns of measured observation. These patterns are known to possible attackers and can be used to their benefit in an attack.
- ▶ Firewalls are computers themselves and are thus prone to programming errors, flaws in rule sets, and inherent vulnerabilities.
- ▶ Firewalls are designed to function within limits of hardware capacity and thus can only respond to patterns of events that happen in an expected and reasonably simultaneous sequence.
- ▶ Firewalls are designed, implemented, configured, and operated by people and are subject to the expected series of mistakes from human error.[4]

There are also a number of management challenges to administering firewalls:

1. No training: Most managers think of a firewall as just another device, more or less similar to the computers already buzzing in the rack; if you get time to read manuals, you are lucky.
2. Firewalls are quite different: You have mastered your firewall and now every new configuration requirement is just a matter of a few clicks in the telnet window; however, the new e-commerce project just brought you a new firewall running on a different OS.
3. Responsible for security: Since you are the firewall guy, suddenly everyone assumes that anything to do with computer security is your responsibility.
4. Daily administration tasks: Being a firewall administrator for a medium or large organization should be a full-time job by itself; however, that's hardly ever the case.[5]

Some of the best practices for firewall use are described below:[6]

- ▶ All traffic from the trusted network is allowed out. This allows members of the organization to access the services they need. Filtering and logging outbound traffic is possible when indicated by specific organizational policy goals.
- ▶ The firewall management interface is never accessible directly from the public network. Almost all management access to the firewall device is denied to internal users as well. Only authorized firewall administrators access the device via secure authentication mechanisms, with preference for a method based on cryptographically strong authentication using two-factor access control techniques.

- Simple Mail Transport Protocol (SMTP) data is allowed to pass through the firewall, but all of it is routed to a well-configured SMTP gateway to securely filter and route messaging traffic.

- All Internet Control Message Protocol (ICMP) data is denied. One common ICMP service, the ping service, is a common method for hacker reconnaissance and should be turned off to prevent snooping.

- Telnet (terminal emulation) access should generally be blocked because it is a clear-text protocol and is trivial to sniff credentials and other confidential information transported over a telnet connection. If internal users need to reach an organization's network from outside the firewall, use a virtual private network (VPN) client or another secure protocol (such as SSH) to support this access.

- When Web services are offered outside the firewall, HTTP traffic is prevented from reaching your internal networks via the implementation of some form of proxy access or DMZ architecture. That way, if any employees are running Web servers for internal use on their desktops, the services will be invisible to the outside Internet. If your Web server is located behind the firewall, you need to allow HTTP or HTTPS (SHTTP) data through for the Internet at large to view it. One solution is to place the Web servers containing critical data inside the network and to use proxy services from a DMZ (screened network segment). It is also advisable to restrict incoming HTTP traffic to internal network addresses such that the originating traffic must also come from an internal address. This restriction can be accomplished through NAT or firewalls that can support stateful inspection or are directed at the proxy server itself. All other incoming HTTP traffic should be blocked. If the Web servers contain only advertising, they should be placed in the DMZ and rebuilt when (not if) they are compromised.

Firewalls in their various forms are important pieces of network plumbing that control the flow of network traffic between trust domains. The general rule for designing the rule sets and other aspects of firewall operations is that only explicitly permitted traffic as required by organization business operations will be permitted. Firewalls allow the network to be segregated into domains of trust where the resources in the domain have similar protection and access constraints.

Like any other security feature, firewalls are not an "install and forget" item because they require continuing maintenance and support to assure that they continue to fulfill their purpose in protecting an organization's assets. Critical to this maintenance are good change control processes that assure that changes to the firewall's configuration are approved and will not effectively lower the protection provided by the device. Choosing the types and locations of firewalls can be a complex decision requiring that many factors (sometimes in conflict) must be considered and weighed.

The Information Security Manager's Checklist

This topic has been fully tested, validated, and integrated into organizational operations with formal performance measures in place (as appropriate).

This topic has been implemented, but not fully tested, validated, and integrated into organizational operations.

The implementation of this topic has begun, but is not yet complete.

The formal planning for this topic has begun, but is not yet complete.

This subject has not formally begun planning, or the organization has made a conscious decision not to pursue this topic.

26. Firewalls	No	Planned	In Progress	In Place	Integrated
Organization determines applicability of firewall					
Organization reviews available firewall technologies					
Organization develops policy for implementation of firewall and modification of firewall rules					
Organization determines logical positioning for firewall—perimeter vs DMZ					
Organization develops rule base for firewall in alignment with business strategy					
Organization installs, monitors, and reports on firewall performance					

For Further Reading

Firewalls: Jumpstart for Network and Systems Administrators by John R. Vacca and Scott Ellis, Digital Press, 2004.

Firewall Fundamentals by Wes Noonan and Ido Dubrawsky, Cisco Press, 2006.

The Best Damn Firewall Book Period, Second Edition, by Thomas W. Shinder, Syngress, 2008.

References

1. Firewall "generations" is a rather nebulous term because there is not a standard agreement on which is what. We include them for completeness but recommend that you remember the names, not the generations.

2. Fred Avolio and Chris Blask. Application gateways and stateful inspection: a brief note comparing and contrasting. *Avolio Consulting Online,* 22 January 1998. Accessed 22 November 2006 from www.avolio.com/papers/apgw+spf.html.

3. Elron Software, Inc. Choosing the best firewall for your growing network. 22 April 2002. Accessed 22 November 2006 from www.e-consultancy.com/knowledge/whitepapers/77864/choosing-the-best-firewall-for-your-growing-network.html.

4. Kevin Day. *Inside the Security Mind: Making the Tough Decisions.* Upper Saddle River, NJ: Prentice-Hall, 2003: 220.

5. Adrian Grigorof. Challenges in managing firewalls. Accessed 22 November 2006 from www.eventid .net/show.asp?DocId=18.

6. Laura Taylor. Guidelines for configuring your firewall rule-set. *Tech Update Online,* 12 April 2001. Accessed 22 November 2006 from techupdate.zdnet.com/techupdate/stories/main/ 0,14179,2707159,00.html.

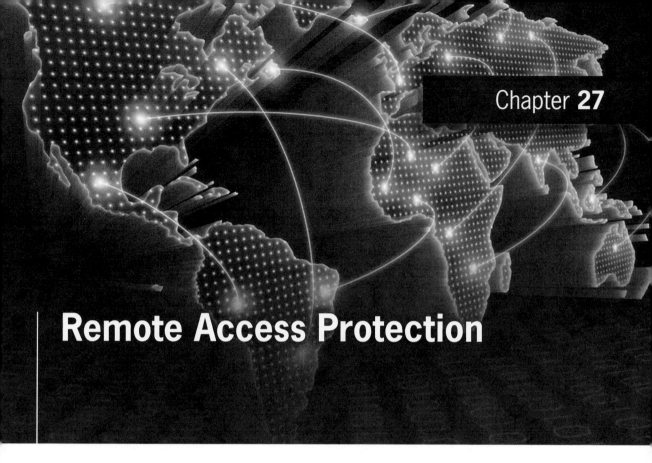

Chapter 27

Remote Access Protection

Prior to the emergence of the Internet, access to information resources was only possible via local access or with the use of a dedicated or leased-line connection. Now, there are significant business and economic incentives to allow access to at least a portion of an organization's information assets (including applications) to a much wider audience. This audience includes customers, business partners, and attackers. The focus of this chapter is on the processes used to provide remote access to authorized users while thwarting that access to potential attackers and other unauthorized users.

Remote access technologies include the familiar dial-up access and the increasingly more common web or virtual private network (VPN) access. While many organizations may scoff at the venerable dial-up access as being both slow and outdated it remains a convenient fall-back method for areas where a fast Internet connection may not be available. In any case, though remote access may be a significant business enabler, it has the potential for abuse unless proper policy and technical controls are imposed and maintained.

Chapter Overview:

▶ First step: policy
▶ Technology selection
▶ Wireless networking protection
▶ Implementation Issues

FIRST STEP: POLICY

The critical first step in managing remote access lies in the policy arena. A remote access policy is one of the most complex issues that must be addressed since it embraces everything from identifying potential users to the technological measures required to manage access and ensure secure operation.

As has been said many times before, the policy process begins with a clear definition of the business goals and functions to be supported by the remote access capability.

Identifying Use Cases

A useful first step is to brainstorm the use cases for remote access. Is it for support of field marketing operations only or does it also include options for remote support by IT personnel (e.g., Irving might not have to drive into the office to resolve a server issue if he can access the server remotely)? Will there be permitted uses for telecommuting?

Mapping out these use cases and their relationships to the overall business process will help management evaluate and understand their alternatives and guide the broad decision-making process that will establish the outlines of the remote access policy.

Consider the Impacts

Remote access is a far-ranging policy area because it is impacted by many other factors. For example, if field marketing representatives are to be issued laptops for use in remote access, what additional policies will need to be developed to assure the confidentiality of

De-perimiterization

The Jericho forum uses the concept of de-perimiterization[1] to reflect the fact that the idea of a clear delineation of an organization's network boundary is fast eroding with the wide availability and use of remote access technologies.

For example, a sales representative's laptop connected to an organization's network through a remote VPN connection becomes a network end point of the internal network. Wireless connections (discussed later in this chapter) potentially extend the limits of the network beyond the physical building to a variety of mobile assets.

Rather than a fixed network boundary that clearly defines "us" and "everyone else," the perimeter is a fluid boundary that expands and contracts based on which devices are connected at a particular point in time.

information on those laptops? Even more troublesome are limits on what types of information will be permitted to reside on those laptops.

If telecommuting is to be supported, what kind of systems will the organization allow to be used for remote access? If an employee's personal home computer is used, what protections (antivirus, etc.) must be in place to protect the organization's assets?

Develop Policies

As mentioned before, policy is the basic expression of what management wants to be done in a particular situation. After defining use cases, winnowing them down to the ones the organization needs to support and then carefully considering the other impacts, policy can be defined to guide the selection and implementation of a remote access solution.

If your organization has already created a home-brew remote access solution in the absence of policy, then a careful analysis of how current operations will be changed by the implementation of policy must be done and a transition plan defined.

TECHNOLOGY SELECTION

With policies developed and approved, the next step is to decide on the appropriate technologies to be applied in providing remote access services.

Dial-up

Dial-up is slower than broadband connectivity but it often finds application in even the most modern remote access solutions. For example, depending on the availability of local infrastructure, customers may not have an Internet connection for the sales representative to use but they will typically always have a telephone.

Unsecured dial-up access represents a substantial exposure to attack. An attacker who suspects that an organization has dial-up lines can use a device called a **war-dialer** to locate the connection points. A war-dialer is an automatic phone-dialing program that dials every number in a configured range (e.g., 555-1000 to 555-2000), and checks whether a person, answering

Unauthorized Access Points

One beneficial application of a war-dialer lies in the detection of unauthorized dial-up connections. Wherever there is an analog telephone line, the potential exists for someone to attach an auto-answer modem to provide an unauthorized access point into the organization. Usually this type of thing occurs with the best of intentions—a developer wants to check the status of overnight test runs or a server administrator wants to be able to make some configuration changes in the wee hours without driving into the office.

Though forbidden by policy, these types of one-time arrangements are fairly common and too often are overlooked until they provide the basis for a compromise.

machine, or modem picks up. If a modem answers, the war-dialer program makes a note of the number and then moves to the next target number. The attacker then attempts to hack into the network through the identified modem connection using a variety of techniques.

Dial-up connections are usually much simpler and less sophisticated than Internet connections. For the most part, simple user name and password schemes are the only means of authentication. Some newer technologies have improved this process, including RADIUS systems, Challenge Handshake Authentication Protocol (CHAP) systems, and even systems that use strong encryption. The most prominent of these approaches are RADIUS and TACACS.

RADIUS and TACACS
RADIUS and TACACS are systems that authenticate the credentials of users who are trying to access an organization's network via a dial-up device or a secured network session. Typical remote access systems place the responsibility for the authentication of users on the system directly connected to the modems. If the dial-up system includes multiple points of entry, such an authentication scheme is difficult to manage. The **Remote Authentication Dial-In User Service (RADIUS)** system centralizes the management of user authentication by placing the responsibility for authenticating each user in the central RADIUS server. When a remote access server (RAS) receives a request for a network connection from a dial-up client, it passes the request along with the user's credentials to the RADIUS server. RADIUS then validates the credentials and passes the resulting decision (accept or deny) back to the accepting RAS. Figure 27-1 shows the typical configuration of a Microsoft remote access server (RAS) system making use of RADIUS authentication.

Similar in function to the RADIUS system is the **Terminal Access Controller Access Control System (TACACS)**. This remote access authorization system is based on a client/server configuration. It makes use of a centralized data service, such as the one provided by a RADIUS server, and validates the user's credentials at the TACACS server. Three versions of TACACS exist: TACACS, Extended TACACS, and TACACS+. The original version combines authentication

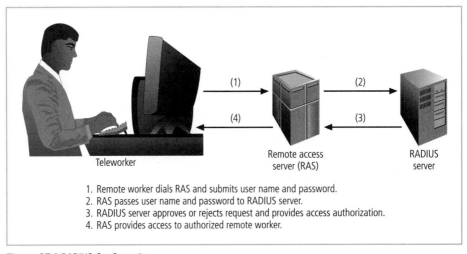

1. Remote worker dials RAS and submits user name and password.
2. RAS passes user name and password to RADIUS server.
3. RADIUS server approves or rejects request and provides access authorization.
4. RAS provides access to authorized remote worker.

Figure 27-1 RADIUS Configuration
Course Technology/Cengage Learning

and authorization services. The extended version authenticates and authorizes in two separate steps, and records the access attempt and the requestor's identity. The plus version uses dynamic passwords and incorporates two-factor authentication.[2]

Managing Dial-up Connections Many organizations that once operated large dial-up access pools are now reducing the number of telephone lines they support, in favor of Internet access secured by VPNs. An organization that continues to offer dial-up remote access must:

- ▶ Determine how many dial-up connections it has. Many organizations don't even realize they have dial-up access, or they leave telephone connections in place long after they have stopped fully using them. This creates two potential problems: (1) The organization continues to pay for telecommunications circuits it is not using; and (2) these circuits may remain connected, permitting unmonitored access to your networks. For example, an employee may have installed a modem on an office computer to do a little telecommuting without management's knowledge. The organization should periodically scan its internal phone networks with special software to detect available connections. It should also integrate risk assessment and risk approval into the telephone service ordering process.

- ▶ Control access to authorized modem numbers. Only those authorized to use dial-up access should be allowed to use incoming connections. Furthermore, although there is no security in obscurity, the numbers should not be widely distributed and the dial-up numbers should be considered confidential.

- ▶ Use call-back whenever possible. Call-back requires an access requestor to be at a preconfigured location, which is essential for authorized telecommuting. Users call into the access computer, which disconnects and immediately calls the requestor back. If the caller is an authorized user at the preconfigured number, the caller can then connect. This solution is not so useful for traveling users, however.

- ▶ Use token authentication if at all possible. Users can be required to enter more than user names and passwords, which is essential when allowing dial-up access from laptops and other remote computers. In this scheme, the device accepts an input number, often provided by the computer from which access is requested, and provides a response based on an internal algorithm. The result is much stronger security.

Virtual Private Networks

Virtual private networks (or VPNs) provide the capability for tunneling a secure network connection over a public insecure network. The VPN connection consists of a client (which may be software or a hardware appliance) and a VPN-gateway (which may be software running on a server or a specialized appliance) that provides entry to the organization's network.

Essentially the client will communicate with the VPN gateway over the Internet and they will negotiate the parameters for a secure connection.

Once the VPN connection is established, the client is functionally "on" the organization network and the communications between it and the gateway is protected from interception and modification by cryptographic means (described in a following chapter).

Authentication of clients is a critical requirement and may make use of RADIUS or TACACS as described earlier.

WIRELESS NETWORKING PROTECTION

The use of wireless network technology is an area of concern for information security professionals. Most organizations that make use of wireless networks use an implementation based on the IEEE 802.11 protocol. A wireless network provides a low-cost alternative to a wired network, because it doesn't require the difficult and often expensive installation of cable in an existing structure. The downside is the management of the wireless network **footprint**—the geographic area within which there is sufficient signal strength to make a network connection. The size of the footprint depends on the amount of power the transmitter/receiver **wireless access points (WAPs)** emit. There must be sufficient power to ensure quality connections within the intended area, but not so much as to allow those outside the footprint to receive them.

Just as war-dialers represent a threat to dial-up communications, so does war driving for wireless. **War driving** is moving through a geographic area or building, actively scanning for open or unsecured wireless access points. In some cities, groups of war-drivers move through an urban area, marking locations with unsecured wireless access with chalk ("war-chalking"). A number of encryption protocols can be used to secure wireless networks. The most common are the Wired Equivalent Privacy (WEP) and Wi-Fi Protected Access (WPA) families of protocols.

Wired Equivalent Privacy (WEP)

Wired Equivalent Privacy (WEP) is part of the IEEE 802.11 wireless networking standard. WEP is designed to provide a basic level of security protection to these radio networks, to prevent unauthorized access or eavesdropping. However, WEP, like a traditional wired network, does not protect users from each other; it only protects the network from unauthorized users. In the early 2000s, cryptologists found several fundamental flaws in WEP, resulting in vulnerabilities that can be exploited to gain access. These vulnerabilities ultimately led to the replacement of WEP as the industry standard with WPA. Even the average home or small office user, for whom the risk of attack is low, will find that WEP will not be sufficient. It is has been widely recommended that all Wi-Fi access points enable WPA or better encryption practices.

Wi-Fi Protected Access (WPA)

Wi-Fi Protected Access (WPA) is a family of protocols used to secure wireless networks that was created by the Wi-Fi Alliance industry group. The protocols were developed as an intermediate solution until the IEEE 802.11i standards were fully developed. **IEEE 802.11i** has been implemented into products as **WPA2**. This is an amendment to the 802.11 standard published in June 2004 specifying security protocols for wireless networks. While WPA works with virtually all wireless network cards, it is not compatible with some older WAPs. WPA2, on the other hand, has compatibility issues with some older wireless network cards. WPA and WPA2 provide increased capabilities for authentication, encryption, and increased throughput as compared to WEP.

Unlike WEP, both WPA and WPA2 can use an IEEE 802.1X authentication server, similar to the RADIUS servers mentioned in the previous section. This type of authentication server can issue keys to authenticated users. The alternative is to allow all users to share a key. The use of these **pre-shared keys** are quite convenient but are not secure compared to other authentication techniques. WPA also uses a Message Integrity Code, a type of message authentication code to prevent certain types of attacks. WPA was the strongest possible mechanism that was backwardly compatible with the older systems. WPA2 introduced newer, more robust security protocols based on the Advanced Encryption Standard (discussed in the cryptography section of this chapter), to greatly improve the protection of wireless networks. The WPA2 standard is currently incorporated into virtually all Wi-Fi devices.

Wi-Max

The next generation of wireless networking is Wi-Max, or WirelessMAN, essentially an improvement on the technology developed for cellular telephones and modems. Wi-Max is a certification mark that stands for *Worldwide Interoperability for Microwave Access* by the WiMAX Forum and was developed as part of the IEEE 802.16 standard.

> *WiMAX is not a technology per se, but rather a certification mark, or "stamp of approval" given to equipment that meets certain conformity and interoperability tests for the IEEE 802.16 family of standards. A similar confusion surrounds the term Wi-Fi (Wireless Fidelity), which like WiMAX, is a certification mark for equipment based on a different set of IEEE standards from the 802.11 working group for wireless local area networks (WLAN). Neither WiMAX, nor Wi-Fi is a technology but their names have been adopted in popular usage to denote the technologies behind them. This is likely due to the difficulty of using terms like "IEEE 802.16" in common speech and writing.*[3]

Managing Wireless Connections

To implement a secure wireless network, there are a number of measures users and organizations can use. These safeguards include the wireless security protocols mentioned earlier, virtual private networks (VPNs), and firewalls. It is also possible to restrict access to the network to a preapproved set of wireless network card MAC addresses. This is especially easy in small or personal networks where all possible users are known.

One of the first management requirements is to regulate the size of the wireless network footprint. The first step to is to determine the best locations for placement of the WAPs. In addition, by using radio strength meters, network administrators can adjust the power of the broadcast antennae, to provide sufficient but not excessive overage. This is especially important in areas where public access is possible.

WEP is usually the first choice in network installation, and there may be a natural tendency to select this option. While this is fine in a home or small office/home office (SOHO) setting, for most professional installations WPA or WPA2 is preferred. The setups of wireless networks are also slightly different than what most users are familiar with. Most smaller wireless networks require the use of a pre-shared key, which is a specific length password (usually 5 or 13 character). On some older equipment, the pre-shared key must be converted into a string of hexadecimal characters that must be entered into both the configuration software used to set up the wireless access point and each associated wireless network access card. This can quickly turn into a labor-intensive process for all but the smallest of networks.

IMPLEMENTATION ISSUES

When we implement remote access, regardless of the mode being used, several issues must be considered such as deployment and training and audit and assurance.

Deployment and Training

Once the technologies are selected, they can be deployed. One critical component of deployment is training the users in the appropriate use of remote access services. When mobile assets (laptops, PDAs, etc.) are involved, this training must branch out beyond the remote access function to include training on protection of assets (even simple things such as don't leave the laptop in your car) to making good decisions about what information to keep on a mobile asset.

Though often overlooked, remote access can be seen as "free Internet service" and training must include appropriate use to assure that the organization does not assume liability for someone's misjudgment while using an organization's network.

When hardening an existing remote access deployment, additional training time must be dedicated to how (and just as importantly why) remote access will be changing to bring it into compliance with security policy.

Audit and Assurance

Remote access is dangerous—it provides a mode of access from the external world into your organization network. For this reason, its deployment and operation must be audited on a regular basis to assure compliance with policy.

Simple lapses in a hardening configuration that might be an inconvenience in other situations can be devastating when they occur in a remote access solution.

This chapter provided an introduction to the important area of remote access and covered the basic sequence of policy development, technology selection, and deployment and training. Remote access can be either a business enabler or an open window of opportunity for an attacker. Good policies, adequate training, and regular audits for policy compliance will help assure that it remains a business enabler.

The Information Security Manager's Checklist

	No	Planned	In Progress	In Place	Integrated
This topic has been fully tested, validated, and integrated into organizational operations with formal performance measures in place (as appropriate).					
This topic has been implemented, but not fully tested, validated, and integrated into organizational operations.					
The implementation of this topic has begun, but is not yet complete.					
The formal planning for this topic has begun, but is not yet complete.					
This subject has not formally begun planning, or the organization has made a conscious decision not to pursue this topic.					
27. Remote Access Protection					
Organization determines applicability of remote access					
Organization reviews available remote access technologies					
Organization develops policies for implementation and use of remote access					
Organization develops access controls for remote access					
Organization installs and configures remote access					
Organization monitors and reports on remote access activity					

For Further Reading

Network Know-How: An Essential Guide for the Accidental Admin by John Ross, No Starch Press, 2009.

Administrator's Guide to VPN and Remote Access, 2nd edition, TechRepublic, 2002.

References

1. Jericho Forum. *The What and Why of De-perimiterization.* http://www.opengroup.org/jericho/deperim.htm, accessed 22 November, 2008.

2. Shon Harris. *CISSP Certification: All in One Exam Guide.* Berkeley: Osborne McGraw-Hill, 2001:163.

3. OECD. The Implications of Wimax for Competition and Regulation. Accessed 22 November 2006 from www.oecd.org/dataoecd/32/7/36218739.pdf.

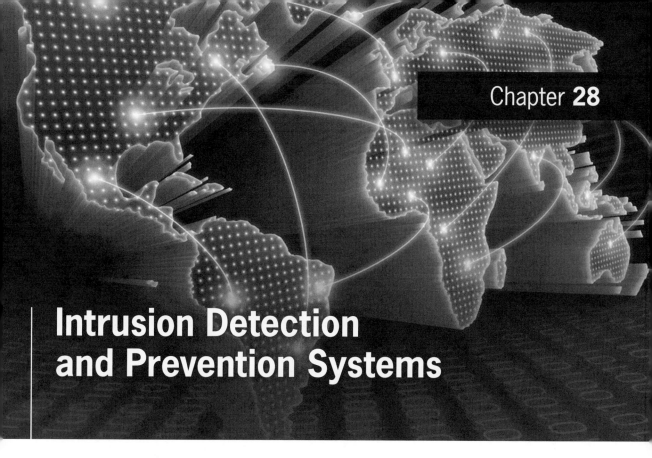

Intrusion Detection and Prevention Systems

Strictly speaking, an **intrusion** occurs when an attacker achieves access to an information asset in violation of security policy. Before something is classified as an intrusion, it is simply an event, an occurrence outside normal operations. In times past, the motivations for intrusion included curiosity, political or social causes, or a general desire to wreak havoc. However, increasingly the motivations for intrusions are focused on profit for the intruder whether the goal is to recruit systems for a botnet, steal personal information for use in identity theft, industrial espionage, etc. Intrusion attempts can be undirected (e.g., a Trojan embedded in a spam e-mail) or targeted at a particular organization.

Chapter Overview:

- ▶ Intrusion detection and prevention system basics
- ▶ Types of IDPS systems
- ▶ Deployment and implementation of an IDPS
- ▶ Honey pots, honey nets, and padded cell systems

INTRUSION DETECTION
AND PREVENTION SYSTEM BASICS

Intrusion *prevention* consists of activities that deter or even block an intrusion. Some important intrusion prevention activities are writing and implementing good enterprise information security policy, planning and performing effective information security programs, installing and testing technology-based information security countermeasures (such as firewalls and intrusion detection systems), and conducting and measuring the effectiveness of employee training and awareness activities. Intrusion *detection* consists of procedures and systems that identify system intrusions. Intrusion *reaction* encompasses the actions an organization takes when an intrusion is detected. These actions seek to limit the loss from an intrusion, and return operations to a normal state as rapidly as possible. Intrusion *correction* activities finalize the restoration of operations to a normal state, and seek to identify the source and method of the intrusion in order to ensure that the same type of attack cannot occur again—thus, reinitiating intrusion prevention.

Information security **intrusion detection systems (IDSs)** became commercially available in the late 1990s. An IDS works like a burglar alarm in that it detects a violation (some system activity analogous to an opened or broken window) and activates an alarm. This alarm can be audible and/or visual (producing noise and lights, respectively), or it can be silent (an e-mail message or pager alert). With almost all IDSs, system administrators can choose the configuration of the various alerts and the alarm levels associated with each type of alert. Many IDSs enable administrators to configure the systems to notify them directly of trouble via e-mail or pagers. The systems can also be configured—again like a burglar alarm—to notify an external security service organization of a "break-in." The configurations that enable IDSs to provide customized levels of detection and response are quite complex. A current extension of IDS technology is the **intrusion prevention system (IPS)**, which can detect an intrusion, and also prevent that intrusion from *successfully* attacking the organization by means of an active response. Because the two systems often coexist, the combined term **intrusion detection/prevention system (IDPS)** can be used to describe current anti-intrusion technologies.

IDPS Terminology

In order to understand IDPS operational behavior, you must first become familiar with some IDPS terminology. The following is a list of IDPS terms and definitions that are standard across the industry:

- ▶ Alert or alarm: An indication (audible signals, e-mail messages, pager notifications, or pop-up windows) that a system has just been attacked or is under attack.
- ▶ Evasion: The process by which an attacker changes the format and/or timing of their activities to avoid being detected by the IDPS.
- ▶ False attack stimulus: An event that triggers an alarm when no actual attack is in progress.
- ▶ False negative: The failure of an IDPS to react to an actual attack event.
- ▶ False positive: An alert or alarm that occurs in the absence of an actual attack.
- ▶ Noise: Alarm events that are accurate and noteworthy but do not pose a significant threat to information security.

- ▶ Site policy: The rules and configuration guidelines governing the implementation and operation of IDPSs within the organization.
- ▶ Site policy awareness: An IDPS's ability to dynamically modify its configuration in response to environmental activity.
- ▶ True attack stimulus: An event that triggers alarms and causes an IDPS to react as if a real attack is in progress.
- ▶ Tuning: The process of adjusting an IDPS to maximize its efficiency in detecting true positives, while minimizing both false positives and false negatives.
- ▶ Confidence value: A value associated with an intrusion indication indicating the assessed likelihood of the indication representing an actual intrusion.
- ▶ Alarm filtering: The process of classifying IDPS alerts in order to make them more meaningful and reduce noise. An IDPS administrator can set up alarm filtering by running the system for a while to track what types of false positives it generates and then adjusting the alarm classifications.
- ▶ Alarm Clustering and Compaction: A process of grouping almost identical alarms that happen at close to the same time into a single higher-level alarm.

Why Use an IDPS?

According to the NIST's documentation on industry best practices, there are several compelling reasons to acquire and use an IDPS:

1. To prevent problem behaviors by increasing the perceived risk of discovery and punishment for those who would attack or otherwise abuse the system
2. To detect attacks and other security violations that are not prevented by other security measures
3. To detect and deal with the preambles to attacks (commonly experienced as network probes and other "doorknob rattling" activities)
4. To document the existing threat to an organization
5. To act as quality control for security design and administration, especially of large and complex enterprises
6. To provide useful information about intrusions that do take place, allowing improved diagnosis, recovery, and correction of causative factors[1]

An additional justification for some form of IDPS is that it is increasingly becoming part of the due diligence organizations are expected to perform in protecting their information assets.

TYPES OF IDPS SYSTEMS

IDPSs operate as network- or host-based systems. A network-based IDPS is focused on protecting networked information assets. Two specialized subtypes of network-based IDPS are the wireless IDPS and the network behavior analysis (NBA) IDPS. The wireless IDPS focuses on wireless networks, as the name indicates, while the NBA IDPS examines traffic flow on a network in an attempt to recognize abnormal patterns like DDoS, malware, and policy violations.

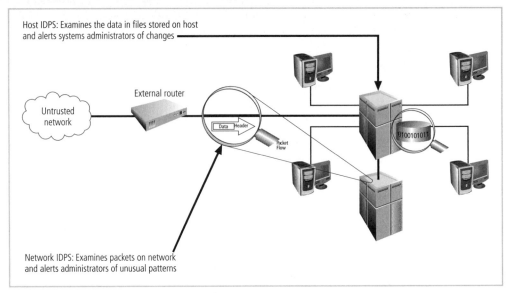

Host IDPS: Examines the data in files stored on host and alerts systems administrators of changes

External router

Untrusted network

Data Header

Packet Flow

01001010101

Network IDPS: Examines packets on network and alerts administrators of unusual patterns

Figure 28-1 Intrusion Detection and Prevention Systems
Course Technology/Cengage Learning

A host-based IDPS protects the server or host's information assets; the example shown in Figure 28-1 monitors both network connection activity and current information states on host servers. The application-based model works on one or more host systems that support a single application and defends that specific application from special forms of attack.

Network-Based IDPS

A **network-based IDPS (NIDPS)** resides on a computer or appliance connected to a segment of an organization's network and monitors network traffic on that network segment, looking for indications of ongoing or successful attacks. When the NIDPS identifies activity that it is programmed to recognize as an attack, it responds by sending notifications to administrators. When examining incoming packets, an NIDPS looks for patterns within network traffic such as large collections of related items of a certain type, which could indicate that a denial-of-service attack is underway, or the exchange of a series of related packets in a certain pattern, which could indicate that a port scan is in progress. An NIDPS can detect many more types of attacks than a host-based IDPS, but it requires a much more complex configuration and maintenance program.

An NIDPS is installed at a specific place in the network (such as on the inside of an edge router) from where it is possible to monitor the traffic going into and out of a particular network segment. The NIDPS can be deployed to monitor a specific grouping of host computers on a specific network segment, or it may be installed to monitor all traffic between the systems that make up an entire network. Since the IDPS must have visibility to all traffic entering or leaving the network, it is typically connected to a monitoring port or active network tap.

To determine whether an attack has occurred or is underway, NIDPSs compare measured activity to known signatures in their knowledge base. This is accomplished by means of a special implementation of the TCP/IP stack that reassembles the packets and applies protocol stack verification, application protocol verification, or other verification and comparison techniques.

While this chapter is titled "intrusion detection," it is important not to overlook useful information that can be derived from the traffic leaving the network.[2] An easily implemented example is looking for use of prohibited protocols. For example, if the Web tier of an organization should only be receiving http, https, and incoming FTP sessions, any instance of an outgoing http or ftp session would be abnormal. Since many successful attacks involve downloading additional tools (port redirectors, root kits, etc.), this can be a very effective tool for detecting that a successful intrusion has occurred.

Host-Based IDPS

While a network-based IDPS resides on a network segment and monitors activities across that segment, a **host-based IDPS (HIDPS)** resides on a particular computer or server, known as the host, and monitors activity only on that system. HIDPSs are also known as **system integrity verifiers**[3] because they benchmark and monitor the status of key system files and detect when an intruder creates, modifies, or deletes monitored files. An HIDPS has an advantage over NIDPS in that it can access information that was encrypted while traveling over the network, and use it to make decisions about potential or actual attacks. Also, since the HIDPS works on only one computer system, all the traffic it examines comes through that system.

An HIDPS is also capable of monitoring system configuration databases, such as Windows registries, in addition to stored configuration files like .ini, .cfg, and .dat files. Most HIDPSs work on the principle of configuration or change management, which means that they record the sizes, locations, and other attributes of system files. The HIDPS triggers an alert when file attributes change, new files are created, or existing files are deleted. An HIDPS can also monitor systems logs for predefined events. The HIDPS examines these files and logs to determine if an attack is underway or has occurred, and if the attack is succeeding or was successful. The HIDPS maintains its own log file so that an audit trail is available even when hackers modify files on the target system to cover their tracks. Once properly configured, an HIDPS is very reliable. The only time an HIDPS produces a false positive alert is when an authorized change occurs for a monitored file. This action can be quickly reviewed by an administrator, who may choose to disregard subsequent changes to the same set of files. If properly configured, an HIDPS can also detect when users attempt to modify or exceed their access authorization level.

IDPS Detection Methods

IDPSs use a variety of detection methods to monitor and evaluate network traffic. Three methods dominate: the signature-based approach, the statistical anomaly approach, and the stateful packet inspection approach.

Signature-Based IDPS A **signature-based IDPS** (sometimes called a **knowledge-based IDPS, or a misuse-detection IDPS**) examines network traffic in search of patterns that match known **signatures**—that is, preconfigured, predetermined attack patterns. Signature-based IDPS technology is widely used because many attacks have clear and distinct signatures, for example: (1) footprinting and fingerprinting activities, described

in detail earlier in this chapter, have an attack pattern that includes the use of ICMP, DNS querying, and e-mail routing analysis; (2) exploits involve a specific attack sequence designed to take advantage of a vulnerability to gain access to a system; (3) denial-of-service (DoS) and distributed denial-of-service (DDoS) attacks, during which the attacker tries to prevent the normal usage of a system, entail overloading the system with requests so that the system's ability to process them efficiently is compromised/disrupted and it begins denying services to authorized users.[4]

The problem with the signature-based approach is that as new attack strategies are identified, the IDPS's database of signatures must be continually updated; otherwise, attacks that use new strategies will not be recognized and might succeed. Another weakness of the signature-based method is that a slow, methodical attack might escape detection, if the relevant IDPS attack signature has a shorter time frame. The only way for a signature-based IDPS to resolve this vulnerability is for it to collect and analyze data over longer periods of time, a process that requires substantially larger data storage capability and additional processing capacity.

Statistical Anomaly-Based IDPS The **statistical anomaly-based IDPS (stat IDPS)** or **behavior-based IDPS** collects statistical summaries by observing traffic that is known to be normal. This normal period of evaluation establishes a performance baseline. Once the baseline is established, the stat IDPS periodically samples network activity, and, using statistical methods, compares the sampled network activity to this baseline. When the measured activity is outside the baseline parameters—exceeding what is called the **clipping level**—the IDPS sends an alert to the administrator. The baseline data can include variables such as host memory or CPU usage, network packet types, and packet quantities.

The advantage of the statistical anomaly-based approach is that the IDPS can detect new types of attacks, since it looks for abnormal activity of any type. Unfortunately, these systems require much more overhead and processing capacity than signature-based IDPSs, because they must constantly compare patterns of activity against the baseline. Another drawback is that these systems may not detect minor changes to system variables and may generate many false positives. If the actions of the users or systems on a network vary widely, with periods of low activity interspersed with periods of heavy packet traffic, this type of IDPS may not be suitable, because the dramatic swings from one level to another will almost certainly generate false alarms. Because of its complexity and impact on the overhead computing load of the host computer as well as the number of false positives it can generate, this type of IDPS is less commonly used than the signature-based type.

IDPS Response Behavior

Each IDPS responds to external stimulation in different ways, depending on its configuration and function. Some respond in active ways, collecting additional information about the intrusion, modifying the network environment, or even taking action against the intrusion. Others respond in passive ways, for example, by setting off alarms or notifications, or collecting passive data through SNMP traps.

IDPS Response Options When an IDPS detects a possible intrusion, it has a number of response options, depending on implementing an organization's policy, objectives, and system capabilities. When configuring an IDPS's responses, the system administrator must exercise care to ensure that a response to an attack (or potential attack) does not inadvertently exacerbate the situation. For example, if an NIDPS reacts to suspected DoS attacks by severing the network connection, the attack is a success, and such attacks repeated at intervals will thoroughly disrupt an organization's business operations.

IDPS responses can be classified as active or passive. An active response is a definitive action automatically initiated when certain types of alerts are triggered and can include collecting additional information, changing or modifying the environment, and taking action against the intruders. Passive response IDPSs simply report the information they have collected and wait for the administrator to act. Generally, the administrator chooses a course of action after analyzing the collected data. The passive IDPS is the most common implementation, although most systems allow some active options that are disabled by default.

The following list illustrates some responses an IDPS can be configured to produce. Note that some of these apply only to a network-based or a host-based IDPS, while others are applicable to both.[5]

- ▶ Audible/visual alarm: The IDPS can trigger a .wav file, beep, whistle, siren, or other audible or visual notification to alert the administrator of an attack.
- ▶ SNMP traps and plug-ins: The Simple Network Management Protocol contains trap functions, which allow a device to send a message to the SNMP management console, indicating that a certain threshold has been crossed, either positively or negatively.
- ▶ E-mail message: The IDPS can e-mail an individual to notify him or her of an event.
- ▶ Page or phone message: The IDPS can be configured to dial a phone number, and produce an alphanumeric page or a modem noise.
- ▶ Log entry: The IDPS can enter information about the event (e.g., addresses, time, systems involved, protocol information, etc.) into an IDPS system log file, or operating system log file.
- ▶ Evidentiary packet dump: Organizations that require an audit trail of the IDPS data may choose to record all log data in a special way. This method allows the organization to perform further analysis on the data and also to submit the data as evidence in a civil or criminal case.
- ▶ Take action against the intruder: It has become possible, although not advisable, to take action against an intruder. Known as trap and trace, back-hacking, or traceback, this response option involves configuring intrusion detection systems trace the data from the target system to the attacking system in order to initiate a counterattack. An organization only owns a network to its perimeter, and conducting traces or back-hacking to systems outside that perimeter may make the organization just as criminally liable as the individual(s) who began the attack.
- ▶ Launch program: An IDPS can be configured to execute a specific program when it detects specific types of attacks.
- ▶ Reconfigure firewall: An IDPS could send a command to the firewall to filter out suspected packets by IP address, port, or protocol. While it may not be easy, an IDPS can block or deter intrusions by one of the following methods:
  - ▶ Establishing a block for all traffic from the suspected attacker's IP address, or even from the entire source network from which the attacker appears to be operating.

- ▶ Establishing a block for specific TCP or UDP port traffic from the suspected attacker's address or source network, blocking only the services that seem to be under attack.
- ▶ Blocking all traffic to or from a network interface (such as the organization's Internet connection) if the severity of the suspected attack warrants that level of response.[6]
- ▶ Terminate session: Terminating the session by using the TCP/IP protocol specified packet *TCP close* is a simple process.
- ▶ Terminate connection: The last resort for an IDPS under attack is to terminate the organization's internal or external connections.

DEPLOYMENT AND IMPLEMENTATION OF AN IDPS

Deploying and implementing an IDPS is not always a straightforward task. The strategy for deploying an IDPS should consider a number of factors, the foremost being how the IDPS will be managed and where it should be placed. These factors determine the number of administrators needed to install, configure, and monitor the IDPS, as well as the number of management workstations, the size of the storage needed for retention of the data generated by the systems, and the ability of the organization to detect and respond to remote threats.

IDPS Control Strategies

An IDPS can be implemented via one of three basic control strategies. A control strategy determines how an organization exerts influence and maintains the configuration of an IDPS. It also determines how the input and output of the IDPS is to be managed. The three commonly utilized control strategies are centralized, partially distributed, and fully distributed.

Centralized Control Strategy As illustrated in Figure 28-2, in a centralized IDPS control strategy all IDPS control functions are implemented and managed in a central location. This is indicated in the figure with the large square symbol labeled "IDPS Console." The IDPS console includes the management software, which collects information from the remote sensors (appearing in the figure as triangular symbols); analyzes the systems or networks monitored; and makes the determination as to whether the current situation has deviated from the preconfigured baseline. All reporting features are also implemented and managed from this central location. The primary advantages of this strategy are related to cost and control. With one central implementation, there is one management system, one place to go to monitor the status of the systems or networks, one location for reports, and one set of administrative management. This centralization of IDPS management supports task specialization, since all managers are either located near the IDPS management console or can acquire an authenticated remote connection to it, and technicians are located near the remote sensors. This means that each person can focus specifically on the assigned task. In addition, the central control group can evaluate the systems and networks as a whole, and since it can compare pieces of information from all sensors, the group is better positioned to recognize a large-scale attack.

Fully Distributed Control Strategy As presented in Figure 28-3, a fully distributed IDPS control strategy is the opposite of the centralized strategy. Note in the figure that

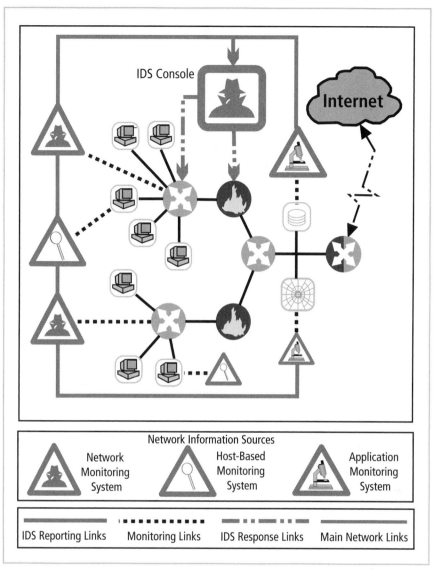

all control functions (which appear as small square symbols enclosing a computer icon) are applied at the physical location of each IDPS component. Each monitoring site uses its own paired sensors to perform its own control functions to achieve the necessary detection, reaction, and response functions. Thus, each sensor/agent is best configured to deal with its own environment. Since the IDPSs do not have to wait for a response from a centralized control facility, their reaction to individual attacks is greatly speeded up.

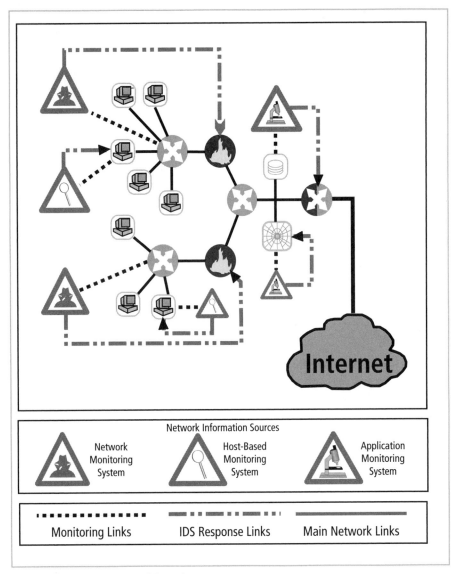

Network Information Sources

| Network Monitoring System | Host-Based Monitoring System | Application Monitoring System |

Monitoring Links   IDS Response Links   Main Network Links

Figure 28-3 Fully Distributed IDS Control
Course Technology/Cengage Learning

Partially Distributed Control Strategy

A partially distributed IDPS control strategy, as depicted in Figure 28-4, combines the best of the other two strategies. While the individual agents can still analyze and respond to local threats, their reporting to a hierarchical central facility enables the organization to detect widespread attacks. This blended approach to reporting is one of the more effective methods of detecting intelligent attackers, especially those who probe an organization through multiple points of entry, trying to scope out the systems' configurations and weaknesses, before they launch a concerted attack. The partially distributed control strategy also allows the organization to optimize for economy

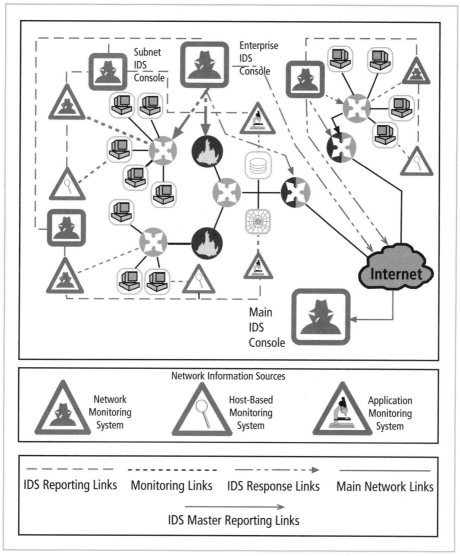

Figure 28-4 Partially Distributed IDS Control
Course Technology/Cengage Learning

of scale in the implementation of key management software and personnel, especially in the reporting areas. When the organization can create a pool of security managers to evaluate reports from multiple distributed IDPS systems, it becomes better able to detect these distributed attacks before they become unmanageable.

IDPS Deployment

Given the highly technical skills required to implement and configure IDPSs and the imperfection of the technology, great care must be made when deciding where to locate the components, both in their physical connection to the network and host devices and in how they are logically connected to each other and the IDPS administration team. Since IDPSs are designed to detect, report, and even react to anomalous stimuli, placing IDPSs in an area where such traffic is common can result in excessive reporting. Moreover, the administrators' monitoring systems located in such areas can become desensitized to the information flow and may fail to detect actual attacks in progress.

As an organization selects an IDPS and prepares for implementation, planners must select a deployment strategy that is based on a careful analysis of the organization's information security requirements and that integrates with the organization's existing IT infrastructure but, at the same time, causes minimal impact. After all, the purpose of the IDPS is to detect anomalous situations—not create them. One consideration is the skill level of the personnel that install, configure, and maintain the systems. An IDPS is a complex system in that it involves numerous remote monitoring agents (on both individual systems and networks) that require proper configuration to gain the proper authentication and authorization. As the IDPS is deployed, each component should be installed, configured, fine-tuned, tested, and monitored. A mistake in any step of the deployment process may produce a range of problems—from a minor inconvenience to a network-wide disaster. Thus, both the individuals installing the IDPS and the individuals using and managing the system require proper training.

NIDPS and HIDPS can be used in tandem to cover both the individual systems that connect to an organization's networks and the networks themselves. To do this, it is important for an organization to use a phased implementation strategy so as not to affect the entire organization all at once. A phased implementation strategy also allows security technicians to resolve the problems that do arise without compromising the very information security the IDPS is installed to protect. In terms of sequencing the implementation, first the organization should implement the network-based IDPS, since they are less problematic and easier to configure than their host-based counterparts. After the NIDPSs are configured and running without issue, the HIDPSs can be installed to protect the critical systems on the host server. Next, after both are considered operational, it would be advantageous to scan the network with a vulnerability scanner like Nmap or Nessus to determine if (a) the scanners pick up anything new or unusual, and (b) if the IDPS can detect the scans.

Deploying Network-Based IDPSs

As discussed above, the placement of the sensor agents is critical to the operation of all IDPSs, but this is especially critical in the case of Network IDPSs. NIST recommends four locations for NIDPS sensors:

Location 1: Behind each external firewall, in the network DMZ (see Figure 28-5, location 1)

Advantages:

- ▶ IDPS sees attacks that originate from the outside world and may penetrate the network's perimeter defenses.
- ▶ IDPS can identify problems with the network firewall policy or performance.
- ▶ IDPS sees attacks that might target the Web server or ftp server, both of which commonly reside in this DMZ.
- ▶ Even if the incoming attack is not detected, the IDPS can sometimes recognize, in the outgoing traffic, patterns that suggest that the server has been compromised.

Location 2: Outside an external firewall (see Figure 28-5, location 2)

Advantages:

▶ IDPS documents the number of attacks originating on the Internet that target the network.

▶ IDPS documents the types of attacks originating on the Internet that target the network.

Location 3: On major network backbones (see Figure 28-5, location 3)

Advantages:

▶ IDPS monitors a large amount of a network's traffic, thus increasing its chances of spotting attacks.

▶ IDPS detects unauthorized activity by authorized users within the organization's security perimeter.

Location 4: On critical subnets (see Figure 28-5, location 4)

Advantages:

▶ IDPS detects attacks targeting critical systems and resources.

▶ Location allows organizations with limited resources to focus these resources on the network assets considered of greatest value.[7]

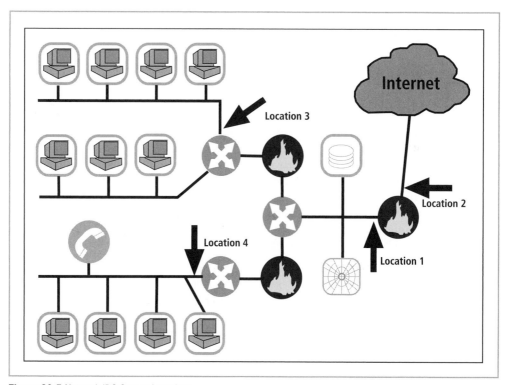

Figure 28-5 Network IDS Sensor Locations
Course Technology/Cengage Learning

Deploying Host-Based IDPSs The proper implementation of HIDPSs can be a pain staking and time-consuming task, as each HIDPS must be custom configured to its host systems. Deployment begins with implementing the most critical systems first. This poses a dilemma for the deployment team, since the first systems to be implemented are mission-critical and any problems in the installation could be catastrophic to the organization. As such, it may be beneficial to practice an implementation on one or more test servers configured on a network segment that resembles the mission-critical systems. Practicing will help the installation team gain experience and also help determine if the installation might trigger any unusual events. Gaining an edge on the learning curve by training on nonproduction systems will benefit the overall deployment process by reducing the risk of unforeseen complications.

Installation continues until either all systems are installed or the organization reaches the planned degree of coverage it is willing to live with, with regard to the number of systems or percentage of network traffic. To provide ease of management, control, and reporting, each HIDPS should, as discussed earlier, be configured to interact with a central management console.

Just as technicians can install the HIDPS in off-line systems to develop expertise and identify potential problems, users and managers can gain expertise and understanding of the operation of the HIDPS by using a test facility. This test facility could use the off-line systems configured by the technicians, but also be connected to the organization's backbone to allow the HIDPS to process actual network traffic. This setup will also enable technicians to create a baseline of normal traffic for the organization. During the system testing process, training scenarios can be developed that will enable users to recognize and respond to common attack situations. To ensure effective and efficient operation, the management team can establish policy for the operation and monitoring of the HIDPS.

HONEY POTS, HONEY NETS, AND PADDED CELL SYSTEMS

A class of powerful security tools that go beyond routine intrusion detection is known variously as honey pots, honey nets, or padded cell systems. **Honey pots** are decoy systems designed to lure potential attackers away from critical systems. In the industry, they are also known as decoys, lures, and fly-traps. When a collection of honey pots connects several honey pot systems on a subnet, it may be called a **honey net**. Because the information in a honey pot appears to be valuable, any unauthorized access to it constitutes suspicious activity. Honey pots are instrumented with sensitive monitors and event loggers that detect attempts to access the system and collect information about the potential attacker's activities.

A **padded cell** is a honey pot that has been protected so that it cannot be easily compromised— in other words, a hardened honey pot. IDPS researchers have used padded cell and honey pot systems since the late 1980s, but until recently no commercial versions of these products were available. It is important to seek guidance from legal counsel before deciding to use either of these systems in your operational environment, since using an attractant and then launching a back-hack or counterstrike might be illegal, and make the organization subject to a lawsuit or a criminal complaint.

Trap and Trace Systems

Trap and trace applications use a combination of techniques to detect an intrusion and then to trace it back to its source. The trap usually consists of a honey pot or padded cell and an alarm. While the intruders are distracted, or trapped, by what they perceive to be successful intrusions, the system notifies the administrator of their presence. The trace is a process by which the organization attempts to determine the identity of someone discovered in unauthorized areas of the network or systems. If the intruder is someone inside the organization, the administrators are completely within their power to track the individual and turn him or her over to internal or external authorities. If the intruder is outside the security perimeter of the organization, then numerous legal issues arise.

Active Intrusion Prevention

Some organizations would like to do more than simply wait for the next attack and implement active countermeasures to stop attacks. One tool that provides active intrusion prevention is known as LaBrea (*http://labrea.sourceforge.net/labrea-info.html*). LaBrea works by taking up the unused IP address space within a network. When LaBrea notes an ARP request, it checks to see if the IP address requested is actually valid on the network. If the address is not currently being used by a real computer or network device, LaBrea pretends to be a computer at that IP address and allows the attacker to complete the TCP/IP connection request, known as the three-way handshake. Once the handshake is complete, LaBrea changes the TCP sliding window size to a low number to hold open the TCP connection from the attacker for many hours, days, or even months. Holding the connection open but inactive greatly slows down network-based worms and other attacks. It allows the LaBrea system time to notify the system and network administrators about the anomalous behavior on the network.

This chapter has introduced the complex area of intrusion detection and prevention. While an organization should have a method for detecting intrusions, the many choices and differing requirements of the various types of solutions can be daunting. A reasoned approach that carefully considers the goals of the intrusion detection program and the resources available to achieve those goals will help assure that the organization makes a wise choice in investment that both improves its security posture and, most importantly, can be supported by the organization over time.

The Information Security Manager's Checklist

	No	Planned	In Progress	In Place	Integrated
This topic has been fully tested, validated, and integrated into organizational operations with formal performance measures in place (as appropriate).					
This topic has been implemented, but not fully tested, validated, and integrated into organizational operations.					
The implementation of this topic has begun, but is not yet complete.					
The formal planning for this topic has begun, but is not yet complete.					
This subject has not formally begun planning, or the organization has made a conscious decision not to pursue this topic.					
28. Intrusion Detection/Prevention Systems (IDPS)					
Organization determines applicability of intrusion detection/prevention systems					
Organization reviews available IDPS technologies					
Organization develops policy for implementation of IDPS					
Organization determines logical positioning for IDPS: host and network					
Organization positions and tunes IDPS					
Organization monitors and reports on IDPS activity					

For Further Reading

Extrusion Detection: Security Monitoring for Internal Intrusions by Richard Bejtlich, Addison-Wesley Professional, 2005.

Practical Intrusion Analysis: Prevention and Detection for the Twenty-First Century by Ryan Trost, Addison-Wesley Professional, 2010.

Security Monitoring: Proven Methods for Incident Detection on Enterprise Networks by Chris Fry and Martin Nystrom, O'Reilly Media, 2009.

References

1. K. Scarfone and P. Mell. Guide to Intrusion Detection and Prevention Systems (IDPS). NIST Special Publication 800-94, 2007. Accessed 21 June 2007 from csrc.nist.gov/publications/nistpubs/800-94/SP800-94.pdf.

2. Richard Bejtlich. *Extrusion Detection: Network Monitoring for Internal Intrusions.* Boston: Addison-Wesley, 2005.

3. R. Graham.FAQ: Intrusion Detection Systems. March 2000. Viewed online on 9 April 2007. Accessed 21 June 2007, from linuxsecurity.com/resource_files/intrusion_detection/network-intrusion-detection.html.

4. Ibid.

5. Ibid.

6. K. Scarfone and P. Mell. Guide to Intrusion Detection and Prevention Systems (IDPS).

7. Ibid.

Scanning and Analysis Tools

Securing a network implies that one has a good knowledge of the risks facing a network. This may sound trivial, but many organizations skip this step. They install a simple perimeter firewall, and then, lulled into a sense of security by this single layer of defense, they relax. To truly control the risk within any computing environment, you must deploy controls using a strategy of defense in depth, which may include technical controls such as intrusion detection/prevention systems (IDPS), active vulnerability scanners, passive vulnerability scanners, automated log analyzers, and protocol analyzers (commonly referred to as sniffers).

Chapter Overview:

- ▶ The scanning and analysis toolbox
- ▶ Port scanners
- ▶ Firewall analysis tools
- ▶ Operating system detection tools
- ▶ Vulnerability scanners
- ▶ Packet sniffers

- ▶ Wireless security tools
- ▶ Insource or outsource

THE SCANNING AND ANALYSIS TOOLBOX

Scanners and other analysis tools can find vulnerabilities in systems, holes in security components, and unsecured aspects of the network. Although some information security experts may not perceive them as defensive tools, scanners, sniffers, and other such vulnerability analysis tools can be invaluable because they enable administrators to see what an attacker sees. Some of these tools are extremely complex and others are rather simple. The tools also range from expensive commercial products to freeware. Many of the best scanning and analysis tools are those developed by the security community (including attackers), and are open source. Good administrators should try to keep up discussions on new vulnerabilities, recent exploits, and common attack techniques. There is nothing wrong with a security administrator using the tools that potential attackers use in order to examine network defenses and find areas that require additional attention (provided such use is permitted by and in accordance with organizational policy). In the military, there is a long and distinguished history of generals inspecting the troops under their command before battle, walking down the line checking out the equipment and mental preparedness of each soldier. In a similar way, the security administrator can use vulnerability analysis tools to inspect the units (host computers and network devices) under his or her control. A word of caution though: Many of these scanning and analysis tools have distinct signatures, and may violate Internet service providers' (ISPs) terms of service. If the ISP discovers someone using hacker tools, it can pull that person's access privileges. It is probably best for administrators first to establish a working relationship with their ISPs and notify the ISP of their plans.

Scanning tools are, as mentioned earlier, typically used as part of an attack protocol to collect information that an attacker would need to launch a successful attack. The **attack protocol** is a series of steps or processes used by an attacker, in a logical sequence, to plan and launch an attack against a target system or network. One of the preparatory parts of the attack protocol is the collection of publicly available information about a potential target, a process known as footprinting. **Footprinting** is the organized research of the Internet addresses owned or controlled by a target organization. The attacker uses public Internet data sources to perform

Legality of Network Scanning

Network scanning can be a contentious issue both legally and ethically.[1] Generally, an organization can usually scan their own network without risk, but scanning another organization's network can lead to unexpected consequences. This commonly arises in the context of business partners where one organization might be tempted to evaluate the security of a partner's network. Before scanning a network, it is critical to assure that the scanning is supported and approved according to organizational policy and is done with the permission of the network owner (and Internet service provider).

keyword searches to identify the network addresses of the organization (e.g., samspade.org). This research is augmented by browsing the organization's Web pages. Web pages usually contain quantities of information about internal systems, individuals developing Web pages, and other tidbits, which can be used for social engineering attacks. The *view source* option on most popular Web browsers allows the user to see the source code behind the graphics. A number of details in the source code of the Web page can provide clues to potential attackers and give them insight into the configuration of an internal network, such as the locations and directories for Common Gateway Interface (CGI) script bins and the names or possibly addresses of computers and servers. In addition, public business Web sites (such as Forbes, or Yahoo Business) often reveal information about company structure, commonly used company names, and other information that attackers find useful. Furthermore, common search engines will allow attackers to query for any site that links to their proposed target. By doing a little bit of initial Internet research into a company, an attacker can often find additional Internet locations that are not commonly associated with the company—that is, Business to Business (B2B) partners and subsidiaries. Armed with this information, the attacker can find the "weakest link" into the target network.

For an example, consider Company X, which has a large datacenter located in Atlanta. The datacenter has been secured, and thus it will be very hard for an attacker to break into the datacenter via the Internet. However, the attacker has run a query on the search engine *www.altavista.com* and found a small Web server that links to Company X's main Web server. After further investigation, the attacker learns that the small Web server was set up by an administrator at a remote facility, and that the remote facility has, via its own leased lines, an unrestricted internal link into Company X's corporate datacenter. The attacker can now attack the weaker site at the remote facility and use this compromised network—which is an internal network—to attack the true target. While it may seem trite or cliché, the phrase "a chain is only as strong as its weakest link" is very relevant to network and computer security. If a company has a trusted network connection with 15 business partners, one weak business partner can compromise all 16 networks.

To assist in the footprint intelligence collection process, you can use an enhanced Web scanner (e.g., Nikto, Wikto, etc.) that, among other things, can scan entire Web sites for valuable pieces of information, such as server names and e-mail addresses.

A tool called "wget" (natively available on Linux but also ported to Windows) allows a remote individual to "mirror" entire Web sites. With this tool, attackers can copy an entire Web site and then go through the source HTML, JavaScript, and Web-based forms at their leisure, collecting and collating all of the data from the source code that will be useful to them for their attack.

The next phase of the attack protocol is a data-gathering process called **fingerprinting**. This is a systematic survey of all of the target organization's Internet addresses (which were collected during the footprinting phase described above); the survey is conducted to identify the network services offered by the hosts in that range. By using the tools discussed in the next section, fingerprinting reveals useful information about the internal structure and operational nature of the target system or network for the anticipated attack. Since these tools were created to find vulnerabilities in systems and networks quickly and with a minimum of effort, they are valuable for the network defender since they can quickly pinpoint the parts of the systems or network that need a prompt repair to close the vulnerability.

PORT SCANNERS

Port scanning utilities, or **port scanners**, are tools used by both attackers and defenders to identify (or fingerprint) the computers that are active on a network, as well as the ports and services active on those computers, the functions and roles the machines are fulfilling, and other useful information. These tools can scan for specific types of computers, protocols, or resources, or their scans can be generic. It is helpful to understand the environment that exists in the network you are using, so that you can use the tool most suited to the data collection task at hand. For instance, if you are trying to identify a Windows computer in a typical network, a built-in feature of the operating system, nbtstat, may be able to get the answer you need very quickly, without the installation of a scanner. This tool will not work on other types of networks, however, so you must know your tools in order to make the best use of the features of each.

The more specific the scanner is, the more useful the information it provides to attackers and defenders. However, you should keep a generic, broad-based scanner in your toolbox as well to help locate and identify rogue nodes on the network that administrators may be unaware of. Probably the most popular port scanner is Nmap, which runs on both Unix and Windows systems. You can find out more about Nmap at *http://www.insecure.org*.

A port is a network channel or connection point in a data communications system. Within the TCP/IP networking protocol, TCP and User Datagram Protocol (UDP) port numbers differentiate the multiple communication channels that are used to connect to the network services being offered on the same network device. Each application within TCP/IP has a unique port number. Some have default ports but can also use other ports. Some of the well-known port numbers are presented in Table 29-1. In all, there are 65,536 port numbers in use for TCP and another 65,536 port numbers for UDP. Services using the TCP/IP protocol can run on any port; however, the services with reserved ports generally run on ports 1–1023. Port 0 is not used. Ports greater than 1023 are typically referred to as ephemeral ports and may be randomly allocated to server and client processes.

Why secure open ports? Simply put, an open port can be used by an attacker to send commands to a computer, potentially gain access to a server, and possibly exert control over a networking device. The general rule of thumb is to remove from service or secure any port not absolutely necessary to conducting business (also known as minimizing the attack surface). For example, if a business doesn't host Web services, there is no need for port 80 to be available on its servers.

FIREWALL ANALYSIS TOOLS

Understanding exactly where an organization's firewall is located and what the existing rule sets on the firewall do are very important steps for any security administrator. There are several tools that automate the remote discovery of firewall rules and assist the administrator (or attacker) in analyzing the rules to determine exactly what they allow and what they reject.

The Nmap tool mentioned earlier has some advanced options that are useful for firewall analysis. The Nmap option called *Idle scanning* (which is run with the -I switch) will allow the Nmap user to "bounce" a scan across a firewall by using one of the DMZ hosts (i.e., a host

TABLE 29-1 Commonly Used Port Numbers

TCP PORT NUMBERS	TCP SERVICE
20 and 21	File Transfer Protocol (FTP)
22	Secure Shell (SSH)
23	Telnet
25	Simple Mail Transfer Protocol (SMTP)
53	Domain Name Services (DNS)
67 and 68	Dynamic Host Configuration Protocol (DHCP)
80	Hypertext Transfer Protocol (HTTP)
110	Post Office Protocol (POP3)
161	Simple Network Management Protocol (SNMP)
194	IRC chat port (used for device sharing)
443	HTTP over SSL
8080	Used for proxy services

Course Technology/Cengage Learning

accessible from the Internet) as the initiator of the scan. More specifically, since some operating systems do not use truly random IP packet identification numbers (IP IDs), if there is a host in the DMZ that uses non-random IP IDs, then the attacker can query the server (server X) and obtain the currently used IP ID as well as the known algorithm for incrementing the IP IDs. The attacker can then spoof a packet that is allegedly from server X and destined for an internal IP address behind the firewall. If the port is open on the internal machine, the internal machine replies to server X with a SYN-ACK packet, which forces server X to respond with a TCP RESET packet (since it didn't really initiate the connection). In responding with the TCP RESET, server X increments its IP ID number. The attacker can now query server X a second time to see if the IP ID has incremented. If it has, the attacker knows that the internal machine is alive and that the internal machine has the queried service port open. In a nutshell, running the Nmap Idle scan allows an attacker to scan an internal network as if he or she were physically located on a trusted machine inside the DMZ. This type of scan is becoming much less practical as most operating system vendors have updated their network operating systems to effectively randomize the IP sequence numbers.

Another tool that can be used to analyze firewalls is Firewalk. Written by noted author and network security expert Mike Schiffman, Firewalk uses incrementing Time-to-Live (TTL) packets to determine the path into a network as well as the default firewall policy. Running Firewalk against a target machine reveals where routers and firewalls are filtering traffic to the target host. More information on Firewalk can be obtained from *http://packetstormsecurity.org/UNIX/audit/firewalk/*.

A final firewall analysis tool worth mentioning is HPING, which is a modified ping client. It supports multiple protocols and has a command-line means of specifying nearly any of the ping parameters. For instance, you can use HPING with modified TTL values to determine the infrastructure of a DMZ. You can use HPING with specific ICMP flags in order to bypass poorly configured firewalls (i.e., firewalls that allow all ICMP traffic to pass through) and find internal systems. HPING can be found at *http://www.hping.org/*.

Incidentally, administrators who are wary of using the same tools that attackers use should remember two important points: Regardless of the tool that is used to validate or analyze a firewall's configuration, it is user intent that dictates how the information gathered is used. In order to defend a computer or network well, it is necessary to understand the ways it can be attacked. Thus, a tool that can help close up an open or poorly configured firewall will help the network defender minimize the risk from attack.

OPERATING SYSTEM DETECTION TOOLS

Detecting a target computer's operating system is very valuable to an attacker, because once the OS is known, all of the vulnerabilities to which it is susceptible can easily be determined. Many tools use networking protocols to determine a remote computer's OS. One specific tool worth mentioning is XProbe, which uses ICMP to determine the remote OS. This tool can be found at *http://sourceforge.net/projects/xprobe/*. When it's run, XProbe sends a lot of different ICMP queries against the target host. As reply packets are received, XProbe matches these responses from the target's TCP/IP stack with its own internal database of known responses. As most OSs have a unique way of responding to ICMP requests, Xprobe is very reliable in finding matches and thus detecting the operating systems of remote computers. System and network administrators should take note of this and restrict the use of ICMP through their organization's firewalls and, when possible, within its internal networks.

The later versions of Nmap include sophisticated algorithms for operating system detection and can determine this information as part of a network scan.

VULNERABILITY SCANNERS

Active vulnerability scanners scan networks for highly detailed information. An *active* scanner is one that initiates traffic on the network in order to determine security holes. As a class, this type of scanner tests for well-known user names (root, administrator, etc.) and common passwords, shows open network shares, and exposes configuration problems and other vulnerabilities in servers. An example of a vulnerability scanner is Nessus, which is a professional utility that determines the hosts available on the network, the services (ports) they are offering, the operating system and OS version they are running, the type of packet filters and firewalls in use, and dozens of other characteristics of the network. Figure 29-1 shows a sample Nessus result screen.

Vulnerability scanners should be proficient at finding known, documented holes. But what happens if the Web server is from a new vendor, or the application was developed by an internal development team? There is a class of vulnerability scanners called *blackbox* scanners, or *fuzzers*. Fuzz testing is a straightforward testing technique that looks for vulnerabilities in a program or protocol by feeding crafted inputs to the program or a network running the protocol. Vulnerabilities can be detected by measuring the outcome of these crafted inputs. One example of a fuzz scanner is SPIKE, which has two primary components. The first is the SPIKE Proxy, which is a full-blown proxy server. As Web site visitors utilize the proxy, SPIKE builds a database of each of the traversed pages, forms, and other Web-specific information. When the Web site owner determines that enough history has been collected to fully characterize the Web sites, SPIKE can be used to check the Web site for bugs—that is, administrators

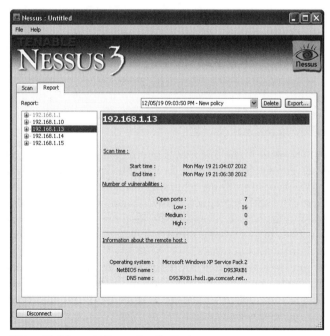

Figure 29-1 Example Nessus Results Display
Course Technology/Cengage Learning

can use the usage history collected by SPIKE to traverse all known pages, forms, active programs (e.g., asp, cgi-bin), etc., and can test the system by attempting overflows, SQL injection, cross-site scripting, and many other classes of Web attacks.

SPIKE also has a core functionality to fuzz any protocol that utilizes TCP/IP. By sniffing a session and building a SPIKE script, or building a full-blown C program using the SPIKE API, a user can simulate and "fuzz" nearly any protocol. The increasing notoriety fuzzers have achieved in identifying zero-day vulnerabilities in closed source software have given rise to their commercial development in products such as those from Codenomicon (*http://www .codenomicon.com/*).

Similar in function, the Nessus scanner has a class of attacks called *DESTRUCTIVE*. If enabled, Nessus attempts common known exploit techniques against a target host. Fuzzers or blackbox scanners and Nessus in destructive mode can be very dangerous tools and should only be used in a lab environment. In fact, these tools are so powerful that even system defenders who use them are not likely to use them in the most aggressive modes on their production networks. At the time of this writing, the most popular scanners seem to be Nessus (a commercial version of Nessus for Windows is available), retina, and Internet Scanner.

Often, some members of an organization require proof that a system is actually vulnerable to a certain attack. They may require such proof in order to avoid having system administrators attempt to repair systems that are not in fact broken, or because they have not yet built a satisfactory relationship with the vulnerability assessment team. In these instances, there exists a class of scanners that actually exploits the remote machine and allows the vulnerability analyst (sometimes called a penetration tester) to create an account, modify a Web page, or view data. These tools can be very dangerous and should only be used when absolutely necessary. Three tools that can perform this action are Core Impact, Immunity's CANVAS, and the Metasploit Framework.

Of these three tools, only the Metasploit Framework is available without a license fee (see *www .metasploit.com*). The Metasploit Framework is a collection of exploits coupled with an interface that allows the penetration tester to automate the custom exploitation of vulnerable systems. For instance, if you wished to exploit a Microsoft Exchange server and run a single command (perhaps add the user "security" into the administrators group), the tool allows you to customize the overflow in this manner.

A **passive vulnerability scanner** is one that listens in on the network and determines vulnerable versions of both server and client software. At the time of this writing, there are two primary vendors offering this type of scanning solution: Tenable Network Security with its NeVO product and Sourcefire with its RNA product. Passive scanners are advantageous in that they do not require vulnerability analysts to get approval prior for testing. These tools simply monitor the network connections to and from a server to obtain a list of vulnerable applications. Furthermore, passive vulnerability scanners have the ability to find client-side vulnerabilities that are typically not found by active scanners. For instance, an active scanner operating without DOMAIN Admin rights would be unable to determine the version of Internet Explorer running on a desktop machine, whereas a passive scanner can make that determination by observing the traffic to and from the client.

Table 29-2 provides World Wide Web addresses for the products mentioned in the vulnerability scanners section.

TABLE 29-2 Vulnerability Scanner Products and Web Pages

PRODUCT	WEB PAGE
Nessus	http://www.nessus.org
Nessus for Windows	http://www.tenablesecurity.com
GFI LANguard Network	http://www.gfi.com/languard Security Scanner
SPIKE - SPIKEproxy	http://www.immunitysec.com
Retina	http://www.eeye.com
Internet Scanner	http://www.iss.net
CANVAS	http://www.immunitysec.com/
Core Impact	http://www.coresecurity.com/
Metasploit Framework	http://www.metasploit.com

Course Technology/Cengage Learning

PACKET SNIFFERS

Another tool worth mentioning here is the packet sniffer. A **packet sniffer** (or network protocol analyzer) is a network tool that collects copies of packets from the network and analyzes them. It can provide a network administrator with valuable information for diagnosing and resolving networking issues. In the wrong hands, however, a sniffer can be used to eavesdrop on network traffic. There are both commercial and open-source sniffers—more specifically, Sniffer is a commercial product, and Wireshark is open-source software. An excellent free, client-based network protocol analyzer is Wireshark (*www.wiresharkWireshark.com*). Wireshark allows the administrator to examine data from both live network traffic and captured traffic. Wireshark has several features, including a language filter and TCP session reconstruction utility. Figure 29-2 shows a sample screen from Wireshark. Typically, to use these types of programs most effectively, the user must be connected to a network from a central location. Simply tapping into an Internet connection floods you with more data than can be readily processed, and may constitute a violation of the wiretapping act. To use a packet sniffer legally, the administrator must: (1) be on a network that the organization owns, (2) be under direct authorization of the owners of the network, and (3) have knowledge and consent of the content creators. If all three conditions are met, the administrator can selectively collect and analyze packets to identify and diagnose problems on the network. Conditions (1) and (2) are self-explanatory. The third, consent, is usually handled by having all system users sign a release when they are issued a user ID and passwords. Incidentally, these three items are the same requirements for employee monitoring in general, and packet sniffing should be construed as a form of employee monitoring.

Many administrators feel that they are safe from sniffer attacks when their computing environment is primarily a switched network environment. This couldn't be farther from the truth. A number of open-source sniffers support alternate networking approaches that can, in turn, enable packet sniffing in a switched network environment. Two of these alternate networking approaches are ARP-spoofing and session hijacking (which uses tools like ettercap). To secure data in transit across any network, organizations must use encryption to be assured of content privacy.

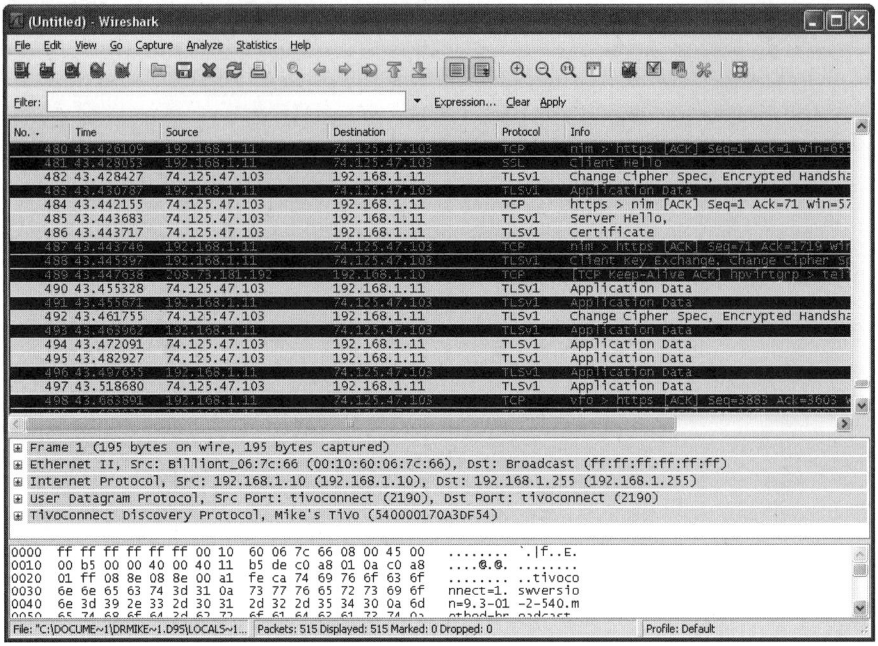

Figure 29-2 Example Wireshark Results Display

Course Technology/Cengage Learning

WIRELESS SECURITY TOOLS

Today, 802.11 wireless networks have sprung up as subnets on nearly all large networks. A wireless connection, while convenient, has many potential security holes. An organization that spends all of its time securing the wired network and leaves wireless networks to operate in any manner is opening itself up for a security breach. As a security professional, you must assess the risk of wireless networks. A wireless security toolkit should include the ability to sniff wireless traffic, scan wireless hosts, and assess the level of privacy or confidentiality afforded on the wireless network. There is a suite of tools from dachb0den labs (*http://www.dachb0den.com/projects/bsd-airtools.html*) called bsd-airtools that automates all of the items noted above. The tools included within the bsd-airtools toolset are an access point detection tool, a sniffer, and a tool called dstumbler to crack Wired Equivalent Protocol (WEP) encryption keys. A Windows version of the dstumbler tool called NetStumbler is also offered as freeware and can be found at *www.netstumbler.org*.

Another wireless tool worth mentioning is AirSnare. AirSnare is a free tool that can be run on a low-end wireless workstation. AirSnare monitors the airwaves for any new devices or access points. When it finds one, AirSnare sounds an alarm alerting the administrators that a new, potentially dangerous, wireless apparatus is attempting access on a closed wireless network.

The tools discussed so far help the attacker and the defender prepare themselves to complete the next steps in the attack protocol: attack, compromise, and exploit. The details of these processes are far too extensive to cover here and the interested reader should consult one of the excellent specialized books such as Wi-Foo.[2]

INSOURCE OR OUTSOURCE

Many of the tools we've discussed are available as Open Source, which gives an organization the option of conducting their own audits and assessments on their networks. This brings up the thorny question of whether or not the organization should do this or whether they should outsource these assessments to a specialized organization.

As has been mentioned earlier, outsourced assessments provide good information but can be quite expensive depending on the specifics. Too many times an organization will contract with an outside organization for an assessment and receive as results the output from one or more of the Open Source tools with no additional explanation or interpretation.

The key to making a good decision in this area is to treat it as any other security investment and carefully weigh the costs and benefits of the investment. If an organization has skilled network administrators with good knowledge of the tools and ways of interpreting their results, it may be a better choice to do most of the assessments themselves. On the other hand, if the organization lacks the time or expertise to conduct reasonable assessments, then outsourcing is a better choice.

When choosing an outsourced organization, carefully consider the specific techniques and deliverables. Outsourcers that will run long lists of tools and deliver raw reports are much less useful than those who will deliver detailed reports that analyze the meaning of the tools' output and make recommendations.

Network security begins with the important step of understanding the weaknesses present before jumping to the process of identifying and applying controls. This chapter has reviewed many of the types of tools that are used by both networking administrators defending a network as well as the attackers seeking to compromise it (i.e., the tools themselves are examples of dual-use technology).

Whether an organization performs the network assessment themselves or outsources to a specialized consulting firm, the critical need is for the assessment to be done on a regular basis in order to ensure that the ongoing changes that occur as part of business operations do not weaken or disable important defensive controls (such as a firewall configuration). Regular assessment also helps to assure that the organization's defenses are adequate to deal with the changing threat landscape of new vulnerabilities and attack techniques.

The Information Security Manager's Checklist

	No	Planned	In Progress	In Place	Integrated
This topic has been fully tested, validated, and integrated into organizational operations with formal performance measures in place (as appropriate).					
This topic has been implemented, but not fully tested, validated, and integrated into organizational operations.					
The implementation of this topic has begun, but is not yet complete.					
The formal planning for this topic has begun, but is not yet complete.					
This subject has not formally begun planning, or the organization has made a conscious decision not to pursue this topic.					
29. Scanning and Analysis (S&A) Tools					
Organization establishes policy on use of S&A tools					
Organization selects appropriate S&A tools					
Organization schedules periodic network scanning for rogue systems					
Organization schedules periodic systems scanning for configuration management (as appropriate)					
Organization schedules periodic systems scanning for system vulnerabilities					
Organization audits systems and network traffic monitoring through log management					
Organization schedules routine archives systems logs and network monitoring results for longitudinal study					
Organization reviews scheduled scans for anomalies and remediation					

For Further Reading

NMAP Network Scanning: The Official Nmap Project Guide to Network Discovery and Security Scanning by Gordon Fyodor Lyon, The Nmap Project, 2009.

Assessing Network Security by Kevin Lam, David LeBlanc, and Ben Smith, Microsoft Press, 2004.

Hacking Exposed Wireless: Wireless Security Secrets & Solutions by Johnny Cache and Vincent Liu, McGraw-Hill Osborne Media, 2007.

References

1. S. Jamieson. The Ethics and Legality of Port Scanning, 2001. Accessed 3 December 2008 from http://www.sans.org/reading_room/whitepapers/legal/71.php.

2. A. Vladimirov, K. Gavrilenko, and Mikhailovsky. *Wi-Foo: The Secrets of Wireless Hacking.* Boston: Addison-Wesley, 2004.

Operational Information Security: Cryptography and Access Controls

Part VIII of *Roadmap to Information Security for IT and InfoSec Managers* will discuss the role and uses of cryptography in information security as well as covering access control. Cryptography is often given great weight by some information security professionals, perhaps to the point of overemphasis. There is no denying that the cryptographic tools built into many of the tools used by the information systems and network systems are critically important, but the degree of mastery needed to use the tools of cryptography is not focused on the number theory or other theoretical aspects of the field, but rather on how to deploy cryptographic tools properly for the intended effect.

Chapters in Part VIII

Chapter 30—"Cryptography in Theory" provides a presentation of the underlying foundations of modern cryptosystems, as well as a discussion of the architectures of those cryptosystems. The chapter begins with an overview of some of the mathematical techniques that comprise cryptosystems, including hash functions.

Chapter 31—"Cryptography in Practice" provides a presentation of implementations of modern cryptosystems and cryptographic algorithms. The chapter extends this discussion by comparing traditional symmetric encryption systems with more modern asymmetric encryption systems and Public Key Encryption systems.

Chapter 32—"Access Controls and Biometrics" examines access control methods and devices commonly deployed through modern operating systems and networks, and new technologies in the area of biometrics that can provide strong authentication to existing implementations.

Chapter 33—"Physical Security" observes that a vital part of any InfoSec process, physical security is concerned with the management of the physical facilities, the implementation of physical access control, and the oversight of environmental controls. From designing a secure data center to the relative value of guards and watchdogs to the technical issues of fire suppression and power conditioning, this chapter examines special considerations for physical security threats.

Chapter 30

Cryptography in Theory

With stories of data thefts and breaches littering the daily press, interest in encryption as a way to protect the confidentiality and integrity of digital information has reached a fever pitch. However, like any other security technique, encryption only works well when it is designed and implemented well. This chapter introduces the basics of encryption with the intent of equipping the security professional to intelligently discuss and evaluate cryptographic products and deployments.

Chapter Overview:

- ▶ Crypto in context
- ▶ Overview of cryptography
- ▶ Using cryptography

CRYPTO IN CONTEXT

Cryptography is not a magic talisman that will make all your security problems disappear. While cryptography is a fairly complex technology, it is not going to solve problems without the proper investment in time, talent, and treasure. It can make a valuable contribution to assuring the confidentiality and integrity of information assets when used wisely and appropriately.

The science of cryptography is not as enigmatic as you might think. A variety of techniques related to cryptography are used regularly in everyday life. For example, open your newspaper to the entertainment section and you'll find the daily cryptogram—a word puzzle that makes a game out of unscrambling letters to find a hidden message. Also, although it is a dying art, many secretaries still use stenography, a coded form of documentation, to take rapid dictation from their managers. Finally, a form of cryptography is used even in the hobby of knitting, where directions are written in a coded form, in such patterns as K1P1 (knit 1, purl 1), that only an initiate would be able to understand. Most of the examples above demonstrate the use of cryptography as a means of efficiently and rapidly conveying information. These aspects are only one important element of the science of cryptography. For the purposes of this chapter, the discussion of cryptography will be expanded to include the confidentiality and integrity of information.

In order to understand cryptography and its uses, you must become familiar with a number of its essential components and some key terminology. The science of encryption, known as **cryptology**, encompasses *cryptography* and *cryptanalysis*. **Cryptography**, which comes from the Greek words *kryptos*, meaning "hidden," and *graphein*, meaning "to write," is the process of making and using ciphers. Cryptanalysis is the process of obtaining the original message (called the **plaintext**) from an encrypted message (called the **ciphertext**) without knowing the algorithms and keys used to perform the encryption (or more commonly the algorithm will be known but the keys are not). **Encryption** is the process of converting an original message into a form that is unreadable to unauthorized individuals—that is, to anyone without the tools to convert the encrypted message back to its original format. **Decryption** is the process of converting the ciphertext into a message that conveys readily understood meaning.

Cryptography has a long history ranging from ancient Egypt where scribes used nonstandard hieroglyphs to conceal a message's contents to the present day where cryptography is ubiquitously used to secure e-commerce transactions. While its details would fill many volumes, the core principle that concerns the security professional is that even though an adversary may have full access to the message itself, they cannot read its contents (confidentiality) or make undetectable modifications to it (integrity).

OVERVIEW OF CRYPTOGRAPHY

Historically, cryptography was used in manual applications, such as handwriting. But with the emergence of automated technologies in the twentieth century, the need for encryption in the IT environment vastly increased. Today, many common IT tools use embedded encryption technologies to protect sensitive information within applications. For example, all the popular Web browsers use built-in encryption features of SSL/TLS that enable users to perform secure e-commerce applications, such as online banking and Web shopping.

Basic Encryption Definitions

To understand the fundamentals of cryptography, you must become familiar with the following definitions:

- **Algorithm**: The programmatic steps used to convert an unencrypted message into an encrypted sequence of bits that represent the message; sometimes used as a reference to the programs that enable the cryptographic processes
- **Cipher** or **cryptosystem**: An encryption method or process encompassing the algorithm, key(s) or cryptovariable(s), and procedures used to perform encryption and decryption
- **Ciphertext** or **cryptogram**: The unintelligible encrypted or encoded message resulting from an encryption
- **Code**: The process of converting components (words or phrases) of an unencrypted message into encrypted components
- **Decipher**: To decrypt or convert ciphertext into the equivalent plaintext
- **Encipher**: To encrypt or convert plaintext into the equivalent ciphertext
- **Key** or **cryptovariable**: The information used in conjunction with an algorithm to create the ciphertext from the plaintext or derive the plaintext from the ciphertext; the key can be a series of bits used by a computer program, or it can be a passphrase used by humans that is then converted into a series of bits for use in the computer program
- **Keyspace**: The entire range of values that can possibly be used to construct an individual key
- **Plaintext** or **cleartext**: The original unencrypted message that is encrypted; also the name given to the results of a message that has been successfully decrypted
- **Work factor**: The amount of effort (usually in hours) required to perform cryptanalysis on an encoded message so that it may be decrypted when the key or algorithm (or both) are unknown

In summary, encryption is the process that transforms an intelligible message (plaintext) into an unintelligible form (ciphertext) with the aid of an algorithm and cryptovariable (key). Decryption is the reverse process of restoring the ciphertext to the plaintext. The keyspace is the range of possible keys that can be used by the algorithm; the more possible keys, the more time an adversary will spend trying to guess which one was actually used (the work factor).

Cipher Methods

A cipher can be applied in basically one of two ways—as a continuous process operating on a plaintext bit at a time (bit stream) or by first chopping up the plaintext into fixed sized blocks and operating on those blocks (block). Bit stream methods most commonly use algorithm functions like the exclusive OR operation (XOR), whereas block methods can use substitution, transposition, XOR, or some combination of these operations, as described in the following sections.

Substitution Cipher
When using a **substitution cipher**, you substitute one value for another. For example, you can substitute a letter in the alphabet with the letter three values to the right. Or, you may substitute one bit for another bit that is four places to its left.

One cryptanalytic attack that can be quite effective with certain ciphers is frequency analysis. Frequency analysis relies on the underlying structure of the plaintext language, which makes certain letters and combinations of letters much more frequent than others. When letters are always replaced by the same substitute (a monoalphabetic substitution cipher), given enough ciphertext, it is fairly easy to restore the plaintext. Caesar reportedly used a three-position shift to the right to encrypt his messages (so A became D, B became E, and so on), thus this particular substitution cipher was given his name—the *Caesar Cipher*.

Ciphers can employ multiple cipher alphabets and combinations of the basic cipher methods in order to make frequency analysis more difficult by assuring that a given plaintext letter seldom, if ever, produces the same ciphertext letter.

A three-character substitution to the right would result in the following transformation of the standard English alphabet:

Initial alphabet	ABCDEFGHIJKLMNOPQRSTUVWXYZ
	yields
Encryption alphabet	DEFGHIJKLMNOPQRSTUVWXYZABC

Within this substitution scheme, the plaintext MOM would be encrypted into the ciphertext PRP.

This is a simple enough method by itself but very powerful if combined with other operations. Incidentally, this type of substitution is based on a **monoalphabetic substitution**, since it only uses one alphabet. More advanced substitution ciphers use two or more alphabets, and are referred to as **polyalphabetic substitutions**.

Transposition Cipher

The next type of cipher operation is the transposition. Just like the substitution operation, the transposition cipher is simple to understand, but it can, if properly used, produce ciphertext that is complex to decipher. In contrast to the substitution cipher, however, the **transposition cipher** (or **permutation cipher**) simply rearranges the values within a block to create the ciphertext. This can be done at the bit level or at the byte (character) level. For an example, consider the following transposition key pattern.

$$\text{Key pattern:} \quad 1{\rightarrow}4, 2{\rightarrow}8, 3{\rightarrow}1, 4{\rightarrow}5, 5{\rightarrow}7, 6{\rightarrow}2, 7{\rightarrow}6, 8{\rightarrow}3$$

In this key, the bit or byte (character) in position 1 (with position 1 being at the far *right*) moves to position 4 (counting from the right), and the bit or byte in position 2 moves to position 8, and so on.

The following rows show the numbering of bit locations for this key: the plaintext message 00100101011010111001010101010100, which is broken into 8-bit blocks for ease of discussion; and the ciphertext that is produced when the transposition key depicted above is applied to the plaintext:

Bit locations:	87654321 87654321 87654321 87654321
Plaintext 8-bit blocks:	00100101|01101011|10010101|01010100
Ciphertext:	00001011|10111010|01001101|01100001

Reading from right to left in the example above, the first bit of plaintext (position 1 of the first byte) becomes the fourth bit (in position 4) of the first byte of the ciphertext. Similarly, the second bit of the plaintext (position 2) becomes the eighth bit (position 8) of the ciphertext, and so on.

Exclusive OR

The **exclusive OR operation (XOR)** is a function of Boolean algebra in which two bits are compared, and if the two bits are identical, the result is a binary 0. If the two bits are not the same, the result is a binary 1. XOR encryption is a very simple symmetric cipher that is used in many applications where security is not a defined requirement.

To see how XOR works, let's consider an example in which the plaintext we will start with is the word "CAT." The binary representation of the plaintext is "01110000 01100101 1000000." In order to encrypt the plaintext, a key value should be selected. In this case, the bit pattern for the letter "V" (10000101) will be used and repeated for each character to be encrypted. Performing the XOR operation on the two bit streams (the plaintext and the key) will produce the following result:

CAT as bits	0 1 1 1 0 0 0 0 0 1 1 0 0 1 0 1 1 0 0 0 0 0 0 0
VVV as key	1 0 0 0 0 1 0 1 1 0 0 0 0 1 0 1 1 0 0 0 0 1 0 1
Cipher	0 1 1 1 0 1 0 1 1 1 0 0 0 0 0 0 0 0 0 0 0 1 0 1

The row labeled "Cipher" contains the bit stream that will be transmitted; when this cipher is received, it can be decrypted using the key value of "V." Note that the XOR encryption method is very simple to implement and equally simple to break. The XOR encryption method should not be used by itself when an organization is transmitting or storing data that needs protection. Actual encryption algorithms used to protect data typically use the XOR operator as part of a more complex encryption process, thus understanding XOR encryption is a necessary step on the path to becoming a cryptologist.

Hash Functions

In addition to ciphers, another important encryption technique that is often incorporated into cryptosystems is the hash function. **Hash functions** are mathematical algorithms that generate a message summary or digest (sometimes called a fingerprint) to confirm the identity of a specific message and to confirm that there have not been any changes to the content. While not directly related to the creation of a ciphertext, hash functions are used to confirm message identity and integrity, both of which are critical functions in e-commerce.

Hash algorithms are publicly known functions that create a hash value, also known as a message digest, by converting variable-length messages into a single fixed-length value. The **message digest** is a *fingerprint* of the author's message that is to be compared with the receiver's locally calculated hash of the same message. If both hashes are identical after transmission, the message has arrived without modification. Hash functions are considered one-way operations in that the message will always provide the same hash value if it is the same message, but the hash value itself cannot be used to determine the contents of the message.

Hashing functions do not require the use of keys, but a **message authentication code (MAC)**, which is a key-dependent and one-way hash function, may be attached to a message to allow only specific recipients to access the message digest. The MAC is essentially a one-way hash value that is encrypted with a symmetric key. The recipients must possess the key to access the message digest and to confirm message integrity.

Because hash functions are one-way, they are used in password verification systems to confirm the identity of the user. In such systems, the hash value, or message digest, is calculated based upon the originally issued password, and this message digest is stored for later comparison. When the user logs on for the next session, the system calculates a hash value based on the user's inputted password. The newly calculated hash value is compared against the stored value to confirm identity.

The **Secure Hash Standard (SHS)** is a standard issued by the National Institute of Standards and Technology (NIST). Standard document FIPS 180-1 specifies SHA-1 (Secure Hash Algorithm 1) as a secure algorithm for computing a condensed representation of a message or data file. SHA-1 produces a 160-bit message digest, which can then be used as an input to a digital signature algorithm. SHA-1 is based on principles modeled after MD4 (which is part of the MDx family of hash algorithms created by Ronald Rivest). New hash algorithms (SHA-256, SHA-384, and SHA-512) have been proposed by NIST as standards for 128, 192, and 256 bits, respectively. The number of bits used in the hash algorithm is a measurement of the strength of the algorithm against collision attacks. SHA-256 is essentially a 256-bit block cipher algorithm that creates a key by encrypting the intermediate hash value with the message block functioning as the key. The compression function operates on each 512-bit message block and a 256-bit intermediate message digest.[1]

A recent method of attack called **rainbow cracking** has generated concern over the strength of the processes used for password hashing. When an attacker can gain access to a file of hashed passwords, it is possible to use a combination of brute force and dictionary attacks to reveal user passwords by applying computer processing time. Many passwords are revealed quickly due to the use of dictionary words and poor password construction rules. Other passwords, especially well-constructed passwords, take a long time to crack even using the fastest current computers. Unfortunately, attackers can use another technique that uses a rainbow table to reduce the time it takes to reverse a hash to almost no time at all. By using a database of precomputed hashes from sequentially calculated passwords, the attacker simply looks up the hashed password and reads out the text version, no brute force required. This type of attack could more properly be classified as a **time memory trade-off attack**.

The defense for this type of attack is to first protect the file of hashed passwords and implement strict limits to the number of attempts allowed per log-in session. Another approach is called password hash salting. Salting is the process of providing a nonsecret, random piece of data to the hashing function when the hash is first calculated. The use of each salt value creates a different hash and when a large set of salt values is used, rainbow cracking fails. The salt value is not kept a secret: it is stored along with the account identifier so that the hash value can be re-created during authentication. This process will make the reverse calculation of the time memory trade-off attack of no value to the attacker.[2]

Cryptographic Algorithms
In general, cryptographic algorithms are often grouped into two broad categories—symmetric and asymmetric—but in practice, today's popular cryptosystems use a hybrid combination of symmetric and asymmetric algorithms. Symmetric and asymmetric algorithms can be distinguished by the types of keys they use for encryption and

decryption operations. The upcoming section discusses both of these algorithms, and includes Technical Details boxes that provide supplemental information on cryptographic notation and advanced encryption standards.

Symmetric Encryption A method of encryption that requires the same **secret key** to encipher and decipher the message is known as **private key encryption** or **symmetric encryption**. Symmetric encryption methods use mathematical operations that can be programmed into extremely fast computing algorithms so that the encryption and decryption processes are done quickly by even small computers. As you can see in Figure 30-1, one of the challenges is that both the sender and the receiver must have the secret key. Also, if either copy of the key falls into the wrong hands, messages can be decrypted by others and the sender and intended receiver may not know the message was intercepted. The primary challenge of symmetric key encryption is getting the key to the receiver, a process that must be conducted out of band (meaning through a channel or band other than the one carrying the ciphertext) to avoid interception.

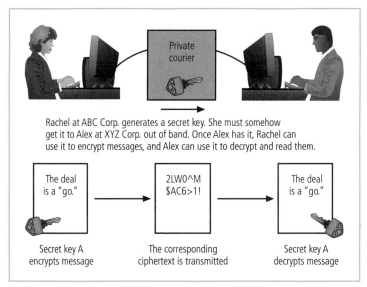

Figure 30-1 Example of Symmetric Encryption
Course Technology/Cengage Learning

Asymmetric Encryption Another category of encryption techniques is asymmetric encryption. Whereas the symmetric encryption systems are based on using a single key to both encrypt and decrypt a message, **asymmetric encryption** uses two different but related keys, and either key can be used to encrypt or decrypt the message. If, however, Key A is used to encrypt the message, only Key B can decrypt it, and if Key B is used to encrypt a message, only Key A can decrypt it. Asymmetric encryption can be used to provide elegant solutions to problems of secrecy and verification. This technique has its highest value when one key is used as a private key, which means that it is kept secret (much like the key of symmetric encryption), known only to the owner of the key pair, and the other key serves as a public key, which means that it is stored in a public location where anyone can use it. This is why the more common name for asymmetric encryption is **public key encryption**.

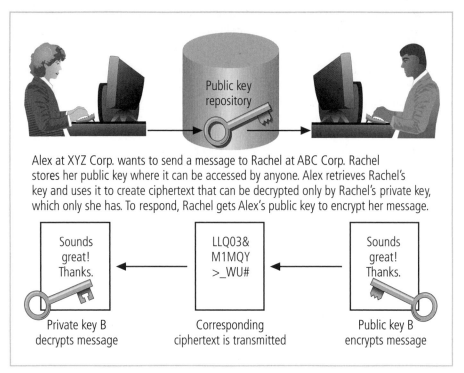

Figure 30-2 Example of Asymmetric Encryption
Course Technology/Cengage Learning

Consider the following example, illustrated in Figure 30-2. Alex at XYZ Corporation wants to send an encrypted message to Rachel at ABC Corporation. Alex goes to a public key registry and obtains Rachel's public key. Remember that the foundation of asymmetric encryption is that the same key cannot be used to both encrypt and decrypt the same message. So when Rachel's public key is used to encrypt the message, only Rachel's private key can be used to decrypt the message and that private key is held by Rachel alone. Similarly, if Rachel wants to respond to Alex's message, she goes to the registry where Alex's public key is held, and uses it to encrypt her message, which of course can only be read by Alex's private key. This approach, which keeps private keys secret and encourages the sharing of public keys in reliable directories, is an elegant solution to the key management problems found in symmetric key applications.

Asymmetric algorithms are usually based on difficult problems in mathematics such as factoring large numbers or discrete algorithms. These mathematical problems are assumed to be practically insoluble in the general case but easily solved in a specific case where one has the "trap door" (or key). For example, if you multiply 45 by 235 you get 10,575. This is simple enough. But if you are simply given the number 10,575, can you determine which two numbers were multiplied to determine this number (in mathematical terms, can you factor it)? Now assume that each multiplier is 200 digits long and prime. The resulting multiplicative product would be up to 400 digits long. Imagine the time you'd need to factor that out. There is a shortcut, however. In mathematics, it is known as a trapdoor (which is different from the software trapdoor).

A mathematical **trapdoor** is a "secret mechanism that enables you to easily accomplish the reverse function in a one-way function."[3] With a trapdoor, you can use a key to encrypt or decrypt the ciphertext, but not both, thus requiring two keys. The public key becomes the true key, and the private key is to be derived from the public key using the trapdoor.

One of the most popular public key cryptosystems is RSA, whose name is derived from Rivest-Shamir-Adleman, the algorithm's developers. The **RSA algorithm** was the first public key encryption algorithm developed (in 1977) and published for commercial use. It is very popular and has been embedded in both Microsoft's and Netscape's Web browsers to enable them to provide security for e-commerce applications. The patented RSA algorithm has in fact become the de facto standard for public use encryption applications.

The problem with asymmetric encryption, as shown earlier in the example in Figure 30-2, is that holding a single conversation between two parties requires four keys. Moreover, if four organizations want to exchange communications frequently, each party must manage its private key and four public keys. In such scenarios, determining which public key is needed to encrypt a particular message can become a rather confusing problem, and with more organizations in the loop, the problem expands.

Asymmetric algorithms are much more computationally intensive than symmetric algorithms and this restricts their use for widespread (or bulk) encryption. One common technique is to use public key algorithms to secure the transmission of a symmetric key (or session key) between the two parties with the remainder of their communications sessions encrypted using this symmetric key, as shown in Figure 30-3. This is a hybrid system that exploits the identity assurance and no requirement for pre-shared key capabilities of public key encryption and the computational efficiency of symmetric algorithms.

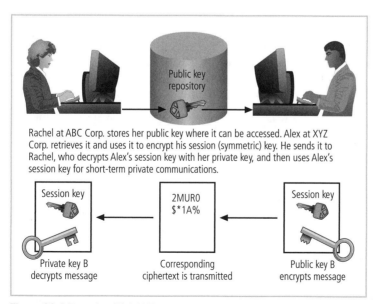

Figure 30-3 Example of Hybrid Encryption
Course Technology/Cengage Learning

Digital Signatures

Another use of public key encryption is to provide the capability for digital signatures. When Alice wishes to send a message to Bob and demonstrate that the message was sent by her and not modified, she can append a digital signature to the message. The digital signature consists of a hash of the message contents (except for the signature), which is then encrypted (signed) with Alice's private key.

When Bob receives the message, he can compute the hash using the same hash algorithm, decrypt the signature hash using Alice's private key, and compare the values. If they are equal, he can have confidence that the message is indeed from Alice and that it was not modified after transmission.

Encryption Key Size

When using ciphers, one of the decisions that has to be made is the size of the cryptovariable or key. This will prove to be very important, because the strength of many encryption applications and cryptosystems is measured by key size. But does the size of the encryption key really matter? And how exactly does key size affect the strength of an algorithm? Typically, the length of the key increases the number of random selections that will have to be guessed in order to break the code. Creating a larger universe of possibilities that need to be checked increases the time required to make guesses, and thus a longer key will directly influence the strength of the encryption.

The length of a key affects the size of the keyspace (the number of possible keys) and thus how much work an adversary will spend when trying to brute force the key. However, for this to be effective, the keys must potentially be drawn from the entire keyspace. In the recent Debian OpenSSL vulnerability,[4] the keyspace was constrained by a software error and a good cryptographic algorithm became vulnerable.

In this vulnerability a simple change to the underlying code weakened the random number generator used in key generation (IOW, the pseudorandom numbers it generated were not as random as they should have been). This led to only a few sections of the potential keyspace being used and made the keys relatively easy to guess.

For a simple example of how key size is related to encryption strength, suppose you have an algorithm that uses a 3-bit key. You may recall from earlier in the chapter that keyspace is the numbers of choices for a key. Also, you may recall that in binary notation, three bits can be used to represent values from 000 to 111, which correspond to the decimal numbers 0 to 7, and thus a keyspace of eight keys. This means that with an algorithm that uses a 3-bit key you have eight possible keys to choose from (the numbers 0 to 7 in binary are 000, 001, 010, 011, 100, 101, 110, 111). If you know how many keys you have to choose from, you can program a computer simply to try all the keys and see if it can crack the encrypted message.

The preceding statement presumes a few things: (1) you know the algorithm, (2) you have the encrypted message, and (3) you have time on your hands. It is easy to satisfy the first criterion. The encryption tools that use the Data Encryption Standard (DES) can be purchased over the counter. Many of these tools are based on encryption algorithms that are standards, as is DES itself; therefore it is relatively easy to get a cryptosystem based on DES that would enable you to decrypt

Secrecy and Encryption

Secrecy and encryption almost seem to be synonyms and it may come as a shock that one of the core principles of a good cryptographic algorithm is that it is public and depends for its efficacy solely on secrecy of the keying materials. This principle, called Kerchoff's Principle, was stated in 1883 and reflects the fact that cryptography is hard to get right. The more an algorithm is exposed to public review and comment, the more confident one can be that the algorithm does not have an undiscovered weakness that an adversary may be able to exploit.

For this reason, most modern cryptographic algorithms are public with their details fully documented (e.g., AES was selected based on an international competition).

an encrypted message if you possess the key. The second criterion requires the interception of an encrypted message, which is illegal, but not impossible. As for the third criterion, the task required is a brute force attack, in which a computer randomly (or sequentially) selects possible keys of the known size and applies them to the encrypted text, or a piece of the encrypted text. If the result is plaintext—bingo! But as indicated earlier in this chapter, it can take quite a long time to exert brute force on the more advanced cryptosystems. In fact, the strength of an algorithm is determined by how long it takes to guess the key. Luckily, however, once set to a task, computers do not require much adult supervision, so you probably won't have to quit your day job.

But when it comes to keys, how big is big? From the example at the beginning of this section, you learned that a 3-bit system has eight keys to guess. An 8-bit system has 256 keys to guess. Note, however, that if you use a 32-bit key, puny by modern standards, you have to guess almost 16.8 million keys. Even so, a modern PC could do this in mere seconds.

Thus cryptography depends on the work factor required to brute force the encryption key. Longer keys increase the keyspace and therefore the number of choices an adversary will have to try. Work factor also depends on breakthroughs in the mathematics underlying the cryptographic algorithm—for example, some algorithms rely on the fact that it is very hard to factor large prime numbers. If a breakthrough in number theory produced a new, highly effective factoring technique, this would dramatically reduce the work factor. The twin vulnerabilities of increasing processor power and possible breakthroughs in mathematics underline the necessity of using only highly regarded and widely reviewed algorithms implemented by trusted sources.

USING CRYPTOGRAPHY

Very few information security professionals will ever write their own encryption algorithms because as Bruce Schneier has pointed out, it's very hard to do correctly.[5] Security professionals will typically find themselves tasked with choosing a particular encryption product and planning its deployment. When planning to use encryption, consider the following:[6]

▶ What you're trying to protect and why—encryption can protect the confidentiality and integrity of information but you need to consider what information you're trying to protect, in what way, and why it matters.

- ▶ Where you will encrypt—will you apply encryption only while information travels across a public network link (transient encryption) or will you encrypt the data while it is stored (permanent encryption)? These choices have significant consequences in complexity and the decision shown may be made in consideration of the particular risks you are seeking to mediate.
- ▶ The pedigree of the encryption—encryption is not magic "crypto faery duste" that will eliminate all your confidentiality and integrity problems when sprinkled over an infrastructure. Assure that you will be using known algorithms whose implementations have been subjected to critical review.
- ▶ How will you manage the keys? Key management is the "Achilles' heel" of cryptographic deployments. Consider how you will control and manage the generation, distribution, and access of cryptographic keying materials. Losing access to the keying material is the same as losing access to the encrypted data. Similarly, disclosure of the keying material neutralizes the confidentiality and integrity protections encryption can provide.
- ▶ Lifetime of the encryption. Encryption algorithms have a lifetime and what may be insoluble today may be practical tomorrow (e.g., DES was considered unbreakable at the time it was developed). For long-lived information, it may be necessarily to re-encrypt it with new algorithms when the current algorithm becomes vulnerable to successful cryptanalysis.

The Information Security Manager's Checklist

	No	Planned	In Progress	In Place	Integrated
This topic has been fully tested, validated, and integrated into organizational operations with formal performance measures in place (as appropriate).					
This topic has been implemented, but not fully tested, validated, and integrated into organizational operations.					
The implementation of this topic has begun, but is not yet complete.					
The formal planning for this topic has begun, but is not yet complete.					
This subject has not formally begun planning, or the organization has made a conscious decision not to pursue this topic.					
30. Cryptography in Theory					
Employees informed of availability and value of cryptosystems					
IT employees trained on organization crypto and crypto threats					
Organization develops policy for unauthorized use of cryptosystems*					

For Further Reading

Cryptography Decrypted: Fifth Edition by H. X. Mel and Doris M. Baker, Addison-Wesley Professional, 2000.

Applied Cryptography: Protocols, Algorithms, and Source Code in C, Second Edition, by Bruce Schneier, John Wiley and Sons, Inc., 1996.

The Code Book: The Science of Secrecy from Ancient Egypt to Quantum Cryptography by Simon Singh, Anchor Press, 2000.

References

1. T. Anderson. "Polyalphabetic Substitution." *Le Canard Volant Non Identifie Online*. 30 January 1999. Accessed 21 June 2007 from cvni.net/radio/nsnl/nsnl010/nsnl10poly.html.

2. S. Varughese. "Rainbow Cracking and Password Security." Palisade Application Security Online. Accessed 21 June 2007 from palisade.plynt.com/issues/2006Feb/rainbow-tables/.

3. National Institute of Standards and Technology. *Data Encryption Standards (DES)*. FIPS PUB 46-3. (25 October 1999).

4. http://www.debian.org/security/2008/dsa-1571, accessed 07 December 2008.

5. B. Schneier. *Snake Oil*. http://www.schneier.com/crypto-gram-9902.html, accessed 07 December 2008.

6. Storage Networking Industry Association. *Encryption of Data at Rest: A Step-by-Step Checklist*. http://www.hds.com/assets/pdf/wp_encryption_steps_checklist_060830.pdf, accessed 10 December 2008.

Chapter 31

Cryptography in Practice

The capabilities to protect the confidentiality of sensitive messages and to verify their integrity while assuring the identities of their senders can be useful in all areas of business. To be actually useful, these cryptographic capabilities must be embodied in tools that allow IT and information security practitioners to apply the elements of cryptography in the everyday world of computing. A number of the more widely used tools that bring the functions of cryptography to the world of information systems are discussed in this section of the chapter.

Chapter Overview:

- ▶ Confidentiality with anonymity
- ▶ Protocols for secure communications
- ▶ Attacks on cryptosystems

CONFIDENTIALITY WITH ANONYMITY

With symmetric encryption, if two entities want to communicate without the risk of interception, they usually must make use of a pre-shared key. This is a severe limitation and was addressed by the Diffie-Hellman algorithm.[1] This algorithm allows two parties to jointly agree on a symmetric session key over an insecure medium (i.e., assuming that an attacker can intercept all their communications).

This was a great step forward but suffered from the significant limitation that the parties were anonymous—that is, the algorithm did not provide any assurances regarding the identity of either party. So although Rachel and Alex could communicate confidentially and be confident that the integrity of their messages was protected, they had no real way of proving to one another who they really were.

Without assurance of identity, there can be no protection against repudiation—Alex might agree to something and then later deny the agreement. The need for nonrepudiation led to the development of the public key algorithms and associated infrastructure that provide confidentiality, integrity, and some assurances of the identities of the communicating parties.

Public Key Infrastructure (PKI)

Public key infrastructure (PKI) is an integrated system of software, encryption methodologies, protocols, legal agreements, and third-party services that enables users to communicate securely. PKI systems are based on public key cryptosystems and include digital certificates and certificate authorities (CAs).

Digital certificates are public key container files that allow computer programs to validate the key and identify to whom it belongs. (Please note that more information about digital certificates is provided in later sections of this chapter.) PKI and the digital certificate registries they contain enable the protection of information assets by making verifiable digital certificates readily available to business applications. This, in turn, allows the applications to implement several of the key characteristics of information security and to integrate these characteristics into business processes across an organization. These processes include the following:

- ▶ Authentication: Individuals, organizations, and Web servers can validate the identity of each of the parties in an Internet transaction.
- ▶ Integrity: Content signed by the certificate is known to be unaltered while being moved from host to host or server to client.
- ▶ Privacy: Information is protected from being intercepted during transmission.
- ▶ Authorization: The validated identity of users and programs can be used to enable authorization rules that remain in place for the duration of a transaction; this reduces some of the overhead required and allows for more control of access privileges for specific transactions.
- ▶ Nonrepudiation: Customers or partners can be held accountable for transactions, such as online purchases, which they cannot later deny.

A typical PKI solution protects the transmission and reception of secure information by integrating the following components:

- A **certificate authority (CA)**, which issues, manages, authenticates, signs, and revokes users' digital certificates, which typically contain the user's name, public key, and other identifying information.
- A **registration authority (RA)**, which operates under the trusted collaboration of the certificate authority and can be delegated to day-to-day certification functions, such as verifying registration information about new registrants, generating end-user keys, revoking certificates, and validating that users possess a valid certificate.
- **Certificate directories**, which are central locations for certificate storage that provide a single access point for administration and distribution.
- Management protocols, which organize and manage the communications between CAs, RAs, and end users. This includes the functions and procedures for setting up new users, issuing keys, recovering keys, updating keys, revoking keys, and enabling the transfer of certificates and status information among the parties involved in the PKI's area of authority.
- Policies and procedures that assist an organization in the application and management of certificates, the formalization of legal liabilities and limitations, and actual business practice use.

Common implementations of PKI include: systems to issue digital certificates to users and servers; directory enrollment; key issuing systems; tools for managing the key issuance; and verification and return of certificates. These systems enable organizations to apply an enterprise-wide solution that provides users within the PKI's area of authority the means to implement authenticated and secure communications and transactions.

The CA performs many housekeeping details regarding the use of keys and certificates within the zone of authority for which it is established. Each user authenticates him or herself with the CA, and the CA can issue new or replacement keys, track keys issued, provide a directory of public key value for all known users, and perform other management activities. When a private key is compromised or when the user loses the privilege of using keys in the area of authority, the CA can revoke the keys used by that user. The CA will periodically distribute a **certificate revocation list (CRL)** to all users that identifies all revoked certificates. Before a party makes use of a certificate, they can make a real-time request to the CA to verify it against the current CRL.

The issuance of certificates (and the keys inside of them) by the CA provides the applications that users employ to perform secure e-business transactions with the ability to take both encryption and nonrepudiation actions. Some applications allow users to generate their own certificates (and the keys inside of them), but a key pair generated by the end user can only provide encryption and cannot be used for nonrepudiation (see the following sidebar on how a web of trust can mitigate this limitation). A central CA can generate cryptographically strong keys that will be considered by all users to be independently trustworthy (or more specifically, as trustworthy as the issuing CA) and can provide services for users such as private key backup, key recovery, and key revocation.

The strength of a cryptosystem relies on both the raw strength of its key's complexity and overall quality of its key management security processes. PKI solutions can provide an organization with several mechanisms for limiting access and possible exposure of the private keys. These mechanisms include password protection, smart cards, hardware tokens, and other hardware-based key storage devices that are memory-capable (like flash memory or PC memory cards). PKI users should select the key security mechanisms that provide a level of key protection appropriate to their needs. Managing the security and integrity of the private keys used for non-repudiation or the encryption of data files is a critical activity for all of the users of encryption and nonrepudiation services within the area of trust managed by the PKI application.[2]

Digital Signatures

Digital signatures were created in response to the rising need to verify information transferred using electronic systems. Currently, asymmetric encryption processes are used to create digital signatures. In its most basic form, a digital signature is a signed hash of a message—Rachel would calculate a hash of her message, encrypt the hash with her private key, and send it with the message to Alex. Alex would recalculate the hash and decrypt the hash in the message with Rachel's public key. If the hashes match, Alex can be fairly confident that the message was sent by Rachel (nonrepudiation) and not modified in transit. Note that this does not protect the confidentiality of the message—Eve could intercept and read the message contents. **Digital signatures** enable messages that can be mathematically proven to be authentic. Note that digital signatures do not provide confidentiality of message contents.

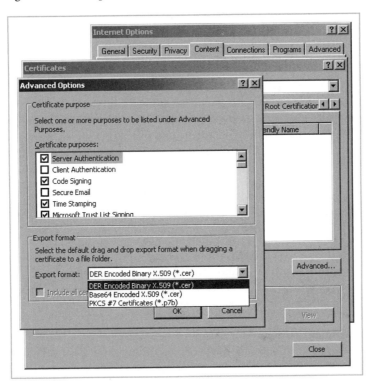

Figure 31-1 Managing Digital Signatures
Course Technology/Cengage Learning

The management of digital signatures has been built into most Web browsers. As an example, the Internet Explorer digital signature management screen is shown in Figure 31-1. In general, digital signatures should be created using processes and products that are based on the Digital Signature Standard (DSS). When processes and products are certified as being compliant with DSS, they have been approved and endorsed by U.S. federal and state governments, as well as many foreign governments, as a means of authenticating the author of an electronic document. NIST has approved a number of algorithms to be used to generate and verify digital signatures. These algorithms can be used in conjunction with the sender's public and private keys, the receiver's public key, and the Secure Hash Standard (described later in this chapter) to quickly create messages that are both encrypted and cannot be repudiated. The process used to accomplish this first creates a message digest using the hash algorithm, which is then input into the digital signature algorithm along with a random number to be used for generating the digital signature. The digital signature function also depends upon the sender's private key and other information provided by the CA. The resulting encrypted message contains the digital signature and will then be verified by the recipient through the use of the sender's public key.

Digital Certificates

As noted earlier in this chapter, a digital certificate is an electronic document or container file that contains a public key value and identifying information about the entity that holds the matching private key. The certificate is often issued by a third party that certifies the authenticity of the information it contains (in other words, this public key really belongs to Rachel). A digital signature is attached to the certificate's container file to certify that this file is from the issuing entity and has not been modified from its original format. As was also noted earlier, a certificate authority is a software agent that manages the issuance of certificates and serves as the electronic notary public by verifying the certificates' worth and integrity. The confidence that can be placed in the certificate's identity assurance depends on the reputation of the issuing certificate authority (e.g., a certificate from Verisign would be more trusted than one from Alex's Discount Certificates and Auto Repair). This process of verification can be seen by users when they download and update software on the Internet. The pop-up window in Figure 31-2 shows, for example, that the files downloaded did in fact come from the purported agency, Amazon.com, and thus can be trusted.

Digital certificates are electronic documents that can be part of a process of identification associated with the presentation of a public key. Unlike digital signatures, which help authenticate the origin of a message, digital certificates authenticate the cryptographic key that is embedded in the certificate. When used properly, these certificates enable diligent users to verify the authenticity of any organization's certificates. This is much like what happens when the Federal Deposit Insurance Corporation issues its "FDIC" logo to banks to help assure bank customers that their bank is authentic. Different client-server applications use different types of digital certificates to accomplish their assigned functions:

- ▶ The CA application suite issues and uses certificates that identify and establish a trust relationship with a CA to determine what additional certificates can be authenticated.
- ▶ Mail applications use Secure/Multipurpose Internet Mail Extension (S/MIME) certificates for signing and encrypting e-mail as well as for signing forms.

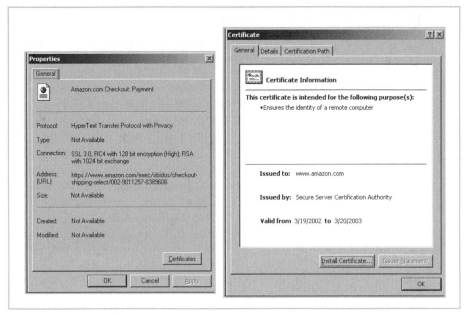

Figure 31-2 Digital Certificate
Course Technology/Cengage Learning

- ▶ Development applications use object-signing certificates to identify signers of object-oriented code and scripts.
- ▶ Web servers and Web application servers use Secure Socket Layer (SSL) certificates to authenticate servers via the SSL protocol (which is described in an upcoming section) in order to establish an encrypted SSL session.
- ▶ Web clients use client SSL certificates to authenticate users, sign forms, and participate in single sign-on solutions via SSL.

Two popular certificate types in use today are those created using Pretty Good Privacy (PGP) and those created using applications that conform to International Telecommunication Union's (ITU-T) X.509 version 3. You should know that X.509 v3 is an ITU-T recommendation that essentially defines a directory service that maintains a database (also known as a repository) of information about a group of users holding X.509 v3 certificates. An X.509 v3 certificate binds a **distinguished name (DN)**, which uniquely identifies a certificate entity, to a user's public key. The certificate is signed and placed in the directory by the CA for retrieval and verification by the user's associated public key. X.509 v3 does not specify an encryption algorithm; however, RSA with its hashed digital signature is recommended.

Hybrid Cryptography Systems

As discussed in Chapter 30, except in the case of digital certificates, pure asymmetric key encryption is not widely used. Asymmetric key encryption is more often used in conjunction with symmetric key encryption—thus, as part of a hybrid encryption system.

Self-Signed Certificates and a Web of Trust

There is another approach to creating and using certificates that does not require a central CA and this is based on the concept of self-signed certificates. These certificates are signed by the private key associated with the public key in the certificate. While they can provide the basis of asymmetric encryption, they do not themselves provide the identity assurance provided by the central CA.

To provide the identity assurance, a web of trust (or reputation system) can be used. If you know and trust Rachel, then you will accept her self-signed certificate. Rachel knows Alex and Eve but they do not know each other. Rachel can assure Alex that the certificate he receives from Eve truly belongs to Eve. After some time of communicating with Eve, Alex may feel confident enough to assure Edward that he too can trust the certificate from Eve.

Over time, these systems can build a complex web of trust that allows use of certificates without the overhead of a central CA. The rather obvious problem occurs when a certificate is compromised (say, Joe manages to get Eve's private key). Without a central CA, it can be difficult for Eve to revoke her current certificate and issue a new one.

Self-signed certificates are often used with devices to support their management via HTTPS where the identity of the device is assured by its physical location (e.g., you can be fairly confident in the identity of device CORE-01-337 because its network address is on an isolated internal management network in a hardened data center). Use of self-signed certificates avoids the overhead of managing device certificates on a central CA.

PROTOCOLS FOR SECURE COMMUNICATIONS

Many of the applications currently used on the Internet and within organizations to keep confidential information private are not true cryptosystems in and of themselves. Instead they are applications to which cryptography-based protocols have been added in order to provide a sufficient level of security. The same could be said for Internet protocols. In fact, some experts have gone further—noting that the Internet and its corresponding protocols were not designed with security in mind at all and that security was added later, as an afterthought. Regardless of whether or not this is true, it can be said that the lack of threats in the environment during the Internet's construction and infancy allowed it to grow rapidly but also enabled it to grow without the advanced security features that are required in the complex threat environment found on the Internet today. As the level of threats grew, so did the need for additional security measures. In other words, the growth of the Internet created the need for Internet security. The following sections overview some of the key protocols that add security to existing applications and protocols used in data communications over the Internet.

Securing Internet Communication with SSL

SSL (Secure Socket Layer) is a protocol designed to enable secure network communications across the Internet.

Netscape developed the original version of the **Secure Socket Layer (SSL)** protocol to use public key encryption to secure a channel over the public Internet, thus enabling secure communications. SSL underwent significant review and public comment during its development through SSL version 3 and the TLS (Transport Layer Security) protocol.[3] Most popular browsers, including Internet Explorer, support the implementation of SSL. In addition to providing data encryption, integrity, and server authentication, SSL can, when properly configured, provide client authentication (this requires a client-side certificate which is relatively rare).

A SSL/TLS session begins with the client initiating a handshake with the server (the actual protocol message is called "Client Hello"). The server responds with its certificate (the actual negotiations between client and server are a bit more complex and involve agreeing on a mutually supported cryptographic suite (key exchange and authentication algorithms, symmetric encryption algorithm and cryptographic hash function—if interested in the gory details, see, for example, the Wikipedia article on TLS[4] or Eric Rescorla's book[5]). The client will encrypt a random challenge (random number) using the server's public key from the certificate, send it to the server and must receive the correct information back before continuing (this is how the client authenticates the server by verifying that the server has the private key matching the public key in the certificate). The client will also verify that the server's certificate is from a trusted CA and has not been revoked (i.e., is not on the CRL). The client and server will then agree on a symmetric encryption key that will be used to secure subsequent communications. Note that while the server's public key could be used to secure communications from the client to the server, asymmetric encryption is very CPU intensive. To reduce the CPU overhead of secure communications and allow for protections of server-client communications in the absence of a client side certificate, the more efficient symmetric encryption will be used.

Securing E-mail with S/MIME, PEM, and PGP

In an attempt to inject some degree of security into e-mail, a notoriously insecure communication medium, a number of cryptosystems have been adapted to work with today's dominant e-mail protocols. Some of the more popular adaptations include Secure Multipurpose Internet Mail Extensions, Privacy Enhanced Mail, and Pretty Good Privacy.

Secure Multipurpose Internet Mail Extensions (S/MIME) builds on the encoding format of the Multipurpose Internet Mail Extensions (MIME) protocol by adding encryption and authentication through the use of digital signatures based on public key cryptosystems. **Privacy Enhanced Mail (PEM)** was proposed by the Internet Engineering Task Force (IETF) as a standard to function with the public key cryptosystems. PEM uses 3DES symmetric key encryption and RSA for key exchanges and digital signatures. **Pretty Good Privacy (PGP)** was developed by Phil Zimmermann and uses the IDEA Cipher for message encoding. PGP also uses RSA for symmetric key exchange and digital signatures. PGP is discussed in more detail in a later section in this chapter.

The first Internet e-mail standard that gained common use was SMTP/RFC 822, also referred to as SMTP, but this standard had problems including a number of security-related shortcomings and limitations, such as the inability to transmit executable files or binary objects, and the inability to handle character sets other than 7-bit ASCII. These limitations made SMTP unwieldy for organizations that wanted to have robust e-mail that supported international character sets and could be used more securely. MIME, the Multipurpose Internet Mail Extension, was developed to address the problems associated with SMTP.

S/MIME, which was created as an extension to improve on and interoperate with MIME, represents the second generation of enhancements to the SMTP standard. MIME and S/MIME share very similar message header fields, except for those added to support new functionality. Like

MIME, S/MIME uses a canonical form format, which allows it to standardize message content type between systems, but it has the additional ability to sign, encrypt, and decrypt messages. It should be mentioned that PGP is functionally similar to S/MIME, incorporates some of the same algorithms, and can, to some degree, interoperate with S/MIME.

Securing Web Transactions with SET, SSL/TLS

Just as PGP, PEM, and S/MIME work to secure e-mail operations, a number of related protocols work to secure Web browsers, especially at electronic commerce sites. Among these are Secure Electronic Transactions (SET), Secure Socket Layer (SSL), Secure Shell (SSH-2), and IP Security (IPSec). SSL was discussed earlier in this chapter.

Secure Electronic Transactions (SET) was developed by MasterCard and VISA in 1997 to provide protection from electronic payment fraud. SET uses DES to encrypt credit card information transfers and RSA for key exchange. SET provides the security for both Internet-based credit card transactions and credit card swipe systems in retail stores. As mentioned, Secure Socket Layer was developed by Netscape in 1994, also to provide security in online electronic commerce transactions. SSL uses a number of algorithms, but mainly relies on RSA for key transfer and IDEA, DES, or 3DES for encrypted symmetric key-based data transfer. Figure 31-2, which was presented earlier, shows the kind of certificate and SSL information that is displayed when you are checking out of an e-commerce site. If your Web connection does not automatically display such certificates, you can right-click in your browser's window and select *Properties* to view the connection encryption and certificate properties.

Securing Wireless Networks with WEP and WPA

Wireless local area networks (also known by the brand name of Wi-Fi or wireless fidelity networks) are thought by many in the IT industry to be inherently insecure. The communication channel between the wireless network interface of any computing device and the access point that provides its services occur using radio transmissions. Without the use of some form of protection, these signals can be intercepted by anyone with a wireless packet sniffer. In order to prevent interception of these communications, the administrators of these networks must use some form of cryptographic security control. Two sets of protocols are currently widely used in attempting to secure wireless transmissions. These are Wired Equivalent Privacy and Wi-Fi Protected Access. Both are designed for use with the IEEE 802.11 wireless networks.

Wired Equivalent Privacy (WEP) WEP was an early attempt to provide security with the 8002.11 network protocol. It is now considered too cryptographically weak to provide any meaningful protection from eavesdropping, but for a time it did provide some measure of security for previous networks used for low-sensitivity tasks. WEP uses the RC4 cipher stream to encrypt each packet using a 64-bit key. This key is created using a 24-bit initialization vector and a 40-bit key value. The packets are formed using an XOR function to use the RC4 key value stream to encrypt the data packet. A 4-byte Integrity Check Value (ICV) is calculated for each packet and then appended.[6] According to many experts WEP is too weak for use in most network settings due to the following:[7]

> ▶ Key management is not effective since most implemented networks use a single shared secret key value for each node. Synchronizing key changes is not easy and is a tedious process without any form of key management defined in the protocol and so keys are seldom changed.

▶ The Initialization Vector is too small, resulting in the recycling of IVs. Once an attacker can reverse-engineer the RC4 cipher stream, he or she can decrypt subsequent packets or can forge future packets. This process was accomplished in 2007 in under 1 minute.[8]

In summary, an intruder who collects enough data can threaten a WEP network in just a few minutes. This can be done by decrypting the data that is being transmitted, or by altering the data being communicated, or by forging the WEP key to gain unauthorized access to the network. WEP also lacks a means of authentication, validating user credentials to ensure that only those who should be on the network are allowed to access it.[9]

Wi-Fi Protected Access (WPA) WPA was created to resolve the issues identified with WEP. In WPA, the key size was increased from 40 bits to 128 bits. Instead of static, seldom changed keys, WPA uses dynamic keys created and shared by an authentication server. WPA accomplishes this through the use of the Temporal Key Integrity Protocol (TKIP).

TKIP is a suite of algorithms that tries to deliver the best security that can be obtained given the constraints of the wireless network environment. The algorithms are designed to work with legacy networking devices. TKIP adds four new algorithms to WEP:

▶ "A cryptographic message integrity code, or MIC, called Michael, to defeat forgeries;

▶ A new IV sequencing discipline, to remove replay attacks from the attacker's arsenal;

▶ A per-packet key mixing function, to de-correlate the public IVs from weak keys; and

▶ A rekeying mechanism, to provide fresh encryption and integrity keys, undoing the threat of attacks stemming from key reuse."[10]

While it offers dramatically improved security over WEP, WPA still is not the most secure wireless protocol design. Some compromises were made in the security design to allow compatibility with existing wireless network components—as a software upgrade for existing hardware. Additional protocols are currently under development as a replacement for TKIP to provide additional security. Table 31-1 provides a summary of the differences between WEP and WPA.

Bluetooth Another wireless technology that should be examined from a security perspective is Bluetooth. Bluetooth is a *de facto* industry standard for short-range wireless communications between devices. It is commonly used to establish communications links between wireless

TABLE 31-1 WEP versus WPA

	WEP	WPA
Encryption	Flawed, cracked by scientists and hackers	Fixes all WEP flaws
	40-bit keys	128-bit keys
	Static—same key used by everyone on the network	Dynamic session keys. Per user, per session, per packet keys
	Manual distribution of keys—hand typed into each device	Automatic distribution of keys
Authentication	Flawed, used WEP key itself for authentication	Strong user authentication, utilizing 802.1X and EAP

Source: http://www.wi-fi.org/files/wp_8_WPA%20Security_4-29-03.pdf

telephones and headsets, between PDAs and desktop computers, and between laptops. It was originally established by Ericsson scientists, and soon involved Intel, Nokia, IBM, and Toshiba. Microsoft, Lucent Technologies, and 3Com joined the industry group shortly after its inception.

The drawback with the protocol is that the wireless communications link can be exploited by anyone within the approximately 30-foot range, unless suitable security controls are implemented. It has been estimated that there will be almost a billion Bluetooth-enabled devices by the end of the decade. In its default implementation the user can select a "discoverable" mode allowing other Bluetooth-enabled systems to detect and connect to it. Users can also select a "nondiscoverable" mode to hide the device from other devices. In discoverable mode, the device can easily be accessed, much as a shared folder can on a networked computer. Even in nondiscoverable mode, the device is susceptible to access by other devices that have connected with it in the past.[11] By default, Bluetooth does not authenticate connections; however, Bluetooth does have some degree of security when accessing some services like dial-up accounts and local-area file transfers. The pairing of devices requires the same passkey be entered on both ends. This key is used to generate a session key, used on all future communications. Unfortunately some attacks can get around this. If a malicious attacker uses a device to simulate a Bluetooth access point, they can trick the device into connecting with it, and open the device up to attack. The fake AP can capture and store all communications, including the passkey submission.

In August 2005, one of the first attacks on Bluetooth-enabled smartphones occurred. At the Athletic's World Championships in Helsinki, a virus called Cabir infected dozens of phones. The virus simply drained the phone's battery, yet demonstrated that even phones are not immune to this type of attack. The virus spread quickly by Bluetooth, prompting users to accept the connection. Many users accepted the connection without thinking, downloading the virus. A Finnish security firm, F-Secure, deployed staff to the event to assist in removing the virus.[12]

About the only way to secure Bluetooth-enabled devices at the current time is to incorporate a twofold approach: (1) Turn off Bluetooth when you do not intend to use it and (2) don't accept an incoming communications pairing request unless you know who the requestor is.

Securing TCP/IP with IPSec and PGP

Internet Protocol Security (IPSec) is an open source protocol to secure communications across any IP-based network such as LANs, WANs, and the Internet. The protocol is designed to protect data integrity, user confidentiality, and authenticity at the IP packet level. IPSec is the cryptographic authentication and encryption product of the IETF's IP Protocol Security Working Group. It is often described as being the security system from IP version 6 (the future version of the TCP/IP protocol), retrofitted for use with IP version 4 (the current version). IP Security (IPSec) is defined in Request for Comments (RFC) 1825, 1826, and 1827 and is widely used to create Virtual Private Networks (VPNs), which were described in Chapter 6. IPSec itself is actually an open framework for security development within the TCP/IP family of protocol standards.

IPSec includes the IP Security Protocol itself, which defines the information to be added to an IP packet as well as how to encrypt packet data; and the Internet Key Exchange, which uses an asymmetric-based key exchange and negotiates the security associations. IPSec works in two modes of operation: transport and tunnel. In **transport mode** only the IP data is encrypted, not the IP headers. This allows intermediate nodes to read the source and destination addresses. In **tunnel mode** the entire IP packet is encrypted and is then placed as the content portion of another IP packet. This requires other systems at the beginning and end of the tunnel to act as proxies and to send and receive the encrypted packets. These systems then transmit the decrypted packets to their true destinations.

IPSec combines several different cryptosystems in its operations:

- ▶ Diffie-Hellman key exchange for deriving key material between peers on a public network
- ▶ Public key cryptography for signing the Diffie-Hellman exchanges to guarantee the identity of the two parties
- ▶ Bulk encryption algorithms, such as DES, for encrypting the data
- ▶ Digital certificates signed by a certificate authority to act as digital ID cards[13]

Within IPSec, IP layer security is obtained by the use of an application header protocol or an encapsulating security payload protocol. The **application header (AH) protocol** provides system-to-system authentication and data integrity verification, but does not provide secrecy for the content of a network communication. The **encapsulating security payload (ESP) protocol** provides secrecy for the contents of network communications as well as system-to-system authentication and data integrity verification. When two networked systems form an association that involves encryption and authentication keys, algorithms, and key lifetimes, they can implement either the AH or the ESP protocol, but not both. If the security functions of both the AH and ESP are required, multiple security associations must be bundled to provide the correct sequence through which the IP traffic must be processed to deliver the desired security features.

Pretty Good Privacy (PGP) is a hybrid cryptosystem originally designed in 1991 by Phil Zimmermann. PGP combined some of the best available cryptographic algorithms to become the open source *de facto* standard for encryption and authentication of e-mail and file storage applications. Both freeware and low-cost commercial versions of PGP are available for a wide variety of platforms. PGP uses RSA/SHA-1 or DSS/SHA-1 for Public Key encryption, and 3DES, RSA, IDEA, or CAST for message encryption.

ATTACKS ON CRYPTOSYSTEMS

Historically, attempts to gain unauthorized access to secure communications have used brute force attacks in which the ciphertext is repeatedly searched for clues that can lead to discovery of the key. These attacks are known as cryptanalytic attacks, and involve an attacker searching for a common text structure, wording, or syntax in the encrypted message that can enable him or her to calculate the number of each type of letter used in the message.[14] This process, known as frequency analysis, can be used along with published frequency of occurrence patterns of various languages and can allow an experienced attacker to crack almost any code quickly if the individual has a large enough sample of the encoded text. To protect against this, modern algorithms attempt to remove the repetitive and predictable sequences of characters from the ciphertext.

Occasionally, an attacker may obtain duplicate texts, one in ciphertext and one in plaintext, which enable the individual to reverse-engineer the encryption algorithm in a **known-plaintext attack** scheme. Alternatively, attackers may conduct a **selected-plaintext attack** by sending potential victims a specific text that they are sure the victims will forward on to others. When the victim does encrypt and forward the message, it can be used in the attack if the attacker can acquire the outgoing encrypted version. At the very least, reverse-engineering can usually lead the attacker to discover the cryptosystem that is being employed.

Most publicly available encryption methods are generally released to the information and computer security communities for testing of the encryption algorithm's resistance to cracking. In addition, attackers are kept informed of which methods of attack have failed. Although the purpose of sharing this information is to develop a more secure algorithm, it has the danger of keeping attackers from wasting their time—that is, freeing them up to find new weaknesses in the cryptosystem or new, more challenging means of obtaining encryption keys.

In general, attacks on cryptosystems fall into four general categories: man-in-the-middle, correlation, dictionary, and timing. These attacks were discussed in detail in earlier chapters and are listed here:

- ▶ A **man-in-the-middle attack** is designed to intercept the transmission of a public key or even to insert a known key structure in place of the requested public key.
- ▶ **Correlation attacks** are a collection of brute force methods that attempt to deduce statistical relationships between the structure of the unknown key and the ciphertext that is the output of the cryptosystem.
- ▶ In a **dictionary attack**, the attacker encrypts every word in a dictionary using the same cryptosystem as used by the target.
- ▶ In a **timing attack**, the attacker eavesdrops during the victim's session and uses statistical analysis of the user's typing patterns and inter-keystroke timings to discern sensitive session information.
- ▶ Once the attacker has successfully broken an encryption, he or she may launch a **replay attack**, which is an attempt to resubmit a recording of the deciphered authentication to gain entry into a secure source.

Defending from Attacks

Encryption is a very useful tool in protecting the confidentiality of information that is in storage and/or transmission. However, it is just that—another tool in the information security administrator's arsenal of weapons against threats to information security. Frequently, unenlightened individuals describe information security exclusively in terms of encryption (regarding it as a form of "magic crypto faery duste"). But encryption is simply the process of hiding the true meaning of information. Over the millennia, mankind has developed dramatically more sophisticated means of hiding information from those who should not see it. No matter how sophisticated encryption and cryptosystems have become, however, they have retained the same flaw that the first systems contained thousands of years ago: If you discover the key, that is, the method used to perform the encryption, you can determine the message. Thus, key management is not so much the management of technology but rather the management of people.

Encryption can, however, protect information when it is most vulnerable—that is, when it is outside the organization's systems. Information in transit through public or leased networks is an example of information that is outside the organization's control. With loss of control can come loss of security. Encryption helps organizations secure information that must travel through public and leased networks by guarding the information against the efforts of those who sniff, spoof, and otherwise strive to interfere with communication. As such, encryption is a vital piece of the security puzzle.

The Information Security Manager's Checklist

This topic has been fully tested, validated, and integrated into organizational operations with formal performance measures in place (as appropriate).						
This topic has been implemented, but not fully tested, validated, and integrated into organizational operations.						
The implementation of this topic has begun, but is not yet complete.						
The formal planning for this topic has begun, but is not yet complete.						
This subject has not formally begun planning, or the organization has made a conscious decision not to pursue this topic.						
31. Cryptography in Practice		No	Planned	In Progress	In Place	Integrated
Organization determines applicability of cryptographic tools						
Organization reviews available cryptographic technologies						
Organization develops policy for implementation of cryptographic and key management						
Organization determines logical positioning for cryptographic solutions—servers, clients, and networking						
Organization installs, monitors, and reports on cryptographic performance						

For Further Reading

Understanding PKI: Concepts, Standards, and Deployment Considerations, 2nd Edition, by Carlisle Adams and Steve Lloyd, Addison-Wesley Professional, 2010.

Implementing SSL/TLS Using Cryptography and PKI by Joshua Davies, John Wiley and Sons, Inc., 2011.

Cryptography Engineering: Design Principles and Practical Applications by Niels Ferguson, Bruce Schneier, and Tadayoshi Kohno, John Wiley and Sons, Inc., 2010.

Public Key Infrastructure: Building Trusted Applications and Web Services by John R. Vacca, Auerbach Publications, 2004.

References

1. W. Diffie and M. E. Hellman. New directions in cryptography. *IEEE Transactions on Information Theory* 22 (1976): 644–654.

2. S. Kelm. The PKI Page. *Secorvo Security Consulting Online.* Accessed 21 June 2007 from www.pki-page .org/.

3. For the network purists, it is more proper to talk about TLS or SSL/TLS rather than SSL. For our purposes, SSL provides a good glimpse into how a secure Web protocol works.

4. Wikipedia. *Transport Layer Security.* http://en.wikipedia.org/wiki/Transport_Layer_Security#Simple_ TLS_handshake, accessed 15 December 2008.

5. E. Rescorla. *SSL and TLS: Designing and Building Secure Systems.* Boston: Addison-Wesley, 2000.

6. WEP (Wired Equivalent Privacy). Accessed 10 April 2007 from www.networkworld.com/details/ 715.html.

7. iLabs Wireless Security Team. What's Wrong with WEP? 9 September 2002. Accessed 9 April 2007 from www.networkworld.com/research/2002/0909wepprimer.html.

8. J. Leyden. WEP key wireless cracking made easy. *The Register.* 4 April 2007. Accessed 30 June 2007 from http://www.theregister.co.uk/2007/04/04/wireless_code_cracking.

9. Wi-Fi Alliance. Wi-Fi Protected Access: Strong, standards-based, interoperable security for today's Wi-Fi networks. 2003. Accessed 9 April 2007 from www.wi-fi.org/files/wp_8_WPA%20 Security_4-29-03.pdf.

10. J. Walker. 802.11 Security Series Part II: The Temporal Key Integrity Protocol (TKIP). Accessed 10 April 2007 from cache-www.intel.com/cd/00/00/01/77/17769_80211_part2.pdf.

11. Bialoglowy, M. "Bluetooth Security Review, Part I: Introduction to Bluetooth" Accessed 15 April 2007 from www.securityfocus.com/infocus/1830

12. J. Leyden. Cabir mobile worm gives track fans the run around. 12 August 2005. Accessed 15 April 2007 from http://www.theregister.co.uk/2005/08/12/cabir_stadium_outbreak/.

13. Cisco Systems, Inc. White Paper: IPSec. *Cisco Online.* 21 November 2000. Accessed 1 July 2002 from www.cisco.com/warp/public/cc/so/neso/sqso/eqso/ipsec_wp.htm.

14. At one point, there was a great struggle between the US CIA and NSA over which agency would have responsibility for the cryptographic intelligence area. The NSA won the struggle and one of the authors asked a CIA operative if that would hinder their mission. The reply was, "Naw, we'll just make a copy on the way to or from the code room." This illustrates an important point about cryptographic protocols and network communications—they only work typically while the message is in transit. The message will be returned to plaintext at the end and is vulnerable to all the usual attacks.

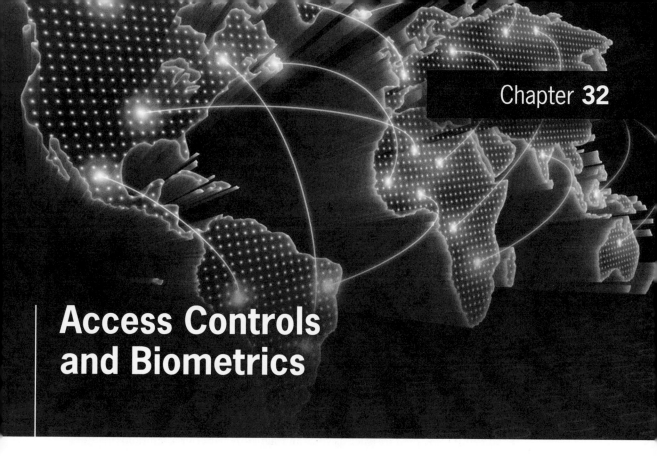

Chapter 32

Access Controls and Biometrics

Access control encompasses four processes: obtaining the identity of the entity requesting access to a logical or physical area **identification**, confirming the identity of the entity seeking access to a logical or physical area **authentication**, determining which actions that entity can perform in that physical or logical area **authorization**, and documenting the activities of the authorized individual and systems **accountability**. A successful access control approach—whether intended to control physical access or logical access—always incorporates all four of these elements.

Chapter Overview:

- ▶ Identification
- ▶ Authentication
- ▶ Authorization
- ▶ Accountability
- ▶ Types of access control
- ▶ Evaluating biometrics
- ▶ Managing access controls

IDENTIFICATION

Identification asserts an identity ("a projection of an actual individual (or application or service) into the computer system"[1]). The entity asserting the identity is commonly called a **supplicant**. The label applied to the supplicant is called an identifier (ID). The identifier must be a unique value that can be mapped to one and only one entity within the security domain being administered. Some organizations use composite identifiers, concatenating elements—department codes, random numbers, or special characters—to make unique identifiers within the security domain. Most organizations use a single piece of unique information, such as name, or first initial and surname.

AUTHENTICATION

Authentication is the process of validating a supplicant's asserted identity. It assures that the entity requesting access is the entity claimed. There are five types of authentication mechanisms:

- Something you *know* (for example, passwords and passphrases)
- Something you *have* (such as cryptographic tokens and smart cards)
- Something you *are* (this includes fingerprints, palm prints, hand topography, hand geometry, and retina and iris scans)
- Something you *produce* (such as voice and signature pattern recognition)
- Somewhere you *are* (for example, at the launch control station of a nuclear missile silo)

Certain critical logical or physical areas require higher levels of access controls and, therefore, use **strong authentication** (or multifactor authentication)—at minimum two different authentication mechanisms (usually something you have and something you know). For example, access to a bank's ATM machine requires a banking card plus a personal identification number (PIN). Such systems are called two-factor authentication, because two separate mechanisms are used. Strong authentication requires that one of the mechanisms be something other than what you know.

The Problem with Shared IDs

Unfortunately access control still carries a lot of baggage from the days when information systems were much less capable. For example, most UNIX systems still have an all-powerful user named root (and Windows still has ADMINISTRATOR). While shared IDs may make some miniscule reduction in storage and trivialize the user provisioning process, they have one glaring problem: when 17 administrators all log into the system as "root," how can you ever trace an action back to the administrator who performed it? As will be discussed later, accountability is a very desirable security feature and shared IDs pretty much toss it out the window.

Something You Know

This authentication mechanism verifies the user's identity by means of a password, passphrase, or other unique authentication code, such as a personal identification number (PIN).

The technical infrastructure for the first type of mechanism—something you know, such as a password—is built into commonly used computer and network operating systems software, and is in use unless it has been deliberately disabled. In some older client operating systems, such as Windows 95 and Windows 98, password systems are widely known to be insecure. Implementing other authentication mechanisms often requires separate supplemental physical devices. Some product vendors offer these hardware controls as built-in features; for example, some laptop vendors include thumbprint readers on certain models.

A **password** is a private word or combination of characters that only the user should know. One of the biggest debates in security focuses on the complexity of passwords. A password should be difficult to guess, which means it cannot be a word that is easily associated with the user, such as the name of a spouse, child, or pet. Nor should it be a series of numbers easily associated with the user, such as a phone number, Social Security number, or birth date. At the same time, the password must be something the user can easily remember, which means it should be short or have an association the user can remember but that is not accessible to others.

A **passphrase** is a plain-language phrase, typically longer than a password, from which a **virtual password** is derived. For example, while a typical password might be 23skedoo, a passphrase could be *May The Force Be With You Always*, from which the virtual password *MTFBWYA* is derived. Another way to create a virtual password is to use a set of construction rules applied to facts you know very well, such as the first three letters of your last name, a hyphen, the first two letters of your first name, an underscore, the first two letters of your mother's maiden name, a hyphen, and the first four letters of the city in which you were born. This may sound complicated, but once memorized, the construction rules are easy to use. If you add another rule to substitute numeric digits for certain letters—1 for L, 0 for O, and 3 for E, and capitalize the first letter of each section, then you have a very powerful virtual password that you can easily reconstruct. Using the preceding rules would create a virtual password for Charlie Moody (born in Atlanta, mother's maiden name Meredith) of *M00-Cha_M3-Atla*, a very strong password.

How important is it to have a long, not obvious password? As shown in Table 32-1, the longer the password, the lower the odds of it being guessed in a brute force attack using random bit combinations (you will learn more about such attacks later in this chapter). A good rule of thumb is to require that passwords be at least eight characters long and contain at least one number and one special character.

Something You Have

This authentication mechanism makes use of something (a card, key, or token) that the user or the system has. While there are many implementations of this mechanism, one example is a **dumb card**, a category that includes ID and ATM cards with magnetic strips containing the digital (and often encrypted) PIN against which user input is compared. A more capable object is the **smart card**, which contains a computer chip that can verify and validate other information in addition to PINs.

Another often-used device is the cryptographic token, a computer chip in a card that has a display. This device contains a built-in seed number that uses a formula or a clock to calculate

TABLE 32-1 Password Power

It is estimated that to brute force crack a password, a computer will need to perform a MAXIMUM of $n\wedge k$ operations (n^k), where n is the length of the character set, and k is the length of the password. On average it will only need to perform HALF that amount.

Using a standard alphabet set (case IN-sensitive) without numbers or special characters) = 26 characters in set, on an average 2008-era dual-core PC performing 30,000 MIPS (million instructions per second)

PASSWORD LENGTH	MAXIMUM NUMBER OF OPERATIONS (GUESSES)	MAXIMUM TIME TO CRACK
8	208,827,064,576	7.0 seconds
9	5,429,503,678,976	3.0 minutes
10	141,167,095,653,376	1.3 hours
11	3,670,344,486,987,780	34.0 hours
12	95,428,956,661,682,200	36.8 days
13	2,481,152,873,203,740,000	2.6 years
14	64,509,974,703,297,200,000	68.2 years
15	1,677,259,342,285,730,000,000	1,772.9 years
16	43,608,742,899,428,900,000,000	46,094.1 years

Using an extended data set with case sensitive letters (upper and lowercase), numbers, and 20 special characters = 82 characters in set on the same 2008-era dual-core PC

PASSWORD LENGTH	MAXIMUM NUMBER OF OPERATIONS (GUESSES)	MAXIMUM TIME TO CRACK
8	2,044,140,858,654,980	18.9 hours
9	167,619,550,409,708,000	64.7 days
10	13,744,803,133,596,100,000	14.5 years
11	1,127,073,856,954,880,000,000	1,191.3 years
12	92,420,056,270,299,900,000,000	97,687.4 years
13	7,578,444,614,164,590,000,000,000	8,010,363.4 years
14	621,432,458,361,496,000,000,000,000	656,849,799.6 years
15	50,957,461,585,642,700,000,000,000,000	53,861,683,563.4 years
16	4,178,511,850,022,700,000,000,000,000,000	4,416,658,052,197.2 years

Course Technology/Cengage Learning

a number that can be used to perform a remote log-in authentication. Tokens may be either synchronous or asynchronous. Once **synchronous tokens** are synchronized with a server, each device (server and token) uses the time to generate the authentication number that is entered during the user log-in. **Asynchronous tokens** use a challenge-response system, in which the server challenges the user with a number. That is, the user enters the challenge number into the token, which in turn calculates a response number. The user then enters the response number into the system to gain access. Only a person who has the correct token can calculate the correct response number and thus log into the system. This system does not require synchronization and does not suffer from mistiming issues.

Something You Are

This authentication mechanism takes advantage of something inherent in the user that is evaluated using biometrics, which you will learn more about later in this chapter. Biometric authentication methods include the following:

- Fingerprints
- Palm scan
- Hand geometry
- Hand topology
- ID cards (face representation)
- Facial recognition
- Retina scan
- Iris scan

Most of the technologies that scan human characteristics convert these images to obtain some form of **minutiae**—that is, unique points of reference that are digitized and stored. Some technologies encrypt the minutiae to make them more resistant to tampering. Each subsequent scan is also digitized and then compared with the encoded value to determine whether users are who they claim to be. One limitation of this technique is that some human characteristics can change over time, due to normal development, injury, or illness. Among the human characteristics currently employed for authentication purposes, only three are considered truly unique:

- Fingerprints
- Retina (blood vessel pattern)
- Iris (random pattern of features found in the iris, including freckles, pits, striations, vasculature, coronas)

DNA or genetic authentication would be included in this category, if it ever becomes a cost-effective and socially accepted technology.

Something You Produce

This type of authentication makes use of something the user performs or produces, for example, a signature or voice pattern. (In some authentication methodologies, this type of authentication is placed within this "something you are" category, since it is sometimes difficult to differentiate biometric output from the biometric feature.) Signature recognition is commonplace. Many retail stores use signature recognition, or at least signature capture, for authentication during a purchase. Customers sign a special pad, using a stylus; the signatures are then digitized and either compared to a database for validation or simply saved. Signature capture is much more widely accepted than signature comparison, because signatures can vary due to a number of factors, including age, fatigue, and the speed with which they are written.

Voice recognition for authentication captures the analog waveforms of human speech and compares these waveforms to a stored version. Voice recognition systems provide the user with a phrase that they must read—for example, "My voice is my password, please verify me. Thank you."

Another pattern-based approach is keystroke pattern recognition. This authentication method relies on the timing between key signals when a user types in a known sequence of keystrokes. When measured with sufficient precision, this pattern can provide a unique identification.

Figure 32-1 depicts some of these biometric and other human recognition characteristics.

Somewhere You Are

This form of authentication relies on physical location. For example, to be able to connect to a router via its serial port, you usually must be physically present at the router's location. This leverages the security measures that control access to the physical location. To access the serial

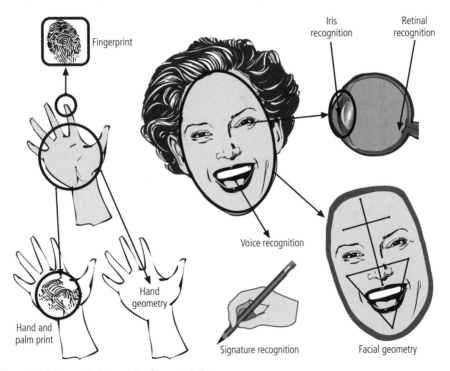

Figure 32-1 Biometric Recognition Characteristics
Course Technology/Cengage Learning

port of a router racked in a hardened data center, one would have to pass all the security measures that control access to the data center. This example can also be extended to a particular computer system—restricting access by MAC or IP address.

AUTHORIZATION

The authorization process begins with an authenticated entity—a person, or a virtual identity like another computer program. In general, authorization can be handled in one of four ways:

- ▶ Authorization for each authenticated user, in which the system performs an authentication process to verify each entity and then grants access to resources for only that entity. This quickly becomes a complex and resource-intensive process in a computer system environment.

- ▶ Authorization for members of a group, in which the system matches authenticated entities to a list of group memberships, and then grants access to resources based on the group's access rights. This is the most common authorization method.

- ▶ Authorization across multiple systems, in which a central authentication and authorization system verifies entity identity and grants a set of credentials to the verified entity. These credentials (sometimes called an **authorization ticket**) are honored by all systems within the authentication domain. Sometimes called **single sign-on (SSO)** or reduced sign-on, this approach is becoming more common, and is frequently enabled using a shared directory structure such as the Lightweight Directory Access (LDAP) protocol.

- ▶ Authorization by role—authorization by role (more commonly known as Role-Based Access Control or RBAC) may at first glance seem similar to authorization by group but there are some subtle differences. Roles are designed to mirror the structure of the organization (for example, in a hospital, there would be physician, pharmacist, nursing, etc., roles) and the access rights assigned to the roles match the capabilities granted to the position in the organization (for example, a member of the physician role could write a prescription).

ACCOUNTABILITY

Accountability assures that all actions on a system can be attributed to an authenticated identity. These actions could be ones that the entity is authorized for, such as looking up or modifying certain data, or might include unauthorized attempts to escalate privileges, or to look at or modify data that is beyond its access level. Accountability is most often accomplished by implementing system logs and database journals, and the auditing of these records. **Systems logs** are records maintained by a particular system that has been configured to record specific information, such as failed access attempts, and systems modifications. Logs have many uses, such as intrusion detection, determining the root cause of a system failure, or simply tracking the use of a particular resource. Some systems are configured to record a common set of data by default; other systems must be configured in order to be activated. To protect the log data, you must ensure that the servers that create and store the logs are secure. Also, you must actively manage log recording systems as follows:

▶ Make sure that data stores can handle the amount of data generated by the configured logging activities. Some systems may generate multiple gigabytes of data for each hour of operation.

▶ Rotate logs when unlimited data storage is not possible. Some systems overwrite older log entries with newer entries to accommodate space limitations. Log rotation settings must be appropriately configured for your system, which may require modifying the default settings.

▶ Archive logs. Log systems can copy active logs periodically to archival storage locations. Log retention, the amount of time logs should be preserved, is a thorny issue because it must somehow find a compromise between the storage space required, organizational data retention policies, legal compliance requirements, and the possible relevance of logs to future legal proceedings.

▶ Secure logs. Archives logs should be encrypted when stored to prevent unwanted disclosure if the log data store is compromised.

▶ Destroy logs. Once log data has outlived its usefulness, it should be securely destroyed.[2]

The process of reviewing the information collected in logs to detect misuse or attempted intrusion is part of a larger process called auditing. Logs are of no value to an organization if their contents are not reviewed periodically and included as part of the records trail used for auditing. Auditing can combine automated and manual mechanisms and can be done internally in an organization or part of an external review that may or may not include financial auditing procedures. Real or near time review of logs is becoming an increasingly important part of security situational awareness and many commercial products are starting to appear that provide this capability.

TYPES OF ACCESS CONTROL

Access controls specifically address the admission of users into a trusted area of the organization. These areas can include information systems, physically restricted areas such as computer rooms, and even the organization in its entirety. Access controls usually consist of a combination of policies, programs, and technologies.

A number of approaches to, and categories of, access controls exist. They can be mandatory, no discretionary, or discretionary. Each category of controls regulates access to a particular type or collection of information, as explained below.

Mandatory Access Controls (MACs)

MACs are required—obviously—and are structured and coordinated with a data classification scheme. When MACs are implemented, users and data owners have limited control over their access to information resources. MACs use a data classification scheme that rates each collection of information. Each user is also rated to specify the level of information that he or she may access. These ratings are often referred to as sensitivity levels.

In a variation of this form of access control called **lattice-based access control**, users are assigned a matrix of authorizations for particular areas of access. The level of authorization may vary depending on the classification authorizations that individuals possess for each group of information assets or resources. The lattice structure contains subjects and objects, and the boundaries associated with each subject/object pair are clearly demarcated. Lattice-based access control then specifies the level of access each subject has to each object, if any. With this type of control, the column of attributes associated with a particular object (such as a printer) is referred to as an **access control list (ACL)**. The row of attributes associated with a particular subject (such as a user) is referred to as a **capabilities table**.

Nondiscretionary Controls

Nondiscretionary controls are determined by a central authority in the organization and can be based on roles—called **role-based controls**—or on a specified set of tasks—called **task-based controls**. Task-based controls can, in turn, be based on lists maintained on subjects or objects. Role-based controls are tied to the role that a particular user performs in an organization, whereas task-based controls are tied to a particular assignment or responsibility.

The role- and task-based controls make it easier to maintain controls and restrictions, especially if the individual performing the role or task changes often. Instead of constantly assigning and revoking the privileges of individuals who come and go, the administrator simply assigns the associated access rights to the role or task. When individuals are subsequently assigned to that role or task, they automatically receive the corresponding access. The administrator can easily remove individuals' associations with roles and tasks, thereby revoking their access.

Discretionary Access Controls (DACs)

DACs are implemented at the discretion or option of the data user. The ability to share resources in a peer-to-peer configuration allows users to control and possibly provide access to information or resources at their disposal. The users can allow general, unrestricted access, or they can allow specific individuals or sets of individuals to access these resources. As an example, suppose a user has a hard drive containing information to be shared with office coworkers. This user can elect to allow access to specific individuals by listing their names in the share control function.

Data Classification Model

Corporate and military organizations use a variety of classification schemes. As you might expect, the **U.S. military classification scheme** relies on a more complex categorization system than the schemes of most corporations. The military is perhaps the best-known user of data classification schemes. It has invested heavily in information security (InfoSec), operations security (OpSec), and communications security (ComSec). In fact, many developments in data communications and information security are the result of military-sponsored research and development.

For most information, the U.S. military uses a five-level classification scheme, defined in Executive Order 12958 and presented below:[3]

- ▶ Unclassified data: Generally free for distribution to the public, and poses no threat to U.S. national interests.
- ▶ Sensitive but unclassified (SBU) data: "Any information of which the loss, misuse, or unauthorized access to, or modification of, might adversely affect U.S. national

interests, the conduct of Department of Defense (DoD) programs, or the privacy of DoD personnel." Common designations include For Official Use Only, Not for Public Release, or For Internal Use Only.

- ▶ Confidential data: "Any information or material the unauthorized disclosure of which reasonably could be expected to cause damage to the national security. Examples of damage include the compromise of information that indicates strength of ground, air, and naval forces in the United States and overseas areas; disclosure of technical information used for training, maintenance, and inspection of classified munitions of war; and revelation of performance characteristics, test data, design, and production data on munitions of war."

- ▶ Secret data: "Any information or material the unauthorized disclosure of which reasonably could be expected to cause serious damage to the national security. Examples of serious damage include disruption of foreign relations significantly affecting the national security; significant impairment of a program or policy directly related to the national security; revelation of significant military plans or intelligence operations; compromise of significant military plans or intelligence operations; and compromise of significant scientific or technological developments relating to national security."

- ▶ Top secret data: "Any information or material the unauthorized disclosure of which reasonably could be expected to cause exceptionally grave damage to the national security. Examples of exceptionally grave damage include armed hostilities against the United States or its allies; disruption of foreign relations vitally affecting the national security; the compromise of vital national defense plans or complex cryptologic and communications intelligence systems; the revelation of sensitive intelligence operations; and the disclosure of scientific or technological developments vital to national security." This classification comes with the general expectation of "crib to grave" protection, meaning that individuals entrusted with top secret information are expected to honor the classification of the information for life, even after they are no longer employed in the role that originally allowed them to access the information.

The military also has some specialty classification ratings, such as Personnel Information and Evaluation Reports, to protect related areas of information. Federal agencies such as the FBI and CIA also use specialty classification schemes, such as Need-to-Know and Named Projects. Obviously, Need-to-Know authorization allows access to information by individuals who need the information to perform their work. Named Projects are clearance levels based on a scheme similar to Need-to-Know. When an operation, project, or set of classified data is created, the project is assigned a code name. Next, a list of authorized individuals is created and assigned to either the Need-to-Know or the Named Projects category.

Most organizations do not need the detailed level of classification used by the military or federal agencies but should implement processes that identify sensitive information and specify the protections that must be applied. Some common labels are:

Public—unlimited distribution both inside and outside the company. This would include information such as product catalogs, etc.

Internal Use Only—information that should be restricted to employees of the organization only. This includes things such as procedures manuals, organizational telephone directories, etc.

Proprietary—sensitive information that could damage the competitive position of the organization. New product designs, proprietary processes or formulas are examples of this type of information.

Restricted—financial information that legally must be protected in advance of its public announcement. Possession of this information also carries restrictions on activities such as trading in the organization's stock (if it is a public company) to avoid liability under insider trading regulations.

The purpose of these labels is primarily to guide people in appropriate use and protection of organizational information.

Security Clearances Another perspective on the data classification scheme is the personnel security clearance structure, in which each user of an information asset is assigned an authorization level that indicates the level of information classification he or she can access. This is usually accomplished by assigning each employee to a named role, such as data entry clerk, development programmer, information security analyst, or even CIO. Most organizations have developed a set of roles and corresponding security clearances, so that individuals are assigned authorization levels that correlate with the classifications of the information assets.

Beyond a simple reliance on the security clearance of the individual is the **need-to-know** principle. Regardless of one's security clearance, an individual is not allowed to view data simply because it falls within that individual's level of clearance. That is, after being granted a security clearance but before viewing a specific set of data, a person must also meet the need-to-know requirement. This extra requirement ensures that the confidentiality of information is properly maintained.

Management of the Classified Information Asset

Managing an information asset includes all aspects of its life cycle, from specification, design, acquisition, implementation, use, storage, distribution, backup, recovery, retirement, to destruction. An information asset, such as a report, that has a classification designation other than unclassified or public must be clearly marked as such. The U.S. government, for example, uses color-coordinated cover sheets to protect classified information from the casual observer. Every classified document should also contain the appropriate security designation at the top and bottom of each page. Classified documents must be available only to authorized individuals, which usually require locking file cabinets, safes, or other such protective devices for hard copies and systems. When an individual carries a classified report, it should be inconspicuous and kept in a locked briefcase or portfolio, and in compliance with appropriate policies (for example, requirements for double-sealed envelopes, tamper-proof seals, etc.).

To maintain the confidentiality of classified documents, managers can implement a risk management policy control known as the clean desk policy. This policy usually meets with resistance because it requires each employee to secure all information in its appropriate storage container at the end of every business day.

When copies of classified information are no longer valuable or too many copies exist, care should be taken to destroy them properly, usually after double signature verification. Documents should be destroyed by means of shredding, burning, or transfer to a service offering authorized document destruction. Policy should ensure that no classified information is inappropriately disposed of in trash or recycling areas. Otherwise, people who engage in **dumpster diving** may retrieve information and thereby compromise the security of the organization's information assets.

EVALUATING BIOMETRICS

Two of the four authentication mechanisms (something you are and something you produce) are **biometric**—literally, life measurement. Biometric technologies are generally evaluated according to three basic criteria:

- ▶ The false reject rate: the percentage of authorized users who are denied access
- ▶ The false accept rate: the percentage of unauthorized users who are allowed access
- ▶ The crossover error rate: the point at which the number of false rejections equals the false acceptances

False Reject Rate

The **false reject rate** is the rate at which authentic users are denied or prevented access to authorized areas, as a result of a failure in the biometric device. This failure is also known as a Type I error or a false negative. Rejection of an authorized individual represents not a threat to security but an impedance to legitimate use. Consequently, it is often not seen as a serious problem until the rate increase is high enough to irritate users.

False Accept Rate

The **false accept rate** is the rate at which fraudulent users or nonusers are allowed access to systems or areas, as a result of a failure in the biometric device. This failure, known as a Type II error or a false positive, represents a serious security breach. Often, multiple authentication measures must be used to back up a device whose failure would otherwise result in erroneous authorization.

Crossover Error Rate

The **crossover error rate (CER)**, also called the equal error rate, is the point at which the rate of false rejections equals the rate of false acceptances. It is the optimal outcome for biometrics-based systems. CERs are used to compare various biometrics and may vary by manufacturer. A biometric device that provides a CER of 1% is considered to be superior to one with a CER of 5%, for example.

Acceptability of Biometrics

A balance must be struck between the acceptability of a system to its users and the effectiveness of the same system. Many of the reliable, effective biometric systems are perceived as being somewhat intrusive by users. Organizations implementing biometrics must carefully balance a system's effectiveness against its perceived intrusiveness and acceptability to users. Note that the rated effectiveness of a system is roughly inverse to its acceptability, as shown in Table 32-2.

TABLE 32-2 Orders of Effectiveness and Acceptance

EFFECTIVENESS OF BIOMETRIC AUTHENTICATION SYSTEMS RANKING FROM MOST SECURE TO LEAST SECURE	ACCEPTANCE OF BIOMETRIC AUTHENTICATION SYSTEMS RANKING FROM MOST ACCEPTED TO LEAST ACCEPTED
▶ Retina pattern recognition	▶ Keystroke pattern recognition
▶ Fingerprint recognition	▶ Signature recognition
▶ Handprint recognition	▶ Voice pattern recognition
▶ Voice pattern recognition	▶ Handprint recognition
▶ Keystroke pattern recognition	▶ Fingerprint recognition
▶ Signature recognition	▶ Retina pattern recognition

Source: Harold F. Tipton and Micki Krause. *Handbook of Information Security Management*. Boca Raton: CRC Press, 1998: 39–41.

MANAGING ACCESS CONTROLS

To appropriately manage access controls, an organization must have in place a formal **access control policy**, which determines how access rights are granted to entities and groups and specifies how those access rights are managed in practice. This policy must include provisions for periodically reviewing all access rights, granting access rights to new employees, changing access rights when job roles change, and revoking access rights as appropriate. Without an access control policy, systems administrators may implement access controls in a way that is inconsistent with the organization's overall philosophy. Once a policy is in place, implementing access controls becomes a technical issue.

Access control is a critical part of the information security program because it specifies the processes responsible for controlling access to the assets. Access control is composed of four related activities: identification, authentication, authorization, and accountability. These four activities function together to assure that users (whether people or automated processes) of assets are uniquely identified, verified (through authentication), authorized to perform the specific activity, and that their performance of important activities can be tracked (accountability).

The Information Security Manager's Checklist

| | | | | This topic has been fully tested, validated, and integrated into organizational operations with formal performance measures in place (as appropriate). |
| This topic has been implemented, but not fully tested, validated, and integrated into organizational operations. |
| The implementation of this topic has begun, but is not yet complete. |
| The formal planning for this topic has begun, but is not yet complete. |
| This subject has not formally begun planning, or the organization has made a conscious decision not to pursue this topic. |

32. Access Controls and Biometrics	No	Planned	In Progress	In Place	Integrated
Organization determines applicability of access controls and biometrics					
Organization reviews available access control and biometrics technologies					
Organization develops policy for implementation of access and biometrics					
Organization determines logical positioning for access controls—coordinated with physical security plan (see Chapter 33)					
Organization installs, monitors, and reports on access control and biometrics performance					

For Further Reading

Mechanics of User Identification and Authentication: Fundamentals of Identity Management by Dobromir Todorov, Auerbach Publications, 2007.

Access Control Systems: Security, Identity Management and Trust Models by Messaoud Benantar, Springer, 2010.

A Guide to Claims-Based Identity and Access Control by Dominick Baier, Vittorio Bertocci, Keith Brown, and Matias Woloski, Microsoft Press, 2010.

References

1. Dobromir Todorov. *Mechanics of User Identification and Authentication: Fundamentals of Identity Management.* Boca Raton: Auerbach, 2007, p. 4.

2. CERT. Managing Logging and Other Data Collection Mechanisms. CERT Security Improvement Modules. Accessed 29 May 2005 from www.cert.org/security-improvement/practices/p092.html.

3. Executive Order 12958. *Classified National Security Information.* Accessed 15 September 2003 from http://www.dss.mil/seclib/eo12958.htm.

Chapter 33

Physical Security

It is a truism in information security that if an attacker can gain physical access to your information asset (i.e., the server), it is not your asset anymore. Though physical security may not be the sexiest area of security, it is one that the information security professional will neglect to his peril. For example, an attacker hardly needs to go to the trouble of mounting a network DoS attack if he or she can simply walk up to the server and pull the power cord.

Chapter Overview:

- ▸ Physical security
- ▸ Physical access controls
- ▸ Fire security and safety
- ▸ Failure of supporting utilities and structural collapse
- ▸ Interception of data
- ▸ Mobile and portable systems
- ▸ Special considerations for physical security threats

PHYSICAL SECURITY

Physical security requires the design, implementation, and maintenance of counter-measures that protect the physical resources of an organization. It includes the physical protection of people, hardware, and the supporting system elements and resources that control information in all its states (transmission, storage, and processing). Most of the technology-based controls discussed up to this point can be circumvented if an attacker gains physical access to the devices being controlled. In other words, if it is easy to steal the hard drives from a computer system, then the information on those hard drives is not secure. Therefore, physical security is just as important as logical security to an information security program.

In his book, *Fighting Computer Crime*, Donn B. Parker lists the "Seven Major Sources of Physical Loss" as follows:

1. Extreme temperature: heat, cold
2. Gases: war gases, commercial vapors, humid or dry air, suspended particles
3. Liquids: water, chemicals
4. Living organisms: viruses, bacteria, people, animals, insects
5. Projectiles: tangible objects in motion, powered objects
6. Movement: collapse, shearing, shaking, vibration, liquefaction, flow waves, separation, slide
7. Energy anomalies: electrical surge or failure, magnetism, static electricity, aging circuitry; radiation: sound, light, radio, microwave, electromagnetic, atomic[1]

Just as with all other areas of security, the implementation of physical security measures requires sound organizational policy. Physical security policies guide users on the appropriate use of computing resources and information assets, as well as on the protection of their own personal safety in day-to-day operations. Physical security is designed and implemented in several layers. Each of the organization's communities of interest is responsible for components within these layers, as follows:

- ▶ General management is responsible for the security of the facility in which the organization is housed and the policies and standards for secure operation. This includes exterior security, fire protection, and building access, as well as other controls such as guard dogs and door locks.
- ▶ IT management and professionals are responsible for environmental and access security in technology equipment locations and for the policies and standards for secure equipment operation. This includes access to server rooms, power conditioning, and server room temperature and humidity controls, as well as more specialized controls like static and dust contamination controls.
- ▶ Information security management and professionals are responsible for risk assessments and implementation reviews for the physical security controls implemented by the other two groups.

PHYSICAL ACCESS CONTROLS

A number of physical access controls are uniquely suited to governing the movement of people within an organization's facilities—that is, controlling their physical access to company resources. While logical access to systems, in this age of the Internet, is a very important subject, the control of physical access to the assets of the organization is also of critical importance. Some of the technology used to control physical access is also used to control logical access, including biometrics, smart cards, and wireless enabled keycards, which can be used to control access to physical locations, information assets, and information system resources.

Before learning more about physical access controls, you need to understand what makes a facility secure. An organization's general management oversees its physical security. Commonly, access controls for a building are operated by a group called **facilities management**. Larger organizations may have an entire staff dedicated to facilities management, while smaller organizations often outsource these responsibilities.

In facilities management, a **secure facility** is a physical location that has in place controls to minimize the risk of attacks from physical threats. The term *secure facility* usually brings to mind military bases, maximum-security prisons, and nuclear power plants, but while securing a facility requires some adherence to rules and procedures, the environment does not necessarily have to be as constrained as in these examples. It is also not necessary that a facility resemble a fortress to minimize risk from physical attacks. In fact, a secure facility can sometimes use its natural terrain, local traffic flow, and surrounding development to enhance its physical security, along with protection mechanisms, such as fences, gates, walls, guards, and alarms.

Physical Security Controls

There are a number of physical security controls that an organization's communities of interest should consider when implementing physical security inside and outside the facility. Some of the major controls are:

- Walls, fencing, and gates
- Guards
- Dogs
- ID cards and badges
- Locks and keys
- Mantraps
- Electronic monitoring
- Alarms and alarm systems
- Computer rooms and network wiring closets
- Interior walls and doors

Some of these areas are discussed here.

ID Cards and Badges One area of access control that ties physical security with information access control is the use of identification cards and name badges. An **identification (ID) card** is typically concealed, whereas a **name badge** is visible. These devices can serve a number of purposes. First, they serve as simple forms of biometrics in that they use an individual's face to identify the person and authenticate his or her access to the facility. The cards may be visibly coded to specify buildings or areas may be accessed. Second, ID cards with a magnetic strip or radio (RFID) chip that can be read by automated control devices allow an organization to restrict access to sensitive areas within the facility. ID cards and name badges are not foolproof, however; even the cards designed to communicate with locks can be easily duplicated, stolen, and modified. Because of this inherent weakness, such devices should not be an organization's only means of controlling access to restricted areas. Another inherent weakness of this type of physical access control technology is the human factor. **Tailgating** occurs when an authorized individual presents a key to open a door, and other individuals, who may or may not be authorized, also enter. Launching a campaign to make employees aware of tailgating is one way to combat this problem.

Electronic Monitoring Monitoring equipment can be used to record events within a specific area that guards and dogs might miss, or in areas where other types of physical controls are not practical. Many retail stores already use cameras to watch employees and customers through video monitoring cameras. Attached to these cameras are video cassette recorders (VCRs) and related machinery that capture the video feed. Electronic monitoring includes **closed-circuit television (CCT)** systems. Some CCT systems collect constant video feeds, while others rotate input from a number of cameras, sampling each area in turn. These video monitoring systems have drawbacks: For the most part, they are passive and do not prevent access or prohibited activity. Another drawback to these systems is that people must view the video output, because there are no intelligent systems capable of reliably evaluating a video feed.

Alarms and Alarm Systems Closely related to monitoring are the alarm systems that notify the appropriate person or system when a predetermined event or activity occurs. Alarms can detect a *physical* intrusion or other untoward event. This could be a fire, a break-in, an environmental disturbance, such as flooding, or an interruption in services, such as a loss of power. To detect intrusions, these systems rely on a number of different types of sensors:

- **Motion detectors** detect movement within a confined space and are either active or passive. Some motion sensors emit energy beams, usually in the form of infrared or laser light, ultrasonic sound or sound waves, or some form of electromagnetic radiation.
- **Thermal detectors** work by detecting rates of change in the ambient temperature in the room.
- **Contact and weight sensors** work when two contacts are connected as, for example, when a foot steps on a pressure-sensitive pad under a rug, or a window being opened triggers a pin and spring sensor. **Vibration sensors** also fall into this category, except that they detect movement of the sensor rather than movement in the environment.

Physical and Environmental Controls for Computer Rooms[2]

The following list of physical and environmental controls for computer rooms is intended to be representative, not comprehensive.

- Card keys for building and entrances to work area
- Twenty-four-hour guards at all entrances and exits
- Cipher lock on computer room door
- Raised floor in computer room
- Dedicated cooling system
- Humidifier in tape library
- Emergency lighting in computer room
- Four fire extinguishers rated for electrical fires
- One fire extinguisher with a combination of a class B and class C fire control rating
- Smoke, water, and heat detectors
- Emergency power shutoff switch by exit door
- Surge suppressor
- Emergency replacement server
- Zoned dry-pipe sprinkler system
- Uninterruptible power supply for LAN servers
- Power strips and suppressors for peripherals
- Power strips and suppressors for computers
- Controlled access to file server room
- Plastic sheets for water protection
- Closed-circuit television monitors

FIRE SECURITY AND SAFETY

The most important physical security concern is the safety of the people who work in the organization. The most serious threat to that safety is fire. Fires account for more property damage, personal injury, and death than any other threat to physical security. As a result, it is imperative that physical security plans examine and implement strong measures to detect and respond to fires and fire hazards.

Fire Detection and Response

Fire suppression systems are devices installed and maintained to detect and respond to a fire, potential fire, or combustion danger situation. These devices typically work to deny an environment of one of the three requirements for a fire to burn: temperature (ignition source), fuel, and oxygen.

While the temperature of ignition, or **flame point**, depends upon the material, it can be as low as a few hundred degrees. Paper, the most common combustible in the office, has a flame point of 451 degrees Fahrenheit. Water and water mist systems work both to reduce the temperature of the flame in order to extinguish it and to saturate some categories of fuels (such as paper) to prevent ignition. Carbon dioxide systems (CO_2) rob fire of its oxygen. Soda acid systems deny fire its fuel, preventing the fire from spreading. Gas-based systems, such as Halon and its Environmental Protection Agency-approved replacements, disrupt the fire's chemical reaction but leave enough oxygen for people to survive for a short time. Before a fire can be suppressed, however, it must be detected.

Fire Detection

Fire detection systems fall into two general categories: manual and automatic. **Manual fire detection systems** include human responses, such as calling the fire department, as well as manually activated alarms, such as sprinklers and gaseous systems. Organizations must use care when manually triggered alarms are tied directly to suppression systems, since false alarms are not uncommon. During the chaos of a fire evacuation, an attacker can easily slip into offices and obtain sensitive information. To help prevent such intrusions, it is a common business practice among fire safety programs to designate an individual from each office area as a floor monitor.

There are three basic types of fire detection systems: thermal detection, smoke detection, and flame detection. **Thermal detection systems** contain a sophisticated heat sensor that operates in one of two ways. In the first, known as **fixed temperature**, the sensor detects when the ambient temperature in an area reaches a predetermined level, usually between 135 degrees Fahrenheit and 165 degrees Fahrenheit, or 57 degrees Centigrade to 74 degrees Centigrade.[3] In the second approach, known as **rate-of-rise**, the sensor detects an unusually rapid increase in the area temperature within a relatively short period of time.

In either case, if the criteria are met, the alarm and suppression systems are activated. Thermal detection systems are inexpensive and easy to maintain. Unfortunately, thermal detectors usually don't catch a problem until it is already in progress, as in a full-blown fire. As a result, thermal detection systems are not a sufficient means of fire protection in areas where human safety could be at risk. They are also not recommended for areas with high-value items, or items which could be easily damaged by high temperatures.

Smoke detection systems are perhaps the most common means of detecting a potentially dangerous fire, and they are required by building codes in most residential dwellings and commercial buildings. Smoke detectors operate in one of three ways. In the first, **photoelectric sensors** project and detect an infrared beam across an area. If the beam is interrupted (presumably by smoke), the alarm or suppression system is activated. In the second, an **ionization sensor** contains a small amount of a harmless radioactive material within a detection chamber. When certain by-products of combustion enter the chamber, they change the level of electrical conductivity with the chamber and activate the detector. Ionization sensor systems are much more sophisticated than photoelectric sensors and can detect fires much earlier, since invisible by-products can be detected long before enough visible material enters a photoelectric sensor to trigger a reaction. The third category of smoke detectors is the air-aspirating detector. **Air-aspirating detectors** are very sophisticated systems and are used in high-sensitivity areas. They work by taking in air, filtering it, and moving it through a chamber containing a laser beam. If the laser beam is diverted or refracted by smoke particles, the system is activated. These types of systems are typically much more expensive than the less effective models; however, they are much better at early detection and more commonly used in areas where extremely valuable materials are stored.

The third major category of fire detection systems is the **flame detector**. The flame detector is a sensor that detects the infrared or ultraviolet light produced by an open flame. These systems require direct line of sight with the flame and compare the flame's light signature to a database of known flame light signatures to determine whether or not to activate the alarm and suppression systems. While highly sensitive, flame detection systems are expensive and must be installed where they can scan all areas of the protected area. They are not typically used in areas with human lives at stake; however, they are suitable for chemical storage areas where normal chemical emissions might activate smoke detectors.

Fire Suppression

Fire suppression systems can consist of portable, manual, or automatic apparatus. Portable extinguishers are used in a variety of situations where direct application of suppression is preferred, or fixed apparatus is impractical. Portable extinguishers are much more efficient for smaller fires, because they avoid the triggering of an entire building's sprinkler systems and the damage that can cause. As described below, portable extinguishers are rated by the type of fire they can combat:

- **Class A fires:** Those fires that involve ordinary combustible fuels such as wood, paper, textiles, rubber, cloth, and trash. Class A fires are extinguished by agents that interrupt the ability of the fuel to be ignited. Water and multipurpose, dry chemical fire extinguishers are ideal for these types of fires.

- **Class B fires:** Those fires fueled by combustible liquids or gases, such as solvents, gasoline, paint, lacquer, and oil. Class B fires are extinguished by agents that remove oxygen from the fire. Carbon dioxide, multipurpose dry chemical, and Halon fire extinguishers are ideal for these types of fires.

- **Class C fires:** Those fires with energized electrical equipment or appliances. Class C fires are extinguished with agents that must be nonconducting. Carbon dioxide, multipurpose, dry chemical, and Halon fire extinguishers are ideal for these types of fires. Never use a water fire extinguisher on a Class C fire.

- **Class D fires:** Those fires fueled by combustible metals, such as magnesium, lithium, and sodium. Fires of this type require special extinguishing agents and techniques.

- **Class K fires:** Those fires fueled by cooking oils or fat. Although technically a subset of Class B, this group has been determined to warrant separate treatment. This type of fires require saponification for extinction. **Saponification** is the reaction of a metallic alkali or base with a fat or oil to form soap. Thus, the use of a base agent like baking soda best extinguishes a fat or oil fire.

Manual and automatic fire response can include systems designed to apply suppressive agents. These are usually either sprinkler or gaseous systems.

Sprinkler Systems

All **sprinkler systems** are designed to apply liquid, usually water, to all areas in which a fire has been detected, but an organization can choose from one of three implementations: wet-pipe, dry-pipe, or pre-action systems. A **wet-pipe** system has pressurized water in all pipes and has some form of valve in each protected area. When the system is activated, the valves open, sprinkling the area. This is best for areas where the fire represents a severe risk to people, but where damage to property is not a major concern. The most obvious drawback to this type of system is water damage to office equipment and materials. A wet-pipe system is not usually appropriate in computer rooms, wiring closets, or anywhere electrical equipment is used or stored.

A **dry-pipe system** is designed to work in areas where electrical equipment is used. Instead of containing water, the system contains pressurized air. The air holds valves closed, keeping the water away from the target areas. When a fire is detected, the sprinkler heads are activated, the pressurized air escapes, and water fills the pipes and exits through the sprinkler heads. This reduces the risk of leakage from the system when it is not activated. Some sprinkler systems are installed as a **deluge system**, in which all of the individual sprinkler heads are kept open, and as soon as the system is activated, water is immediately applied to all areas. It is not, however, the optimal solution for computing environments, because there are other more sophisticated systems that can both suppress the fire and maintain the integrity of computing equipment.

A variation of the dry-pipe system is the **pre-action system**. This approach has a two-phase response to a fire. The system is normally maintained with nothing in the delivery pipes. When a fire has been detected, the first phase is initiated, and valves allow water to enter the system. At that point, the system is in a state identical to that found in a wet-pipe system. The pre-action system does not deliver water into the protected space until the individual sprinkler heads are triggered, at which time water flows only into the area of the activated sprinkler head.

Water mist sprinklers are the newest form of sprinkler systems and rely on ultra-fine mists instead of traditional shower-type systems. The water mist systems work like traditional water systems in reducing the ambient temperature around the flame, therefore minimizing its ability to sustain the necessary temperature needed to maintain combustion. Unlike traditional water sprinkler systems, however, these systems produce a fog-like mist that, because the droplets are much less susceptible to gravity, stays buoyant (airborne) much longer. As a result, a much smaller quantity of water is required; also the fire is extinguished more quickly, which causes less collateral damage. Relative to gaseous systems (to be discussed shortly), water-based systems are low cost, nontoxic, and require minimal retrofit for an existing sprinkler system.

Gaseous Emission Systems

Gaseous (or chemical gas) emission systems can be used in the suppression of fires. They are often found protecting chemical and electrical processing areas, as well as facilities that house computing systems. Gaseous fire suppression systems are either self-pressurizing or must be pressurized with an additional agent. Until recently there were only two major types of gaseous systems: carbon dioxide and Halon. Carbon dioxide extinguishes a fire by removing its supply of oxygen. Unfortunately, any living organisms that also rely on oxygen are similarly extinguished. As a result, carbon dioxide systems are not commonly used in residential or office environments where people or animals are likely to be present. The alternative is Halon. Halon is one of a few chemicals designated as a **clean agent**, which means that it does not leave any residue after use, nor does it interfere with the operation of electrical or electronic equipment. Unfortunately, the EPA has classified Halon as an ozone-depleting substance, and therefore new installations of the controlled types of Halon are prohibited in commercial and residential locations. There are a number of alternatives:

- ▶ FM-200 (very similar to Halon 1301) is safe in occupied areas.
- ▶ Inergen is a high-pressure agent composed of nitrogen, argon, and carbon dioxide.
- ▶ Carbon dioxide, although riskier than Halon, is an acceptable alternative.
- ▶ FE-13 (trifluromethane) is one of the newest and safest clean agents.

A typical physical security plan requires that every building have clearly marked fire exits and maps posted throughout the facility. It is important to have drills to rehearse fire alarm responses and designate individuals to be in charge of escorting everyone from the location and ensuring that no one is left behind. It is also important to have fire suppression systems that are both manual and automatic, and that are inspected and tested regularly.

FAILURE OF SUPPORTING UTILITIES AND STRUCTURAL COLLAPSE

Supporting utilities, such as heating, ventilation and air-conditioning, power, water, and other utilities, have a significant impact on the safe operation of a facility. Extreme temperatures and humidity levels, electrical fluctuations and the interruption of water, sewage, and garbage services can create conditions that inject vulnerabilities in systems designed to protect information. Thus, each of these utilities must be properly managed in order to prevent potential damage to information and information systems.

Heating, Ventilation, and Air-Conditioning

Although traditionally a facilities management responsibility, the operation of the heating, ventilation, and air-conditioning (HVAC) system can have dramatic impact on information and information systems operations and protection. Specifically, the areas within the HVAC system that need to be adjusted to reduce risk to information-carrying systems are temperature, filtration, humidity, and static electricity.

Temperature and Filtration Computer systems are electronic and as such are subject to damage from extreme temperature and particulate contamination. Temperatures as low as 100 degrees Fahrenheit can damage computer media, and at 175 degrees Fahrenheit, computer hardware can be damaged or destroyed. At the other end of the thermometer, when the temperature approaches 32 degrees Fahrenheit, media is susceptible to cracking, and computer components can actually freeze together. Rapid changes in temperature, from hot to cold or from cold to hot, can produce condensation, which can create short circuits or otherwise damage systems and components. The optimal temperature for a computing environment (and for people) is between 70 and 74 degrees Fahrenheit.

Humidity and Static Electricity **Humidity** is the amount of moisture in the air. High humidity levels create condensation problems, and low humidity levels can increase the amount of static electricity in the environment. With condensation comes the short-circuiting of electrical equipment and the potential for mold and rot in paper-based information storage. **Static electricity** is caused by a process called **triboelectrification**, which occurs when two materials are rubbed or touched and electrons are exchanged, and results in one object becoming more positively charged and the other more negatively charged. When a third object with an opposite charge or ground is encountered, electrons flow again, and a spark is produced. One of the leading causes of damage to sensitive circuitry is **electrostatic discharge (ESD)**. Integrated circuits in a computer are designed to use between two and five volts of electricity, and any voltage level above this range introduces a risk of microchip damage. Static electricity is not even noticeable to humans until levels approach 1,500 volts, and the little blue spark can't be seen until the level approaches 4,000 volts. Moreover, a person can generate up to 12,000 volts of static current by merely walking across a carpet.

As a result, it is imperative to maintain the optimal level of humidity, which is between 40% and 60%, in the computing environment. Humidity levels below this range create static, and levels above create condensation. Humidification or dehumidification systems can assist in the regulation of these conditions.

Power Management and Conditioning

Electrical power is another aspect of the organization's physical environment that is usually considered within the realm of physical security. As discussed in earlier chapters, not only is electrical quantity (the voltage level and the amperage rating) of concern, but the quality of the power (the frequency, noisiness, and grounding) is of importance as well. **Grounding** ensures that the returning flow of current is properly discharged to the ground. If the grounding elements of the electrical system are not properly installed, anyone touching a computer or other electrical device could act as a ground source, which would cause damage to equipment and injury or death to the person.

Uninterruptible Power Supply (UPS) The primary power source for an organization's computing equipment is most often the electric utility that serves the area where the organization's buildings are located. This source of power can experience interruptions. Therefore, organizations should identify the computing systems that are vital to their operations (in other words, the systems that must continue to operate during interruptions) and make sure those systems are connected to a device that assures the delivery of electric power without interruption—that is, an **Uninterruptible Power Supply (UPS)**.

This section describes the following basic configurations: the standby, line-interactive, standby online hybrid, and double conversion online (also known as true online).

A **standby** or **offline UPS** is an offline battery backup that detects the interruption of power to the power equipment. When the power stops flowing to the equipment, the UPS activates a transfer switch that then provides power from batteries, through a DC to AC converter, until the power is restored or the computer is shut down. Because this type of UPS is not truly uninterruptible, it is often referred to as a standby power supply (SPS). The advantage of an SPS is that it is the most cost-effective type of UPS. However, the significant drawbacks, such as the limited run time and the amount of time it takes to switch from standby to active, may outweigh the cost savings. Switching time may also become an issue because very sensitive computing equipment may not be able to handle the transfer delay, and may reset and even suffer data loss or damage. Also, SPS systems do not provide power conditioning, a feature of more sophisticated UPSs (discussed below). As a result, an SPS is seldom used in critical computing applications and is best suited for home and light office use.

The **line-interactive UPS** has a substantially different design than the previously mentioned UPS models. In the line-interactive UPS, the internal components of the standby models are replaced with a pair of inverters and converters. The primary power source, as in both the SPS and the ferroresonant UPS, remains the power utility company, with a battery serving as backup. However, the inverters and converters both charge the battery and provide power when needed. When utility power is interrupted, the converter begins supplying power to the systems. Because this device is always connected to the output as opposed to relying on a switch, this model has a much faster response time and also incorporates power conditioning and line filtering.

In a **true online UPS**, the primary power source is the battery, and the power feed from the utility is constantly recharging this battery. This model allows constant use of the system, while completely eliminating power fluctuation. True online UPS can deliver a constant, smooth, conditioned power stream to the computing systems. If the utility-provided power fails, the computer systems are unaffected, as long as the batteries hold out. The online UPS is considered the top-of-the-line option and is the most expensive. The only major drawback, other than cost, is that the process of constantly converting from the AC feed from the utility to the DC used by the battery storage and then converting back to AC for use by the systems generates a lot of heat.

Selecting the best UPS can be a lesson in electrical engineering, because you must calculate the load that the protected systems require from the UPS. This can be quite complex and proves challenging in practice. Fortunately, many UPS vendors provide sample scenarios that can help you select the optimal device. Because a high-quality UPS large enough for many applications may cost several thousand dollars, it is advisable to select the smallest UPS necessary to provide the desired effect.

Maintenance of Facility Systems

Just as with any phase of the security process, the implementation of the physical security phase must be constantly documented, evaluated, and tested; also once the physical security of a facility is established, it must be diligently maintained. Ongoing maintenance of systems is required as part of the systems' operations. Documentation of the facility's configuration, operation, and function should be integrated into disaster recovery plans and standard operating procedures. Testing provides information necessary to improve the physical security in the facility and identifies weak points.

INTERCEPTION OF DATA

The interception of data is also a security concern. There are three methods of data interception: direct observation, interception of data transmission, and electromagnetic interception. The first method is *direct observation*, where an individual must be close enough to the information to breach confidentiality. Incidences of interception, such as shoulder surfing, can be avoided, if employees are either prohibited from removing sensitive information from the office or required to implement strong security at their homes.

The second method, *interception of data transmissions*, has become easier in the age of the Internet. If attackers can access the media transmitting the data, they needn't be anywhere near the source of the information. The challenges (such as sniffers) and solutions (such as VPNs) to these problems were discussed in earlier chapters.

The third method of data interception, *electromagnetic interception*, sounds like it could be from a *Star Trek* episode. For decades, scientists have known that electricity moving through cables emits electromagnetic signals (EM). It is possible to eavesdrop on these signals, and therefore to determine the data carried on the cables without actually tapping into them. In 1985, scientists proved that computer monitors also emitted radio waves, and that the image on the screens could be reconstructed from these signals.[4] Regardless of whether the threat from eavesdropping on electromagnetic emanations is real, many procedures that protect against emanations also protect against threats to physical security.

MOBILE AND PORTABLE SYSTEMS

Mobile computing requires even more security than the average in-house system. Most of these mobile computing systems—laptops, handhelds, and PDAs—have valuable corporate information stored within them, and some are configured to facilitate user access into the organization's secure computing facilities. Forms of access include VPN connections, dial-up configurations, and databases of passwords.

For maximum security, laptops should be secured at all times. If you are traveling with a laptop, you should have it in your possession at all times. Special care should be exercised when flying, because laptop thefts are common in airports. The list below comes from the Metropolitan Police of the District of Columbia and outlines steps you can take to prevent your laptop from being stolen or carelessly damaged:

▶ Don't leave a laptop in an unlocked vehicle, even if the vehicle is in your driveway or garage, and never leave it in plain sight, even if the vehicle is locked—that's just inviting trouble. If you must leave your laptop in a vehicle, the best place is in a locked trunk. If you don't have a trunk, cover it up and lock the doors.

▶ Parking garages are likely areas for thefts from vehicles, because they provide numerous choices and cover for thieves. Again, never leave your laptop in plain sight; cover it or put it in the trunk.

▶ Do be aware of the damage extreme temperatures can cause to computers.

▶ Carry your laptop in a nondescript carrying case, briefcase, or bag when moving about. Placing it in a case designed for computers is an immediate alert to thieves that you have a laptop.

▶ Going to lunch, or taking a break? Don't leave a meeting or conference room without your laptop. Take it with you, or you run the risk that it won't be there when you return.

▶ Lock the laptop in your office during off-hours. Don't have your own office? Use a cable lock that wraps around a desk or chair leg. Or put the laptop in a locked closet or cabinet.

▶ Don't let unaccompanied strangers wander around in your workplace. Offer assistance and deliver the visitors to their destinations.

▶ Apply distinctive paint markings to make your laptop unique and easily identifiable. Liquid white-out is a good substance to apply.

▶ Consider purchasing one of the new theft alarm systems specially made for laptops.

▶ Be aware that if your computer is stolen, automatic log-ins can make it easy for a thief to send inappropriate messages with your account.

▶ Back up your information on disks today, and store the disks at home or the office.[5]

SPECIAL CONSIDERATIONS FOR PHYSICAL SECURITY THREATS

There are a number of special considerations for physical security threats that you should consider. The first of these is the decision to develop physical security in-house or to outsource it. As with any aspect of information security, the make-or-buy decision should not be made lightly. A number of qualified and professional agencies provide physical security consulting and services. The benefits of outsourcing physical security include gaining the experience and knowledge of these agencies, many of which have been in the field for decades.

Another physical security consideration is social engineering. As discussed in previous chapters, social engineering involves using people skills to obtain confidential information from employees. While most social engineers prefer to use the telephone or computer to solicit information, some attempt to access the information more directly.

While physical security may seem like one of the less interesting domains of information security, it is absolutely foundational since without adequate physical security, other information security practices are of doubtful value.

Physical security includes many classic techniques such as fences, guards, etc., but is becoming an increasingly technical area with the addition of biometric physical access controls, multifaceted electronic alarms, and so on. With the rise of telecommuting and remote workers, the challenges of physical security have reached out to include employees on the go and employees at home.

The Information Security Manager's Checklist

	No	Planned	In Progress	In Place	Integrated
This topic has been fully tested, validated, and integrated into organizational operations with formal performance measures in place (as appropriate).					
This topic has been implemented, but not fully tested, validated, and integrated into organizational operations.					
The implementation of this topic has begun, but is not yet complete.					
The formal planning for this topic has begun, but is not yet complete.					
This subject has not formally begun planning, or the organization has made a conscious decision not to pursue this topic.					
33. Physical Security	No	Planned	In Progress	In Place	Integrated
Keys inventoried and managed					
Critical information locations identified					
Critical information locations keycard access with auditability					
Nonemployees escorted in facilities					
Appropriate fire control systems implemented and tested periodically					
Power backup supply implemented and tested					
Data communications infrastructure checked periodically for interception					

For Further Reading

Effective Physical Security, Third Edition, by Lawrence Fennelly, Butterworth-Heinemann, 2003.

Design and Evaluation of Physical Protection Systems, Second Edition by Mary Lynn Garcia, Butterworth-Heinemann, 2007.

Physical & Technical Security: An Introduction by Robert Gruber, Delmar Cengage Learning, 2005.

References

1. Donn B. Parker. *Fighting Computer Crime* (New York: John Wiley and Sons Inc., 1998), 250–251.

2. Marianne Swanson. *Guide for Developing Security Plans for Information Technology Systems* (December 1998). National Institute of Standards and Technology SP 800-18, 30. Accessed 05 July 2007 from *http://csrc.nist.gov/publications/nistpubs/800-18-Rev1/sp800-18-Rev1-final.pdf.*

3. Nick Artim. *An Introduction to Fire Detection, Alarm, and Automatic Fire Sprinklers.* Emergency Management, Technical Leaflet 2, sec. 3. Middlebury: Fire Safety Network.

4. Wim Van Eck. "Electromagnetic Radiation from Video Display Units: An Eavesdropping Risk?" *Computers & Security* 4 (1985): 269–286.

5. Metropolitan Police of the District of Columbia. "Tips for Preventing Laptop Computer Theft." *Government of The District of Columbia Online.* Accessed 7 July 2007 from *mpdc.dc.gov/mpdc/cwp/view,a,1237,q,543203,mpdcNav_GID,1548.asp.*

Part **IX**

Appendix

Part IX of *Roadmap to Information Security for IT and InfoSec Managers* provides a set of security self-assessment checklist as well as guidance as regards two dominant professional certifications—those from ISC[2] and ISACA.

Appendix A—Information Security Self-Assessment Checklists provides a security self-assessment checklist, based in part on two dominant industry standards: ISO 17799 (soon to become ISO 27002) and NIST SP 800-27. This appendix will provide guidance on performing a continuous improvement assessment program, along with guidelines on implementing and interpreting the results of such an assessment.

Appendix B—Information Security Certification Guidelines—The CISSP/SSCP contains information for those professionals interested in using the material contained in this book as a foundation for a self-study program in pursuit of one of the two (ISC)[2] certifications: the CISSP and the SSCP. While the book makes no claims as to the level of preparation of a prospective certification candidate, it will serve as a starting point to

449

determine what areas the reader should continue to focus on to optimize their chance of success with the process.

Appendix C—Information Security Certification Guidelines—The CISM continues the examination of dominant certification standards, mapping the content to the other preferred industry certification standard ISACA's CISM. The text again will provide a guide to preparing for this certification.

Information Security Self-Assessment Checklists

This part of the appendix provides a security self-assessment checklist, based in part on two dominant industry standards: ISO 27002 and NIST SP 800-27. This appendix will provide guidance on performing a continuous improvement assessment program, along with guidelines on implementing and interpreting the results of such an assessment.

ISO 27000

The following checklist—loosely based on the ISO 27000 series, can be used as a scoring mechanism to determine the extent to which an organization's information security management structure is complete. For each of the following Security Management Domains, evaluate the state of information security in your organization. For each of the items specified, indicate as to whether your organization is:

- ▶ Fully compliant: The standard objective has been fully implemented at the organization. Results in a score of 10 for the objective.

- ▶ Partially compliant: The standard objective has been partially implemented at the organization. Results in a score of 5 for the objective.

- ▶ Planned: The organization has made definite plans to implement the standard objective. Results in a score of 2 for the objective.

- ▶ Not compliant or planned: The standard objective has not been implemented (even partly) and there are no plans to implement it. Results in a score of 0 for the objective.

- ▶ Not applicable: The objective does not appear to apply to the organization. No score is given and the potential score of 10 is not incorporated in the calculation of the total score, as if the objective was not included in the index.

For each Domain, score up to 10 points for each item (e.g., 1a, 1b, etc.) and divide by the total points possible for each domain (e.g., by 60 for Domain I). The resulting scores for each domain can then be averaged to develop an overall "grade" for information security management in the organization.

I. Security Policy (___ points out of 60 total possible)

1. Information Security Policy—The current information security policies within your organization:

   a) Define information security objectives and illustrate the importance of security.

   b) Provide a statement of management's intentions to support information security.

   c) Define general responsibilities for employees.

   d) References other appropriate documents: regulations, laws, and policies.

2. Information Security Policy—When reviewing, evaluating, and distributing security policies, your organization:

   a) Specifies a distinct information security owner who has the responsibility for update and maintenance of those policies.

   b) Requires a review by business owners, legal, and HR.

II. Risk Management (___ points out of 70 total possible)

1. Risk Identification and Assessment—In determining the current level of threat against organizational information assets the organization:

   a) Identifies and prioritizes threats to information assets.

   b) Identifies and prioritizes information assets in the organization.

   c) Identifies vulnerabilities in information assets that could be exploited by threats.

   d) Identifies current levels of controls protecting assets from threats.

2. Risk Management—Once risk identified, organization makes appropriate determination if current levels of protection are sufficient:

   a) For each evaluated Threat–Vulnerability–Asset set, selects appropriate level of additional controls relative to risk appetite: Accept, Transfer, Mitigate, or Further apply controls.

   b) Repeats risk management process periodically to ensure controls continue to provide acceptable levels of protection.

   c) Follows established risk management approach that provides sustainable continuous improvement, and a generally accepted methodology.

III. Organizational Security (___ points out of 120 total possible)

1. Information Security Infrastructure—Your organization's information security infrastructure is supported by a(n):

   a) Enterprise-wide security steering committee.

   b) Information security representative from each business unit.

   c) Allocation of information security responsibilities.

d) Information security advisor (for expert advice) or coordinator (to coordinate security knowledge sharing).

e) Documented points of contact with law enforcement, standards setting organizations, and service providers for both incident response support and security advice.

f) Autonomous oversight of information security policy implementation.

g) Performing risk assessments before granting access to external parties.

h) Management review and approval for the development or implementation of any new information technologies.

2. Security of Third-Party Access—Third-party access is controlled in your organization by:

a) Documenting the organization's security policy in the third-party contract.

b) Educating third parties on the information classification program.

3. Outsourcing—Outsourcing is controlled in your organization by:

a) Communicating legal requirements for protecting your organization's information and information technologies and services.

b) Educating outsourcers on their liabilities in regards to the security of your organization's information, technologies, and services.

IV. Asset Classification & Control (___ points out of 30 total possible)

1. Accountability for Assets—Your organization accounts for key information technology assets by:

a) Recording the information and business ownership.

2. Information Classification—Safeguarding information within your organization includes:

a) A simple, effective guideline that indicates the degree of protection for each type of information asset.

b) Handling and labeling procedures for physical media.

V. Personnel Security (___ points out of 90 total possible)

1. Security in Job Definition and Resourcing—Your organization has policies and procedures in place that require:

a) Information security roles and responsibilities included in all company job descriptions.

b) All candidates for employment be adequately screened to ensure that their qualifications are accurate.

c) All employees sign a confidentiality (nondisclosure) agreement to ensure that they understand their information handling responsibilities.

2. User Training—An organization-wide training program is in place for:

a) Information security policy and procedure awareness and comprehension.

b) Informing personnel of their legal responsibilities for security.

c) Correct usage of information technologies including business applications.

3. **Responding to Security Incidents and Malfunctions**—In response to a security incident or malfunction, a formal process exists in your organization that:

   a) Instructs employees on the correct method of handling security incidents.

   b) Instructs employees on the proper method for preserving the evidence necessary for forensic investigations.

   c) Disciplines employees who have violated security policies and procedures.

VI. **Physical and Environmental Security** (___ points out of 120 total possible)

   1. **Secure Areas**—Facilities are properly secured by:

      a) Adequately establishing and monitoring a physical perimeter.

      b) Logging and supervising physical entry by visitors.

      c) Taking precautions (including proper layout and site selection) to secure against natural or man-made disasters.

      d) Adequately controlling personnel or third parties working in secure areas.

      e) Controlling delivery and loading areas and if possible, isolating them from information processing facilities.

      f) Protecting equipment from power failures and other electrical anomalies.

   2. **Equipment Security**—Equipment is properly secured by:

      a) Protecting power and telecommunications cabling from interception or damage.

      b) Correctly maintaining equipment to ensure its continued availability and integrity.

      c) Physically destroying storage devices containing sensitive information or securely overwriting sensitive data when disposing of those storage devices.

   3. **General Controls**—Your organization prevents the compromise or theft of information and information-processing facilities by requiring:

      a) A clear desk policy for papers and removable storage media, and a clear screen policy for information-processing facilities.

      b) Equipment or information taken off-site to be removed only with authorization, and proper logging is in place to control removal.

VII. **Communications & Operations Management** (___ points out of 120 total possible)

   1. **Operational Procedures and Responsibilities**—Your organization ensures the correct and secure operation of information technologies by using:

      a) Documented standard operating procedures including processing information, scheduling, error handling, support, and recovery.

      b) A change management process.

      c) An incident management process.

      d) An enforceable segregation of duties policy.

      e) A separation between the development and operational (production) facilities.

   2. **System Planning and Acceptance**—Your organization minimizes the risk that essential systems will fail by using acceptable:

      a) Capacity planning.

3. Protection Against Malicious Software—Your organization protects the integrity and security of essential software and information by:

   a) Using a policy requiring compliance with software licenses.

   b) Using a policy for obtaining files and software from third parties.

   c) Installing and regularly updating antivirus detection and repair software.

   d) Checking any files, electronic mail attachments, or downloads of uncertain origin for viruses before use.

4. Housekeeping—Your organization maintains the integrity and availability of essential information processing and communication services by:

   a) Implementing a backup and recovery process.

   b) Logging operator commands.

   c) Logging network and system faults.

5. Network Management—Your organization ensures the protection of networks and supporting infrastructure by:

   a) Establishing special controls to safeguard the confidentiality and integrity of data passing over public networks.

   b) Separating operational responsibility for the networks from the computer operations where possible.

6. Media Handling and Security—To prevent asset damage and business activity interruption, your organization's media should be controlled and physically protected by:

   a) Procedures for managing removable computer media such as CDs, disks, and printed reports.

   b) Securely storing system documentation.

7. Exchanges of Information and Software—Your organization prevents loss, modification, or misuse of information exchanges between organizations by utilizing the appropriate:

   a) Agreements between organizations for the exchange of information.

   b) Security precautions for electronic commerce.

   c) Security precautions for electronic mail.

   d) Security precautions for electronic office systems such as voice mail, mobile communications, video, and postal services.

   e) Security precautions for publicly available systems such as Web servers.

VIII. Access Control (___ points out of 190 total possible)

   1. Business Requirement for Access Control—Your organization controls access to sensitive information by:

      a) Documenting policy and business requirements for controlling access to each business application.

      b) Establishing access control rules that grant permissions to each group of users.

2. User Access Management—Your organization prevents unauthorized access to information systems by:
   a) Using a formal user registration and de-registration procedure for granting access to all multi-user information systems.
   b) Controlling password allocation through a formal management process.
3. User Responsibilities—To prevent unauthorized user access, your organization requires users to:
   a) Follow good security practices in the selection and use of passwords.
   b) Ensure that unattended equipment automatically logs users out or securely locks the system from unauthorized use.
4. Network Access Control—The protection of networked services is enforced by:
   a) Authenticating all users from external connections.
   b) Requiring authentication for an automatic connection to a network, such as in trust relationships between computers.
5. Operating System Access Control—All access to computer resources is restricted by operating system controls that:
   a) Authenticate connections using terminal identification when it is important to ensure logins occur only from specific locations and/or computers or terminals.
   b) Require a unique, nondescript identifier for all authorized users.
   c) Employ effective password management systems that ensure quality passwords.
   d) Restrict and log all use of system utilities.
   e) Permit time-of-day connection limits to high-risk or sensitive applications.
6. Monitoring System Access and Use—All access and use of computer systems is monitored to detect unauthorized activities by:
   a) Recording all relevant security events in audit logs.
   b) Reviewing audit logs through an effective and routine process.
   c) Documenting and implementing procedures for monitoring the use of information technologies.
   d) Using a process to ensure that all system clocks are synchronized with an agreed standard.
7. Mobile Computing and Teleworking—Your organization has information security policies and procedures documented and implemented to control:
   a) The use of all mobile computing facilities including physical protection, access controls, cryptographic techniques, backups, and virus protection.
   b) All activities related to working remotely from a fixed site not located within your organization.

IX. Systems Development and Maintenance (___ points out of 90 total possible)
   1. Security Requirements of Systems—Your organization specifies security requirements and specifications that:
      a) Reflect the business value of the information assets involved.

b) Follow a risk assessment and risk management process to determine the acceptable controls.

2. Cryptographic Controls—Your organization uses cryptographic systems and techniques to protect the confidentiality, authenticity, or integrity of information by:

   a) Considering regulatory restrictions that may apply to the use of cryptographic algorithms in different parts of the world.

   b) Applying digital signatures to any form of legal or business document being processed electronically.

   c) Implementing a system for the management of cryptographic keys.

3. Security of System Files—System files are secured during IT projects and support activities by:

   a) Controlling program source libraries in the development process to restrict possible corruption or tampering.

4. Security in Development and Support Processes—In order to minimize the corruption of information systems, your organization controls the implementation of changes by:

   a) Using access controls to restrict the movement of programs and data from development into production.

   b) Testing the application system when a change in the operating system occurs to ensure that there is no adverse impact on operation or security.

   c) Conducting source code reviews to eliminate possible security vulnerabilities.

X. Business Continuity Management (___ points out of 40 total possible)

1. Aspects of Business Continuity Management—Your organization has a business continuity planning process in place that:

   a) Has produced a current, comprehensive, documented, and routinely maintained business continuity plan for the entire organization.

   b) Requires the completion of a business impact analysis that identifies events and their associated risks.

   c) Requires a current prioritization of all business processes and supporting functions, including computer systems and applications.

   d) Ensures that the business continuity plan is routinely tested using effective techniques to assure that the plan is viable.

XI. Compliance (___ points out of 70 total possible)

1. Compliance with Legal Requirements—Your organization has implemented policies and procedures to ensure compliance with legal requirements that specifically address the:

   a) Data protection and privacy of personal information.

   b) Acceptable use of information technologies.

   c) International usage or transport of cryptographic controls.

2. Reviews of Security Compliance and Technical Compliance—Compliance procedures are in place that require the:

   a) Departmental managers to perform routine self-assessments to ensure that their areas comply with security policies and standards.

   b) Technical checking of information systems by independent experts for compliance with security standards and leading practices.

3. System Audit Considerations—Audit procedures are in place that require:

   a) Review of all operational systems to minimize the risk of business process disruptions.

   b) Restricted access to system audit tools to prevent misuse or compromise.

XII. Governance (___ points out of 130 total possible)

1. Board of Directors' Responsibilities—The board of directors for your organization has indicated the importance of information security in the organization by:

   a) Instilling a culture that recognizes the importance of information security to the organization.

   b) Ensuring that the information security strategic planning is aligned with the organizational strategies and the current risk environment.

   c) Ensuring that an effective information security management program is developed, implemented, and periodically assessed.

   d) Requiring periodic reports from the appropriate responsible individuals on the effectiveness and adequacy of the information security program.

2. Information Security Governance Implementation—Organization seeks to implement effective security governance through executive leadership that ensures the organization:

   a) Conducts annual information security evaluations and reports results to top executive management.

   b) Conducts periodic risk management evaluations, as part of a formal risk management program, and reports results to top executive management.

   c) Implements and enforces effective information security policies.

   d) Develops information security strategies in alignment with strategies of the organization, its business units, and the information technology function.

   e) Integrates information security into development life cycles.

   f) Provides effective security training and awareness to all employees.

   g) Develops, implements, and tests incident response plans.

   h) Develops, implements, and tests disaster recovery and business continuity plans.

   i) Bases information security management efforts on established methodologies and standards. Reviews and ensures compliance with all applicable regulations, policies, and practices.

This checklist is derived from a number of resources, including "ISO/IEC FDIS 27001 Information technology—Security techniques—Information Security management systems—Requirements", as well as Praxiom's "ISO IEC 27001 2005 Translated into Plain English" and also the work of the Human Firewall Council, 2005–2007, among others.

Information Security Certification Guidelines—The CISSP/SSCP

This part contains information for those professionals interested in using the material contained in this book as a foundation for a self-study program in pursuit of one of the two (ISC)² certifications: the CISSP and the SSCP. While the book makes no claims as to the level of preparation of a prospective certification candidate, it will serve as a starting point to determine what areas the reader should continue to focus on to optimize their chance of success with the process.

When pursuing one of these certifications it may help to have another perspective or different view on the subject. These mappings include the general subject areas of these exams, with references to the chapter and major heading the content can be found in.

NOTE

This book does NOT claim to be a certification preparation guide, nor does it claim to cover the material in sufficient breadth or depth of material to guarantee success on the described exams. It can, however, provide a good basis for beginning one's study of the material, and with sufficient supplement, assist the reader in obtaining this certification.

The CISSP Certification

The Certified Information Systems Security Professional (CISSP) is still considered by many to be the preeminent certification for Information Security professionals. The challenges in obtaining this certification are considerable. This section provides a brief overview of the certification requirements, and then maps the general domains of the CISSP common body of knowledge against this book.

Offered by the International Information Systems Security Certification Consortium (ISC)², the CISSP exam test the applicant's knowledge of 10 domains:

- ▶ Access Control
- ▶ Application Security
- ▶ Business Continuity and Disaster Recovery Planning
- ▶ Cryptography
- ▶ Information Security Governance and Risk Management
- ▶ Legal, Regulations, Investigations, and Compliance
- ▶ Operations Security
- ▶ Physical and Environmental Security
- ▶ Security Architecture and Design
- ▶ Telecommunications and Network Security

CISSP® candidates must meet the following requirements prior to taking the CISSP examination:

- ▶ Have a minimum of 5 years of direct full-time security professional work experience in two or more of the ten domains of the (ISC)² CISSP common body of knowledge, or 4 years of direct full-time security professional work experience in two or more of the ten domains of the CISSP CBK with a college degree. Alternatively there is a 1-year waiver of the professional experience requirement for holding an additional credential on the (ISC)²-approved list.
- ▶ Complete the Candidate Agreement, attesting to the truth of his or her assertions regarding professional experience and legally commit to adhere to the (ISC)² Code of Ethics.
- ▶ Successfully answer questions regarding criminal history and related background.

Upon successfully passing the CISSP examination, you must submit a properly completed and executed endorsement form. The endorser attests that the candidate's assertions regarding professional experience are true to the best of their knowledge, and that the candidate is in good standing within the information security industry.[1]

Individuals who pass the certification exam but have not completed their industry experience can qualify for the Associate of (ISC)² program. These individuals earn the Associate Certification, and upon completion of their industry experience (and submission of the endorsement form) receive the full CISSP certification.

Once you earn the CISSP certification, the work's not over. All CISSPs must either recertify every 3 years by either retaking the exam or submitting at least 120 continuing professional education (CPE) credits—with a minimum of 20 CPEs per year. CISSPs must also pay annual maintenance fees. For more information on the CISSP certification, visit www.isc2.org/cissp.

The following table maps the major headings of each Domain to the appropriate sections of this book. If a particular header is not covered in this text, N/A (not available) will be shown. When a topic is covered in a large number of places, it has been tagged as 'Pervasive'. In some cases a list of chapter numbers is provided. The topics included in this table were developed based on the chapter outlines of the *Official (ISC)² Guide to the CISSP CBK*.[2]

CISSP DOMAINS AND MAJOR TOPICS	ROADMAP—MAPPINGS
I. Access Controls	
a. Definitions and Key Concepts	32-Whole chapter, 9-Access Controls
b. Access Control Principles	32-Whole chapter
c. Access Control Requirements	32-Whole chapter
d. Access Control Categories	32-Types of access controls, 9-Access Controls
e. Access Control Types	32-Types of access controls
f. Access Control Models and Methodologies	32-Managing access controls
g. System Access Control Strategies	32-Managing access controls
h. Identity Management	32-Identification, 32-Authentication
i. Access Control Technologies	Pervasive in Chapters 27, 32, 33
j. Data Access Controls	Pervasive in Chapters 31, 22, 33
k. Intrusion Detection and Prevention Systems	28-Intrusion Detection and Prevention System Basics 28-Types of IDPS systems
l. Threats	Pervasive in Chapter 32
II. Application Security	
a. Definitions and Key Concepts	N/A
b. Applications Development Concepts and Protection	N/A
c. Software Protection Mechanisms	N/A
d. Audit and Assurance Mechanisms	N/A
e. Malicious Software (Malware)	N/A
f. Databases and Data Warehousing	N/A
g. Web Application Environment	N/A
III. Business Continuity and Disaster Recovery Planning	
a. Project Initiation and Management	Pervasive in Chapters 21, 22, 23, and 24
b. Executive Leadership Support	Pervasive in Chapter 21
c. DR/BC Planning Benefits	24-The Business Continuity Plan
d. Policies and Standards	23-DR Policy, 24-BC Planning Policy Statement
e. Legal and Regulatory Requirements	N/A
f. DR/BC Practice Areas	N/A
g. Business Impact Analysis	21-Business Impact Analysis
h. Selecting a DR/BC Strategy	24-Continuity Strategies

(Continued)

CISSP DOMAINS AND MAJOR TOPICS	ROADMAP—MAPPINGS
i. Managing DR/BC Communications	
j. Testing and Training	21-Testing Contingency Plans
k. Roles and Responsibilities	23-DR Policy, 24-BC Planning Policy Statement
l. Threats	2-Threat categories, 8-Threats
IV. Cryptography	
a. Definitions and Key Concepts	Pervasive in Chapter 30
b. Encryption Systems	30-Cryptographic Algorithms, 31-Confidentiality with Anonymity
c. Message Integrity	30-Hash Functions
d. Digital Signatures	30-Using Cryptography, 31-Digital Signatures
e. Key Management	30-Using Cryptography
f. Attacks on Cryptosystems	30-Rainbow cracking, 31-Attacks on Cryptosystems
g. Use of Cryptosystems	30-Using Cryptography
V. Information Security Governance and Risk Management	
a. Definitions and Key Concepts	1-Information Security Defined, 17-Definitions
b. Information Security Policy	17-Information Security Policy, Standards, and Practices, 18
c. Information Security Best Practices	17-Information Security Policy, Standards, and Practices, 12-The ISO 27000 Series
d. Information Security Frameworks and Standards	17-Information Security Policy, Standards, and Practices, 12-The ISO 27000 Series
e. Information Security Department Reporting Structures	1-The responsibility for Info Security
f. Planning for Information Security	4-The role of planning
g. Information Security Personnel Issues	8-Identifying People, Procedure, Assets
h. Security Education, Training, and Awareness Programs	5-Credentials for Info Security Professionals, 13-Information Systems Security Certification and Accreditation 20-Security Education
i. Risk Management: Risk Identification and Assessment	8-Risk Management (whole chapter), 9-Risk Management 8-Identifying People, Procedure, Assets
j. Risk Management: Risk Control	9-Identify Possible Controls, 10-Risk Control Strategies
k. Information Security Metrics	4-Metrics
l. Ethics	Pervasive in Chapter 16
VI. Legal, Regulations, Investigations, and Compliance	
a. Definitions and Key Concepts	Pervasive in Chapter 14
b. Laws and the Legal System	14-Law versus Policy, Types of Law, 15-Key Laws for Every IT Security Manager
c. Computer Related Laws and Regulations	14-Privacy of Customer Information, 15-General Computer Crime Laws
d. Incident Response Planning	22-Incident Response Planning
e. Digital Investigations and Forensics	8-Data Destruction, Digital Forensics, and e-Discovery

CISSP DOMAINS AND MAJOR TOPICS	ROADMAP—MAPPINGS
VII. Operations Security	
a. Definitions and Key Concepts	Pervasive in Chapter 1
b. Controlling Access	7-Access Controls, 9-Access Controls
c. Identity and Access Management	7-Identification and Authentication Controls
d. Security Services	N/A
e. Managing Information Security Technical Controls	9-Technical controls
f. Data Backup and Recovery Procedures and Fault Tolerance	23-Planning for Disaster
g. Change, Configuration, and Patch Management	7-Configuration Management Controls, 25-Configuration and Change Management
h. Security Audits	7-Audit and Accountability Controls
VIII. Physical and Environmental Security	
a. Definitions and Key Concepts	33-Physical Security
b. Site and Facility Considerations	6-Does size matter?, 33-Physical Access Controls, 33-Maintenance of Facility Systems
c. Closed-Circuit Television Monitoring and Physical Intrusion Detection Systems	28-Intrusion Detection and Prevention System Basics
d. Guards	33-Physical Security Controls
e. Gates, Doors, and Locks	33-Physical Security Controls
f. Biometrics	32-Evaluating Biometrics, Acceptability of Biometrics
g. Special Requirements for Secure Facilities	33-Physical and Environmental Controls for Computer Rooms
h. Security Considerations for Environmental Controls	33-Physical and Environmental Controls for Computer Rooms
IX. Security Architecture and Design	
a. Definitions and Key Concepts	Pervasive in book
b. Secure Software Design	13-Information systems certification and accreditation
c. Security in the Systems Development Life Cycle	N/A
d. Security of System Types (Mainframe, Mini, Desktop, etc.)	Pervasive in book
e. Security in Computer Architectures	Pervasive in book
f. Common Vulnerabilities and Exploits	3-Attacks, exploits, and vulnerabilities
X. Telecommunications and Network Security	
a. Definitions and Key Concepts	25-Networking Fundamentals
b. Physical Layer Security	25-The Physical Layer
c. Data Link Layer Security	25-Data Link Layer
d. Network Layer Security	25-Network Layer
e. Transport Layer Security	25-Transport Layer
f. Session Layer Security	25-Session Layer
g. Presentation Layer Security	25-Presentation Layer
h. Application Layer Security	25-Application Layer

The SSCP Certification

While the CISSP is considered to be a pinnacle certification in information security, (ISC)[2] and others consider the Systems Security Certified Professional (SSCP) certification an excellent stepping stone to more advanced certifications and security responsibilities. Also offered by the (ISC)[2], the exam test the applicant's knowledge of seven Domains:

- ▶ Access Control
- ▶ Cryptography
- ▶ Malicious Code and Activity
- ▶ Monitoring and Analysis
- ▶ Networks and Communications
- ▶ Risk, Response, and Recovery
- ▶ Security Operations and Administration

"SSCP candidates must meet the following requirements prior to taking the SSCP examination:

- ▶ Subscribe to the (ISC)[2] Code of Ethics.
- ▶ Have at least 1 year of cumulative work experience in one or more of the seven domains in information security.

To remain in good standing with (ISC)[2], you must recertify every 3 years to maintain your SSCP credential. This is primarily accomplished by acquiring 60 continuing professional education (CPE) credits every 3 years, with a minimum of 10 CPEs earned each year after certification. You must also pay an annual maintenance fee. For more information on the CISSP certification, visit www.isc2.org/sscp.[3]

The following table maps the major headings of each SSCP domain to the appropriate sections of this text. If a particular header is not covered in this text, N/A (not available) will be shown. The topics included in this table were developed based on the chapter outlines of the *Official (ISC)[2] Guide to the SSCP CBK.*[4]

SSCP DOMAIN AND MAJOR TOPICS	ROADMAP—MAPPINGS
I. Access Controls	
a. Definitions and Key Concepts	Pervasive in Chapters 9, 32
b. Logical Access Controls	32-Managing access controls
c. Access Control Technologies	Pervasive in Chapters 27, 32, 33
d. Access Control Concepts and Models	32-Managing access controls
e. Access Control Types	32-Types of access controls
f. Operating System Hardening	N/A
g. Access Control Models and Methodologies	32-Managing access controls
II. Cryptography	
a. Definitions and Key Concepts	Pervasive in Chapter 30
b. Encryption Algorithms	30-Cryptographic Algorithms

SSCP DOMAIN AND MAJOR TOPICS	ROADMAP—MAPPINGS
c. Encryption Methods	30-Cipher Methods
d. Message Integrity and Hash Functions	30-Hash Functions
e. Public Key Infrastructure	30-Cryptographic Algorithms
f. Cryptographic Attacks	31-Attacks on Cryptosystems
g. Key Management	30-Using Cryptography
h. Secure Protocols	31-Protocols for Secure Communications
III. Malicious Code and Activity	
a. Definitions and Key Concepts	3-Attacks, exploits, and vulnerabilities
b. Malicious Code Examples	3-Attacks, exploits, and vulnerabilities
c. Network Exploits	3-Attacks, exploits, and vulnerabilities
d. Application Exploits	3-Attacks, exploits, and vulnerabilities
e. Social Engineering	3-Attacks, exploits, and vulnerabilities, 33-Special Considerations for Physical Security Threats
f. Incident Detection Tools and Techniques	22-Incident Detection
g. Antivirus and Anti-malware software	Pervasive in Chapter 2
IV. Monitoring and Analysis	
a. Definitions and Key Concepts	Pervasive in Chapter 26
b. Information Security Auditing	Pervasive in Chapter 17
c. Security Frameworks and Blueprints	12-Whole chapter
d. Security Analysis and Monitoring Controls	29-Whole chapter
e. Security Testing: Vulnerability Assessment and Penetration Testing	29-Whole chapter
f. Auditing Data Sources	N/A
g. Intrusion Detection and Prevention Systems	28-Intrusion Detection and Prevention System Basics
h. Information Security Monitoring Methods and Tools	Pervasive in Chapter 17
i. Anti-Monitoring and Analysis Techniques	N/A
V. Networks and Communications	
a. Definitions and Key Concepts	25-Networking Fundamentals
b. The OSI Reference Model	25-OSI Reference Model and Security
c. TCP/IP Protocols	25-The Internet and TCP/IP
d. Networking Topologies	25-Networking Fundamentals
e. Wide Area Networks	25-Networking Fundamentals
f. Networking Protocols	31-Protocols for Secure Communications
g. Networking and Communications Infrastructure	25-Networking Fundamentals
h. Communications Devices	25-Managing Communication
i. Virtual Private Networks	31-Protocols for Secure Communications
j. Wireless Networking	29-Wireless Security Tools, 31-Securing Wireless Networks with WEP and WPA
k. Network and Communications Attacks	3-Attacks, exploits, and vulnerabilities

(Continued)

SSCP DOMAIN AND MAJOR TOPICS	ROADMAP—MAPPINGS
VI. Risk, Response, and Recovery	
a. Definitions and Key Concepts	9-Risk Management
b. Risk Management	9-Risk Management
c. Disaster Recovery and Business Continuity Planning	24-The Business Continuity Plan
d. Incident Response Planning	22-Incident Response Planning
e. Digital Investigations	8-Data Destruction, Digital Forensics, and e-Discovery
f. Computer Forensics	8-Data Destruction, Digital Forensics, and e-Discovery
VII. Security Operations and Administration	
a. Definitions and Key Concepts	1-Information Security
b. Goals of Information Security	1-Information Security
c. Information Security Policy	17-Information Security Policy, Standards, and Practices, 18
d. Security Best Practices	12-The ISO 27000 Series
e. Security in the Systems Development Life Cycle	12-Other models
f. Secure Software Development	N/A
g. Security Requirements and Certification and Accreditation Standards	5-Certifications, 13-Information Systems Security Certification and Accreditation
h. Risk Assessment	8-Risk Management (whole chapter), 9-Risk Management
i. Personnel Security Practices	8-Security clearance, 19-Personnel and Security
j. Data Classification	8-Data classification model
k. Identity Management	7-Identification and Authentication Controls
l. Change and Configuration Management	7-Configuration Management Controls, 25-Configuration and Change Management
m. Security Education, Training, and Awareness Programs	20-Security Education Training and Awareness
n. Security Management Planning	4-The role of planning

Information Security Certification Guidelines—The CISM

This appendix continues the examination of dominant certification standards, mapping the content to the other preferred industry certification standard ISACA's CISM. The text again will serve as a guide to preparing for this certification.

The Certified Information Security Manager (CISM) is a well-recognized and respected certification for those information security professionals who have experience as a manager. The challenges in obtaining this certification are considerable. This section provides a brief overview of the certification requirements, and then maps the general domains of the CISM common body of knowledge against this book.

NOTE

This book does NOT claim to be a CISM study guide, nor does it claim to cover the material in sufficient breadth or depth of material to guarantee success on the CISM exam. It can, however, provide a good basis for beginning one's study of the material, and with sufficient supplement, assist the reader in obtaining this certification.

The CISM Certification

The Certified Information Security Manager (CISM) is a very well-recognized and respected certification for those information security professionals who have experience as an information security manager. The challenges in obtaining this certification are considerable. This section provides a brief overview of the certification requirements, and then maps the general domains of the CISM common body of knowledge against this book. Offered by ISACA (formerly known as the Information Systems Audit and Control Association), the CISM exam tests the applicant's knowledge of five domains:

- ▶ Information Security Governance (23%)
- ▶ Information Risk Management (22%)
- ▶ Information Security Program Development (17%)
- ▶ Information Security Program Management (24%)
- ▶ Incident Management and Response (14%)

In order to earn the CISM designation, you will be required to:

- ▶ Successfully pass the CISM exam.
- ▶ Adhere to ISACA's Code of Professional Ethics.
- ▶ Agree to comply with the Continuing Education Policy.
- ▶ Demonstrate work experience in the field of information security.
- ▶ Submit an Application for CISM Certification.

The work experience requirement for the exam requires you to submit verified evidence of a minimum of 5 years of information security work experience, with a minimum of 3 years of information security management work experience in three or more of the job practice analysis areas. The work experience must be gained within the 10-year period preceding the application date for certification or within 5 years from the date of originally passing the exam.

The CISM also has a maintenance fee and a minimum of 20 contact hours of CPE annually. In addition, a minimum of 120 contact hours is required during a fixed 3-year period.[5]

The following table maps the major headings of each job practice area to the appropriate sections of this text. If a particular header is not covered in this text, N/A (not available) will be shown. The topics included in this table were developed based on the CISM Exam Job Practice Areas section of the ISACA website.[6]

CISM DOMAIN AND MAJOR TOPICS	ROADMAP—MAPPINGS
I. Information Security Governance (23%)—Establish and maintain a framework to provide assurance that information security strategies are aligned with business objectives and consistent with applicable laws and regulations.	
a. Information Security Concepts	1-Information Security Defined, 17-Definitions
b. Information Security Governance	Pervasive in Chapter 4
c. Information Security Steering Group	4-Strategic planning
d. Information Security Management Roles and Responsibilities	Pervasive in Chapter 5
e. Information Security Strategy Alignment with Business Goals and Objectives	4-Strategic planning

CISM DOMAIN AND MAJOR TOPICS	ROADMAP—MAPPINGS
f. Information Security Strategy Alignment with Corporate Governance	4-Strategic planning
g. Business Cases Development Justifying Investment in Information Security	4-Planning for implementation
h. Legal and Regulatory Requirements Affecting Information Security	Pervasive in Chapters 14 and 15
i. Drivers Affecting the Organization (e.g., Technology, Business Environment, Risk Tolerance, Geographic Location) and Their Impact on Information Security	10-Managing risk
j. Senior Management Commitment to Information Security	4-The role of planning
k. Information Security Roles and Responsibilities	6-The organization
l. Internal and External Reporting and Communication Channels that Support Information Security	6-The organization
m. Information Security in Third-Party Relationships	Pervasive in Chapter 19
n. International Standards for Information Security Management	12-The ISO 27000 series, 13-ISO 27002 guidance on systems certification and accreditation
o. Centralized and Distributed Methods of Coordinating Information Security Activities	4-Strategic planning
p. Methods for Establishing Reporting and Communication Channels Throughout an Organization	4-The roles of planning
II. Information Risk Management (22%)—Identify and manage information security risks to achieve business objectives.	
a. Information Asset Classification and Ownership	8-Creating an inventory of information assets
b. Components of Information Ownership Schema (Including Drivers of the Schema such as Roles and Responsibilities)	32-Types of access control
c. Systematic and Structured Information Risk Assessment Process	9-Approaches to risk assessment
d. Business Impact Assessments	21-Components of contingency planning
e. Threats, Vulnerabilities, and Exposures Evaluations	8-Threat identification, vulnerability assessment
f. Evaluation of Information Security Controls and Countermeasures to Mitigate Risk to Acceptable Levels	9-Percentage of Risk Mitigated by Current controls
g. Integration of Risk, Threat, and Vulnerability Identification, and Management into Life-Cycle Processes	8-Threat identification
h. Information Resource Valuation Methodologies	9-Approaches to risk management
i. Risk Assessment and Analysis Methodologies	8-Approaches to risk assessment
j. Quantitative and Qualitative Risk Assessment Methods	8-Approaches to risk assessment
k. Baseline Modeling	12-Baselining and best business practices
l. Information Security Controls and Countermeasures	32-Management of the Classified Information Asset
m. Risk Mitigation Strategies Used	10-Risk control strategies

(Continued)

CISM DOMAIN AND MAJOR TOPICS	ROADMAP—MAPPINGS
n. Gap Analysis and Generally Accepted Standards of Good Practice for Information Security Management	10-Managing risk
o. Cost-Benefit Analysis Techniques in Assessing Security Options	10-Cost-benefit analysis
III. Information Security Program Development (17%)—Create and maintain a program to implement the information security strategy. This job activity area focuses on the development and implementation of the following:	
a. Information Security Strategy Implementation	Pervasive in Chapter 12
b. Information Security Program Activities	Pervasive in Chapter 12
c. Information Security Program and Other Assurance Functions Alignment	Pervasive in Chapter 12
d. Information Security Program Resources	Pervasive in Chapter 12
e. Information Security Architectures Development	Pervasive in Chapter 12
f. Information Security Awareness, Training and Education Program Development, and Implementation	20-Security Education Training and Awareness (SETA)
g. Information Security Metrics and Performance Measures Development and Implementation	4-Metrics
h. Plans for Implementing Information Security	4-The role of planning
i. Information Security Program Activities	4-Whole Chapter
j. Information Security Program Implementation	4-Whole Chapter
k. Information Security Controls Planning, Designing, Developing, Testing, and Implementing	4-The role of planning
l. Information Security Resource Acquisition	4-Whole Chapter
m. Information Security Architectures	Pervasive in Chapters 5, 6, and 7
n. Security Technologies and Controls	Pervasive in book
o. Information Security Policies, Standards, Procedures, Guidelines, and Other Documentation Development and Implementation	17-Information Security Policy, Standards, and Practices
p. Information Security Requirements Integration into Organizational Processes (e.g., Change Control, Mergers, and Acquisitions)	Pervasive in book
q. Life-Cycle Methodologies and Activities	4-The security life cycle
r. Third-Party and Service Agreement Security Assessment and Control	Pervasive in Chapters 5 and 19
s. Implementation of Information Security Metrics	4-Metrics
t. Compliance Certification and Accreditation	Pervasive in Chapters 13, 14, and 15
u. Information Security Controls Testing and Evaluation	Pervasive in Chapter 29

CISM DOMAIN AND MAJOR TOPICS	ROADMAP—MAPPINGS
IV. Information Security Program Management (24%)— Oversee and direct information security activities to execute the information security program. This job activity area focuses on the **management** of the following:	
a. Internal and External Resources (e.g., Finances, People, Equipment, Systems) Required to Execute the Information Security Program	Pervasive in book
b. Information Security Maintenance in Third-Party and Service Agreements	Pervasive in Chapter 5
c. Information Security as an Integral Part of the Systems Development Process	Pervasive in Chapter 7
d. Information Security Maintenance Throughout the Organization's Processes and Life-Cycle Activities	Pervasive in book
e. Information Security Awareness, Training, and Education Program Management	20-Security Education Training and Awareness (SETA)
f. Information Security Policy Management	17-Information Security Policy, Standards, and Practices, Pervasive in Chapter 18
g. Information Security Controls and Policies Monitoring and Compliance Testing	Pervasive in book
h. Information Security Administrative Processes and Procedures	Pervasive in book
i. Information Security Metrics and Performance Measures	4-Metrics
j. Change and Configuration Management Activities	Pervasive in Chapter 7
k. Internal and External Information Security Reviews and Audits	Pervasive in Chapter 7
l. External Vulnerability Reporting Sources	Pervasive in Chapter 29
m. General Line Management Techniques Including Budgeting, Staff Management, and Facilities	Pervasive in book
V. Incident Management and Response (14%)—Plan, develop, and manage a capability to detect, respond to, and recover from information security incidents.	
a. Incident Detection, Identification, Analysis, and Response Components	22-Incident Response Planning
b. Information Incident Management Practices	22-Incident Response Planning
c. Notification and Escalation Processes for Effective Security Management	22-Incident Response Planning
d. Business Impact Analysis	21-Business Impact Analysis
e. IR, DR, and BC Rules and Responsibilities	23-DR Policy, 24-BC Planning Policy Statement

(Continued)

CISM DOMAIN AND MAJOR TOPICS	ROADMAP—MAPPINGS
f. Recovery Time Objective (RTO) and Recovery Point Objective (RPO)	22-Incident Response Planning
g. Recovery Planning and Business Continuity Planning	24-Continuity Strategies
h. Plans and Processes for Information Security Incidents	22-Incident Response Planning
i. Information Security Incidents Investigation (e.g., Forensics, Evidence Collection and Preservation, Log Analysis, Interviewing)	Pervasive in Chapters 22, 23, 24
j. Information Security Incident Response Plans and Disaster Recovery (Dr) and Business Continuity Plan (BCP) Integration	Pervasive in Chapters 22, 23, 24
k. IR, DR, BC, and Crisis Internal and External Communications	Pervasive in Chapters 22, 23, 24

References

1. http://www.isc2.org/uploadedFiles/Credentials_and_Certifcation/CISSP/CISSP_for%20 Professionals.pdf

2. H. F. Tipton (ed). *Official (ISC)² Guide to the CISSP CBK*, 2nd Edition. Boca Raton, FL: CRC Press, 2010.

3. http://www.isc2.org/uploadedFiles/Credentials_and_Certifcation/SSCP/SSCP_for%20Practitioners .pdf

4. Contesti et al. (eds). *Official (ISC)² Guide to the SSCP CBK*. Boca Raton, FL: CRC Press, 2007.

5. ISACA. *Candidate's Guide to the CISM® Exam and Certification*. WWW Document viewed 5/3/2010 from http://www.isaca.org/AMTemplate.cfm?Section=CISM_Exam_Info&Template=/ ContentManagement/ContentDisplay.cfm&ContentID=54213.

6. ISACA. *Job Practice Areas for the CISM*. WWW Document viewed 5/3/2010 from http://www.isaca.org/ Template.cfm?Section=Job_Practice_Areas1&Template=/ContentManagement/ContentDisplay .cfm&ContentID=49296#TheTop.

Glossary

Access control encompasses four processes: obtaining the identity of the entity requesting access to a logical or physical area (identification), confirming the identity of the entity seeking access to a logical or physical area (authentication), determining which actions that entity can perform in that physical or logical area (authorization), and documenting the activities of the authorized individual and systems (accountability).

Access control list (ACL) is the column of attributes associated with a particular object.

Access control policy determines how access rights are granted to entities and groups and specifies how those access rights are managed in practice.

Accountability exists when a control provides assurance that every activity undertaken can be attributed to a named person or automated process.

Accreditation authorizes an IT system to process, store, or transmit information.

Acquired value refers to the value that an information asset has in the context of the organization that possesses and uses it. It may be higher than the intrinsic value of the asset and its components.

Active vulnerability scanners scan networks for highly detailed information. An *active* scanner is one that initiates traffic on the network in order to determine security holes.

Acts of human error or failure include acts performed without intent or malicious purpose by an authorized user.

Acts of information extortion occur when an attacker or trusted insider steals information from a computer system and demands compensation for its return, or for an agreement not to disclose the information.

Acts of sabotage or vandalism involve the deliberate sabotage of a computer system or business, or acts of vandalism to either destroy an asset or damage the image of an organization.

Acts of theft are the unauthorized taking of another's property.

Acts of trespass and espionage is a well-known and broad category of electronic and human activity that can breach the confidentiality of information.

Administrators operate and administrate the security tools and the security monitoring function and continuously improve the processes, performing all the day-to-day work.

Adware is any software program intended for marketing purposes such as that used to deliver and display advertising banners or popups to the user's screen or tracking the user's online usage or purchasing activity.

After-action review (AAR) entails a detailed examination of the events that occurred from first detection to final recovery.

Aggregate information is created by combining pieces of nonprivate data—often collected during software updates, and via cookies—that when combined may violate privacy.

Agreement on Trade-Related Aspects of Intellectual Property Rights (TRIPS), created by the World Trade Organization (WTO), and negotiated over the years 1986–1994, introduced intellectual property rules into the multilateral trade system.

Air-aspirating detectors are very sophisticated fire-detection systems and are used in high-sensitivity areas. They work by taking in air, filtering it, and moving it through a chamber containing a laser beam. If the laser beam is diverted or refracted by smoke particles, the system is activated.

Alert message is a scripted description of the incident and consists of just enough information so that each responder, SIRT or otherwise, knows what portion of the IR plan to implement without impeding the notification process.

Alert roster is a document containing contact information on the individuals to be notified in the event of an actual incident.

Algorithm is the programmatic steps used to convert an unencrypted message into an encrypted sequence of bits that represent the message; sometimes used as a reference to the programs that enable the cryptographic processes.

Annualized loss expectancy (ALE) is the estimated losses per year based on the current risk and control environments. It is not necessarily an estimate of expected losses but is, rather, a comparative value allowing decisions to be made about the relative risk of various information assets.

Annualized rate of occurrence (ARO) is the probability of a threat occurring and depicted as a table that indicates how frequently an attack from each threat type is likely to occur within a given time frame (for example, once every ten years).

Application header (AH) protocol provides system-to-system authentication and data integrity verification, but does not provide secrecy for the content of a network communication.

Application-level firewalls often consist of dedicated computers kept separate from the first filtering router (called an edge router); they are commonly used in conjunction with a second or internal filtering router.

Asset is the organization's possession or thing of value that the organization wants to (or must) protect.

Asset valuation is the process of assigning financial value or worth to each information asset.

Asymmetric encryption uses two different but related keys, and either key can be used to encrypt or decrypt the message.

Asynchronous tokens use a challenge-response system in which the server challenges the user with a number.

Attack means an act that takes advantage of a *vulnerability* to damage, steal, disclose, render unusable or available, or modify without the authorization of an asset.

Attack profile is a detailed description of the activities that occur during an attack.

Attack protocol is a series of steps or processes used by an attacker, in a logical sequence, to plan and launch an attack against a target system or network.

Attack scenario end case describes multiple outcomes of how a situation may exist if and when an attack is made against an information asset. This may be done as worst-case, best-case, or likely-case constraints and is useful when developing plans for recovery and resumption.

Attack success scenario describes how a situation may exist if and when an attack is successfully made against an information asset. This may be done as worst-case, best-case, or likely-case constraints and is useful when developing plans for recovery and resumption.

Authentication occurs when a control provides proof that a user possesses the *identification* that he or she claims.

Authenticity verifies the information must be real. What if a regulatory agency received two differing sets of financial records for a company? Authenticity would assure them which set was the real set of records.

Authorization is a process that ensures that the user (person or a computer) has been specifically and explicitly authorized by the proper authority to perform an action.

Authorization ticket is authorization across multiple systems, in which a central authentication and authorization system verifies entity identity and grants a set of credentials to the verified entity.

Availability is the characteristic of information that enables user access to information without interference or obstruction and in a useable format.

Availability disruption is any circumstance that causes systems to be unavailable for the intended use by the users of the system.

Avoidance is the risk management strategy that directs the organization to avoid those business activities that introduce uncontrollable risks.

Back door is a virus or worm that can have a payload that installs a back door or trapdoor component in a system, which allows the attacker to access the system at will with special privileges.

Bastion host represents a single, rich target for external attacks, and should be very thoroughly secured.

Behavioral feasibility, see "operational feasibility."

Behavior-based IDPS, see "statistical anomaly-based IDPS."

Benefit is the value to the organization of using controls to prevent losses associated with a specific vulnerability.

Biometric means having to do with using the measurement of human biological characteristics as part of an authentication process.

Blackout is a complete loss of power for an extended period of time.

Bot (an abbreviation of robot) is an automated software program that executes certain commands when it receives a specific input.

Bottom-up approach describes a planning process that starts from the lower levels of the organization with users or first-line supervisors.

Brownout is a prolonged period of time when voltage levels are lower than usual.

Brute force attack is an attempt to try every possible combination of options for a password.

Builders are the real techies, who create and install security solutions.

Business continuity planning (BCP) ensures that critical business functions can continue if a disaster occurs.

Business impact analysis (BIA), the first phase in the CP process, provides the CP team with information about systems and the threats they face.

Business resumption plan (BR plan) is a plan that combines the DR (disaster recovery) and BC (business continuity) plans.

Cache servers (or a caching proxy) are network devices that include storage units that keep current copies of frequently accessed Web-based content in order to reduce the quantity of data transmitted over wide-area network links.

Capabilities table is the row of attributes associated with a particular subject.

Certificate authority (CA) issues, manages, authenticates, signs, and revokes users' digital certificates, which typically contain the user's name, public key, and other identifying information.

Certificate directories are central locations for certificate storage that provide a single access point for administration and distribution.

Certificate revocation list (CRL) is a list of certificates issued by a specific key server that are no longer valid and have been revoked.

Certification (system) is defined as the comprehensive evaluation of the technical and non-technical security controls of an IT system to support the accreditation process that establishes the extent to which a particular design and implementation meets a set of specified security requirements.

Champion is a term used to describe a member of the management team that has sufficient stature to marshal resources and heighten visibility for critical projects.

Change management is the administration of changes in the strategy, operation, or components of the information security program.

Chief information security officer (CISO or CSO) is typically the top information security officer in the organization (or, if physical security, executive protection, loss prevention, etc., are also included as duties, the title of chief security officer or CSO is common).

CIA triplet is the three characteristics of information that give it value: *confidentiality*, *integrity*, and *availability*. Noted author Don B. Parker adds three additional attributes: *utility*, *authenticity*, and *possession*.

Cipher or cryptosystem is an encryption method or process encompassing the algorithm, key(s) or cryptovariable(s), and procedures used to perform encryption and decryption.

Ciphertext is an unintelligible encrypted or encoded message resulting from encryption.

Civil law represents a wide variety of laws that govern a nation or state and deal with the relationships and conflicts between organizational entities and people.

Class A fires are fires that involve ordinary combustible fuels such as wood, paper, textiles, rubber, cloth, and trash.

Class B fires are fires fueled by combustible liquids or gases, such as solvents, gasoline, paint, lacquer, and oil.

Class C fires are fires with energized electrical equipment or appliances.

Class D fires are fires fueled by combustible metals, such as magnesium, lithium, and sodium.

Class K fires are fires fueled by cooking oils or fat.

Clean agent does not leave any residue after use, nor does it interfere with the operation of electrical or electronic equipment.

Cleartext, see "plaintext."

Clipping level is the level of IDPS traffic that triggers a specific set of actions.

Closed-circuit television (CCT) is a system of cameras, recording devices, and displays that allows motion picture images to be managed for surveillance or distribution of programming.

Code, or encode is the process of converting components (words or phrases) of an unencrypted message into encrypted components.

Cold site provides only rudimentary services and facilities.

Communities of interest are the three distinct groups of decision makers in the process of securing information assets of an organization: information security managers and professionals, information technology managers and professionals, and nontechnical general business managers and professionals.

Competitive intelligence is a legal technique that threat-agents use to access information assets.

Computer Fraud and Abuse Act of 1986 (CFA Act) is the cornerstone of many computer-related federal laws and enforcement efforts. It was amended in October 1996 by the National Information Infrastructure Protection Act of 1996, which modified several sections of the previous act and increased the penalties for selected crimes.

Computer Security Act of 1987 was one of the first attempts to protect federal computer systems by establishing minimum acceptable security practices.

Computer virus is segments of code that perform malicious actions.

Confidentiality ensures that only those with authorization and a business-relevant need are allowed access to the *assets*.

Configuration management is the administration of the configuration of information security program components.

Contact and weight sensors work when two contacts are connected as, for example, when a foot steps on a pressure-sensitive pad under a rug, or a window being opened triggers a pin and spring sensor.

Contingency planning (CP) is the overall process of preparing for unexpected events.

Contingency planning management team (CPMT) is the combined group of staff and consultants responsible for designing, planning, creating, and operating the contingency planning process.

Contract employees are typically hired to perform specific services for the organization.

Control, see "countermeasure."

Correlation attacks are a collection of brute force methods that attempt to deduce statistical relationships between the structure of the unknown key and the ciphertext that is the output of the cryptosystem.

Countermeasures are the methods that are imposed to mitigate (or reduce the effect of) *vulnerabilities*.

Criminal law addresses violations harmful to society and is actively enforced by the state.

Crisis management is the action steps that affect the people both inside and outside the organization that are taken during and after a disaster.

Crossover error rate (CER), also called the equal error rate, is the point at which the rate of false rejections equals the rate of false acceptances.

Cryptogram, see "ciphertext."

Cryptography, which comes from the Greek words *kryptos*, meaning "hidden," and *graphein*, meaning "to write," is the process of making and using ciphers.

Cryptology is the science of encryption.

Cryptosystem, see "cipher."

Cryptovariable, see "key."

Cultural mores are moral attitudes or customs of a particular group.

Database right is the United Kingdom's version of Directive 95/46/EC.

Database security encompasses the specific concerns arising from the storage of large amounts of information in a database store.

Database shadowing combines electronic vaulting with remote journaling, by writing multiple copies of the database simultaneously in two separate locations.

Decipher is to decrypt or convert ciphertext into the equivalent plaintext.

Decryption is the process of converting the ciphertext into a message that conveys readily understood meaning.

De facto standards are standards that may be informal or part of an organizational culture.

Defense in depth is a strategy of having multiple, independent layers of controls that provide redundant layers of protection for critical information assets.

Definers provide the policies, guidelines, and standards.

De jure standards are standards that may be published, scrutinized, and ratified by a group.

Deluge system is when all of the individual sprinkler heads in a sprinkler system are kept open, and as soon as the system is activated, water is immediately applied to all areas.

Demilitarized Zone (DMZ) is an intermediate area between a trusted network and an untrusted network.

Denial-of-service (DoS) occurs when the attacker sends a large number of connection or information requests to a target that will either crash or overload the system and cannot respond to legitimate requests for service.

Desk check is the simplest kind of validation during test contingency planning where copies of the plan are distributed to all individuals who will be assigned roles during an actual incident and they review the plan and create a list of correct and incorrect components.

Deterrence is the best method for preventing an illegal or unethical activity.

Deviations in services can disrupt an organization's information system since it requires the successful functioning of many interdependent support systems, including power grids, telecom networks, parts suppliers, service vendors, and even the janitorial staff and garbage haulers.

Dictionary attack is a variation of the brute force attack that narrows the field selecting specific target accounts and using a list of commonly used passwords (the dictionary) instead of random combinations.

Digital certificates are public key container files that allow computer programs to validate the key and identify to whom it belongs.

Digital Millennium Copyright Act (DMCA) is the American contribution to an international effort by the World Intellectual Properties Organization (WIPO) to reduce the impact of copyright, trademark, and privacy infringement, especially when accomplished via the removal of technological copyright protection measures.

Digital signatures enable messages that can be mathematically proven to be authentic.

Directive 95/46/EC added protection for individuals with regard to the processing of personal data and the use and movement of such data.

Disaster recovery planning (DRP) entails the preparation for and recovery from a disaster, whether natural or human-made.

Distinguished name (DN) uniquely identifies a certificate entity to a user's public key.

Distributed denial-of-service (DDoS) attack is an attack in which a coordinated stream of requests is launched against a target from many locations at the same time.

Dry-pipe system is designed to work in areas where electrical equipment is used. Instead of containing water, the system contains pressurized air. The air holds valves closed, keeping the water away from the target areas.

Due care is the existence of a program to assure due diligence.

Due diligence requires that an organization make a valid effort to protect others and continually maintain this level of effort.

Dumb card, a category that includes ID and ATM cards with magnetic strips containing the digital (and often encrypted) PIN against which user input is compared.

Dumpster diving is the act of looking in discarded materials for information or objects of use that can assist in an attack using social engineering or acquired knowledge.

Dust contamination is a *force of nature* of excessive presence of foreign material on hardware preventing normal operation or impeding function.

Dynamic packet filtering firewall allows only a particular packet with a specific source, destination, and port address to pass through the firewall.

Earthquake is a *force of nature* that causes foundational stress that either weakens the structure within which the information assets and systems or destroys it. Volcanic activity is also included in this category.

Economic Espionage Act (EEA) attempts to prevent trade secrets from being illegally shared.

Electronic Communications Privacy Act of 1986 is a collection of statutes that regulate the interception of wire, electronic, and oral communications.

Electronic vaulting is the bulk batch-transfer of data to an off-site facility.

Electrostatic discharge (ESD) is a *force of nature* of a mild static shock we receive when walking across a carpet and can be costly or dangerous when it damages costly electronic components. Static electricity can draw dust into clean-room environments or cause products to stick together.

Elite hacker, see "expert hacker."

Encapsulating security payload (ESP) protocol provides secrecy for the contents of network communications as well as system-to-system authentication and data integrity verification.

Encipher is to encrypt or convert plaintext into the equivalent ciphertext.

Encroachment of Intellectual Property, see "theft."

Encryption is the process of converting an original message into a form that is unreadable to unauthorized individuals—that is, to anyone without the tools to convert the encrypted message back to its original format.

Enterprise information security policy, see "information security policy."

Ethics define socially acceptable behaviors.

European Council Cyber-Crime Convention provides for the creation of an international task force to oversee a range of security functions associated with Internet activities for standardized technology laws across international borders.

Event-driven is a response to some event in the business community, inside the organization, or within the ranks of employees, customers, or other stakeholders.

Exclusive OR operation (XOR) is a function of Boolean algebra in which two bits are compared, and if the two bits are identical, the result is a binary 0.

Exit interview is used to remind the employee of contractual obligations, such as nondisclosure agreements, and to obtain feedback on the employee's tenure in the organization.

Expert hacker is a person who develops software scripts and program exploits for personal use or sale to criminal organizations.

False accept rate is the rate at which fraudulent users or nonusers are allowed access to systems or areas, as a result of a failure in the biometric device.

False reject rate is the rate at which authentic users are denied or prevented access to authorized areas, as a result of a failure in the biometric device.

Fault is a brief interruption in power quality, either voltage or noise.

Federal Privacy Act of 1974 regulates government agencies and holds them accountable if they release private information about individuals or businesses without permission.

File hashing ensures information *integrity*. It is a special algorithm that evaluates the bits in a file and then computes a single representative number called a *hash value*; that is, essentially converting a variable length input into a fixed-length output, typically ranging from 56 to 256 bits.

Financial Services Modernization Act or Gramm-Leach-Bliley Act of 1999 contains a number of provisions focusing on facilitating affiliation among banks, securities firms, and insurance companies.

Fingerprinting is a systematic survey of all of the target organization's Internet addresses (which were collected during the footprinting phase); the survey is conducted to identify the network services offered by the hosts in that range.

Fire is a *force of nature* that damages a building and/or computing equipment that comprises all or part of the information assets, as well as smoke damage and/or water damage from sprinkler systems or firefighters.

Fixed temperature is where the sensor detects when the ambient temperature in an area reaches a predetermined level, usually between 135 degrees Fahrenheit and 165 degrees Fahrenheit, or 57 degrees Centigrade to 74 degrees Centigrade.

Flame detector is a sensor that detects the infrared or ultraviolet light produced by an open flame.

Flame point is the temperature of ignition.

Flood is a *force of nature* where the overflow of water causes direct damage to all or part of the information system, or to the building that houses all or part of the information assets.

Footprint is the geographic area within which there is sufficient signal strength to make a network connection.

Footprinting is the organized research of the Internet addresses owned or controlled by a target organization.

Forces of nature also known as *force majeure*, or acts of God, can present some of the most dangerous threats because they usually occur with little warning and are beyond the control of people.

Fourth Amendment of the U.S. Constitution protects individuals from unlawful search and seizure.

Fraud and Related Activity in Connection with Identification Documents, Authentication Features, and Information (Title 18, U.S.C. § 1028), which criminalizes creation, reproduction, transfer, possession, or use of unauthorized or false identification documents or document-making equipment.

Freedom of Information Act allows any person to request access to federal agency records or information not determined to be a matter of national security.

Full-interruption in the testing of contingency planning is where the individuals follow each and every procedure, including the interruption of service, restoration of data from backups, and notification of appropriate individuals.

General business community is focused on achieving the organization's objectives (making a profit, remaining competitive, in other words, "running the business"). In the final analysis, it is this community that largely controls the information security program through its setting of overall policy goals and control of the budget.

Georgia Computer Systems Protection Act seeks to protect information, and establishes penalties for the use of information technology to attack or exploit information systems.

Gramm-Leach-Bliley Act of 1999, see "Financial Services Modernization Act."

Grounding ensures that the returning flow of current is properly discharged to the ground.

Hackers are "people who use and create computer software [to] gain access to information illegally."

Hardware failures or errors are faults that occur when a manufacturer distributes equipment containing a known or unknown flaw.

Hash algorithms are publicly known functions that create a hash value, also known as a message digest, by converting variable-length messages into a single fixed-length value.

Hash functions are mathematical algorithms that generate a message summary or digest (sometimes called a fingerprint) to confirm the identity of a specific message and to confirm that there have not been any changes to the content.

Hash value is the value resulting from a hashing calculation and will be different for each combination of bits.

Health Insurance Portability and Accountability Act Of 1996 (HIPAA), also known as the **Kennedy-Kassebaum Act**, protects the confidentiality and security of health care data by establishing and enforcing standards and by standardizing electronic data interchange.

HIDS is an acronym for host intrusion detection system. These are devices installed on a computer system that monitor the status of files stored on that system to protect them from *attacks*. This technology is sometimes referred to as a host intrusion and prevention system (HIDPS).

Hoaxes with an attached virus are a more devious attack on computer systems since the transmission of a virus hoax also adds a social engineering aspect to the attack to get the victim to act along *with a real virus attached*.

Honey net is a collection of honey pots that connects several honey pot systems on a subnet.

Honey pots are decoy systems designed to lure potential attackers away from critical systems.

Host-based IDPS (HIDPS) resides on a particular computer or server, known as the host, and monitors activity only on that system.

Hot site is a fully configured computer facility, with all services, communications links, and physical plant operations.

Humidity is the amount of moisture in the air.

Hurricane or typhoon is a *force of nature* that is a severe tropical storm usually involving heavy rains and hurricane gale forces that will cause damage to the building, disrupt electrical services, or completely destroy an organization's physical complex.

Identification means that an information system is able to recognize individual users.

Incident occurs when an attack (natural or human-made) affects information resources and/or assets, causing actual damage or other disruptions.

Incident candidate is a possible incident.

Incident classification is the process of examining a possible incident and determining whether it constitutes an actual incident.

Incident damage assessment is the immediate determination of the scope of the breach of confidentiality, integrity, and availability of information and information assets.

Incident response (IR) is a set of procedures that commence when an incident is detected.

Incident response plan (IR plan) comprises a detailed set of processes and procedures that anticipate, detect, and mitigate the effects of an unexpected event that might compromise information resources and assets.

Incident response planning (IRP) is a plan preparing for an event.

Industrial espionage is when threat-agents employ techniques that cross the threshold of the legal or ethical boundary.

Information security community guides the protection of the organization's information assets from the many threats they face.

Information security policy provides rules for the protection of the information assets of the organization.

Information Systems Security Association (ISSA) (*www.issa.org*) is a nonprofit society of information security professionals and its primary mission is to bring together qualified practitioners of information security for information exchange and educational development.

Information technology community supports the business objectives of the organization by supplying and supporting information technology appropriate to the business' needs.

Information warfare (IW) involves the use of information technology by a sovereign state to conduct organized and lawful military operations.

Integrity is the quality or state of being whole, complete, and uncorrupted.

Internet Protocol Security (IPSec) is an open source protocol to secure communications across any IP-based network such as LANs, WANs, and the Internet.

Intrinsic value is the essential worth.

Intrusion occurs when an attacker achieves access to an information asset in violation of security policy.

Intrusion detection/prevention system (IDPS) is a system that acts as a burglar alarm for information systems that may also be able to take certain corrective action to limit damages in the event of an intrusion.

Intrusion detection system (IDS) work like a burglar alarm in that it detects a violation (some system activity analogous to an opened or broken window) and activates an alarm. This alarm can be audible and/or visual (producing noise and lights, respectively), or it can be silent (an e-mail message or pager alert).

Intrusion prevention system (IPS) can detect an intrusion and also prevent that intrusion from *successfully* attacking the organization by means of an active response.

Ionization sensor is a smoke detector that measures the level of ionization present in the particles of smoke.

Issue-specific security policy, or **ISSP**, (1) addresses specific areas of technology, (2) requires frequent updates, and (3) contains a statement on the organization's position on a specific issue.

Job rotation or task rotation is the requirement that every employee be able to perform the work of another employee.

Jurisdiction is the court's right to hear a case if the wrong was committed in its territory or involving its citizenry.

Kennedy-Kassebaum Act, see "Health Insurance Portability and Accountability Act of 1996 (HIPAA)"

Key or **cryptovariable** is the information used in conjunction with an algorithm to create the ciphertext from the plaintext or derive the plaintext from the ciphertext; the key can be a series of bits used by a computer program, or it can be a passphrase used by humans that is then converted into a series of bits for use in the computer program.

Keyspace is the entire range of values that can possibly be used to construct an individual key.

Knowledge-based IDPS, see "signature-base IDPS."

Known-plaintext attack is when an attacker may obtain duplicate texts, one in ciphertext and one in plaintext, which enable the individual to reverse-engineer the encryption algorithm.

Landslide or mudslide is a *force of nature* that can directly damage all or part of the information system or, more likely, the building that houses it.

Lattice-based access control is when users are assigned a matrix of authorizations for particular areas of access.

Laws are rules that mandate or prohibit certain behavior in society; they are drawn from ethics.

Least privilege is a control measure that provides employees with the minimal amount of information for the minimal amount of time necessary for them to perform their duties.

Liability is the legal obligation of an entity that extends beyond criminal or contract law; it includes the legal obligation to make restitution.

Lightning is a *force of nature* of an abrupt, discontinuous natural electric discharge in the atmosphere. Lightning usually damages all or part of the information system and/or its power distribution components. It can also cause fires or other damage.

Line-interactive UPS is when the internal components of the standby models are replaced with a pair of inverters and converters.

Long arm jurisdiction is the long arm of the law reaching across the country or around the world to pull an accused individual into its court systems.

Mail bomb is a DoS attack in which large quantities of e-mail are routed to the targeted system through either social engineering or by exploiting various technical flaws in the Simple Mail Transport Protocol (SMTP).

Malicious code is an attack program that exploits multiple vulnerabilities in commonly used software.

Malware, see "malicious code."

Managerial controls cover security processes that are designed by the strategic planners and performed by security administration of the organization.

Managerial guidance SysSP is created by management to guide the implementation and configuration of technology as well as to address the behavior of people in the organization in ways that support the security of information.

Man-in-the-middle (MITM) is a form of attack that allows an intruder to become an intermediary in the communications between two parties.

Manual fire detection systems include human responses, such as calling the fire department, as well as manually activated alarms, such as sprinklers and gaseous systems.

Message authentication code (MAC) is a key-dependent and one-way hash function that may be attached to a message to allow only recipients to validate the content of the message as being authentic and having integrity.

Message digest is a *fingerprint* of the author's message that is to be compared with the receiver's locally calculated hash of the same message.

Methodology is an approach to solving complex problems that is well documented and assures repeatability of results.

Minutiae are unique points of reference that are digitized and stored.

Mission statement explicitly declares the business of the organization and its intended areas of operations. It is, in a sense, the organization's identity card.

Misuse-detection IDPS, see "signature-based IDPS."

Monoalphabetic substitution is cipher substitution using only one alphabet.

Motion detectors detect movement within a confined space and are either active or passive. Some motion sensors emit energy beams, usually in the form of infrared or laser light, ultrasonic sound or sound waves, or some form of electromagnetic radiation.

Mutual agreement is a contract between two organizations in which each party agrees to assist the other in the event of a disaster.

Need-to-know is a principle of security that requires the recipient of classified data to not only have the proper clearance but also have a work-related need to access the specific data.

Network-address translation (NAT) is a method of converting multiple real, valid, external IP addresses to special ranges of internal IP addresses.

Network-based IDPS (NIDPS) resides on a computer or appliance connected to a segment of an organization's network and monitors network traffic on that network segment, looking for indications of ongoing or successful attacks.

Network security addresses the protection of an organization's data networking devices, connections, and contents, and the ability to use that network to accomplish the organization's data communication functions.

NIDS is the acronym for network intrusion detection system. It is a collection of devices that work together to monitor and assess network activity for possible *attacks*.

Offline UPS, see "standby."

Operational feasibility refers to user acceptance and support, management acceptance and support, and the system's compatibility with the requirements of the organization's stakeholders.

Operations security focuses on securing the organization's ability to carry out its operational activities without interruption or compromise.

Packet filtering firewalls are simple networking devices that filter packets by examining every incoming and, in some cases, outgoing packet header.

Packet monkeys, see "script kiddies."

Packet sniffer is a device or software program that enables monitoring of all traffic that passes by that network location.

Padded cell is a honey pot that has been protected so that it cannot be easily compromised—in other words, a hardened honey pot.

Parallel testing during test contingency planning is where individuals act as if an actual incident occurred, and begin performing their required tasks and executing the necessary procedures, without interfering with the normal operations of the business.

Passive vulnerability scanner is one that listens in on the network and determines vulnerable versions of both server and client software.

Passphrase is a plain-language phrase, typically longer than a password, from which a virtual password is derived.

Password is a private word or combination of characters that only the user should know.

Password attacks are those attacks that exploit weaknesses in authentication practices that rely on passwords for authentication.

Password cracking is an attempt to reverse-calculate a password.

Permutation cipher, see "transposition cipher."

Pharming is an attack for implementing an MITM attack where the host's file on the client system is modified to resolve the target address to the address of the hostile intermediary.

Phishing are hybrids that combine both social engineering and malicious software.

Photoelectric sensors project and detect an infrared beam across an area.

Physical security encompasses strategies to protect people, physical assets, and the workplace from various threats including fire, unauthorized access, or natural disasters.

Plaintext The original unencrypted message that is encrypted; also the name given to the results of a message that has been successfully decrypted.

Plan-driven is the result of a carefully developed planning strategy.

Policies are a body of expectations that describe acceptable and unacceptable employee behaviors in the workplace.

Policy administrator is the policy champion and manager.

Political feasibility analysis considers what can and cannot occur based on the consensus and relationships among the communities of interest.

Polyalphabetic substitutions are more advanced substitution ciphers using two or more alphabets.

Polymorphism is a threat that over time changes the way it appears to antivirus software programs, making it undetectable by techniques that look for preconfigured signatures.

Port scanners are tools used by both attackers and defenders to identify (or fingerprint) the computers that are active on a network, as well as the ports and services active on those computers, the functions and roles the machines are fulfilling, and other useful information.

Possession means control over the data or *asset*.

Post mortem, see "after-action review."

Pre-action system in a sprinkler system has a two-phase response to a fire. The system is normally maintained with nothing in the delivery pipes. When a fire has been detected, the first phase is initiated, and valves allow water to enter the system. The pre-action system does not deliver water into the protected space until the individual sprinkler heads are triggered, at which time water flows only into the area of the activated sprinkler head.

Pre-shared key is a secret value that has been shared by two or more users or devices to access a secured communication channel. It requires out-of-band communication of the key value.

Pretexting is the use of a false premise to gain the confidence of a subject in an investigation. It is a critical element of social engineering.

Pretty Good Privacy (PGP) was developed by Phil Zimmermann and uses the IDEA Cipher for message encoding.

Privacy means that when data is collected, used, and stored by an organization, it can only be used for the purposes stated by the data owner at the time it was collected. It governs what the organization can or cannot do with the information given.

Privacy Enhanced Mail (PEM) was proposed by the Internet Engineering Task Force (IETF) as a standard to function with the public key cryptosystems. PEM uses 3DES symmetric key encryption and RSA for key exchanges and digital signatures.

Privacy of Customer Information Section of the common carrier regulation states that any proprietary information shall be used explicitly for providing services, and not for any marketing purposes, and that carriers cannot disclose this information except when necessary to provide their services.

Private key encryption, see "symmetric encryption."

Private law regulates the relationship between the individual and the organization, and encompasses family law, commercial law, and labor law.

Project manager leads the project, putting in place a sound project planning process, guiding the development of a complete and useful project, and prudently managing resources.

Proxy server, named so, because it serves as a proxy for external service requests to internal services.

Public key encryption, see "asymmetric encryption."

Public Key Infrastructure (PKI) is an integrated system of software, encryption methodologies, protocols, legal agreements, and third-party services that enables users to communicate securely.

Public law regulates the structure and administration of government agencies and their relationships with citizens, employees, and other governments.

Operational controls deal with the operational functionality of security in the organization.

Rainbow cracking is when an attacker can gain access to a file of hashed passwords and use a combination of brute force and dictionary attacks to reveal user passwords by applying computer processing time.

Rapid-onset disasters occur suddenly, with little warning, possibly taking the lives of people and destroying the means of production. Rapid-onset disasters may be caused by earthquakes, floods, storm winds, tornadoes, mud flows, or even an especially virulent worm that affects a majority of the organization's systems before it can be contained.

Rate-of-rise is where the sensor detects an unusually rapid increase in the area temperature within a relatively short period of time.

Recovery point objective (RPO) is the point in the past to which the recovered applications and data at the alternate infrastructure will be restored.

Recovery time objective (RTO) is the amount of time that passes before an infrastructure is available once the need for BC is declared.

Registration authority (RA), which operates under the trusted collaboration of the certificate authority and can be delegated to day-to-day certification functions, such as verifying registration information about new registrants, generating end-user keys, revoking certificates, and validating that users possess a valid certificate.

Remote Authentication Dial-In User Service (RADIUS) system centralizes the management of user authentication by placing the responsibility for authenticating each user in the central RADIUS server.

Remote journaling involves online activities on a systems level, much like server fault tolerance, where data is written to two locations simultaneously.

Replay attack is an attempt to resubmit a recording of the deciphered authentication to gain entry into a secure source.

Residual risk is a combined function of (1) a threat less the effect of threat-reducing safeguards; (2) a vulnerability less the effect of vulnerability-reducing safeguards; and (3) an asset less the effect of asset value-reducing safeguards.

Restitution is to compensate for wrongs committed by an organization or its employees.

Risk is the probability of an unwanted or undesirable event occurring, commonly used as an expression of potential loss.

Risk appetite (also known as risk tolerance) describes the quantity and nature of risk that organizations are willing to accept, as they evaluate the trade-offs between the limits of perfect security (e.g., sealed in a concrete shell and sunk to the bottom of the Marianas Trench) and unlimited accessibility.

Risk tolerance, see "risk appetite."

Risk transfer attempts to shift the risk elsewhere (usually outside the organization).

Role-based access controls are nondiscretionary controls determined by a central authority in the organization and can be based on roles.

Rolling mobile site is an approach to business continuity that makes use of a mobile office space that can be delivered to the user's premises in the event the primary space is unusable.

Rootkits take their name from their historical development as malicious replacements for common UNIX administrative tools (thus, their name as "rootkits" since the default administrative user on a UNIX system is root).

RSA algorithm was the first public key encryption algorithm developed (in 1977) and published for commercial use.

Sacrificial host, see "bastion host."

Safeguard, see "control."

Sag is when voltage levels are momentarily low.

Saponification is the reaction of a metallic alkali or base with a fat or oil to form soap.

Script kiddies are hackers of limited skill who use expertly written software to attack a system who "ape" experts in using automated exploits to engage in distributed denial-of-service attacks.

Secret key is a key value that is not shared with any other than those who need to use it to decode encrypted information. The same key is used to encrypt and decrypt the message.

Secure Electronic Transactions (SET) was developed by MasterCard and VISA in 1997 to provide protection from electronic payment fraud. SET uses DES to encrypt credit card information transfers and RSA for key exchange.

Secure facility is a physical location that has in place controls to minimize the risk of attacks from physical threats.

Secure Hash Standard (SHS) is a standard issued by the National Institute of Standards and Technology (NIST).

Secure Multipurpose Internet Mail Extensions (S/MIME) builds on the encoding format of the Multipurpose Internet Mail Extensions (MIME) protocol by adding encryption and authentication through the use of digital signatures based on public key cryptosystems.

Secure Socket Layer (SSL) uses public key encryption to secure a channel over the public Internet, thus enabling secure communications.

Security and Freedom through Encryption Act of 1999 provides guidance on the use of encryption, and provides measures of protection from government intervention.

Security blueprint is a plan for implementing information security improvements.

Security education, training, and awareness (SETA) program is the responsibility of the CISO and is designed to reduce the incidence of accidental security breaches by members of the organization, including employees, contractors, consultants, vendors, and business partners who come into contact with its information assets.

Security framework is an outline of the overall information security strategy for the organization and a roadmap for planned changes to the information security environment of the organization.

Security incident response team (SIRT) is the group of people who react to security incidents to evaluate them and take the appropriate responses.

Security managers are accountable for the day-to-day operation of all or part of the information security program.

Security policy is the enabling guidance from management that identifies the security mission of the organization and empowers them to act on the behalf of management to protect information assets.

Security technicians are the technically qualified individuals tasked to configure firewalls, deploy IDSs, implement security software, diagnose and troubleshoot problems, and coordinate with systems and network administrators to ensure that an organization's security technology is properly implemented.

Selected-plaintext attack is sending potential victims a specific text that they are sure the victims will forward on to others.

Self-insurance is the control approach that attempts to reduce, by means of contingency planning and preparation, the damage caused by the exploitation of vulnerability, or the approach to acknowledge that some risk may not be controllable and the loss from them will be absorbed should they occur.

Self-protection attempts to prevent the exploitation of the vulnerability.

Separation of duties is used to reduce the chance of an individual violating information security and breaching the confidentiality, integrity, or availability of information.

Service bureau is a service agency that provides a service for a fee.

Service Level Agreement (SLA) is a contract provision between a service provider and the client that defines what is to be done, and how quickly it must be done.

Signatures are preconfigured, predetermined attack patterns.

Signature-based IDPS (sometimes called a knowledge-based IDPS, or a misuse-detection IDPS) examines network traffic in search of patterns that match known signatures.

Simulation during test contingency planning is where each person works individually, rather than in a group setting, to simulate the performance of each task.

Single loss expectancy (SLE) is a function used to estimate or calculate a value associated with the most likely loss from a single attack.

Single sign-on (SSO) is a technique used to reduce the number of user credentials each system user is required to use to the minimum possible—one of possible.

Slow-onset disasters occur over time and slowly degrade the capacity of an organization to withstand their effects. Hazards causing these disaster conditions typically include droughts, famines, environmental degradation, desertification, deforestation, and pest infestation.

Smart card contains a computer chip that can verify and validate other information in addition to PINs.

Smoke detection systems are perhaps the most common means of detecting a potentially dangerous fire, and they are required by building codes in most residential dwellings and commercial buildings.

Sniffer is a program or device that monitors data traveling over a network.

Social engineering is a process that convinces systems insiders that an attacker is a legitimate and authorized entity.

Software failures or errors are often threats since large quantities of computer code are written, debugged, published, and sold before all their bugs are detected and resolved. Sometimes, combinations of certain software and hardware reveal new bugs.

Software threats are those that deal with the computer programs that are developed intentionally for the purpose of damaging, destroying, or denying service to your company's systems and/or information assets and are called malicious code or malicious software, or sometimes malware.

Spam is the receipt of unsolicited commercial e-mail.

Spike is when voltage levels experience a momentary increase.

Spoofing is a class of attacks used to gain unauthorized access to computers by pretending to be another person or computer.

Sprinkler systems are designed to apply liquid, usually water, to all areas in which a fire has been detected.

Spyware is any technology that aids in gathering information about a person or organization without their knowledge.

Standards are detailed statements of what must be done to comply with policy.

Standby or offline UPS is an offline battery backup that detects the interruption of power to the power equipment.

State tables track the state and context of each exchanged packet by recording which station sent which packet and when.

Stateful inspection firewalls keep track of each network connection established between internal and external systems using a state table.

Static electricity is a discharge of excess electricity from lack of humidification.

Statistical anomaly-based IDPS (stat IDPS) or behavior-based IDPS collects statistical summaries by observing traffic that is known to be normal.

Storage security deals with the specialized techniques for securing information stored in storage area networks (or SANs).

Strategic planning lays out the long-term business direction to be taken by the organization.

Strategy, see "strategic planning."

Strong authentication (or multifactor authentication) uses at minimum two different authentication mechanisms.

Structured review or *reality check* takes place at the end of each phase of system projects, during which the team and its management-level reviewers decide whether the project should be continued, discontinued, outsourced, or postponed until additional expertise or organizational knowledge is acquired.

Structured walk-through is where all involved individuals walk through the steps they would take during an actual event in test contingency planning.

Substitution cipher is substituting one value for another.

Sunset clause is a policy's expiration date.

Supplicant is an unauthenticated user who has proposed an identity in an access control transaction.

Surge is when voltage levels experience a prolonged increase.

Symmetric encryption methods use mathematical operations that can be programmed into extremely fast computing algorithms so that the encryption and decryption processes are done quickly by even small computers.

Synchronous tokens are synchronized with a server and each device (server and token) uses the time to generate the authentication number that is entered during the user login.

System integrity verifiers, see "host-based IDPS."

Systems development life cycle (SDLC) is a methodology for the design and implementation of an information system in an organization.

Systems logs are records maintained by a particular system that has been configured to record specific information, such as failed access attempts and systems modifications.

Tailgating occurs when an authorized individual presents a key to open a door, and other individuals, who may or may not be authorized, also enter.

Task-based controls are specified set of tasks.

Task rotation, see "job rotation."

TCP hijacking is where an attacker monitors (or sniffs) packets from the network, modifies them, and inserts them back into the network.

Team members should be the managers or their representatives from the various communities of interest: business, information technology, and information security who will function as subject matter experts supplying the detailed knowledge of their particular areas.

Technical controls address those tactical and technical issues related to designing and implementing security in the organization.

Technical feasibility is the argument about whether or not an organization has the technical means to accomplish a proposed project.

Technological obsolescence can occur when antiquated or outdated infrastructure leads to unreliable and untrustworthy systems.

Terminal Access Controller Access Control System (TACACS) is a remote access authorization system based on a client/server configuration. It makes use of a centralized data service, such as the one provided by a RADIUS server, and validates the user's credentials at the TACACS server.

Thermal detection systems is a smoke detection sensor that uses the heat produced by a fire as a triggering event.

Thermal detectors work by detecting rates of change in the ambient temperature in the room.

Threat is a category of possible "bad things" that can happen to an *asset*. The use of the term *threat* means that the action has not yet occurred, but that the possibility of it occurring is within reason and experience (known as risk).

Threat agents are specific instances of threat categories, including human attackers who seek to access or damage *assets* for financial gain or other reasons.

Threat identification is the assessment of potential weaknesses in each information asset.

Time-memory trade-off attack is using a database of precomputed hashes from sequentially calculated passwords. The attacker simply looks up the hashed password and reads out the text version, no brute force required.

Time-share operates like one of the three sites: hot, warm, or cold, but is leased in conjunction with a business partner or sister organization. It allows the organization to provide a disaster recovery/business continuity option, while reducing its overall costs.

Timing attack exploits the contents of a Web browser's cache and stores a malicious form of cookie on the client's system.

Top-down approach is a method of planning where directives are passed from the top of the organization to lower ranking staff, often with the allocation of resources for the assigned work.

Tornado or severe windstorm is a *force of nature* that can cause electrical disruption to the information systems, or partially or completely damage the building in which the information assets are housed.

Transposition cipher (or permutation cipher) simply rearranges the values within a block to create the ciphertext.

Trap and trace applications use a combination of techniques to detect an intrusion and then to trace it back to its source. The trap usually consists of a honey pot or padded cell and an alarm.

Trap door, see "back door."

Triboelectrification occurs when two materials are rubbed or touched and electrons are exchanged, and results in one object becoming more positively charged and the other more negatively charged.

Trojan horses are software programs that hide their true nature and reveal their designed behavior only when activated.

True online UPS is when the primary power source is the battery, and the power feed from the utility is constantly recharging this battery.

Tsunami is a *force of nature* caused by an underwater earthquake or volcanic eruption. These events can directly damage all or part of the information system or, more likely, the building that houses it.

Two-man control is the requirement that two individuals review and approve each other's work before the task is categorized as finished.

Uninterruptible Power Supply (UPS) is when systems are connected to a device that assures the delivery of electric power without interruption.

United Nations Charter makes provisions for information security during information warfare.

Unskilled hacker, see "script kiddie."

U.S.A. PATRIOT Act of 2001 modified a wide range of existing laws to provide law enforcement agencies with broader latitude in order to combat terrorism-related activities.

U.S.A. PATRIOT Improvement and Reauthorization Act made permanent fourteen of the sixteen expanded powers of the Department of Homeland Security and the FBI in investigating terrorist activity.

Utility means that the data must be available in a useful form.

Vibration sensors detect movement of the sensor rather than movement in the environment.

Violations of intellectual property is defined as "the ownership of ideas and control over the tangible or virtual representation of those ideas."

Virus and worm hoaxes are notices from well-meaning individuals who distribute e-mail warnings concerning fictitious viruses or worms.

Vision statement expresses what the organization wants to become.

Vulnerabilities are the "windows of opportunity" that allow threats to become a reality and affect assets.

War-dialer is an automatic phone-dialing program that dials every number in a configured range (e.g., 555–1000 to 555–2000) and checks whether a person, answering machine, or modem picks up. If a modem answers, the war-dialer program makes a note of the number and then moves to the next target number.

War driving is moving through a geographic area or building, actively scanning for open or unsecured wireless access points.

Warm site provides many of the same services and options as the hot site, but, typically, software applications are not included or are not installed and configured.

Water mist sprinklers are the newest form of sprinkler systems and rely on ultra-fine mists instead of traditional shower-type systems. The water mist systems work like traditional water systems in reducing the ambient temperature around the flame, therefore minimizing its ability to sustain the necessary temperature needed to maintain combustion. Unlike traditional water sprinkler systems, however, these systems produce a fog-like mist that, because the droplets are much less susceptible to gravity, stays buoyant (airborne) much longer.

Wet-pipe system has pressurized water in all pipes and has some form of valve in each protected area. When the system is activated, the valves open, sprinkling the area.

Wi-Fi Protected Access (WPA) is a family of protocols used to secure wireless networks that was created by the Wi-Fi Alliance industry group.

Wired Equivalent Privacy (WEP) is part of the IEEE 802.11 wireless networking standard and is designed to provide a basic level of security protection to these radio networks, to prevent unauthorized access or eavesdropping.

Wireless access points (WAPs) is a device that connects a local area network to wireless devices in the immediate vicinity of the radio signals it emits.

Work factor is the amount of effort (usually in hours) required to perform cryptanalysis on an encoded message so that it may be decrypted when the key or algorithm (or both) are unknown.

Worms are named for the tapeworm in John Brunner's novel *The Shockwave Rider*. A worm is a malicious program that replicates itself independently, without requiring another program.

WPA2 is the second, improved iteration of the WPA protocol.

INDEX

I